READER'S DIGEST

ALL-AMAZING
GARDEN
SECRETS

Thousands of expert tips for growing a fabulous garden

READER'S DIGEST

ALL-AMAZING GARDEN SECRETS

Thousands of expert tips for growing a fabulous garden

Published by the Reader's Digest Association Limited
London   New York   Sydney   Montreal

Contents

Special features

FOREWORD

Here, in easily accessible form, is the concentrated know-how of top plant experts, presented as nuggets of information so you can make the best of your own plot – be it country acres or a city window box. The book's aim is to supply entertaining, inspirational and often unexpected hints and tips – to novice gardeners and experts alike.

Its advice is set out in a simple alphabetical format, with entries ranging from Acid soil to Zinnias. By using the cross-references and index, you'll have access to many related topics as well. For example, if you want to grow superb vegetables, you'll consult not only the entry on each vegetable type but also Vegetable gardens, Mulches and Compost, Organic gardening and other topics as well. Similarly, Alpines could lead you to Rock gardens, Lawn care takes you to Scarifying, and Hedges will also direct you to Topiary.

The advice and recommendations of the book's expert contributors will enable you to choose and grow the finest plants to fill the borders, the best trees and shrubs to screen the garden, the loveliest trailing plants for window boxes and the brightest selection of flowers, foliage, stems and fruits for year-round colour. In addition, they provide useful, money-saving tips, such as ways of turning eggshells into seed pots or a dustbin into an ornamental shrub container. There are tips about theme gardens, water gardens and children's gardens and on matters as disparate as plant photography, what to grow in shade and the best ways to maintain tools.

Within the alphabetical framework, too, there are informative features on all kinds of gardening-related topics from wildlife to period and stately gardens to vintage vegetables, roses and wild flowers.

Scattered throughout *All-Amazing Garden Secrets*, you will also find panels of background information. Some are concerned with the curious origins of plants, others with the uses to which they were once put. Another group explores the role of plants in folklore and legend. All of which adds a browsing ingredient to the book, making it a welcome companion for a winter evening as well as an invaluable helper in the garden.

Acid soil

The acid test

You can find out whether or not your soil is acid by testing the pH level with a soil testing kit. If the pH is less than 7 (neutral), the soil is acid. Take a look, too, at some of the weeds prevalent in your garden or in the surrounding area. Bittercress, creeping buttercups, daisies, docks, plantains and thistles are all indicators of an acid soil. (See also **Soil analysis**)

Added sweetener

A wide range of plants thrive in a slightly acid soil (pH 6.5). If your soil has a pH level of 6 or less, you will need to add lime. In autumn or winter, or – if your soil is sandy – in spring, spread the lime onto freshly dug ground and leave it to be washed in by the rain.

Plant selection

Make the most of an acid soil by growing plants that prefer a pH range of 4–6.5. Those that like very acid soil include azaleas and rhododendrons, callunas, gaultherias, kalmias, pernettyas and pieris. If you are adding lime to the garden to 'sweeten' it, leave a few areas untreated, where you can grow a selection of these and other acid-lovers.

Frequent feeding

Apply fertilisers, especially those containing phosphates and potash, more frequently than usual if you have an acid soil. Soil acidity affects the availability of key nutrients to the plants. The best method is to divide the recommended application into two or three equal parts and to apply at intervals of about six weeks.

Soil check

Some fertilisers, such as sulphate of ammonia and sulphate of potash, can have an acidifying effect on the soil. If you apply such fertilisers regularly, check the pH of your soil every year to ensure that it remains within the pH range that is required by your plants.

Mulching care

When applying an annual mulch to soil in which acid-loving plants are grown, avoid using mushroom compost. Although this compost is high in organic matter, it contains large quantities of lime that will cause severe damage to the plants. (See also **Mulching**)

Growing know-how

Sweetening the soil

The addition of the following amounts of limestone or ground chalk will raise an acid soil's pH to 6.5.

Soil	Present pH	g/m² (oz/sq yd)
Sand	6.0	140 (4)
	5.5	240 (7)
	5.0	440 (13)
	4.5	620 (18)
Loam	6.0	200 (5)
	5.5	380 (11)
	5.0	620 (18)
	4.5	960 (28)
Clay	6.0	240 (7)
	5.5	480 (14)
	5.0	820 (24)
	4.5	1200 (35)

Alpine plants

Chilling seeds

The seeds of some alpine plants need a period of exposure to cold to help them to germinate. In their natural environment this ensures that they germinate in the spring rather than at the onset of winter. In summer or autumn, as soon as the seeds are available, sow them in pots and leave them in a cold frame or in a sheltered corner of the garden to overwinter. If sowing them in spring, put the pots in the bottom of the refrigerator for eight weeks before moving them outside. Do not allow them to dry out.

Mixing the right soil

Most alpines will do well in a good loam combined with plenty of sand and gravel to ensure adequate drainage. Add lime to this mixture if you want to grow varieties that need an alkaline soil. For acid-lovers, add flowers of sulphur. Within a rock garden, you can then provide planting pockets of 'specialised' soil modified in this way to meet the individual needs of each plant. Pack the soil in between the rocks in place of your garden's natural soil.

Room for the kitchen sink

Create an alpine garden in an old 'butler-style' kitchen sink. Set the sink on bricks, place a flat stone over the plug hole, then cover the bottom with crocks or gravel. Add a mixture, in equal parts by volume, of soil, peat and grit. Choose small alpines, such as dwarf campanulas, dianthus, saxifrages and sedums. A dwarf conifer will add height, while a few stones among the plants will create a natural effect.
(See also **Containers**)

Grow in manageable beds

Don't make alpine beds wider than 1.2m (4ft). It is difficult to plant and maintain beds where plants cannot be reached easily from the surrounding paths.

A warning about watering

Water your alpine garden in periods of drought only, or when watering in a new plant. Water plants slowly and carefully to ensure that they are not dislodged.

Feed once a year

Alpine plants do not require much feeding but they will benefit from the application of a small amount of general fertiliser each year. Apply 30g per m² (1oz per sq yd) each February.

Winter protection

Some alpines, especially those with silver foliage and those that grow into tight cushion shapes, can be damaged by the cold and damp of British winters. The leaves and stems rot and the plants may die. To minimise the damage, use bricks or blocks of wood placed on each side of the plant to support a sheet of glass that should then be held down with a stone or tied down with twine. This will protect the plant from rain while allowing in light and air.

Protect the foliage

Cover the soil beneath cushion-forming, ground-hugging plants, such as phloxes and saxifrages, with a layer of fine gravel. During periods of rain, this covering will protect the foliage from the damp soil and will also deter slugs and snails.

Keeping plants in shape

Unless you want to harvest the seeds of alpine plants, cut down the flowers, using scissors or shears, when the blooms have faded. This will keep the plants compact and the alpine garden tidy. Some plants may be encouraged to bloom again, less spectacularly than the first time but still enough to create a colourful splash at the end of the season.

A tool from the cutlery drawer

Keep an old table fork among the tools for the alpine garden. It can be used as a hoe to aerate the soil without damaging roots.

Pot essentials

When potting alpines in clay or plastic pots, begin by covering the bottom of each pot with a layer of broken crocks or gravel. This provides good drainage, which is essential for all alpines. The growth of mosses and liverworts on the surface of the compost can be prevented by adding a top dressing of gravel to each pot.

Avoid overcrowding

Do not plant alpines too close together; nine average-sized plants in a square metre or square yard of soil is sufficient. Protect the stems and leaves from rotting by spreading a 2.5cm (1in) layer of gravel round each plant.

Spring show

For a pretty spring display, put single alpines like campanulas or pasque flowers in 13cm (5in) pots of gritty compost and stand them in a sunny, sheltered place outdoors.

See also **Rock gardens**

Amaryllis

The right choice

There are two types of amaryllis, one that can be grown indoors or outdoors in warmer parts of the country and one that must be grown in a pot indoors. The hardier variety is *Amaryllis bella-donna*. The indoor varieties, which have much larger flowers, are hybrids in the genus Hippeastrum.

In the fresh air

Though tender, Hippeastrums will survive outdoors during mild spells. Sink their pots into the border to make them easy to lift again before colder weather moves in.

Border fanfare Hippeastrum's large trumpet-like flowers make a spectacular show. A single plant may be enough indoors, but an entire outdoor border is a striking sight.

A second flowering

To encourage further blooming, feed amaryllis with a high-potash liquid fertiliser (tomato fertiliser is ideal). When you are deadheading, remove only the top of the flower spike. The nutrients in the stem are then taken back into the bulb to provide energy for new flowers the following season.

The bigger the better

When buying amaryllis, it is best to choose large bulbs. Although these are more expensive than smaller ones, each bulb will often produce two or even three spikes, making it worth the additional cost.

Planting tips

Any good potting compost can be used for an amaryllis, but a soil-based one, such as John Innes No. 3, is preferable because it drains quickly. When planting, leave the top third of the bulb exposed. Covering it completely will cause it to rot.

Southern spot

Plant *Amaryllis bella-donna* bulbs at the foot of a south-facing wall, where they will bask in the maximum summer sunshine. The young leaves that appear in late winter and early spring will be sheltered from the elements by the wall.

Do not disturb

Leave your outdoor amaryllis bulbs undisturbed. Over the years new bulbs will form, creating an attractive clump of plants.

Outdoor companions

Plants that enjoy the same well-drained and sunny conditions as amaryllis include other autumn-flowering bulbs, such as nerines and zephyranthes. Plant three or more species together for an interesting autumn display.

Annuals

Where to plant

Annuals provide short-lived, readily changeable colour schemes in beds, borders, pots and boxes. They are also excellent in mixed borders, where their blooms bridge the gaps between perennial flowering times. In newly planted shrub borders they can be used to great effect in the spaces that the developing shrubs will eventually spread to fill. Annuals are not particular about soil type and most will grow in chalk, clay or sand, but all of them require good drainage.

Ideal arrangement

Many of the commonly grown annuals make excellent cut flowers. However, if they are taken from your main display it can result in gaps in the overall design. Instead of picking the flowers from a showpiece border or bed, plant some in rows in the vegetable garden just for cutting. Calendulas, godetias, larkspurs and love-in-a-mist are all good choices.

Importance of colour

Before planting annuals, give some thought to colour schemes. A single colour makes a strong

Make the right choice

Hardy and half-hardy annuals

Annuals flower, seed and die in one year, and can be divided into two types: hardy and half-hardy. Hardy annuals can be sown outdoors in March or April. Half-hardy annuals are sown under glass and the seedlings are planted out when all danger of frost is past.

Hardy annuals	Flower colour	Half-hardy annuals	Flower colour
Alyssum	Lavender, pink, white	Antirrhinum	Pink, red, white, yellow
Calendula	Orange, tan, yellow	Begonia	Pink, red, white
Centaurea	Blue, pink, red, white	Callistephus	Lavender, pink, purple, red, white
Chrysanthemum	Pink, red, white, yellow		
Clarkia	Pink, purple, red, white	Dahlia	Pink, red, yellow
Convolvulus	Blue, pink, white	Impatiens	Pink, red, white
Delphinium	Blue, pink, red, white	Lobelia	Blue, pink, red, white
Eschscholtzia	Apricot, orange, red, yellow	Nemesia	Orange, pink, red, yellow
Godetia	Pink, red, white	Nicotiana	Green, pink, red, white
Lavatera	Lavender, pink, white	Pelargonium	Pink, red, salmon, white
Linum	Blue, pink, red	Rudbeckia	Orange, red, yellow
Matthiola	Lavender, pink, purple, white	Salvia	Pink, purple, red, white
		Tagetes	Orange, red, rust, white, yellow
Mimulus	Pink, red, yellow	Verbena	Apricot, pink, purple, red
Nigella	Blue, pink, white	Zinnia	Green, pink, purple, red, yellow

statement but if you prefer a multicoloured display, choose harmonious shades or variations on a single theme rather than clashing contrasts. White, yellow and pink flowers are at their best in the evening and early morning. (*See also* **Colour, A Gardener's Palette** *pp. 64–67, A Year of Glory in the Garden pp. 108–11*)

Mixed borders
When choosing annuals to plant in a mixed border, always make a note of the colour of established plants so that you can choose tones that are in harmony.

A packet of surprises
A wide range of seeds can be bought in mixtures based on themes like 'flowers for butterflies' or 'fragrant flowers'. The enormous variety, sometimes a hundred in one packet, makes the results rather unpredictable. Those subdivided by height, in packets labelled 'tall', 'medium' or 'short', are more practical.

Some for the shade
Few hardy or half-hardy annuals will do well in total shade, but *Begonia semperflorens* and both upright and trailing varieties of lobelia will bring colour to the most overcast corner. Busy lizzies, foxgloves, fuchsias, nemophilas, pansies and violas thrive in partial shade.

Trick planting
If you sow hardy annuals in straight lines it will make it easier to distinguish them from weeds and to thin them out to the required spacing. However, since straight lines of flowers can give a rather regimented appearance to your beds, try marking out the area into overlapping semicircles, with one semicircle for each variety. Draw the drills in one semicircle at a different angle from those in the next. As the plants grow and spread, the lines of the drills will blur and you will achieve natural-looking drifts of flowers.

Careful rearing
As soon as seedlings begin to grow, treat them with tender, loving care. Hand-weed carefully between the plants and water generously but gently, using a fine rose on the watering can. A good way to provide a little support for taller varieties is to surround them with short, twiggy sticks, which the developing foliage will soon cover.

Spacing out seeds
If you do not have any of the very small grow-pots that are available, use a seed tray covered with a piece of 1.3cm (½in) mesh wire. Plant one seed through each hole to obtain well-spaced seedlings. Remove the mesh after sowing.

A good soak
Soak the roots before planting potted annuals. Plunge the pots into a basin of water or water them from above. Drain well, remove the plants from their pots and place them in the soil, making sure that each planting hole has been watered well and allowed to drain.

Preparation is the key
If the soil is too hard or dry, annual seeds will have difficulty in germinating. Work the soil well before sowing, raking it down until the surface is a fine, crumbly tilth. Then water the drills well, before and after sowing. This will speed germination and help the roots to grow deeply and strongly.

Waste not
When the seedlings are about 2.5cm (1in) tall, thin them out to approximately half the final spacing recommended on the seed packet. With a little care, most thinnings, with the exception of plants that develop tap roots (lupins and poppies, for example), can be transplanted successfully in another part of the garden. Make the final thinning when the plants have grown to about 5cm (2in).

Pinching out
To encourage bushy growth, pinch out the growing tips of young plants, just above the topmost pair of leaves. This encourages the plants to produce side shoots and more flowers. Pinching out is particularly recommended for clarkias, cosmos, godetias and sweet peas.

Propagating method
For a fresh supply of flowers next year, collect the seeds from annuals before pulling them up in autumn and scatter these round the garden. Alternatively, sow in pots, trays or seedbeds and plant out in spring. Seeds from F1 hybrids, however, will not breed true.

Ants

Assault on a hill
To kill ants, dust the ant hill with a proprietary ant killer, following the manufacturer's instructions. During showery weather, repeat the application when necessary.

Garden secrets

Ant survival
Ant colonies range from groups of a few insects to nests of millions. They do harm but also good in the garden.

- There are more than 40 species of ants in Britain. Some, having been imported accidentally, can only survive indoors.
- Most ants 'herd' aphids, which excrete a food source called honeydew. Ants may protect aphid eggs during the winter, then place them on plants to hatch in spring.
- If wood ants (*Formica rufa*) are threatened, they exude formic acid, an irritant to predators and humans.
- Slave-maker ants (*F. sanguinea*) steal the larvae and pupae of other ants (usually those of *F. fusca*). When they are fully developed adults, these ants become workers for their new 'masters'.
- Some plants, such as violas, use ants to disperse their seeds. The seeds, which have a food source attached, are carried away by the ants, who eat the food and leave the seeds to germinate.
- Their burrowing activities help to aerate heavy soil and improve drainage.

Aphids

The right diet

Aphids, sap-sucking insects about the size of a pinhead, can cause severe damage in the garden. Not only do they stunt the growth of plants but they also spread viral diseases. Aphids can be an indication of the soft, sappy growth that is caused by an excess of nitrogen. Using balanced fertilisers in moderate amounts will ensure healthy plants that are less prone to aphid attack.

Multicoloured marauders

Blackfly and greenfly are the most familiar types of aphid but they come in orange, red, yellow and many other colours, too. Some are very specific about the plants they attack, while others will target a wide variety of hosts. The one thing all aphids have in common, however, is that they can be killed by the same chemical. A spray containing pirimicarb, which is harmless to beneficial garden insects such as hover flies, should be your first choice.

Bitter remedy

If the trees in your garden are regularly attacked by aphids, it is worth sowing rue at their bases. This plant is thought to produce a bitter ingredient that passes into the sap, making the trees distasteful to aphids.

Ladybird welcome

Plant *Artemisia absinthium* (wormwood), either bordering a pathway or in a flowerbed. This plant will serve as an early season stopping-off point for ladybirds and other insects that will then eat any aphids that are also attracted to the wormwood's silvery grey foliage, before they spread to the rest of your garden.

Apples

Something for everyone

Whether your garden is large or small, or even if you have nothing more than a narrow balcony on which to cultivate your plants, you have room to grow at least one apple tree. A few varieties are self-pollinating and a single tree like this is all you need to harvest an excellent crop of fruit. Specialist tree nurseries or good garden centres will be able to advise you on which are the most suitable types of tree for your garden.

Space-saver

A 'Ballerina' or 'Minarette' type in a container is an excellent way to grow apples on a small patio or balcony. The slim, columnar shapes of these trees mean that they require less space than some large pot plants.

A walkover

Allow yourself to be led down the garden path by an edging of 'step-over' trees. Grafted onto strongly dwarfing rootstocks, these tiny trees are nursery trained to grow along a single wire support no more than 60cm (2ft) high. The longer your garden path, the more trees you will be able to accommodate and, of course, the greater the variety of apples you will be able to enjoy. (See also **Cordons**)

Small pollinator

To increase your apple harvest, or if your garden has space for only one apple tree, you can plant a crab apple tree as a pollinator. Reliable varieties that are also very attractive include 'John Downie', which has white flowers in May and large conical yellow fruits that can be used to make very good jelly, and the very dwarf 'Evereste', which produces pink flowers followed by small, orange crab apples.

Upright growth

In a narrow garden, choose fans, cordons and espaliers that allow you to grow your fruit upwards instead of outwards. The tree's eventual height will be restricted only by the height of the wall or fence that supports it.

Single specimen

Freestanding trees are available in heights from 1.2m (4ft) to 5m (17ft), with round, goblet or pyramid-shaped heads. A single tree makes an excellent specimen for the centre of a lawn, or a miniature orchard can be created with a few dwarf pyramid varieties.

Suit the climate

If you live in the north of England or in Scotland, plant late-flowering, frost-resistant varieties such as 'Edward VII' or 'Howgate Wonder'. In the wetter, western areas 'Laxton's Superb' and 'Discovery' are good choices as they both tolerate moist conditions. (See also **Frost**)

Growing know-how

Easy picking

To make your own fruit picker, you will need a pole about 3m (10ft) long, a large empty tin, two pieces of wire, each about 15cm (6in) long, and a small nail.

Make two holes, side by side and about 1.3cm (½in) apart, near the top of the tin. Directly below these, near the bottom of the tin, make a second pair of holes. Thread one length of wire through the top pair of holes, wind it round the pole and, using pliers, twist the ends together, making sure the top of the tin is level with the top of the pole. Do the same through the bottom holes with the other piece of wire. Tap the nail into the pole just below the top loop of wire, to stop the tin slipping.

Line the tin with a piece of foam rubber or bubble polythene to prevent the fruit from bruising, then simply position the tin under the ripe fruit and nudge it gently to dislodge it from the tree.

Thin the fruit

In May or June, apple trees usually drop some of their fruit. This is known as the June drop and it ensures that the apples that remain will grow to a reasonable size. Thinning the clusters even more will result in large, well-formed fruit. Remove the smallest fruitlets from each cluster. Do this by carefully teasing out some of the apples. On bush trees, it is best to remove all but the largest fruitlets from each cluster. If the crop is very heavy, remove complete clusters to leave eating apples that are 10–15cm (4–6in) apart and cooking apples 15–23cm (6–9in) apart. On cordon trees, you should thin the young fruitlets to one or two to each cluster.

Removing a parasite

Most people would be delighted to discover that mistletoe is developing on their apple trees. If, however, you want to get rid of this parasite, the best method is to cut it out with a sharp pruning knife. Heavily infested branches can be cut off completely. (See also **Mistletoe**)

Correct picking

Apples on individual trees ripen at different times, so pick them over a few weeks. Fruit is ready if it parts with a gentle lift and twist.

Cutting out canker

Canker attacks the branches of certain apple trees, such as 'Cox's Orange Pippin' and 'James Grieve'. Remove severely affected branches. Less severe cankers can be removed using a sharp knife. Cut back affected parts until healthy wood is reached. Burn the diseased wood.

Killing off larvae

In July, place corrugated cardboard strips, 25cm (10in) wide, with the corrugations facing inwards, round the trunks of apple trees. Hold the strips in place with string. Larvae of codling moth, which feed on the fruit, will hibernate in the ridges of the cardboard. In winter, burn the cardboard to destroy the hibernating larvae.

Ways with woolly aphids

Woolly aphids, which form colonies in cracks in the bark of apple trees, are recognised by their distinctive white, fluffy coating. It is difficult to kill these pests with insecticides and the best and most effective method is to spray the affected trees with a tar oil winter wash.

Delicious when dried

To dry apples, peel and core them and slice into rings 6mm (¼in) thick. To prevent the rings from browning, drop them into a bowl of water to which a little lemon juice has been added. Thread the rings onto a length of string and then suspend them over a warm radiator by attaching the string to broom handles or wooden poles that are leant against the wall. After several days, when the rings are completely dry, you should store them in paper bags. When you wish to use the rings, presoak them and then add to dried-fruit compotes and crumbles.

Keeping apples crisp

To prevent apples wrinkling and softening during storage, place them carefully between layers of dry moss peat, or a substitute such as coir compost, in cardboard boxes. Keep the boxes in a cool, dry place, like a garage, where the temperature never falls below 3°C (37°F).

Make the right choice

Partners for pollination

Because few apple trees are self-pollinating, choose varieties that flower at the same time, so that bees can transfer the pollen from one to the other, otherwise you won't get a crop of fruit. Pick partners from the groups below, though note that 'Crispin' is a triploid, and requires two pollinators.

Flowering	Variety	Description	Use
Early	Egremont Russet	Brown, dessert	October to December
	George Cave	Juicy red and yellow, dessert	August
	George Neal	Yellow-orange, cooking	August to October
Mid season	Cox's Orange Pippin	Dull red, dessert	November to January
	Crispin	Golden-yellow, dessert	December to February
	Grenadier	Large green-yellow, cooking	August and September
	James Grieve	Pale yellow- and red-streaked, dessert	September
	Sunset	Gold-speckled, dessert	October to December
Late	Ellison's Orange	Red-yellow, dessert	September and October
	Lane's Prince Albert	Yellow-green and red-streaked, cooking	November to March
	Orleans Reinette	Golden-yellow and russet, dessert	January and February

Apricots

Up the wall

Apricots can be grown outdoors as bush trees in large, sheltered gardens, only in the mildest parts of the country. In Scotland and northern England, apricots will usually thrive only when grown under glass but, in other areas and in small gardens, they can be fan-trained against a south- or west-facing wall. In the British climate, fruiting will be sporadic and, in some years, your tree may not produce a crop. (*See also* **Fan-training**)

Room to grow

Make sure that you give apricot trees sufficient space in which to grow. They are vigorous plants and the head of a mature tree, grown in the open, can reach a diameter of 4.5m (15ft) and cover an area greater than 15m^2 (200sq ft). Fan-trained trees need less space but to grow well require a wall at least 2.5m (8ft) high.

Dangers of frost

Apricot blossom appears in February, so the tree needs protection from frosts that prevent pollination and kill fruitlets. It is hard to cover a large, mature specimen growing in an open spot, but young trees, and those growing against walls, can be draped with horticultural fleece. (*See also* **Frost**)

When to water

In dry summers, apricots will be larger and juicier if the tree is given four or five heavy waterings between mid May and September. Water an area of soil round the tree that is equal to the spread of its branches.

Be wary of weeds

Apricot trees do not do well if their trunks are surrounded by weeds or grass, which compete for water and nutrients. Provide the best conditions by leaving a circle of bare soil round the base of the trunk, or mulch with a layer of bark or wood chips, leaving a narrow strip of bare soil close to the trunk. The mulch will suppress weeds but allow the roots to breathe.

Arbours

Trellis for the sides

The best support for the open sides of arbours is wooden trellis with diamond or rectangular-shaped latticework. This is ideal for supporting climbing plants such as clematis, honeysuckle or roses. Wire mesh will do the job but is less attractive. (*See also* **Trellises**)

Firm fixing

Because the plants that grow up the trelliswork of arbours will eventually become large and heavy, make sure that the poles that support the trellis are fixed firmly in the ground. Otherwise, strong winds could lead to the whole structure being blown down.

A longer life

Rustic poles, with one end ready-sawn to a point, can be used as uprights for arbours. These are sold by many garden centres and fencing firms. To prolong the life of the poles, immerse the pointed ends, to a depth of 40–45cm (15–18in) in a bucket of wood preservative and leave them to soak for at least 48 hours. Drive them into the ground to 2.5cm (1in) below the preservative mark.

Scented sideshow

Select two one-year-old apple trees and train them up opposite sides of an arbour so that you can enjoy the sweet scent of apple blossom in spring and a feast of fresh fruit in autumn. The varieties 'Sunset' and 'Discovery' cross-pollinate well.

Make the right choice

Golden fruits of summer

Apricots grow best in a sunny position, well protected from icy winds and from the early morning sun, which can damage the flowers. In most areas they are best trained on a sunny wall. They prefer a slightly alkaline soil to which large amounts of organic matter have been added.

Alfred Early blossoming variety that produces juicy, orange-pink fruit in early August. It is resistant to dieback, a common disease.

Early Moor Park An early-fruiting form of 'Moor Park', which is especially suitable for colder areas.

Farmingdale Produces a high yield of red-tinged, yellow fruit in late July. Some resistance to dieback.

Goldcot Vigorous and hardy variety from the United States. A late-flowering tree that produces medium to large fruit with thick, golden skins in August.

Moor Park A popular and reliable specimen that produces juicy, sweet, brownish-orange fruit in August. This variety is best grown as a fan-trained tree in the south and in the greenhouse in the north. It is susceptible to dieback.

Extra aroma

To create an aromatic hideaway, plant lavender, rosemary and sweet cicely close to the edges of the path that leads to the arbour, and lawn camomile, creeping thyme or corsican mint under the seat.

Arches

How to site an arch

A garden arch must have a purpose; it is no good putting it all alone in the middle of a lawn – it should always appear to lead somewhere, or should be used in a corner of the garden where it can highlight a fountain, a statue or an attractive specimen shrub.

Enhancing the entrance

If the entrance to your garden is lined by hedges on either side, you can create an attractive archway from the greenery. Buy, or make, a wooden or metal arch and secure it firmly to suitable branches in the hedges or to metal stakes driven into the ground. As the hedge grows, tie the new shoots into the arch. It will take two to three years for the hedge to grow thick enough to hide its support.

Getting the size right

When erecting an archway in your garden, make sure it is wide enough and tall enough to allow you to walk through it or stand under it comfortably. A minimum width of 1.2m (4ft), combined with a height of at least 2m (7ft), will allow room for climbers to grow through the sides and top without their branches obstructing the path or catching on your clothes or hair.

A restful spot

After a hard day's weeding, a garden seat beneath an archway that is smothered in sweet-smelling roses and summer jasmine makes an ideal spot to rest from your labours. Sit here quietly and enjoy the scents and sounds of summer.

Winter check

High winds can damage even the most strongly built and solid arch, especially when it is clothed in bushy climbers. You should check arches every winter and replace any posts that have rotted. Make sure, too, that all crosspieces are fixed firmly together.

Artichokes

Double joy

The globe artichoke is worth growing, not only for its culinary delights but also for the ornamental value of its large leaves. In the vegetable garden it is grown for its fleshy, scaled, edible flower heads. These should be cut with a sharp knife when they are young and tender, just as the outside scales of the buds are beginning to open but before the flowers come into bloom.

Saving for next season

When growing globe artichokes, leave only four to six flowers on each of your plants. By limiting the number of artichokes you harvest, you will be preparing for the following season and ensuring that the plants will not be exhausted. Add a mulch of well-rotted compost during April.

Water well for tenderness

To ensure a tender crop the buds of globe artichokes must grow quickly. Encourage vigorous growth by watering abundantly and frequently, especially in dry weather, and mulch with compost or manure.

Replenishing the stock

Artichokes are short-lived perennials, being productive for only four or five years. It is not necessary, however, to buy new plants or to grow them from seed as they can be replaced with suckers (side shoots) that are taken from established plants in April and May and planted at least 1m (3ft) apart.

Protecting plants for winter

In late autumn, after harvesting the heads, cut off the outer leaves of globe artichokes and wrap the crowns with dry bracken or straw held in place with a sheet of sacking or pliable cardboard, tied tightly to the plant. Pile up sand, sawdust, dead leaves or ashes round the cardboard or sacking to protect the plants against very harsh frosts.

Water storage

Eat globe artichokes as soon as possible after picking. However, they can be kept fresh for two to three days by standing the stems in a jar of clean water.

Making a statement

An architectural plant is one that can be used in a garden landscape, either singly or in small groups, for emphasis or statement. To fulfil these functions, it needs to have bold foliage, a defined shape, or a distinct habit. Although many architectural plants are trees or shrubs, they can also be found amongst annuals, herbaceous perennials, grasses and even bulbs. As long as they qualify for the job in hand, then they can be considered as architectural.

Acacia Avenue The slender trunks and pom-pom heads of *Robinia pseudoacacia* form an elegant guard of honour drawing attention forward down the grassy verge towards a focal point – the glass-doored entrance and the decorative brickwork framing it.

Stately plants

Plants of tight, formal habit are useful for flanking a path. Space fastigiate (narrowly erect) trees and shrubs at equal distances on either side and the eye is immediately drawn to what might be found at the far end. If you want to draw attention to a particularly stunning view, it is not even necessary to have a path as such leading the eye towards it; two parallel lines of suitable species set in the lawn will immediately take the eye to the feature or vista you want to emphasise. It is essential that all the plants should be the same variety and well matched, otherwise the effect will be lost. As they grow, they may need some pruning or clipping to keep their matching shapes, but if the right varieties were used in the first place, this work should be minimal. Suitable plants are *Juniperus scopulorum* 'Skyrocket' and *Taxus baccata* 'Fastigiata' (two very slim conifers); *Fagus sylvatica* 'Dawyck Gold' and 'Dawyck Purple' (two narrow, reasonably slow-growing forms of beech); *Sorbus aucuparia* 'Fastigiata' (a mountain ash with tightly ascending branches); and *Ulmus* 'Lobel' (a slow-growing, very narrow elm with golden foliage).

Narrow shrubs may also be used as taller accent plants in borders of low-growing plants, especially in scree and alpine gardens. Slow-growing conifers, such as *Juniperus communis* 'Compressa' and *Taxus baccata* 'Standishii', and the upright form of purple barberry (*Berberis thunbergii* 'Helmond Pillar' are particularly suited to this use; in larger schemes a group of three can be more effective than a single specimen.

Spiky plants

Plants with spiky or thick, strap-like leaves, such as yucca, phormium and cordyline, have become increasingly popular as architectural plants in the past few years. A few decades ago, most of these were considered not to be reliably hardy in the British Isles and required planting in a container and moving to a frost-free situation for the winter. Today's warmer winters have made it possible for many of them to remain outdoors throughout the cold weather with little or no damage, and they can now be planted in the ground permanently to add architectural interest to all kinds of planting arrangements, from shrub and mixed beds, and herbaceous borders to bedding schemes and even gravel gardens.

Spiky architectural plants are still ideal specimens for containers, however, and where there is only room for one pot or tub, a yucca or cordyline should be the first plant to consider. Certain grasses can be used to similar effect, especially in low-maintenance gardens. While

Exotic landscape Warmer winters have meant that cultivating spiky plants such as these – furcraea, echiums, and cordylines – is increasingly feasible in many parts of Britain.

yuccas and similar plants require full sun and good drainage, if conditions are not so perfect a certain variety of grass or sedge may make an ideal substitute. For example, *Carex pendula* makes a lovely architectural specimen for dry shade, while *Typha shuttleworthii* is a dwarf form of reed mace that is suitable for planting at the edge of small pools.

Weeping trees

Weeping trees are nearly always most effective when planted singly as an architectural feature, either in a lawn or gravel with no other taller plants close by, or near water, where the full benefit of the weeping form can be obtained in the reflection. The weeping willow (*Salix* x *sepulcralis* 'Chrysocoma') is the tree that most often springs to mind, though it is really a parkland tree and is too big for small gardens.

For the modern plot, a flowering tree such as Prunus 'Pendula Rubra', Malus 'Sun Rival' or Laburnum anagyroides 'Pendulum' is much more suitable. In a very small space, a spreading shrub, such as Cotoneaster 'Coral Beauty', grafted onto a straight trunk to make a miniature weeping standard, can have a similar effect.

Bold plants

Bold architectural plants combine well with different foliage shapes and sizes, but in a mixed planting will always be the dominant feature, so those that surround them should be chosen to emphasise the attributes of the bold ones, not to compete with them. For example, large-leaved herbaceous species like gunnera, rodgersia, rheum and acanthus are best combined with light, feathery plants such as flowering grasses, some ferns, cut-leaved varieties of elder, and hardy geraniums, which accentuate the boldness of the large leaves while retaining a delicate quality of their own.

'Dot' plants

These were very fashionable in the elaborate bedding schemes of a century or so ago, and are now beginning to regain popularity. They are, essentially, taller plants used in a ground cover of lower ones, to give height and contrast. They are perhaps used most often as architectural plants in bedding schemes, and the ones most frequently used are cannas, *Eucalyptus globulus*, abutilons, kochias, standard fuchsias, marguerites and pelargoniums, and some young conifers.

Weeping splendour A magnificent weeping willow provides an effective backdrop to a toadstool hut and island beds of herbaceous perennials.

Ashes

A log fire bonus
Never throw away ashes from wood fires as they can be used throughout the garden. If you cannot use the cooled ashes immediately, store them in a plastic sack or in a covered bucket and keep it in a dry place.

Bonfire nutrients
Ashes from a bonfire or domestic log fire contain 5–10 per cent potash. They make excellent plant food, particularly as a top dressing for fruit bushes. (See *also* *Potash*)

Protecting fragile plants
Coarse bonfire ashes, mixed with pulverised bark, can be heaped up round the crowns of frost-tender plants such as fuchsias and ferns to protect them in very cold periods.

The right sort
Use the ashes from burnt wood or bonfire ash rather than coal or coke ash, which may contain harmful toxins that can cause plant damage. It is better to save the coal or coke ash to use as foundation material when laying patios or paths.

Slug deterrent
Surround plants that are attractive to slugs and snails, such as hostas, with ash from wood fires. Spread the ash in a circle round the plants. Slugs and snails will avoid it as they find its gritty texture unpleasant. The ash can be sieved first, and the coarse pieces used as a base below the soil in a cold frame.

Keeping your feet
If paths become icy during winter, scatter ashes over them to reduce the risk of slipping. They can also be spread over the driveway to improve your car's traction.

Asparagus

The prolific sex
Male asparagus plants have a higher yield than female ones. As the plants look similar, the only way of distinguishing between them is to wait until the females have berried. If you are growing asparagus from seed, keep the plants in the seedbed for two years, by which time the females will be identifiable and can then be discarded. A faster way to grow asparagus, which can bring the process ahead by a year, is to sow the seeds in February at 13–16°C (55–60°F). Prick out the seedlings into pots and plant them out in June.

All male plants
A simple way of ensuring a high yield is to select those F1 hybrids that produce only male plants. These include the specimens 'Franklim', 'Pacific 2000', 'Lucullus' and 'Blacklim'. You can buy one-year-old crowns that will crop lightly in their second year, becoming more prolific in subsequent years.

Improving with sand
The life of a well-tended asparagus bed can be up to 20 years. Good production depends on the soil, which should be very light, or can be made lighter by adding coarse sand. The seeds should be sown in March or April, in a separate

Garden secrets

Compost heap
Bonfire ashes are particularly good for the compost heap. As well as being a source of potash and other elements, they will help to speed up the process of decomposition. Include ash from indoor wood fires and pure charcoal fires, too. However do not add ashes from coal or coke fires, or those made with charcoal briquettes, as they contain sulphur dioxides and chemicals.

Make the right choice

Asparagus varieties

Because asparagus takes so long to raise from seed, purchase one-year-old crowns. Do not harvest until the second year. Prepare the asparagus bed before the crowns arrive so that they can be planted out before the roots dry out.

Ariane A German-bred variety producing an early flush of large spears.

Cito A modern hybrid variety that crops early and heavily, producing delicious long spears.

Connover's Colossal A popular and reliable old variety with tender-tipped spears that are tinged with purple. Will crop fully from the fourth year.

Franklim An F1 hybrid variety, producing dark green spears of excellent size and flavour early in the season.

Guelph Millennium A Canadian variety with good cold tolerance and a later harvest. Can be planted in either autumn or spring.

Martha Washington Well-known American variety that has large, purple-tinged spears of good quality that are produced during May and June. Resistant to rust.

Purple Pacific More tender and sweet than many green varieties. The spears can be eaten raw or steamed lightly to preserve their colour.

bed, 2.5cm (1in) deep in drills 30cm (12in) apart. When they are large enough to handle, thin out the seedlings to 23cm (9in) apart. They can then be planted in a permanent bed in late autumn or, preferably, during the following spring.

Making use of space
Plant in blocks of three rows, each 30cm (12in) apart, with 1m (3ft) between the blocks. Sow lettuces in the gaps.

Keeping roots fresh
The roots of new asparagus plants must be kept moist. If you cannot put them in the ground immediately, cover with a bag, floor cloth or damp sand. After planting, spread with a protective mulch of well-rotted manure or compost.

Tender asparagus
Cook asparagus in a covered pan, in a little boiling water to which salt and some sugar has been added. Boil for 3 to 4 minutes, take the pan from the heat and let it stand, uncovered, for 10 minutes.

First harvest
Wait until the second year to harvest, then cut only some of the thicker spears from the plant. Scrape away the soil round the plant and cut the spears 2.5cm (1in) below the surface. Use a

sharp, narrow blade, taking care not to damage roots or new stems. Never cut after mid June as this prevents the plant from regaining strength for the next year. Cut foliage when it yellows in late autumn, then dress with well-rotted manure or compost.

A golden addition to dried flowers
Keep asparagus leaves to combine with dried flowers. By autumn they will have turned golden yellow. Do not decimate the plant, however, as the green fern feeds the roots for next year's crop. Cut the ferns down in autumn.

Aubergines

Tropical temperatures required
Because aubergines are tropical plants they need a temperature of at least 21°C (70°F) to germinate and a warm climate in which to grow. So, unless your vegetable garden is exceptionally well protected, or you use cloches, they must be grown in a greenhouse.

Deep planting
Aubergines should be planted deep, with the first leaf at soil level. Make a depression in the soil at the foot of each plant to help the roots to absorb sufficient water.

Prick out with care
When you are pricking out the delicate aubergine seedlings, make sure that you handle them by their seed leaves only. Otherwise, you may bruise the stems, which will be fatal to the seedlings.

Plenty of fruit
To increase the quantity of fruit from an aubergine plant, you should pinch out the growing tip above the fifth leaf when the new plant has grown six or seven leaves. This will encourage lateral buds, which bear flowers and fruit. Then pinch out each shoot above the first or second leaf that follows the second flower. (See also **Pinching out**)

No more than four
Unless you are growing your aubergines in a heated greenhouse, or they are small-fruited varieties, restrict each plant to a maximum of four fruits, allowing only one on each branch.

Avoiding problems
The main enemies of aubergines are low temperatures and too little water, which restrict growth, and a hot, dry atmosphere, which encourages red spider mite. To avoid these conditions, do not ventilate the greenhouse on cool days, water the plants well and feed them with a high-potash fertiliser every ten days. Spray the plants and the greenhouse paths twice a day in hot weather to keep the atmosphere moist.

Taking out the bitterness
Pick aubergines as soon as the skins are firm and glossy, because the fruits may taste bitter if they are left on the plants for too long. To enjoy the aubergines at their best, slice them in half lengthways, sprinkle with salt and lay them, cut side down, on a wire rack to drain. This prevents them from absorbing too much oil while they are cooking, and also helps to eliminate any bitterness in the flavour.

Purple rows
If you have a south or west-facing balcony, grow aubergines in 25cm (10in) pots in a row along the house wall. Their large, violet flowers and glossy, deep purple fruit are attractive.

Autumn colours

Making sure they are seen
Make the most of plants with colourful autumn foliage by planting them on both sides of a well-travelled path or in areas that can be seen from the windows of your house. These plants are at their best between mid October and late November, when you are unlikely to spend long periods in the garden.

Keeping the hues alive
Autumn colours will be especially brilliant after a hot summer, but they may not last as long as in a less extreme year. You can make sure that the colours are prolonged by severely restricting the water supply to any plants that start to develop colour after the end of August. Do not, however, let them dry out completely. Plants that colour well in October need moisture in early September.

Bright bulbs, corms and tubers
For instant effect, autumn-flowering bulbs, corms and tubers are unsurpassed. If planted in late summer, many will flower within a month, bringing a fresh blush of colour. Grow clumps of the violet-blue *Crocus speciosus* 'Oxonian' alongside bright yellow *Sternbergia lutea* or pure white *Cyclamen hederifolium* 'Album' with the pink- and purple-chequered *Colchicum bivonae*. For delicate pink flowers, try *Cyclamen hederifolium*.

Late-season perennials
Few perennials can offer the variety of colours and shapes as charm, Korean and spray chrysanthemums. They brighten beds and borders and are delightful for autumn arrangements. For a fiery touch, grow *Kniphofia* hybrids (red-hot pokers), or *Aster ericoides* 'Pink Cloud', which has small, pink, daisy-like flowers.

See also **Bark, Colour, Persimmons**

Leafy splendour The Japanese maple, *Acer palmatum*, is particularly suitable as a garden tree and produces an impressive display of colour every autumn.

Make the right choice

Shrubs and climbers for a colourful backdrop

A well-positioned shrub or a climber scaling a wall makes an eye-catching feature for autumn and, after leaf-fall, the tracery of branches will provide some interest during winter.

Name	Leaf colour and requirements
Azaleas (deciduous)	Red to yellow; the lighter the flower, the more yellow the foliage
Berberis thunbergii	Brilliant red; unsurpassed for its colour in autumn
Cornus 'Eddie's White Wonder'	Scarlet autumn colour; best in acid soil
Cotinus coggygria	Red; among the best of all the autumn shrubs
Enkianthus perulatus	Rich crimson/purple; needs an acid soil
Fothergilla major	Glowing gold; only for lime-free soil
Parthenocissus tricuspidata 'Veitchii'	Brilliant red; self-supporting Virginia creeper for a tall wall
Rhus glabra 'Laciniata'	Orange and yellow; suitable for any soil
Vitis coignetiae	Rich crimson and scarlet; needs space to be appreciated

Make the right choice

Trees for autumn colour

Make a tree the centrepiece of an autumn garden and enjoy the spectacular leaf colours.

Name	Leaf colour
Up to 6m (20ft)	
Acer capillipes	Orange, red
A. cappadocicum 'Aureum'	Golden/yellow
A. palmatum 'Osakazuki'	Scarlet, orange
Cornus kousa	Red/purple
Crataegus persimilis 'Prunifolia'	Orange/scarlet
Malus tschonoskii	Crimson/purple
Nyssa sylvatica	Crimson
Prunus 'Okame'	Yellow, orange
P. sargentii	Orange, crimson
Sorbus alnifolia	Scarlet/orange
S. commixta	Copper-red
Stuartia pseudocamellia	Orange, red
Taxodium distichum	Copper-brown
Up to 9m (30ft)	
Acer pensylvanicum	Butter yellow
Betula aibo-sinensis var. septentrionalis	Yellow
Fagus sylvatica 'Dawyck Gold'	Rich copper-brown
Liquidambar styraciflua 'Worplesdon'	Orange/scarlet/purple
Sorbus 'Embley'	Orange/crimson

Balcony gardens

Playing safe with pots

To avoid accidents in windy weather, always ensure that pots and containers are kept a safe distance from the edge of the balcony. This is particularly important where the balcony overhangs another or where it overlooks a public area used by passers-by. As an added safety measure, fit a strip of sturdy wire mesh to any space between the floor of the balcony and the rails.

Sheltering from the wind

To shelter a balcony from the wind, line the open part that faces into the wind with bamboo canes tied closely together or adapt a screen made from split bamboo. Also plant shrubs the leaves of which are evergreen such as *Aucuba*, *Buxus* (box), *Prunus lusitanica* (Portugal laurel) and *Ligustrum* (privet).

Although this is a longer term solution, eventually these shrubs will grow into an attractive glossy-leaved hedge.

Bags of blooms

A hanging manger large enough to hold a growing bag can be attached by brackets to a balcony wall, and ornamental plants, such as fuchsias and pelargoniums, or culinary delights such as strawberries, tomatoes or herbs, can be grown in it. The manger can be lined with hay or moss before the growing bag is inserted. Make holes in the underside of the bag and insert trailing plants to give a colourful cascade in the summer. (See also **Hanging baskets**)

Scent and height

Fragrant *Jasminum officinale* (white jasmine) produces an exuberant tracery of flower-studded shoots in summer and is a decorative and accommodating climber, twining with neighbouring plants on a balcony to create a unified display. Plant it in a large container.

Flowery focus

Choose a dainty clematis, such as *Clematis alpina*, that will not climb too high or overwhelm other plants. The violet-blue, cup-shaped flowers provide a delightful display in April and May. The many forms of *C. viticella* in pinks, reds and purples are also suitable for containers and will flower from July into autumn. (See also **Clematis**)

A dark, velvety accent

The dark petals of *Viola* 'Bowles' Black' make a bold impact when planted in a container to peep through the petals of a white verbena. Plant up twin pots for pleasing symmetry.

Protecting plants on the balcony

Plants that are kept out on the balcony during winter should be placed close to the wall, which will provide shelter from the cold. If heavy frosts are forecast, cover the pots with bubble polythene or straw, held in place with garden twine. Wrap a little insulating material round any very exposed parts of the plants. Insulate between the pots and the cold floor with square pieces of wood or polystyrene.

Storing exotic plants during winter

If you do not have a warm, well-lit area in which to store exotic plants, such as bougainvilleas, daturas and tibouchinas, try overwintering them at the other extreme – in a cool, shady place in a temperature of 5–10°C (40–50°F). The plants will remain dormant and will therefore require less light.

Winter cover-up

Small perennials, bulbs and dwarf shrubs on the balcony can be sheltered in winter by being placed in a cardboard box lined with straw. Shelter any climbers by placing screens of split bamboo in front of them.

Bagging a specimen plant

To protect a large balcony shrub that you do not want to move indoors in winter, lift the pot into a large, heavy-duty paper bag – the sort in which potatoes are delivered to greengrocers. Fill the bag with straw or wood shavings and tie the top loosely.

Garden secrets

Lighten the load

Containers will be much lighter and easier to move from one part of your balcony to another – or to move indoors if necessary for protection in winter – if you allow the compost to dry out until it is only just slightly damp before you attempt to lift the pot.

Rustic planter

Plant up a half-barrel, available from garden centres, to bring some rustic charm to your balcony garden. Drill a few holes in its base and fill the first few inches with large stones or crocks to ensure good drainage. Use a good potting compost but do not choose a loam-based one as these are very heavy and make containers difficult to move.

See also **Container gardening, Containers**

Bamboos

The right conditions

Container-grown bamboos can be planted at any time of year, except during periods of frost or drought. They grow best when sheltered from cold winds and the roots should not be allowed to dry out. Add a mulch of garden compost to moist soil in spring.

Bamboo well-being

Spread dry leaves as a mulch round the base of any new bamboo you plant. This will help to retain moisture in the soil and to protect the roots from the sun. Once the shoot is growing, leaves that fall naturally from the plant will be sufficient to keep it healthy.

The beauty of bamboo

A bamboo can overwhelm a very small garden, but a tall-growing, evergreen specimen makes a striking display in a medium-sized plot. Plant it in a well-drained spot in partial shade.

A brief history

All in a name

In recent years, bamboo experts have been changing the names of many species so some familiar names have disappeared and new names are now in use. The name changes can be confusing – a few of them are listed below.

Old name	New name
Arundinaria fargesii	Bashania fargesii
A. japonica	Pseudosasa japonica
A. murieliae	Fargesia murieliae
A nitida	F. nitida
A. palmata	Sasa palmata
A. pygmaea	Pleioblastus pygmaeus
A. variegata	P. variegatus
A. viridistriata	P. auricomus
Sasa tessellata	Indocalamus tessellatus

Growing for canes

Harvest canes when they have reached just over the length you require, and use them to support other plants. Autumn is the best time to cut them. With sharp secateurs, cut each cane as close to the ground as possible. Store the canes flat or hanging from a string in a cool dry place, so that they dry straight. A garage or shed would be ideal.

Propagating bamboo plants

If you want to propagate a bamboo plant, increase your chances of success by digging out four to six three-year-old stems in early spring before growth commences. Transplant the stems quickly to the same depth in a sheltered position in the garden, without letting the soil dry out. Water amply, then cut the stems down by a third.

Foliage cascades

Bamboos provide a dazzling green screen or backdrop and will also frame the view of the garden from a window.

Fighting the invaders

If certain bamboos are planted outside, watch out for an invasion. The rhizomes that spread horizontally underground from the plant can quickly take over a whole area of a garden. *Pleioblastus humilis* var. *pumilus*, *P. pygmaeus* and *Sasa veitchii* are especially invasive and should be planted only where they have plenty of space to spread.

To contain a bamboo, dig a trench 50cm (20in) deep around the plant and hammer in sheets of rigid plastic of the same depth. When they hit the barrier, the rhizomes will make their way to the surface, where they can be cut off.

Brightening a balcony

On a balcony or a patio, a tuft of bamboos is a magnificent sight.

Growing know-how

Invasive or clump-forming?

When planting bamboos it is important to plant the right type in the right place – distinguishing between vigorous and clump-forming types is a valuable first step.

Vigorously spreading types

Indocalamus tessellatus, Pleioblastus humilis var. pumilus, P. pygmaeus, Sasa veitchii

Moderately spreading types

Phyllostachys aurea, P. nigra, Pleioblastus variegatus

Clump-forming types

Arundinaria gigantea, Chusquea culeou, Fargesia murieliae, F. nitida, Shibataea kumasasa, Sinarundinaria intermedia

Choose a species that does not grow too tall and is resistant to cold – *Shibataea kumasasa* would be a good choice. Grow it in a large pot and water regularly.

Bigger pots for bamboo

If you want to grow a tall bamboo, such as *Fargesia murieliae* or *F. nitida*, in a pot for dramatic effect, be sure to plant it in a heavy pot or container so that it does not become top-heavy and blow over in the wind. Avoid pots that taper towards the base, as these will be less stable than straight-sided containers or boxes. Some bamboos will grow fast and you may find that plants need to be transplanted to a bigger pot each year.

Winter protection

Protect bamboos in pots from frost by wrapping the plants and the pots in several thicknesses of bubble polythene, loosely tied in place. Cover the soil with a thick layer of straw or dead leaves.

Barbecues

Dangers of sudden breezes
Be careful when using a mobile barbecue or planning to build a permanent barbecue in your garden. If the barbecue is placed too near a wall, wind eddies can make lighting difficult or fan flames unexpectedly. Always stand with your back to the wind when cooking.

Never position your barbecue near plants or trees – especially resinous trees such as pines, firs and spruces – or underneath a pergola.

A way to improvise
If you do not have a conventional barbecue, you can make a temporary one out of building blocks or bricks. Build two stacks 50cm (20in) apart, laying bricks face down or standing blocks on their sides. Lay two metal rods between the stacks and set a grill on top. Spread the charcoal on a steel tray underneath the rods, or construct a brick hearth on the ground.

Don't gamble with safety
Each year, careless use of barbecues causes serious accidents and even deaths. Wear leather gloves and use long-handled implements when cooking in order to keep a safe distance from the coals. Never start a fire with petrol or methylated spirit. Use barbecue lighting fluid, small pieces of dry wood or a firelighter cube, which should be placed underneath the charcoal. Do not let children play near the barbecue while it is alight, and keep a can of water beside it. To avoid the danger of embers flaring up on the barbecue after the food has been cooked, sprinkle some ashes over them.

Easy lighting
Punch holes round the base of a 1kg (2lb) coffee tin, then discard the lid and remove the bottom end with a tin opener. Place the tin, base down, in the middle of the barbecue and put a layer of crumpled newspaper inside. Add charcoal, then light the paper through the punched holes. The tin will act as a flue, drawing the flames up through the charcoal pieces. Once these are aglow, use the tongs to lift the tin and spread hot charcoal over the barbecue.

Bark

Make room for the birch
If you have a reasonably large garden, make the most of the decorative bark of birch trees. *Betula albo-sinensis*, which has an orange to orange-brown bark, *B. ermanii*, the beautiful peeling orange-brown bark of which changes to cream-white, or *B. utilis* var. *jacquemontii* (Himalayan birch) with its white bark make eye-catching features, particularly in winter. The smaller-growing *B. papyrifera* var. *kenaica* has white bark tinged with orange.

Bark for winter colour
Silver birch trees are renowned for their attractive bark, but many other shrubs and trees have branches that are equally colourful. The shrub *Rubus cockburnianus* has stems that are white with a tinge of blue in winter, while *R. thibetanus* has off-white stems. The olive-green stems of *Cornus stolonifera* 'Flaviramea' and *C. alba* 'Sibirica', which has coral-red stems, also offer vivid winter colour. (*See also* **Willows**)

Colour renewal
To enjoy vividly coloured rubus and willow stems in the garden in winter, cut down all the stems to ground level early in spring. They will renew themselves and produce fresh, strong colour.

Striped bark
Acers are frequently grown for their brilliant autumn foliage, but the bark of some species is equally striking. For example, the white-striped, green bark of either *Acer capillipes* or *A. pensylvanicum* (snake bark maple), makes a striking feature in the garden. Keep an eye out for green algae that may appear on the trunk. If this mars the appearance of the bark, wash it off with soapy water.

Flaking bark
Apart from striped-bark acers, eye-catching species include *Acer griseum*, the glossy bark of which peels off in paper-thin flakes to reveal light orange-brown bark, and *A. palmatum* 'Sango-kaku', which has remarkable coral-red bark, especially on young growth.

Startling bark The pinkish-orange bark of *Betula nigra*, known as the river birch or red birch, becomes ridged and brown on old trees and peels away in large strips.

Bay trees

Conditions for growing a bay tree
Although usually hardy in Britain, the bay tree's place of origin is the Mediterranean region. It should therefore be planted in a warm, sheltered position in the garden to protect it from harsh winters. The leaves may be seared by cold winds. If a cold snap is forecast, wrap the foliage with canvas and cover the soil at the base of the tree with a carpet of dead leaves or straw.

Secateurs not shears
A bushy, standard bay tree with its glossy, aromatic leaves clipped into a perfect ball is as decorative in the garden as it is useful in cooking. Always use secateurs when pruning to shape your bay tree to maintain its visual appeal. Although shears will complete the job faster, they will cut through the leaves, creating a rather messy appearance.

Training a standard
A bay tree can be grown as a standard in a container and will thrive best against a south-facing wall. To train it, cut off the lowest branches when the plant is about 75cm (2½ft) high. This will encourage growth at the top. When the central leading shoot has reached the height you want your bay tree to be, pinch out the tip. Thereafter prune in spring and summer to keep growth compact and to shape the head.

Growing more plants
Propagate bay by taking 10cm (4in) heel cuttings – a heel is a short portion of old wood at the base of a stem on a side shoot – during August or September. Insert them in equal parts of peat and sand in a cold frame and transfer them to pots in April.

Fresh is best
Fresh bay leaves have a better flavour than dried leaves. If possible, pick leaves early in the morning for a stronger flavour. Do not cut them off; pull downwards to break them off.

Beans

Soaking for seeds
To speed up germination, soak beans in warm water for one night before sowing them in soil that is moist. Sow them 2.5–5cm (1–2in) deep. Gardeners of old used to say that beans should be planted near to the surface 'where they can see the gardener leaving'.

Nitrogen at the roots
Bean roots are a rich source of nitrogen. After harvesting, cut back the stems and leave the roots in the soil where they will release this valuable plant nutrient.

Preparing the ground
Dig the ground deeply and work in well-rotted manure or compost during late autumn before replacing the topsoil in preparation for sowing or planting beans.

Soya beans
New varieties, such as 'Ustie', have been recently introduced for the British climate. The plants are self-pollinating and the leaves feed the pods, which are harvested fresh in the autumn, or the beans can be shelled and stored indefinitely in airtight containers. They do not suffer from pests and diseases, so are a good crop for the organic gardener.

See also **Broad beans**, **French beans** *and* **Runner beans**

Make the right choice

Know your beans
There are four basic types of bean, all with their own special features and cultural requirements. Heaviest yields result from picking beans regularly once they have attained their maximum length but before the seeds begin to bulge within the pods.

Runner beans
The easiest beans to grow well, runner beans are vigorous climbers with red or white flowers. Plant them in full sun where their shade can be of benefit to other vegetables, such as lettuces.

Broad beans
Broad beans are tough, hardy and very easy to grow in any good garden soil in a sunny place. They grow to about 1m (3ft) tall.

Dwarf french beans
Grown on a bush with a neat habit, the beans are generally stringless and have a fine flavour. They thrive in rich soil and full sun. Pick them small, top and tail, then steam for a few minutes.

Climbing french beans
Flowers set without insect pollination, which makes them more reliable than runner beans. Their flavour is often stronger than that of dwarf french beans and they crop for longer.

Gardener's potpourri

Bean selection

The Greeks used beans as voting tokens during elections. The Roman usage was somewhat less serious. During Saturnalia, celebrated in December and an occasion for unrestrained revelry, the master of the festivities was selected by drawing beans. The custom survived until more recent times in a form adapted to Christianity: the traditional cake eaten on Twelfth Night (January 6) often contained a bean. Whoever found it was king for the night.

Bedding plants

Knowing what they are

Almost all bedding plants are treated as annuals – usually raised from seed, brought on in a greenhouse or cold frame and planted out for summer display. Then, after a few months of glory, they are consigned to the compost heap. But they can also include some biennials (plants with a two-year life cycle) and some half-hardy perennials.

Making the best buys

Bedding plants are sold in boxes, pots or cellular trays in late spring and early summer. The best ones are those with green foliage, short branching stems, set in a slightly moist compost and having a good root system. Avoid plants that are pale, have over-long foliage or

roots bunched in drainage holes. Also avoid those set in dry compost that is pulling away from the container's edges or plants set in compost covered with algae or weeds.

Hardening off

If you are growing bedding plants from seed, sow them indoors in March–April and harden off the plants before transplanting them to the flowerbeds. If they have been grown in the greenhouse, put them outside every day in fine weather and return them at night. If the plants are raised in a cold frame, open the top of the frame as soon as possible – leaving it open a little more as the weeks go by.

Getting the colour right

Before buying, check a plant's colour by examining the buds. The colour shown on plant labels may sometimes vary considerably from the actual colour of the plant.

Avoiding flowering plants

Try to choose bedding plants that have not yet flowered – the plants will last longer and bloom later. If some already have flowers, snip them off. This will stimulate growth and the formation of new buds.

Window boxes for beginners

If you are decorating a balcony for the first time and are unsure about choosing bedding plants, ready-planted window boxes are sold by many garden centres. Everything is included – from the box filled with compost to the correct selection of plants. If you already have window boxes, ready-to-plant mixtures are also available.

Planting to a plan

To avoid any disappointment with a display of bedding plants, make a plan of your flowerbed before planting. Make allowances for the height and spread of each plant you wish to include. Use felt-tipped pens to map out a colour scheme on the plan. Like wearing expensive jewels, the mingling of hardy and half-hardy annuals and biennials in the garden requires care if harmony is to be achieved. Balance a focal point of scarlet petunias, say, with a pastel

blend of hardy annuals, and combine purple *Heliotropium* (cherry pie) with violet Canterbury bells.

Watering before planting

Before setting out bedding plants in their final positions, submerge their pots for a few minutes in a washing-up bowl half-filled with water to thoroughly moisten the compost. This will help the plants to become established and to grow faster and flower earlier.

Adding height

Give your flowerbeds height and interest by including a few large pot plants, such as fuchsias, lilies or even tomatoes. Place the pots in the centre or at the rear of the beds.

Wait for warm weather

Do not be tempted to plant too early. Bedding plants found in garden centres in early spring are often forced in greenhouses and will not take kindly to the chill of spring. Wait until mid or even late May to plant them out in the north and east.

Different ways to plant

Try to avoid planting in straight lines. It is far more attractive and natural-looking to plant in staggered rows, to make curves, or to establish clumps of colour and foliage.

Outsmart the slugs

If slugs are a problem, protect your bedding plants from the time of planting by leaving a single slug pellet alongside each plant immediately after watering in.

Watering after planting

Regular watering of any new bedding plant is necessary at first. However, once a plant has started active growth and begins forming leaves, watering can vary according to the amount of rainfall.

Helping plants to bloom

To grow bedding plants that are admired by your neighbours, deadhead the plants frequently and feed them every two to three weeks with liquid tomato feed, diluted as directed on the container. Plants in pots should be fed every eight to ten days.

See also **Annuals**, **Biennials**, **Planting**, **Sandy soil** *and* **Sowing**

Beds and borders

Get the most from your beds

Following just two principles of design when planning a flowerbed or border will help you to create a pleasing effect.

First, put most of your tall plants at the back of borders or in the centre of beds that have been cut out of the lawn. This offsets smaller plants positioned at the front of the border or round the edge of the bed. Do not be too rigid in your planting patterns, though, as a couple of taller plants mixed with small ones can make a striking focus and add extra depth.

Second, always group an odd number of flowering or foliage plants together. Groups of three, five or seven plants will give a more natural effect in a planting scheme than groups of two, four or six.

Weird and wonderful

Add height and excitement to a low-lying flowerbed by growing annuals over structures made from bamboo or wire mesh. Spheres, cones or even animal-shaped structures will be covered quickly by *Cobaea scandens* (cup and saucer vine), nasturtiums, sweet peas or other climbers to give the flowerbed an unusual appearance.

Year-round interest

Make your flowerbed a centre of interest throughout the year by choosing plants that flower or produce decorative foliage at different times. Include bulbs that will bloom at the end of winter and in early spring, and add some late-flowering perennials to brighten up your garden in autumn and early winter. (*See also* **A Gardener's Palette** *pp. 64–67 and* **A Year of Glory in the Garden** *pp. 108–11*)

Comfortable beds

Make sure that plants in borders and beds get sufficient nutrients by making a barrier against the roots of nearby hedges or trees. Bury a sheet of rigid plastic, 40–500cm (16–20in) high and as long as the bed, in the ground 40–50cm (16–20in) from the hedge or tree roots. This will ensure that bedding plants do not have to compete with their stronger neighbours for food and water.

Final check

Avoid creating a bed that is too large or appears awkwardly shaped by first covering the area with a light sprinkling of sand. This will enable you to see what the bed will look like before you sacrifice lawn space. To help you to decide where best to place your plants, insert stakes or canes into the ground to represent tall species and use pots for the smaller plants. This will give you an impression of the finished shape your planned flowerbed will have.

Cutting out a straight edge

To cut a straight border, lay down a plank and, using the edge as a guide, cut through the soil with a sharp edging iron. Even if you are standing on the plank, the pressure applied by the edging iron being levered backwards to define the edge can still move the plank out of position. To stop this happening, stabilise the plank by hammering a long nail into the ground through each end.

Neat edges

To avoid having to clip the edges of the lawn by hand, surround your flower borders or beds with a cordon of paving stones, bricks or old railway sleepers. This will allow you to mow right up to the edge of the lawn without damaging any of your plants.

Make the right choice

Tall plants for the back of a border

Make an impressive display at the back of a large border by selecting stately plants that will stand above their neighbours. Pick and choose from the selection below, complementing the colours and shapes of other plants in the border. Include some tall grasses and some foliage plants such as bronze fennel, green *Artemisia lactiflora***, silver** *A. arborescens* **and** *Onopordum acanthium***.**

Name	Flower colour	Height
Aruncus dioicus	Creamy white	1.2–1.8m (4–6ft)
Crambe cordifolia	White	1.8m (6ft)
Crocosmia 'Lucifer'	Red	1.2m (4ft)
Delphinium hybrids	White, blue, purple	1.2–2.4m (4–8ft)
Eupatorium cannabinum 'Flore Pleno'	Rose pink	60cm–1.2m (2–4ft)
Filipendula kamtschatica	White, pale pink	1.2–2.4m (4–8ft)
Helianthus salicifolius	Golden yellow	1.8–2.4 m (6–8ft)
Kniphofia 'Wrexham Buttercup'	Yellow	1.2m (4ft)
Leucanthemella serotina	White	1.2–1.5m (4–5ft)
Macleaya microcarpa 'Kelway's Coral Plume'	Pink	1.5–2.4m (5–8ft)

Edging a path

If you want to put a flowerbed next to a path made of gravel or bark chippings, it is best to separate them by an edging of stones, bricks, tiles, strips of treated timber or low-growing shrubs and perennials to prevent the gravel or bark from spreading into the bed.

Cutting a smooth curve

To cut a curved or shaped border, lay a hose on the ground to trace a shape. Cut out the shape with a lawn edging tool by following the contours of the hose.

Decorative surround

Create an attractive surround for a flowerbed or border with frost-resistant bricks. Dig a narrow trench about 15cm (6in) deep round a circular bed or at the front of the border. Then set the bricks in at an angle, positioning each one carefully. Take your time – a hasty job will look ragged.

Walking the plank

A heavy, sticky soil will become compacted if you stand on it. Prevent this by laying a plank on the ground whenever you need to work on the beds. Your weight will be spread more evenly and the soil will be less compressed.

Shady character

A damp, shady border can be a blot on an otherwise bright and cheerful garden scene, but with careful selection even the most unpromising site can produce vivid summer colour. Plant deep violet *Geranium ibericum* with yellow *Iris pseudacorus* 'Golden Queen' or 'Variegata', which has yellow-striped leaves. Add frothy rose-pink *Astilbe* x *arendsii* 'Hyazinth', multicoloured *Mimulus* (monkey flower) and deep red *Astrantia major* var. *rubra*. To give height to the planting scheme, include clumps of yellow *Ligularia* 'The Rocket'.

Holding plants back

Invasive plants, such as *Hypericum calycinum* (rose of Sharon) and *Vinca* (periwinkle), have a tendency to grow beyond their flowerbeds and onto the lawn. If you do not want to pull up the plants or cut them back, they can be kept in check by driving slates or flat tiles vertically into the soil, side by side, at the edge of the border. To make it easier to drive in the slates, dig a narrow trench for them around the edges of the flowerbed and firm them in well.

Fill the gaps

While you are waiting for perennials and shrubs to reach maturity, fill the spaces in the beds with annuals, biennials and bulbs.

Willow-twig edgings

Unusual and elegant border edgings were made out of willow by old-time gardeners. Their technique was simple and is easily replicated: drive wooden stakes about 45cm (18in) long into the ground at 15cm (6in) intervals along the intended border, leaving 20–25cm (8–10in) of each stake exposed, depending on the height of edging required. When all the stakes are in position, intertwine willow twigs between the stakes, as if weaving a basket.

Willow edging looks very attractive round small herb gardens and flowerbeds. Willow lengths suitable for creating this type of border can be bought from basket makers or local conservation organisations.

Creative colour

For a cohesive look when choosing colour for a flowerbed, pick a dominant colour and build a contrasting or complementary scheme round it. Add some white if you wish to highlight the colours. Stronger tints work best at the front of a bed with paler ones farther back. This trick will make your beds look larger than they really are.

Bright and bold

Create a border of vibrant colour, mixing reds and bronzes, blues and oranges, and yellows and purples. Use green, white, cream and silver-grey to separate the vivid partnerships.

Flowers of contrast

Give flowerbeds variety and life by contrasting flowers that are spiked, such as lupins, with daisies and other plants that have flat-topped or rounded blooms.

Accommodating vegetables in your borders

Make the most of a small garden by growing a few herbs and vegetables in your borders. Chives, carrots and parsley all have attractive foliage. Red cabbages, purple Brussels sprouts, bronze fennel and red-stalked ruby chard all make colourful splashes.

Bees

The great pollinators

Bees carry pollen from flower to flower, helping to fertilise many edible and ornamental plants. Some bumblebees can take nectar from tubular flowers by biting a hole in the back.

Choosing the right plants

Be nice to bees. Without insects, many garden plants would not produce fruits or berries, or set seeds. Several kinds of flies, beetles and wasps help to pollinate flowers, but bees play the greatest role. To attract bees to your garden, grow campanulas, clover, comfrey, *Cotoneaster microphyllus*, heathers, lilies of the valley, lungwort, *Antirrhinum* (snapdragon), sweet woodruff, teasels, thyme and many of the hardy geraniums.

Avoiding daytime spraying

To avoid harming pollinating insects, confine spraying plants in flower to the evening, when bees are less active, and try not to spray the flowers themselves. You will be helping to conserve the native bee population, which has declined significantly as a result of massive changes in agricultural practice, including the destruction of hedgerow habitats and the widespread use of pesticides and herbicides.

Removing a bee sting

Never try to remove a bee sting with your fingers – you can easily squash the sting, causing the venom to penetrate more deeply. Remove it quickly by scraping it off with a knife or your fingernail.

Taking the pain out of a sting

To ease the pain of a bee sting, there are many folk remedies that have been handed down through the ages – among them, rubbing the area with a slice of onion or with the leaves of a leek. While these two remedies can be very helpful, neither is as effective as a paste made from sodium bicarbonate and water. Applied early enough, it neutralises acid from the sting and prevents swelling. Some people can have serious allergic reactions to stings, resulting in a rapid and severe swelling, accompanied by difficulty in breathing. If this happens, take the victim to the accident and emergency department of the nearest hospital, or call an ambulance.

Beetroot

Crop failure

In some seasons it seems as if few seeds have germinated and you may get a poor beetroot crop. In fact, sparrows may have pulled the seedlings out and eaten them. Prevent this by protecting the seedlings with net.

Beets with the best flavour

For the best taste and quality in beetroot, pick them as soon as they reach the size of a golf ball. For this size of beetroot, you should sow seeds thinly and thin to 5cm (2in). Allow 10cm (4in) for larger roots.

Growing the earliest crop

If you want young beetroot in late May or early June, sow early varieties in pots in February and place in a warm greenhouse with a minimum temperature of 13°C (55°F). When the plants are about 5cm (2in) high harden them off over two weeks and set them outside under polythene sheets or cloches with 5cm (2in) between each plant, allowing 30cm (12in) between the rows.

Diagnosing problems

If your beetroot is woody and lacking in flavour, it could be due to a number of factors. The soil may be too rich or have been dressed with fresh manure: beetroot is best grown on a plot that was manured for a previous crop. The soil may be too acid: if it is below pH 6, apply lime to compensate. The soil may be too dry: water well in dry spells. Or the seedlings may have been thinned leaving them too far apart: check the seed packet for advice. (See *also* **Acid soil**, **Soil analysis**)

Making a meal of beetroot

After pulling, the youngest, tenderest beetroot, leaves can be kept and served in a salad, or cooked like spinach. Boil the beetroot and rub off the skins. Serve hot or let them cool and then pickle in vinegar, or grate or dice for inclusion in a salad.

Wiping stains away

If your fingers are stained with beetroot juice, rub them with the juice or rind of a lemon to remove the stain.

Twisting off the leaves

Late varieties of beetroot will keep for several months, provided that you harvest them during October before the frosts. Choose a dry day and let the beetroot dry on the ground. Twist off – rather than cut – the leaves to prevent bleeding.

Storing beetroot for the winter

Beetroot left in the ground will not keep as well as those that have been lifted and stored. To keep beetroot fresh for the winter, store in layers with the stalks uppermost, in boxes filled with slightly damp sand or peat. Do not let the roots touch each other, and make sure that the top layer is covered. Left like this in a dry, frost-free shed or garage, the roots will remain firm until small shoots start forming on them in March.

Overwintering in the ground

In mild areas, beetroot may be left in the ground. Draw up soil over the roots and cover with straw if severe weather is forecast.

See also **Vegetable gardens**

Begonias

Sowing seeds

When sowing begonia seeds, in February or March, use clean trays and fresh seed compost. The seeds are susceptible to fungal diseases in compost. Never firm the compost too much as this impedes drainage, which increases the danger of fungal attack. Mix the tiny seeds with dry fine sand and sow on the surface. Do not cover with compost or the young seedlings may be smothered. Cover the tray with Cling Film, then stand it in a dish of water to absorb moisture – watering with a can may disturb the seeds. When the surface of the compost darkens with the moisture, remove the tray and let it drain, then place it in a heated propagator at a temperature of 20°C (68°F).

The choice with tubers

Never skimp on quality when buying begonia tubers – the bigger a tuber is, the more flowers it will produce. The largest flowers are produced on individually named varieties but these can be difficult to find. As an alternative, buy mixed sorts such as 'Giant Doubles' with large flowers in a variety of colours, 'Non Stop' with smaller flowers but in larger quantities, and the trailing 'Sensation' for hanging baskets.

This way up

Make sure tubers are planted the right way up: the tops are concave and the bases convex. Look for the beginnings of the first shoots in the hollow tops and plant with these uppermost. Start tubers into growth in February and March at a temperature of 18°C (64°F), in boxes of moist peat or coir. Do not bury the tubers but let them protrude from the growing medium.

When in doubt

If you are unable to identify the concave top of begonia tubers, plant them on their sides. The shoots will grow upright.

The time to plant

Begonias cannot stand frost, so wait until you are certain the cold is gone before planting them out. To be safe, plant around late May in the south or early June in the north.

Getting rid of mildew

In dry seasons, the leaves of begonias may be attacked by powdery mildew, a disease that spreads small, white, dusty patches on the leaves. Many varieties may be attacked in bad seasons. Treat affected plants with a fungicide obtainable from garden centres. Repeat the treatment every three weeks.

Prolong the season

Later in the year, when frosts are forecast, bring in potted begonias in the evening and leave them overnight in a cool room.

Make the right choice

Know your beetroot

There are two main types of beetroot, round beetroot and long beetroot; both grow successfully in any well-drained soil in a sunny place. Beetroot seeds are actually clusters containing three or four seeds, so thinning is essential, although modern, more convenient varieties with just one seed have been developed.

Type	Description	Good varieties
Long	Good for storing for winter use and for slicing for salads. They need a longer season than round beetroot. All long varieties are red fleshed.	Cheltenham Green Top (long-rooted, excellent flavour) Cheltenham Mono (tapering, single-seeded) Forono (cylindrical, stores well)
Round	Best for using straight from the ground. Most are deep red but there are also yellow and white-rooted types. Round varieties are quick to develop and many are resistant to bolting.	Action (red, quick, harvest at 2.5cm/1in in diameter) Albina Vereduna (round, white, tasty) Burpee's Golden (yellow, foliage edible) Motown (red, quick, single-seeded)

Vivid blooms Plant colourful begonias as a quick means of brightening up a dull or shady corner in summer.

Looking after plants indoors
Water begonias sparingly. They are extremely susceptible to root rot and prefer a temporary dryness to a temporary dampness. Use water at room temperature to prevent shock.

Extended flowering
At the end of the summer, repot some of your most vigorous fibrous-rooted begonias in compost. Take them indoors where they will continue to bloom for several months.

Storing tubers
After digging tubers from the soil in autumn, make sure that they are properly dry by laying them for a few days on shelves covered with newspaper. If they are stored for winter while still damp, they may rot. Store them in a cool environment, at a temperature of about 4–10°C (39–50°F), buried in dry peat.

Propagation from a leaf
There are easy ways of taking cuttings from begonias. Select a variety with large leaves, *Begonia rex*, for example, and take the healthiest mature leaf. Cut off the stalk and turn the leaf over on a cutting board so that the back faces upwards. Use a razor blade to make a number of incisions through the leaf so that the main veins are severed. Place the leaf, face up, on a tray filled with damp compost. Keep the leaf flat by placing stones round its edges and place the tray somewhere light, in a temperature of 18°C (64°F). Within a few weeks, roots will appear at some of those places where the incisions were made.

Short cut to cuttings
An even simpler method of taking cuttings is by removing the leaf and chopping it into small pieces – square, oblong or triangular, it does not matter. Each piece must include a section of the leaf's veins. With the outer edge of the leaf facing upwards, press these pieces upright into, or lay them onto, a tray of compost and, within a few weeks, roots should develop at the base of the leaf pieces where the vein ends have come into contact with the compost.

See also **Cuttings**

Berberis

Tolerant and hardy
Berberis is a useful shrub for gardeners because it will tolerate most soils. All species thrive in sunny positions, though evergreens will tolerate a degree of shade.

A thorny shrub
Make sure you keep a thorny berberis well away from pathways and doors as it tends to ensnare anything that passes it. For this reason some species of berberis, such as *Berberis* x *frikartii*, will make excellent barrier hedging.

On the ground
For unusual ground cover, try growing *Berberis wilsoniae*. This dwarf, deciduous shrub turns brilliant red in autumn.

Biennials

Making a spring show
By mixing biennials with bulbs, you will achieve beautiful spring displays. Choose low-growing, early-flowering biennials, such as wallflowers and forget-me-nots, and mix them with tulip, daffodil and hyacinth bulbs. In autumn, plant the biennials, then plant the bulbs between them. The bulb stems will push through the carpet of biennials.

How to recognise biennials
Biennials are plants that germinate and grow in their first year and flower, seed and die in their second year. If they are sown at the beginning of summer, they will have developed stems and leaves by winter and be ready for blooming the following spring.

Rooting power
Do not sow wallflowers before August. Sowing too early results in large plants with stringy roots that do not transplant or establish well.

Garden secrets

Giving hollyhocks a longer life
As soon as the flowering season is over, cut down hollyhocks to 15cm (6in). In this way you may keep the plants for several years, although rust may occur. If you let them go to seed, the parent plants will become exhausted and die – though you may well have hollyhock offspring scattered about.

A helping hand for foxgloves

Cut off the main spikes of foxgloves once they have flowered. This will encourage the flowering side shoots to increase in size.

Ideal places for cultivation

Late-flowering biennials, such as *Bellis perennis* (daisy), Brompton stocks, Canterbury bells, foxgloves and sweet williams, intended for indoor displays, can be grown at the back of the vegetable garden or in a discreet corner of their own. There, they will not be disturbed when you plant out the summer bedding.

Easy does it

Make an attractive wild garden by planting biennials that re-seed themselves, such as evening primroses, forget-me-nots, foxglove and honesty. If you have a dry and stony patch, the gigantic candle shapes of *Verbascum* (mullein) will do well there. Give the plants time to set and drop their seeds before pulling them up.

Harvesting seeds

Introduced as a garden flower from North America, evening primroses now grow wild on sandy dunes and waste ground. Collect and sow the seeds. Although it is highly invasive, this plant is ideal for a wild garden and will provide a wealth of large, sweetly scented, yellow flowers throughout the summer.

Striking foliage

Biennials are usually grown for their flowers, but it is worth growing *Euphorbia lathyris* (caper spurge), *Onopordum acanthium* (Scotch thistle) and silver-leaved *Galactites tomentosa*. All have spectacular foliage.

Planting lines

Sow seeds of biennial plants in rows as this will help you to distinguish between the emerging seedlings and the weeds. Forget-me-nots and evening primroses are among those that may cause confusion.

A distinctive display

In August, cut the dried stems of *Lunaria annua* (honesty) to make an attractive, indoor decoration. Rub the pods lightly between finger and thumb. The pale brown exterior will fall away, leaving a silvery centre.

See also *A Year of Glory in the Garden* pp. 108–11

Bindweeds

Tackling a robust weed

Calystegia sepium (large bindweed), a strong-growing twining weed, can quickly strangle garden plants. It grows from fairly shallow underground stems and digging out is sometimes possible. Tree roots are often in the way, however, and small pieces will always be left to grow again. Weedkiller is usually the only complete answer.

Painting individual leaves

When bindweed is entangled with other plants, making treatment difficult, use a branch as a stake and insert it near the bindweed's root. The stem will soon attach itself to this support. Once the weed has been isolated, its individual leaves can be daubed with a systemic weedkiller (see above), which will be drawn down to the root, killing the plant. A second dose may be necessary.

A way to use weedkiller

On a cultivated plot, where using weedkiller can be difficult, untwine hedge bindweed stems, lay them on bare ground, then carefully spray a glyphosate weedkiller over them. Alternatively, place a plastic drainpipe or an old, bottomless plastic bucket over the stems and spray down inside it. The weaker but deeper growing *Convolvulus arvensis* (small bindweed) can be treated similarly.

Watch out and keep out

Bindweed is found in all types of soil. Check that no pieces of fleshy, underground stem are hidden in any manure or topsoil brought into your garden and check again in spring for signs of shoots or seedlings.

See also *Weedkillers*

Cover up Conceal an ugly wall or fence behind a colourful screen of tall-growing, stately biennials, such as foxgloves and Canterbury bells.

Biological controls

Balancing act

Instead of chemical treatments, designed to eradicate garden pests, you can use biological control agents that reduce the number of pests to an acceptable level without upsetting the balance of nature. Their actions are very specific and they are harmless to other creatures. Because the control agents cannot survive without the pests on which they feed, there is no danger that today's predators may become tomorrow's pests.

Cuckoo in the nest

Parasitic pest controls utilise insects that lay their eggs in the larvae of other insects. For example, whiteflies are dealt with in this way by the parasitic wasp *Encarsia formosa*. When the eggs hatch, the parasites eat their hosts before they emerge as adults to recommence the cycle.

Nematode action

If slugs or vine weevils are destroying your garden, send for the nematodes (parasitic worms), available from garden centres. Unlike some nonbiological remedies, such as slug pellets, these tiny worms will act without endangering the lives of hedgehogs or birds. They should be used only when the soil temperature is above 15°C (59°F).

Moth traps

Pheromone, a synthetic sex hormone, attracts male codling and plum moths into a sticky trap from which they cannot escape. Hang traps in fruit trees in May. One trap will protect up to five trees.

Damage limitation

Bacillus thuringiensis is a deadly bacterium that infects caterpillars. Apply this biological control agent as a spray solution to brassicas.

Birds

Building a bird table

Build a bird table by sawing a circular piece of wood about 4cm (1½in) thick from a log. Nail it through the centre to a sturdy wooden post 1.5m (5ft) long that has been hammered into the ground. To stop the wood from splitting as the nail is being driven through, first drill a pilot hole slightly smaller than the nail's diameter. In addition to seed, place a couple of stones on the table – the birds like to stand on them – and a saucer of water for them to drink.

Making a table with a roof

If you have the time, build birds a proper 'house' by making the bird table square, adding a plywood roof supported by two struts (as illustrated) and with a plywood rim nailed round the edge of the table to prevent the seeds from falling to the ground. As a deterrent to predators, fit a circular piece of wood to the post about 30cm (12in) beneath the table top. To get the full pleasure from a bird table, always position it near your house so that you can watch the birds feeding.

Make the right choice

Biological control agents

Agents are available by mail order. Biological control cards can be bought at garden centres and sent to the appropriate supplier as soon as a pest becomes apparent. Some agents are for use in the greenhouse, others for use outdoors.

Pest	Control agent	Type (* Suitable for outdoor use)
Aphids	*Aphidoletes aphidimyza*	Predatory midge larva
	Aphidius matricariae	Parasitic wasp
Caterpillars	*Bacillus thuringiensis*	Bacterium*
Codling moths	Pheromone	Trap*
Flower thrips	*Amblyseius cucumeris*	Predatory mite
Leaf miners	*Dacnusa sibirica*	Parasitic wasp
	Diglyphus isaea	Parasitic wasp
Mealybugs	*Cryptolaemus montrouzieri*	Predatory beetle
Plum moths	Pheromone	Trap*
Red spider mites	*Phytoseiulus persimilis*	Predatory mite
Scale insects	*Metaphycus helvolus*	Parasitic wasp
Sciarid flies	*Hypoaspis miles*	Nematode
Slugs	*Phasmarhabditis hermaphrodita*	Nematode*
Vine weevils	*Steinernema carpocapsae*	Nematode*
	Heterohabditis megidis	Nematode*
Whiteflies	*Encarsia formosa*	Parasitic wasp

Food that birds like best

Avoid clipping too closely those shrubs or hedgerows that produce berries or hips, such as hollies, pyracanthas, rugosa roses and snowberries. Birds always prefer naturally grown food and will be encouraged to visit a garden that has a plentiful supply of food, shelter and fresh water.

Keeping predators away

Remove the bird-table top and slip a length of plastic drainpipe about 75cm (30in) long over the post so that it drops to the ground. The drainpipe will defeat cats or other predators wanting to scale the post. Another deterrent is a thorny climbing rose bush planted at the foot of the post.

Encouraging birds with seeds

Spread a mixture of seeds on the bird table to encourage different species of birds. Most birds will find something they like in the selection of seeds; greenfinches, which seem to like everything, may be the most regular visitors. Other diners may include the occasional goldfinch, blue tits, great tits, coal tits and nuthatches. Collared doves and chaffinches may also pay visits, but these usually prefer to eat from the ground.

Giving birds other food

To complement the seeds, add cereals, dried fruits, crumbled cheese, wholemeal breadcrumbs and leftover cake crumbs to the bird table. Whole nuts, including unsalted peanuts, are suitable if put in a feeder. Lumps of fat can be hung out to attract tits. Do not put out raw meat or mouldy bread and never offer dehydrated coconut as it may swell in a bird's crop and cause it to choke.

Letting nature help

On cold or snowy winter days, get out into the garden and turn over the top of your compost heap. Compost hides millions of insects, which will provide a feast for many small birds.

Power of the sunflower

Birds are attracted by seeds that are rich in oil and protein. Their favourite among these is sunflower seeds. Whether sprinkled on the ground, placed on a seed table or even put in a wire-mesh feeder basket, you will find birds flocking to your garden to eat them.

Starting with small portions

Avoid putting out too much food when trying to attract birds into your garden – uneaten seeds will quickly become damp and mouldy. Put out small quantities of seeds to begin with, increasing the amount gradually as more birds begin to appear and the food is consumed more quickly.

Installing a birdbath

A birdbath should be shallow – 5–10mm (¼–½in) deep. Because it is so shallow, it will need to be refilled at least once a day. Place a few stones in the water for the birds to stand on. Position the birdbath where it will benefit from full sun, and not too far from a hedgerow or bushes where the birds can perch to dry out after bathing. A birdbath on a short pedestal will attract more species than one on a tall pedestal but, whatever its height, it must be out in the open where predators cannot approach unseen.

Instant bird-proof tunnels

To protect seedlings and young plants from birds, cut flexible PVC-coated 13mm (½in) mesh wire netting into lengths suitable to fit along the rows, then bend each length into a tunnel shape to fit over the young plants.

Slip-proof netting

When netting a fruit bush to protect its crop, place a cane at each corner. Make a small slit in several tennis or ping-pong balls and put one over the top of each cane. Slide the net over the balls. These will keep the net in position and prevent it from snagging on the canes.

Helping birds with building

A mesh net, such as a greengrocer's fruit bag, can be used to supply birds with building materials for their nests. Fill an empty net with lengths of string, hairs recovered from brushes, and pieces of wool and cotton and suspend the net from a branch.

Garden secrets

Foiling birds

Hang pieces of aluminium foil on a length of thread attached to the branches of a fruit tree. The foil will frighten off birds as it gleams in the sun or makes a noise as it twists in the wind. The free CDs given away with newspapers also make good deterrents. Remove from their covers and hang on lengths of string. Birds will become accustomed to these scarers after a while and you will need to try something new.

Keeping birds at bay

While birds can bring a lot of pleasure to a garden, they also have destructive ways and can be a source of irritation – particularly to a vegetable gardener. To protect newly sown seeds from birds, insert small wooden stakes into the ground at each side of the seeded area. Fit lengths of string, pulled taut, to stakes opposite each other. Along the strings, lay pieces of prickly branches that have been pruned from holly and thorn bushes, or from roses. The string and branches may look unsightly, but they will stop your vegetable crops from being destroyed.

Cassette-tape deterrent

As a temporary measure to protect raspberries from birds, take the tape out of an unwanted audio cassette and tie one end to the top of one of the raspberry canes, letting the remainder hang free. The sound of the tape twisting in the wind will frighten off invaders.

See also **Cherries, Hanging baskets, Onions, Red and white currants**

Blackberries

Painless picking
Make blackberry picking a pain-free experience by planting thornless blackberry varieties such as 'Merton Thornless', 'Oregon Thornless' or the late-cropping variety, 'Loch Ness'. Climbing thornless varieties, including 'Waldo', which fruits in July and August, could also make an unusual covering for an archway or pergola.

Growing fruit on wires
Train blackberry plants – one of the most prolific and easily grown fruits – on wires. This is more satisfactory than a system of growing against posts. Using 10 or 12 gauge wire, stretch lengths horizontally between posts, setting them 30cm (12in) apart up to a height of 1.8m (6ft).

Training blackberries – one way
One simple way to train blackberries is in a fan shape on horizontal wires. Train the branches out on both sides of the rootstock, spacing them evenly on the wires. During summer these branches will flower and then produce fruit. At the same time new branches will be produced from the rootstock and these can be tied in vertically, in a loose bundle in the centre of the fruiting canes. After fruiting, cut out at the base all the branches that have carried fruit. Untie the new shoots and tie them in to replace those cut away. They will fruit the following year.

Training blackberries – another way
Some gardeners find the method described above difficult to manage, but there is another way that separates the stems more clearly. Tie all the branches out on the wires on one side of the rootstock then, as the new growth develops, tie these young branches to the wires on the other side. All the fruit will then be carried on the branches on one side and after fruiting these branches should be cut out. In the following year the blackberries will be carried on the branches on the other side.

Water well
Before the blackberries ripen, keep the plants thoroughly watered during dry summer weather to ensure plump and healthy fruit.

Beetle drive
The raspberry beetle affects blackberries as well as raspberries. Keep the fruits grub-free by spraying with fenitrothion after flowering.

Protection from frost
In frost-prone areas, tie up the canes in a bundle along the bottom wire in autumn. In spring, untie and train the canes out.

Natural layering
The tip of a blackberry bush stem will take root if it touches the soil. Make use of this natural layering by selecting longer stems and burying them. After a year, you can cut off and transplant the new plant to a suitable position. If it is not removed, the existing bush will become larger. (See also **Layering**)

Thorny problem
Some blackberry bushes have vicious thorns. Choose a planting site for them that is well away from pathways, children's play areas and the washing line. Always wear thick clothing and heavy-duty gardening gloves when you are handling or pruning the canes to avoid getting scratched, and never throw the prunings onto the compost heap unless they have been well shredded beforehand.

Defensive hedging
Grow blackberry bushes that have a dual purpose – to provide fruit and to protect your property from intruders or animals. Put up a fence and at its foot plant varieties of blackberries, wild brambles and spiny climbing roses, which will scramble over and through it to create a thorny 'burglar-proof' hedge.

Improving yields
Blackberries respond well to a moisture-retentive soil. Improve yields by applying an annual mulch of compost, spent hops or farmyard manure. Do not be tempted to use mushroom compost as it contains large quantities of lime. This is an unsuitable material for application to blackberries, which grow best in an acid soil.

Potash boost
Feeding blackberries regularly will also improve yield. In March, feed blackberry plants with 30g (1oz) sulphate of potash for every square metre (square yard). Add 60g (2oz) superphosphate every third year.

Gardener's potpourri

Blackberry lore
According to folklore, the devil stamps on blackberries at Michaelmas, September 29, and they should not be gathered after that day. Another belief is that he spits on them on October 10. The origin of both tales may be that by this time of year, brambles and cultivated blackberry varieties begin to turn mushy and tasteless. The culprit is not the devil but pests, such as bluebottles and houseflies, that abound in late summer and dribble digestive juices over the berries.

Blackcurrants

Encourage growth
Plant a blackcurrant bush deeply – at least 7.5cm (3in) below the soil surface. This helps to encourage growth at the base of the plant.

Controlling the size
If your garden is small and you are worried by the size to which some bushes may grow, keep them under control by cutting out branches that are more than three years old (as opposed

to the normal four years). Choose new varieties which grow into smaller, upright bushes. 'Ben Connan' and 'Ben Sarek' grow to little more than 1m (3ft) high and can be planted 1.2m (4ft) apart. Larger varieties need to be about 1.8m (6ft) apart.

When to prune

Pruning old branches keeps blackcurrant bushes young and vigorous so that they continue to produce abundant crops each year. Since young branches – those that grew in the previous year – produce the best fruits, the main aim of pruning is to make space for the young branches to develop by cutting out the older ones. Bushes should be pruned in autumn after the leaves have fallen, cutting out all of the

Make the right choice

Know your blackcurrants

For a long blackcurrant season, plant early, mid-season and late varieties.

Season	Variety	Description
Early	Boskoop Giant	Large, sweet berries; prone to spring frosts
Mid	Ben Connan	Very large berries; compact growth
	Ben Lomond	Crops heavily; some resistance to frost
	Ben Sarek	Large berries; heavy crop, compact growth
	Wellington XXX	Sweet berries; heavy cropping and vigorous
Late	Ben More	Upright growth; avoids spring frost

branches that have fruited; leave between eight and ten older branches. Cut down to the ground any outside branches that are hanging at an angle of less than 45 degrees, followed by any dead, diseased or broken branches.

Regular mulching

Blackcurrants benefit from a regular mulch, applied every autumn. It will help to improve the soil, feed the plants and keep down any weeds. Use well-rotted garden compost or well-rotted manure. Black polythene will smother weeds very effectively, but as it provides no nutrients it should be laid over the compost or manure.

Making a tree from a bush

A blackcurrant bush can be turned into a blackcurrant tree. Start with a cutting 60–70cm (24–28in) long. Plant it 15cm (6in) deep in the soil and secure it with a wooden stake. Rub off, or use a knife to cut off, all the buds with the exception of three or four at the top – these will form the tree's future branch system. After three years you will have an attractive little blackcurrant tree, although it may not produce as much fruit as a blackcurrant bush.

Taking cuttings

Choose the straightest, youngest branches when taking cuttings from blackcurrant bushes. Take the cuttings in October and cut them into 25cm (10in) long segments, trimmed just above a bud at the top and below a bud at the bottom. Insert them into the soil 20cm (8in) deep and 15cm (6in) apart. They will start to grow in spring.

Blanching

Blackout

Take care that light is totally excluded when blanching vegetables. If exposed to light, chicory, endives, Florence fennel and leeks form chlorophyll that turns the

Garden secrets

Inner cleanliness

When earthing up vegetables for blanching, take care to prevent particles of soil from falling inside the leaves, as they are difficult to remove before the vegetables are cooked. Slip a rubber band round the top of each plant to hold the leaves tightly together. Another way of keeping soil particles out and protecting the plant is to slip a loo roll or kitchen roll tube over the plant while it is young.

vegetables green and detracts from their taste. It is well worth the effort, therefore, to ensure that all appropriate parts of the plants are properly covered so that the stems remain white. When blanching vegetables under upturned pots, use stones to cover the drainage holes completely.

Bog gardens

Choose the place

If an area of your garden has naturally poor drainage, dedicate this to plants that thrive in damp soil. If no such area exists, create an artificial bog garden. Dig a hole, at least 30cm (12in) deep and as large as you require, and line it with heavy-duty plastic, pierced in a few places to aid slow drainage. Fill with garden soil mixed with water-retentive organic matter, such as compost or peat. Water the bog garden frequently.

Garden in a bowl

Make a small bog garden by burying a container, such as a washing-up bowl, that is filled with soil and has two or three drainage holes pierced in it. Hide the container's edges so that it does not protrude above soil level.

Natural plantings

Moisture-loving plants for a bog garden include hostas, water irises, marsh marigolds and bog rush, especially *Juncus effusus* 'Spiralis' with its corkscrew-shaped leaves. Exotic-looking *Matteuccia struthiopteris* (ostrich feather fern) or *Osmunda regalis* (royal fern) are other plants that will adapt well to life in a bog garden.

Colour for winter

Do not forget to include some plants that will provide interest in winter. Colourful shrubs that tolerate boggy conditions include *Cornus alba* 'Sibirica', which has coral-coloured winter stems, and shrubby willows such as *Salix alba* var. *vitellina*, the stems of which are yellow when young.

Primulas for bog gardens

Many primulas thrive in moist soil. Species such as *Primula japonica* (Japanese primrose) and *P. pulverulenta* will quickly self-sow and produce a variety of flower colours. Other good species include *P. bulleyana*, *P. florindae* (giant cowslip) and *P. sikkimensis* (Himalayan cowslip).

High drama

Leave room for a few tall plants to add dramatic effect. *Ligularia dentata* 'Desdemona' (golden rays), for example, is a bog-loving plant that has towering stalks of orange-red flowers and leaves that are flushed with red-purple.

Easy steps

Put stepping-stones alongside and through a large bog garden so that you can tend the plants without getting your feet wet.

See also **Water gardens**

Bone meal

A boost for trees and shrubs

To give your trees and shrubs a long-lasting boost, scatter a handful of bone meal into the planting hole and fork it in. This slow-release fertiliser provides a rich source of phosphate, which helps development of roots, while the nitrogen in it provides food for leaf growth.

Protect your hands

While modern steamed bone meal is perfectly safe to use, always wear rubber gloves as an added precaution when handling it and spreading it on the soil.

Bonfires

Safety first

Choose the site for your bonfires with care. It should be well away from any buildings or fences and, in addition to the ground round the bonfire, the space above must be completely clear to avoid the heat from flames damaging trees or foliage. Never leave a smouldering fire unattended.

What and what not to burn

Vegetable waste, such as potato or apple peelings, cauliflower and cabbage leaves, should never be put on a bonfire; save them for the compost heap. Candidates for a bonfire include diseased plants, perennial weeds, prunings from trees and bushes, and most paper and cardboard household packaging but exclude polythene or plastic items, which could give off toxic fumes. Put the latter into the dustbin for collection.

Sensible precautions

Avoid upsetting your neighbours by choosing carefully when to light a bonfire in the garden. A still, overcast day during the week may be more suitable than a sunny weekend when neighbours are sitting or eating outside.

Look out for wildlife

Before lighting an autumn or winter bonfire that has stood for some weeks, check that there is no hibernating wildlife underneath.

See also **What the Law Says pp. 170–1**

Bonsai trees

Finding the right shape

One of the best ways to find a suitable subject for bonsai is to keep your eyes open in your garden, or in the gardens of generous friends, for a tree seedling that has an interesting shape. In autumn, dig up the seedling carefully, pot it and leave it to establish itself for one year. The following spring, take the plant out of its pot, prune any thick roots and pinch off vigorously growing shoots. Repeat the process in the second year. In its all-important third year, the plant can be placed in its permanent container. Trim the roots by up to a third to fit and continually pinch out unwanted shoots.

Wired for shape

Plastic-coated wire, spiralled round branches, helps to train young bonsai into a natural shape. Deciduous trees are most pliable in spring and evergreens in autumn. Check wires regularly and loosen if necessary.

Giving bonsai fresh air

There are two kinds of bonsai trees – indoor and outdoor. The indoor types come from tropical climates and with a little care will adapt to the atmosphere of a house far better than British trees, which do better growing outdoors. But indoor bonsai still like to be exposed to the fresh air from time to time when the weather is mild – either place them in the garden for a few hours in semi-shade or stand them on a ledge by an open window.

A brief history

What bonsai means

The word 'bonsai' is formed from the Japanese word 'bon' meaning 'wide tray', and 'sai' meaning 'tree' – which in combination add up to 'a tree cultivated in a pot'. The bonsai-tree culture began in China in the third century AD.

In later years, the art of bonsai was developed by Japanese Buddhist monks, who grew the different forms for their aesthetic qualities, maintaining that the tree and its pot cannot be separated – the balance of plant and pot representing a harmonious reproduction of the balance of nature.

Making the right choice

When choosing a specimen, always check carefully that the roots of the tree are spread out evenly round the trunk and have not become entangled. Look for a tree structure that rises naturally and has an elegant habit. Plants with small leaves, fruits and flowers make the best bonsai as the reduced height will be in proportion.

Choosing the right spot

An indoor bonsai tree does not like being moved from one room to another in the house. The pot should be kept in a permanent place, away from draughts and radiators. The plant needs light but should be protected from direct sun. When watering bonsai, use only rainwater if possible, but if you do not have any and your tap water is hard, leave it to stand for a couple of days before use.

Providing a humid atmosphere

A bonsai tree grown indoors needs a humid environment. Stand the pot on a tray of gravel, half-filled with water. In summer, spray with water, using an atomiser. Do not do this in full sun as the leaves may become scorched.

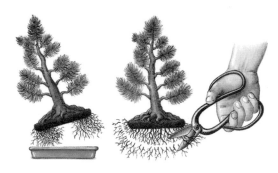

The time to repot

Repot a bonsai every two to five years, depending on its age, in early spring. Change the soil and cut off a third of the plant's roots to restrict its growth. The older the tree, the less often it needs repotting.

Looking after outdoor plants

An outdoor bonsai should never be brought into the house or warm greenhouse in winter. Sudden warmth can start the sap circulating, upsetting the plant's natural cycle.

Protecting a bonsai against frost

When frost is forecast, wrap the pot in several thicknesses of newspaper, bubble polythene or straw, to protect the bonsai's roots. Remove the protection once the danger has passed. If your outdoor bonsai is covered with snow, leave it round the pot as snow is an excellent natural insulator, but shake any excess from the branches.

Time for a soaking

Excessive moisture is harmful to bonsai roots so do not stand the pot in a saucer of water for long periods. If the soil becomes extremely dry, soak the pot in a pan of water, then allow it to drain by standing it at an angle, resting one edge of the pot on a brick before returning it to its normal position.

When to fertilise

Bonsai need regular feeding during the growing season. Leave four to six weeks after repotting, then use a liquid house plant fertiliser at regular intervals until autumn.

Keeping a bonsai in shape

Unless a new branch is required, bonsai trees should be kept in shape by pinching back soft new growth during spring and summer. On vigorous-growing plants pinching back may be necessary several times during the growing season.

Making major cuts

Major structural cuts to a bonsai tree should be made during late winter to prevent the sap loss that would occur if it were pruned during the growing season. No sealing compound is necessary on completion of pruning – the plant will heal naturally.

Oriental appeal Bonsai trees, a fascinating blend of the miniature and the mature, make an eye-catching display when grouped together.

Box

Dividing the garden

Give your garden an air of formality by surrounding flowerbeds and vegetable gardens with low box hedges. Box is an ideal plant for such hedges because it does not mind constant hard clipping and because it provides the neatest edging.

Preparing to plant a box hedge

Box hedges are long-lived and can be in place for very many years so prepare the ground well. In autumn or spring, dig a trench the depth and width of a spade, removing the soil to one side. Then fork over the base, adding plenty of organic matter such as garden compost or well-rotted manure together with bone meal. Mix some organic matter with the soil from the trench, replace it and firm it well. Do not overfirm a clay soil.

Keeping the hedge straight

To be sure of planting in a straight line, drive a stake into the ground at each end of the proposed hedge area and stretch a string between them. Place the young box plants 30–45cm (12–18in) apart, then water well and snip off the tops with shears.

Intricate edging Box of different colours can be planted to striking effect in front of a patio.

all the new ones will be the same or buy young plants from a specialist who will raise plants only from cuttings. To achieve the illustrated bicoloured effect, keep the sets of cuttings or plants separate.

When to prune

Clip hedges and topiary specimens into the chosen shape in August and September. Although box thrives on clipping, be careful not to clip it too much at one time. This could retard its growth.

Box choice

When planting box, it pays to choose the right variety for a particular purpose. For low box hedges to edge flowerbeds, choose 'Suffruticosa' or 'Elegantissima'. 'Myrtifolia' is a good choice for taller hedges and screens and an excellent specimen for topiary is the variety 'Handsworthiensis'.

See also **Topiary**

A uniform hedge

It is inadvisable to grow a box hedge or edging from seed, since it is unlikely that all the plants will be the same colour and equally vigorous. Instead, take cuttings from a single plant so that

Broad beans

Dealing with aphids

To get rid of aphids on broad bean plants, pinch out the tops once the beans start to form, or try luring the pests away from the beans by growing nasturtiums among them. Once the nasturtium shoots are infested, cut them off and burn them.

Beans at their best

Broad beans, one of the first vegetables to be sown in the gardening year, are actually at their best when the pods are 6cm (2½in) long and the beans are about the size of peas. Do not shell them, but cook them as they are – pods and all. If you prefer them shelled, harvest them when the beans are about as big as 10 pence pieces. After that, they begin to develop leathery skins.

Putting beans into storage
Broad beans can be put into suspended animation by allowing them to ripen, then taking as many pods as you require together with the stems on which they grow. Hang the beans upside-down in a dry shed or wrap them in newspaper. Shell them when you want to eat them, although they will be tougher than fresh broad beans.

Freezer tactic
Broad beans will freeze well if you follow these steps. Shell the beans and blanch them in a saucepan of boiling water for 1 minute. Cool them immediately in iced water, then put them into small bags – each containing a single serving – and place them in the freezer. Eat the beans within 12 months.

Broccoli

Check the variety
When buying broccoli seeds, look carefully at the type you are choosing. Sprouting broccoli produces small heads but once the first ones are cut a succession of heads develop for many weeks afterwards to give a long cropping season. Other types, usually known as calabrese, produce a few, much larger heads over a shorter period.

An angled cut
Always use a sharp knife to harvest broccoli heads, making an angled cut into each shoot. This will prevent rain or other moisture from collecting and causing rot.

Pinch off flowers
Examine broccoli regularly to stop the plants from flowering. Do not let them to go to seed.

Plant props
Broccoli develops into tall, heavy plants that can collapse under the weight of snow or in a gale. Earth up the stems to about 15cm (6in) in the growing season to encourage root growth.

Brussels sprouts

Tight buttons
If sprouts are to form tight buttons, the seedlings must be planted in soil that has been deeply dug and well manured the previous autumn. If the soil is heavy and needs forking over immediately before planting, tread it well to firm it, then rake the surface level. To ensure that the roots become well established, use a dibber to make the planting hole.

Short and steady
In exposed gardens, winds can be a problem. Mounding a little soil around each stem and tying each plant to a stake should help. Shorter varieties, such as 'Peer Gynt', are more able to withstand being buffeted by the wind.

Overlay with underlay
Foam underlay for carpets can help to deter the cabbage root fly from laying her eggs on the plants. In spring, cut discs or squares, about 15cm (6in) across, and make a slit from the edge to the centre of each. Tuck the shields carefully round the base of the stems, leave them in position until late September.

Harvesting the stem tops
Sprouts develop first at the bottom of the stem. When these are ready to harvest, encourage those at the top of the stem to develop by cutting off the leaves, which can be cooked and eaten in the same way as cabbage.

Growing red sprouts
For a touch of colour in the vegetable garden and on the table grow 'Falstaff', the red sprout.

Make the right choice

Colourful sprouting broccoli
Before the flowers open, cut sprouting broccoli shoots, about 5cm (2in) from the base. A second crop of shoots, produced from lower side shoots, usually follows.

Type	Description	Good varieties
Purple broccoli	Hardy and tolerates poor soil. Crops for several weeks.	Early Purple Sprouting (harvest from late February or early March), Late Purple Sprouting (harvest from late March).
White broccoli	Usually tastier than purple varieties but not as hardy.	Early White Sprouting (matures in March and April), Late White Sprouting (best in April and May).
Calabrese	A form of green sprouting broccoli. Less hardy than purple varieties, calabrese varieties mature between July and November.	F1 Belstar (early variety with large, domed head), F1 Tendergreen (bright green heads with tender, edible stems), F1 Fiesta (large bright heads), Waltham (late maturing variety, with many side shoots).

Bulbs

Memory jogger
In February, take a good look at your garden and make notes or take photographs of any areas that need cheering up. Refer to the photographs in autumn to remind you where to plant spring-flowering bulbs.

Making a better show
Whether planting bulbs outdoors or in pots, do not plant just a single layer – try planting two, or even three layers. This way you will have a much denser showing and will enjoy the flowers for a longer period. Keep each layer 4–5cm (1½–2in) apart with a layer of soil and avoid planting the bulbs directly above each other. Use the same variety of bulb so that all the flowers will bloom together, or at least within a few days of each other.

Increasing the season
You will lengthen the duration of your display if you plant bulbs that have successional flowering periods. Mix them with biennials, low perennials or creeping plants that later help to hide any yellowing leaves. (See also **A Year of Glory in the Garden** pp. 108–11)

A lawn of flowers
Scatter clumps of bulbs in the lawn as well as in the flowerbeds to create a cheerful spring garden. Wait until the foliage dies down before mowing to ensure that the bulbs have absorbed the nutrients they need to flower again the following year. (See also **Lawn care**)

Garden secrets

Money-saving storage
Recycle old tights and stockings as useful containers for bulbs that need to be stored over winter. Knot them between bulbs and groups of bulbs. They can be hung from hooks in the shed. Not only is this convenient but the synthetic fibres in the material will deter attacks by rodents.

Growing know-how

Bulb power
Although when first purchased bulbs are a powerhouse of energy with their embryo flower buds in place just waiting to burst into growth, they still benefit from feeding. Traditionally, bulbs have been fed after flowering but recent experiments indicate that better results come from applying a liquid fertiliser frequently – from the emergence of the flower buds until the tips of the leaves start to yellow. Use one rich in potash, such as a liquid tomato feed.

Avoiding empty spaces
As a general rule, a bulb should be buried to a depth of at least twice its height. There are exceptions, however: lilies that have roots on their stems must be buried three or four times deeper than their height, while *Lilium candidum* – the white madonna lily – is planted almost on the soil surface. When planting a bulb, make sure that it does not become lodged at an angle against the side of the planting hole as this may create an air pocket round the bulb. To grow properly the base of the bulb must be in contact with the soil. (See also **Lilies**)

Stakes before planting
To avoid bruising or splitting bulbs, insert stakes for weighty flowers, such as lilies, before you plant the bulbs. If the bulbs are small, mark the planting area of each with a twig or small stake.

Easy ways to lift
Instead of planting your bulbs individually in the soil, plant them directly into a colander or cheap plastic box with holes drilled in the bottom and sides. Fill the box or colander with soil removed from the hole where you want the bulbs to flower, adding compost. Place it into the hole, with its top level with the surrounding earth. After the bulbs have flowered and the leaves start to yellow, lift out the improvised basket and store it ready for

'replanting' next year. An alternative quick and easy method of lifting bulbs that need storing over winter is to line the planting hole with wire netting, angling the edges of the material towards the surface of the ground, before planting the bulbs on top. When it is time to store your bulbs, simply pull the two edges of the netting gently together and lift up.

Layered effect
Because bulbs contain all the nutrients that the plants need to flower, they can be grown in any medium that provides anchorage. For a decorative effect, plant some bulbs closely together in a glass container filled with alternate layers of sand, marbles, compost and gravel. Keep the base filled with water.

Saving energy
Always deadhead flowers when they fade in order to conserve the energy of the bulbs for next year's display.

Garden secrets

Keeping mice away
If you are worried that mice may get at your bulbs, lay wire netting with a 1.3cm (½in) mesh above the bulbs. Mothballs placed near the bulbs when planting them can also be a good deterrent against mice.

Conventional storage
When storing bulbs in open wooden boxes, keep them in layers of dry peat, sand or sawdust, making sure the bulbs do not touch each other. Some gardeners think it is best to keep delicate bulbs, such as lilies, in cold ashes from wood fires. Pour and spread the ashes slowly to avoid creating clouds of dust.

Butterflies

Grow a butterfly nursery

Butterflies will be encouraged to breed in your garden if there is a supply of food plants for their caterpillars. Most butterflies will lay their eggs only on plants that are in full sun, so if you hope to have a garden of beautiful butterflies, such as small tortoiseshells, peacocks, red admirals and commas, provide them with generous clumps of stinging nettles in the sun. (See also panel, below)

Live and let live

Bear in mind that when you create a butterfly-friendly environment in your garden, you are also issuing an invitation to butterflies to lay eggs. These will become plant-eating caterpillars. For example, cabbage white butterflies, which you may enjoy seeing flit about in your garden, produce caterpillars that feed on brassicas and nasturtiums. A possible solution is to plant so many cabbages and nasturtiums that you can spare a few to share with the caterpillars. Luckily, most other caterpillars are not excessively greedy. At worst, they munch a few leaves without doing much damage – a small price to pay for the pleasure of the decorative, transient presence of butterflies in your garden.

Growing the right plants

Make sure you grow the sort of plants that attract butterflies to your garden (see panel, right). If you want to encourage more butterflies, note which plants are visited by them during summer and grow more of these plants the following year.

Showy blooms

Butterflies are attracted by purple, orange, yellow and red flowers. Remember that nectar is more accessible to a butterfly in single than in double blooms – some of which may produce no nectar – and that butterflies find it hard to sip from flowers that hang downwards or have ruffled petal edges.

Fluttering over windfalls

While plants that contain a rich store of nectar are often the main food source for butterflies, fallen fruits can be just as enticing. Leave windfall apples, pears and plums where they have landed. Butterflies, particularly red admirals, will turn up in large numbers to feast on the fermenting fruit.

Big and beautiful

The name 'aristocrat' covers the largest and most striking butterflies in Britain, including the painted lady, peacock and red admiral.

Keeping track of butterflies

If you are interested in monitoring butterflies in your area, the Institute of Terrestrial Ecology runs a scheme in which amateur naturalists can send in weekly counts of butterflies they see while on their regular walks. The Institute's address is: Monks Wood, Abbots Ripton, Huntingdon PE17 2LS; the telephone number is 01487 773381.

The first 'butterfly'

Grow ivy to provide the brimstone butterfly with a hibernation site. The word butterfly is thought to have been used originally to denote only this butter-coloured flying insect, before it acquired its 'brimstone' forename and butterfly became a more general term. The brimstone may be the first and last butterfly to be seen each year as it can be in flight from February until November. It drinks nectar from wild flowers and its caterpillars are dependent for their food on buckthorn and alder buckthorn.

Make the right choice

Food plants for caterpillars

Below are some of the plants where female butterflies like to lay eggs.

Plant	Butterfly
Alder buckthorn	Brimstone
Bird's-foot trefoil	Common blue, dingy skipper
Cock's foot	Large skipper
Cuckoo flower	Green-veined white, orange tip
Garlic mustard	Orange tip
Grasses	Meadow brown, gatekeeper, ringlet, small heath, small skipper, speckled wood
Holly	Holly blue
Hop	Comma
Horseshoe vetch	Dingy skipper
Sorrel	Small copper
Stinging nettle	Comma, painted lady, peacock, red admiral, small tortoiseshell
Thistle (spear or marsh)	Painted lady

Make the right choice

Plants to attract butterflies

Encourage butterflies with plants that produce nectar throughout the year.

Season	Plant
Spring	Alyssum saxatile, Aubrietia, Erysimum (wallflower), Matthiola (stock), Primula (polyanthus, primrose), Prunus spinosa (blackthorn), Viola odorata (sweet violet)
Early summer	Arabis, Armeria (thrift), Dianthus (pink), Iberis (candytuft), Lunaria (honesty), Myosotis (forget-me-not), Scabiosa (scabious)
Late Summer	Buddleja, Hyssopus (hyssop), Lavandula (lavender), Lonicera (honeysuckle), Nepeta (catmint), Verbena
Autumn	Aster novae-angliae (Michaelmas daisy), Sedum spectabile (ice plant), Solidago (golden rod)

Cabbages

Early care
Transplant cabbage seedlings from the nursery bed to the vegetable garden once they have sprouted between three and five leaves. Prevent early dehydration by dipping the roots in water before planting.

Deep planting
Plant cabbages deeply, covering the first two leaves. New roots will grow from the buried stems, resulting in more stable plants.

Small and tender
To have early spring greens before your spring cabbages have hearted up, set the plants 10cm (4in) apart and cut two out of every three from April onwards, leaving the remaining plants at 30cm (12in) intervals. They will develop hearts later in spring.

Cool storage
Handle winter cabbages carefully when lifting for storage. The roots can be left intact or, if it is more convenient, they can be cut leaving a stump of about 15cm (6in). Store at a temperature close to freezing, in a place where they will not dry out. Laying them on slatted shelves or on a layer of straw in a garage or unheated shed is usually suitable.

A splash of colour
Brighten up the winter vegetable garden with decorative varieties, such as the blue-green F1 'Rodeo', or Savoy cabbages with their attractive foliage. In autumn and winter, non-hearting, ornamental cabbages make a colourful contrast, and you can eat their tender young leaves.

Keeping pests at bay
Cabbage butterflies may look pretty but their caterpillars can cause enormous damage to your brassicas. Help to keep them away by planting aromatic herbs, such as camomile, mint, rosemary, sage and thyme – butterflies hate the smell of these – or by covering the plants with muslin or horticultural fleece. Biological control methods are also effective. (*See also* **Biological controls, Caterpillars**)

Prevent club root
Club root, the cabbage's worst enemy, is a serious disease that causes swollen roots and yellow, wilting leaves. Help to prevent it by

Garden secrets

A second harvest
When harvesting a spring or summer crop, use a sharp knife to cut each cabbage at the base of the head, then make a cross-shaped notch 1cm (⅜in) deep in the top of the stump. A healthy crop of greens will grow. Once harvested, pull up the stumps, pulverise them with a hammer, discard the roots, then add them to the compost heap.

Make the right choice

Know your cabbages
With all the varieties available it is easy to have fresh cabbages all year. Note sowing dates on seed packets to ensure continuity and correct timing.

Season	Name	Description	Ready
Summer crops	Derby Day	Round head, dark green	June to October
	Golden Acre	Round head, good flavour	June to October
	Greyhound	Conical head, medium size	June to October
	F1 Hispi	Conical head, crisp	May to October
	F1 Sherwood	Slow to run to seed, disease resistant	June to October
Autumn and winter crops	F1 Minicole	Small, good for small plots	September to January
	F1 Tundra	Very hardy, savoy/white cabbage cross	November to March
	F1 Savoy King	Vigorous growth, good flavour	November to March
	January King Hardy	Flat, round heads last well	November to March
Spring crops	F1 Excel	Compact, good mini-veg variety	April to May

ensuring that lime levels in the soil are high. Test the soil, using a kit from a garden centre, and add lime, according to the advice on the packet, to bring the pH up to at least 7. Rotate crops to ensure that brassicas are never grown on the same plot more than once in four years and ensure that drainage is good. In addition, remove weeds of the crucifer family, such as shepherd's purse, and flowers such as stocks and wallflowers, which are susceptible to club root. (See also **Acid soil, Soil analysis, Vegetable gardens**)

Pick Chinese cabbage seedlings
Sow a fast-growing variety of Chinese cabbage and pick the seedlings about four weeks later. The stems will regrow if you cut the leaves 2.5cm (1in) above ground level.

Cultivate tender hearts
White, tender hearts will develop in taller varieties of Chinese cabbages if you hold the leaves together with elastic bands.

See also **Vegetable gardens**

Cacti and succulents

Growing from seed
In spring, sow cacti in a tray of moist but well-drained seed compost. Place the tray in a warm, semi-shaded place until the seeds germinate, then move it to a sunny room and keep the soil moist. After a year, pot the cacti in cactus compost or in a mixture of equal quantities of grit, peat or coir and leafmould.

Give cacti a cold spell
A cold period helps to induce flowering in many cacti. Keep them in a light, frost-free, dry place throughout the winter, then begin to feed and water them in March or April. In June, when the weather is warm, the cacti can be put outside.

Growing know-how

Where do they come from?
Some cacti and succulents originate from areas of semi-desert, while others come from tropical forests. Each requires different growing conditions, so it is important to know the backgrounds of your plants.

Habitat	Origin	Examples	Treatment
Desert plants	American semi-deserts	*Cereus, Mammillaria, Opuntia, Rebutia*	Plenty of sun. South or western window ledge. Little or no water between October and March
Forest plants	Forests of Central and South America. Grown among trees	*Epiphyllum, Rhipsalidopsis, Schlumbergera*	A bright but sunless situation, which is shaded during the hottest part of the day. A north or east-facing window ledge is ideal

All-round light
Cactus growth can be distorted if the plant receives insufficient or uneven light. To ensure that your plant keeps its shape, place it on a sunny window ledge and give it half a turn every few days.

Winter watering
Many cacti and succulents need little or no water in winter and should be watered only when the compost begins to shrink from the sides of the pot. In summer, both cacti and succulents should be watered thoroughly whenever the top few centimetres of compost have dried out.

Water with care
When watering a cactus, avoid splashing water onto the plant because it leaves unsightly marks. Stand the container in a shallow basin of water until the compost is saturated, then remove it from the basin and let it drain. The greatest danger to a cactus is overwatering. A basic rule is to check water requirements once a week in summer and once a month in winter, or less if the average room temperature is below 10°C (50°F).

Select the right pot
When repotting, the new pot should be big enough to allow room for root growth. Its diameter should be equal to that of the plant, including its spines. If the plant is columnar, allow for a pot diameter that is equal to half the height of the plant. Never use a pot that is too large.

New cacti from leaves

Cacti that have leaves can be propagated without difficulty. Any healthy leaves that fall should root easily as long as you make sure that they are potted up immediately and watered well.

Growing know-how

Propagating a cactus

If your cactus is one such as *Opuntia*, that has branches or stems, detach one or two, using a sharp knife or razor blade. If it is the columnar type, take one or two 7.5cm (3in) slices from the top and leave them in a warm, dry place until the cut surfaces have dried out. Then insert the stems or slices into damp, sandy compost that consists of one part of potting compost and three parts of sand or grit. Take care that the cuttings are inserted bottomside down. Columnar cacti from which slices have been cut will grow branches that will supply further material for propagation.

Repotting brittle cacti

Succulents, such as crassulas, echeverias and sedums, can be difficult to repot because they are brittle and can snap easily when being moved. This can be avoided if you stop watering the plant a week or so before you intend to repot it. As the lack of moisture causes the plant's leaves to gradually crinkle and wilt, they will become more flexible and less likely to snap.

Protection from prickles

When you need to handle a cactus, to repot or move it, protect your hands from injury and prevent damage to the spines by wrapping a band of thickly folded newspaper round it.

Picking out spines

If spines do stick in your fingers when you are tending a cactus, remove them by applying a piece of adhesive tape to the area and then peeling it off again sharply. Alternatively, for really stubborn ones, use tweezers.

Top-heavy plants

Terracotta pots are heavier than plastic ones and provide a more stable base for cacti, which can become top-heavy – especially when the compost has dried out in winter. If your cactus is tall or heavy, before adding the potting compost, put a large pebble or other weight in the bottom of the pot. This will counterbalance the weight of the top growth and prevent the plant from toppling over.

Stop the mealybugs

White, woolly patches on your cactus mean that mealybugs have struck. These pests live underneath a covering of warm wool, sucking the sap and weakening the cactus. Kill them by spraying the plant with an insecticide recommended for house plants, but first check the label carefully for the manufacturer's instructions.

Christmas cactus

Flower buds on Christmas cacti begin to form as the days become shorter. If your Christmas cactus is to flower each year, it needs only 8 to 10 hours of light during autumn and early winter. If the plant is positioned near artificial light, move it each evening to an unlit room where the temperature does not fall below 16°C (60°F). Once it is in bud, however, avoid moving it frequently, as this will cause the newly formed buds to drop off.

Bud drop

A sudden drop in temperature, lack of water, or a sudden change in light levels can cause Christmas cacti to drop their buds before the flowers open. Keep them away from draughts and never put them next to the window behind the curtains at night. Water them well with tepid water whenever the surface of the

compost dries out, and avoid changing their position once the flower buds have formed.

Feed wisely

When feeding cacti, never use fertilisers that are rich in nitrogen, as they encourage foliage growth at the expense of flowers. Stimulate flowering by using a fertiliser that is rich in potash. A liquid tomato fertiliser is ideal.

Camellias

Growing camellias in limy soil

Although camellias are lime-haters, it is possible to grow them in slightly alkaline clay soils. Make the bed more suitable for growing camellias by adding flowers of sulphur at the rate of 136–271g per m² (4–8oz per sq yd). If your soil is very limy, create homes for the shrubs in pots, raised beds or trenches filled with leafmould or ericaceous compost. (*See also Chalky soil, Soil analysis*)

Cutting back

It is unnecessary to prune camellias, although straggly shoots may be shortened in April. In addition, should your camellia grow too large, cut back branches in early spring. The shrub will regenerate even from thick, leafless stems.

The key to success

Camellias flower best if they are mulched with well-rotted, lime-free organic matter every autumn. This not only provides a steady supply of nutrients to the plants, but also improves the soil and helps to prevent the plants from drying out in hot weather. (*See also **Mulching***)

Preventing frost damage

Camellias grown in pots can suffer during prolonged periods of frost because the roots of container-grown plants have less protection than those grown in the garden. In late autumn, transfer the pots to a protected place such as a light, airy porch or a cold greenhouse. If this is impossible, put the plants in a sheltered spot in the garden and wrap the containers overall in bubblewrap.

Successful sowing

Speed up the germination of camellia seeds by sowing them in autumn before the outer coat hardens. Alternatively, pour boiling water over the seeds to soften them. Leave them to soak for 24 hours while the water cools, then sow in ericaceous compost. Cover the compost with a layer of 3–6mm (⅛–¼in) grit and place in a cold frame. Prick out the seedlings when the first true leaves appear. Then prepare to wait – it may take seven years for them to flower.

Water, water everywhere

In summer, water camellias frequently to encourage budding. From September onwards, water them during dry periods. If possible, use rainwater from a butt, or fill the watering can from the tap and leave the water to stand for several hours.

Campanulas

Provide good drainage

Most dwarf perennial campanulas are alpines and need a well-drained soil. They may rot during winter if they are in heavy, wet ground. Plant them in gritty soil, at the edge of stony paths or in rock gardens.

Double display

Deadhead tall border campanulas when the flowers have faded, and water the plants generously to encourage a second blooming.

Divide and grow

Perennials, such as *Campanula glomerata* and *C. takesimana*, which have more than one crown can be divided in March, April or October. This is the only way to propagate the *C. persicifolia* varieties that do not come true from seed. Add some compost to the planting hole and spread some round the collar of the plant to promote growth.

Grand bouquets

Choose tall perennial campanulas to add height to flowerbeds. *Campanula lactiflora* 'Loddon Anna', has pale pink flowers; *C. latifolia* has big, violet-blue or white bells, and *C. persicifolia* has open, blue or white bells close to the stem.

Tall campanulas These give height to beds and borders and are delightful in bouquets.

Carrots

Fast-growing carrots

Stump-rooted varieties of carrots, such as 'Amsterdam Forcing 3' and 'Nantes 2', can be sown in late July and early August. They will yield a tender harvest of young roots in November and December. Cover the rows with cloches in October to protect them from the worst of the winter weather.

Varieties for most soils

Carrots grow best in deep, light loam but there are varieties that will suit most soils. 'Chantenay Red Cored' and F1 'Honey Snack' are medium-sized and excellent choices for stony or heavy soils; 'Paris Market' or 'Parmex', with almost round roots, will suit shallow, heavier soils.

Growing in heavy soils

A series of ridged beds will enable you to grow a crop of medium-sized carrots in even the heaviest of clay. First, break up the soil with a fork and work in some well-rotted organic matter. Then rake the soil into a series of ridges about 10cm (4in) high and no more than 30–40cm (12–16in) wide, so that you can work on them without standing on the soil. Alternatively, provide a deep bed system for the whole vegetable garden so that other crops will benefit from the improved drainage. (See also **Deep beds**)

Easy lifting

Flooding the carrot patch lessens the effort of harvesting. In a light soil, some say that gently pushing carrots into the ground will break root hairs, making lifting trouble-free.

Deterring carrot fly

Carrot fly maggots wreak havoc on carrot roots, so it is essential to prevent infestation. Grow the carrots under horticultural fleece, fine-mesh anti-insect nets or old net curtains. Make sure that the crop is well protected by burying the edges of the covers in the soil. Alternatively, erect a 61cm (2ft) high barrier of clear polythene round the carrots. The barrier prevents the low-flying carrot fly from gaining access to the bed. Water the crop before and after thinning out. The varieties 'Fly Away', 'Resistafly' and 'Sytan' have some resistance to attack.

Good companions

Grow aromatic plants such as garlic and onions next to your carrots. Carrot flies will be confused by the smells and may miss the crop. (See also **Companion plants, Rosemary**)

Outsmart the fly

The year's first generation of carrot flies hatches in early June. The maggots spend their first months feeding on, and destroying, the tender roots of early carrots. By delaying sowing until late May or early June, the crop should escape attack because the seedlings will not develop until after the danger period.

Store in the ground

Store carrots in boxes, between layers of sand or pulverised bark, in a cool place. Alternatively, leave them in the ground and cut off the foliage or leave the tops to die down. Place strips of wire netting over the rows and cover with layers of dead leaves or straw. Lift the covers and dig up the carrots as required. They will keep until April or May.

See also **Vegetable gardens**

Growing know-how

What can go wrong

In the right conditions, carrots need little care. Incorporate well-rotted manure to improve soil structure before planting. Minor problems are often easily solved.

Symptoms	Causes and solutions
Forked roots	Your soil is too stony or contains too much unrotted manure or compost. Plant stump-rooted varieties or use a site that has been manured for a previous crop.
Short roots	You have not left enough space for carrots to grow. Next year, leave 2.5–5cm (1–2in) between each plant. Compacted soil may also be a cause.
Split roots	A dry spell has been followed by too much water. Apply a mulch and water regularly in dry weather.
A hard and woody heart	Not enough water or a variety unsuitable for late harvesting used. Water well; pull early carrots when they are young, while sowing maincrop varieties for later.
Lack of flavour	A variety for late planting has been sown too early.

Make the right choice

Know your carrots

Whatever the soil type, there are carrot varieties that can be grown.

Early varieties

Sow early carrot varieties in frames or under cloches in February and early March for pulling in June and July. Alternatively, sow outside in March, as soon as soil conditions allow, for harvesting in July. Continue to sow successively during spring for pulling later in summer.

Amsterdam Forcing 3 The earliest. Good for greenhouse borders, frames, cloches, or in the open

Early Nantes 5 Old favourite, good for successional sowing

Parmex Round rooted, ideal for shallow soil. Can be grown in window boxes or containers

Dual-purpose varieties

These varieties can be pulled young for eating or left in the ground to mature for storage. Sow dual-purpose varieties from March to May.

F1 Artemis Can be sown to produce baby carrots from mid-July and more mature roots from August to April

F1 Sugarsnax 54 Exceptionally sweet, good disease resistance

F1 Favor Sweet and juicy, can be grown at high density as mini-veg

Maincrop varieties

Sow maincrop carrots in May and early June for eating or storing in autumn

Autumn King 2 Vita Longa Large, stump-rooted variety, good for storing in the ground

F1 Harlequin Nantes-type, roots in a mixture of purple, orange, yellow and white

F1 Kingston Large, long roots, stores well and good for show bench

Caterpillars

Birth control

When removing caterpillars from your plants, look for clusters of eggs on the undersides of leaves and destroy them before they hatch into a second generation of caterpillars.

Biological power

Deal with caterpillars safely by spraying susceptible plants, such as brassicas and nasturtiums, with a lethal bacterium, *Bacillus thuringiensis*. It destroys caterpillars but is harmless to people, pets and insects.

Bird sanctuary

Encourage birds to come to your garden by putting nesting boxes in trees where they are inaccessible to cats. The birds and their young will eat insect pests, including caterpillars, by the thousand.

Cats

A garden for your cat

Make a special place in the garden where your cat can play or bask in the sun by allocating a raised corner of the flowerbed to its favourite plants. Try growing catmint, Chinese gooseberries and mugwort; cats love the smell of all these plants.

Discourage soiling

A cat will soil freshly dug, bare earth in preference to any other type of garden terrain, so keep borders and flowerbeds well covered with flowers and foliage.

Seedling protection

To protect seedlings and young plants from the attentions of cats, cover the beds with arches of protective wire mesh. Rusty wire will do, as it will be less noticeable against the soil. A covering of horticultural fleece, wire hoops draped with netting, or small barricades of twigs or pea sticks are alternative means of protection. Use sheets of chicken wire to cover

Garden secrets

Detestable deterrents

Cats hate wet soil, so water your flowerbeds last thing at night. They also dislike the smell of citrus peel, camphor and eucalyptus, so sprinkle some orange or lemon rinds or a few mothballs, or even some old tea bags sprinkled with eucalyptus oil, round the garden. Pay particular attention to areas where cats congregate.

the flowerbed and, as the seedlings develop, they will grow up through the holes. Prunings from prickly shrubs, such as holly or mahonia, make good deterrents. Lay clippings of these round the seed bed or between the rows.

Blocking tactics

When ventilating a tunnel cloche, block the open ends with pieces of wire or plastic mesh to prevent cats from using it as a warm and sheltered sleeping place. You may also find it useful to construct a rough wooden frame covered with mesh that can be used to block the open door of a greenhouse or the top of a cold frame.

Guard your pots

To deter cats from scratching in the soil in your pots, cover the surface with pebbles or damp moss.

Cauliflowers

Hardening off seedlings

It is essential to harden off February and March greenhouse-grown cauliflower seedlings before planting out. A sudden change in temperature can cause severe stress to the plants and result in stunted growth. At least two weeks before planting out, transfer the seedlings to a cold frame and keep it closed for the first few days, covering it with old carpet, sacking or other insulating material at night if there is any risk of frost. After that, you can open the frame during the warmest part of the day, gradually increasing the length of time it is open.

Put your foot down

If the mature vegetables are to form compact curds, cauliflower seedlings must be planted in firm ground. Unless the soil was dug over in winter and has had time to settle, dig it before planting and tread it down firmly by shuffling over the bed twice, the second time at right angles to the first, and pressing down the soil with your heels. Rake the ground gently to level it before planting, and firm the soil round each seedling after planting.

Root room

Use a trowel or dibber to make planting holes for the seedlings. If the soil is heavy, a trowel is preferable because a dibber will compact the sides of the holes, restricting root development.

Keep them warm and watered

Newly planted cauliflower seedlings must be watered well in dry weather. If a sudden drop in temperature is forecast before they have had a chance to establish themselves in their new positions, cover them with cloches to keep them growing well. When the weather improves and the temperature rises, the cloches can be removed.

A dose of soot

The application of a little soot round each plant will help the soil to absorb more heat from the sun while providing a little extra nitrogen to boost growth. Never use fresh soot for this purpose as it is caustic and will burn the plants' stems. Store it under cover for at least six months before use.

Lack of boron

If your cauliflowers have underdeveloped brown curds, stunted brittle leaves and brown stems these may be indications that your soil is either acid or deficient in boron. If the pH of your soil is less than 6.5, add lime to bring it up to the correct level. This will release the boron that becomes locked up in acid soil, and inaccessible to the plants. If the soil already has a pH of 6.5 or over, it may be deficient in boron and should be treated with an application of borax at the rate of 30g per m² (1oz per sq yd) before planting next season. Mixing the borax with a small quantity of sand in a bucket will make it easier to sprinkle evenly on the soil. (*See also* **Acid soil, Soil analysis**)

Make the right choice

A succession of cauliflowers

Choose the varieties listed here and you will be able to cut fresh cauliflowers from March until November. Divide a few heads into florets and pop them into the freezer to bridge the gap between the autumn and spring harvests.

Season	Sowing and harvesting times	Varieties
Early summer crops	Sow under cloches in early October and thin the seedlings to about 5cm (2in) apart, or sow in February in a propagator. Prick out the seedlings into pots and plant out 51cm (20in) apart each way in late April. Cut in June and early July.	All the Year Round, F1 Gypsy, F1 Mayflower, F1 Avalanche, F1 Nessie
Summer crops	Sow in a seedbed under cloches or in a sheltered spot in March. Plant out in mid May, spacing the plants 51cm (20in) apart each way. Cut in August and early September.	All the Year Round, Andes, F1 Cheddar (orange curd), F1 Graffiti (violet curd)
Early autumn crops	Sow in a seedbed in late April, thin to 5cm (2in) apart and plant out 51cm (20in) apart each way in mid June. Cut in late August and September.	F1 Candid Charm (can be grown as a mini-veg), F1 Clapton, Avisto, all Romanesco varieties
Autumn crops	Sow in a seedbed in mid May, thin to 5cm (2in) apart and plant out 64cm (25in) apart in late June. Cut in October and November.	All Romanesco varieties, F1 Moby Dick, Violet Queen, Igloo
Winter/spring crops	Sow in a seedbed outside in late May, thinning to 7.5–10cm (3–4in). Plant out 75cm (30in) apart each way in mid July. Cut from March to June.	Walcheren Winter 3-Armado, F1 Haddin, F1 Deakin, Purple Cape

Sun shield

Protect cauliflower curds from scorching in the summer sun by covering them with a few outer leaves. To do this, pull the leaves upwards round the curds and clip the leaf tips together with a clothespeg. Alternatively, use a piece of aluminium foil to protect the curds, holding it down with stones at the corners.

Keep them firm

Once harvested, cauliflowers will keep for up to three weeks if their roots have most of the soil shaken off and they are then hung upside-down in a cool frost-free place. Alternatively, the curds can be separated and kept for up to a week in polythene bags in the salad compartment of the refrigerator, or blanched and stored in the freezer until required.

Celeriac

Sowing seeds

Sow celeriac, also known as turnip-rooted celery, indoors in small pots of seed compost in February or March. The seeds will take two weeks or more to germinate at a temperature of 15°C (59°F) and, once planted out, need between 16 and 20 weeks to develop.

Lifting the crop

Harvest the roots before hard frosts set in and store them in boxes of sand. In milder areas, they can be left in the ground and covered with straw, but care should be taken to protect them against slugs.

Celery

Tender stems

Make sure that trench celery is tender and well blanched by shading the stems from the sun. When they are 30–38cm (12–15in) high, encase the stems of the plants with cardboard or black plastic tied with string, leaving only the leafy tips exposed. Alternatively, you can save yourself the trouble by buying the self-blanching green or golden varieties, including 'Golden Self-Blanching 3', 'Greensnap', 'Lathom Self-Blanching' or 'Victoria'.

To blanch or not to blanch

Self-blanching golden and green celery varieties are easier to grow than trench celery because they do not require earthing up. They are planted on a flat bed, and there is no need to dig a trench. However, these varieties are not frost-hardy and can be cropped between August and October only. Trench celery is fully hardy and is harvested from October to February. The extra effort involved in its production often results in plants that are larger and crisper than the self-blanching golden and green varieties.

Beware of the celery fly

Newly planted celery, both trench and self-blanching varieties, is susceptible to attack from celery-fly maggots. Examine the plants regularly for signs of these pests. Pick off and burn infested leaves as soon as they appear and spray plants with malathion. Grow celery alongside parsnips and celeriac as these vegetables, too, can be attacked by celery-fly maggots. All three can be treated together.

All year round

Grow a clump of cutting celery or 'Par-Cel' in the herb garden. This tall, hardy biennial produces a large quantity of very tasty leaves. These can be added to soups and stews or chopped finely and sprinkled on salads or cheese dishes.

Chalky soil

Test for chalk

Chalky soil is pale in colour, finely textured and often rich in pebbles, flint or pieces of chalk. If you think that the soil in your garden is chalky, you can test it by dropping a little vinegar onto a dry clod. If the vinegar fizzes, the soil is chalky.

Weeds and trees

If indicator plants, such as clovers, Clematis vitalba (old man's beard) and small scabious, are common in your area and there are trees such as native juniper and Sorbus aria (whitebeam), it is likely that you have a chalky soil. The absence of popular lime-haters, such as camellias, heathers and rhododendrons, is further confirmation that your soil may have a pH of more than 7.

Make the right choice

Two types of celery – all a question of taste

By weighing up the pros and cons of both types of celery, you will be able to decide if the superior taste of trench celery merits the extra effort involved in its production.

Type	Description	Good varieties
Self-blanching golden and green celery	Frost-tender, mild-flavoured varieties that do not require earthing up	Golden Self-Blanching 3, Greensnap. Lathom Self-Blanching, Victoria
Trench celery	Hardy white, pink or red varieties that need to be grown in a trench and earthed up	Giant Red, Giant White, Hopkins Fenlander, Martine, Solid Pink, Solid White, Unrivalled Pink

Make the right choice

Plants for chalky soil

Make the most of your chalky soil by selecting from this list of lime-tolerant plants, which includes something for all areas and situations in the alkaline garden.

Alpines
Anthemis, Arabis, Dianthus, Gypsophila, Saxifraga, Thymus (creeping varieties)

Annuals and biennials
Campanula, Cheiranthus, Chrysanthemum, Convolvulus tricolor, Dianthus, Echium, Nemesia, Papaver, Petunia, Phacelia, Rudbeckia, Salvia, Verbena

Bulbs
Allium, Crocus, Cyclamen, Galanthus, Lilium candidum, Muscari

Climbers and wall shrubs
Ceanothus, Chimonanthus, Clematis, Forsythia, Lathyrus, Lonicera

Ground-cover plants
Bergenia, Campanula, Cotoneaster, Euonymus, Hypericum, Sarcococca, Vinca

Perennials
Campanula, Dianthus, Dicentra, Kniphofia, Linaria, Lupinus, Paeonia, Scabiosa

Shrubs
Buxus, Cornus mas, Elaeagnus, Hebe, Mahonia, Sambucus, Viburnum, Weigela

Trees
Cedrus, Crataegus, Fagus, Malus, Populus alba, Prunus, Sorbus

Succeeding with lime

It is possible to neutralise a limy soil by reducing its pH value. The process requires the application of very large amounts of peat or a sulphur treatment, either of which will involve time, trouble and expense. Neither treatment will make a permanent change to the soil and either one will need to be repeated on a regular basis if the new pH is to be maintained. It is much easier to make the best of what you have, and grow lime-tolerant plants, such as beeches, box, campanulas, clematis, cotoneasters, crab apples, dianthus, forsythias, gypsophilas, honeysuckles and viburnums.

Cabbages before celery

If your soil is shallow, do not plant vegetables such as celeriac and celery, which need a rich, moist soil. Plant beans, brassicas, peas and salad crops instead. Club root, the serious disease that infects the cabbage family, is rarely a problem on chalky soils.

Stony soil

Work only the top layer of very stony soils. Digging any deeper will bring more stones to the soil surface.

Protect roots

Take care that the roots of shallow-rooted plants grown in chalky soils do not become exposed in repeated rains or freeze-thaw cycles. Pack soil round each plant's collar in order to provide protection.

Root-forking problems

The stones in chalky soil may cause root vegetables to fork, though this does not affect the taste of the vegetables. Remove any large stones when you are digging over the plot to minimise the problem but you will not be able to eradicate it completely. Another solution is to grow stump-rooted varieties.

Lime-haters on alkaline soil

If your soil is so alkaline that growing lime-hating plants in the garden is impossible, use large containers filled with ericaceous compost or lime-free soil. Stand them in partial shade and make sure that they never dry out.

Autumn planting

Unless a plant is recommended for spring planting only, try to plant in autumn rather than spring. This will give the plants time to root firmly before the summer drought.

Raising the ground

Create a raised bed to grow lime-haters such as azaleas, camellias and rhododendrons. Use wood or bricks to build the walls, making them at least 30cm (12in) higher than the surrounding soil. Put a thick layer of lime-free drainage material in the bottom, cover with landscape fabric, available from garden centres, and fill with ericaceous compost.

Trench tactic

As an alternative to the raised-bed, dig a trench 40–51cm (16–20in) deep, add a layer of drainage material such as lime-free grit or small stones and cover it with landscape fabric, available from garden centres. Cover the sides of the trench with plastic sheeting to prevent any seepage from the surrounding soil. Fill the prepared trench with lime-free soil or ericaceous compost, plant your lime-hating plants and water with lime-free water. Collect rainwater for the lime-haters in your garden, because your tap water is likely to be as alkaline as your soil. Alternatively, boil tap water and leave it to cool before watering.

Organic aids

Add well-rotted compost, leafmould or manure, liberally and frequently, to a chalky soil. Bulky organic matter helps the soil to retain nutrients, but it decomposes quickly.

Chard

Chard and spinach

Spinach is an annual vegetable which comes only in a green-leaved form. Leaf beets, often used as alternatives to spinach, belong to the beetroot family. They include chard – Swiss chard, which is also known as sea kale beet or silver chard, and ruby chard. Chard is biennial and therefore lasts longer than spinach before running to seed. The stalks are either red or white, and these can be eaten separately from the leaves. Chard leaves are less tender than those of spinach.

A full harvest

Pick only one or two leaves at a time from each plant to encourage the growth of new foliage throughout the summer. Be generous with applications of well-rotted compost, as more Swiss chard will be produced if the plants are fed regularly.

Garden ornament

Ruby chard's distinctive red leaf stalks make it a colourful and unusual addition to the vegetable garden. Assemble an eye-catching display by growing it with nasturtiums or decorative vegetables, such as ornamental cabbages. Chard also looks attractive when grown alongside purple basil.

Easy weed control

To keep weeds at bay, grow Swiss chard through holes in black polythene. Space the plants at 38cm (15in) intervals.

Pick by hand

Always use your fingers to pick the leaves from Swiss chard. Cutting the leaves with a knife may damage the central crown and prevent the plants from re-growing.

Chemicals

Stop and think

Garden chemicals of all kinds should be treated with great care and respect, used strictly in accordance with the manufacturer's instructions and only as a last resort. Before you reach for the weedkillers, insecticides, fungicides or fertilisers, ask yourself if they are absolutely necessary. Very often there may be equally effective, or better, ways to deal with the problem that do not require the use of garden chemicals.

Cause or effect

If your plants lack vigour, it is likely that the soil is poor and unable to provide a balanced diet. A fast-acting chemical fertiliser will make the plants look healthy but unless you deal with the cause of the problem, their vitality will be short-lived and they will soon display the symptoms of starvation. Enriching the soil regularly with well-rotted organic matter will improve soil structure and increase moisture and nutrient retention. With fungal infections, too, it is preferable, having removed and destroyed the affected parts of plants, to deal with the causes before resorting to chemical treatment.

Weigh up the pros and cons

Dandelions on the lawn can be removed immediately with the aid of a small weeding tool. They take much longer to disappear if treated with a weedkiller, and you may have the inconvenience of having to keep children and pets off the lawn while the chemical dries. Spraying cabbages with an insecticide is an effective way of getting rid of caterpillars but this may mean waiting for several days before it is safe to harvest and eat the vegetables. If you want to eat the cabbages right away, remove the caterpillars by hand.

Sensible spraying

Most insecticides kill all insects, helpful and harmful alike. To minimise risk to beneficial creatures such as ladybirds, lacewings, bees and beetles, spray in the early morning or late evening when fewer of them are active. Spray only when there is little or no wind, and restrict treatment to plants where a pest or disease is visible. Use a small sprayer, and mix no more chemical than is required to do the job. If there is any left over, spray it onto a piece of bare ground or a gravel path. Do not leave it in the sprayer for another time and do not use it on plants that do not require treatment.

To each their own

Labels on containers state clearly which pests or diseases the contents are intended to treat and the plants for which they are suitable. Always match the treatment to both the problem and the plant. Failure to do this could result in an unsolved problem and a damaged or dead plant.

Added detergent

Most manufacturers add detergents to their products to help them to adhere to the leaves. There is, therefore, no need to add more and risk upsetting the carefully balanced formula. Doing so could render the spray ineffective or could cause severe damage to plants.

Hazardous hoarding

Most garden chemicals have a relatively short shelf life, so check all bottles and packages from time to time and consult your local council's environmental health department about any you no longer need: their details will be online or in the telephone directory. Never pour chemicals down the drain. Do not use empty chemical containers for storing other things and never store chemicals in containers other than those in which they were supplied. Keep them well away from children and animals.

Lethal mixtures

Never mix different chemicals, either in the sprayer or by spraying the same plant with a second chemical immediately after the first. Allow a day for the first spray to dry. Where the label states that the chemical may be mixed with another, follow the instructions to the letter. Use the mixture immediately, because the chemicals may be compatible for a short time only.

See also **Fertilisers, Fungicides, Insects**

See also Fertilisers, Fungicides, Insects

Make the right choice

Know your chemicals

When you are choosing a chemical remedy, consider its mode of action and the situation in which it is to be used.

Insecticides and fungicides
Contact action
The chemical comes into direct contact with the pest or germinating fungus spores. Effective against pests that chew.

Systemic action
Absorbed by the foliage and transported through the plant by the sap. Effective against sap-sucking pests and fungi.

Weedkillers
Non-residual contact action
This type kills only the foliage that it touches and is effective on annual weeds.

Non-residual systemic action
Absorbed through the leaves, this type is then passed to the roots. It is effective on annual and perennial weeds.

Residual
Applied to the soil and absorbed by roots. It can remain active for months. Good for paths and for clearing ground.

Selective
Used on lawns to kill broad-leaved weeds without harming grasses. Some kill grasses but not broad-leaved plants.

Cherries

Sizing down

Most sweet cherry trees can reach heights of 12m (40ft), making them too large for the average garden. If you like cherries but have a small garden, choose the sweet Stella Compact or an acid variety such as Morello, which has been grafted onto semi-dwarfing rootstock. Morello is self-pollinating: one tree will provide a good crop.

Tree in a tub

Growing a cherry tree in a tub will constrict its roots, which will help to keep the tree to a manageable size. Choose a container that has a height and width of at least 50cm (20in) and plant the young tree in John Innes No. 3 potting compost. Constricting the roots of any tree means you have to water frequently, especially in summer, to ensure that the compost never dries out.

Clear the way

Cherry trees will not tolerate competition for water. Plant your tree in a cleared patch, removing any weeds, plants or grass within 1.2–1.5m (4–5ft) of the trunk.

A substitute drinking place

Thirst is one of the main reasons that birds steal cherries. Positioning a birdbath or other container filled with water near the trees will help to save the crop. If the birds have a constant source of water to drink, they will eat less of your fruit.

Scaring birds away

Do not install bird-scaring devices before the cherries ripen, because they will lose their effect after a few days. Aluminium foil, noise-making string and balloons can help to frighten birds away. Vary the types of devices and their positions so that the birds do not have time to become accustomed to them.

Split cherries

Split cherries are a sign of overwatering following a period of drought. As soon as the fruits appear, water the tree liberally every two to three weeks to keep the roots uniformly moist at all times.

Make the right choice

Know your cherries

Choose a sweet cherry that may be eaten straight from the tree, or an acid variety for preserving in syrup.

Lapins Heavy cropper with large fruits

Morello Acid variety that can be trained on a north wall

Nabella Acid variety with dark fruits

Stella Popular choice; dark red fruits

Stella Compact Dwarfing form of Stella

Sunburst Early fruiter that has large, sweet cherries

Take care with netting

Covering a cherry tree with netting is the best way to discourage birds from pecking at the ripe fruits. But remember that the birds can become entangled in the netting. To minimise this danger remove the netting as soon as it has served its purpose.

A bad sign

It your cherry tree begins to shed its fruits before they are ripe, it may indicate an attack by plum sawflies. If grubs are present in the fruits, act quickly next season to prevent further infestation. Spray the tree with fenitrothion a week after petal fall and again three weeks later. (See also **Fruit drop**)

Bacterial canker

When the trunk or branches of a cherry tree develop flat lesions that exude a sticky gum, the cause is bacterial canker. This disease enters the tree at the points where the leaf stalks separate from the twigs, when leaves fall in autumn. In spring, the buds may fail to open and the affected branches may die back during the summer. Leaves may also be attacked. If so, they will develop circular brown spots that become holes. Severely affected branches and dead wood should be cut out and burned. Kill the bacteria, which live on the leaves, by spraying the affected trees with copper oxychloride or another copper fungicide in mid August, mid September and again in mid October.

Chervil

A year's leaves

For fresh leaves throughout the summer, sow chervil outside in a prepared bed four to six times in succession between March and August. During the rest of the year, grow chervil in 15cm (6in) pots on a sunny window ledge. Encourage healthy growth by watering often.

Early crop

To provide an early spring harvest, keep chervil covered with cloches throughout the winter or move potted plants to a cold frame.

Self-seeding crop

For a second year's crop of chervil, let a few plants run to seed in early autumn. Seeds will fall and germinate naturally and the plants will develop without attention. Prevent them from taking over the herb bed by removing unwanted seedlings.

Remove flowering stems

Chervil will produce young, tender leaves for a much longer period if the flowering stems are removed. This diverts the energy normally used in seed formation to the production of fresh young growth.

See also **Herbs for flavour and aroma pp. 144–8**

Chicory

Alternative chicory

Try the red variety (radicchio). Its flavour is not as strong as that of other types of chicory and it does not need blanching. Radicchio looks attractive in borders before it is ready to eat, and will add a touch of colour to salads. The crisp, inner leaves of the plant are less bitter than the outer foliage.

Winter warming to produce chicons

During November, lift roots of 'Witloof' types sown in March and April. Cut off the leaves 2.5–5cm (1–2in) above the root. Leave outside for a few days to expose them to frost. This helps to produce chicons (hearted heads of leaves) when the roots are forced. Plant up a few at a time in a soil-filled box. Cover the box with black polythene and keep it at a temperature of 18°C (64°F). After three to four weeks the chicons will be succulent and ready to eat.

'Rossa di Treviso'

This chicory is hardier than many other varieties, and is able to withstand all but the most severe weather. It does not form a heart and its slender, red leaves are very decorative.

Sugar-loaf chicory

Unlike traditional chicories, sugar-loaf chicory is not forced. If planted in a sunny place, it can be grown outdoors during winter and may be harvested several times when grown as a cut-and-come-again crop.

Surplus seedlings

If you have more chicory seedlings than you can accommodate in the vegetable garden, plant the leftovers 23cm (9in) apart in a clump in the flower border. In June and July you will be rewarded with tall, bright blue or pink flowers. Because these seedlings closely resemble dandelions they should be labelled so that they are not mistaken for weeds and removed inadvertently. To flower well, they need a fertile soil.

Children

A garden of their own

Encourage children to take up gardening by giving them a patch where they can cultivate easy-to-grow flowers and vegetables. Separate it from the rest of the garden by marking out walkways or putting up a small fence.

Bulb appeal

Young children are fascinated by the way that plants grow. A bulb, such as a hyacinth, growing in a pot on a child's window ledge may awaken an early interest in gardening.

A flowering den

Create a children's hideaway – and a bright addition to your garden – by making a teepee of annual climbing nasturtiums, convolvulus, runner beans or sweet peas. Use canes for the structure and involve your children by letting them sow these easy-to-grow annuals that can be trained over the teepee.

Gardening projects for children

For swift and spectacular results, put a 2.5cm (1in) layer of mung beans in a jar of water. Drain and seal with an old stocking. The beans

Garden secrets

Mini-greenhouses

Cut a large, transparent plastic bottle in half lengthways, make a few holes in one half, and fill it with seed compost. Help your child to sow a few seeds of tomatoes, or other plants that enjoy warmth, in the compost. Use the other half of the bottle as a roof which can be opened and closed as required. The seeds need warmth and sunlight to germinate, so place the mini-greenhouse on a window ledge where the child can watch the seedlings develop and feed and water them when necessary. When the first true leaves appear, pot up the seedlings in 8cm (3in) pots.

will produce moisture as they grow, so lay the jar on its side to aid drainage. Rinse the beans twice daily for three to six days, after which they should sprout. Salad cress can be sprouted on damp paper towels and tree seedlings grown from apple, lemon and orange pips.

A green-haired friend

Wash the shell from a boiled egg, fill it with potting compost and sprinkle some salad cress seeds on top. Using a felt-tipped pen, draw a face on the shell and stand it in an egg cup. After a few days, your children will be delighted to find they have a new friend with long, green hair.

Alyssum monogram

Ask your children to draw their initials in the soil, using a short length of cane or a small stick. They can then sow seeds of alyssum in the drills and watch as their initials appear, picked out in flowers.

Avocado tree

Children will enjoy growing plants from avocado stones. Insert three cocktail sticks just above the base of each stone, then suspend it over water with the base of the stone immersed. After several weeks, each stone should produce roots and a shoot, at

Small jobs For small hands: encourage your child to enjoy the garden with easy, 'fun' tasks.

which time it should be potted up. To encourage bushy growth, pinch out each growing tip when it is about 15cm (6in) high.

Floral giants

Your children and their friends can each plant a sunflower seed, then enjoy the excitement of waiting to see whose will grow the tallest. They will be intrigued to see their plants grow taller than themselves.

Save the grass

If your children have an inflatable paddling pool or plastic sandpit on the lawn, move it regularly and water the flattened area beneath to prevent the grass from dying. Never allow the pool or sandpit to stand on the same spot for more than a week. Solid surfaces provide more permanent homes for pools and sandpits and, to avoid damage to the polythene or plastic, they should be placed on a 5cm (2in) layer of sand.

Tools of the trade

For a young child, an old dessert spoon and ladle can double as a trowel and spade, while a washing-up-liquid bottle with extra holes can

Make the right choice

Make the right choice

Plants for children

Select colourful and fast-growing plants for children to enjoy.

Bulbs
Crocuses, daffodils, snowdrops and tulips

Flowers
Dwarf and climbing convolvulus, cosmos, love-in-a-mist, marigolds, nasturtiums, sunflowers and sweet peas

Vegetables
Courgettes, lettuces, ornamental gourds, radishes, runner beans, salad cress and greenhouse tomatoes

become a watering can. Turn a plastic bowl into a miniature garden, plant seeds in ice-cream cartons and make a mini-greenhouse out of a clear plastic egg box.

Sand play
To make a sandpit, dig a hole, add drainage material, cover the base and sides with tiles or bricks and pave the border. Alternatively, use planks or bricks to build a sandbox above the ground. Fill the pit or box with special playground sand, which is available from large toy shops and garden centres. Do not use orange-coloured builder's sand, which will stain clothes and can cause an allergy rash. Make a lid from polythene-covered plywood to protect the sand from rain and to keep out the neighbourhood cats.

A movable scarecrow
Children can help to make a scarecrow with a cane (for arms) tied across a pole and an old ball for a head. They can dress it up with colourful cast-off clothing and an old straw hat. The birds will not be scared off for long, so move the scarecrow from place to place in the garden and change its clothing periodically.

Chives

A whiff of garlic
Add a flavour of garlic to salads and cooked dishes, and some pretty, star-shaped, white flowers to the herb or vegetable garden, by growing garlic chives. They grow to about 46cm (18in) in height, which is a little taller than common chives, and come up every year. Their leaves are a little broader than those of the more familiar, pink-flowered, onion-flavoured variety of chives. Garlic chives can be grown from seed in the same way as common chives.

Avoid yellowing
Never harvest chives by plucking the tops of the leaves. Use a knife to cut off whole leaves at the base of the plant. As well as keeping the chives green and tender, this will encourage new leaves to grow. Fortnightly liquid feeding with a tomato fertiliser will help to stimulate new growth.

Keep them compact
Clumps of chives should be divided every three or four years, preferably in autumn. Lift the clumps with a fork. Each new portion should consist of not more than about six shoots. Add well-rotted manure or compost to the bed and replant the chives 30cm (12in) apart. If you divide the chives in summer, cut them right back to the base as this will help them to root.

Delicious and decorative
Make the most of the blue-green foliage and attractive pink flowers by planting some chives in your flower borders. The herb looks particularly attractive when alternated with campanulas or carnations.

Flowers from the herb garden
Both the flowers and leaves of chives may be used in the kitchen. If only the leaves are required, remove the flowers. If they remain on the plant, they will reduce the flavour of the leaves and will eventually turn to seed. This will reduce the number of young leaves available for culinary purposes.

Window cropping
A sunny window ledge in the kitchen is the perfect place for a pot of chives that will supply your needs throughout the winter. In September, pot up a clump from the garden in a 13cm (5in) pot of good potting compost. Be sure to keep the compost moist and feed the plant every three weeks with a liquid house-plant fertiliser.

The giant chive
If you are prepared to take the time and trouble to grow chives from seeds you will find a greater choice of varieties available than those offered for sale for planting out. *Allium schoenoprasum* var. *sibiricum* (giant chive) produces very large, purple flowers and, although it is less well flavoured than the familiar, pink-flowered, culinary *A. schoenoprasum*, it makes a striking addition to the flower border.

Fine leaves for fine garnishes
For something a little unusual in both garden and kitchen, look out for seeds of extra-fine-leaved chives. Their grass-like leaves are thinner than those of other chive varieties and they can be chopped finely for use in delicate fresh garnishes.

The rarest of all
True chive connoisseurs may wish to seek out the once popular, but now rarely seen, red-flowered chives. If you know a gardener who grows them, it is well worth asking for a clump. Separate it into smaller clumps and plant them out in a bed to which some well-rotted manure or compost has been added.

Britain's Changing Climate

Soil is a key factor in determining the vegetation of a country or locality. But even more important is climate, and that of Britain is neither as constant nor as temperate as is often thought.

There seems to be little doubt that Britain's climate is changing. Over the past 150 years, there has been a gradual increase in air temperatures right across the globe, with the past two decades showing the steepest rise. However, the year-on-year upward trend has not been constant — cold spells have hit most countries at different times.

Too cold for gardeners

The last Ice Age ended in Britain some 7,000 years ago and was succeeded by a warm period. As the ice and snow retreated, almost all of Scotland and much of northern England became forested. At that time, temperatures were much as they are today — or perhaps a little warmer.

About 2,500 years ago this warm spell came to an end. Colder weather again brought widespread snow and ice during the winter, and summers too were cooler. Trees largely disappeared from Scotland, and large parts of the north-west Highlands became peat bogs.

Too little Dry rivers, lakes and reservoirs have become a regular summer feature.

By the time of the Roman occupation, the British climate had altered once more, to one not unlike that of present-day southern Italy and France. This culminated in severe droughts during the Saxon era, gradually yielding to more temperate conditions, though as late as the 12th and 13th centuries, vineyards were flourishing as far north as York. During the next 200 years, however, a further reversal took place, bringing in its wake failed harvests and famine.

The 16th century again saw ice sheets covering much of Scandinavia, Iceland and Greenland, while in the Scottish Highlands snow lingered all year. With no more than a few breaks, this very cold weather persisted until 1850, and is known to climatologists today as the 'Little Ice Age'. From all these variations it is apparent that changes in climate are nothing new.

Knowing your local climate

Britain today has a relatively warm maritime climate — but one in which differences are nevertheless apparent from north to south and west to east. We know, for instance, that gardens do not particularly thrive on the cold, north-facing slopes of the Scottish Highlands or in places where drying, continental winds inhibit growth.

There are, too, some distinct climatic differences between regions, that dictate growing success or failure. For example, western districts are on average two or three times wetter in a 'normal' year than those in the

Too much Widespread flooding is by no means unusual due to Britain's recent pattern of mild, wet winters.

Hoar frost Sharp frosts are mostly short-lived today.

east. It is certainly warmer and, for the most part, less windswept in the south than in the north, while a garden's location in relation to sea and mountains are additional factors that govern gardening practice.

In short, your location in terms of soil type and regional climate is vital. Know and understand your local climate and you begin to understand exactly what will thrive in your garden. Even more importantly, you will also come to understand what will not grow, which will prevent you from making expensive mistakes.

The influence of a microclimate

Beyond regional climates there are two other meteorological factors that gardeners should take into consideration. The first is microclimate, the climate that affects a small area. It could refer to the climatic influences that prevail in a city or town, an estate or village, a road or street – or simply the confines of a particular garden. For a simple example, gardens facing south receive a greater share of sunshine and therefore tend to be warmer – especially during summer months. It follows that scorching and drought will occur more readily in south-facing gardens than in those facing east, west and, particularly, north.

Another example of a microclimate is that of a frost pocket. A well-known example is Rickmansworth in Hertfordshire, which lies on chalk soil surrounded by the higher ground of the Chilterns. On clear winter nights, cold air drops down into Rickmansworth from the surrounding hills so that by morning the town is three to four degrees colder than, say, neighbouring Watford. However, on bright days, the Rickmansworth frost pocket also traps incoming sunshine, so giving rise to a startling range of diurnal temperatures.

There are many kinds of microclimate, some so local that only the householder might be aware of them. A few, like extra moisture in the air near a garden pond, could be to the gardener's advantage; others, such as barren rain shadows caused by the house or a garden shed, could be a positive hindrance.

The long-range forecast

Whatever the importance of microclimates, it is Britain's general climate that provides the major influence on the performance of our gardens. Here the future is uncertain. The planet is definitely undergoing a warm phase, which may be natural, man-made, or a combination of the two. In Britain, our weather over recent years has tended to be more Mediterranean in style. Warm, dry summers and mild, wet winters have become more commonplace – especially in the past decade.

Statistical pointers would seem to indicate that the next decade will bring a greater than average occurrence of summer droughts and winter floods. Occasional violent storms and higher than average day and night temperatures will probably figure prominently. Add to that a general lack of winter snow (except in the Scottish Highlands) and the kind of climate we may find ourselves getting used to might be more familiar to the inhabitants of Bordeaux.

Arguments about global warming, the depletion of the ozone layer and the greenhouse effect will undoubtedly ebb and flow with every weather-related event over the next decade and beyond. Whatever the truth of the matter, if the omens are to be believed, then our climate is destined to take a route it has not followed since the 14th century. How gardeners – and garden centres – respond will provide the great horticultural excitements of the years ahead.

Winter wonderland In many parts of Britain, heavy snows that settle are no longer an annual event but usually just the stuff of Christmas cards.

Chlorosis

How to recognise chlorosis
The iron deficiency chlorosis turns leaves yellow or white, sometimes only between the veins, and is most noticeable on young leaves. It is usually caused by essential minerals being locked up in the soil. Chlorosis frequently affects acid-loving plants grown on chalky soil, but evergreen trees and shrubs in any type of soil may also develop it. In alkaline soil, applications of bark will help to alleviate the problem.

Give a boost
To release nutrients locked up in the soil, water with sequestered iron or apply a granular formulation.

Christmas trees

Naturally decorative
Decorating a tree in the garden at Christmas time creates a festive atmosphere that can be enjoyed not only by your family and your guests, but also by neighbours and passers-by. A traditional conifer is ideal, but any bare-branched, deciduous tree or large shrub is also suitable. Choose a tree of good shape that can be seen from both the street and the living room. Hang fairy lights decoratively from the branches but be sure that you are using the correct outdoor variety.

Many happy returns
If you buy a rooted tree to pot up in the garden after Christmas, put it into a pot, at least 25cm (10in) in diameter, filled with John Innes No. 3 compost. Gradually acclimatise the tree to the warmth of the house, and keep it inside for no longer than ten days. After Christmas, stand it outdoors, putting it into a shed or garage at night for a couple of weeks. Then bury the pot up to its rim in a sheltered, partially shaded spot. Next year, you can dig up the potted tree without disturbing its roots.

Warm gently
Just as a container-grown tree must be acclimatised to the cold before being returned to the garden after Christmas, so must it also

be allowed gradually to become accustomed to the indoor temperature it will be forced to withstand during the festive season. About three weeks before Christmas, lift the pot carefully from its place in the garden and bring it into a cool room such as a garage or outhouse, where there is some light.

Preventing needle drop
A centrally heated room can reduce your Christmas tree to a pathetic heap of needles long before the festivities are over. To keep the tree looking fresh until Twelfth Night, spray it with an anti-transpirant before bringing it indoors. Available from garden centres, the spray contains a coating agent and pine oil, and prevents the moisture loss that causes needle drop. Once dry, it is harmless and invisible.

Watering needs
During its time indoors, the tree will need up to 1.15 litres (2 pints) of water each day, depending on its size and the size of the container. Before adding the decorations, stand it on a drip tray, which can then be concealed, along with the pot, with a covering of crepe paper. If possible, place the tree in a well-lit part of the room, away from sources of intense heat, such as a fire or a radiator.

Chrysanthemums

Handle with care
It is important to firm in chrysanthemums well but gently, so that their roots make good contact with the surrounding soil and quickly start to absorb moisture. If the roots are surrounded by air spaces, they will dry out.

Overwintering temperature
Too much heat in the greenhouse can cause the shoots that sprout from overwintering stools (root clumps) of both garden and greenhouse varieties to become spindly and pale. The optimum temperature is 4°C (40°F). Increase this to between 13°C (55°F) and 16°C (60°F) about three weeks before you intend to take cuttings from the shoots.

A brief history

A tree for Christmas
The custom of illuminating a conifer at Christmas originated in northern Europe, and was taken to North America by George III's Hessian troops during the War of Independence. It did not reach Britain until 1829, when Princess Lieven gave a Christmas party for children in Hertfordshire, though German merchants imported the idea to Manchester not long after. But it was the decorated tree that Prince Albert set up at Windsor Castle in 1841 that really made the custom an integral part of the festive season. A high point today is the tree in Trafalgar Square, an annual gift from Oslo to London.

Growing know-how

Flowers for cutting

All chrysanthemums are good for cutting for the house. They come in a wide range of colours and flower types, with varieties for growing indoors and outside. Outdoor spray chrysanthemums develop a head of flowers naturally, and do not need to be disbudded. Early chrysanthemums are also grown outdoors and should be restricted to six stems a plant. For the largest flowers, all the buds except the topmost one should be pinched out when they are small. Spray chrysanthemums should have the topmost centre bud removed to allow the side buds to extend more evenly to provide a good spray. Indoor decoratives are disbudded in the same way as early chrysanthemums, to provide a single, large flower on each stem.

Small blooms to enjoy at the season's end

As soon as flowering is over, cut back the main stems of early border varieties of chrysanthemum to between 20cm (8in) and 30cm (12in). This will encourage new growth and will also produce some small blooms for cutting late in the season.

Out with the old

For maximum success with outdoor chrysanthemums, make sure you dig the border deeply each year and incorporate well-rotted compost or manure. Replace ageing plants with cuttings taken from them. (*See also* **Cuttings**)

Space for healthy plants

When plants are overcrowded, they are much more vulnerable to attacks by pests and diseases. When planting out in the border, depending on variety, leave 30–46cm (12–18in) between the plants, and spray them regularly to keep them healthy.

Vigorous blooms

Application of a high-potash fertiliser in July will encourage chrysanthemums to grow strongly and to develop large flowers. (*See also* **Potash**)

Autumn beds

Make a cheering display in the garden with late-flowering perennial chrysanthemums. Their vibrant colours, in shades of orange, red, rust, terracotta, yellow and white, are perfectly suited to the mood of autumn. (*See also* **Autumn colours**)

Charms from seeds

If you cannot overwinter chrysanthemum stools, you can have a beautiful display each year by growing 'Charm' chrysanthemums from seeds instead. These are normally grown in containers. They grow to a height of about 46cm (18in) and flower from late September until November, with masses of tiny blooms. 'Charm' chrysanthemums can also be grown in the open, to provide late interest when the garden begins to lose its summer colour. An early sowing date is necessary to ensure success in the first season.

Fantastic balconies

Plant a number of 'Charm' chrysanthemums in a trough on a balcony or windowsill and attach

Blankets of colour Create magnificent drifts of late colour in the garden by planting the smaller-growing 'Charm' chrysanthemums.

each plant to a cane. Move the canes gradually outwards as the plants grow so that they are trained to slant progressively downwards. Remove the canes just before the plants flower. Your reward will be a hanging curtain of blooms.

Clay soil

A colourful tree for clay soil

Amelanchier lamarckii (snowy mespilus) is a small tree that does well in clay soil, and can withstand high winds. In spring it is covered in white blooms which are followed by edible, black fruits. The leaves turn to gold in autumn.

Concrete clay

If the surface of your soil becomes as hard as concrete in dry weather, it is a sign that it is lacking in organic matter. Digging in well-rotted compost or manure regularly and in the largest quantities you can find will solve the problem. However, it may take some years, particularly if the soil is heavy.

Improving drainage

On clay soil, drainage can be improved by digging two spits deep – a spit is the depth of a spade's blade (see panel, overleaf). This will also help roots to penetrate more deeply. Because this double digging is extremely hard work, it is worth first experimenting on a small part of the plot to judge if the results are worth while. (*See also* **Drainage**)

Treatment for cracks

If cracks appear in the lawn and flowerbeds after a period of drought, watering the area thoroughly should cure the problem. However, if this does not work, fill the cracks with a gritty soil to which a little general fertiliser has been added.

Making sure of a clean cut

If using a rotary tiller on virgin clay soil, always use pick-tyne or L-shaped blades on the machine, and never attempt to rotavate soil if it is wet or frozen.

Try a potato crop

One of the best ways to break up a heavy clay soil is to grow a crop of potatoes. Unlike most other vegetables, seed potatoes do not need to be sown in a fine tilth. Earthing them up two or three times in early summer will help to break down the clay while keeping the weeds down.

Helping hand for new plants

When planting shrubs and perennials in clay soil, dig grit, sharp sand or granular organic matter such as fine-grade bark, into the planting area. This will open up the soil and improve drainage. When planting bulbs in clay soil, use only grit to blend with the clay. In addition, place a 2.5–5cm (1–2in) layer of grit under each bulb.

Leave it to the frost

Autumn, after the crops have been harvested, is the best time to double dig a clay soil. The winter frosts will break up the clods and the soil will be easier to work in spring. Do not dig deeply in spring or summer, as this will bring unbroken lumps of clay to the surface.

Warm clay in spring

Put cloches out in early March, or cover beds with heavy-duty black polythene to speed up the warming process. Clay is slow to warm up and lettuces, radishes and spring onions will fail if sown directly into cold soil in early spring. Alternatively, lettuce seeds can be started off in a greenhouse or propagator and planted out in April, by which time the soil should be warm.

Clematis

Perfect pairing

Two clematis growing together and flowering either simultaneously or in succession are very attractive, but never plant the two in the same planting hole. If clematis wilt attacks one of the plants, the disease could spread to the other. Plant the clematis at least 1.8m (6ft) apart and train the branches so that they intermingle.

Early flowers

Unless winters are severe in your area, try growing *Clematis cirrhosa* for winter flowers. This variety grows to between 1.8–2.4m (6–8ft) and will give you a succession of early flowers from January to March.

Training and support

Clematis stems need to grow on a support. A trellis or wire framework is best. Provide support when the clematis is planted by guiding the main stem through a terracotta or plastic drainpipe placed over the plant. This will also help to prevent rodents from damaging the bark.

Growing know-how

The technique of double digging

On clay soils, do not attempt to double dig until the soil is dry enough to be walked on without it sticking to your boots or becoming compacted.

1 Mark out the plot down each side, using a garden line. At one end, dig a trench one spade deep and 46cm (18in) wide, taking thin slices of soil onto the spade each time. Thin slices will be easier to lift than soil that is heaped high on the spade. Wheel the soil to the far end. If the plot is very wide, divide it in half lengthways and place the excavated soil at the end of the adjacent section. Do not work too quickly at this stage or you will soon tire.

2 Fork over the bottom of the trench, to the depth of the fork, to break it up and improve the drainage, then spread a 5–7.5cm (2–3in) layer of well-rotted organic matter on top. Remove the soil from the second trench and place it, upside-down, on top of the manure in the first trench. Continue in this way until you reach the end of the plot.

3 When you have dug the final trench, forked the bottom and added the organic matter, use the soil from the first trench to fill it in. If you have divided the plot in half, fill the final trench on the first section with the soil from the first trench on the second section. Work your way back down to where you started and refill the last trench with the soil that was taken right at the beginning from the first trench.

Growing support Use bamboo as a natural prop for your clematis; it complements the climber's beautiful flowers perfectly.

Garden secrets

A torrent of water

Before planting a clematis, plunge it, up to the rim of the pot, in a bucket of water and leave it for an hour. Fill the planting hole with water, let drain, then plant the clematis and firm the soil.

Beware of slugs

If you are growing an herbaceous clematis, protect young spring shoots from slugs and snails by using pellets, traps or a barrier. (See also **Slugs and snails**)

Sun and shade

A clematis should have its head in the sun and its roots in the shade. When planting, protect the roots with a thick mulch of compost or cover the soil round the stem with tiles or slates. Plant a low bush, such as a hebe, lavender or rue, at the foot of the clematis — the cool shade it will provide will help the clematis to establish itself, as well as making a pleasing companion.

Propagating a climbing clematis

In late spring and early summer, take cuttings 5–7.5cm (2–3in) long, with buds at the top, and trimmed midway between the nodes. Push the base of each, to a depth of 2.5cm (1in), into a pot or tray containing a mixture of peat or coir and sharp sand. Cover with a plastic bag and keep in a warm place, out of direct sunlight. After six to eight weeks, when the cuttings have rooted, pot separately in 8cm (3in) pots of John Innes No. 1 compost; overwinter in a greenhouse or cold frame. In spring, you can transfer the plants to 10cm (4in) pots and stand them outside. In late spring, plant out the clematis in their permanent homes. (See also **Cuttings**)

Cuttings from herbaceous types

Propagate herbaceous clematis species in April or May by taking 7.5cm (3in) basal cuttings (shoots from the base of an established plant). Set the cuttings in pots in a mixture of equal parts of peat or coir and sand. Place in a cold frame or cover with plastic bags. When the cuttings have rooted, pot them up into 9cm (3½in) pots of John Innes No. 1 compost and place in a cold frame or in a sheltered spot outside. Transplant in October. (See also **Cuttings**)

Success with seeds

Many of the climbing clematis that are grown in gardens are hybrids and will not come true from seed. Some, however, produce good plants. The best varieties are *Clematis alpina*, *C. campaniflora*, *C. rehderiana* and *C. tangutica*. Sow the seeds in autumn in trays of John Innes seed compost and leave them in a shady spot in the garden until spring, then bring the trays into a warm greenhouse. As soon as the seedlings emerge, prick them out into 8cm (3in) pots, and treat them in the same way as cuttings.

Clematis wilt

If flowers and leaves turn brownish-black and stems wilt, do not pull up the plant. It is suffering from wilt, but you may be able to save it. Cut back affected stems and leave for several months. It may recover.

Growing know-how

Pruning guide for clematis

Clematis varieties fall into one of four groups, each of which requires a different method of pruning.

Group 1 (Early-flowering species and their varieties)
Prune immediately after flowering to remove dead shoots and to keep plants within bounds.

Group 2 (Early and mid-season large-flowered varieties)
Remove dead wood in early March. Cut back remaining shoots to just above the topmost, fat, green buds and retie evenly.

Group 3 (Late-flowering varieties)
Prune hard in March, taking the previous year's growth back to a strong pair of buds just above the base.

Group 4 (Evergreen varieties)
Prune to remove dead or diseased wood. Cut back *Clematis armandii* hard after flowering if space is limited.

Unusual displays

Clematis are usually seen covering walls, but there are many more situations in which they can be cultivated. For instance, you could try training a clematis plant to grow over an arch, a bower, a tree stump or a pillar. A beautiful, flowering clematis will also cheer up a drab hedge, a conifer or an isolated apple tree. If you have an old discarded garden umbrella, you could use it to create a particularly unusual display. Simply strip the umbrella of its fabric, then drive a metal pipe into the ground and slip the umbrella handle into it. Plant two clematis at the base, and they will quickly grow up to cover the frame, and will soon be trailing their flowers and stems down the spokes in a cascade of colour.

Climbing plants

Natural shading and plenty of water

When planting a climbing plant to grow against a wall, dig in plenty of organic matter and place the roots 30cm (12in) from the wall's base. Insert a length of drainpipe into the soil so that one end is close to the roots and the other is just above ground level. Spread a layer of mulch round the root area to help to retain moisture and water the roots directly through the drainpipe. To provide cool shade for the roots in summer, plant an evergreen shrub at the base of the climber.

Wire supports

Horizontal wires provide stronger supports than vertical ones for climbing plants. Set the wires 30–46cm (12–18in) apart and tie in the plant stems as they grow. Pull the wires taut or they will sag under the weight of the plants.

In trees

A mature tree is the ideal host for a climber. Beneath a tree that has an upright habit and a narrow crown, a climber is best planted close to the trunk. Dig a hole between the tree's roots and plant the climber, refilling the hole with potting compost. Feed the new plant and water it frequently until it is established, or it may suffer competition from the roots of the tree. A climber that is required to grow through a tree with a dense, spreading crown is best planted in line with the periphery of the tree's crown and trained up a rope or a heavy stake that has been tied to a stout branch.

Hinged support

Climbing plants are an attractive way of covering a wall but they pose a problem when the wall needs to be repainted. By using hooks and hinges to fix a trellis to the wall, both trellis and plants can be moved, without disturbance to roots, then replaced when the paint is dry.

A climber for shaded spots

Grow the climbing *Hydrangea anomala* ssp. *petiolaris* on a north, east or partly shaded wall. It needs three or four years to become established but, once it has done so, it will attach itself to any support without guidance and will withstand harsh winds. It produces attractive, white flowers in early summer. (See also **Hydrangeas**)

Large spaces

If you need fast-growing plants to cover a large surface, such as an unsightly wall or fence, plant two or three climbers of the same variety 61–91cm (2–3ft) apart, and train the stems across the surface as they grow.

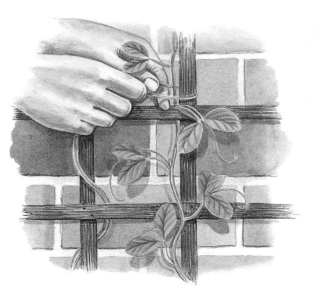

Tying in to prevent damage

Tie in side shoots on climbing plants before gusts of wind snap them. Do not tie too tightly. Always allow for thickening of the stems as the plants mature. Use raffia or soft garden string that will not damage the plants.

Good companions

An old apple tree can be given fresh beauty if clothed with a vigorous rambling rose. *Rosa filipes* 'Kiftsgate', which can reach a height of 18m (60ft) and has huge trusses of single, white, fragrant flowers in midsummer, is particularly suitable in such a situation.

See also **Dead tree trunks, Trellises, Wall planting**

Cloches

Make your own

Save some money by making your own cloches for use in the garden. Nail pieces of wood together to make a square frame and fix two crossed hoops of strong wire onto it. Stretch a piece of clear polythene over the wire hoops and staple this onto the wooden frame. You can make a series of cloches of different sizes. They can be stacked easily together when they are not required.

A vital helper
Use transparent cloches made from glass or plastic to protect seedlings, cuttings and young plants from cold and rain, heat up the ground before sowing and maintain humidity.

Cloche succession
Protect crops that mature in late autumn, then cover those sown to overwinter. Follow these by covering early outdoor sowings, then use the same cloches to cover early plantings of half-hardy vegetables.

Classy cloches
Demijohns make elegant cloches, reminiscent of stylish Victorian bell jars. They can be bought sometimes for a few pence at car boot sales or jumble sales. Using a glass-cutter, score a line round the bottom of the demijohn, then fill it with iced water up to the level of the line. Pour a little very hot water into a plastic bowl and lower the demijohn gently into it. The bottom should come away cleanly, leaving a perfect bell jar. If necessary, use a piece of coarse sandpaper to smooth any sharp edges on the bottom of the jar. Wear a pair of leather gardening gloves to protect your hands and take great care as you work.

Adapt a pot
An empty flowerpot, filled with straw or dead leaves and turned upside-down, is a good way of protecting a small plant in a harsh winter. Watch out for slugs and snails and put down pellets or traps if necessary. Remove the pots when the weather warms up.

Floating cloches
Lay horticultural fleece, or sheets of clear polythene with slits or perforations, over plants or soil to keep in warmth. Hold down the edges of the covering with some large bricks or planks of wood, leaving it slack and 'floating' to allow enough room for the plants to grow.

Covered with style Bell-jar cloches like this were a common sight in the Victorian vegetable garden.

Coastal areas

Spring planting for safety
Plant in spring so that the young plants will not have to withstand winter storms and wind before they are established.

Beneficial windbreaks
In coastal areas, help the growth of newly planted shrubs and saplings by protecting them with windbreaks for two to three years. Use special plastic netting that is available from garden centres.

Hose down after a storm
Evergreens and conifers are particularly susceptible to salt burn. As soon as possible after a storm, remove the salt from the foliage by hosing it down with clean water, using a fine rose.

Multi-purpose seaside shrub
For a shrub with many uses, it is hard to find a more versatile plant than *Ulex europaeus* (gorse). Easily raised from seed, it will withstand sea spray and wind and will fill the air with the sweet scent of its yellow blossoms on warm spring days. Its thorny branches make it an excellent deterrent to potential intruders.

A simple support
Staking will prevent a prevailing wind from causing damage to a young tree's roots. Drive the stake in at an angle, reaching as high up the tree trunk as possible, on the side opposite the direction of the prevailing wind. Fasten the stake to the trunk with a tree tie and spacer to prevent direct friction between the stake and the bark of the tree. Adjust the spacer and retie regularly to prevent the stake from working loose and to protect the bark from suffering damage as the trunk thickens.

A gardener's palette

The following charts will enable you to unite your plants in ever-changing, year-round harmonies of colour to enhance the garden as a whole or to make subtle nooks with shades that will soothe or cheer the beholder.

Colour is the gardener's trustiest tool and staunchest friend. It defines the seasons with the pale golds of spring, the opulent tapestry of summer, the glorious russets and yellows of autumn and the dark green, crimson and scarlet livery of winter. The gardener uses it to set moods, to attract or divert attention, to make corners of special interest or link one season with another. Pyracanthas, for example, might unite their crimson berries with the purple leaves of bergenias in winter or couple their foamy white blossom with the blue of delphiniums in summer. In a woody setting, bluebells and Welsh poppies could be joined with hostas and ferns, while in a favourite spot for an evening stroll there might be planted tall, pale lupins to catch the last of the light.

The chart that follows will help you to select the plants that you need to compose the colour schemes of your choice, month by month, through the year. The horizontal bars provide a check on the colour value of the plants listed, whether flowers, leaves, bark or fruits. The vertical columns show whether the plants are herbaceous (annual, biennial, perennial or bulbous), or woody shrubs and trees and tell you the months when the colours are at their best.

Use the chart to compose your own colour schemes, whether for border, vista, town patio or window box. An even better idea would be to ally it with the 'A Year of Glory in the Garden' charts on pp. 108–11 to help you to make the very best choice of plants while at the same time using the palette to make your overall colour plan.

Summer's essence
Few British summers are so tropical that they will not be enhanced by a border full of hot colours, including those of dahlias, montbretias, golden rod, sunflowers, redhot pokers and lavatera.

January/February

	Herbaceous plants	Shrubs and trees
WHITE	Crocus sieberi 'Bowles' White' Galanthus 'Atkinsii' Helleborus niger H. orientalis Pulmonaria rubra albocorollata Viola Ultima Series White	Abeliophyllum distichum Betula utilis var. jacquemontii Erica carnea 'Springwood White' Lonicera fragrantissima Sarcococca confusa Viburnum tinus
PINK	Bergenia × schmidtii Crocus tommasinianus 'Rose' Cyclamen coum roseum Helleborus orientalis Vinca difformis bicolor 'Jenny Pym' Viola Universal Series Rose	Daphne mezereum Erica carnea 'Foxhollow' E. × darleyensis 'Darley Dale' Prunus mume Rhododendron 'Praecox' R. 'Rose Mundii' Viburnum × bodnantense 'Dawn'

VIOLET	Crocus sieberi 'Violet Queen'
	Helleborus orientalis ssp.
	  abchasicus Early Purple Group
	Iris reticulata 'Pauline'
	I. unguicularis 'Mary Barnard'
	Viola Universal Series Violet
	  with Blotch
		Erica carnea 'Ann Sparkes'
		E. c. 'King George'
		Rhododendron dauricum
		Salix acutifolia 'Blue Streak'
		S. irrorota

BLUE	Crocus chrysanthus 'Blue Pearl' C. sieberi ssp. atticus Euphorbia characias 'Blue Hills' Hepatica nobilis Iris reticulata 'Cantab' I. unguicularis 'Walter Butt' Viola Ultima Series Marina	Elaeagnus macrophylla Hebe pinguifolia 'Pagei' Ruta graveolens 'Jackman's Blue' Teucrium fruticans
GREEN	Euphorbia × martinii Helleborus argutifolius H. odorus Iris foetidissima Polystichum setiferum	Daphne laureola Garrya elliptica Pleioblastus pygmaeus Viburnum rhytidophyllum V. tinus
YELLOW	Adonis amurensis Crocus ancyrensis Eranthis hyemalis Helleborus orientalis Iris danfordiae Narcissus 'February Gold' Viola Ultima Series Yellow	Acacia dealbata Chimonanthus praecox Cornus mas Hamamelis mollis 'Pallida' Jasminum nudiflorum Mahonia × media 'Charity' Ulex europaeus

ORANGE	Crocus angustifolius
	C. chrysanthus 'Zwanenburg
	  Bronze'
	C. gargaricus
	Viola Ultima Series Orange
	V. Ultima Series Orange
	with Blotch
		Acer griseum
		Hamamelis × intermedia
		  'Jelena'
		H. × i. 'Winter Beauty'
		Prunus maackii 'Amber Beauty'

RED	Bergenia 'Eric Smith' B. 'Jo Watanabe' Cyclamen coum Pulmonaria rubra Viola Ultima Series Scarlet	Cornus alba 'Sibirica' Erica carnea 'Nathalie' E. c. 'Vivellii' E. × darleyensis 'Kramer's Rote' Hamamelis × intermedia 'Diane'

March

Herbaceous plants	Shrubs and trees
Anemone blanda 'White Splendour'	Camellia 'Alba Plena'
Crocus vernus ssp. albiflorus 'Jeanne d'Arc'	Chaenomeles speciosa 'Nivalis'
Galanthus nivalis	Clematis armandii
Helleborus orientalis	Daphne mezereum alba
Saxifraga × burserana	Lonicera × purpusii
	Rhododendron 'Snow Lady'
	Viburnum × burkwoodii

Herbaceous plants	Shrubs and trees
Anemone blanda 'Pink Star'	Camellia 'Donation'
Bergenia 'Bressingham Salmon'	Clematis montana
Helleborus orientalis	Erica erigena 'Brightness'
Primula denticulata	Prunus glandulosa 'Sinensis'
P. rosea 'Grandiflora'	P. padus 'Pandora'
Tulipa 'Heart's Delight'	P. triloba 'Multiplex'
T. humilis var. pulchella	Rhododendron 'Cilpense'

Herbaceous plants	Shrubs and trees
Aubrietia (many)	Daphne mezereum
Crocus vernus ssp. albiflorus 'Purpureus Grandiflorus'	Erica carnea 'Ann Sparkes'
Ipheion 'Froyle Mill'	E. c. 'King George'
Iris reticulata 'Purple Gem'	Rhododendron ciliatum
Tulipa humilis Violacea Group	R. dauricum
Viola odorata	

Herbaceous plants	Shrubs and trees
Chionodoxa forbesii	Calluna vulgaris 'Silver Queen'
C. luciliae Gigantea Group	Hebe pinguifolia 'Pagei'
Crocus vernus ssp. albiflorus 'Queen of the Blues'	Rhododendron 'Blue Tit'
Primula Rainbow Series Blue Shades	Ruta graveolens 'Jackman's Blue'
Scilla sibirica 'Spring Beauty'	Teucrium fruticans

Herbaceous plants	Shrubs and trees
Euphorbia × martinii	Daphne laureola
Helleborus argutifolius	D. pontica
H. odorus	Elaeagnus pungens
Iris foetidissima	Olearia × macrodonta
Polystichum setiferum	Ribes laurifolium
Sedum rupestre	

Herbaceous plants	Shrubs and trees
Crocus × luteus 'Golden Yellow'	Azara microphylla
Eranthis Cilicica Group	Corylopsis pauciflora
Lysichiton americanus	Forsythia (many)
Narcissus (many)	Hamamelis (many)
Primula vulgaris	Mahonia × media
Tulipa 'Golden Emperor'	Rhododendron 'Chink'
T. 'Jeantine'	Stachyurus praecox

Herbaceous plants	Shrubs and trees
Narcissus 'Jetfire'	Acer griseum
Primula Rainbow Series Orange Shades	Hamamelis × intermedia 'Jelena'
Tulipa urumiensis	H. × i. 'Winter Beauty'
Viola Ultima Series Orange	Pinus sylvestris 'Gold Coin'
	Prunus maackii

Herbaceous plants	Shrubs and trees
Anemone blanda 'Radar'	Camellia 'Adolphe Audusson'
Helleborus orientalis	Chaenomeles × superba 'Crimson and Gold'
Primula Rainbow Series Scarlet	C. × s. 'Rowallane'
Pulmonaria rubra	Erica carnea 'Myretoun Ruby'
Tulipa 'Lilliput'	Rhododendron sanguineum
T. 'Showwinner'	

April

Herbaceous plants	Shrubs and trees
Erythronium californicum 'White Beauty'	Camellia (many)
Fritillaria meleagris alba	Magnolia stellata
Leucojum aestivum	Pieris (many)
Primula 'Schneekissen'	Prunus avium 'Plena'
Pulmonaria 'Sissinghurst White'	Rhododendron 'Beauty of Littleworth'
Tulipa 'Concerto'	Spiraea thunbergii

Herbaceous plants	Shrubs and trees
Bellis perennis Carpet Series Pink	Camellia (many)
Myosotis 'Carmine King'	Daphne odora
Primula rosea 'Grandiflora'	Erica australis
Pulmonaria 'Dora Bielefeld'	Magnolia × loebneri 'Leonard Messel'
Saxifraga 'Cranbourne'	Pieris japonica 'Valley Rose'
Tulipa 'Apricot Beauty'	Prunus 'Fire Hill'

Herbaceous plants	Shrubs and trees
Fritillaria persica 'Adiyaman'	Clematis alpina 'Pamela Jackman'
Hyacinthus 'Purple Dream'	Magnolia × soulangeana 'Rustica Rubra'
Iris 'Church Stoke'	Rhododendron 'Susan'
Lewisia rediviva	R. yungningense
Muscari comosum	
Pulsatilla vulgaris	
Tulipa 'Striped Sail'	

Herbaceous plants	Shrubs and trees
Anemone nemerosa 'Allenii'	Ceanothus impressus
Hyacinthus orientalis 'Blue Jacket'	Clematis alpina
Muscari azureum	Rhododendron 'Blue Diamond'
Myosotis (many)	R. 'Blue Tit'
Pulmonaria officinalis Cambridge Blue Group	Rosmarinus officinalis

Herbaceous plants	Shrubs and trees
Euphorbia characias ssp. wulfenii	Daphne laureola
Foeniculum vulgare	D. pontica
Fritillaria pontica	Elaeagnus pungens
Ranunculus ficaria 'Green Petal'	Pittosporum tenuifolium 'Silver Queen'
	Ribes alpinum
	R. laurifolium

Herbaceous plants	Shrubs and trees
Aurinia saxatilis	Acer platanoides
Doronicum 'Spring Beauty'	Cytisus × praecox 'Allgold'
Erysimum 'Cloth of Gold'	Forsythia × intermedia 'Lynwood'
Erythronium 'Pagoda'	F. suspensa 'Nymans'
Euphorbia polychroma	Fothergilla major
Narcissus (many)	Kerria japonica 'Pleniflora'

Herbaceous plants	Shrubs and trees
Erysimum 'Orange Bedder'	Berberis darwinii
Fritillaria imperialis	B. linearifolia
Tulipa 'Orange Princess'	B. × lologensis 'Apricot Queen'
T. praestans 'Fusilier'	B. × stenophylla 'Etna'
T. 'Prinses Irene'	Chaenomeles × superba 'Boule de Feu'

Herbaceous plants	Shrubs and trees
Anemone coronaria	Chaenomeles × superba 'Knap Hill Scarlet'
Dicentra spectabilis	Magnolia liliiflora 'Nigra'
Erysimum 'Fire King'	Malus 'Eleyi'
Pulsatilla 'Eve Constance'	M. 'Liset'
Tulipa 'Carlton'	Rhododendron Elizabeth Group
T. 'Red Riding Hood'	

May

Herbaceous plants	Shrubs and trees
Allium neapolitanum Cowanii Group	Camellia japonica 'Primavera'
Convallaria majalis	Magnolia × kewensis 'Wada's Memory'
Phlox subulata 'Maischnee'	Malus 'John Downie'
Polygonatum × hybridum	Rhododendron (many)
Tulipa 'White Triumphator'	Syringa vulgaris 'Madame Lemoine'
Zantedeschia aethiopica	

Herbaceous plants	Shrubs and trees
Convallaria majalis var. rosea	Clematis montana var. rubens
Lychnis alpina	C. 'Pink Champagne'
Oxalis adenophylla	Crataegus laevigata 'Rosea Flore Pleno'
Tulipa 'China Pink'	Deutzia discolor 'Rosalind'
T. 'Clara Butt'	Kolkwitzia amabilis 'Pink Cloud'
	Rhododendron 'Pink Pearl'

Herbaceous plants	Shrubs and trees
Erysimum 'Bowles' Mauve'	Clematis 'Mrs Cholmondeley'
Euphorbia amygdaloides 'Purpurea'	Paulownia tomentosa
Iris 'Brannigan'	Rhododendron 'Purple Splendour'
Tulipa 'Queen of Night'	Syringa vulgaris 'Katherine Havemeyer'
Vinca minor 'Atropurpurea'	Wisteria sinensis

Herbaceous plants	Shrubs and trees
Ajuga reptans 'Braunherz'	Ceanothus impressus
Brunnera macrophylla	C. thyrsiflorus var. repens
Corydalis flexuosa	Clematis 'H.F. Young'
Iris 'Florentina'	Rhododendron 'Blue Peter'
Muscari armeniacum 'Heavenly Blue'	Rosmarinus officinalis
Viola 'Maggie Mott'	

Herbaceous plants	Shrubs and trees
Angelica archangelica	Ailanthus altissima
Asplenium scolopendrium	Griselinia littoralis
Athyrium filix-femina	Hedera maderensis
Dryopteris filix-mas	Lonicera nitida
Tulipa 'Spring Green'	Parthenocissus tricuspidata
Viola 'Irish Molly'	

Herbaceous plants	Shrubs and trees
Hyacinthus orientalis 'City of Haarlem'	Camellia 'Jury's Yellow'
Iris 'Mary McIlroy'	Cytisus × beanii
Primula prolifera	C. × kewensis
Tulipa 'Golden Duchess'	Potentilla fruticosa
T. 'Silver Wedding'	Rhododendron 'Princess Anne'
Uvularia grandiflora	

Herbaceous plants	Shrubs and trees
Euphorbia griffithii 'Dixter'	Berberis darwinii
Primula chungensis	B. linearifolia
Trollius 'Feuertroll'	Buddleja globosa
Tulipa 'Dillenburg'	Chaenomeles × superba 'Boule de Feu'
T. linifolia Batalinii Group 'Bronze Charm'	Cytisus 'Killiney Salmon'
	Rhododendron Fabia Group

Herbaceous plants	Shrubs and trees
Dodecatheon media	Chaenomeles × superba 'Knap Hill Scarlet'
Heuchera 'Red Spangles'	Magnolia liliiflora 'Nigra'
Iris 'Cherry Gardens'	Malus 'Eleyi'
Primula japonica 'Miller's Crimson'	M. 'Liset'
Tulipa 'Flying Dutchman'	Rhododendron Carmen Group

June — Herbaceous plants	June — Shrubs and trees	July — Herbaceous plants	July — Shrubs and trees	August — Herbaceous plants	August — Shrubs and trees
Clarkia 'Snowflake' Delphinium Southern Maidens Group Dianthus 'Haytor White' Iris 'Cliffs of Dover' Paeonia lactiflora 'White Wings' Papaver orientale 'Black & White'	Cornus kousa var. chinensis Exochorda x macrantha 'The Bride' Pyracantha 'Mohave' Rosa (many) Viburnum plicatum 'Lanarth' Wisteria venusta	Astilbe 'Deutschland' Brachyscome 'White Splendour' Campanula latifolia alba Gypsophila paniculata 'Bristol Fairy' Phlox paniculata 'Fujiyama' Romneya coulteri	Carpenteria californica Cistus ladanifer 'Albiflorus' Clematis 'John Huxtable' Convolvulus cneorum Daboecia cantabrica alba Hebe albicans Rosa (many)	Anaphalis margaritacea var. cinnamomea Cortaderia selloana Galtonia candicans Leucanthemum maximum Penstemon 'White Bedder' Phlox paniculata 'Fujiyama'	Buddleja davidii 'White Profusion' Calluna vulgaris 'Alba Plena' Hydrangea paniculata 'Grandiflora' Rosa (many) Solanum jasminoides 'Album'
Armeria maritima Clarkia 'Appleblossom' Delphinium Southern Aristocrats Group Heuchera 'Rachel' Lupinus 'The Chatelaine' Papaver orientale 'Mrs Perry'	Clematis 'Comtesse de Bouchaud' Daphne x burkwoodii 'Somerset' Escallonia 'Donard Star' Kalmia latifolia Rosa (many) Weigela 'Florida Variegata'	Campanula 'Elizabeth' Dianthus 'Doris' Geranium endressii Gypsophila paniculata 'Flamingo' Petunia (many) Phlox paniculata 'Eva Cullum' Potentilla nitida	Ceanothus x pallidus 'Perle Rose' Cistus 'Silver Pink' Clematis 'Hagley Hybrid' Erica cinerea 'C.D. Eason' Potentilla fruticosa 'Princess' Rubus ulmifolius 'Bellidiflorus'	Geranium cinereum 'Ballerina' Linaria purpurea 'Canon Went' Monarda 'Fishes' Penstemon 'Evelyn' Phlox paniculata 'Prospero' Stachys macrantha	Abelia x grandiflora Buddleja davidii 'Pink Delight' Clematis 'Miss Crawshay' Hydrangea macrophylla (many) Rosa (many) Tamarix ramosissima 'Pink Cascade'
Delphinium Southern Consort Group Digitalis purpurea Iris sibirica 'Blue Burgee' Nepeta x faassenii Papaver orientale 'Blue Moon' Phacelia 'Lavender Lass'	Clematis 'Lasurstern' Daboecia cantabrica 'Atropurpurea' Hebe 'Youngii' Lavandula angustifolia 'Hidcote' Rosa 'Reine des Violettes' Wisteria sinensis 'Caroline'	Iris latifolia Malva sylvestris 'Brave Heart' Nepeta x faassenii Petunia 'Purple Wave' Phlox paniculata 'Border Gem'	Clematis 'Gipsy Queen' Daboecia cantabrica 'Atropurpurea' Hebe 'Amy' Lavandula angustifolia 'Hidcote' Rosa 'Wise Portia' Salvia officinalis 'Purpurascens'	Heliotropium 'Marine' Hosta ventricosa Penstemon 'Alice Hindley' Salvia farinacea 'Victoria' S. x superba 'Superba' Verbena 'Imagination'	Buddleja davidii 'Nanho Purple' Clematis 'Jackmanii' C. viticella 'Purpurea Plena Elegans' Hebe 'Autumn Glory' Hibiscus syriacus 'Meehanii'
Delphinium Southern Countrymen Group Iris sibirica 'Papillon' Lupinus 'The Governor' Meconopsis betonicifolia Nemophila menziesii Polemonium caeruleum	Ceanothus 'Puget Blue' Clematis 'Perle d'Azur' Hebe x franciscana 'Blue Gem' Rosmarinus 'Benenden Blue' R. officinalis 'Severn Sea' Teucrium fruticans	Delphinium (many) Echinops ritro Geranium 'Johnson's Blue' Laurentia axiliaris 'Blue Stars' Lithodora diffusa Lobelia (many)	Ceanothus x delileanus 'Gloire de Versailles' Clematis x durandii C. 'Perle d'Azur' Hebe x franciscana 'Blue Gem' Rosa 'Blue Moon' Teucrium fruticans	Ageratum (many) Campanula 'Kent Belle' Geranium 'Buxton's Blue' Lithodora diffusa Lobelia (many) Scabiosa caucasica 'Clive Greaves'	Ceanothus x delileanus 'Gloire de Versailles' Clematis 'Perle d'Azur' Hibiscus syriacus 'Oiseau Bleu' Hydrangea macrophylla 'Blue Wave' Solanum crispum 'Glasnevin'
Alchemilla mollis Angelica archangelica Asplenium scolopendrium Athyrium filix-femina Dryopteris filix-mas Hosta 'Royal Standard' Viola 'Irish Molly'	Acer japonicum 'Vitifolium' Ailanthus altissima Aralia elata Hydrangea quercifolia Magnolia grandiflora Paulownia tomentosa Rosa x odorata 'Viridiflora'	Alchemilla mollis Hosta 'Royal Standard' Moluccella laevis Nicotiana 'Lime Green' Ocimum basilicum	Acer japonicum 'Vitifolium' Ailanthus altissima Aralia elata Hydrangea quercifolia Liriodendron tulipifera Paulownia tomentosa Rosa x odorata 'Viridiflora'	Bassia 'Evergreen' Galtonia viridiflora Hosta 'Royal Standard' Moluccella laevis Nicotiana langsdorffii N. 'Lime Green' Zinnia 'Envy'	Ailanthus altissima Hydrangea quercifolia Itea ilicifolia Liriodendron tulipifera Magnolia grandiflora Paulownia tomentosa Rosa x odorata 'Viridiflora'
Aquilegio 'Yellow Star' Asphodeline lutea Bartonia aurea Coreopsis 'Early Sunrise' Lilium 'Connecticut King' Lupinus 'Chandelier' Sisyrinchium striatum	Helianthemum 'Wisley Primrose' Laburnum x watereri 'Vossii' Paeonia delavayi var. ludlowii Potentilla fruticosa 'Elizabeth' Rosa (many) Spartium junceum	Anthemis tinctoria 'E.C. Buxton' Carex elata 'Aurea' Geum 'Lady Stratheden' Hemerocallis (many) Hypericum olympicum Tagetes Zenith Series	Cytisus battandieri Fremontodendron 'California Glory' Potentilla fruticosa 'Primrose Beauty' Rosa (many) Santolina chamaecyparissus	Helianthus annuus Kniphofia 'Little Maid' Lysimachia punctata Oenothera fruticosa ssp. glauca Rudbeckia 'Goldsturm' Tagetes Zenith Series Viola 'Sunbeam'	Choisya ternata 'Sundance' Clematis 'Bill Mackenzie' Hypericum 'Hidcote' Koelreuteria paniculata Phygelius aequalis 'Yellow Trumpet' Rosa (many)
Calendula 'Orange King' Eschscholzia 'Orange King' Lilium 'Enchantment' Papaver 'Curlilocks'	Buddleja globosa B. x weyeriana 'Golden Glow' Eccremocarpus scaber Helianthemum 'Ben More' Potentilla fruticosa 'Tangerine' Rosa 'Just Joey'	Hemerocallis (many) Lilium 'Festival' Meconopsis cambrica var. aurantiaca Nemesia 'Orange Prince' Pelargonium 'Orange Appeal' Tagetes 'Safari Tangerine'	Buddleja x weyeriana 'Golden Glow' Campsis x tagliabuana 'Madame Galen' Eccremocarpus scaber Potentilla fruticosa 'Sunset' Rosa 'Just Joey'	Cosmos 'Sunny Orange-Red' Crocosmia 'Star of the East' Mimulus 'Magic Yellow' Rudbeckia 'Marmalade' Tagetes 'Sarafi Tangerine' Verbascum 'Cotswold Queen' Viola 'Padparadja'	Buddleja x weyeriana 'Golden Glow' Campsis grandiflora Eccremocarpus scaber Potentilla fruticosa 'Sunset' P. f 'Tangerine'
Centranthus ruber Dianthus barbatus 'Blood Red' D. 'Houndspool Cheryl' Iris sibirica 'Ruffled Velvet' Lupinus 'The Page' Paeonia lactiflora 'Inspecteur Lavergne'	Cornus florida rubra Crinodendron hookerianum Cytisus 'Killiney Red' Escallonia rubra 'Crimson Spire' Potentilla fruticosa 'Red Robin' Rosa (many)	Centranthus ruber Geum 'Mrs J. Bradshaw' Nemesia 'St George' Pelargonium (many) Polygonum amplexicaule Potentilla atrosanguinea	Clematis 'Niobe' Crinodendron hookerianum Escallonia rubra 'Crimson Spire' Potentilla fruticosa 'Red Robin' Rosa (many)	Crocosmia 'Lucifer' Lobelia 'Compliment Scarlet' Monarda 'Cambridge Scarlet' Penstemon 'Chester Scarlet' Salvia 'Red Arrow' Tagetes 'Red Seven Star' Verbena 'Lawrence Johnston'	Calluna vulgaris 'Dark Beauty' Clematis 'Niobe' C. texensis 'Sir Trevor Lawrence' Erica cinerea 'Stephen Davis' Fuchsia 'Riccartonii' Hydrangea 'Preziosa'

September

Herbaceous plants	Shrubs and trees
Anemone × hybrida 'Honorine Jobert' Colchicum speciosum 'Album' Cyclamen hederifolium album Nicotiana sylvestris Phlox paniculata 'Fujiyama' Viola cornuta Alba Group	Abelia × grandiflora Clematis 'Alba Luxurians' Clethra alnifolia Erica tetralix 'Alba Mollis' Magnolia grandiflora Pileostegia viburnoides
Aster amellus 'Pink Zenith' Centaurea hypoleuca 'John Coutts' Colchicum agrippinum C. 'Waterlily' Cyclamen hederifolium Dierama pulcherrimum Physostegia virginiana	Calluna vulgaris 'H.E. Beale' Clematis 'Hagley Hybrid' C. 'Margot Koster' Erica vagans 'Mrs D.F. Maxwell' Hebe 'Great Orme' Hydrangea macrophylla 'Mariesii'
Aster amellus 'King George' A. × frikartii 'Mönch' Colchicum 'Lilac Wonder' Crocus karduchorum C. speciosus 'Oxonian' Viola cornuta 'Prince Henry'	Buddleja 'Black Knight' Clematis 'Jackmanii' C. viticella 'Etoile Violette' Hebe 'Alicia Amherst' H. 'Amy' H. 'Autumn Glory' Indigofera heterantha
Agapanthus 'Bressingham Blue' Crocus speciosus Echinacea purpurea 'Robert Bloom' Gentiana farreri G. sino-ornata Sisyrinchium angustifolium	Caryopteris × clandonensis 'Kew Blue' Ceanothus 'Autumnal Blue' Ceratostigma willmottianum Hibiscus syriacus 'Oiseau Bleu' Perovskia atriplicifolia 'Blue Spire' Teucrium fruticans
Acanthus mollis Hosta (many) Humulus lupulus Moluccella laevis Nicotiana langsdorffii N. 'Lime Green' Zinnia 'Envy'	Ailanthus altissima Chamaerops humilis Hedera colchica Itea ilicifolia Magnolia delavayi M. grandiflora
Helenium 'Waldtraut' Helianthus 'Lemon Queen' Hemerocallis 'Stella d'Oro' Kniphofia 'Little Maid' Solidago 'Spätgold' Sternbergia lutea	Acer palmatum Clematis 'Bill Mackenzie' Colutea arborescens Eccremocarpus scaber 'Aureus' Grevillea juniperina f. sulphurea Hypericum 'Hidcote'
Crocosmia 'Jupiter' Dendranthema 'Mary Stoker' Helenium 'Coppelia' Helianthus annuus Kniphofia 'Bressingham Comet' Physalis alkekengi	Campsis grandiflora C. × tagliabuana 'Madame Galen' Eccremocarpus scaber Oxydendrum arboreum Potentilla fruticosa 'Sunset'
Aster novae-angliae 'Red Cloud' Dahlia 'Bishop of Llandaff' Dendranthema 'Ruby Mound' Helenium 'Feuersiegel' Imperata cylindrica 'Rubra' Persicara amplexicaulis 'Firetail' Schizostylis coccinea	Clematis 'Madame Julia Correvon' Desfontainia spinosa Fuchsia 'Riccartonii' Lonicera × brownii 'Dropmore Scarlet' Sambucus racemosa

October

Herbaceous plants	Shrubs and trees
Aster pringlei 'Monte Cassino' Cyclamen hederifolium album Saxifraga fortunei Scabiosa caucasica 'Mount Cook' Sedum spectabile 'Iceberg' Zephyranthes candida	Calluna vulgaris 'White Star' Erica tetralix 'Alba Mollis' Euonymus fortunei 'Silver Queen' Pileostegia viburnoides Symphoricarpos × doorenbosii 'White Hedge'
Amaryllis bella-donna Aster novae-angliae 'Andenken an Alma Pötschke' Dendranthema 'Clara Curtis' D. 'Mei-Kyo' Nerine bowdenii Sedum 'Herbstfreude'	Erica cinerea 'Pink Ice' Gaultheria mucronata 'Pink Pearl' Hebe 'Great Orme' Lespedeza thunbergii Symphoricarpos × doorenbosii 'Mother of Pearl'
Aster novi-belgii 'Storm Clouds' Colchicum atropurpureum Crocus medius C. speciosus Salvia patens 'Chilcombe' Tricyrtis formosana	Callicarpa bodinieri var. giraldii 'Profusion' Gaultheria mucronata 'Mulberry Wine' Symphoricarpos × doorenbosii 'Magic Berry' Vitex agnus-castus
Aconitum carmichaelii Gentiana asclepiadea Liriope muscari Salvia guaranitica 'Blue Enigma' S. patens Scabiosa caucasica 'Clive Greaves'	Caryopteris × clandonensis 'Kew Blue' Ceanothus 'Autumnal Blue' Ceratostigma willmottianum Hibiscus syriacus 'Oiseau Bleu' Perovskia atriplicifolia 'Blue Spire' Symplocus paniculata
Acanthus mollis Helleborus foetidus Iris foetidissima Miscanthus (many) Rudbeckia occidentalis 'Green Wizard'	Aucuba japonica f. longifolia Fatsia japonica Magnolia grandiflora Mahonia × media 'Charity' Trachycarpus fortunei
Dahlia 'Yellow Hammer' Dendranthema 'Enbee Sunray' D. 'Golden Seal' D. 'Nantyderry Sunshine' Helianthus salicifolius	Acer (many) Clematis 'Bill Mackenzie' Cotoneaster salicifolius 'Rothschildianus' Fagus sylvatica Pyracantha 'Soleil d'Or' Sorbus aucuparia 'Xanthocarpa'
Dahlia 'David Howard' Dendranthema 'Bronze Elegance' D. 'Doctor Tom Parr' D. 'Paul Boissier' Kniphofia galpinii	Cercidiphyllum japonicum Fothergilla major Pyracantha (many) Rhus typhina 'Laciniata' Sorbus (many) Vitis coignetiae
Aster novi-belgii 'Crimson Brocade' Dahlia 'Preston Park' Dendranthema 'Duchess of Edinburgh' Zauschneria californica	Acer (many) Cotoneaster (many) Disanthus cercidifolius Euonymus alatus Gaultheria mucronata 'Crimsonia'

November/December

Herbaceous plants	Shrubs and trees
Crocus niveus Cyclamen hederifolium album Galanthus caucasicus var. hiemalis Helleborus niger Schizostylis coccinea alba	Arbutus unedo Betula utilis var. jacquemontii Elaeagnus × ebbingei Erica × darleyensis 'Silberschmelze'
Cortaderia selloana 'Rendatleri' Cyclamen cilicium Helleborus niger Blackthorn Group Nerine bowdenii Schizostylis coccinea 'Jennifer' Viola Universal Series Rose	Erica carnea 'Foxhollow' E. c. 'R.B. Cooke' Gaultheria mucronata 'Pink Pearl' Prunus × subhirtella 'Autumnalis' Rosa × odorata 'Pallida' Viburnum × bodnantense 'Dawn'
Crocus medius C. serotinus ssp. clusii Iris unguicularis 'Mary Barnard' Liriope muscari 'Royal Purple' Ophiopogon planiscapus Viola Ultima Series Purple Wing	Callicarpa bodinieri var. giraldii 'Profusion' Gaultheria mucronata 'Mulberry Wine' Salix acutifolia 'Blue Streak' Symphoricarpos × doorenbosii 'Magic Berry'
Crocus niveus C. speciosus Elymus magellanicus Iris unguicularis 'Walter Butt' Liriope muscari Scilla lingulata ssp. ciliolata Viola Ultima Series Marina	Ceratostigma willmottianum Clerodendrum trichotomum var. fargesii Picea pungens 'Hoopsii' Symplocos paniculata Viburnum davidii V. tinus 'Gwenllian'
Asplenium scolopendrium Bergenia 'Ballawley' Iris foetidissima Juncus effusus 'Spiralis' Luzula sylvatica Polystichum setiferum	Garrya elliptica Hedera maderensis Ilex aquifolium 'Ferox' Magnolia grandiflora Mahonia × media 'Charity' Viburnum davidii V. rhytidophyllum
Dendranthema nankingense Deschampsia cespitosa 'Goldschleier' Pennisetum alopecuroides Sternbergia sicula Viola Ultima Series Primrose	Chimonanthus praecox Cornus stolonifera 'Flaviramea' Cotoneaster salicifolius 'Rothschildianus' Hamamelis mollis 'Pallida' Pyracantha 'Soleil d'Or' Sorbus aucuparia 'Fructo Luteo'
Carex comans bronze Dendranthema 'Mary Stoker' Iris foetidissima Uncinia uncinata Viola Ultima Series Orange V. Ultima Series Orange with Blotch	Calluna vulgaris 'Golden Feather' C. v. 'Sunrise' Hamamelis × intermedia 'Jelena' Prunus maackii 'Amber Beauty' Pyracantha 'Saphyr Orange' Thuja occidentalis 'Rheingold'
Bergenia 'Eric Smith' Dendranthema 'Emperor of China' Phormium 'Dazzler' Schizostylis coccinea Viola Ultima Series Scarlet	Calluna vulgaris 'Fairy' C. v. 'Robert Chapman' Cornus alba 'Sibirica' Cotoneaster (many) Euonymus europaeus 'Red Cascade'

Cold frames

A place in the sun

The best place for a cold frame which is to be used for growing plants rather than seeds is facing south in full sun, where there is some protection from north or east winds in winter. If possible, ventilate the frame on the side away from the prevailing wind.

Hot and cold

Use pieces of old carpet or sacking to protect plants from frost. Covering the frame before sunset will help to trap the day's warmth inside. In summer, use plastic netting or shading paint to protect plants from sunscorch and overheating. Ventilate the frame fully in very hot weather by opening the lid as wide as possible or by removing it altogether. But remember that when the lid is removed, the plants will still need to be shaded from the sun.

Sturdy seedlings

To prevent seedlings in a cold frame from becoming leggy in their efforts to reach the light, raise pots and trays on bricks to bring them as close as possible to the top of the frame. Do not allow the plants to touch the glass as they may scorch or become deformed. Turn the trays and pots every few days to ensure even growth.

Warmth in the cold frame

In a small cold frame, a nightlight will protect plants from early, light frosts. To help to spread the heat evenly round the frame, place the nightlight under an upturned tin with holes punched all round it. Alternatively, line the sides of the cold frame with offcuts of polystyrene sheeting, which will keep plants warm by night and reflect the light by day.

Reclaim and frame

Old window frames and bricks can often be bought cheaply at reclamation yards and can easily be made into excellent cold frames. Measure the length and width of each window then construct the walls of the frame to match these dimensions, making the back wall higher than the front to maximise light penetration and to assist the run-off of rainwater. A frame measuring 1.8m (6ft) from front to back should have a front wall approximately 30cm (12in) high and a back about 46cm (18in) high. Instead of bricks, old railway sleepers, thick planks of wood or breeze blocks can be used to construct the walls, if preferred.

Kill off fungus spores

Microscopic fungus spores can thrive in the framework of a wooden cold frame. Protect plants from disease by washing the frame thoroughly using a garden disinfectant. Keep the frame free of old debris such as broken pots and old wood. These items can harbour woodlice, slugs and snails.

Making a hot bed

Transform a cold frame into a heated propagator and get your seeds off to a flying start in spring on a hot bed. To make the bed you will need equal quantities by volume of very fresh horse manure and dead leaves. Mix them together and stack them in a heap. Turn the heap three or four times during the following two weeks. Meanwhile, dig a hole 1m (3ft) deep and 46cm (18in) wider all round than the frame. Fill the hole with the prepared mixture, firming it down in layers. Level the surface and place the frame on top, then cover the mixture with a 15–20cm (6–8in) deep layer of fine soil. Close the frame and do not use it for at least a day to allow the heat to build up.

Using a hot bed

Never sow or plant directly into the soil of a hot bed, as young roots could be damaged by the powerful mixture. Sow or plant in trays or pots, then bury them, up to their rims, in the soil. Open the frame when the temperature reaches 21°C (70°F).

Colour

Throw a little light

Plants, furniture and even pathways can help to brighten up a dull corner. Grow plants with silver or pale leaves and white, yellow or pink flowers. Paint trellises, fences and garden furniture white and construct walkways using pale-coloured bricks or paving stones. White gravel will reflect the light and make an attractive pathway.

Deceiving the eye

You can make a small garden appear larger by placing soft colours farthest from the main viewing area and vivid colours in the foreground. Broaden a long, narrow garden by growing bright flowers in the background with paler plants at the front.

Mood swings

Colour combinations can help to create moods. Use yellow, orange or red to illuminate a dark backdrop, or unite pastel shades of pink, blue, yellow or mauve with cream or white for a peaceful effect.

Separating pastel and bright colours

Use the neutrality of white to separate uncomplementary colour schemes. Vivid colours, in particular, should be kept away from pastels as they make the paler shades appear lifeless. Soften large areas of blue with orange, which is blue's complementary colour, and offset the effect of an abundance of red with areas of green.

Gardener's potpourri

Black magic

The truly black tulip is a myth, but breeders have come close to creating it with 'Queen of Night' and 'Recreado'. Some varieties of other plants are also dark, providing vivid contrasting colour schemes for a garden.

Flowers

Alcea rosea 'Nigra'
Cosmos atrosanguineus
Dianthus 'Black and White Minstrels'
Fritillaria camschatcensis
F. persica
Nemophila menziesii 'Pennie Black'
Viola 'Bowles' Black'

Foliage

Corylus avellana 'Fuscorubra'
C. maxima 'Purpurea' (purple hazel)
Cotinus coggygria 'Royal Purple'
    (smoke tree)
Fagus sylvatica Atropurpurea Group
(purple beech)
Foeniculum vulgare 'Purpureum'
    (bronze fennel)
Heuchera 'Palace Purple'
Ophiopogon planiscapus 'Nigrescens'
    (lily turf)
Phormium tenax Purpureum Group
    (New Zealand flax)
Pittosporum tenuifolium 'Atropurpureum'
Vitis vinifera 'Purpurea' (grape vine)

Colourful autumn containers

Patios and balconies need not become dreary, neglected areas as the days shorten. A pot or tub planted up in late summer with an eye-catching mixture of red and white hardy chrysanthemums, all edged with variegated trailing ivies, will be ready to burst into flower as the first autumn leaves fall from the trees. When the chrysanthemums eventually die down, they can be planted in the garden to provide further flowers the following year. (See also **Balcony gardens**)

Contrasting foliage

Use plants with variegated or yellow foliage to add contrast to those with green leaves. Some plants with yellow leaves, such as *Lysimachia nummularia* 'Aurea' (creeping jenny), lose their brightness if grown in shade. Others, such as *Aucuba*, *Elaeagnus*, *Euonymus* and *Philadelphus coronarius* 'Aureus' (mock orange) keep their colours better.

Winter colour

Get more from your garden in winter by growing colourful evergreens within view of windows and doors. Try planting *Aucuba japonica* 'Rozannie' or 'Variegata', or *Pyracantha coccinea* 'Lalandei', both of which have cheerful red berries in winter.

Memory tip

It is easy to forget the colours of plants when they are not in leaf or flower. Tie pieces of nylon yarn that match exactly the shades of the flowers or foliage onto the stems of the plants. Then, when moving plants to new positions or adding new ones, you can make sure that the new colours will complement established schemes, and avoid repetition of tones and hues.

See also **Autumn colours**, **A gardener's palette pp. 64–67**, **A year of glory in the garden pp. 108–11**

Columnar trees

Backyard orchard

To grow a crop of apples in a small garden, plant a few Minarette or Ballerina apple trees in separate containers. Adult trees are tall and slim and produce fruit on short branches, thus providing both decoration and nourishment. Keep them well watered in summer.

Dignified design

Columnar trees add dignity to the garden and are ideal for framing a view, accentuating a natural slope or providing a boundary without obscuring what lies beyond. Avoid placing them in a regimented straight line by planting the trees alternately on either side of a line.

Shapely pruning

Take care not to remove the growing point when pruning a columnar tree, as this will alter its shape. Trim only outward-pointing shoots. When using a telescopic pruner, do not cut through branches that are thicker than 7.5cm (3in) as the blade may get stuck in a branch. Use a bow saw to remove thicker branches.

See also **Silhouettes and styles pp.300–303**

Companion plants

Friends and foes
Gardeners have noticed for generations that some plants appear to have a direct effect on others growing near them. In some cases the effect is beneficial but in others it is detrimental. Roses, for example, seem to be more sweetly scented and less prone to disease when surrounded by garlic, and less troubled by aphids when lavender is grown underneath them. Beans, however, do not seem to do well when grown near onions.

Social climbers
Flowers that attract pollinating insects can increase the yields from some other crops. Morning glory or sweet peas and runner beans are good companions in this way, and also look extremely attractive scrambling up bean poles together in both flower and vegetable gardens.

Aphid control
Hover fly larvae are among the most voracious of aphid eaters. To help to reduce aphid damage to your plants, encourage adult hover flies to lay their eggs in the garden by planting *Convolvulus minor*, *Fagopyrum esculentum* (buckwheat) and *Limnanthes douglasii* (poached egg plant), which is known to attract over 30 species of hover fly.

Weed beaters
Few weeds grow in pine woods because secretions from the trees prevent them from germinating. A mulch of pine needles on the strawberry bed will suppress weeds and may also improve the flavour of the fruits. Similarly, *Rhododendron ponticum* produces secretions from its leaves which prevent seeds in the soil nearby from germinating, and the leaves of dandelions give off a gas that appears to have the same effect.

Subtle protection
Plant onions with carrots to confuse both onion flies and carrot flies and plant french beans with members of the cabbage family to keep away their respective pests. *Nicotiana sylvestris* (tobacco plant) protects other plants from whiteflies, by trapping the pests on its sticky leaves.

Sunshades
Use plants that thrive in the sun to shade other more delicate species. *Santolina* (cotton lavender), for example, will give protection to the heat-sensitive roots of clematis, while delicate lilies will thrive when grown through small evergreens such as daphnes.

Chives and apples
Any member of the allium family planted beneath an apple tree will reduce attack on the fruit from scab and other fungal diseases. Chives, in particular, fulfil a protective role.

Garden secrets

Mixed planting benefits
Plants of different species, when grown together, compete less with each other than those of the same species, and make it more difficult for pests and diseases to spread. Planting broad beans and potatoes together in the same bed can increase the yields from both crops.

Space savers
Make good use of space in the vegetable garden by planting shallow-rooting vegetables alongside deep-rooting ones. Carrots and radishes do well together and occupy less space when planted together than when planted in separate rows.

Just a little is enough
Stinging nettles give off secretions that, in small quantities, can be beneficial to other plants. A small patch of nettles in the herb garden can help to increase the oil content of the herbs, making them more aromatic. Too many nettles inhibit the herbs' development.

Disease resistance
Some plants can increase others' ability to resist disease. Camomile, for example, is known as the plant physician; foxgloves and *Tanacetum parthenium* 'Aureum' (golden feverfew) are helpful to plants nearby, summer savory benefits beans, and onions can prevent mould on strawberries.

Groundwork
Prepare the ground for a vegetable plot by planting potatoes. The methods involved in growing them help to break down the soil, while earthing them up destroys weeds as they germinate, thus preventing them from re-seeding the plot. The following year, the area will be suitable for other vegetables.

See also **Vegetable gardens**

A brief history

Perfect combination
Companion planting, the art of growing plants together in mutually beneficial combinations, can be traced back to pre-Christian times, when Marcus Varro, a Roman scholar who lived around 116–27 BC, wrote in his treatise on agriculture that vines and cabbages did not thrive when grown together. In AD 77, the Roman writer and administrator Gaius Plinius Secundus, Pliny 'the Elder' (23–79), noted in his voluminous encyclopedia of natural history that chickpeas, when grown with cabbages, protected them from caterpillars. Almost 2000 years later, in 1890, E.A. Ormerod, in her *Manual of Injurious Insects and Methods of Prevention*, advocated the planting of celery as an effective deterrent against the same pests.

Compost

Which compost?

The term compost is used to describe two different materials. Garden compost is made by rotting down vegetable matter and is used to improve the soil. It should not be used for sowing seeds or potting plants. Seed and potting composts are special formulations, often based on peat, coir or loam, specifically for sowing seeds or potting plants. (*See also* **Potting compost**)

Setting up the site

Choose the site for your compost heaps carefully. You will need a corner of the garden that has easy access for a wheelbarrow and is hidden from general view.

Ready-made bins

In a small garden where everything is on view, a makeshift compost heap may be an eyesore. Fortunately, there are some fairly attractive plastic bins on the market. They have walls that are, preferably, insulated, a lift-up panel and a weatherproof top, and will produce usable compost in three to four months in summer and six to eight months in winter.

Making your own bins

If you have room, it is best to have a pair of compost bins, so that the contents of one can be left to mature while the other is being filled.

Bins of 1m³ (35 cu ft) should supply sufficient compost for the average garden. It is easy to build your own bins out of secondhand materials. Begin with six 1.2m (4ft) fence posts. If they have not been treated, paint them with a solvent-based wood preservative. Drive them into the ground, 1m (3ft) apart, to a depth of 30cm (1ft). Using galvanised nails, attach planks across the back, sides and centre of the structure. The planks can be old floorboards or scaffolding planks; alternatively, strip them from wooden pallets. Paint them with preservative. The front of each bin should be made of wooden bars or palings, secured between struts nailed to the posts, that can be lifted out so that you can get to the compost.

Natural camouflage

Hide composting areas with deciduous and evergreen bushes about 1m (3ft) from the bins. Alternatively, grow *Lavatera* (mallow) a sprawling, exuberant shrub that quickly reaches a height of 1.8m (6ft).

Compost-making

Good compost is made from a mixture of suitable materials added in small amounts. There is no need to add accelerators or water providing there is a balance between green, damp materials and drier, more woody ones, and if the bin is properly insulated, it is best not to turn the compost as this will cool it down and slow up rotting. There is also no need to ventilate the container as air will enter with the waste, and it is not necessary to add soil as micro-organisms will be introduced on the roots of plants. To ensure the finished compost is not too acid, 140g/sq m of garden lime may be sprinkled over the surface at 30cm intervals.

What to compost?

All plant material will make compost, but some types will do so more swiftly than others. Lawn mowings, vegetable peelings and, if your carpets are made from natural fibres, the dust from the vacuum-cleaner, break down quickly. Coarser items, such as hedge clippings and tree prunings, are best shredded before being added to the heap. Mix bulky waste, such as cabbage leaves and shredded or crushed woody stems

or brassica stumps, with fine material, such as lawn mowings, before adding. Leaves should be stored separately in an uncovered mesh container, until they turn into leafmould.

Separate mowings

Lawn mowings should not be put directly onto the compost heap. They will pack down to form a slimy, airless mass. Mix them with other materials before adding them to the heap.

Plant a summer crop

If your compost heap is unlikely to be disturbed after May, it is a good place to plant a marrow or a couple of courgettes. However, watch out for slugs and snails.

Make the right choice

Waste not, want not

A lot of organic material can go back into the soil via the compost heap.

Things you can use

Annual weeds and plants • Coffee grounds and tea leaves • Eggshells • Hair from humans and pets (spread out) • Lawn mowings • Litter from rabbit hutches and bird cages • Manure • Paper and card (torn into small pieces) • Rhubarb leaves • Small feathers • Straw and hay • Stable litter • Spent potting compost • Spent bedding plants • Vacuum-cleaner dust (only from natural-fibre carpets and rugs) • Vegetable peelings and raw vegetable waste • Withered perennials or partly decomposed leaves and stems • Shredded branches • Wood and bonfire ash

Things you should avoid

Colour magazines • Detergents and chemical products • Diseased plant material • Dog and cat faeces • Meat scraps • Perennial weeds • Scraps of food that may attract vermin • Thick paper or cardboard

will need about 100 brandling worms to start your compost 'factory'. If you already have a conventional compost heap, they can be taken from there. Add the worms to the bin, cover them with a thin layer of compost or manure, then cover the bin. After about two weeks, add some kitchen waste such as vegetable or fruit peelings, coffee grounds and tea bags. When the worms have partially digested this layer, add more kitchen waste. Repeat this process until you have a bin full of rich, fertile compost. In colder areas, keep the bin in a frost-free place in winter.

Keep compost working

The presence of ants in the compost heap may be an indication that it is too dry and, therefore, will not rot down properly. Dampen each new layer of materials as you add it to the heap, using a watering can or the garden hose.

A compact alternative

If you have difficulty in finding enough materials to make a compost heap, but have regular, small supplies of kitchen waste, it may be worth while setting up a wormery. The compost produced in this way is very fertile and a wormery provides an ideal way of recycling kitchen waste where space for conventional compost heaps is limited.

Brandlings – compost makers

These small manure or compost worms, *Eisenia foetida*, which can live and breed in the rotting vegetation of compost heaps, are popular as bait with fishermen. If you need some brandlings to start off your wormery, they can be bought from fishing-tackle shops.

Make your own wormery

Heat a metal skewer that has a heat-resistant handle and use it to make two rows of holes round the base of a plastic dustbin, the first row about 7.5cm (3in) from the bottom, and the second about 7.5cm (3in) away from the first. Put a layer of gravel in the bottom of the bin and a 7.5cm (3in) layer of well-rotted garden compost or manure on top. Add water until it begins to seep out of the drainage holes. You

Conifers

Careful buying

Choose your conifer with care. The tree should be well balanced, so walk all round it to check that the branches are symmetrical and the stem is straight. Fallen needles around the base can indicate an unhealthy plant or one suffering from severe root damage caused by drought.

Strong stem for healthy growth

To grow properly, a conifer needs one strong main stem. If yours develops two stems, cut off the weaker one. If the main stem breaks, train up the nearest young shoot so that it can take over. If necessary, support the young growth by tying it to a stake.

Turning brown

Many conifers are showing signs of browning. This can be due to stress, which regular feeding and watering will combat, but it may be due to damage by conifer aphids or mites. Spray with an insecticide from mid spring, and if the branch is not dead, it will put out new growth that will eventually hide the bare parts. Where a conifer hedge has died in patches, light trimming will encourage adjacent healthy shoots to grow out into the dead areas.

Brighter aspect

The foliage of a tall imposing conifer can appear sombre in summer. Brighten it up by training a climber, such as a clematis or honeysuckle, on its sunny side to illuminate its dark branches. (*See also* **Climbing plants**)

Changing colours

Plant conifers with foliage that changes colour. *Cryptomeria japonica* 'Elegans' changes from green to purple or bronze-red in winter and the green foliage of *Thuja orientalis* 'Rosedalis' turns purple in winter and yellow in spring.

Impose a shape on a steep bank

Slim conifers can bring visual focus to a steep bank. When planting, create a level, water-retaining terrace at the base of each tree.

See also **Dwarf plants, Silhouettes and styles pp.300–303, Snow**

Green and gold A group of prostrate and upright conifers brings constant colour and texture to the garden all year round.

Conservatories

Choose the aspect
A south-facing conservatory can be a pleasant place in which to sit in winter but may become unbearably hot in summer. One with a northern aspect, while cooler in summer, may need to be heated in winter. An east or west-facing aspect is best, but whatever its position, the conservatory should be fitted with an efficient system of shading. It will also need ventilating panels in the roof. The panels should have a combined area equal to about a quarter of the overall floor space.

Choose the materials
Select the construction material for a conservatory carefully. Each material has its advantages and disadvantages. Aluminium requires less maintenance than wood but looks less attractive. Wood will need to be treated every two to three years with oil or wood preservative but wooden conservatories remain a degree or two warmer in winter than aluminium ones. The widely available plastic and polythene models require no maintenance - merely an annual wash down.

Choose the style
Conservatory furniture should be comfortable and resistant to damp. Its style should be in keeping with the style of the conservatory and the plants. Cane furniture looks particularly attractive surrounded by large-leaved plants such as *Ficus lyrata* (fiddle-back fig) and *Chamaedorea elegans* (parlour palm). In an Edwardian-style conservatory, try wrought-iron furniture surrounded by fuchsias, pelargoniums,

and the scented flowers, such as *Heliotropum* (cherry pie), that were popular at the beginning of the 20th century.

Colourful walls
Make good use of the conservatory walls and ceiling. Grow crimson bougainvillea and purple-leaved vines alongside blue and white *Passiflora caerulea* (passion flower) or sky-blue *Sollya heterophylla*. For scent, grow Jasminum polyanthum and allow ivy-leaved pelargoniums to trail from hanging baskets, window ledges and shelves. (*See also* **Hanging baskets, Window boxes**)

Planting areas
Plants that enjoy humidity will do best in pots on the conservatory floor. Reserve high shelves where the air circulates more freely for plants, such as African violets and begonias, that do not enjoy high levels of humidity. After watering, make sure that water is not left to stagnate in saucers under the pots.

Cut the heating bills
Choose Mediterranean plants for the conservatory to keep heating bills down. In winter these plants survive at 6°C (43°F), a much lower temperature than that required by some of the exotics. In summer, they can be placed outdoors, then they can be returned to the conservatory before the first frosts.

Summer cleaning
When you take your conservatory plants out into the garden in summer, take advantage of their absence to give the conservatory a thorough clean. Wipe the small shelves and glass with disinfectant. Pay particular attention to where the panes of glass overlap. Clean the dirt from these with a small knife.

Container gardening

Stop soil from escaping
Always ensure that drainage holes in flowerpots are covered with a layer of netting, stones or shells. Otherwise, potting compost will be washed out through the holes when the plants are watered. This layer also aids drainage as it prevents the compost from blocking the holes.

Make the most of leafmould
Use leafmould mixed with an equal quantity of potting compost when potting up woodland plants in containers. This mixture will provide the correct level of nutrients and the moisture retention required by plants such as trilliums, cyclamens and uvularias.

Grouping for impact
Instead of positioning containers individually around the garden, make a greater impact by displaying them in a collection and varying the height of the display by standing some of the pots on top of upturned pots or piles of bricks.

Keep planters well drained
To prevent waterlogging in a planter, spread a layer of gravel, coarse sand or pieces of broken clay pots over the bottom and cover with garden felt, an old floor cloth or other porous material. When replanting, if you are careful when removing the soil, you can leave the drainage layer in place. It can also be used to support pots of spring-flowering bulbs placed in the planter to provide a colourful display. (*See also* **Drainage**)

Growing plants in a narrow jar

It can be a striking feature but a tall earthenware jar with a narrow neck needs special treatment if it is to be used to grow plants successfully. Many of these jars do not have drainage holes and may break if you attempt to drill through them. To provide the plants with adequate drainage, cover the base of the jar with a 5–7.5cm (2–3in) layer of gravel. Then, push a cardboard tube – about 3.8cm (1½in) in diameter and the same length as the jar – into the centre of the gravel. Fill the tube with gravel, and hold it upright while you fill the jar with potting compost. Withdraw the tube when the compost is in place. This central drainage channel and the gravel layer at the base of the jar will help to keep the roots of the plants well drained.

Colour throughout the year

The container garden need never look dull. As one pot of plants finishes flowering, move it to a hidden area of the garden and replace it with a pot filled with up-and-coming plants. Use the panel, below, to plan combinations of colours.

Container plants for shade

Containers can bring colour to even the shadiest of areas. In a sunless spot, grow euonymus, pansies, periwinkles, pieris and dwarf rhododendrons in spring; begonias, busy lizzies, foxgloves, fuchsias, lobelias, pansies and tobacco plants in summer. For later colour, plant up containers with chrysanthemums, cyclamens and heathers. Box, fatsias, ivies and skimmias will remain green throughout the year, providing interest when the flowers have faded.

Heavyweight pots

A tall and bulky plant in a pot may topple over in the wind. Guard against this by placing a few heavy stones or weights in the bottom of the pot before adding the compost. They will act as ballast and help the container to withstand the elements.

Repositioning a heavy planter

If you want to move a planter to a new position but find it too heavy to carry, lift it onto a few round logs and roll it into place. To avoid splinters or grazing, wear gloves when moving containers.

Keep the compost in place

When you're repotting a plant, you can line the bottom of the pot with a coffee filter or a used

Make the right choice

Four seasons of container plants

When planted in containers, the following shrubs, climbers, perennials, bedding plants and bulbs will provide a succession of flower and foliage colour throughout the year.

Plants	Winter	Spring	Summer	Autumn
Shrubs	Box, dwarf conifers, daphnes, hamamelis, some dwarf rhododendrons, viburnums	Camellias, daphnes, forsythias, rhododendrons, dwarf weeping willows, willows	Abelias, hebes, hydrangeas, dwarf lilacs, philadelphus, potentillas, roses	Cotoneasters, euonymus, fatsias, fothergillas, hardy fuchsias, hebes, pyracanthas
Climbers and wall shrubs	Chimonanthus, *Clematis cirrhosa*, garryas, winter jasmines	Ceanothus, clematis, honeysuckles, wisterias	Clematis, honeysuckles, climbing hydrangeas, jasmines, passion flowers, solanums	Campsis, clematis, Chilean glory flowers, solanums, vines
Perennials	Hellebores, periwinkles, early primroses	Bergenias, irises, primroses, pulmonarias, pulsatillas	Belladonna delphiniums, bellflowers, diascias, hostas, irises, peonies, pinks	Asters, hardy chrysanthemums, sedums
Bedding		Forget-me-nots, pansies, polyanthus, wallflowers	Begonias, impatiens, nicotianas, pelargoniums, petunias, salvias	
Bulbs	Winter aconites, early crocuses, snowdrops	Wood anemones, crocuses, grape hyacinths, hyacinths, narcissus, tulips	Galtonias, lilies	Colchicums, autumn crocuses, hardy cyclamens

Mineral supplement

The cooking water from vegetables and boiled eggs, and fish tank water are all rich in minerals that are good for container-grown plants. Make sure that cooking water is allowed to cool completely before it is used.

tumble-drier sheet to keep the compost from leaking out through the drainage holes.

Natural windbreaks

If you have an exposed terrace or balcony, you will need to protect delicate plants from harsh

winds. Plant dwarf conifers, facing into the wind, at the back of containers. These hardy plants make excellent windbreaks.

Protection for outdoor plants

Plants in pots that stand outside in the winter need protection from sharp frosts. First, carefully remove the plant and its soil from its existing pot, then line a pot, one size larger than the old one, with bubble polythene round the sides and over the bottom. Perforate the polythene at the bottom so that water can drain through. Put the plant in its new pot and fill any gap between the rootball and the bubble polythene with fresh potting compost. The bubble polythene lining will keep the plant's roots warm.

Clever cover-up

The black or brown plastic pots commonly used for commercially grown plants tend to be less attractive than clay or terracotta pots, which are often ornamental. To hide the more mundane plastic pot and avoid the need to repot, place it inside a slightly larger ornamental clay or terracotta one, then fill the gap with moss or sand.

A guide to watering

To protect a large plant's roots from drying out in a big container, cover the top of the compost to help it to retain moisture. Use either some fine, light-coloured gravel or add a ground-cover plant such as *Ajuga reptans* (bugle) or *Lamium* (dead nettle). The dryness of the gravel or the limp appearance of the ground-cover plant is an indication that the compost in the container is in need of watering. (*See also* **Ground cover**)

Stopping root rot

A container that stands in a saucer should have a layer of gravel or sand, about 1.3cm (½in) deep, placed between the base of the container and the saucer. This will prevent water from becoming trapped in the bottom of the container and causing the roots of the plant to rot. It will also prevent the growth of algae on the container and the saucer.

Break up the surface

Every few weeks take a kitchen fork and break up the crust of soil that forms on the surface of pots after heavy rain or a dry spell. This impenetrable skin can prevent water from seeping in and saturing the compost.

Container plants need nutrients

Six weeks after planting, start feeding container-grown flowering plants with a high-potash feed, such as a tomato fertiliser. Alternatively, use a granular, controlled-release fertiliser, which will feed the plants until late summer.

Fresh nutrients

Each spring, remove 2.5cm (1in) of the old growing medium from the tops of your containers. Replace it with fresh potting compost, leaving at least 1.3cm (½in) between the top of the new compost and the rim of the pot. Watering will diffuse the nutrients contained in the new compost throughout the container. If the plant's roots have become compacted, cut them vigorously with a sharp knife in March, leaving the largest intact. The nutrients in the added compost will encourage new roots to grow. Repot the plant whenever it becomes pot-bound and its roots begin to appear through the holes in the bottom of the container.

See also **Peat**, **Planting**

Containers

A second life

Salvage items such as old chimneys and earthenware pipes – they make splendid tall containers for outdoor plants. Discarded Belfast and butler sinks can be transformed into miniature alpine gardens, and buckets and metal watering cans make eye-catching pots. Where necessary, drill a few holes in the bottoms for drainage. Add a layer of gravel and cover with newspaper before adding the compost. Old metal containers should be lined with perforated polythene before adding compost.

From sink to stone

Create a 'stone' container from an old Belfast or butler sink by using imitation rock (hypertufa). Mix two parts sand, two parts peat or coir and one part cement by bulk, then add water until the mixture has the consistency of stiff porridge. Using an old chisel, and wearing gloves, score the glaze of the sink and apply a layer of epoxy glue before coating it with the hypertufa. Spread it 1.9cm (¾in) thick; leave the surface slightly rough to give the appearance of stone. After a week, when the surface has set, scrub it with a wire brush. Paint it with liquid seaweed to encourage moss and algae.

Treating wooden containers

Wooden tubs and half-barrels need to be treated against rot if they are to stand outdoors, but some preservatives, before they have dried thoroughly, are harmful to plants. Allow treated tubs to stand for a week before planting, or put the plant into a plastic pot that fits inside the tub.

Wooden planters

When constructing a wooden planter, always use a hardwood, such as oak, or a pressure-treated wood, which should be guaranteed for ten years. These woods resist dampness but, for additional protection, pot up the plant in a plastic pot and then stand it on a saucer inside the planter. (See also **Dead tree trunks**)

A soaking before planting

Never put a plant into a new earthenware pot without first soaking the pot thoroughly. Otherwise, initial waterings will be swallowed up by the porous sides of the pot and not by the plant. Fill a bowl with water and keep the pot immersed in it until bubbles stop rising to the surface.

Getting rid of chalk marks on pots

Do not try to rub off the white chalk marks that often stain earthenware pots. Fill a large container with ground bark, adding water to dampen it. Bury the pot completely in the moistened bark, letting it stand overnight. By the morning, the chalk marks will either have disappeared or will be easily removed by rubbing with a cloth.

Saving pots from breaking up

A cracked earthenware pot will eventually disintegrate with the effects of both weather and watering. Save it by encircling it under its rim with a length of strong wire. Use pliers to twist the ends of the wire together.

Checking for cracks

Before buying an earthenware pot, always check that it is sound by flicking it with your fingernail. A clear sound means that there are no cracks in the pot.

Picking up a pot's pieces

Never throw away the pieces of broken earthenware pots. They will make excellent drainage layers at the bottom of other pots and tubs that are to be planted up. If necessary, use a hammer to break them up into smaller pieces, and store in a bucket.

Cleaning self-watering planters

If the sizes of plants allow it, self-watering planters should be emptied every two or three years and washed thoroughly, inside and out, with a solution of warm water and a garden disinfectant. Use a mixture of vinegar and warm water to remove any chalky deposits from the bottoms of the planters, and rinse the planters thoroughly before putting the plants back. Some planters have flotation chambers. If a planter has a detachable chamber, immerse in a sterilising solution to remove algae, following the manufacturer's instructions.

Suspending earthenware pots

Like a hanging basket, a hanging earthenware pot makes an attractive display on a wall. Hold the pot in three metal chains suspended from a ring, attaching the chains by a hook to a bracket on the wall. Alternatively, make a sling for the pot. Cut out a square, the corners of which extend just beyond the base of the pot, from a piece of wood. Drill a hole in each of the four corners. Thread a length of waxed cord through a pair of holes on one side of the wood and another length through the two holes opposite. Place the pot on the wooden square, and tie the ends of the waxed cord to the bracket.

Burning holes in a plastic pot

To make or enlarge drainage holes in the bottom of a plastic flowerpot, heat an old, slim screwdriver or a metal skewer with a heat-resistant handle. Twisting it gently, push it carefully through the base of the pot. Do this outdoors to disperse any noxious fumes.

Drilling drainage holes

If planting directly into a container that has few or no drainage holes, make holes in the base before planting up. For a wooden container, make the holes with a hand or electric drill, working slowly to widen the holes gradually. If the container is made of clay or glazed terracotta, use a carbide-tipped masonry bit in the drill. To avoid cracking the container, do not apply too much pressure to the drill, and withdraw the bit slowly at frequent intervals to prevent overheating.

Choosing the right depth

When buying a container make sure the depth is suitable for the plants you intend to grow. Alpines need a depth of at least 15cm (6in). For most bedding plants, a depth of 20–30cm (8–12in) is sufficient. Taller plants such as shrubs, small conifers and small climbers will need pots between 30cm (12in) and 40cm (16in) deep. Small trees and more vigorous climbers need deeper pots.

Out of shape

Containers with narrow necks and wider middles can look attractive. However, it is unwise to use them for small trees or shrubs whose roots will spread inside, making it impossible for the plants to be removed. Plant, instead, with annuals or tender perennials that can be removed each year.

See also **Balcony gardens, Hanging baskets, Window boxes**

Cordons

Cordons and step-overs

Cordons are single-stemmed trees, usually trained at an angle against a wall or fence. If they are trained horizontally at a height of about 40cm (16in) they are referred to as step-over trees, and can be grown on wire supports alongside paths. A vertical cordon is often called a minarette or pillarette. It is an ideal choice where space is tight, and makes a good height feature. Minarettes are pruned in the same way as other cordons, and need staking firmly for years, until a strong enough trunk has formed.

Small but abundant

Cordons provide the best way to grow apples or pears in a small garden. They take up little space, are easy to manage and have a reasonably high yield for their size. When training against a wall, place the roots at least 15cm (6in) away and at a slight angle, so that the stems lean towards the wall.

Step-over trees

Beginning with young, grafted cordons is the least expensive way to create step-over trees. Plant them 1.8m (6ft) apart, then cut each tree at a height of about 40cm (16in), at a point just above a bud. In spring, one or two branches will start to form and these should be trained along horizontal wires. In July or August, prune back the laterals to two buds.

Using wall space

Cordons grown at a 45-degree angle will have a higher yield than those grown horizontally, and will enable you to make the most of the available space along a wall or fence. Stretch three horizontal wires 1m, 1.5m and 2m (3ft, 5ft and 7ft) above the ground. Plant the trees about 1m (3ft) apart, training them up the wires until the top of each tree leans over the base of its neighbour.

Keeping them in shape

To get a heavy crop, always prune cordon trees in summer. This also helps the trees to keep their shape. Between late July and September each year, cut back all the laterals to one good leaf from the base, ignoring the cluster of basal leaves. Cut all sub-laterals back to one or two buds. When the main shoot has reached the top wire, cut it back in May to the previous year's growth, and trim any additional growth to 2.5cm (1in) when pruning in summer.

See also **Espaliers**, **Pruning**

Miniature orchard Step-over trees provide a maximum of fruit in a minimum of space.

Coriander

Two of the best

There are two main types of coriander. 'Cilantro' is the variety to grow for the fresh leaves which make an unusual addition to salads. Grow 'Morocco' coriander if you want the seeds, which are delicious when crushed and added to curries or pork dishes. The seeds of both are wildly available, or you can grow 'Morocco' coriander by planting the seeds that are sold for culinary use.

Aroma on the doorstep

Grow a tub of 'Cilantro' by the kitchen door and harvest the leaves, as required, for salads and other dishes. Coriander leaves do not dry well but you can chop them finely and freeze them in small quantities in polythene bags or in an ice-cube tray.

Collecting seeds

Harvest the seeds from 'Morocco' coriander when they are plump but before they ripen fully and begin to drop from the plant. Alternatively, lift the plants carefully before the seeds ripen and hang them upside-down over a newspaper in a cool, shady place. As the seeds ripen, they will fall onto the paper and can be gathered without difficulty. Store them in an airtight, dark-coloured glass jar.

Save and sow

Coriander seeds remain viable for up to six years if stored in a dry, shady place. Save enough to sow next year and allow one or two plants of the 'Cilantro' variety to produce seeds to provide next year's crop of leaves.

Corn salad

Successful sowing

Before sowing this delicious, soft-leaved salad vegetable, rake the soil well to remove weeds and water well. Mix the seeds with sand to separate them, then sow them in 1.3cm (½in) deep drills or broadcast them over the bed. Rake gently, then water them in using a watering can with a fine rose.

Staggered production

Corn salad, also known as lamb's lettuce, can be sown throughout the growing season. Sow in March and April for cropping from June, and from May to July for cropping from August to October. The main crop is sown in August and September for cropping from late autumn through to spring. In hot summers, corn salad may run to seed before it develops sufficiently to provide a crop. For a high quality spring crop, sow in a cold greenhouse between October and December after crops such as tomatoes have been harvested.

Salads without effort

If you allow corn salad to run to seed in spring, there will be no need to sow more, as it will seed itself prolifically.

Make the right choice

Two types of corn salad

The two kinds of corn salad are not always differentiated in seed catalogues. Large-seeded types are more productive, develop large pale leaves and are suited to spring and summer sowing for summer and early autumn crops. Varieties to look out for include 'Broadleaved English' and 'Italian Large-Leaved'. Small-seeded varieties make smaller plants with thicker, dark green leaves and, as they thrive in cooler conditions, are suited to later sowing. Look out for 'Verte de Cambrai' and 'Vit'.

Courgettes

A good turn

If you are sowing courgettes in pots, place them on a warm, sunny window ledge. Give each pot a half-turn every day to ensure that the light is evenly distributed. The seedlings will grow up straight as a result.

On the heap

Make the most of a binful or heap of old, well-rotted compost in the garden by planting courgettes on top. Fresh, unrotted compost is not a suitable medium for growing courgettes because it is rich in nitrogen and encourages excess leaf production at the expense of fruits.

Food supply in poor soil

If you are growing courgettes on a sandy or poor soil, make a central source of food for several plants. Pierce the sides and bottom of an old plastic bucket and bury it so that the rim is level with the surface of the soil. Fill the bucket with manure and plant four seedlings in the bed, in a circle, 1m (3ft) in diameter, round the bucket. Water directly into the bucket, so that the nutrients from the manure are passed to the plants.

A helping hand

If the weather is wet and windy, and bees and other pollinating insects are discouraged from flying and pollinating your courgette flowers, you can pollinate them yourself. First, identify the female flowers: they each have a small, embryo fruit behind the petals. Pick a male flower, gently remove its petals and push it into the trumpet of the female flower. You can use one male flower to pollinate several females.

Garden secrets

Soak and plant

Soak courgette seeds overnight before planting. The water will soften the outer coating and speed up germination. Plant two seeds, on their edges, in each pot or planting hole. If both seeds germinate in a pot or hole, remove the weaker seedling.

Be generous

Modern courgette varieties produce huge crops on compact plants, and unless you want large surpluses, you may find that only three or four plants will be more than enough for the needs of your household. Your neighbours may welcome your spare plants, or you can pass them on at a charity bring-and-buy event.

Green screen

If you want a quick and temporary screen, grow a trailing marrow such as 'Long Green Trailing' and tie it into a trellis. Pick the fruits when they are about 10cm long, and cook as courgettes.

Watch the water

Overwatering encourages leaf growth. Unless the plants are suffering, do not water liberally until the fruits begin to form, then give each plant 9 litres (2 gallons) of water daily.

Pick them all

Be vigilant when picking the crop. If you leave just one fruit to turn into a marrow, further courgette production will be slowed down.

Flower food

Courgette flowers stuffed with rice make delicious party snacks. They can also be dipped in batter and deep fried in oil, stuffed or served raw in a salad.

See also **Marrows**

Creeping plants

Using climbers as creepers
Cover a bare, weedy or unattractive slope in the garden with climbing plants but allow them to spread along the ground instead of providing them with supports on which to climb. Many climbers, including clematis, early and late-flowering honeysuckles, ivies, winter-flowering jasmines and roses, will succeed very well in such situations.

Clean and tidy
At the end of winter, tidy up your creeping plants by pruning out dry, damaged or weak stems, cutting back any that are too long and dividing the clumps if necessary. Any plants that are left over when the clumps have been divided can be replanted elsewhere, either as creepers or as climbers.

Rejuvenating old plants
If the centre of a creeping plant starts to thin out, spread some soil, or old compost from a growing bag or container, on top of the balding stems. This will encourage the stems to take root in the soil and to send out new shoots to thicken up the plant.

Care with prostrate roses
Unless you are prepared to prune them regularly, avoid planting prostrate roses close to the edges of paths because their thorny stems can cause injury and damage clothing. These roses may also trap wind-blown litter.

Make the right choice

Climbers that will creep

Many plants that commonly drape walls and fences will, if given no support, creep along the ground, providing a dense carpet of colour. But, growth will often be much less in the prostrate position than when the plants are trained on a wall.

Name	Description
Akebia quinata	Purple, heavily scented flowers in spring followed by purple, sausage-shaped fruits
Clematis alpina	Blue or pink flowers in spring, fluffy seed-heads in summer
C. montana	White flowers with yellow anthers in late spring
Fallopia baldschuanica (Polygonum)	Rampant, creeping plant with panicles of white flowers in summer and autumn
Hedera helix	Large and small-leaved varieties, with green or variegated leaves
Hydrangea petiolaris	Large, lacy clusters of small, white flowers in summer
Jasminum nudiflorum	Bright yellow flowers from November to April
Lonicera japonica 'Halliana'	Semi-evergreen honeysuckle. Fragrant white/yellow flowers from June to October
L. peridymenum 'Belgica'	Purple-red and yellow flowers in May and June
L. p. 'Serotina'	Red-purple flowers with cream-white inside from July to October
Parthenocissus tricuspidata	Deciduous creeping plant with brilliantly coloured foliage in autumn
Rosa 'Breath of Life'	Modern rose, bearing medium-sized blooms in an attractive shade of pinky apricot
R. 'Felicite Perpetue'	Semi-evergreen rose with fragrant, pale pink flowers
R. 'Grouse'	Prostrate rose with fragrant, blush-pink flowers

Cucumbers

Planting cucumbers
From late April to mid June, sow outdoor types in a protected place, such as a cold greenhouse. Plant them out from mid May onwards, using cloches or portable frames covered with clear polythene until all risk of frost is past. In colder areas, keep them covered until well established.

Early crops
You can harvest cucumbers from May onwards by sowing seeds of indoor varieties in the greenhouse in February and keeping them at a temperature of about 18°C (64°F). Grow them on in a greenhouse bed of rich, moist compost, raising the temperature to 21°C (70°F).

A question of pollination
If you are growing greenhouse cucumbers, prevent pollination of the female flowers, which gives cucumbers a bitter taste, by pinching out the male flowers. The latter are easily distinguished from the female flowers because they do not have a small embryo fruit behind each bloom. Outdoor (ridge) varieties need to be pollinated, so male flowers should be left on the plants. However, all-female varieties of greenhouse and ridge cucumbers are available. There is no need to remove the flowers and none of the cucumbers will be bitter.

Space-saving support
Save space by training outdoor cucumber plants upwards on supports. This will produce more fruit, check rot and help longer-fruited varieties to grow straighter.

Garden secrets

Perfectly formed
If you want to grow perfectly shaped cucumbers for the show bench, you can ensure that they are straight by slipping transparent plastic tubes over the fruits as soon as they begin to swell. The tubes should be about 10cm (4in) in diameter and about 30cm (12in) long. Transparent plastic bottles with the ends cut off will make suitable tubes.

In the frame
If you do not have a greenhouse or if you prefer to use it for more tender crops, you can grow greenhouse cucumbers well in a cold frame by training the plants to trail along the ground instead of to climb. Encourage the plants to form side shoots (laterals) by pinching out the growing tips as soon as four to six leaves have formed. Similarly, when the laterals have each made four to six leaves, pinch them out in the same way. Spread the laterals along the floor of the cold frame. You should remove the male flowers (those without an embryo fruit behind the bloom) as soon as they appear and then pinch out the fruiting shoots two leaves beyond the first fruit. (*See also* **Cold frames**)

Varieties for small gardens
Cucumbers grow on long stems, and each plant needs an area of about 1m² (11sq ft). If you do not have the space, train the plants on wires or grow compact, non-running varieties such as 'Bush Champion'. One of these plants will fit into a plot of about 40cm² (4sq ft), and can even be grown in a container on a balcony.

Harvest before your holiday
Before you go on holiday, pick all cucumbers, even small ones, growing either outdoors or in a greenhouse or frame. During your absence, other cucumbers will form and will be ready to pick when you return. Give each plant a good soaking before you depart, as this will help the production of new fruits. On outdoor crops, place a few slug pellets or traps round the plants.

Make the right choice

Know your cucumbers
Choose between greenhouse and outdoor varieties, or grow some of each.

Greenhouse varieties
'Galileo' All-female F1 variety that produces two female plants per leaf and therefore more than one cucumber per leaf axil.

'Femspot' All-female F1 variety, disease-resistant and early maturing

'Landora' Early-producing F1 variety which grows in a cold greenhouse or cold frame.

'Passandra' All-female F1 mini-cucumber, resistant to powdery mildew

'Petita' All-female F1 variety, produces heavy crop of fruit, 20–23cm (8–9in) long

'Telepathy' Improved F1 'Telegraph' type, tolerant of a wide range of temperatures.

Ridge (outdoor) varieties
'Burpless Tasty Green' Prolific, mildew-resistant variety

'Bush Champion' Space-saving plant that can be raised in growing bags

Cut flowers

Early picking
Cut flowers in the morning when they are turgid. This will help them to retain moisture after they have been cut.

Clean-cut stems
When cutting flowers, always use scissors or a knife. This will prevent damage to the stems and make a clean cut through which the flowers can absorb water.

A bucket for blooms
To prevent cut flowers from drying out while being carried back to the house, carry a bucket half-filled with water and plunge the flowers into it as soon as they are cut.

The kindest cut
When preparing cut flowers for a vase, remove any leaves that will be below the water line. Then, holding it under water, cut the end of each stem at an angle to leave a large area. This enables the flower to absorb the maximum amount of water.

Crushing blow
Using a sharp knife, slice the base of the hard stems of woody plants such as lilacs, roses and viburnums, then crush the wound with a hammer to aid the penetration of water.

Bottoms up
Flowers with large, hollow stems, such as delphiniums and amaryllis, should be turned upside down and have their stems filled with water. Use pieces of damp cotton wool to plug the stems and immediately stand the flowers upright in a vase of water.

Longer blooming
Before arranging flowers, give them a long drink by plunging their stems, right up to the blooms, in a bucket of water and leaving them to stand overnight. This helps the arrangement to last longer. Other aids said to prolong the life of cut flowers include crushed aspirin, sugar or a copper coin added to the water.

Garden secrets

Homemade flower food
All cut flowers benefit from a feed. A good homemade mix can be made by blending 2 tablespoons of sugar and 1 litre (1¾ pints) of warm water together with 1½ teaspoons of household bleach.

Supporting stems
Tulips and other long-stemmed flowers may droop after cutting. Keep them upright by placing a piece of chicken wire, folded several times, into the neck of the vase. Slip the stems through the holes in the mesh.

Refresher course
Revive wilted flowers by cutting off the ends of their stems and plunging them into a bucket of hot water for half an hour. Fill the vase with fresh cold water and return the flowers to it. If the room is hot, add ice cubes to the water and spray with a misting spray to help to rejuvenate the petals. Alternatively, move the display to a cooler room, a balcony or a windowsill.

A sense of occasion
Make a table arrangement for a special occasion by cutting out the shape of an appropriate letter or number from florist's

foam. Soak in water until saturated, then cover completely with short-stemmed flowers. Stand in a shallow container. (See also **Florist's foam**)

Look after the stems
If flowers are to look their best for as long as possible after they have been cut, they require special treatment according to their variety. Stand clematis stems in about 3.2cm (1¼in) of boiling water for 30 seconds before putting them in cold water. Pick poppies while they are in bud, then seal the ends of the stems with a candle flame or dip them into boiling water. Stand peonies and violas in deep water for several hours.

The time to cut
The best time to cut flowers varies according to variety. Cut daffodils when they are in bud and peonies when the buds are just showing colour. Never cut dahlias until the flowers have opened, and wait for the first gladiolus floret, at the base of the stem, to open. It is not uncommon for the topmost bud on a gladiolus to remain closed and if this happens, the bud can be trimmed off carefully with scissors.

Watertight vases
If a favourite vase is cracked or porous, make it watertight with paraffin wax. Heat the wax to melting point, then pour a little into the vase and rotate it quickly, making sure that the inside is completely coated. Pour away the excess wax and leave the remainder to set before using the vase.

Fragrant flowers
Some of the prettiest flowers lack fragrance but you can cheat by adding some yourself. Sprinkle a few drops of your favourite essential oil onto a small piece of cotton wool or paper towel and tuck it between the stems of fresh or dried flowers.

Rose revival
If roses or other woody-stemmed flowers begin to droop, they may perk up if you trim about 1.3cm (½in) from the bottom of each stem, then stand them in 2.5cm (1in) of boiling water before returning them to a vase of fresh water.

Protect the flowers and leaves from the steam by wrapping them in a cloth.

Keep flowers in the dark
When transporting flowers in a car in hot weather, wrap the stems in damp newspaper, slip them into a polythene bag and put them into the boot where they will be shaded.

Gardener's Potpourri

The language of flowers
The idea that flowers have different meanings is embedded in folklore. Any bouquet makes a beautiful and much appreciated gift, but if the flowers are selected to convey a secret message to the recipient, they take on an added significance.

Flower	Meaning
Amaryllis	Pride
Aster	A first step
Begonia	Ethereal love
Buddleja	Refinement
Calendula	Tenacity
Candytuft	Peace
Chrysanthemum	Truth
Clematis	Pure in mind
Daffodil	Chivalry
Forget-me-not	Fidelity
Gladiolus	Strength of character
Honeysuckle	Sweet disposition
Hyacinth	Play
Iris	Message
Lavender	Chastity
Lilac	First love
Lily of the valley	Purity
Magnolia	Dignity
Marigold	Happiness
Primrose	Sadness
Rose	Love
Sunflower	Haughtiness
Sweet pea	Gentleness

Cuttings

New plants from old

The most popular method of propagation is by cuttings. Part of a plant is removed and grown so that it becomes a new plant that is a clone (genetic copy) of its parent. Provided that cuttings are taken from healthy plants and have warmth, moisture and light and a suitable growing medium, new plants can be produced at almost no cost.

Hormone rooting powder

When applied sparingly to some stem cuttings, hormone rooting powder can encourage the cuttings to put out roots. If the cuttings are taken at the right time and from healthy plants, rooting powder should not be necessary. But if previous attempts to root untreated cuttings have been unsuccessful, you may wish to try again using rooting powder. Only the smallest amount is necessary. Too much will inhibit, rather than promote, root formation. Dip only the base of the cutting into the powder, then tap it lightly to remove the excess. Sufficient powder will remain on the stem. Rooting powder is not suitable for leaf or root cuttings.

Top and tail

Once a hardwood cutting is stripped of its leaves, it can be difficult to know which end is which. To prevent mistakes, trim the top of the cutting at an angle and cut the bottom straight across.

Propagation in water

The stems of some house plants, such as *Coleus blumei* or *Fuchsia* and short-lived perennials such as *Impatiens* (busy lizzie), will put out roots if left to stand in a container of water. Cover the top of a container with foil. Make small holes in the foil with the point of a knife and push the cuttings gently through the holes, making sure that any leaves remain above the foil. Keep the water topped up, and replace it if it turns green. When roots appear, pot up the cuttings in moist compost. Cuttings struck in water can be slow to become established.

Propagating papyrus

Cut a stem from a papyrus plant and trim the leaves until they are about 5cm (2in) long. Stand the stem, leaves downwards, in a jar or bottle of water. Keep the water level topped up and, when roots appear from the nodes round the leaves, pot up the cutting in a pot of moist compost.

Make a clean cut

When taking hardwood cuttings with a knife, position the blade below the branch and cut in an upward direction. With secateurs, position the sharp cutting blade flush with the main stem of the parent plant. If the secateurs are reversed, a snag will be left.

Poisonous plants

The sap of some plants is an irritant or even poisonous and great care must be taken to prevent both sap and fragments of such plants from coming into contact with the skin or eyes. Cuttings of poisonous plants should not be prepared on household surfaces, while hands, tools and work surfaces should be washed down thoroughly. Plants that require caution include codiaeums, *Dieffenbachia* (leopard lily), *Euphorbia* (spurge), x *Fatshedera* (tree ivy), hoyas, philodendrons and *Sinningia speciosa* (gloxinia).

Heel cuttings

Cuttings with a heel (a woody piece of tissue from the main stem) can be taken to form semi-hardwood cuttings, particularly from hollow-stemmed plants.

Select a suitable side shoot and remove it from the parent plant by holding it between your thumb and finger and pulling down sharply while supporting the main stem of the plant with the other hand. Trim the heel and remove the lower leaves from the stem. Take several cuttings in the same way, then insert them in a small pot of cuttings compost or an equal mixture by bulk of peat or coir and coarse sand. Cuttings that root better in a humid environment can be protected from excess moisture loss by covering with a plastic bag. To keep the bag from resting on the cuttings, use several short sticks, or a length of wire with one end bent into a hoop, to support the bag.

Make the right choice

Timing for taking cuttings

The best time of year for taking cuttings depends on the type of plant to be propagated, and its stage of growth. See below for plant types and timings.

Plants	Type of cutting	Time
House plants, half-hardy perennials	Softwood	February to July
Shrubs, trees, conifers, heathers	Semi-hardwood Hardwood	July to September October to March
Herbaceous perennials, shrubs and trees with fleshy roots, plants which produce suckers	Root cuttings	When plant is dormant

Wounding
Some plants, including rhododendrons, can be difficult to propagate from cuttings because their stems have a sheath of material between the bark and the wood which can inhibit root development. To increase the chance of success, use a sharp knife to make a shallow cut about 1.9cm (¾in) long at the base of the cutting before inserting it in its pot.

Propagation from leaves
Cuttings taken from the stems of leaves, known as leaf petiole cuttings, are a simple and reliable way of propagating house plants such as *Saintpaulia* (African violet) and begonias (with the exception of *Begonia rex*). Fill a tray or other shallow container with cuttings compost or a mixture of equal parts by bulk of sifted peat and grit. Select an undamaged leaf and, using a sharp knife, sever it from the parent plant, taking about 5cm (2in) of the stalk. With a fine dibber, make a hole in the compost, just deep enough to hold the cutting. Insert the leaf at an angle so that its blade lies almost flat. Firm the compost gently round the cutting and water well using a fine rose on the watering can. If you wish, add fungicide to the water.

A DIY propagator
A polystyrene tray is an efficient propagator in which to root cuttings. Remove the hooks from three wire coat hangers and bend the lengths of wire into hoops. Insert one at each end of the tray and the third in the middle. Fill the tray with cuttings compost, insert the cuttings and wrap clear polythene over the wires and round the base. Close each end with plastic-covered wire.

CABILLAUD LORIENT

Coloured stems
Cornus (dogwood) and *Salix* (willow), many varieties of which are grown for their coloured stem effects, can be propagated easily by taking hardwood cuttings between November and March. Cut the stems into 30cm (12in) sections, following the advice in **Top and tail** on page 82.

Striking cuttings outdoors
Hardwood cuttings taken from some plants, such as blackcurrants, buddlejas or roses, can be rooted in borders in the shade of shrubs or perennials that are watered regularly in the winter. Insert the cuttings in the soil and leave them undisturbed until the following autumn, then, when they have rooted, lift them and plant them out in their permanent positions.

First make a planting hole
Always use a dibber to make a hole in the compost before inserting a softwood cutting. If the cutting is forced into the compost the delicate base may be damaged.

Testing for roots
Always allow enough time for cuttings to take root (this will vary according to the plant and the time of year). Examine the plants for signs of growth, such as new leaves or shoots, or roots showing through the bottoms of the pots. Alternatively, grip the base of the cutting between your thumb and finger and pull it very gently. Resistance is a sign that roots have formed.

Potting up
Before potting up rooted cuttings, stand them, in their pots, in a bowl of water and leave them to soak until the compost is thoroughly wet and bubbles no longer rise to the surface. This will help to separate any roots which may have become tangled where several cuttings were rooted in the same pot.

Root cuttings
Some herbaceous perennials, shrubs and trees, such as *Anchusa azurea*, *Chaenomeles* species, *Primula denticulata* (the drumstick primula), *Rhus* and *Romneya coulteri*, can be propagated from root cuttings. When the parent plant is fully dormant, remove the surrounding soil to expose the roots. Cut off some young roots close to the crown, then replace the soil round the parent plant. Wash the young roots well, then, using a sharp knife, cut them into sections 5cm (2in) long. Fill a pot with moist, sandy potting compost, make holes in the compost, then insert the cuttings, pushing them down until their tops are level with the compost surface. Stand in a frost-free place and do not water until shoots appear.

See also **Sand**

Dahlias

Enviable early colour

To dazzle the neighbours with a show of July-flowering dahlias, start them off in mid March. Take some of your stored tubers, or begin with new ones from the garden centre, and pot them up into 13cm (5in) pots of good potting compost. Water them well and keep them in a greenhouse or other well-lit, frost-free place, at a temperature of 10–12°C (50–54°F). Tall, strong-growing varieties may need potting up into 18 or 20cm (7 or 8in) pots. In early May, you can begin to harden them off by standing them outside in a sheltered spot during the day and taking them indoors at night. Plant them

out in late May in the south, or early June in the north, when all danger of frost is past. If a cold snap is forecast, protect the young plants by covering them with sheets of newspaper.

Starting with seed

Most of the largest and most spectacular dahlias are bought as tubers from garden centres and then propagated by cuttings, but dahlias can also be raised from seeds. The best seed-raised dahlias are the shorter bedding types that reach a height of just 30–38cm (12–15in). The seeds can be sown in March or April in a heated propagator and the seedlings pricked out into 9cm (3½in) pots. Harden off, and plant out at the end of May in the south or early June in the north. The dahlias should be in flower by July and will continue to flower right through until the first frosts. Mixtures to look out for include the semi-double 'Rigoletto', the collerette-flowered 'Dandy' and the bronze-leaved 'Diablo'. A few single colours, such as red, pink, yellow and white, are also available.

Dahlias in mixed borders

Dahlias are often grown in beds of their own where they make a spectacular display, but many varieties can be grown in mixed or herbaceous borders. Choose those that produce a number of small blooms, rather than the large-flowered varieties, because these will blend more successfully with other plants. Varieties with bronze foliage are especially effective in mixed borders – among good

examples are 'Redskin', in mixed colours, and the scarlet-flowered 'Bishop of Llandaff'. Another wide-ranging mixture, from white through yellows to reds, is 'Disco Mixed'. They flower early and long and make an excellent display.

Doubling up on dahlias

To increase your stock of dahlias, take out the stored tubers in February or March and put them into trays of moist compost. Water well, and keep them at a temperature no lower than 13°C (55°F). After three or four weeks, new shoots will develop. When they are about 7.5cm (3in) long, cut off each one just above its base and trim back to just below a leaf joint. Dip the bottoms of the shoots in a hormone rooting powder, then carefully insert them about 2.5cm (1in) deep, in 9cm or 3½in pots of sandy compost, allowing four shoots to each pot. Put the pots into a propagator and leave them for two or three weeks. When they have rooted, pot up the cuttings individually into 9cm or 3½ in pots of potting compost. Keep them in a frost-free greenhouse then gradually harden them off. Plant them out when all danger of frost is past.

Showy blooms

For exhibition flowers, choose the giant decorative or cactus dahlia strains that are intended to carry only three or four blooms in

A brief history

The obliging dahlia

The astonishing range of colours and forms available in modern border hybrids, plus a reasonable ease of cultivation, have introduced a high degree of competition into dahlia growing. Some gardeners concentrate on size, producing blooms 30cm (12in) across and more, others on filling the garden with as dazzling a spectrum as possible. Although the varieties obtainable seem almost limitless, they are probably all descended from a single species, *Dahlia pinnata*, that was introduced into Europe from Mexico in 1789 and named in honour of Anders Dahl, a Swedish botanist. But despite the present array of hues that span pinks and crimsons, creams and lilacs, mauves and purples, no one has as yet produced a blue dahlia, which has come to be a symbol of something unobtainable.

one season. Ensure that each plant produces no more than this number by pinching out the weakest stems at soil level when they are about 10cm (4in) long. On each shoot, pinch out all but the crown (central) bud. This should result in extra-large blooms.

Staking

All tall dahlias need support. They make a great deal of foliage that can be caught easily by the wind and, when they flower, the sheer weight of the blooms can lead to broken stems unless the plants are staked well. The simplest method is to use three or four thick bamboo canes or square dahlia stakes to each plant. Push the canes or stakes into the ground round the plant, leaving 1–1.2m (3–4ft) above ground, then run twine from cane to cane to support the dahlia.

Dahlias are thirsty plants

Prevent dahlias from wilting in hot, dry summers by copious watering. The plants are largely composed of water and, to ensure maximum development, each should be given at least 9 litres (2 gallons) of water every other day during dry spells in August and September, the growing period.

Bright blooms Clumps of small-flowered dahlias bring dazzling colours to the late summer garden.

A longer, brighter life

Dahlias look fresher and will last longer if cut early in the morning when they are full of sap. Cut the stems at an angle; this prevents them from sitting flat on the bottom of a vase and allows them to take up more water. They will flourish better, too, if the vase is placed out of direct sunlight.

Go gently with tubers

When taking up dahlia tubers for winter storage, do not tug on the stems as this may cause damage. The best way is to loosen the soil carefully, then gently lift the whole clumps with a fork. Leave them to dry in the open – preferably in the sun – for a day, before putting them under cover. After a further ten days, when the tubers have dried thoroughly, shake them vigorously to remove the soil trapped between them. Cut back the old stems to short stubs, then turn the tubers upside-down so that any water in the old stems can drain away before storage.

Dry bases

Standing dahlias upside-down not only removes water from the old stems, but also allows any damp to evaporate from the base.

Indoor storage

Trim off all roots that are less than 1.3cm (½in) thick from lifted and dried dahlia tubers to leave small, compact tubers. Immerse them in a fungicide and put them in shallow wooden boxes of peat that is almost, but not quite, dry. Wrap the boxes in fine gauge wire mesh to protect the tubers from mice and rats, then store them in a cool but frost-free place. (See also **Labelling**)

Outdoor storage

If you have no suitable indoor storage space for dahlia tubers, store them in a well-drained spot in the garden. Dig a hole about 60cm (24in) deep and large enough to contain all of the tubers. Line the bottom of the hole with a 25cm (10in) layer of straw and lay the tubers on top, roots downwards. Cover them with another 25cm (10in) layer of straw, then replace and mound up the soil.

Dandelions

Clearing up the lawn

Dandelions, like other broad-leaved weeds on the lawn, will yield quickly to a selective weedkiller, but removing them can leave bare patches that will rapidly be colonised by other weeds. In March, before dealing with the dandelions, apply a proprietary lawn food, according to the manufacturer's instructions, followed by regular mowings once a week with the blades set high. This will encourage strong growth by both grass and weeds. After about a month, apply the selective weedkiller, as the grass should then be growing vigorously and will fill the gaps. Make a second application of weedkiller after a month, if necessary. (See also **Lawn care**)

Spring harvest

It is a good idea to encourage a few dandelions to grow in a wild corner, or to plant them in a row in the vegetable garden. In spring, cut the young, pale leaves and mix them with chives and parsley in a side salad, garnished with oil and lemon juice. For a sweeter taste, blanch the leaves by placing inverted pots over the plants for a few days before cutting. Remove all the flower heads before the plants set seeds.

Dead leaves

The simple approach

In large gardens, gathering up leaves to make a heap of leafmould can be a tiresome chore. Instead, rake or sweep the leaves onto the borders and leave them spread evenly among the shrubs. This replicates what happens in nature when trees and shrubs shed their leaves. Gradually, the worms pull them under, where they rot and improve the texture of the soil.

Winter topcoat

Use autumn leaves to make winter overcoats for tender plants, particularly those in pots. Spread leaves generously over roots and round stems, where they will provide excellent protection against cold and frost. Firmly anchored plastic mesh or wire netting can be used to hold the leaves in place, if necessary.

Mechanised leaf clearance

If the fallen leaves do not lie too thickly on your lawn, set the blade of your rotary mower high and use the machine to sweep them up. You may have to empty the box fairly frequently, but it saves the time and effort of raking them up.

A leaf-free lawn

Leaves, if left on the lawn, will cause the grass to turn yellow, so sweep or rake them up frequently. On large areas, it may be worth borrowing or buying a mechanical sweeper or a vacuum cleaner designed to blow them into a heap or suck them up. These can also be used to clear leaves from flowerbeds.

Disease carriers

When sweeping up autumn leaves, watch out for those showing signs of diseases such as black spot or rust. These diseases can overwinter and flare up again in spring. They can also survive for years in the leafmould heap. Either put them in the middle of the compost heap, where the heat will kill the spores, or bury them deep in the ground. Alternatively, you can put them into bags and take them to your local rubbish tip.

A leafy substitute

Gather fallen, disease-free leaves and put them into a bin or a container made from four stakes driven into the ground and surrounded by plastic mesh or wire netting. Keep the leaves moist and press down to compact them. They will eventually break down and become leafmould, which is an excellent substitute for peat. Dig the leafmould in to improve the texture of the soil, or use it as a mulch.

Beware autumnal overflows

Keep an eye on gutters, and downpipes that have open entrances and exits. Scooping out accumulated leaves and other debris will prevent blockages that can lead to overflows and flooding. Even better, fit wire cages over the tops of downpipes. As well as preventing blockages, these will discourage birds from building their nests in the pipes in spring.

Dead tree trunks

A treasure to be cherished

Sometimes, even a dead tree has a place in the garden. The shape can be attractive, and the tree can become an important habitat for a variety of creatures, creating interest in your garden. Birds such as owls, redstarts, coal tits and nuthatches may nest in its holes and hollows; insects, small rodents and toads may also find homes in the tree. However, you should remove the tree if it stands near a building, wall or fence that could be damaged if the tree were to fall onto it. Also cut the tree down and burn it if it begins to sprout fungus.

A home for climbers

If a dead tree has begun to shed its bark, you can compensate by growing climbing plants round its base. Choose climbers in keeping with the size and shape of the tree. On small trees, *Clematis rehderiana* or *C. cirrhosa* var. *balearica* are ideal.

Safety cuts

To make more of a dead tree, prune it to present an attractively striking silhouette. Remove all the small branches and keep only a few of the larger ones. In this way, the tree will have less wind resistance and will add more character to the garden.

A new life for ivies

Plant three or four ivies at the base of a dead tree and within a few years they will grow to cover the trunk completely. When the tree eventually rots away, the ivies will be established sufficiently to continue to grow without any support.

Nature's flower trough

Before you have an old, half-rotted tree trunk removed, think about giving it a new, if temporary, life. Cut the top flat, scrape out the rotten wood from the centre and line the cavity with a thin coating of cement. Drill a drain hole from the outside of the trunk to the bottom of the cavity and fill the cavity with a mixture of soil and compost. You will then have a rugged and attractive planter that will last until the trunk finally rots away.

Honey fungus

One of the most likely causes of death in trees is honey fungus. Loss of vigour and dieback are two of the initial symptoms. Honey fungus spreads from infected trees through the soil by means of rhizomorphs (black thread-like growths) to infect healthy trees. After a few years, honey-coloured fungal growths appear beneath the bark at ground level. Where houses have been built on arable land, there is little risk of infection, but gardens near woodlands are particularly vulnerable and it may be wise to remove dead trees.

Decking

A sunny spot
Give your decking a dry, sunny spot in the garden. Avoid areas under the drip of trees or that are likely to flood in periods of wet weather, as this will considerably shorten its life.

Installation know-how
When installing decking, lay the joists on a sheet of landscape fabric. This will prevent weeds growing through the boards and will also help to control rotting at the base of the joists, as most fabrics allow moisture to seep through into the soil but prevent it returning to the surface. Make sure the decking boards slope slightly to one side so that water can run off onto the garden.

Prevent slips
All timber surfacing becomes slippery when wet, and the problem gets worse if algae are allowed to grow on it. Use a decking cleaner, which usually contains an algaecide, regularly – before the problem becomes apparent. You may need to do the job several times a year, particularly in warm, wet weather. Don't forget the winter months, even if the decking is not often used, as the worse it gets, the more difficult it will be to clean the green slime off when you want to use it again.

A sunny spot
When constructing a wooden deck, butt the boards together, or provide a small gap only for ventilation, rather than leaving a large space between them, which can severely affect the safety of the feature as rubbish may start to collect in the void beneath and become a fire hazard. High heels may also get lodged in a gap more than a few millimetres wide, and rats can squeeze through gaps and take up residence in the cosy area under the boards.

Fire alarm
Treated timber is always a fire hazard in certain circumstances. If your family or friends smoke, try to persuade them to be careful with smoking materials in the vicinity of the decking – better still, ask them not to smoke at all in that area. Check, too, that stray fireworks have not fallen onto the boards, and never light fires where sparks or burning materials could fall onto the boards. You should also have a fireproof barbecue area if your patio is made from decking.

Preserve and protect
Well-maintained decking, like any other wood product, will last much longer than that which is forgotten about once laid. Use a decking preservative regularly to delay rotting, particularly in the joists and other upright members; a pressure sprayer will apply the preservative much more efficiently than painting it on with a brush. Remove some of the boards to access the timber that is covered; at the same time check for any rot that has started, cut it out and paint the sound timber with a wood hardener before replacing with new wood that has first been treated with a preservative.

Raise your pots
If you want to stand containers on decking, always raise them on pot feet so the boards beneath can dry out, otherwise they will start to rot.

Keep weeds at bay
However careful you are with construction, weeds will eventually start to grow, either in the detritus under the boards, or in the dust that collects in the cracks and joints. Treat with a path weedkiller as soon as you notice them – once established, they will be so much more difficult to remove.

Decorative fruits

Balancing the sexes
If a spectacular display of berries is your ideal way of rounding off the gardening year, make sure that you get the right balance of sexes. Species whose male and female flowers are carried on separate plants include *Aucuba japonica* (spotted laurel), *Ilex* (holly), *Skimmia* and *Hippophae rhamnoides* (sea buckthorn). To facilitate pollination, plant one male plant to every three females. The male plants will not produce berries. (*See also* **Holly**)

Avoiding mess
The brightness of fruits and berries can add much to the charm of a garden path, but this is not necessarily the case when the fruits and berries fall. Some, such as the berries from *Cotoneaster*, *Sambucus* (elder), *Sorbus aucuparia* (rowan) and damsons and greengages, can make a mess when they hit flagstones or when carried indoors on footwear, so plant them well back from the path. Do not allow hawthorn branches to arch over the place where you

Winter brilliance Evergreen *Cotoneaster lacteus* bears dense clusters of red berries well into winter.

park the car. Left to themselves, the berries will do little damage, but they become almost indelible when they have been eaten by birds and become part of their droppings.

Berry pyrotechnics
Display fruits and berries to their best advantage by making a hedge from berry-bearing shrubs, or by placing a single specimen in front of some evergreens. Alternatively, plant a *Pyracantha* (firethorn) or *Cotoneaster* at the foot of a brick or stone wall and, as it grows, train the arching sprays to decorate the wall. (*See also* **Shrub**)

Leafy back-up
Red, amber or yellow berries standing out against dark green, glossy leaves make evergreen hollies supremely decorative plants. And, among trees that lose their leaves in autumn, varieties of crab apple also offer outstanding crops of ornamental yellow fruits flushed with red or purple.

Make a good show
Plant *Euonymus europaeus* 'Red Cascade' close together in groups of two or three to ensure a good show of berries.

Deep beds

Grow more
If your garden is too small to produce all the vegetables that your family needs, a deep-bed system can solve the problem. This method of growing produces a large crop, even allowing for the space taken by the paths between the beds. Vegetables are spaced equally in all directions and, as their foliage meets, the weeds are smothered.

Made to measure
Once dug, deep beds should not be walked on, as this will compact the soil. So, before digging the beds, make sure that they will not be too wide. You must be able to reach the crops in the centre of the bed while standing on one of the paths. A width of 1.2m (4ft) suits most gardeners, but if you are shorter or taller than average, you can adjust the width to suit your reach.

Once and for all
The initial effort required to prepare deep beds will be more than amply rewarded for years to come. Whatever your type of soil, begin by double digging the beds and include plenty of bulky organic matter. All that is required thereafter is the addition of well-rotted compost or manure, either applied as a mulch or forked in lightly every season. (*See also* **Clay soil**)

Make the right choice

Trees with bright berries

Fruit-bearing trees are decorative in autumn and winter.

Name	Colour
Crataegus x *lavalleei* 'Carrierei' (ornamental thorn)	Orange-red
Ilex aquifolium 'Bacciflava'	Yellow
I. aquifolium 'J.G van Tol' (English or common holly)	Red
Malus x *robusta* 'Red Sentinel' (crab apple)	Scarlet
Sorbus aucuparia (rowan, mountain ash)	Orange-red
S. cashmiriana	White
S. sargentiana	Scarlet

Growing know-how

How far apart?

For some spacing suggestions for deep-bed vegetables, see below.

Vegetable		Spacing	
Artichokes		46cm	(18in)
Beans	(broad)	30cm	(12in)
	(french)	30cm	(12in)
	(runner)	38cm	(15in)
Beetroot		15cm	(6in)
Brussels sprouts		46cm	(18in)
Cabbages	(spring)	30cm	(12in)
	(summer/winter)	38cm	(15in)
Carrots		15cm	(6in)
Cauliflowers		61cm	(24in)
Celeriac		30cm	(12in)
Celery	(self-blanching)	23cm	(9in)
Chicory	(blanching)	20cm	(8in)
	(non-blanching)	25cm	(10in)
Courgettes		61cm	(24in)
Cucumbers	(ridge)	61cm	(24in)
Garlic		10cm	(4in)
Leeks		23cm	(9in)
Lettuces	(early sowings)	15cm	(6in)
	(later sowings)	23cm	(9in)
Marrows	(bush)	61cm	(24in)
Onions	(sets)	15cm	(6in)
Parsnips		15cm	(6in)
Peas	(dwarf)	46cm	(18in)
Potatoes	(earlies)	30cm	(12in)
	(others)	38cm	(15in)
Spinach		15cm	(6in)
Sweetcorn		46cm	(18in)
Tomatoes	(cordon/bush)	46cm	(18in)

Paths and edges

Ideally, the paths between the beds should be wide enough for your wheelbarrow, but if space is very limited, make every alternate path wide enough for the barrow, and the others about 46cm (18in) wide. Edge the beds all round with old railway sleepers, planks or paving stones standing on end.

Delphiniums

Cuttings or seeds

The best delphiniums are named varieties, which are propagated by division in spring, or by taking cuttings. These plants have tall, majestic spikes in rich colours and large, semi-double flowers. It is easy to raise delphiniums from seeds and the Southern series of seed-raised varieties will produce plants of the same quality as those raised from cuttings. Seeds collected from the garden produce variable results.

The richer the better

All delphiniums need a deep, rich, well-drained soil and a sunny position. Dig in plenty of bulky organic matter before planting in early spring, then mulch with well-rotted compost. Do not allow the soil round the roots to dry out. Given this treatment, they will, for a time, flourish even in shallow, chalky soil, although they prefer richer conditions.

Height needs help

Tall delphiniums will need staking. Tie in each stem to a stout bamboo cane or surround the plant with canes spaced 15–20cm (6–8in) apart and link them with wire, strong twine or a herbaceous support, available from garden centres.

Best for show

Among varieties of *Delphinium consolida* (larkspur), the Giant Imperial type, which stands 1.2m (4ft) tall and is available in a wide range of striking colours, is best for the border and for fresh and dried flower arrangements. For large, early-flowering plants, sow the seeds *in situ* in autumn and protect the seedlings with cloches during the winter. If a later display is required, delay sowing until April.

Focus on flowering

Stagger flowering by pinching out the tips of some young plants when they are 15cm (6in) high. Once the first flowering is over, encourage a second display by cutting the plants back to 10–20cm (4–8in) above the basal leaves.

Water low

When watering delphiniums, soak the soil at the base of the plants. Do not sprinkle them from above, as water on the leaves can encourage disease.

Dianthus

When planting dianthus, bury only the bottom 6mm (¼in) of the stem, making sure that the lower leaves are above soil level. Deeply planted dianthus is more susceptible to stem rot.

Bushy growth

If young pinks do not put out side shoots, pinch out the top of the main shoot in March or April, if possible early in the morning on a damp day. This will delay blooming but is essential for strong, bushy growth.

Simple to grow

For trouble-free dianthus, choose border carnations or garden pinks rather than the perpetual-flowering varieties, which are better grown in a greenhouse. Pinks, in particular, are easy to grow as they rarely need staking and never require disbudding.

Autumn colour

Most modern pinks can be encouraged to flower throughout the summer if the flowers are snipped off as they fade. However, some pinks, especially older varieties, will produce only one flush of flowers in early summer. These may be encouraged to flower a second time if the plants are trimmed back when the flowers fade.

Stopping and disbudding

Perpetual-flowering carnations produce the best flowers if they are first stopped and then disbudded. Stopping means pinching out the tip of the main shoot when it has eight to ten pairs of leaves so that six pairs of leaves are left. A number of new shoots will then appear lower down the plant. As the flower buds start to develop, the topmost bud on the shoot is encouraged to grow larger by the removal of smaller buds just underneath. This is called disbudding and ensures that all the plant's energy goes into producing one large flower on each stem. If you prefer a spray of smaller flowers, pinch out the main bud instead.

A brief history

What's in a name?

Dianthus have been valued since classical times, for both their scent and their beauty. Such high regard over so long a period has given rise to a great variety of common names that sometimes meant one species and sometimes another. Coronation (carnation), gillyflower and pink, which got its name from a Dutch word for Whitsun, are dianthus. So are clove pinks and sops-in-wine, which was perhaps derived from the practice of drinking vinegar in which pinks had been steeped as a preventative of plague. Sweet william became associated with William, Duke of Cumberland after his victory at Culloden in 1746, although the defeated Jacobites retaliated by christening the malodorous common ragwort 'Stinking Billy'.

Layering carnations

Border carnations should be propagated every three or four years, depending on variety. The simplest way to do this is by layering in July or August. Choose a stem 20–25cm (8–10in) long that has not flowered and, leaving it attached to the plant, strip off all but the top three or four pairs of leaves. Make a shallow, lengthways cut about 2.5cm (1in) long, at a position halfway down the stem just below a joint. Prise open the cut with your fingers, then bend the stem, cut side down, into a shallow hole filled with a mixture of soil, sharp sand and peat. Leave the tip protruding above the soil and pin the stem down with a large hairpin or piece of bent wire. After six weeks, check if the stem has rooted by gently brushing away the soil round the hairpin or wire. If roots are visible, re-cover them with soil and cut the stem on the plant side of the hairpin or wire. After two more weeks, lift the cutting and plant it in its permanent position.

Cutting it fine

The narrow stems of pinks make layering difficult, so they are better propagated by cuttings. Do this at any time after flowering until the end of August. Cut off side shoots at the base, then cut just below a pair of leaves to make 7.5–10cm (3–4in) cuttings. Strip off the bottom foliage, leaving three or four pairs of leaves at the top of each stem. Insert the cuttings in pots containing a mixture of moss peat and sharp sand and place in a cold frame. After three or four weeks, when the cuttings have rooted, they can be potted individually into small pots of John Innes No. 1 compost.

Keeping up appearances

Gardeners used to believe that if different varieties of pinks were planted together, the flower shapes would deteriorate and the colours would change over the years. This is a myth, but even if you grow a single variety, and the plants are not deadheaded, seeds may drop and germinate round the plant. Since the seedlings of pinks are rarely the same as the parent plant it may appear that the original plant has changed when, in fact, a new seedling is growing beside the original. Regular deadheading of pinks will avoid this problem.

Digging

Spade choice

When choosing a spade, make sure the shaft is a suitable length for you, in order to avoid back strain when digging. Test whether a D-shaped, Y-shaped or T-shaped handle feels the most comfortable, although the T-shaped handle may not be readily available. A spade is the ideal tool for digging, unless the soil is so wet or heavy that it would stick to the blade, in which case a strong fork may make a more suitable choice.

Digging technique

Begin digging by inserting the blade of the spade into the ground, at right angles to the line of the trench. Press the spade home to about a quarter of its depth, then align the blade to the trench and press it firmly into the soil to its full depth. As you pull the handle of the spade backwards and downwards, you will lift out a neat cube of soil.

The best method

Start by marking out with pegs and string the area of the garden you intend to dig. Take out a trench, one spade deep, across one end of the

plot, put the soil into a wheelbarrow and move it to the other end. Working backwards, dig a second trench, depositing the soil in the first trench. When you have dug the final trench, fill it with the soil taken from the first.

Comfort and health

If possible, always dig in mild weather, since wind and cold tend to chill the muscles and can increase fatigue. Be careful not to overdo it, taking out only small amounts of soil at a time. Never dig when the ground is frozen, very wet or covered with snow. On clay soil, use a strong fork rather than a spade, and avoid straining by keeping your back as straight as possible and bending at the knees. This will put less pressure on your arms and shoulders and help to prevent injury.

Economise on spadework

If you dig the soil deeply and incorporate plenty of organic matter, such as well-rotted compost or manure, you will not need to do much work in future. In subsequent years, just spread a thick layer of organic matter over the ground in autumn and allow the worms to pull it in. Avoid compacting the soil by working from a plank when sowing or planting. (*See also* **Clay**, **Mulching**, **No-dig gardening**)

Avoid back strain when lifting soil

In addition to keeping your back straight and bending at the knees while digging, make sure that the quantity of soil on your spade is manageable before lifting it.

Clean up the soil

When digging, remove all large stones and perennial weeds from the plot, making sure that no fragments of the roots of weeds, such as

dandelions, docks and thistles, are left in the ground, as these will quickly regrow. Annual weeds will rot away if buried, so skim them off the surface, then turn them upside-down in the bottom of the trench and cover them with soil as you dig.

Time the digging

If your soil is heavy clay, dig it over in the autumn, leaving it rough for the frosts to break down. If the soil is light and free-draining, dig it in the spring to prevent the winter rain from washing out the nutrients

Dill

Getting started

Grow dill in well-drained, fertile soil in a sunny position. Sow the seeds in shallow drills 23–30cm (9–12in) apart and thin the seedlings to 10–15cm (4–6in) apart if wanted for leaf production, or 23cm (9in) apart if wanted for both leaves and seeds. Keep the plants well watered.

Non-stop summer supplies

Monthly sowings of dill seeds from March to July will result in a continuous summer supply of fresh leaves. The leaves are ready for use six to eight weeks after sowing.

Strong plants

Self-sown dill often results in more vigorous plants than those that are produced by hand sowing. Seedlings adapt well to being moved from one part of the garden to another, so distribute them as you wish.

Decorative dill

Dill flower heads contain masses of tiny flowers, and these look delightful in flower arrangements. For fresh displays, cut off the flower heads before they begin to brown; for dried arrangements, however, allow the heads to mature. The fresh, lacy, blue-green leaves are also pretty when used as a foil for other flowers.

Division

Get the timing right

Most plants should be divided in the autumn, but some, such as *Anthemis*, *Aster*, *Chrysanthemum*, *Delphinium*, *Helenium*, *Kniphofia*, *Lobelia*, *Pyrethrum* and *Viola*, are best left until spring. If, however, your soil is heavy clay, and particularly if you live in a cold area, it may be wise to divide all your plants in spring when the soil has warmed up.

Benefit from division

When dividing a plant into smaller ones you should take the opportunity to enrich the soil while the ground is clear. Have plenty of bulky organic material, such as well-rotted compost or farmyard manure, standing by, mixed with a little bone meal or other slow-acting organic fertiliser. Fork it into the soil before replanting the divisions.

A job for two forks

When separating a large clump of perennials, use two border forks. Push them into the clump back-to-back, with the handles about 38cm (15in) apart. First bring the handles together, then push them apart. You will find this much easier than holding part of the root with one hand and trying to break it in half using a single fork.

Keeping the pieces that count

When dividing an old plant, keep only the strongest, vigorous young shoots from the outer edge of the clump and reject the old, woody centre, which is past its best. If possible, use only the divisions that have good, strong root systems, as the weaker ones may take a long time to establish and may never produce a good display. It is better to have young plants with a good root system and little top growth than prolific growth on a puny root system.

Saving time with smaller clumps

Do not pull up a whole plant if you want to separate only one or two fragments for replanting elsewhere. Remove the soil on one side of the plant and, using a garden fork, loosen the stems and roots as far down into the soil as possible. Use a knife to remove the pieces you require, then replace the soil firmly round the remaining roots. Be careful not to do this too often, however, because, by continually removing strong, outer shoots and retaining the weaker ones in the centre, the plant will become weak and may eventually fade away completely.

Handling hostas
Hostas have tough, tightly packed roots that can be difficult to divide. The simplest method is to use a sharp spade to remove a V-shaped piece from the edge of the clump. Fill the space with old potting compost and plant the smaller piece of the hosta elsewhere.

A new lease of life
To make sure of success when dividing plants, replant the divisions immediately and water them in. If there are any pieces that you cannot attend to straightaway, heel them into a shallow trench. This will provide a temporary home until permanent planting can be carried out. Cover the roots with soil and firm them in well. Divisions from larger plants should be heeled in at an angle so that the wind cannot blow them over, while any plants that you intend to give away should be potted up and their roots kept moist.

Healthy stock
Take divisions from healthy plants only. If you propagate from diseased stock, infection will be passed on to the young plants. Before replanting divisions, inspect the roots carefully to make sure that no pests are concealed among them.

Dogs

Thorny barriers
To keep dogs out of your garden, surround it with hollies, pyracanthas, roses and other thorny shrubs. Make sure that dustbin lids are kept firmly closed so that dogs are not attracted by the smell of food

Pepper protection
Some dogs love to gnaw at wood and can damage trees and bushes, leaving them vulnerable to infection. If your pet likes to chew your garden plants, try sprinkling the plants with pepper dust or spraying with a little pepper diluted in water to discourage them.

Defence for vegetables
A picket fence can help to deter small dogs from scratching up seedlings in the vegetable patch. The fence can be covered with bright, climbing annuals such as nasturtiums.

Wander no more
An invisible electronic boundary will keep your dog or cat from straying, whether your frontier is a garden gate or the perimeter of a small estate. It will also keep pets away from swimming pools and vegetable plots. When the animal approaches the boundary, a warning bleep is transmitted. If this is ignored, the animal receives a mild but effective correction. Companies that install the system advertise in country magazines.

Keeping the lawn green
Canine urine can cause yellow patches on the lawn. Bitches are usually responsible, because they empty their bladders in one spot, while male dogs tend to distribute their urine round the garden in small amounts. Once a patch of grass has yellowed, it will soon turn brown and will almost certainly die. The only treatment is to dilute the urine with water as soon as it is deposited. If you are too late and the grass has died, give the dead patch a good soaking and resow with grass seed, or repair the area with a square of turf of a similar grade.
(See also **Lawn care**)

Doorways

Mobile highlights
Create seasonal changes around your front door by setting out a succession of new pot plants and containers. Pots of bright spring bulbs can give way to fragrant drifts of nicotianas and puffs of candytuft spilling from a half-barrel in summer. For autumn impact, follow with a pot of fatsia, whose strong outlines, glossy leaves and white flower clusters make an exciting contrast to the season's reds and golds. Then winter can be cheered with baskets of pansies and trailing ivies hanging round the door.

Making an entrance

Bring the doorway into focus with flowering climbers such as clematis and honeysuckle, arresting stands of hollyhocks and lilies, boxes of plants such as blazing pink petunias or pelargoniums on nearby windowsills and hanging baskets brimming over with fuchsias, petunias and trailing lobelia.

Colour harmony

Choose the right plants to complement the exterior of your house. Dark red and blue blooms can appear dull against new, raw brickwork, where pale flowers would stand out with heightened clarity. Keep the darker flowers as a foil for a mellow wall. For the white entry to a town house, you might provide a pair of pots containing blue hydrangeas. Alternatively, a pair of flowering evergreens, such as skimmias, choisyas or hebes will look good all year round.

Formal approach

Place a clipped shrub or tree, such as a box or bay, in an elegant urn or Versailles tub on each side of the front door. Plant variegated ivies to trail attractively over the edges.

(See also **Climbing plants**, **Container gardening**, **Containers**, **Hanging baskets**)

Lift up your bed

Most herbs require a well-drained soil. A small herb bed that is badly drained can be improved and turned into a feature if it is raised within a retaining wall two bricks high with at least a couple of drainage holes on each side. Fill with well-rotted garden compost or farmyard manure mixed with grit. When the mixture has settled, the bed should drain well and the herbs should flourish.

Land drain

You may have a mature tree or shrub in the garden that is suffering from the effects of badly drained soil. Improve drainage by digging a circular trench, one spade wide and 12.5cm (5in) deep, in the soil surrounding the tree or shrub, in line with the outer edge of the foliage. Shovel a thick layer of gravel into the bottom of the trench and top up with a mixture of garden soil, grit and well-rotted garden compost or farmyard manure.

Drainage

Combating clay

If the soil in your garden is heavy clay, and water is slow to drain away after a downpour, there are several remedies. The most effective, but most expensive and labour-intensive, is to install a drainage system. Alternatively, dig in autumn to penetrate any compacted layers and allow frost to break the soil down in winter. Or add lime to help to bind the clay into granules through which water can drain more easily. Otherwise fork plenty of horticultural grit and organic matter into the soil. This helps to separate the clay, allowing the water to drain through.

Garden secrets

Crocks in high places

Finding stones or fragments of flowerpots to aid drainage in containers is easy for most gardeners, but it can be a problem for city flat-dwellers with balcony or roof gardens. The well-washed shells of mussels or cockles will work just as well, as will corks, beer-bottle tops, nutshells, small pieces of polystyrene or little balls of aluminium foil.

Dried flowers

Stopping petals from falling

To prevent flowers from losing their petals while they are drying, pick them before they are in full bloom and leave at least 15cm (6in) between the hanging bunches.

Supporting flowers

Flowers can be wired before drying. If the stem is hollow, make a small hook at one end of a length of florist's wire, and push the other end down through the centre of the flower into the stem. On flowers with solid stems, twist the wire round the stem. The wire will be concealed by the flower.

The best way to dry flowers

The best way to dry freshly cut flowers is to hang them upside-down. They should be picked in mid morning after any dew has evaporated, and grouped into small bunches. To preserve the colours of the flowers, hang them in a well-ventilated, dry place with little light, such as a garage or cellar.

Dried to perfection To preserve their colours, hang flowers in bunches to dry immediately after picking.

Dealing with large heads

Flowers such as alliums, artichokes and globe thistles, which have large, heavy heads, need to stand upright while they are drying. Staple a piece of chicken wire across the top of a cardboard box, then simply slip the flower stems through the holes in the wire.

Striking seedpods

Do not deadhead the blooms of *Nigella damascena* (love-in-a-mist). Instead, leave the flowers to form their seedpods. These are pale brown with red bars and are complemented by the finely cut foliage of the plants. The seed heads can be dried to make, or add to, an unusual arrangement, or coloured with spray paints for even greater effect.

Drying roses

To dry roses, pick them either when they are in bud or just as they begin to open and hang them in bunches, or leave them in the oven, at an extremely low heat and with the door left open, for about 5 hours. Pink roses, when dried, keep their colour best. Reds, yellows and oranges darken with drying, and creams and whites turn beige.

Pressed into action

Use an old directory or mail order catalogue to press stems, flowers or leaves. Slip your chosen specimens separately between the absorbent pages, then add extra weight by laying a heavy object on top. Pressed material is fragile, so avoid needless disturbance by tagging pages or sections of an album with the plants' names.

Preventing colours from fading

Preserve the colours of large leaves from trees such as chestnuts, beeches and limes by ironing them with a moderately hot iron. In the case of smaller leaves, slip them, still attached to their stems, between a double thickness of newspaper and press gently with a slightly hotter iron.

Freshening-up arrangements

Check dried flower arrangements from time to time for faded or dusty blooms. Remove them carefully and fill the resultant gaps with newly dried replacements.

Using desiccants

Silica gel crystals, silver sand or borax, obtainable from chemists, floral suppliers, glass merchants and DIY stores, can all be used for drying flowers, such as carnations or roses, that have fragile petals. Place the flower heads, spaced well apart, in a container and cover them with the desiccant. If using silica gel, which completes the drying process quickly, check the flowers every two or three days.

Drying with salt

Fill a vase with coarse-grain salt and add a couple of tablespoons of water to moisten it slightly. Flowers, such as aconitums (monkshood) and members of the delphinium genus that have rigid stems, can be dried by plunging the stems into the salt.

See also **Potpourri**

Drought

Beating the hosepipe ban

Prepare in advance for the times when drought occurs and the use of hosepipes is banned. Place water butts in strategic positions near the house, greenhouse, shed and garage – anywhere there is a downpipe that can be led into a butt.

Second-hand water

Recycled bath water is perfectly good for the garden, and it saved the lives of thousands of plants in the hot, dry summers of 1976 and 1995. Siphon it out through the bathroom window and into a water butt. Alternatively, you can buy a small pump for this purpose, which is driven by a power drill. Water saved from defrosted freezers and the rinsing water from washing machines and dishwashers can also be used, but water containing detergents or salt should be avoided.

How much water?

In dry conditions, it is best to water plants and soil thoroughly or not at all. If only the top couple of centimetres or so of the ground is dampened, plants will develop roots in this shallow layer where they are even more vulnerable to the drying effects of the sun. Try to moisten the soil to a depth of at least 30cm (1ft). Roots will then be encouraged to grow downwards, into a layer of soil that is insulated from the sun and will, consequently, remain damp for much longer.

Mulch to retain moisture

If you are worried that your holiday may coincide with a period of dry weather, you should make preparations in advance. While the soil is moist, cover beds and borders with a rich organic mulch, at least 10cm (4in) thick. Such material, as well as being of benefit to plants and soil, is water retentive. (*See also* **Holidays**, **Mulching**)

Waste not

To reduce wasteful surface evaporation, direct water to the places where it is needed most. Sink clay pots close to the roots of plants that

require large amounts of water. At each watering, fill the pots and allow the water to drain directly down into the soil.

Catching every drop

Even in the most extreme drought conditions, rain may fall overnight. Put saucers under every potted plant in your garden and stand your watering can and other empty containers in the open before you go to bed. On some mornings, you may be surprised to see how much water has accumulated.

Make the right choice

Plants for dry soil

Your garden should flourish and watering can be reduced to a minimum, even in very dry summers, if you plant a selection of drought-tolerant plants. Most are undemanding and look their best with the minimum amount of water.

Trees and shrubs
Berberis, Buddleja, Ceanothus, Choisya, Cistus, Cotoneaster, Deutzia, Escallonia, Euonymus, Fatsia, Genista, Hebe, Ilex, Juniperus, Lavandula, Ligustrum, Phlomis, Potentilla, Ribes, Robinia, Rosmarinus, Rubus, Santolina, Senecio, Sorbaria, Symphoricarpos, Syringa, Tamarix

Perennials
Acanthus, Achillea, Anchusa, Artemisia, Campanula, Dianthus, Echinops, Eryngium, Euphorbia, Gaillardia, Gypsophila, Linum, Malva, Nepeta, Platycodon, Rudbeckia, Stachys, Stipa

Bulbs, corms and tubers
Allium, Alstroemeria, Chionodoxa, Crocosmia, Cyclamen, Gladiolus, Hyacinthus, Nerine, Ornithogalum, Tulipa

Annuals
Antirrhinum, Calendula, Campanula, Clarkia, Cosmos, Dianthus, Helianthus, Nigella, Papaver, Pelargonium, Petunia, Scabiosa, Tagetes

Let the lawn look after itself

In times of drought, either mow your lawn with the mower blades set high, or do not mow it at all. The more grass that is left on the lawn, the longer it will take to turn yellow. You may not think so at the time, but however brown it becomes, it will quickly turn green again after the first rains.

Select specialised plants

If some long-range forecasts are correct, and northern Europe is to experience a run of dry summers, it might be as well to plan for them. One way to combat drought is to put in plants that relish dry conditions, such as those of Mediterranean origin, and those with grey and silvery foliage covered with fine hairs. (See also *Plants for dry soil, p.95*)

Build up some pressure

Manufacturers have realised that many garden watering appliances – even hand-held sprinklers – will not work on the low pressure from a water butt, and have produced submersible pumps that are capable of producing a pressure that makes it as easy to water from a butt as from the mains water supply. To be really satisfactory, you need the largest butt or tank you can accommodate; if space is limited, you might find it more convenient to join several smaller butts together – devices are available from garden centres and hardware shops that make this easy to do.

Shop around

Large tanks are now available that will hold several hundred litres/pints – even a cubic metre or more (over 35ft³) – of rainwater, but these are expensive. The alternative is to look out for a metal-reinforced, translucent plastic tank that has held agricultural or other chemicals and generally has a capacity of one cubic metre. These are often sold second-hand; check local newspapers and sales publications for what is available. Prices vary – some firms give these away for collection – but make sure it has been cleaned out before you install it. You may need to modify your downpipe to get the rainwater through the hole in the top, but this should be a simple job.

Lovely lavender The many lavender varieties all do well in dry conditions, producing fragrant flowers in exquisite shades from white to deepest purple throughout summer.

Keep the weeds away

Unwanted plants require just as much soil moisture as your most precious garden specimens, so make sure beds, borders, the vegetable plot and the fruit garden are kept clear of weeds at all times.

Hoe regularly

Gardeners used to say that 'a good hoeing is worth more than a shower of rain', and it is still true today. This is because breaking up the surface of consolidated soil interrupts the capillary attraction of the particles, and prevents moisture from the root area of the plants from gradually being drawn up to the top, where it will continue to evaporate until all the soil is completely dry. A light hoeing after every heavy shower will therefore considerably reduce the necessity for watering .

Automatic watering

Watering with a can or hosepipe can waste water, especially where containers are concerned, as much of the water runs off to where it is not needed. An automatic or semi-automatic watering system that delivers a required amount when it is needed can conserve water substantially if it is properly set up. If the system is based on drippers, the drippers and the time they are allowed to drip should be adjusted so that large amounts of water do not run out of the base. This will vary according to weather conditions and the time of day and year, so automatic watering is not an excuse for neglect.

Let your hose seep

Overhead watering with a hosepipe or watering may put more water on the foliage than it does on the ground, and wetting the foliage is not always necessary. Running a length of perforated (seep) hose along each row, or making a ring round plants that may require watering in times of drought, will get the water to the soil above the roots, exactly where it is needed. Check periodically that the hose does not become blocked with soil or limescale; if this happens, wash it in soapy water and treat limescale with a household scale remover, rinsing thoroughly afterwards.

Add organic matter

Soil containing plenty of organic material will hold moisture much longer than that which is lacking in humus. A mulch of garden compost or farmyard or stable manure will enrich the earth as the soil organisms pull it down; the mulch should be topped up regularly.

Lay a carpet

Weed-control fabric is used regularly by landscape contractors to prevent weeds growing through paving, but it is also an ideal way to prevent water loss from beds and borders. A small cut is made in the fabric where each specimen is planted and the fabric is adjusted after planting so it covers the surface right up to the base of the plant. The best materials allow water to pass through to the soil but regulate the amount that returns to the atmosphere, so the ground always stays damp but not waterlogged. Avoid polythene, which does not let the earth breathe and can produce a sour and infertile soil in time.

Cuddle up

Close planting can actually reduce the amount of watering that is needed as the foliage shades the soil and prevents drying out. Young, closely spaced plants should be mulched well, but will provide their own protection once mature.

Dustbins

Hiding a wheelie bin

Wheelie bins are much larger – and possibly even less attractive – than dustbins. In addition, most households these days are obliged to have several, usually of different and often garish colours, to contain landfill, recyclable and compostable waste, with the result that unless there is adequate space for them in a large shed, they can become the most dominant feature in the garden. Construct a small paved area at the edge of a border, adjacent to a firm path leading easily to the front of the property where the bins are placed for emptying, and make a designated hard standing for your wheelie bins here.

Cover up

Plastic covers are available with flower and foliage designs printed on them. While these can make the bins stand out even more if they are sited in an area of paving or gravel, or against the front wall of the property, if situated among plants the camouflage effect is more successful. Obtain floral or leaf-patterned covers for each bin, and you will be surprised just how well they blend into the scenery. The covers are sometimes sold at garden centres and hardware shops, but more often through mail-order catalogues and on the internet.

Make life easy for yourself

Wheeling a full wheelie bin over gravel can be extremely hard work. If you are forced to move your bin along a shingle path or down a gravel drive, lay a line of slabs in the gravel on which to move your bins. It will make like easier, and can make an attractive contrast to the rest of the path or driveway.

Dwarf plants

Deceptive dwarfs

The term 'dwarf' can sometimes be a misnomer. Many so-called dwarf conifers, for example, are really slow-growing forms of normal trees, which means that, in time, they will grow as big as the standard forms. Since the standard forms of many conifers are forest giants, smaller versions can grow into alarmingly big trees. To make sure the dwarf conifer you buy will stay that way, go to a reputable garden centre that will guarantee the eventual height and spread of the tree.

An orchard on the patio

If space is short for growing fruit trees, grow them in pots on the patio. A few varieties are naturally dwarfing, and ideally suited to large pots. But any apple or plum tree that has been grafted onto a dwarfing or semi-dwarfing rootstock can be grown in a pot. A pot-grown apple tree on the semi-dwarfing rootstock M26 will thrive and fruit when very young, while a plum tree grafted onto Pixy rootstock will also stay small. Or you can use the naturally dwarfing cherry 'Compact Stella'. The peach 'Bonanza' and the nectarine 'Nectarella' each reach a maximum height of about 1.2m (4ft) and will thrive on a sunny, sheltered patio. All need large pots, 46cm (18in) in diameter, and John Innes No. 3 compost.

Unexpected growth

Do not be surprised if a small, potted chrysanthemum develops long stems in time. Growers often treat flowering house plants such as chrysanthemums and poinsettias with a dwarfing chemical so that they retain their compact shapes and flower early. After a few months, they resume normal growth patterns.

A mini-forest

You can imitate the appearance of a forest in your living room by grouping together carefully chosen house plants and dwarf varieties of some garden plants. The colourful flowers of compact evergreen azaleas such as Rhododendron 'Vuyk's

Scarlet' or R. 'Hino-mayo', miniature roses, such as Rosa 'Baby Masquerade' or R. 'Rise 'n' Shine', Saintpaulia (African violet) and the white, waxy spikes of Spathiphyllum combine well with the contrasting leaf shapes and textures of ferns, Peperomia, Pilea cadierei 'Nana' (aluminium plant) and the creeping fig, Ficus pumila 'Minima'. (See also **House plants**)

Golden foliage 'Nana Aurea' is an appealing dwarf form of Chamaecyparis obtusa (Hinoki cypress).

Earthing up

Keep early shoots warm
A mild spell in winter or early spring may prompt perennials to send up early shoots. Protect these from the frosts by covering them with a thick layer of peat or coir compost. Apply this carefully. Do not press down or you may bruise the shoots.

Winter protection
Some plants, such as fuchsias, are not hardy enough to withstand a harsh winter. Mound up a mixture of pulverised bark and pebbles round the bases to protect them.

Help brassicas to root
Earth up the stems of winter cabbages and cauliflowers. At the same time, stake the taller-growing Brussels sprouts and cauliflowers. This will prevent the plants from rocking in the ground in strong winds, which disturbs the roots.

Blanch vegetables
Earthing up is the easiest way of blanching vegetables such as celery, Florence fennel and leeks. Simply draw the soil round the bases as the stems develop.

Protecting potatoes
Tubers exposed to light turn green and become poisonous. Prevent this by earthing up, starting when the foliage appears above ground. A gutter on top of the mound will improve water absorption.

Earthworms

Encourage friends
Earthworms are indispensable in the garden because they aerate the soil, pull down and digest decomposing organic matter and create humus. Encourage them to take up residence by keeping the soil moist, mulched and manured.

Dressing for lawns
Leave wormcasts to dry on the lawn, then use a besom broom to brush them over the grass. They make a nutritious top dressing.

Cast out the culprits
Never apply a lawn dressing that contains worm killer. The benefit of worms in the lawn far outweighs the inconvenience of a few wormcasts. If the problem is severe, apply sulphate of ammonia to the lawn to increase the acidity of the soil – cast-forming worms prefer alkaline soils.

Fertility check
Dig a spadeful of soil and count the number of earthworms it contains. Six or more indicate a fertile soil in which plants should thrive. If there are only a few, dig plenty of organic matter into the soil to improve its fertility.

Prevent scab
Enlist the help of worms to keep fruit trees free from scab, a fungus disease that causes black or brown blotches on the leaves and fruit of apples and pears. The fungus grows on dead leaves and releases its spores around Christmas time. Run a mower over the leaves in autumn to chop them small. Worms can then easily pull them underground before the scab spores have a chance to infect healthy trees.

Foreign peril
Everyone recognises the value of earthworms in the garden, but flatworms are foes rather than friends. In fact, while earthworms are invaluable in improving the soil, flatworms actually feed on earthworms. Flatworms arrived in this country from New Zealand and are easy to identify. While all types of earthworms have the familiar round profile, flatworms are – as their name implies – noticeably flat. They grow up to 18cm (7in) long, are dark in colour and have a pale stripe running down each side of their body. They are also rather sticky.

Garden secrets

The incredible earthworm
Invaluable to gardeners, earthworms are also vital for the survival of many other creatures, such as badgers, slugs beetles, birds, moles and hedgehogs.

- Up to 8 million earthworms may live in a hectare (2½ acres) of grassland, even more in deciduous woodland.

- Worms can live for up to ten years.
- There are some 25 species of British earthworm, of which *Lumbricus terrestris*, the common earthworm, is the most often seen. It usually measures between 9 and 23cm (3½–9in) in length.
- Worms are sensitive to vibration, which they associate with rainfall. Drumming on the soil will bring them to the surface in search of moisture.
- Charles Darwin estimated that the worms in a single acre will, between them, shift 8–18 tons of soil a year.
- *Microchaetus microchaetus*, the world's largest species of earthworm, is found in South Africa. It can grow to 7m (23ft) long.

Dealing with flatworms

Though birds devour earthworms by the million, they shun flatworms. Not only are the creatures sticky and unpalatable, they also tend to emerge at night, when most birds are asleep. There are no chemical controls against flatworms, but you can sometimes trap them by laying down an old carrier bag or polythene sheet in a cool, sheltered spot and weighing down the corners with stones. Check the underside every day and you may well find them underneath. A stamp of the foot usually kills them but make sure the head is crushed. Alternatively, drop them into a bucket of salty water.

Regional differences

Flatworms are slowly spreading throughout the UK but you are much more likely to find them in your garden if you live in damp areas, such as Scotland, Ireland, Wales and western parts of England, rather than in the generally drier south and east.

Edible flowers

The edible garden

Mingle edible flowers and culinary herbs with vegetables in the kitchen garden to create an eye-catching and edible display. The flowers and herbs will bring delightful fragrances and colours to the vegetable garden.

Container flowers

Grow edible flowers in a window box, hanging basket or tub for a bright display. Heartsease, nasturtiums and marigolds will all flower more vigorously if they are frequently deadheaded. Combine these with the attractively frilled foliage of 'Lollo Rosso' lettuce, which has red-tinged leaves, and the short-rooted carrot variety called 'Early French Frame'.

Eat with caution

Eat only flowers that you can definitely identify as edible – and those you can be certain have not been contaminated with either insecticide or weedkiller.

Small doses

Some people may suffer an allergic reaction to certain species of edible flowers. It is always advisable to eat only a small quantity of a flower if you have never eaten it before. It is certainly inadvisable to eat the flowers of *Calendula officinalis* (pot marigold) or thyme during pregnancy.

Petal-strewn salads

Use the peppery-tasting nasturtium and *Calendula officinalis* to bring prominent splashes of scarlet, orange or yellow to green salads. You can also add a subtle flavour and visual impact to fruit salads by using petals from heartsease, roses or sweet violets.

Culinary herb flowers

Culinary herbs are an excellent source of edible flowers. Herbs such as borage, camomile, chervil, chives, wild garlic, lavender, wild marjoram, mint, sage, thyme and lemon verbena all produce flowers that have a similar taste to the plants' leaves and can be used as garnishes. The blue, star-shaped flowers of borage are particularly appealing.

Vegetable flowers

Both runner beans and peas produce edible flowers, but picking them will prevent pods from forming; therefore you need to choose between edible flowers and vegetables for your table. The male flowers of courgettes can, however, be picked without preventing the fruit from growing. They are particularly prized as

edible flowers because their pale yellow, showy trumpets are ideal for either stuffing or turning into delicate fritters. (*See also* **Courgettes**)

A sweeter scent

The sweeter the scent of an edible flower, the stronger its taste will be. This is particularly true of roses, so pick only the blooms of scented varieties. Before eating a rose petal, pinch out its base as this can taste bitter.

Preparing ahead

If flowers are not eaten straight after being washed and patted dry, put them in a bag and store in the refrigerator. They will keep for a few days.

Floral sugar

Pick six heads of lavender or the petals of three large roses or six scented dianthus and dry for a few hours. Place them in a jar with 450g (1lb) of icing or caster sugar. The sugar absorbs the flavour and can be used to add an unusual taste to icings or fools.

Edible ice

Fill an ice-cube tray with water and place one small edible flower in each compartment to make enticing, year-round floral decorations for your drinks.

Eggshells

Keep slugs at bay
Eggshells baked in the oven then crushed and spread round the base of a plant make an effective barrier against slugs and snails, which dislike travelling over rough surfaces.

Nature's seed boxes
Save your eggshells and use them as fun containers for seedlings or cuttings. With a pin, pierce three or four drainage holes in the base of each shell. Fill the shells with seed or cutting compost and sow one seed in, or insert one cutting into, each of them. When the young plants are large enough to handle, crack the shells and transfer the seedlings or cuttings to more permanent homes. An advantage of using eggshells as pots is that there will be little root disturbance to the plants when they are removed.

Compost booster
Eggshells can be added to the compost heap or worked directly into the soil. Provided that you first crush them in your hand, they will quickly break down, adding some extra calcium to the soil.

Endives

Blanch before eating
Endives need to be blanched before they are harvested as the leaves are bitter if left exposed to the light. Once the plants have matured, make sure the leaves are dry – to minimise any danger of rotting. Then, either bind the entire plant loosely with raffia or string so that the outside leaves block light from the inner leaves, or place an upturned flowerpot over each plant, covering the drainage hole with a stone. (See also *Earthing up*)

Ready to eat
Blanch only a few plants at a time, allowing 10–14 days for the blanching process. Depending on the variety that you are growing, the colour of the leaves will be either pale green, pink, creamy white or pale yellow. When the plant has reached this stage, it is ready for eating and can be lifted. The flatter varieties of endives can be blanched by simply covering the whole plant with a large dinner plate.

Refrigerator storage
Ideally, endives should be eaten soon after they are picked because the leaves quickly toughen and wither after they are harvested. However, surplus leaves can be slightly moistened and placed in a polythene bag. They will stay fresh for several days if kept in the refrigerator.

Cut and come again
Sow endives with spinach, lettuce, corn salad, chervil and purslane to harvest a mixed crop of 'cut and come again' salad vegetables. At regular intervals between March and August, sow the seeds in a broad drill. Then, once the seedlings

Growing know-how

The winter salad
Between late summer and early winter, endives make an excellent alternative to lettuce. Two groups of endives can be grown – those with curled leaves, which are called chicorée frisée, and those with plain leaves, known as Batavians. You can enjoy this vegetable throughout its seasons by planting 'Moss Curled' (ready to eat from August onwards if sown in May), 'Sally' (late summer onwards) and 'Batavian Broad Leaved' (autumn and winter).

have reached 10cm (4in) in height, cut the leaves back to about 2.5cm (1in) from the ground. By doing so, it is sometimes possible to obtain one or two more crops.

A sweeter flavour
Even after blanching, endives still have a slight bitterness. If they are not to your taste, try one of the newly introduced varieties, such as 'Riccia Pancalieri' or 'Wallonne'. These are predominantly self-blanching and have a sweeter taste.

Espaliers

Space-saving fruit
Make the most of your wall space by using it for an espalier, a fruit tree with 'tiers' of three or more horizontal branches trained to grow flat against a support. This type of cultivation is particularly useful for growing apples and pears in small gardens, where every centimetre of space needs to be used effectively.

Easy espaliers
Buy an espalier fruit tree that already has two tiers in place. The juvenile shaping has been done by an expert whose skill enables you to begin harvesting earlier.

Planting angle

Before planting a two-tiered espalier tree, stretch three or more wires horizontally along the wall at about 45cm (18in) intervals, but matching the lower two wires to the two tiers already established. When planting, place the roots about 23cm (9in) away from the wall to allow for future growth and lean the stem slightly inwards to make it easier to attach the branches to the wires.

Strong support

When growing espaliers on wires, check the supporting posts are sturdy, pressure-treated with preservative and driven well into the ground. Use galvanised wires, fix them to the posts with vine eyes and ensure they are taut by using tensioning bolts.

Training the branches

In the first winter after planting, cut back the main stem to just below the third wire from the ground, at a point where there are buds growing alternately on either side of the stem. As the buds develop into new branches, begin training by tying them into canes. Gently lower the canes, so that by the following autumn, the branches have been trained down to the wires, to which they are tied and the canes discarded. Ensure that the branches grow to the same length and girth by raising the canes to stimulate growth, or by lowering them to check it.

Taller trees

If you want an espalier of more than three tiers, cut the main stem to a bud just above the third supporting wire. As it grows, use a cane to train it upwards while training two lower buds out along the wire as before. Five tiers are usually the maximum, with branches about 1.8m (6ft) long. However, you can create an espalier fruit tree that has as many as ten tiers if you keep the total width of the tree branches to no more than 1.8m (6ft).

Disease prevention

If you have a warm, south or south-west facing wall, and you live in the balmier parts of the country, there is no better way of using it than to grow an espaliered peach tree. Harvests can be excellent, but there is a risk of the plant becoming infected by peach leaf curl. This is often due to poor air circulation round the plant, and to soil being splashed up onto it by rain. You can guard against the disease by fixing battens that stand out by 15–25cm (6–10in) to the wall and, in winter, nailing or stapling polythene sheeting to them. This will protect the plant without impeding the air flow.

Early fruit

To secure an earlier harvest, try planting espalier fruit trees against a south or west-facing wall, where they will be protected from cold winds and will benefit from the heat that is stored by the wall.

Line a pathway

If you have a large garden, create an unusual edging for a pathway by growing single-tier espaliers along each side. These trees, which are also known as step-over trees, can be bought ready-trained from the nursery. Alternatively, train the trees onto a wire supported by posts at each end. You could also use espaliers to cover post-and-wire fences or as a surround to the vegetable garden by training them in exactly the same way.

Standing alone

If you have room for only one espalier, make sure that you choose a self-pollinating variety. Alternatively, choose a 'family' tree where two or three varieties are grafted onto the same stock, although these can be difficult to find in nurseries.

Eucalyptus

Strong start

You should plant a young eucalyptus in late spring, ideally when it is 23–30cm (9–12in) tall, and certainly before it reaches a height of 1m (3ft). Attach it to a split cane to provide initial support. Eucalyptus are rapid growers and a tall plant may become unstable during its first season. If this happens, cut the main stem back to 46cm (18in) above the ground the following spring. This will help to stabilise the plant.

Forever young foliage

Eucalyptus gunnii (cider gum) produces appealing silver-blue foliage in its first one or two years. Encourage the plant to continue producing this juvenile growth by stooling – pruning the stems back almost to ground level – or by cutting the stems back to a main stem, 1.2–1.5m (4–5ft) from the ground, in early spring each year.

Spring rebirth

In chilly districts, protect the base of eucalyptus stems with straw or a mulch during their first winter. If a eucalyptus seems to have died before spring, give it a second chance. Provided that the roots and the base of the stem are still living, new shoots should appear in May.

Evergreens

Making a choice

The roots of evergreens should never be allowed to dry out. This makes bare-rooted plants a risky purchase, so always choose those that are container-grown or ball-rooted.

Garden secrets

Deciduous versus evergreen

Evergreen leaves either have dense, glossy surfaces or they are small and needle-like. These are adaptations the plants have made to reduce moisture loss during the winter months when water uptake is at its lowest. Evergreen leaves also curl over during cold weather, thus reducing moisture loss still further. Deciduous plants generally have larger, less waxy leaves that if retained during the winter would cause grave loss of moisture. They are therefore shed during the autumn.

Make the right choice

Shrubs with a difference

The evergreen shrubs below can be planted to provide specific effects.

Variegated foliage
Elaeagnus x *ebbingei* 'Gilt Edge', *E. pungens* 'Maculata', *Euonymus fortunei* 'Emerald 'n' Gold', *Ilex aquifolium* 'Handsworth New Silver', *Leucothoe fontanesiana* 'Rainbow', *Pittosporum* 'Garnettii', *Viburnum tinus* 'Variegatum', *Vinca major* 'Variegata'

Gold foliage
Chamaecyparis pisifera 'Filifera Aurea', *Lonicera nitida* 'Baggesen's Gold', *Ozothamnus ledifolius*

Silver foliage
Artemisia 'Powis Castle', *Chamaecyparis pisifera* 'Boulevard', *Cistus* 'Silver Pink', *Convolvulus cneorum*, *Hebe albicans* 'Red Edge', *Lavandula angustifolia* 'Hidcote'

A time for planting

Gardeners who have a light soil can plant container-grown evergreens from autumn through to spring, provided the ground is not waterlogged or frozen. On heavy soils the operation is best left until spring. But if, for some reason, early planting is essential, cover the ground with polythene sheeting in advance to maintain an adequate moisture level and soil temperature.

Protection from the wind

Provide a winter windbreak for evergreens by wrapping them in sacking. If you have a small group of evergreens growing in the garden, drive four stakes into the ground round the plants and attach fine-mesh netting or sacking to the stakes. Further protection from drying winds can be given by putting a heavy layer of composted bark round the roots before constructing the windbreak.

Turn away from the east

Avoid planting evergreens in an east-facing position. Only the toughest species, such as *Mahonia aquifolium*, *Calluna vulgaris* and *Euonymus fortunei*, could escape the leaf damage inflicted by bright morning sunshine following a frost. But if there is an east-facing wall nearby to radiate a little heat, a much wider range of evergreens can be grown.

Cold comfort

Plant in spring if your area experiences harsh winters. Protect any young plants from frost by covering them with horticultural fleece.

Controlling weeds

To control weeds, lay a black polythene sheet over the ground before planting, using stones to hold it in place. Cut a cross in the sheet and plant the evergreen. Then spread a bark or gravel mulch round its base.

Scented evergreens

Evergreens grown for their scent should be planted in an open, sunny position where the foliage will be warmed, helping to release their fragrance into the air. Evergreens belonging to this useful category include *Choisya ternata*, *Daphne odora*, *Magnolia grandiflora*, *Mahonia japonica*, *Pittosporum tobira*, *Sarcococca* (which does well in shade) and *Viburnum* x *burkwoodii*.

Aromatic leaves

Some scented, evergreen shrubs release their fragrance when their leaves are brushed against or crushed in the hand. Among them are *Artemesia*, *Cistus ladanifer*, *Lavandula angustifolia*, *Myrtus communis*, *Rosmarinus officinalis* and *Thuja plicata* 'Stoneham Gold'. Grow these by the edge of a path, or on a corner where people will come into contact with them as they walk past. The slightest disturbance of the leaves will delightfully perfume the air round about.

Rejuvenating cuts

A number of ageing and straggly evergreens will develop new and youthful growth if cut back severely in spring. Among those that will respond well are camellias, mahonias, viburnums and yews. When pruning is complete, apply some liquid fertiliser to the soil round the plant.

Careful chippings

If you have access to a garden shredder, do remember that not all wood chippings are suitable for mulches. Be especially careful with rhododendron remains whose chippings can release harmful toxins that can be absorbed through dogs' paws, while chipped laurel wood and foliage give off cyanide. To be on the safe side, when you are operating a shredder, always work in short bursts in an open, well-ventilated place.

Make the right choice

A constant presence

Evergreen shrubs are a garden constant, providing colour, texture and interest throughout the year. Below is a guide to the flowering times of some attractive evergreen shrubs, which can be combined with gold and silver-leaved varieties (*see panel, left*) to make a stunning show.

Month	Shrub in flower
January	*Sarcococca hookeriana*
February	*Garrya elliptica*
March	*Camellia japonica* cultivars
April	*Berberis darwinii*
May	*Ceanothus*
June	*Cistus*
July	*Escallonia*
August	*Phygelius*
September	*Abelia* x *grandiflora*
October	*Osmanthus heterophyllus*
November	*Mahonia* x *media*
December	*Viburnum tinus*

Fan-training

A good start

Fan-training is the best way of growing apricots, nectarines or peaches. Make use of the expertise of your nurseryman and buy a fan-trained tree that has its two main ribs (trained branches) in place so that you do not have to tackle the specialist job of creating the initial shape. Plant the tree against a sunny wall.

Keep the shape

A fan-trained tree needs pruning each winter to help it to produce regular crops and high-quality fruit. Cut out some overcrowded spurs completely and cut back others to reduce their size. For summer pruning, wait till new growth is woody, is at least 23cm (9in) long and has dark green leaves. Then cut back to one leaf beyond the cluster of leaves at the base of each new shoot.

Checking growth

If a branch begins to outgrow the available space, cut it back to a strong side shoot and tie this to the wire.

Growing know-how

Training a tree into a fan shape

Fan-training is a highly decorative way to shape a fruit tree but needs a great deal of wall space. All trees are trained in the same way as the apricot, below.

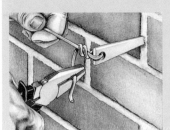

Positioning wires

Before planting a year-old fan-trained tree, attach six to eight horizontal wires to the wall at 23cm (9in) intervals. A fan height of about 1.8m (6ft) is usually sufficient. Attach the first wire 38cm (15in) above ground level, ensuring that the base of the tree's two main branches is just below it. Use vine eyes to fix it to the wall as these create space allowing air to circulate behind the tree, thus helping to prevent fungal diseases.

Planting space

Plant the tree, setting its base about 15cm (6in) from the wall, and lean the stem slightly towards the wall to make it easier to attach the branches to the wires. The first winter after planting, prune the two main branches back to 30–46cm (12–18in); cut just above a growth bud. Attach the main branches to canes fixed to the wires.

Summer training

The following summer, attach the extension growth from each bud to the cane. Then, on each branch, select two evenly spaced shoots on the upper side and one on the lower. Remove all the rest with secateurs or pinch them out with your thumb and forefinger. As the chosen shoots grow, attach them to canes and train them, fan-wise, outwards.

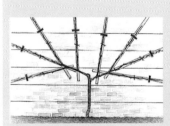

The following winter

Prune all new branches back to 61–76cm (24–30in), just above a growth bud. In summer, train the new growth from the end buds along canes. Choose two shoots on the upper side and one on the lower to develop as branches. Cut back other mature shoots to three leaves from the basal cluster.

Tie to the wires

The 24 new branches should be tied to canes as soon as they are long enough. The fan will now have 32 branches, usually enough to cover the wall. Once they have become woody, remove their canes and tie them directly to the wires.

Fencing

Keeping out the elements

When purchasing wood, make sure that it has been treated with a preservative, or paint it with timber preservative yourself, to protect it from the elements.

To the point

You need to prevent water from collecting on the top of wooden fence posts as this will cause the wood to rot. If the posts are hardwood, trim the tops to a slant or point. However, if they are made from softwood, you will need to cover them with either wooden or metal caps.

On the slope

Make sure that any batten on top of the fence is cut at an angle, rather than flat. This will ensure that rain runs off and does not cause damage to the wood.

Perfect posts

The simplest way of fixing posts is to use spikes with sockets, which are hammered into the ground. As high winds can loosen the spikes, they are suitable for use only in a sheltered spot. If you are erecting a fence in an exposed site, set the posts in concrete, with a rubble base to ensure good drainage. Slope the top of the concrete so that rainwater drains off. Concrete posts set in concrete are ideal for long life, and those with slots to accommodate fencing panels make it easy to replace panels when necessary.

Maintain wooden fences

Regular upkeep of a wooden fence will make it last much longer, saving you time and money in the long run. Every two or three years, cut out and replace any sections that have rotted. Close-boarded fences need a gravel board to protect the panels from dampness in the soil. Leave a space between the bottom of the fence or gravel board and the ground to enable air to circulate underneath and thus reduce the risk of further rotting. Paint the new sections with an outdoor wood preservative.

Fences at risk

On exposed sites with high winds, keep close-board fencing below 1.2m (4ft). For privacy, add height with trellis and climbing plants. Wind can penetrate trellis, so secure plants such as climbing roses with ties. Do not weave rose stems through the trellis; as they grow they will put pressure on the supporting timber, causing damage that is hard to repair.

Cope with a slope

To put up a fence on a slope, erect it section by section, stepping down the height of the posts evenly. Place a spirit level onto a length of timber laid between two posts, then use a wooden block at the lower post end to raise the levelling timber to the height of the higher post. Dig out or build up areas of soil at the base of the fence to leave an even gap under each section.

Climbing camouflage

Camouflage an unattractive wire mesh fence by training climbing plants to cover it. You will find that the mesh serves as an efficient trellis. Choose one of the many ornamental ivies, which give cover without taking up too much space. These are particularly useful for fences that can be seen from the windows, and give a pleasant aspect in winter.

Securely attractive

If you need to erect a wire mesh fence – to improve security or to keep animals in or out of your garden – grow an evergreen hedge through it. This will hide the unsightly mesh and provide a greater degree of privacy.

Make the right choice

Deciding between a fence, hedge or wall

Fences

Both wooden and wire fences are quick to erect and take up the minimum of space. Wooden fences are more attractive than wire but need regular maintenance. Wire mesh fences can be used to restrain livestock and poultry, or to keep animals out of the garden. The appearance of most fences can be improved with a covering of climbing or trained plants.

Hedges

Patience is needed with hedges as they take time to grow. Hedges take up more space than fences and walls but have a more natural and attractive appearance, particularly in winter, if evergreen plants are used. For wildlife, they can be a good source of shelter, as well as food, if a berry-bearing variety of hedging is chosen, and they make an effective windbreak.

Walls

The most solid barriers, walls need little upkeep if they are properly erected. Building a wall requires some skill, and materials can be expensive. New walls may look unattractive, but can be covered with climbing plants if a trellis is attached. In a small garden, walls are useful as supports for espalier, fan-trained or cordon trees.

Fennel

Edible decoration

The attractive, feathery foliage of biennial *Foeniculum vulgare* (fennel), grown for its leaves and seeds, and annual *F. v. var. dulce* (Florence fennel), grown for its edible bulb and leaves, make these plants at home in a flower border. Alternate both with lavender and roses, or plant among decorative *Anthemis*, hostas, irises or sedums to create an unusual display.

Earth up stems

To ensure that the swollen stems of Florence fennel are white and tender, they should be earthed up. As the bulbs start to swell, draw soil round them to about half their depth; do not cover them completely. Keep the plants well watered to prevent bolting.

Ferns

Spring cleaning

Do not prune the old growth of a fern in autumn or winter. The fronds help to protect the base of the plant from frost and cold weather, as well as looking attractive. Wait until new shoots appear in spring before you cut back the fern.

Feed your ferns

A restorative brew will help your ferns, gardenias and other acid-loving house plants to thrive. Substitute black tea from time to time when watering or work wet tea leaves into the soil to give the plants a luxurious shine.

Divide and grow

If a fern grows too large for its place in the garden, wait until spring to divide it. Lift the clump then use a saw or, if very large, two forks.

Push these, back-to-back, into the centre of the clump, then lever them apart. Plant the spare section in an area with room for it to grow.

Mulch to reduce watering

At the end of each winter, spread about 5cm (2in) of leafmould or well-rotted compost over the base of the fern. This helps the soil to retain moisture and the fern will then need watering only during dry spells.

Make the right choice

The shade lovers

As a general rule, ferns prefer a shady spot and a moist, well-mulched soil.

***Adiantum pedatum* (maidenhair fern)**
Hardy, with graceful, drooping fronds. *A. p. subpumilum* grows to 15cm (6in) in height; ideal for a rock garden.

***Asplenium scolopendrium* (hart's tongue)**
Evergreen, with single fronds. Good for planting with other ferns or bluebells, or in a shady rock garden. Select ruffled or tufted varieties for extra interest.

***A. trichomanes* (maidenhair spleenwort)**
Semi-evergreen dwarf fern that prefers limy soil. Suitable for an alpine or rock garden, it has bright green pinnate fronds with black mid-ribs.

***Athyrium filix-femina* (lady fern)**
A hardy native fern with delicate green fronds; it prefers light shade. Plants of the Cruciatum Group are particularly attractive.

***Dryopteris* (buckler fern)**
Grows in acid or alkaline soil, with the exception of *D. aemula*, which needs acid or neutral soil. *D. erythrosora* has broad, triangular, pinnate fronds that turn from copper to dark green. *D. affnis* 'Crispa Congesta' is a compact form, good for rock gardens. Its crinkled, congested fronds are deep green.

***Matteuccia struthiopteris* (ostrich feather or shuttlecock fern)**
Hardy and moisture-loving; ideal planted near water. Arching fronds are like ostrich feathers.

***Osmunda regalis* (royal fern)**
Good for a damp position in sun or partial shade. *O. r. purpurascens* has copper-pink fronds that turn copper-green with purple ribs.

***Polystichum setiferum* (soft shield fern)**
Evergreen, with mid green, divided fronds. Prefers a cool, woody position. Reaches its full spread of up to 1.2m (4ft) in autumn. The compact 'Plumoso-divisilobum' is a good choice.

Stately backdrop The arching fronds of the elegant ostrich feather fern make a dignified show in the border.

Propagating moves

In the autumn, cut a healthy frond and leave it to dry on a sheet of paper for two or three days. After this time a fine dust of spores should have fallen onto the paper. Fill a pot with moist, sterile soil or compost. Put a saucer beneath, filled with water. Gently remove the frond and, using the point of a knife, pick up a few spores and sprinkle them on the potting compost.

Growing on

After sowing spores, cover the pot with cling film or glass to help to keep the soil moist, and keep the saucer full of water. Three to twelve weeks later, depending on variety, heart-shaped growths will emerge. Remove the cover to allow air circulation. Once the plants are big enough to handle, replant in individual pots filled with moist compost.

Fertilisers

Long life

Extend the life of fertilisers by storing them in plastic bags or sacks that are raised off the ground on wooden slats. Make sure too that the bags are closed firmly after use to prevent the chemicals in the fertiliser from coming into

contact with moist air. Keep the bags in a dry but airy place, such as a garage that is used frequently. Most fertilisers stored in this way will keep for up to four years.

Chemical reaction

Store fertilisers that contain weedkillers well away from other types of fertiliser, and keep all lime well away from ammonium nitrate, ammonium sulphate, nitro-chalk and superphosphate, to avoid a chemical reaction.

Food and water

Apply granular fertilisers when the ground is wet as moisture aids absorption and the release of nutrients. Water thoroughly if there is no rainfall within two days of application. Take care to follow the manufacturer's directions exactly, because an excessive amount of fertiliser may burn the roots of the plants.

The right time

When applying a fertiliser to plants, do so only before and during the growing period. Never add a fast-acting fertiliser to trees or shrubs when they are about to become dormant and their growth is slowing down.

Make your own sieve

If you are spreading a granular or powdered fertiliser by hand rather than with a garden spreader, a sieve will help you to control the

Garden secrets

Household waste

Recycle household liquids such as stale beer, cold tea and even the water from an aquarium to use in the garden. All these contain some nutrients and can be poured round the roots of plants. Keep a special container, such as a bucket with a lid, outside your kitchen door and use it to collect household waste, such as coffee grounds, tea leaves and vegetable and fruit peelings. When the bucket is full, transfer the contents to the compost heap.

Make the right choice

Choosing a fertiliser

Fertilisers come in a variety of forms.

Complete or compound fertilisers

These are also known as general fertilisers and contain the three main plant foods – nitrogen, phosphorus and potassium – plus trace elements essential for plant growth. Some are specially mixed to suit individual plant needs, such as tomatoes or roses.

Organic fertilisers

Derived from wholly natural sources, some are quick-acting while others release nutrients over a period of time. They are generally used as dressings before sowing, or as top dressings for growing crops.

Inorganic fertilisers

These are derived from non-natural sources and may consist of a single chemical that stimulates growth in part of the plant, or a compound of two or more chemicals. Some give an instant boost while others are effective for as long as 18 months.

Farmyard manures

Consisting mainly of animal dung, these contain plant foods, are rich in organic matter and improve soil condition.

Liquid feeds

Once diluted, these can be applied as foliar feeds, or watered into the roots to provide a regular supply of plant foods and help to correct nutrient deficiencies. They are particularly beneficial to container plants.

Controlled-release fertilisers

These are specially formulated to release nutrients over a long period. Some are for summer baskets and tubs and provide nutrients for up to six months; others, for more general use, can last up to 18 months.

flow and distribute it evenly. Make your own by piercing several holes in an old tin can, then simply measure in the required amount of fertiliser and shake it over the soil.

Quick boosts
Plants that are languishing can be given a quick boost by spraying the foliage or watering the roots with a liquid fertiliser. Alternatively, scatter a fast-acting granular fertiliser round the base of the plant.

Feeding new plants
Mix a slow-release fertiliser, such as bone meal, which is rich in phosphates, into the soil when planting a tree, shrub or perennial, or work it into the potting compost when planting up containers. (See also **Bone meal**)

Green lawns
Lawn fertilisers should be spread evenly, according to the manufacturer's instructions, and watered in if the weather is dry. Aerating the lawn before applying fertiliser helps the nutrients to penetrate the soil, as well as improving the surface drainage and preventing compaction. (See also **Lawn care**)

Tree time
To feed a tree, spread a general fertiliser in the area beneath the edges of the leaf canopy. Alternatively, make holes in the ground directly below the canopy edges and fill these with the fertiliser. As with lawn fertiliser, unless the weather is rainy, you will need to water the fertiliser into the soil.

Extreme measures
Apply fertiliser more frequently than usual to very acid or very chalky soils. Phosphates and potash become more soluble in an acid soil, making them more likely to be washed away by rain, while phosphate becomes insoluble when mixed with the calcium in chalky soils. Use the manufacturer's recommended application but divide it into two or three lots and apply at intervals throughout the growing season.

Less for clay soils
The more clay your soil contains, or the more organic matter that you dig into it, the less fertiliser you will need to apply. This is because both substances act as reservoirs, trapping the nutrients and releasing them to plants over a period of time.

Using liquid
It is important to apply liquid fertilisers when plants are actively growing – that is, usually late spring and summer. If used earlier, nutrients will be washed away; if used later, the fertiliser will not have an effect. During these times, apply a solid fertiliser, which lasts longer.

More for light soils
Re-apply fertilisers, particularly those that are nitrogen-based, more frequently if your soil is light and free-draining. These soils, which are usually sandy in composition, lose nutrients more quickly than other types, particularly during rainy spells

See also **Manures, Nitrogen, Phosphates, Potash, Seaweed**

Growing know-how

The three principal elements of fertilisers

Fertiliser must contain at least one of three elements – nitrogen, phosphorus and potassium – that promote healthy growth in different ways. In the UK, fertiliser packages indicate the ratio of each one of these elements to the others.

Nutrient	Uses	Application	Effects of shortage
Nitrogen (N)	Encourages leafy growth and formation of stems and branches. Plants most in need of nitrogen include grass and leafy vegetables such as cabbage and spinach.	Nitrogenous fertilisers are quickly washed out of the soil by rain, and need to be renewed annually.	Stunted growth, weak stems and yellow or discoloured leaves.
Phosphorus (P)	Essential for seed germination and root development. Needed particularly by young plants, fruit and seed crops, and root vegetables such as carrots, swedes and turnips.	Phosphates remain in the soil for two or three years after application. Add at planting or top-dress during growth periods.	Stunted growth, dull or purplish leaves and a low fruit yield.
Potassium (K)	Promotes flower and fruit production and is vital for maintaining growth and giving plants resistance to disease. Helps to build up starch and sugar in vegetables and fruit, especially carrots, parsnips, beetroot, tomatoes and apples.	Potash usually lasts in the soil for two or three years. It can be applied as a top dressing or as a liquid feed.	Low resistance to disease, low fruit yield, poorly coloured fruits or flowers and scorching of leaves.

A year of glory in the garden

Enjoy beds and borders ablaze with colour and interest for 12 months of the year, every year. The secret to all-season delight is knowing when each species is at its best and in coordinated planting.

Each plant in your garden has its moment of triumph, the magic time in the year when flowers or foliage, fruits, bark or scent are at their very best. The chart on the following pages reveals when this moment occurs in the lives of many species. More importantly, it shows how, by coordinating groups of trees, flowering shrubs, perennials, bulbs and annuals, you can have a star-studded cast on your garden stage throughout the year with still more getting ready in the wings.

Though the chart tells you the months when particular species are at the height of their powers, regional variations in climate mean that some may give their best performance a little earlier or later than shown and many will continue in their prime for weeks afterwards.

The plants are listed according to the major types that occur in the garden: annuals (for planting in spring), biennials (mainly for planting in summer or autumn), bulbs including corms and tubers (to be planted in spring or autumn), and perennials, shrubs and trees that flourish without disturbance for years.

The list does not include all the plants available to the gardener, but if it is used in conjunction with the colour chart on pp. 64–67, it will ensure that your garden is full of interest all year round.

Informal appeal
Climbing roses, with campanulas, cerastiums and potentillas, make a charming summer herbaceous border in various shades of white.

January/February

Annuals/biennials
Brassica 'Winter Beauty' (ornamental cabbage), see right, *Viola* Ultima Series Mixed and Universal Series Mixed (winter pansy)

Bulbs
Chionodoxa (glory of the snow)
Crocus imperati (crocus)
Galanthus nivalis (snowdrop)

Perennials
Bergenia (elephant's ears)
Eranthis hyemalis (winter aconite)
Helleborus niger (Christmas rose)
H. orientalis 'Early Purple' (Lenten rose)
Iris unguicularis (winter iris)
Sempervivum (houseleek)

Shrubs
Azara petiolaris
Chimonanthus praecox (winter sweet)
Daphne mezereum
Erica carnea (winter heather)
Hamamelis (witch hazel)
Jasminum nudiflorum (winter jasmine), see left,
Lonicera fragrantissima and *L. standishii* (winter honeysuckle)
Mahonia

Trees
Betula ermanii (birch)
Corylus colurna (Turkish hazel)
Eucalyptus gunnii
Prunus serrula
P. × *subhirtella* 'Autumnalis' (winter cherry)

March

Annuals/biennials
Viola Ultima Series Mixed and Universal Series Mixed (winter pansy)

Bulbs
Anemone blanda
Chionodoxa (glory of the snow)
Crocus
Iris reticulata (dwarf iris)
Leucojum vernum (snowflake)
Narcissus (daffodil), see right,
Puschkinia scilloides
Scilla (squill)
Tulipa

Perennials
Bergenia (elephant's ears)
Helleborus niger (Christmas rose)
H. orientalis (Lenten rose)
Primula auricular
P. vulgaris (primrose)
Saxifraga × apiculata 'Gregor Mendel' (saxifrage)

Shrubs
Camellia japonica, see left
Chaenomeles japonica (Maule's quince)
C. speciosa (japonica)
Forsythia
Mahonia
Ribes sanguineum (flowering currant)
Skimmia, see above

Trees
Alnus incana 'Aurea'
Prunus (flowering cherry)

April

Annuals/biennials
Bellis perennis (daisy)
Erysimum cheiri (wallflower)
Lunaria annua (honesty)
Myosotis (forget-me-not)
Primula (polyanthus), see right

Bulbs
Anemone nemerosa
Hyacinthus, below
Ipheion uniflorum
Muscari botryoides (grape hyacinth)
Narcissus (daffodil)
Ornithogalum umbellatum (star of Bethlehem)
Tulipa

Perennials
Anemone narcissiflora
Aubrieta
Aurinia saxatilis 'Gold Dust' (rock alyssum)
Epimedium (barrenwort)
Primula vulgaris (primrose)
Pulmonaria (lungwort)

Shrubs
Camellia
Daphne tangutica
Laurus nobilis (bay laurel)
Magnolia × soulangeana, *M. stellata*
Osmanthus delavayi
Rhododendron (including azaleas)
Viburnum

Trees
Amelanchier lamarckii (snowy mespilus)
Malus (crab apple)
Prunus 'Kansan' (flowering cherry)
Pyrus calleryana 'Chanticleer' (ornamental pear)

May

Annuals/biennials
Campanula medium (Canterbury bell)
Dianthus barbatus (sweet william)
Myosotis sylvatica (forget-me-not)
Papaver (poppy), see right

Bulbs
Fritillaria imperialis (crown imperial)
Muscari botryoides (grape hyacinth)
Tulipa

Perennials
Dianthus, see right
Geranium Paeonia lactiflora (peony)
Phlox subulata (moss phlox)
Saxifraga × urbium (London's pride)
Tanacetum (pyrethrum)
Verbascum

Shrubs
Cytisus (broom)
Pieris
Rhododendron (including azaleas)
Syringa vulgaris (common lilac)
Viburnum
Weigela

Trees
Aesculus hippocastanum (horse chestnut)
Caragana arborescens (pea tree)
Cercis siliquastrum (Judas tree)
Crataegus laevigata (hawthorn, may)
Davidia involucrata (pocket handkerchief tree)
Fraxinus (ash)
Malus (crab apple)
Paulownia tomentosa
Sorbus aucuparia (rowan, mountain ash)

June

Annuals/biennials

Campanula, right
Clarkia
Delphinium
Echium vulgare
Eschscholzia californica
(California poppy)
Godetia
Iberis umbellata
(candytuft)
Impatiens walleriana (busy lizzie)
Lathyrus odoratus (sweet pea)
Limnanthes (poached egg plant)
Malcolmia maritima (Virginian stock)
Matthiola (stock)
Papaver (poppy)

Bulbs

Allium (ornamental onion)
Iris
Ixia (corn lily)
Lilium (lily)

Perennials

Aquilegia vulgaris – hybrids
(columbine, granny's bonnet)
Campanula
Delphinium
Dianthus (carnations, pinks and
sweet williams)
Gypsophila paniculata
Papaver (oriental poppy),
see left.
Scabiosa

Shrubs

Clematis
Hydrangea
Passiflora caerulea (passionflower)
Philadelphus (mock orange)
Rosa
Viburnum opulus (guelder rose)
V. plicatum tomentosum (Japanese snowball)

Trees

Crataegus persimilis 'Prunifolia' (hawthorn)
Laburnum
Robinia pseudoacacia

July

Annuals/biennials

Antirrhinum (snapdragon)
Begonia semperflorens (fibrous begonia)
Convolvulus tricolor
Coreopsis (tickseed)
Digitalis purpurea (foxglove)
Helianthus annuus (sunflower)
Heliotropium × hybridium (heliotrope, cherry pie)
Iberis umbellata (candytuft)
Impatiens (busy lizzie)
Lathyrus odoratus (sweet pea)
Mesembryanthemum criniflorum
(Livingstone daisy)
Petunia
Scabosia atropurpurea (sweet scabious)
Schizanthus pinnatus (butterfly flower)
Tagetes (African/French marigolds)
Tropaeolum majus (nasturtium)

Bulbs

Galtonia (summer hyacinth)
Gladiolus
Lilium (lily) – various hybrids, left

Perennials

Aquilegia vulgaris – hybrids
(columbine, granny's bonnet)
Clematis integrifolia
Delphinium – large-flowered hybrids
Dianthus (old-fashioned pinks)
Kniphofia (red-hot poker) – hybrids
Penstemon
Phlox maculata and *P. paniculata* (border phlox)
Potentilla (cinquefoil) – garden hybrids

Shrubs

Buddleja (butterfly bush), see right
Caryopteris
Clematis
Hydrangea paniculata
Lavandula (lavender)
Rosa
Yucca filamentosa

Trees

Koelreuteria paniculata
(golden rain tree)
Liriodendron tulipifera (tulip tree)

August

Annuals/biennials

Althaea rosea (hollyhock)
Amaranthus caudatus (love-lies-bleeding)
Begonia × tuberhybrida, B. semperflorens
Centaurea cyanus (cornflower)
Helianthus annuus (sunflower)
Impatiens (busy lizzie)
Lavatera trimestris
(mallow), see right
Limonium sinuetum
(sea lavender, statice)
Malcolmia maritima
(Virginian stock)
Phlox (annual phlox)
Rudbeckia hirta (black-eyed susan)
Salvia farinacea, S. splendens
Tagetes (African/French marigolds)
Verbena × hybrida

Bulbs

Begonia (tuberous begonia)
Cardiocrinum giganteum (giant lily)
Crocosmia × crocosmiiflora (montbretia)
Galtonia candicans (summer hyacinth)
Gladiolus

Perennials

Anemone × hybrida
Clematis heracleifolia
Leucanthemum × superbum
Phlox paniculata

Shrubs/Climbers

Calluna vulgaris (heath)
Ceanothus
Eucryphia × nymansensis
Fuchsia – various
Hebe, see right
Hibiscus syriacus
Hydrangea
Hypericum 'Hidcote'
Lonicera japonica
(honeysuckle)
Potentilla

Trees

Catalpa bignonioides (Indian bean tree)
Magnolia grandiflora

September

Annuals/biennials
Begonia (fibrous begonia)
Callistephus chinensis (China aster)
Canna × generalis
Cleome (spider flower)
Helianthus annuus (sunflower)
Impatiens (busy lizzie)
Petunia
Tagetes (African/French marigolds)

Bulbs
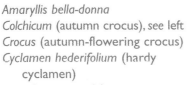
Amaryllis bella-donna
Colchicum (autumn crocus), see left
Crocus (autumn-flowering crocus)
Cyclamen hederifolium (hardy cyclamen)
   Dierama pulcherrimum
   Gladiolus
   Leucojum autumnale
Nerine bowdenii

Perennials
Anemone hupehensis
A. × hybrida
Aster novae-angliae and *A. novi-belgii* (Michaelmas daisy)
Dendranthema (chrysanthemum)
Gentiana sino-ornata (gentian)
Penstemon
Sedum spectabile (ice plant)

Shrubs/Climbers

   Abelia Calluna vulgaris (heather)
   Clematis
   Euonymus europaeus 'Red Cascade' (spindle tree)
   Hydrangea
   Parthenocissus (Virginia creeper)
   Perovskia (Russian sage)
   Rosa

Trees
Cotoneaster lacteus, see above
Sorbus aucuparia 'Beissneri' (mountain ash)

October

Annuals/biennials
Callistephus (aster)
Helianthus annuus (sunflower), see far right
Helichrysum (everlasting flower), see near right

Bulbs
Amaryllis bella-donna
Anemone × hybrida
Colchicum (autumn crocus)
Crocus speciosus (autumn-flowering crocus)
Cyclamen hederifolium (hardy cyclamen)
Nerine bowdenii
Schizostylis coccinea
Sternbergia lutea

Perennials
Anemone hupehensis
Aster novae-angliae and *A. novae-belgii* (Michaelmas daisy)
Cortaderia selloana (pampas grass)
Dendranthema (chrysanthemum)
Echinacea purpurea
Gentiana sino-ornata (gentian)
Liriope muscari (lily turf)
Saxifraga fortunei

Shrubs
Ceratostigma
Cotoneaster
Hebe × andersonii 'Variegata'
Rosa moyesii
Skimmia japonica

Trees
Acer capillipes and *A. japonicum* (maple)
Arbutus unedo (strawberry tree)
Cotinus coggygria (smoke bush)
Liquidambar, see above
Malus 'Golden Hornet' (ornamental crab apple)
Nyssa sylvatica

November/December

Annuals/biennials
Viola × wittrockiana (winter-flowering pansy)

Bulbs
Amaryllis bella-donna
Colchicum (autumn crocus)
Crocus speciosus
Cyclamen species, see below
   Iris unguicularis (winter iris)
   Nerine bowdenii

Perennials
Bergenia (elephant's ears)
Persicaria vacciniifolia (knotweed)
Saxifraga fortunei (saxifrage)

Shrubs
Arundinaria (bamboo), see below
Elaeagnus × ebbingei
Erica carnea
Gaultheria mucronata (pernettya)
Jasminum nudiflorum (winter jasmine)
Pyracantha 'Watereri' and *P. rogersiana* (firethorn)
Viburnum betulifolium
V. × bodnantense

Trees
Fraxinus excelsior 'Jaspidea'
Ilex (holly)
Malus × robusta 'Red Sentinel' and *M.* 'Yellow Siberian' (crab apple)
Prunus subhirtella 'Autumnalis' (flowering cherry)
Salix babylonica var. *pekinensis* 'Tortuosa'

Figs

Wall-trained for warmth
Native to Mediterranean countries, the fig tree needs warmth. In the UK it can be grown outside only in the south and west and even in these areas a severe winter or poor summer can ruin the crop. For the best possible chance of success, plant in March when the tree is dormant and the worst of the frosts are over. Train the tree against a south or west-facing wall to ensure that it receives the maximum amount of sunshine and warmth.

Root restriction
A fig tree that is planted outside should have its roots restricted to prevent the production of excess, unfruitful wood. To do this, dig a hole 60cm x 60cm and 1m deep (about 2ft x 2ft and 3ft deep). Line the sides with stone slabs, concrete or bricks, and cover the bottom with a 30cm (12in) layer of brick rubble, rammed down hard. Fill the hole with some good garden soil to which 225g (8oz) of bone meal has been added.

Potted fig
An easy way to contain fig roots is to grow the tree in a 38cm (15in) pot. Fill the container with potting compost, and bury it to the rim. Every year, lift the pot and prune roots that protrude through the drainage holes.

Northern solution
Gardeners who live north of the Trent can cultivate the fig outside only as an ornamental tree. To produce edible fruit it will need to be container-grown in a greenhouse.

Keep young fruits warm
Figs take two years to mature, overwintering as embryo fruits. As only the smallest fruits will survive the cold temperatures, remove any that are larger than a pea at the end of September. Protect the remaining fruits by covering them with straw held in place with netting, or by tying horticultural fleece round the shoots.

Protect yourself
The sap produced by the fruit, stems and leaves of fig trees contains a substance that may irritate the skin and eyes. Wear gloves when working on the tree, and do not allow sap to come into contact with your eyes.

Ready to eat
To recognise that a fig is ripe, look for a slight cracking of the skin or the appearance of some sticky nectar at the base. Because the stem weakens as the fruit ripens, the fig may also drop down from its horizontal position when it is ready to eat.

Florist's foam

Colour code
Green florist's foam absorbs water to hold fresh stems; brown foam does not absorb water and is used to hold dried or artificial stems. Soak a green block in a bowl or bucket of water until it is saturated and sinks by its own weight.

Imaginative arrangement
You can display flowers in many imaginative settings rather than simply using conventional vases. Florist's foam makes it easy to use unusual containers, such as a casserole dish, champagne bucket, jug or a basket with a plastic box inside.

Flowering plants

Check plants daily
In summer, make a daily inspection, cutting off any fading flowers, watering where necessary and supporting weak stems with canes.

To dig or not to dig
Once flowering plants have become established, do not dig the soil round them. If you cut through the surface roots, the plants will have to use up their energy in renewing them. Use a hoe to get rid of weeds or apply a weedkiller or mulch. (See also **Weeding, Weedkillers**)

Save the ashes
If you like an open fire and burn logs in your home, save the ashes and scatter them around flowering plants. Wood ash contains 5–10 per cent potash, which promotes flowering. (See also **Potash**)

A brief history

Cottage flower gardens
Medieval peasants grew vegetables for subsistence and little else, but the Reformation provided them with the riches of the deserted monastery gardens in the shape of medicinal herbs, such as borage and comfrey, sweet-smelling herbs, such as lavender and rosemary, and flowers, such as flag and golden rod, for dyes. There were lilies, too, that had decorated Easter altars. The cottage gardener supplemented these with oddities from the hedgerow – double primroses and plants to ward off witchcraft – as well as granny's bonnets, peonies, and stonecrop. Thus, among the vegetables there now stood a charming profusion of flowers, much added to in the 18th century when formal gardens of the gentry were abandoned in favour of the landscapes advocated by Capability Brown.

Prolong blooming
For a longer flowering period, remove flowers as soon as they fade. Deprived of its chance to produce seed and thus ensure its survival, the plant will produce new blooms. After the first flush of flowers, apply a complete fertiliser and water frequently, particularly if the weather is hot and dry, to encourage further blooming.

Tidy clipping
When deadheading, use a pair of secateurs to make the task easier. Remove the stem as well as the flower to give a tidier appearance.

Deadheading technique
If there are no new flower buds on a stem, cut it off at ground level to redirect the plant's energy. If buds are developing farther down the stem, cut it off above the top bud.

Staying power
Some flowering plants produce long-lasting blooms or a succession of flowers. *Coreopsis* can last from July to October; *Pelargonium* from early summer to first frosts, *Tagetes patula* (French marigold) from June to late autumn; *Viola* (pansy) blooms all year round.

Fast flowers
While it can take time for many seed-raised plants to flower, a few will bloom in just a few weeks. For fast flowers, sow *Malcolmia maritima* (Virginian stock), which produces red, pink, mauve, white and cream flowers as quickly as ten weeks after a spring sowing, or the variously coloured annual varieties of *Mimulus* (monkey flower), which, if treated as half-hardy annuals, flower 10–12 weeks after sowing and bloom throughout the summer. If planted in summer, many autumn crocuses will produce their pink and white goblets a few weeks later, before their leaves appear.

See also **A year of glory in the garden pp. 108–11**

Flowering trees

Small specimens
There are many flowering trees, grown for their stunning blooms, that are ideal for small gardens. If lack of space is a problem in your garden, choose a single specimen that will have a low to moderate eventual height, such as lilac, magnolia or an ornamental cherry.

Extra attraction
An advantage gained from having flowering trees in the garden is that the blooms are often followed by attractive berries in late summer and autumn. *Sorbus aucuparia* (mountain ash) bears eye-catching white flower heads in May and June, then produces large bunches of globular, orange-red berries that ripen from August onwards. Other flowering trees that have attractive berries include *Amelanchier lamarckii* (snowy mespilus), *Malus* (crab apple) and whitebeams.

Effective filling
Take advantage of the space available in a large garden to plant several trees that flower at different times to extend the season of interest. Choose from (in order of flowering) ornamental cherries, magnolias, ornamental pears, crab apples, mountain ash, laburnums, robinias and catalpas.

Restrained pruning
Do not be tempted to overprune a flowering tree: this will reduce the number of blossoms. Prune in spring, cutting out only the damaged wood and weak or crossed branches.

City flowers
If you live in a city, choose a reasonably tough species that will be able to withstand air pollution. Ideal are sorbus trees, and ornamental thorns, such as *Crataegus oxycantha* varieties, which produce clusters of white flowers in May followed by attractive, bright scarlet haws.

Make the right choice
Flowering trees
Select flowering trees suitable for the space in your garden. If you only have room for one, make sure that you choose something extra special.

Amelanchier lamarckii **(snowy mespilus)**
Height and spread about 3m (10ft). White flowers in May, followed by black berries. In autumn, the tree has copper-red leaves, covered with silky hairs.

Magnolia denudata **(yulan tree)**
Height and spread 3–4.6m (10–15ft). In maturity, a small, spreading tree that produces hundreds of lemon-scented blossoms in April.

M. x kewensis **'Wada's Memory'**
Height 3–4.6m (10–15ft), spread 1.8–3m (6–10ft). An ideal tree for a small garden as it is small and upright in form. The white flowers with curved petals are produced in April and May. They are followed by the leaves unfurling.

Malus **(crab apple)**
Height and spread 3.7–7.5m (12–25ft). Pink, white, or purplish flowers (depending on variety) are borne in late spring, while the small, apple-like fruits, ranging from green to yellow tinged with shades of red, ripen in September and October.

Prunus mume **'Bene-chidori' (Japanese apricot)**
Height 2.4–3m (8–10ft), spread 1.8–2.4m (6–8ft). Fragrant, pink flowers grow in abundance along the delicate stems, emerging as early as February and lasting until April. These trees are best given wall protection in all but the mildest areas.

Forcing

The garden indoors

Branches of flowering shrubs can be forced to provide early blooms to display indoors. A month before flowering time, cut a few supple stems bearing well-formed buds that have points of colour. Place the stems in a vase filled with water and put it in a well-lit room at 16–18°C (61–64°F). The buds will bloom within two or three weeks. *Chaenomeles* (Japanese quince), *Daphne mezereum* (mezereon), *Forsythia*, *Hamamelis* (witch hazel) and *Jasminum nudiflorum* (winter-flowering jasmine) can all be forced.

Bulbs for Christmas

Many spring-flowering bulbs, if forced, will flower as early as Christmas. Pots of specially prepared bulbs, including varieties such as crocuses, grape hyacinths, hyacinths, narcissi and tulips are widely available.

Force your own

To force your own bulbs, wait until September, then plant the bulbs close together in a large pot filled with bulb fibre or a mixture of potting compost and sharp sand. Water well, then put the pot in a cold, dark place or cover it with a black plastic bag and store it in a cellar or garage for two months, keeping the compost slightly damp. When the shoots grow to between 1.9cm (¾in) and 5cm (2in), depending on the bulb, move the pot into the house.

Acclimatisation process

Acclimatise forced bulbs by placing them in a cool place at 10–15°C (50–59°F) then, as each bud begins to show a tinge of colour, move the plants to a warm, well-lit room at a temperature of about 21°C (70°F).

Prolong blooming

Make sure that bowls of forced bulbs are kept in a cool room at night as this will extend their blooming period.

Fountains

Choose gentle droplets

Moving water helps to oxygenate a pond, but large, falling droplets can harm water lilies and other delicate ornamental plants, and floating plants can be sucked under water by the force of the pump. To minimise the danger, install the pump well away from vulnerable plants and protect water lilies by choosing a fountain with a bell jet that produces a gentle cascade of water.

Keep the jet low

A jet that is too powerful can cause water to flow over the edges of the pond, turning the surrounding garden into a bog. To prevent this, regulate the fountain so that the jet is no higher than half the width of the pond. This will ensure that the water is contained.

Prevent blockages

The pump's filter can become blocked by the dead leaves and debris that accumulate at the bottom of the pond. To prevent this, lay a couple of bricks next to each other and place the pump on top to raise it above the base.

Match the style

Choose a fountain that complements the style of your garden. If it is formal, a traditional fountain may well suit it best. In a natural or wild-flower garden, a rock waterfall may be more appropriate than a fountain.

A child-proof water feature

Gardeners with children do not have to forgo the pleasure of a water feature in the garden because of fears about safety. Danger to children can be minimised if a bubble fountain is installed in a millstone or bed of pebbles, through which the water can drain into an underground reservoir.

A touch of the Orient

To create an oriental-style water spout, make a 45° cut at one end of a wide, hollow bamboo cane and fit the other end into the output pipe from a small water pump. Using another two canes, make an X-shaped support for the spout. This simple ornament will look best in a corner of the pond among foliage. (See also **Ponds**)

French beans

Firm support

Make sure that climbing french beans are firmly supported or else you may find that you get a smaller crop. Like runner beans, the plants, which can reach up to 2m (7ft) in height, may be grown up strings or canes, or on netting supported by a vertical pole at each end. Whichever support you use, make sure that it is firmly anchored and secure enough to prevent it from waving about in the wind. (*See also* **Runner beans**)

Pod picking
Pick pods regularly, when they are young and tender. This encourages more flowers and a heavier yield. Remove old, bulging pods and put them on the compost heap.

Haricots and flageolets
Grow your own flageolet or haricot beans. Both are types of french bean, but only the dried seeds are eaten, not the whole pods. Flageolets are picked when the seeds inside the pods are soft and usually pale green; haricots are picked after they have ripened to white, pale green, red, light brown or bicoloured, according to variety. French and runner beans are among the few vegetables that must not be eaten raw; always cook thoroughly before eating. For an interesting dual-purpose crop, plant 'Chevrier Vert'. This variety of beans can be harvested as flageolets or, if left to dry to a green-white colour on the plant, as haricot beans.

Garden secrets

The time to sow beans
It is best never to sow dwarf french beans until the temperature of the soil is at least 16–18°C (61–64°F). Or, as you may hear some old gardeners say, do not sow until the hawthorn is in flower and you can walk around the garden barefoot without your feet feeling the cold.

Watching the watering
Although beans require plenty of water, take care when watering dwarf varieties. Their flowers are near to the ground and can be damaged by water from a watering can or spray. It is best to let water flow gently from a perforated hosepipe placed between the rows of beans.

See also **Vegetable gardens**

Frost

Plant protection
To protect vulnerable shrubs, insert four stakes into the ground round each one, then wrap a piece of hessian or heavy-duty polythene round the stakes. Fill the space between the covering and the shrub with leaves, bracken or polystyrene granules.

Caring for evergreens
Evergreens that are susceptible to frost cannot be covered up during periods of cold weather because they need light to thrive. If long periods of frost are forecast, erect hessian screens round the plants. This makeshift shelter allows sufficient light to reach the plants while protecting them from frost and damaging icy winds.

Container cover
Protect terracotta planters that cannot be moved indoors in frosty weather by enclosing them in boxes made from old cratewood, and packed with straw.

Make the right choice

Climbing and dwarf french beans
Crisp and juicy french beans can be enjoyed from July to October if you sow successively between May (or mid April under cloches) and late July. As french beans fertilise their own flowers, you can get an early crop: sow a few seeds in a warm greenhouse, minimum 13°C (55°F), during February for a bean crop in May.

Type	Description	Good varieties
Climbing	Can be flat or round-podded types, in green, purple or yellow	**Blue Lake** (green, round, stringless); **Goldmarie** (yellow, flat, stringless); **Hunter** (green, flat, prolific); **Purple Podded** (purple, round)
Dwarf french beans	Purple and yellow-podded types are available as well as the more common green-podded varieties. Most are round-podded, though a few are flat	**Annabel** (heavy cropper, good flavour, hardier than most); **Masterpiece Stringless** (flat-podded, stringless); **Purple Teepee** (purple pods held above foliage, very heavy cropper); **Slenderwax** (yellow-podded, round)

Shade early buds
Early-morning spring sunshine can cause the buds of early-flowering shrubs to thaw out rapidly, often with fatal results. Plant any vulnerable shrubs in sheltered locations in the garden where the flowers can thaw out slowly and without damage.

Blanket of straw

Ground frost can affect half-hardy dormant bulbs, such as gladioli, and tender perennials like lobelias. Avoid damage by covering the soil round susceptible plants with a thick, protective blanket of leaves or straw, weighed down with old tiles, pipes or stones.

Pot plants

Frost is especially harmful to pot plants as their roots are more exposed than those of plants in the ground, and terracotta pots, unless frost-proof, may crack. In winter, move pots to a frost-free greenhouse or a sheltered porch, or bring them inside the house. Alternatively, bury them up to their rims in the ground.

Cover up fruit crops

A spring frost can destroy fruit crops by killing the blossom. If your trees are trained against a wall, cover them with old net curtains or horticultural fleece. To do this, screw some hooks a few centimetres, or inches, above the tops of the trees, then attach the material with eyelets or loops. Canes leant against the wall will prevent the covers from sagging, and stones can be used to keep the ends weighed down. These versatile shelters can be put up easily at night and removed during the day.

Insulate greenhouses

Plants in an unheated greenhouse or conservatory can suffer if there is a severe drop in temperature. Ensure that leaves are kept away from cold glass, and line the inside of the walls and roof with bubblewrap. If your greenhouse or conservatory is heated, the polythene insulation will reduce your fuel bills.

Gravel and rock

Alpine plants are at risk of drying up during the winter months because freeze-thaw cycles can cause the soil round their roots to loosen. Help to anchor these plants securely by piling gravel gently round them. If this is done carefully, it will not damage the plants.

A quick cure

Never pour warm water or blow hot air on a frozen plant. This will kill it. Instead, wrap the plant in leaves or hessian so that it can thaw slowly and recover.

Remove icicles from trees

One of the most beautiful sights of winter is glistening icicles hanging from tree branches. However, icicles are heavy and should be removed if they appear to be weighing down branches. Shake them off by gently pushing up the branches with a rake, the lightest long-handled tool in the shed. Snow that collects on conifer branches should be removed to stop it distorting the tree's shape.

Fruit drop

June drop

Falling fruit at the end of June is a natural phenomenon that enables the tree to get rid of poorly pollinated or badly positioned fruit. Well-fed trees can support more fruit, so feeding in March and watering regularly from about the beginning of April will reduce the amount of fruit that the tree will shed.

Cherry partners

Cold or rain can cause cherries to fall prematurely, but the cause may be poor pollination. If you have room for only one cherry tree, you need a self-fertile variety, such as the sweet 'Lapins', 'Stella' or 'Sunburst' or the acid 'Morello'. Where there is space for two trees, plant varieties that produce flowers at the same time.

Trap the codling moth

Falling apples and pears may provide an early warning that the codling moth is about. The caterpillars of this pest burrow into fruit, ruining the crop, so it is well worth taking quick action

---

Growing know-how

How cold can help your garden

The cold is not always an enemy of your garden. It helps some plants to grow and protects others from pests.

Spring bulbs
The cold stimulates bulbs into growth. Do not protect them until their first shoots begin to show.

Fruit tree flowers
Frost and ice can protect buds from the rapid changes in temperature caused by frosty nights and clear, sunny days. Professional growers sometimes spray cold water onto the buds to protect their future crop from temperature variation.

Easy digging
Freeze-thaw cycles in winter help to break down lumps in freshly dug heavy soils. This improves the soil texture and makes it easier to work in the spring.

Pest control
Cold kills off many harmful insects and disease spores in the garden

against them. Hang a pheromone trap, available from garden centres, on your tree to attract and capture the male moths. This will prevent many of the females from mating and subsequently laying their eggs. In addition, the presence of codling moths in the trap is a sign that it is time to use insecticide.

Fruit trees

Coping with damp soils

Fruit trees need a well-drained soil if they are to thrive. A heavy soil can become waterlogged, causing roots to die and the shoots to wilt. If you cannot improve the drainage, you can try raising the roots above the waterlogged area as a last resort. First, create a small mound of soil then plant the tree so that the upper part of the roots are about 10–20cm (4–8in) above ground level. (See also **Drainage**)

Shoots not blooms

After planting a fruit tree, encourage the growth of new shoots by rubbing off any flowers that appear in its first season.

Root out grass

Remove competition for water and nutrients by keeping the soil round the bases of young trees free of grass and weeds. Leave circles of bare soil equal in size to the spread of the branches until the trees are established. After three or four years, you can allow grass to grow under the trees, leaving a 15cm (6in) ring of bare ground close to each trunk to discourage collar rot.

Feeding fruit trees

Give fruit trees a general fertiliser at the end of winter, at the rate of 70–140g per m² (2–4oz per sq yd) of ground beneath the spread of the tree. If the soil is cultivated, spread the fertiliser evenly, leaving it for the rain to wash down into the soil. Otherwise, use a bulb planter to make a circle of holes in the ground 30cm (12in) apart to match the outer extent of the branches above. Fill the holes with fertiliser, mixed with a 10cm (4in) pot filled with old potting compost or good soil. Fruit trees will also benefit from a further mulch of well-rotted compost, manure or spent mushroom compost in April or May.

Take the strain

Fruit trees may produce more fruit than they can support. A heavy crop may lead to a harvest of small fruit, stunt the tree's growth or cause branches to break. Wait until the June drop, the summer phenomenon when the tree rids itself of badly pollinated, diseased or surplus fruit, before you do the necessary thinning. If the crop is still over-heavy, cut off any damaged or stunted fruits. Leave one or two of the best to ripen on each fruiting spur.

Keep on picking

The fruits on a tree mature at different rates. This means picking should be carried out on several occasions, harvesting only the mature fruits from the tree each time.

Potted fruit

There are fruit trees for even the smallest garden. Apples, apricots, peaches, nectarines and quinces can all be bought ready-grafted onto a semi-dwarfing rootstock, making them suitable for growing in containers. Plant your choice in a terracotta pot rather than a plastic one as terracotta is sturdier, more pleasing to the eye and gives a better degree of protection from frost. (See also **Columnar trees**, **Dwarf plants**)

Fruit stains

The dark red fruits of the *Morus nigra* (black mulberry) are delicious, but if you are thinking of planting one, be careful where you site it. The juice from the fruit is very difficult to remove from paving stones or car roofs.

A home for birds

All tits are gardeners' friends because they have voracious appetites for the insect pests that plague fruit trees. Encourage a family of tits to take up residence in

your garden by putting a nesting box among the branches of susceptible trees. A circular opening in the front of the box, with a diameter between 2.5 and 3.2cm (1in and 1¼in), is large enough for the tits to pass through but too small to admit sparrows. Make sure that the box is securely fixed in position and in a place that cats cannot reach.

Let cold air flow

Never plant a hedge at the bottom of a sloping orchard. Cold air will be trapped, creating a frost pocket that can have a disastrous effect on the fruit blossom.
If you must erect a barrier, choose a slatted wooden fence or use wire mesh so that the air flow is not impeded. Alternatively, plant late-flowering fruit trees that are less susceptible to frost.

Make the right choice

The form to suit the fruit and your garden

The taste of freshly picked fruit from your own garden is matchless. Although few gardens can accommodate an orchard, most have room for at least one tree even if it has to be grown in a container. Before buying, check the eventual size and choose the shape that best suits your garden and the type of fruit that you want to grow. You can train the tree yourself, or buy a ready-trained specimen.

Half-standard/standard
Height: 3.7–6m (12–20ft). Slower to fruit than cordons or bushes, but more prolific.

Bush
Height: 2.4–3.7m (8–12ft). Quick to produce fruit, bushes are easy to prune and manage.

Dwarf pyramid
Height: 2.4–3m (8–10ft). Needs careful pruning but quickly produces fruit that is easy to harvest.

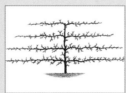

Espalier
Tiers of horizontal branches, usually grown against a wall. This form is suited to small spaces.

Fan
This attractive form takes up a large amount of wall space but produces a good crop.

Cordon
Space-saving form that provides a high yield; commonly used for apples and pears.

Fuchsias

Cold comfort for hardy plants

Hardy fuchsias can be left outside during the winter, but they need to be protected from frost. In spring, when all danger of frost is past, set out young, well-hardened plants, burying them deep to give extra protection to the crowns. In autumn, when they have finished flowering, leave the stems unpruned and pile dead leaves or earth over the bases of the plants as an added defence against frost. The following spring, cut back any stems that have been affected by frost.

Overwintering fuchsias

Half-hardy fuchsias need to be overwintered in a frost-free place such as a garage, greenhouse or shed. Before bringing them inside, prune each stem back to just above the third joint. Until April, water only if the stems appear to be drying up, then increase watering to restart growth. Keep the plants inside until all danger of frost has passed, then harden them off before planting out.

A second chance

If the stem of a standard fuchsia dies, save the plant by training a new shoot up from the base, using a cane as a support.

Create a frost-free area

If you lack a frost-free place to overwinter half-hardy fuchsias, cut them back to 15cm (6in), pot them up and bury them in the garden. Make sure that the tops of the pots are at least 23cm (9in) below ground level, then cover with a layer of straw and one of soil. Mark each spot as a reminder.

Fuchsias for foliage

Although most fuchsias are grown for their attractive, long-lasting flowers, a few are worth growing for the beauty of their foliage alone. Among the hardier ones are 'Genii', which has bright yellow leaves and attractive purple and red flowers; *Fuchsia magellanica molinae* 'Sharpitor', which has cream-edged leaves and pale pink blooms; and *F. m. gracilis* 'Variegata'

Make the right choice

Hardy and half-hardy fuchsias

In mild areas, hardy fuchsias can even be used for hedging but only grow. half-hardy types outdoors in summer.

Hardy varieties

Corallina Strong-growing fuchsia with dainty red and purple blooms; attractive in baskets and window boxes

Madame Cornelissen Showy red and white flowers; an excellent choice for bedding schemes

Riccartonii Small purple and red blooms; the ideal hedging fuchsia

Tennessee Waltz Attractive bush or standard fuchsia with pink and lilac flowers

Tom Thumb Dwarf plant with red and mauve blooms; useful for rock gardens

Half-hardy varieties

Auntie Jinks Small, purple and white flowers, ideal for hanging baskets

Celia Smedley Adaptable fuchsia that can be used for bushes, standards or pyramids; large pink and red flowers

Golden Marinka Popular basket plant with red blooms and golden foliage

Thalia Bedding fuchsia with tubular, orange-red flowers

Ting-a-Ling Profusely flowering fuchsia with white, shapely blooms; an attractive summer bedding plant

with grey-green, yellow-edged leaves and small, red flowers. For the greenhouse, conservatory or summer containers, try half-hardy varieties such as 'Autumnale', which has golden leaves overlaid with red; the variegated form of 'Golden Swingtime', one of the most popular fuchsias for hanging baskets; or 'Tropic Sunset', with bronze foliage and blue and red blooms.

Growing new plants

Fuchsias grow easily from cuttings, which can be taken at any time of year. Cut about 5cm (2in) from the tip of a non-flowering shoot. Cut just below a joint and remove the lower pair of leaves. Dip the base of the cutting in hormone rooting powder and pot it in cutting compost or John Innes No. 1. Water well, and stand in a warm place, out of direct sunlight. Keep the compost moist and, in a few weeks, the cutting will have rooted and can then be potted on into potting compost. (See *also* **Cuttings**)

Fungicides

Use fungicides sparingly

An overdose of fungicide can be fatal to plants, so always follow the manufacturer's instructions to the letter. When using either an aerosol or a sprayer, hold it at arm's length and first make sure that the spraying nozzle is directed at the plant. Spray from the bottom of the stem upwards, and be sure to coat the undersides of the leaves where most diseases occur.

Growing know-how

Limiting the use of fungicide

Plants will be far less prone to fungal diseases if you follow these tips:

- Choose plant varieties that have some in-built resistance.
- Give plants the amount of light, space and food that they require.
- Always rotate your crops in the vegetable garden.
- Be scrupulous about garden hygiene, picking up and burning diseased leaves, weeds or fruits.

Sensitive plants

Some plants can be sensitive to certain chemicals used in fungicides. For example, some gooseberries are sulphur-shy. The leaves may drop, or develop various spots and scorches. Always check the label for warnings about plants known to be susceptible. Do not spray in bright sunlight, in very hot weather or when plants are dry at the roots. If in doubt, test a small area of plant first. Where you have a group of plants to treat, try the chemical on one first.

Take quick action

Fungi reproduce themselves by means of airborne spores – minute, dust-like bodies composed of a single cell. Most fungicides do not actually kill fungi, but prevent the spores from spreading. At the first signs of a fungal disease such as rust or mildew, prompt spraying of the whole plant and any others of the same type standing nearby should provide adequate protection against infection.

Prevention before cure

Apply preventive spray early in the season to any plants, such as roses, that may be susceptible to attack. A protective coating of fungicide on the leaves will ensure that any fungus spores that land do not infect the plants.

(See *also* **Chemicals**)

Garages

Make a virtue out of a necessity

Practical rather than pretty, the garage can, nevertheless, be transformed into an eye-catching feature that will make a valuable contribution to the garden as a whole. You might, for example, replan the drive, uniting it with the front path and giving it a more interesting curve. A 1–1.2m (3–4ft) beech hedge, that draws the eye inwards from the gateposts, enhances a front garden and provides a welcoming entry to the house.

Scented approach

You could erect a pergola over the driveway to the garage to support clematis, wisteria or perhaps a thornless rose such as 'Zéphirine

Drouhin'. Choose your favourites and match and harmonise the colours of the plants and their flowers with the paintwork on the house and garage.

The potting option

If your garage has a concrete surround and a long, blank wall jutting out from the house, improve it by painting the wall a warm colour, then fix a row of flat trellis arches along it, painting the centre of each arch in a contrasting colour. Position an evergreen shrub in a pot in front of every arch and underplant the shrubs with polyanthus, pansies and small bulbs in winter and spring followed by colourful summer-bedding plants.

Matching pair

Where the garage is at a lower level than the house, the slopes on each side of the drive can be developed into rock gardens. Since about a ton of rock is required for every 4m² (43sq ft) of garden, the initial labour can be arduous, but the end result is worthwhile. Put the rocks in place, then plant alyssums, arabis and aubrietas. Add miniature bulbs such as *Leucojum* (snowflake), *Muscari* (grape hyacinth) and *Narcissus triandrus* var. *triandrus* (angel's tears) for a splash of early-season colour. Plant *Helianthemum* (rock rose), which has evergreen or grey leaves and delicate flowers, to continue the interest through the summer. (*See also* **Rock gardens**)

Floral trail

Build a low retaining wall alongside the drive, back-fill with good soil, then plant with low shrubs and trailing plants. If the wall is in the sun, plant an aromatic lavender such as *Lavandula angustifolia* 'Hidcote'; in the shade, choose shiny-leaved evergreens, such as *Lonicera pileata*, or a fragrant, winter-flowering *Sarcococca* underplanted with ivy. Hanging baskets along garage walls provide colour all through summer; on a shady wall, baskets of busy lizzies, trailing fuchsias and small-leaved ivies give a charming display. Water-retentive granules and a slow-release fertiliser reduce aftercare and will help to keep the plants healthy when you are away.

Garden design

Plotting and planning

Using a pencil, draw to scale the outline of your garden on a large piece of graph paper. Then mark in the features you wish to include, such as flowerbeds, greenhouse, pool, vegetable garden and lawn. Include any existing features that you want to retain and indicate the proposed positions of others, such as dividing hedges, steps and paths that you wish to create. Rub out and revise the plan until you are fully satisfied with it.

A photographic guide

To help you to design the layout of a new garden, take photographs of the garden from different angles and have them enlarged. Draw your planned layouts on tracing paper and lay them over the photographs. This will help you to decide which design you prefer.

Jigsaw design

When designing your garden, experiment by drawing each feature on a separate piece of paper; as your ideas change, you can move the pieces around as you would in a jigsaw until they match the ideas in your mind's eye.

Allow for subsidence

Always allow for the soil's natural subsidence when carrying out any back-filling in a redesigned garden. Soil that has been dug up and moved to a new area will gradually pack itself down, with its overall height being reduced by approximately 20 per cent.

Initial simplicity

To create your first small garden, do not be tempted to use too many different plants. Focus instead on a striking group of the same plants, such as a clump of lilies or irises, to make a strong impact.

Lawn or stone?

When designing a new garden, think carefully before establishing a lawn. A gravel, or paved, area may be more suitable, particularly if you want to be spared the bother of mowing.

Unite house and garden

Integrate the house and garden by training climbers up the walls and round doorways, or erect a flower-covered pergola over the drive.

Careful curving

Curves are an effective way of creating interesting borders and separating different areas of the garden. Lay out a hosepipe or a piece of rope to give an idea of how the curve will look. View the shape from different areas of the garden and from an upstairs window in the house. Use broad sweeps rather than tight curves, which are more difficult to maintain. Do not overdo it. An excess of curves can look fussy.

Growing know-how

The six steps to follow when transforming a garden

Alongside the tips on these pages, these are the six major steps you should follow if planning to transform your garden. After making a list of the plants you want to grow and drawing rough sketches of a design plan, work logically towards the improvements.

1 Clear up the garden. If it is established, remove all unwanted plants, rotting fences and unwanted debris; if it is new, clear away any rubble that may have been left behind by the builder.

   Put bricks, lumps of concrete and old stones to one side for possible use later as paths, edging or foundations for any walls and patios.

2 Dig over the ground, where necessary removing pieces of brick, weeds, old timber and rotting tree roots. Install or renovate the boundary walls, fences and hedges.

   Carry out any earth-moving necessary for making raised beds, changes of level, steps, banks or pools.

3 Make or repair any permanent features that you are incorporating – internal walls, pools, paths, steps, seating areas, garden buildings and play areas.

   Install any outside plumbing and electrical fittings, or make future provision for them by laying conduits before constructing paths and paved areas.

4 Mark out and double-dig the planting areas, removing all weeds and incorporating organic material, such as peat or peat substitutes, leafmould, garden compost or well-rotted manure.

   Allow time for any soil you have dug or moved to settle naturally before planting hedges, trees, the larger shrubs and key plants (using tree stakes and ties where necessary).

5 Mark out the lawn areas, dig over, remove weeds and stones and rake level. Firm down, then rake again and apply a general fertiliser before seeding or turfing.

   Keep off a new lawn or use boards if you have to walk on it.

6 Add the finishing touches. Position any statues and wall ornaments, wall fountains, containers and garden furniture.

   At the appropriate time of the year, plant the smaller shrubs, herbaceous perennials, annuals and bulbs. Clean and fill the garden pool, adding plants after one week and any fish two weeks later.

Protecting trees

If you plan to carry out major works, such as land clearance, excavation or building in your garden, protect trees and plants that you wish to retain by encircling them with planks of wood or covering them with canvas or polythene.

A hilltop house

A bare lawn makes a house on a hill stand out like a sore thumb. Avoid this by planting trees, shrubs and perennials along at least two sides to soften the lines of the hill and to merge the house with the garden or the surrounding landscape.

Avoid hard, straight lines

If there is a narrow, uninviting space instead of a garden between your house and its boundaries, add elements to give it shape and interest. A winding path bordered by a light-reflecting pool and beds of plants of graduating height are very effective. Add a flower-covered archway and train climbing or rambling plants on trellises to hide prominent, unsightly walls.

Bring interest to a dull landscape

Avoid growing columnar trees in isolation in a wide expanse of featureless garden. Their rigid appearance will only help to accentuate a landscape that is bare. Instead, choose a few spreading shrubs and trees such as *Liquidambar* (sweet gum), *Malus* (crab apple), *Parrotia persica*, *Viburnum rhytidophyllum* and *V. tinus*.

Making a garden appear longer

If your garden is short, create an illusion of length by making a path that narrows slightly as it runs away from the house. On each side, plant a row of trees or shrubs of graduating heights – the tallest nearest the house, the smallest at the far end. Topiary globes, cones or spirals would be an excellent choice.

A place in which to relax

Make the bottom of your garden an intriguing little haven. It may be the ideal place for a scented floral arbour in which to relax. Alternatively, provided there are no young children who could be scratched by the thorns, surround a garden seat with gooseberry, blackcurrant and raspberry bushes whose tasty fruits you can reach for and pluck while you are relaxing.

Design highlights

Objects chosen to enhance your garden can be made more effective by careful placing. Fill containers with striking plants such as a spiky yucca or a large-leaved fatsia, setting them at an angle of the garden or against a back wall; hang a wall fountain on a shady wall and frame it with bamboos, ivies and ferns; or set a classical statue within a plant-smothered arch. If the object is visible from the house, add lighting so it can be seen at night. (See also **Garden lighting**)

Plant choice

If you want to create a new garden without having to wait too long for it to look its best, plant some fast-growing perennials. The varied growth habits of stately delphiniums and lupins, prolific geraniums, knotweed, bergamots and billowing gypsophila will complement each other. Ground-cover plants such as ivies, London pride and periwinkles will rapidly cover the bare soil between these plants. Finally, try sowing a few quick-flowering annuals, such as alyssums, calendulas, nasturtiums, poached egg plants and Virginian stocks.

Bring a garden to life

Enhance your garden with highlights such as a gushing fountain in a quiet corner, a secluded summerhouse or a collection of herbs planted in an old cartwheel.

*See also **Architectural plants pp.16–17, Perspectives***

Garden furniture

Instant antiquity

There is no doubt that a stone bench or table can lend an air of quiet dignity to your garden, particularly if it is made in an antique style. The initial stark appearance of the stone will soon mellow as it weathers. A stone nymph, a sundial or an urn filled with trailing pelargoniums makes an interesting focal point at the end of a path, particularly when it is set against a background of climbers.

Faster ageing

Accelerate the ageing process of a stone bench or table by using a proprietary compound or by painting it with a mixture of 1 part yoghurt in 10 parts of water.

Plant-friendly wood preservative

Protect wood in the garden with a non-toxic wood preservative rather than with creosote. Creosote will kill any plants that it touches and its fumes can damage nearby plants.

Choosing the site

Take care with the siting of your garden seat. The top of a flight of steps or the end of a path are places worth considering, as is a site in front of a warm wall. The seat can be in sun or shade and may be a focal point, or tucked away in a secluded corner. For greater effect, place the seat on a raised half-circle of granite cobbles mixed with gravel, which will dry out quickly after rain. Plant with aromatic thyme and sweet alyssum. In shade, plant lady's mantle and creeping campanulas.

Rest and be thankful

A wooden bench seat makes a good focal point and, if properly sited, can draw attention to your garden's best view. Those made from teak, from managed plantations,

Sitting pretty A stone bench makes an attractive feature in a corner of the garden. Cushions can be spread on the seat to make it more comfortable.

are the most expensive, but are by far the best buy. The seat will last a lifetime and become even more attractive as it weathers and ages. It can be left outdoors throughout the year, requiring only a quick scrub at the end of each winter. Make the bench even more of a feature by enclosing it within an arch covered with clematis or a long-flowering succession of roses, and flank the approach with a low hedge of lavender or clipped rosemary.

Movable garden furniture

If you need a bench that can be moved easily, buy one that has handles at both ends or one that is fitted with a wheel at one end. These benches, sold by some garden centres, can be moved round the garden whenever you fancy a different position or view.

Room with a view

If you have space, consider erecting a gazebo, a building rather like a summerhouse that was much loved by the Victorians. It can be surrounded by climbing scented plants, and will give shelter from the rain and shade from the sun, while offering views of the entire garden from its windows. Inside, you can install a few wicker chairs, and a table to support the drinks tray on a summer evening. Gazebos can be bought ready-made or in kit form from many garden centres.

Rustic comfort

An attractive garden seat need not be expensive. A simple heavy baulk of timber fixed to a couple of well-embedded logs can be most effective, especially when it has a well-clipped hedge as a backdrop.

Avoiding wear and tear

If you want a garden seat on the lawn, stand it on flat stones or blocks of wood to keep it level and to prevent the legs from sinking into the ground. Lay stones in front of the seat to avoid an ugly worn patch in the lawn.

Cleaning wicker furniture

When summer is over, bamboo, cane or wicker furniture can be cleaned by sponging gently using warm water with a little washing-up liquid.

Painting to effect

Garden furniture will stand out if painted to contrast with house walls. For a unified effect, paint the furniture to match the woodwork – doors, window frames and tubs.

Versatile seating

Car boot sales, junk shops and antiques fairs are all places where you may find old wooden chairs going cheaply. They need not be a matching set as you can paint them to complement different areas of the garden.

A circular seat

Provide a shady retreat by constructing or buying a wooden seat that will fit round the trunk of a favourite tree. If there is grass beneath the tree, avoid an unsightly worn area by laying a bed of bricks or small, flat pebbles. This effective, protective carpet will add to the attraction and charm of your tree seat.

Seat of softness

In a less formal garden, a seat that is made from timber, weathered bricks or old railway sleepers is more fitting than one made from metal. If constructing a brick seat, choose a suitable place and construct the seat as you would a low, raised bed, making it about 1m (3ft) long and 46cm (18in) wide. When building the frame to the necessary height, be sure to leave drainage holes at the base. Infill with good garden soil, firm it well, then cover with a layer of fine turf. Alternatively, you can plant creeping thyme or 'Treneague' camomile. These will not withstand wear as well as grass, but both release a delightful aroma when crushed. .

Make the right choice

Choose your wood wisely

It may be worth investing in furniture made from more expensive woods, such as teak, as last longer than cheaper woods. As timber is a diminishing natural resource, always ensure that what you buy comes from a managed plantation.

Wood	Type	Advantages	Disadvantages
Cedar	Softwood	Resistant to rot and insects. Natural reddish-brown colour	Easily dented. Does not hold nails well. Colour likely to fade, but oils are available that maintain the colour
Iroko	Hardwood	Cheaper than teak but equally hard-wearing. Suitable for garden furniture	Coarse-textured
Larch	Softwood	Resistant to rot. Holds nails well	Difficult to work
Meranti	Hardwood	A good, much cheaper alternative to mahogany. Suitable for garden furniture	Lacks the rich colour and natural lustre of mahogany
Oak	Hardwood	Strong and durable	Expensive. Difficult to work. Splits easily when nailed
Redwood	Softwood	Easy to work. Easy to stain or paint	Little resistance to rot
Teak	Hardwood	Resistant to rot, water and fire. Excellent for garden furniture	Expensive. Diminishing natural resource, so check labels to ensure supplier is approved

Garden hygiene

Cleaning canes
After clearing crops such as peas and runner beans, always be sure to clean the canes. Brush off the soil, remove plant debris and dislodge any insects that may be hiding. Overnight, soak the ends that were in the soil in a bucket of household detergent or horticultural disinfectant. Rinse, allow to dry, then store them in a dry place.

A clean-up following pruning
Once you have finished pruning, clean the pruning tools by rubbing a cloth dipped in bleach along the blades. Wear rubber gloves when using neat bleach.

Grooming plants
Grooming is not just for pets: the regular removal of dead, diseased or pest-infested leaves will make plants look more attractive and is good for their general health as it also helps to prevent diseases from taking hold.

A tidy garden
While there are some areas of your garden that can safely be left untended to encourage wildlife, never leave piles of rubble and accumulations of dead leaves and prunings lying around. They will soon harbour pests such as earwigs, which damage flower petals, woodlice, which feed on seedlings, and vine weevils, which attack at night taking notches out of the leaf edges of plants such as camellias, clematis, cyclamen, rhododendrons and also plants in pots.

Hygiene in the vegetable plot
Always ensure that the vegetable plot is kept free of weeds. Some weeds, such as chickweed and groundsel, can be carriers of viral diseases. (*See also* **War on weeds pp. 324–5**, *Weeding, Weedkillers*)

Garden lighting

Safety first with outside lights
The safest form of lighting for the garden is a low-voltage system in which a transformer reduces power to 12 or 24 volts. With this arrangement, submersible lights are available for use in ponds. These provide white light, but coloured lenses are also available. It will be quite simple, too, with this method, to change the position of any light. A permanent system, which requires the installation of weatherproof, underground cables, must be installed by a qualified electrician. Cables carrying 240 volts should never be run along fences or buried shallowly in the ground.

By candlelight
Outdoor candles give off soft light and help to create a pleasant atmosphere in the garden. As an additional bonus, some candles contain natural additives that act as insect deterrents. To protect the flame from wind or breeze, stand the candle in a tall glass bottle or jar, fixing it to the base with melted wax. Flares, available from garden centres, are another useful form of outdoor lighting and need no protection from wind.

Working to a plan
When a permanent lighting system is part of a new garden plan, think about your lighting requirements at the planning stage. You may need to run cables under walls, along paths or beneath the lawn. It is less disruptive and more cost-effective to install these before constructing the garden. When the cables are in place, draw a detailed diagram showing their positions. If in the future you want to extend the lighting, you will know exactly where the cables have been laid.

Fitting lights and cables
There are various forms of low-voltage lights available – for setting in the ground, fixing on standard holders or siting on trees. After you have positioned these where you want them, you can then lay the cables. If necessary, the cables can be left on the surface or, preferably, threaded through nearby undergrowth. Full instructions will be provided with the installation packs, the most important of which will be to ensure that the transformer is sited in a dry place. Security lights are also available. These are usually plugged into an existing socket in the house and are controlled by passive infrared detectors. They can be adjusted for sensitivity.

Money-saving bulbs
For all garden lighting, you will find it well worth investing in energy-saving 11 or 13-watt bulbs, which have the equivalent light output of

Magical transformation Low-voltage lighting, which is relatively easy and cheap to install, can bring a fairy-tale atmosphere to a summer evening.

Lights round the garden

A number of small lights will be more effective than a single spotlight and, as a general rule, a warm light is best. The exceptions may be when lighting a patio or barbecue or at party time or Christmas. Then, strings of weatherproof outdoor lights or lanterns may be used. These will usually include various coloured bulbs, which may also be used to illuminate a pond. Note, however, that Christmas tree lights intended for indoor use should never be used outdoors.

Brighter is not better

When is comes to the garden, don't assume that brighter is always better. A bulb stronger than 100 watts will actually just accentuate the 'black hole' of unlit spaces behind it, and will draw attention to the darkness of the garden. What's more, it may annoy your neighbours if it is shining in their direction.

Make use of free energy

Solar power has taken the gardening industry by storm in the last few years, and lighting has become so sophisticated that there is no need for an electrician nowadays if you want to install an outdoor lamp or even a whole array of garden lights. They are easy to find, inexpensive, and designs are so varied and refined that only the tiny panel on the top confirms that the light is not only energy-efficient but kind to the environment as well. Instead of waiting days or weeks for a professional to fit you in, solar garden lighting takes a matter of minutes and your whole garden can be transformed the same day as you buy your lights.

60-watt bulbs. Although they are more expensive to purchase, their life expectancy is up to ten times longer.

Focus on a special feature

Up-lights, down-lights and side-lighting can be used to great dramatic effect to illuminate various features – specimen trees and plants, for instance, or an ornament or a statue. It is worth spending some time experimenting with lights in different positions to see what looks best.

Ways of switching

Outdoor lights can be controlled by standard switches. Alternatively, you might consider incorporating a photoelectric cell unit in the circuit so that the lights come on at dusk. This can be useful from a security point of view with lanterns and bulkhead fittings. And if these incorporate energy-saving bulbs, it becomes more economical to leave certain lights on all night.

Garden ornaments

In harmony with the plants

Whatever the style of your garden and plants, complement them with appropriate ornaments. Terracotta pots on patios and terraces will enhance a Mediterranean arrangement, classical statues and fountains belong in a formal setting, while a statue of an oriental divinity and a bamboo waterspout will effectively evoke a Japanese garden.

Distracted by a statue

An ornamental urn or a statue placed slightly off-centre at the end of the lawn will make the garden appear larger and draw attention away from any shortcomings it may have.

Features to surprise

Some elements of surprise are welcome in any garden. A birdbath or a bird table, for example, installed at a turning in a path, can be particularly eye-catching. For a touch of humour, place statues and ornaments in out-of-the-way and out-of-the-ordinary places. Tuck a tall bird away behind a clump of bamboos, and let bronze frogs, snakes and hedgehogs cross a terrace or lurk in low ground cover. Allow a few jolly clay piglets to tumble down a flight of steps. For a touch of romance, a shy nymph looks especially charming when glimpsed through sprays of roses and ivy.

A Mediterranean ambiance Add beauty and a feeling of sunshine to the garden with a simple stone vase.

Creating a background
An evergreen backdrop to a statue or a fountain will make it stand out. Ivy, yew and box are especially effective.

Frost resistance
Unless your containers are frostproof, bring them inside in winter. Those with garland decorations are particularly vulnerable, as water can seep behind the garlands and freeze. (See *also* **Containers**)

Raising the level
When standing a potted plant inside a deep terracotta jar, raise it to the required height by standing it on an upturned flowerpot hidden inside.

Instant patina
Stand reconstituted stone or concrete statues or ornaments in a cool and shady place. Soon, algae will spread over them and soften their starkness. Give them one or two coats of liquid manure to speed up the process.

Garlic

Go Continental
Perhaps due to a knowledge of its importance in Mediterranean cookery, people tend to think that garlic doesn't flourish in Britain. In fact, this invaluable culinary plant, which can be included in an ornamental garden, is totally hardy and thrives even in northern counties.

Growing hints

Choose a sunny spot in which to plant garlic. It requires a cold spell to grow well so, in November, divide bulbs into cloves and plant about 15cm (6in) apart in drills 7.5cm (3in) deep. Cover the nose with a thin layer of soil. They need little attention other than watering during dry spells. If the soil is very heavy, plant the cloves in February or March.

Deadhead quickly
Pick off the flowers as soon as they appear. This will ensure that nourishment is not diverted away from the bulb.

Harvest time
Harvest garlic in late summer, when the leaves have turned yellow and dry. Dig up the plants, leaves and all, and leave them in the sun to dry off the surface moisture. Then, put them under cover until the bulbs have dried. Use the leaves to plait the bulbs together and hang the bunches in a cool, dry place. Do not hang garlic in the kitchen. as it will not dry properly because the moisture from kettles and cooking softens it.

Continuing the crop
When harvesting, leave two or three bulbs in the ground where they will overwinter. Then, when the green shoots start to show above the soil, dig up the bulbs, split them into cloves and replant them in a different section of the garden. Because these cloves have already

A brief history

The bulb that helped to build the pyramids
Garlic, thought to have originated in the Kirghiz Desert in Central Asia, has been cultivated in Mediterranean countries since the earliest times. Together with radishes, onions, peas and cucumbers, it was the staple diet of the workers who built the pyramids, some of whom valued it so highly that they carved its likeness on the Great Pyramid at Giza.

The Romans introduced garlic to Britain, but by the time the Anglo-Saxons arrived, its culinary use seems to have been largely forgotten, though it was still highly regarded as a cure for constipation. Medieval housewives included it in their vegetable potages or stews, but it was not until the advent of Continental holidays . that the British again began to use it in their cooking. The French have always considered garlic to be indispensable, even using its juice as a disinfectant on wounds in the First World War.

rooted, they will grow quickly and produce a particularly fine crop.

Good for you and the garden
Some gardeners claim that garlic grown between other plants will help to ward off pests and diseases. Roses, particularly, appear to benefit from the proximity of garlic, which is said to give them a sweeter scent and also a greater resistance to disease. Garlic may also help to deter aphids and other garden pests. Garlic is good for people as well as plants because it contains chemicals that aid digestion and help to purify the blood. Its constituents are also said to be antiseptic and anti-inflammatory, and it is reputed to help fight dysentery, typhoid and, more practically, the common cold. (See also **Medicinal plants**, **Rodents**)

Gherkins

Defining the gherkin

The gherkin is a variety of cucumber whose stumpy, spiny fruits are particularly suitable for pickling. Grow gherkins as you would any other outdoor cucumber and harvest them when they are 7.5–10cm (3–4in) long. Dependable varieties include 'Conda', an F_1 hybrid, and 'Venlo Pickling'.

A settled start

Gherkins may take some time to settle if their roots have been disturbed, so when starting them off in the greenhouse or frame, plant the seeds in peat pots. These can be put straight into the ground where the roots will grow through the pots without interruption. Prior to planting out – between the beginning and the middle of June, depending on whether you live in the north or the south of the UK – acclimatise the seedlings for a few days by standing them outside under a cloche or beneath bell jars.

Net-trained

One of the best ways to grow gherkins is to train them up a net that has been hung from posts about 1.2m (4ft) high. Raised in this way, the fruit will be clean, well shaped, uniformly green and easy to pick.

Morning fresh

If at all possible, pick your gherkins before the sun is high and the fruits have warmed up. You will find that the gherkins are firmer then and will, therefore, keep for longer.

Small and select

If you like your gherkins about 5cm (2in) long, pick them every two or three days. If you prefer longer, thicker gherkins, leave them to grow for an extra few days.

Gladioli

Summer-long supply

Plant the first batch of corms between mid March and mid April in well-manured soil and in a sunny position. Three or four further batches, planted at fortnightly intervals, will give a steady supply of flowers throughout the summer. Gladioli grown for cutting should be planted in rows 30–38cm (12–15in) apart.

Stem support

In windy areas, or places where the soil is light, plant the corms more deeply than usual, at least 10cm (4in) into the ground. This will give the flower stems more support.

Place a stake

Insert a stake into the soil at planting time and place it on the side of the plant from which the wind usually blows. Never tie the upper part of the spike to the cane as it will simply be snapped off during a strong wind.

Decorative value

If gladioli figure highly in any of your flower arrangements, grow the showiest hybrids possible. Try the orange 'Saxony', the pink 'My Love', the red 'Hunting Song' and the lime-green 'Green Woodpecker'.

Winter survivors

Delightful though the big hybrid gladioli are, the corms will not survive if left in the ground through a British winter. An alternative is to grow some of the hardier species, which work very well both in a mixed border or against a south or west-facing wall where they can be left to look after themselves from year to year. Among the toughest is *Gladiolus byzantinus*, which produces spikes of crimson flowers 61cm (2ft) tall, while the sulphur-yellow *G. tristis* is hardy in many southern gardens. All gladioli prefer a warm, sunny place in rich soil.

Plan ahead

Give gladioli a thorough watering two days before cutting for inclusion in flower arrangements. Select flowers on which the bottom florets are just starting to open, and cut them first thing in the morning.

A brief history

The flower named after a Roman sword

The gladiolus gets its name from the similarity of its leaves to the gladius, the sword of the Romans and weapon of the gladiator. However, southern Europeans were familiar only with the wild species that is native to Mediterranean countries; the larger, showier species originated in South Africa. These were first brought to northern Europe more than 250 years ago. They were hybridised by the British and Belgians, and this gave rise to many of the brilliant, large-flowered, modern varieties that have been popular for so long. The smaller, more natural-looking varieties are easier to grow.

Early flowers

Gladioli will flower up to three weeks earlier, depending on the variety, if you put the corms in the greenhouse in February or March. Place them in empty trays in a well-lit spot and at a temperature of 12°C (54°F). Once they have sprouted, plant them outdoors in the usual way.

Lift and dry

Leave the corms of hybrid gladioli in the ground until the first frosts blacken the foliage as this helps to seal the tissues of the corms against fungal diseases. Chop off the frost-damaged foliage and spread the corms out to dry in shallow trays in an airy shed or garage, turning them upside-down to drain any moisture that may be in the stems.

Preparation for storage

When lifted corms are thoroughly dry, gently twist off the old, shrivelled corm at the base of the new, and discard. Peel away the tough outer skins of each large corm, then carefully break off the tiny cormlets at the base and store them in a paper bag. Remember to name each bag. You may also find it useful to note down the flower colour and plant height.

High storage

Put the corms in a net and suspend them from the shed roof to allow the air to circulate freely. If you have only a few corms, you can put them in an old pair of tights.

Propagating gladioli

Gladioli can be increased from cormlets or seeds, although any hybrids that are grown from seed may not grow true to colour or type. When planting cormlets, space them 30cm (12in) apart and 5–7.5cm (2–3in) deep in drills. They should be put in a well-drained soil to which some well-rotted compost has been added. Place a layer of sand below and above the cormlets to help growth and to ease lifting. Keep the cormlets well watered and weed-free, then, when the foliage has died down, lift and store them in the same way as adult corms. Most cormlets will flower in their second year, but some may take up to three years to bloom.

Gooseberries

Two for one

If you are undecided between dessert or culinary varieties, choose one of the dual-purpose gooseberries, such as 'Invicta', 'Jubilee' or 'Whinham's Industry'. These useful and flavoursome fruits can either be eaten raw or used for cooking.

Weed control

Never dig the soil round a gooseberry bush – you may disturb the plant's shallow roots. Keep weeds at bay by shallow hoeing, or by applying a mulch or a proprietary weedkiller.

Cordon gooseberries

Train gooseberries as cordons to make effective use of a small area. Single cordons are rather uneconomical as you will need to buy several plants to get a reasonable crop. However, a U-shaped cordon, with two vertical branches, will not only give you a large amount of fruit but its open centre allows air to circulate and thus helps to prevent fungus diseases taking hold.

Thinning out

Thin out gooseberry bushes in late May to help the remaining fruits to develop. Use the small, immature gooseberries that you remove for bottling or cooking.

Firm them in

Gooseberry bushes are shallow-rooting, which means frosts can cause the roots of newly planted bushes to lift out of the soil. Check regularly during the winter months

Make the right choice

Gooseberries for the table and the kitchen

Choose from the following varieties of gooseberries that are ideal for eating raw, serving in pies or using in jam-making:

Greenfinch A newly developed variety, good for cooking, which ripens earlier than 'Invicta'. Mildew-resistant.

Invicta Produces a heavy crop of large pale green fruit with a good flavour. Excellent for culinary purposes, and can also be used for dessert. Mildew-resistant.

Keepsake Large gooseberries with a delicious flavour. Can be picked early for cooking, or left to ripen.

Leveller A popular choice, with juicy, yellow fruits. A mid-season cropper.

Lord Derby Has exceptionally large, dark red berries with a wonderful flavour and excellent quality.

Whinham's Industry Produces masses of dark red berries that are ideal for desserts and preserves. Prone to mildew.

Whitesmith A good, reliable variety, with lots of pale, juicy fruit and a delicious flavour. Pick early for culinary use, or leave to ripen for eating raw.

A brief history

Gorgeous gooseberries

In the 18th century, there was a passion for growing exhibition gooseberries rather akin to that for growing giant parsnips now. The hand-loom weavers of the Manchester area formed clubs that exhibited 722 varieties at dozens of shows. Today, only a few clubs are left, the oldest of which (formed in 1800) is the Egton Bridge Old Gooseberry Society of Yorkshire. It holds its show each August.

and firm in the soil round any plants that appear to be loose.

Clear a space

Gooseberry buds are particularly attractive to sparrows so make sure that you net the bush as soon as the buds start to form in early winter. Use a cage to ensure that the netting is kept well clear of the branches, otherwise the birds will still be able to reach some of the buds. If you do not have a fruit cage, it is best to

delay pruning until bud break. Do not leave it any later than late March or this will delay or reduce the crop

Gourds

Moist berth

As the plants start to grow, make an indentation in the soil round them to aid watering. Mulch generously with lawn mowings or well-rotted compost.

Good for young gardeners

Though they are native to tropical America, these half-hardy inedible annuals grow well in Britain. Plant the seeds in pots at the end of April or the beginning of May, or in an open, sunny spot outdoors in late May. Train the plants that develop up a fence, tripod or trellis. The odd shapes and bright colours of the fruits will appeal to children and are an excellent way to introduce youngsters to the joys of gardening.

Fun with gourds

Allow the gourds to ripen on the plants until they are quite hard and the foliage begins to die back, then sever them from the stalks with a sharp knife, wipe them clean and leave them to dry for a few weeks. When fully dry they become much lighter and the seeds rattle inside. Then you should apply a coat of clear varnishm which allows them to develop thick skins and deep colours.

Grafting

Elastic to the rescue

If you are in the middle of a grafting operation and run out of raffia, do not despair. An elastic band will bind just as tightly and will last for between two and four weeks. Another alternative is 1.3cm (½in) clear polythene strips cut from freezer bags.

Beware of birds

Grown grafts are susceptible to damage by birds, who push them aside or break them. Protect them by bending a flexible twig over the top and lashing it firmly in position. Birds can use this as a perch without doing any damage to the graft.

Thinking ahead with deciduous plants

If planning grafts on deciduous plants in spring, start well in advance. Cut the scions on a sunny day in winter, tie into bundles of ten and bury them in a box of fine sand. They will remain in good condition until spring.

The versatile pencil

Sometimes, if the stock is vigorous, it becomes difficult to insert the scion without the aid of a wedge. A well-sharpened pencil is excellent for carrying out the task. Simply tap it into the slit and, when the scion is in place, remove it.

Selecting the right rootstock

Make sure you visit an expert nurseryman when choosing the correct rootstock for an apple tree. For normal garden use, the rootstock known as M9 is recommended for dwarf trees, and MM106 for apple trees that grow to a medium size.

Growing know-how

The where, how and when of grafting

Success with grafting relies on the matching cuts being made quickly and cleanly. Practise your technique on branches that can be cut easily, such as willow, using a budding or grafting knife.

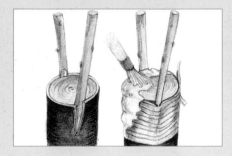

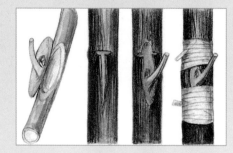

Crown graft Try to avoid large wounds as they take a long time to heal. It is better to insert new scions into two smaller limbs than one large one. Method for autumn or late winter:

1 Take shoots from the variety you wish to propagate and make slanting cuts at the lower end of each. Prune the upper ends just above a bud.

2 Using a hammer or mallet, insert a sharp wedge obliquely (taking care to ensure that it does not extend across the branch) into the top of the rootstock. Then insert the scions, checking to make sure that they make good contact.

3 Tie the graft in with raffia and paint over with sealant

Shield graft (budding) A way to propagate roses, fruit trees and some ornamental shrubs. Requires no more than a single bud for the scion. Method from mid to late summer:

1 Remove shoots from the rootstock. Prune to 30cm (12in) in July or August. Insert a knife beneath the selected bud on a well-ripened shoot of the plant to be propagated and cut behind it, making a 5cm (2in) slice to remove it. Leave about 1.3cm (½in) of the leaf stalk to hold when inserting the bud.

2 Make a T-shaped cut in the rootstock, just penetrating the bark, and peel flaps back. Insert scion, trim the top flush with T.

3 Tie in with 1.3cm (½in) tape until bud takes in early winter.

Approach graft Used on camellias, magnolias and citrus trees, on which other forms of grafting often fail to take. Method is best carried out in spring before growth begins:

1 Stock and scion are grown side by side in separate pots. Make a shallow, slicing wound in both stems.

2 The wounds are put together and bound in place with raffia.

3 When the two are united, the top of the stock and the base of the scion are cut and removed.

4 Keep in a closed frame in a greenhouse to maintain humidity and aid healing.

A less usual technique is apical wedge grafting, which involves a slightly different method:

Used for *Hibiscus syriacus*, wisteria and many trees or shrubs. For late winter/early spring:

1 Select a suitable rootstock, ideally a one to two-year-old seedling grown in a container. Cut off the top of the stem and leave a length of 10cm (4in). Make a single, vertical cut about 3.8cm (1½in) long through the middle of the stem.

2 Select a one-year-old scion about the diameter of a pencil and cut into sections with two or three buds. On each section, make two cuts 3.8cm (1½in) on either side to form a wedge.

3 Insert the wedge into the rootstock and bind it tightly in place using 1.3cm (½in) wide polythene tape, ensuring that the cambium (rind) is matching. Place in a cold frame and remove the tape when the graft starts growing.

Grapevines

Grapevines in Britain

It is virtually impossible to grow top-quality dessert grapes outdoors in Britain, but some hardy dessert and wine-making varieties will yield a reasonable crop in the south (see panel, right). A vine is well worth growing anyway, as an autumn attraction. The leaves turn red and purple, making a spectacular show. A vine grown against a south-facing wall can reach a height and spread of 3–4.6m (10–15ft).

The greenhouse conundrum

There are two ways to plant a grapevine in a greenhouse – one with the plant indoors, the other with the roots outdoors and the plant stems inside. Both methods have advantages; outdoor roots obtain more moisture and nutrients, but their exposure to frost can lead to reduced growth. In the warmer south and west of Britain, it is probably best to plant the vine outside, leading the stem inside through a hole in the wall. In the north and east, it is better to grow the entire plant indoors.

Vines on the patio

If your balcony or patio is sufficiently sheltered, a couple of vines would make an unusual decoration. Grow them in 36–40cm or 14–16in pots, filled with John Innes No. 3 potting compost. Select young plants and provide frames for them to grow on. You will be rewarded with rich autumn colours as well as some delicious fruit. Protect the vines from frost by moving the pots indoors at the onset of the cold weather. Repot every two years to ensure vines remain vigorous.

Training technique

The simplest way to train a vine is on a permanent framework, such as a trellis. In the first summer, one stem only should be allowed to grow. In the dormant December season, this should be shortened by two thirds of its length. In the following year, laterals should be stopped at five leaves in the summer then cut to two buds in December. The main stems should be shortened by two thirds of their length each December until they fill the desired space.

Best of the bunches

When grapes have reached the size of small peas, protect fruit from fungal diseases and from pests, such as birds and wasps, by using clear plastic bags or some cheesecloth to cover bunches. As the grapes begin to swell, remove the bags and cut out overcrowded fruit. This will help to concentrate growth.

Make the right choice

Grapes that grow best indoors and outdoors

Different grape varieties are suitable for outdoor and indoor sites but outdoor grapes can be grown only in the warmer, southern half of the UK.

Outdoor
Brandt Small, black, eating grapes. A reliable cropper. Spectacular autumn colour

Leon Millot Vigorous, prolific, black grape for eating or wine making. Mildew-resistant. May also be grown under glass

Müller-Thurgau Golden grape that can be used to produce Moselle-type wine, also good to eat. Only for warm areas.

Seyval Blanc Dependable white grape for making a light wine

Indoor
Black Hamburgh Sweet, black dessert grape, easy to grow and highly popular

Chasselas Reliable variety, thin-skinned, pinkish fruit. May also be grown outdoors

Foster's Seedling Heavy-cropping variety, juicy amber grapes

Madresfield Court Large, rather thick-skinned black grapes. Prone to splitting

Muscat of Alexandria White-bloomed, sweet grape, needs a heated greenhouse

Green energy

Help the environment

Your compost bin, however well insulated, gives off heat and carbon dioxide as the materials in it break down. You can make use of this heat by leaving a hole in the lid and making a structure on top from wire loops and clear, horticultural grade polythene, rather like a miniature tunnel house. The area inside can be used to germinate seedlings and take cuttings – the air will be several degrees warmer, and the enriched CO_2 atmosphere gives the young plants a boost. There will still be a little heat given off the compost during winter, so replace the clear polythene with bubble insulation sheeting, and you can overwinter slightly tender plants such as pelargoniums, fuchsias, osteospermums and marguerites. You may have to increase the height of the supports, as any major cutting back should wait until the spring, when the plants start into growth again.

Top of the heap

A few years ago, gardeners would grow marrows, cucumbers and other non-hardy vegetables on top of the compost heap, and this is still a good way of cultivation to save energy. Instead of putting all your compostable material into the compost bin, dig a trench, 30–45cm (12–18in) deep, in the vegetable garden or a bit of spare ground in late summer, and add kitchen and garden waste until the trench is full. In mid spring, cover with 20–30cm (8–12in) of the soil from the trench, which will soon start to warm up from the heat produced by the rotting rubbish. Half-hardy vegetables, such as runner beans, outdoor tomatoes, peppers, cucumbers and courgettes, can be planted into this after the last frost, and will get off to a flying start, and the nutrients released from the trench will help to feed them, although regular liquid feeds should still be given as normal.

Solar power

Make life easy and help the environment by buying solar-powered fountain pumps and garden lights. These are no more expensive than conventional examples, but utilise free energy and save you pounds in installation costs. A solar panel on the shed roof can be used to top up batteries for mowers and similar pieces of garden equipment.

Harness the wind

Consider a small wind turbine for heating and lighting greenhouses. As well as utilising free energy, you will get your investment back quite quickly. Some larger DIY superstores now stock these and can give advice on installing and using them.

Waste not water

Never let rainwater go to waste. Downpipes can be re-routed into water butts easily and inexpensively. Surplus rainwater can also be channelled into the garden pond or used to create an attractive bog garden. (See also **Watering**)

Re-use your buckets

Re-use old plastic buckets as large flower pots and planters. Make holes in the bottom for drainage and use for growing tomatoes, or plant up with bedding plants for a summer display. Colour co-ordinate the plants with the buckets to produce a really effective feature.

Recycle polystyrene

Although expanded polystyrene (the material often used for packing electrical and other fragile equipment) is recyclable, most councils commit it to landfill as there are insufficient remunerative outlets for reprocessing it. However, it can be recycled to good effect in the garden. Crumble it up and use it as drainage material in the bottom of containers, or float a piece in the pond in winter. If you make a hole in the piece before you put it in the pond, you will find the water here does not freeze over as quickly as it does in the open pool, allowing toxic gases that otherwise might build up under the ice to escape.

Greenhouse hygiene

Don't accumulate rubbish

The best way to control pests and diseases in the greenhouse is to make sure that it is kept scrupulously clean. Do not use the area under the staging as a store for spent potting compost, empty fertiliser bags, unwashed seed trays and pots or decaying vegetation, all of which can become desirable residences for insects and breeding grounds for diseases.

Be greenhouse proud

Treat all tools, trays and pots as you would your household cutlery and crockery. Wash them up, dry them thoroughly and put them away. If you do not have a garden shed or other suitable storage area outside the greenhouse, pack all the items carefully in clean boxes or polythene sacks and stand them neatly under the staging, where they can remain until they are needed.

A turnout for the best

At least once a year, either in autumn or spring, give the inside of the greenhouse a thorough clean. Remove all plants and stored bulbs, corms and tubers before you begin. Take any very tender plants indoors and stand the others in a sheltered spot in the garden.

Washing up

Use hot water, a little household detergent or horticultural disinfectant and a nailbrush to remove dried-on soil and chemical residues from trays and pots. Soak clay pots in a bucket of dilute disinfectant or detergent.

Fixtures and fittings

Check door hinges, window catches, screws and nuts and bolts for signs of rust and general wear and tear. Replace badly rusted hinges and treat less affected ones with a tannate-based rust destroyer. Apply a thin film of oil to all sound fixtures and fittings, and deal with any automatic window and ventilator openers according to the manufacturer's instructions.

Crevice clean-up

When cleaning inside the greenhouse, pay attention to crevices in the framework where insects can hide. Use a solution of warm water and horticultural disinfectant or household detergent, and a small, stiff brush on wooden structures, wire wool on aluminium ones. A sprayer with a long nozzle will help you to reach otherwise inaccessible corners.

Get under the overlap

Where the panes of glass overlap, dirt and algae can build up, causing dark bands that reduce the level of light. Scrape this hard-to-reach dirt away by slipping a plastic or metal plant label between the panes, sliding it gently up and down and being careful not to crack the glass. Take care not to dislodge any of the glazing clips in the process.

Greenhouses

Think big
When choosing a greenhouse, buy the biggest you can afford; its larger volume of air will help to control the growing environment. Your enthusiasm for cultivation, too, will grow and a small structure will only cramp your efforts.

Space-saving shelves
If it is possible, fit shelves as well as staging into your greenhouse to take seed trays and potted plants. Then you will be able to tend all your seedlings and plants without bending over and have the added advantage of leaving floor space free. Take care to position trays in such a way that, when watering, drips of muddy water do not land on the plants below.

Year-round brightness
To ensure that a greenhouse receives maximum light in winter, place it in full sunlight, well away from the shade of overhanging trees.

Shading a greenhouse
A greenhouse needs to be shaded from the hot sun during the summer months. If your greenhouse is not fitted with blinds, coat the glass with a white shading that becomes fairly translucent during wet, dull weather, and resists rain for several months. It is available from most garden centres. Apply it with a brush in the spring, but sponge it off in the autumn. Never use white acrylic paint or any other type of domestic paint.

Greenhouse insulation
Protect plants from winter cold by insulating the roof, sides and ends with bubblewrap. For aluminium frames, use special studs to fit this 1.9cm (¾in) from the glass.

Miniature model
If you fancy growing flowers and produce under glass but do not have room in your garden for a full-size greenhouse, buy a mini version, which could be attached to the side of the house. Although these can prove difficult to heat, they are perfectly suitable for growing hardy seeds, cuttings and plants.

Winter sparkle
Light levels are low in winter, so ensure that as much as possible reaches your plants by regular cleaning of the greenhouse glass. You can use a brush that attaches to your hosepipe to make the job easier.

Winter water
Whether rainwater or tap water, always keep a supply inside the greenhouse in winter. This will ensure that delicate plants are supplied with water of the right temperature.

All round the house
Careful maintenance of the exterior of the greenhouse is just as essential as that of the interior. Pay particular attention to any guttering that your greenhouse may have, because an overflow of rainwater could result in rotting wood in the framework as well as algal growth on the glass.

Automatic ventilation
If you are away from home for most of the day, ask your supplier about automatic openers for windows and ventilators. These openers, which can also be bought at some garden centres, work on the principle of thermal expansion, opening and closing in line with the changes in temperature.

Preventing breakage
Build the base of an aluminium greenhouse perfectly square at its corners. This stops the frame twisting and shattering the glass.

Make the right choice

The greenhouse for you
Before buying a greenhouse, make sure you choose one that suits your needs – and your pocket.

Aluminium
Alloy greenhouses require little maintenance and the slender glazing bars admit plenty of light, especially at ground level. Bought in kit form, their many parts can make them difficult to erect. You will need the help of another person.

Wood
Usually supplied in large sections that are bolted together, wooden greenhouses are easier to erect than aluminium ones. They are also more decorative, but the wood needs to be treated every two or three years, and even rot-resistant cedar has to be treated with preservative from time to time. Wooden greenhouses need a base of brick or concrete.

Plastic
Polythene tunnels, constructed from ultraviolet-inhibiting sheeting stretched across metal hoops, are relatively inexpensive. However, polythene, even when treated with an ultraviolet-light inhibitor that slows down the rate at which sunlight attacks the plastic, has a short life span, rarely lasting more than three years. It is easily punctured or torn.

What shape?
A greenhouse with vertical sides has more headroom at the eaves than one with sloping sides and is, therefore, more suitable for tall plants. A Dutch light greenhouse, with sides sloping outwards like a tent, offers less resistance to wind in exposed positions and lets in plenty of low-angled winter sunlight.

Growing know-how

Greenhouse buyer's checklist

A greenhouse is a major purchase so choose one that suits your future as well as current needs. Check the following:

- Before ordering your greenhouse, try to see a similar one already erected.
- Find out if the price includes base, staging, guttering and delivery, and what, if any, blinds can be supplied as extras.
- Buy a greenhouse large enough for your future needs, or a model that can be extended later.
- Make sure there are enough vents. The roof ventilation area should not be less than 20 per cent of the floor space.
- Check that the doors open widely enough to admit your wheelbarrow and that the door sill is not so high as to obstruct it.
- Enquire whether your supplier will erect the greenhouse for you. You will, however, probably have to install the base yourself or get a builder to do it.

Draught exclusion

A draughty greenhouse is bad for your pocket as well as your plants. Shrivelled foliage and soaring fuel bills can be prevented by the sealing of all cracks and gaps. There will already be an 8 per cent heat loss through the floor, so replace any worn seals round doors and windows and repair any louvre windows that do not close properly. Small cracks or gaps in the glass can be sealed with transparent waterproof tape, but cracked or broken panes will need to be replaced.

Make your glazing needs clear

When replacing any cracked or broken panes from the greenhouse, make a note of the measurements for each piece of glass. If possible, make a template of any pieces that have an awkward shape, such as triangular glass.

In addition, take a piece of the existing glass, wrapped in newspaper or bubble polythene to protect it, to show the glazier the exact thickness of the replacement glass you require.

Keep the greenhouse damp

During hot, dry weather, dampen the benches and paths in the greenhouse twice a day to increase the amount of humidity available to the plants. Alternatively, wet an old towel and hang it in the greenhouse with the lower end dangling in a container of water. The towel will stay wet as it constantly draws up water.

Winter vegetables

Make the most of an unheated greenhouse by growing lettuces over the winter. Sow seeds in late August and plant out the seedlings in the greenhouse border in late September. In exceptionally hot weather, sow in trays in a shaded area outside, to ensure the seeds germinate, and then transfer the seedlings to the greenhouse. Use only those varieties recommended for greenhouse growing.

Advancing the seasons

Anemones, Peruvian lilies and gladioli are suitable for growing in a cold greenhouse. As long as the temperature in your greenhouse does not fall below 10°C (50°F), you will be able to grow chrysanthemums to pick from October to January and be sure of a supply of perpetual carnations and early freesias. It is advisable to grow the chrysanthemums in large

Make the right choice

Heating options

The main sources of power for heating the greenhouse are paraffin, electricity and natural and bottled gas. Each choice has its advantages and disadvantages.

Paraffin

Gives off moisture as it burns, which can encourage diseases, but it also produces carbon dioxide, which encourages growth. The heaters are relatively inexpensive but cannot be thermostatically controlled. They also need refilling regularly and if they run out of fuel the greenhouse may be filled with acrid, black smoke.

Electricity

Usually trouble-free. The heat is dry, helping to prevent diseases in winter. Fan heaters are more expensive than paraffin ones, but are usually thermostatically controlled to help cooling in summer. Laying on the power can be expensive and there is the danger of power cuts.

Bottled gas

Worth considering if the greenhouse is some distance from the electricity supply. Gas heaters cost about the same as electric ones and are thermostatically controlled. They give out a damp heat. The cylinders are heavy and ideally you need two, with a cross-over valve, to be sure of a continuous supply.

Garden secrets

String up climbers

Before potting up, and as an alternative to using stakes for climbers in pots, coil one end of a long piece of nylon string in the bottom of the pot. Then add the compost and the plant, which will keep the string in place. Attach the other end of the string to hooks in the roof of the greenhouse. As the plant grows, it will twist round the string.

pots you can leave outdoors in summer, then bring them into the greenhouse before the start of the frosty weather. The perpetual-flowering carnations will crop winter after winter when planted in 18cm (7in) pots, while new plants can be raised from cuttings in spring.

Next year's tulips

In early summer, when the foliage has withered, lift tulip and hyacinth bulbs and leave them to ripen in the greenhouse, then store them in boxes under the staging until you plant them out in autumn.

Giving foliage air

Check that the overhanging foliage of a potted plant in the greenhouse does not reach to the bottom of a pot. It will soon spoil if left to lie on the surface where the pot is standing. Place the pot on a second, upturned pot so that air can circulate under the foliage.

Ground cover

Choosing the plants

A strong start

Give ground cover a fighting chance by using selective weedkillers to kill as many weeds as possible before planting. Use spot treatment, if necessary, after planting. Choose a weedkiller suited to the most prevalent and persistent weeds. (See also **War on weeds**, **Weedkillers**)

Take on the weeds

Plant ground-cover plants in autumn so that they will be well established in spring when weeds raise their heads and begin to compete for nutrients and moisture.

Planting for succession

Drifts of single varieties of ground-cover plants can be uninteresting. Try a mixture of deciduous and evergreen plants to give year-round variety, then underplant with spring bulbs, such as narcissi and tulips, to brighten the patch from late winter, and white alliums and lilies for a display later in the year.

Look after the pennies

Save money by selecting ground-cover plants that can be divided into smaller pieces for planting. These include the rock-garden plant *Cerastium alpinum*, which bears white, star-shaped flowers, the hardy, evergreen perennial *Tolmiea* and the yellow-flowered perennial *Waldsteinia ternata*.

Pretty yet ruthless

Among hardy perennial ground-cover plants, the self-seeding *Alchemilla mollis* (lady's mantle) is an excellent choice, covering the ground with distinctive foliage between spring and autumn and displaying frothy green flower heads during summer. Although it is not evergreen like many other ground-cover plants, it will smother weeds throughout the growing season.

Low-level display

For eye-catching ground cover, plant prostrate conifers such as *Juniperus horizontalis* and *J. procumbens*. Prostrate roses too, such as the rich pink 'Max Graf' and the pale pink 'Nozomi', are very effective. Prostrate conifers are particularly suited to acid soils, as are heathers. Some varieties of heather, such as *Erica carnea*, will tolerate an alkaline soil. Some brooms will fan out over the ground.

Suit the situation

Make sure that you choose plants that will thrive in the particular soil and site (see **Pick of the plants for ground cover, pp. 136**).

Most ground-cover plants will fill out within one to three years. In the meantime, plant colourful flowering annuals such as *Limnanthes douglasii* (poached egg plant) and *Tropaeolum majus* (nasturtium). These will provide an attractive display and also help to keep the weeds in check.

Planting aftercare

Compost cover-up

Once you have planted your ground cover, mulch the areas of soil between the plants with a thick layer of well-rotted compost or bark chips. These will suppress the weeds until your plants have spread sufficiently to smother them with their foliage.

Curbing enthusiasm

Some ground-cover plants are so good at the task that they will, if unrestricted, romp all over the garden. Restrain them by sinking slates, or plastic or metal strips, edge down into the ground at the frontier of their territory. These defences, though hidden, will stop root spread.

Winter warmer

Spread a layer of well-rotted compost round the roots of deciduous ground-cover plants during the winter. This will help to promote new growth in spring and to smother weeds until the new leaves take over.

Fast clip

In a wild garden, promote new growth by trimming back dead and leafless stalks on such rampant evergreens as yellow archangel and lesser periwinkle. To do the job properly, clip them hard – particularly if you have other plants growing in the patch.

Drying-out danger

Make sure you keep plants well watered, especially if you are attempting to establish them under trees, where less moisture than usual will have penetrated the ground. If new plants are left for just a few days in dry conditions, they will quickly wither and die.

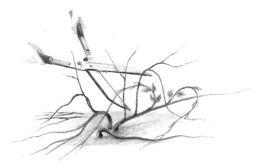

Summer sprucing

Deadhead ground-cover plants as soon as flowers fade. Use shears on tall plants but try a rotary lawn mower, with blade set high, on lower species such as strawberries, *Alchemilla* (lady's mantle), *Lamium* (dead nettle), *Diascia* and *Viola cornuta*. Give the same treatment to *Hypericum* (St John's wort) in winter.

Under trees

With soil in mind

The choice of plants that will grow under trees is limited to those shade-lovers that will survive competition from the trees' roots. The soil type needs to be taken into consideration as well, though there is usually some variety of ground cover that will grow, even in the most unpromising sites (see **panel**, **right**).

Choosing for dry lime

If you have a soil that is dry, poor and limy, a mingling of the variegated forms of *Lamium galeobdolon* 'Florentinum' (yellow archangel)

along with ivies, *Pachysandra terminalis* and *Vinca minor* (lesser periwinkle) will make a strikingly handsome carpet.

Plants for loam

If the soil under your trees is a rich, deep loam, you have a wide choice of ground cover. Try the blue-flowered *Omphalodes cappadocica*, *Symphytum grandiflorum* (comfrey), *Tiarella*

cordifolia (foam flower), some of the weed-defying epimediums (barrenworts), and even a selection of the shade-loving Araceae, such as *Arum maculatum* and its variants.

Planting under trees

Use a fork to break up soil between the roots when planting ground cover under a tree. Then, for extra nutrients, work in well-rotted compost.

Make the right choice

Pick of the plants for ground cover

The many varied ground-cover plants fulfill all kinds of roles, from filling in shady crannies to making an exposed slope a colourful attraction all year round. Choose a type and colour, and note the suitable growing conditions from the list below.

Name	Description and pointers
Acaena buchananii	Tiny grey-green leaves and spiky burrs; for rockeries and between stones.
Ajuga reptans	Blue flowers and variously coloured foliage; ideal for damp spots.
Calluna vulgaris	Various flowers; tolerates poor, acid soils and exposed sites.
Cotoneaster dammeri, C. horizontalis and C. microphyllus	Rich red berries in autumn. C. h. is deciduous; foliage also turns red. All grow in most soils; good for covering banks, bare rocks, even walls.
Euonymus fortunei	Grows well even in chalk soil; excellent for wall and ground cover.
Geranium macrorrhizum	Aromatic leaves, pink flowers; good in most soils. Tolerates shade.
Hebe pinguifolium 'Pagei'	Spikes of white flowers, small glossy leaves; best in full light.
Hypericum calycinum	Dense and compact, with golden-yellow flowers; good for a dry bank.
Juniperus horizontalis 'Douglasii'	Blue-green foliage that becomes rich purple in autumn; needs good light.
Lamium maculatum	Silver-striped green leaves, purple flowers; vigorous and shade-loving.
Lonicera pileata	Small yellow-green flowers; ideal for covering large areas.
Mahonia aquifolium	Yellow flowers and blue-black berries; tolerates sun, shade and wind.
Pulmonaria	Pink-violet flowers; useful in the front of a border and rock gardens.
Thymus praecox ssp. Arcticus	Mat-forming thyme with aromatic leaves; good for full sun.
Tolmiea menziesii 'Variegata'	Yellow-splashed leaves; suitable for most soils in sun or light shade.
Vinca major 'Variegata' and V. minor	Long-lasting blue or white flowers; good under trees or on steep banks.
Waldsteinia ternarta	Leaves in rosettes, creeping stems, yellow flowers; tolerates some shade.

Covering a slope

Planting for strength
To prevent erosion on a slope, choose plants whose roots will help to bind the soil together. Among those suitable are the tough evergreen *Rubus* 'Kenneth Ashburner', *Vinca major* (greater periwinkle) and the prostrate cotoneasters. Plant at the bottom of steep slopes and train the stems upwards. Alternatively, make planting holes in the slope, and reinforce the holes by laying logs beneath them, across the slope. The logs can be removed once the plants are established.

Sacking solution
Another method of preventing erosion is to place some old sacking over the soil before planting your ground cover. This will prevent the rain from washing soil down the slope. After laying the sacking, cut holes in it and insert the plants into the ground through these. By the time the ground cover has become well established, the sacking will have rotted away. If you wish, you can anchor the sacking more firmly in place by laying large stones or bricks round its edges.

The right plant
Generally speaking, a slope is not an appropriate place for drought-sensitive and low-growing plants such as *Pulmonaria* (lungwort). However, in addition to prostrate roses, cotoneasters and periwinkles, there are a number of other species that will flourish quite happily on a sloping surface. These include *Genista pilosa*, a spreading, mat-forming broom, *Hypericum* (St John's wort), prostrate junipers, ivies or *Rubus tricolor*, an ornamental raspberry.

The vegetable and fruit garden

Soil cover
Traditionally, vegetables were grown in rows with a greater space between the rows than between the plants. This meant there were areas of soil between the rows where weeds could develop. For maximum use of space, light, water and nutrients, it is better to space the plants evenly in both directions but stagger the rows. This also suppresses weeds.

Keep on cropping
Bare soil in the vegetable garden encourages weeds to grow so, to avoid this, always plant a second crop or sow green manure as soon as the first crop has been harvested. (*See also* **No-dig gardening**)

Intercropping
Vegetables, like sprouts, that take a long time to mature may not cover the soil and smother weeds until some months after planting. In the meantime, grow quick-maturing crops, such as lettuce, to keep the soil covered.

Fill the gaps
However well you plan the vegetable garden there always seem to be spaces where weeds can take hold. You can fill these gaps with *Calendula officinalis* (pot marigold), *Viola tricolor* (heartsease) and nasturtiums, whose flowers can be used in salads, and French marigolds and *Limnanthes douglasii* (poached egg plant), which attract beneficial insects, and annual herbs for the kitchen.

Among the fruit bushes
Plant strawberries, especially wild ones, as ground cover round gooseberry and currant bushes, unless these have been heavily mulched.

All strawberries appreciate light, composted soil and their shallow roots mean they will not compete with the bushes.

Plants in containers

Outdoor pots
If you have plants such as azaleas, bay trees or fuchsias growing in pots outdoors, a little ground cover will help to prevent the soil from drying out, although some watering is still necessary. Plant alyssums, lobelias, small-leaved ivies or trailing fuchsias round the edges of the containers.

In the house
Establish some small, undemanding ground-cover plants, such as *Tradescantia* (wandering jew), *Ficus pumila* (creeping fig) or the pretty, trailing *Plectranthus oertendahlii* (Swedish ivy) that produces racemes of white or pale mauve flowers. Choose companions that have the same water and light requirements as each other and, if possible, plant them all at the same time.

Growing bags

Reusing growing bags
Crops such as cucumbers, melons, radishes, beans, lettuces and herbs can be cultivated in growing bags in which tomatoes were raised the previous year, as long as roots are removed and old fertiliser salts are washed out by flushing the bags with rainwater before planting. Peppers and aubergines, which are related to tomatoes, should not be grown in the same compost.

Recycling growing bags
After a growing bag has been used a second time, it is generally not suitable for growing further crops. Never throw away the contents, as they can be used as a first-class mulch or soil conditioner. However, if the compost is really solid with roots, it is better to put it in the compost bin, where it will soon break down and add texture to material already in there.

Transporting a growing bag

Try not to move a growing bag after planting. If it has to be moved, gently ease it onto a wide wooden plank, then lift and carry plank and bag together.

Toning it down

Camouflage the garish colours of bags by enclosing the sides with bricks and covering the exposed plastic with chipped bark.

Deepen the compost

Some people have trouble growing tomatoes in growing bags and end up with problems such as blossom end rot (a watering disease) and poor fruit set. This can be due to an insufficient depth of compost, and devices are available to address the problem. These usually resemble bottomless pots that are placed over a hole in the growing bag cover where the tomato would normally be planted, the idea being to increase the depth of compost. It is easy to make your own, similar piece of equipment by cutting the bases out of old 20 or 25cm (8 or 10in) plastic pots. Then cut a hole of similar diameter in the polythene cover and insert the bottomless pot into this, working the sides a little way into the compost for stability. Fill with a good, soil-less compost to about 2.5cm (1in) below the rim and plant your tomatoes into this. Make sure the compost in both the pots and the growing bag are kept damp but not soggy. The plant roots will soon work their way into the growing bag and produce good crops. You can also use this method with cucumbers.

Pay a little more

As with many things in life, you get what you pay for with a growing bag. Cut-price bags frequently contain poor-quality compost, often of insufficient depth to produce good crops. If in doubt, stick to branded names you recognise.

Read the instructions

At one time, all growing bags contained compost based on peat. Nowadays, many manufacturers are replacing some or all of the peat with a suitable substitute, and although you should get just as good results, it is essential to read the instructions on watering and feeding thoroughly, as they can be very different from what you may have been used to with growing bags in the past.

Lend some support

Supporting plants in a growing bag can be a problem, especially if the bag is placed on a hard surface. You can buy purpose-designed frames, but they are often not tall enough to support plants such as tomatoes. In a greenhouse, support can easily be provided by tying garden twine around the base, close to the plants needing support, and running it up to a convenient point, such as a structural bracket, near the apex. The plants can be wound round the twine if they are pliable, or otherwise tied in .

Tomatoes on the patio

You will get quicker and heavier tomato crops when growing on the patio if you place the growing bag near a warm, sunny wall. The plants can be easily supported by attaching a piece of trellis of a suitable height to the wall, and tying them in to this at intervals.

Be more successful

The reason why half-hardy vegetables, including peppers, aubergines, tomatoes and cucumbers, sometimes produce less satisfactory crops than those grown in the greenhouse border or vegetable garden, is often that too many plants are grown in one bag. Although the recommendation is usually three plants per bag for most crops except cucumbers, you will usually get better yields and produce healthier plants if you grow two plants per bag (one for cucumbers). Growing too many in one bag is a false economy and often leads to disappointment.

Water wise

Once the crop has become established and the compost is full of roots, a growing bag can be difficult to water. The solution is to sink three small plastic plant pots into the compost at equal distances and water into these. The water will gradually soak into the compost without running off the top, and the bags will always be evenly moist.

Make a miniature herb garden

All culinary herbs grow well in a growing bag and you can have a collection of all your favourites in a sunny spot near the kitchen door, right where you need them. Thyme, marjoram, oregano, sage, lavender, parsley and rosemary are just a few that you can put together to make both a useful and attractive growing bag. If these are cut or pruned back regularly, they will stay fresh and bushy for at least two years. Mint is best grown in a bag on its own, and will last indefinitely in a growing bag if kept well watered and fed regularly throughout summer.

Sun-ripening tomatoes A glorious crop of tomatoes enjoys its warm, sunlit position against a garden wall.

Hanging baskets

Making a head start
To enjoy an early display, plant up hanging baskets in March or April and keep them in a greenhouse or conservatory until the end of May. Harden them off by taking them outside during the day and putting them back under cover at night for two weeks or so, then hang them in their permanent positions.

Too close for comfort
Because plants in hanging baskets are grown close together, always examine the plants carefully before planting up to ensure they are free of pests and diseases. In a basket, aphids and fungal spores can spread from plant to plant easily and rapidly.

Lighten the look
When planting up a basket for the conservatory, achieve a striking effect by offsetting broad-leaved plants with the feathery foliage of ornamental asparagus or *Adiantum* (maidenhair fern).

Avoid a colour clash
Think carefully about the colours of both foliage and flowers before planting up a hanging basket. Aim for a mix that will harmonise with walls and paintwork, and avoid those that clash.

Strong means of support
A large, well-filled and well-watered basket can weigh 11kg (25lb) or more so it is essential to ensure that hooks and brackets are designed to withstand the weight and that they are fixed securely to the wall. Never attach brackets to crumbling brickwork or rotting wood.

The right site
Wind and strong sunlight, especially sunlight that is reflected off a white wall, will cause baskets to dry out even more rapidly than usual. If possible, choose a site that is sheltered from wind, and where the baskets will receive some shade for at least part of the day. Once they have dried out completely, it can be difficult, if not impossible, to water baskets adequately with a watering can or lance. The only remedy is to take them down and stand them in a container of water until the compost is thoroughly wet.

A longer display
Extend the life of your hanging basket arrangement by sowing a few nasturtium seeds in midsummer. These attractive trumpet-like flowers will provide an eye-catching and attractive display when the other plants are coming to an end.

Swinging salads
Hanging baskets filled with flowers are a delight but, for something a little different, you can plant a few baskets with herbs, such as marjoram, chives, basil and a tightly curled, dark green variety of parsley, such as 'Envy'. Add a splash of colour with the tomato 'Tumbler', which was bred specially for hanging baskets and has small, tasty fruits.

Strawberry flair
Strawberries do especially well in hanging baskets. Any variety will be successful, but 'Temptation', which does not produce long runners, is particularly suitable.

Waiting in the wings
Although hanging baskets are generally associated with summer, they can be used to provide a welcome touch of colour all year round. While the summer display is still at its best, prepare another basket with winter-flowering pansies and heathers to put in place when the glory of the summer basket is over. Then, you can replant the first basket with miniature bulb varieties, such as *Narcissus* 'Tête-à-Tête', for a spring display before planting up again for the summer.

Garden secrets

Solving the watering problem
Keeping hanging baskets moist is essential if the plants are to look attractive throughout the summer. It is important to use a water-retentive compost with a peat or coir base or a compost specially formulated for hanging baskets. Granules that absorb and retain water can be added to composts to improve their water retention. They are available at most garden centres. Basket liners made of compressed paper, plastic, sponge or moss all help to retain moisture. After fitting the liner in the basket, place a saucer or a circle of polythene about the size of a dinner plate on top of it. This will form a valuable water reservoir.

Bottle trick
As an aid to watering hanging baskets, cut a plastic bottle in half, leaving the screw cap in place. With a heated skewer or nail, make holes all round the bottle and bury it, cap end down, in the compost. To water, fill the bottle and allow the water to seep through the holes.

Charcoal in the basket
If you are lining a hanging basket with moss, put several lumps of charcoal into the base. They will help to retain moisture.

Balancing baskets

The rounded bases of hanging baskets make them awkward to maintain and replant. The job is made easier if you stand the baskets on large, empty buckets or plant pots when attending to them.

Automatic watering

Hanging baskets often need watering more than once a day. If you do not have enough time to manage this, consider installing one of the irrigation systems that are available from garden centres. You can even include an electronic timer for periods when you are going to be absent for more than a day.

One for the birds

Use a hanging basket as a feature to attract birds. Plant up a basket with trailing plants round the edge, create perches by inserting a few sturdy twigs through the sides, and place a dish of water in the centre, on top of the compost. This will provide birds with a suspended dining table where they will reward your efforts by consuming the unwelcome insects on your plants.

New life for an old basket

An old shopping basket can be converted into an attractive and unusual plant container to hang by the front door. Line the inside with transparent plastic film, or clear polythene, pierced at the base. Evaporation will take care of excess moisture. Before planting up, give the outside of the basket two coats of spray varnish to protect it from the weather, allowing at least 24 hours for it to dry between coats. To soften the outline of the basket, choose plants with dense foliage and a bushy habit, such as fuchsias, pelargoniums and petunias.

A welcome feast

Use an old hanging basket as a bird feeder. Scrape out the compost and lining, and place a clean saucer or other small container on the base of the basket. Fill this with seeds and hang the basket in a tree, or other place that is inaccessible to cats. Make sure that you refill the saucer or container regularly, especially during the cold winter months.

Flower cage

Look out for an old birdcage in junk shops or antique markets and transform it into an unusual hanging basket. Place either one large pot, or several small ones, containing a mixture of upright and trailing plants, on the floor of the cage and train the plants through the bars. Alternatively, attach chains to an old colander, line it with perforated polythene and plant it up with cherry tomatoes, herbs, or decorative plants.

Hazels

Easy to please

Corylus avellana (common hazel) is undemanding in its requirements for soil type or aspect. Its excellent adaptability means that it will grow happily on cold or exposed sites, in chalk, clay or sand, in sun or shade. It is sometimes grown as a single-stemmed tree, reaching a height of 6m (20ft) with a spread of 4.6m (15ft). Coppicing (regularly cutting back the shoots to the base) will produce a multistemmed shrub. As a bonus, growing a native hazel is an excellent way of attracting birds, mammals and beneficial insects to the garden.

Beat the weevil

Hazels are prone to attack by weevils, whose grubs leave telltale holes in the shells when they emerge from the nuts in summer. Apply grease bands to the trunks as weevils cannot climb over the bands to reach the nuts.

Nuts for the table

Hazelnuts are among the most flavoursome of our native nuts and are best prepared by removing the husks and leaving them to dry in a warm place, preferably in the sun, for at least a week. If dried insufficiently, they will become mouldy when stored.

Pick of the stakes

Hazel provides the best brushwood for staking peas and hardy perennials. The branches develop in flat sprays, making them ideal supports when positioned round the outside of clumps of plants.

Increase your hazels

Hazel trees are welcome in the garden, for their nuts and attractive catkins and foliage. They can be propagated easily by taking a few healthy cuttings from young branches in November. Each cutting should be about 30cm (12in) long and slightly thicker than a pencil. Insert the cuttings in trenches, leaving a third of each exposed. They will start to sprout in the spring, when they can be either planted out in the garden in a light soil or potted on. The following autumn, transfer them to their permanent positions in the garden.

Heathers

Heaths and heathers

Plants commonly referred to as heathers can be divided into two main groups, *Calluna* and *Erica*. Although similar in appearance, *Calluna* is heather and *Erica* is heath.

The lime problem

With the exception of some winter-flowering varieties, heathers require an acid soil and if planted in alkaline conditions will turn yellow and die. Soil acidity can be increased by the addition of sulphur but it usually needs to be done frequently as soil has a tendency to revert back to its natural state after treatment. Test the acidity of your soil using a kit from a garden centre. A pH of between 5.5 and 6 is ideal for most heathers. (See also **Acid soil, Soil analysis**)

Designer beds

Provide perfect conditions for heathers, whatever the pH of your garden soil. Make raised beds with good drainage and fill them with ericaceous compost. Keep the soil well watered in summer.

Suitable situations

All heathers need an open position in full sun. They dislike light, sandy soils and heavy, clay soils, but both can be improved to suit heathers. Lighten heavy soil with sharp sand, well-rotted garden compost and acid organic matter, such as spent hops. Mushroom compost is alkaline and unsuitable. Acid organic matter will also improve light soil.

A sumptuous palette

For a really joyful display of heathers, plant groups of different colours, leaving a space of 20–51cm (8–20in) between each plant, depending on their vigour. Each group should consist of at least five plants. It will take up to three years for the plants to form into big cushions but, even while they are developing, they will be very attractive.

Plant in partnership

Set off the beauty of heathers by grouping them with dwarf conifers, *Salix lanata* (woolly willow) or a dwarf birch, such as *Betula nana*. Other pleasing companions include the bell-flowered *Andromeda polifolia* and *Gaultheria mucronata*, the female varieties of which have enduring pink, red, purple and white berries.

Winter colour on chalk

Some of the most colourful heathers are the winter-flowering varieties *Erica carnea* and *E. x darleyensis*. Both will tolerate an alkaline soil and will give a warming blaze of colour during the winter months.

Combine colour and height

The compact, winter-flowering heathers are ideal for a window box. Combine them with a conical dwarf conifer or some dwarf bulbs, such as *Narcissus* 'February Gold', to add some height. (See also **Window boxes**)

Keep plants compact

To promote growth and maintain their cushion-like appearance, cut back winter and spring-flowering heathers after flowering. Prune summer-flowering plants the following spring.

Wise watering

If you have a water butt in the garden, save the water to use on your heathers. Most tap water contains lime, which these plants dislike (see **The lime problem, pp. 140**). If you have to use tap water, let it stand for several hours before putting it on the garden. This will allow the lime to settle at the bottom of the container and you can then scoop water from the top.

Rejuvenating old plants

When heathers begin to look straggly or leggy, you can rejuvenate them by digging them up in spring and replanting in soil that has been treated with acid organic matter. Make sure that you bury the base of the stems deeply, so that only new growth appears above soil level.

Winter bonus

The dead flower heads of many of the summer-flowering heathers, such as *Erica cinerea* or *E. vagans*, the blooms of which fade to an attractive russet-brown, look ornamental and may be left on the plants for a pleasing winter display. In spring, clip off the old stems close to the foliage to ensure growth remains bushy.

Propagate by layering

Large heathers can be propagated by layering. In March, select healthy stems on the outsides of the plants, bend them down and bury them in the soil, leaving only the tips above the surface. Hold the stems in place with bent wires or stones. After a year, they will have rooted and can be severed from the parent plants and moved to their permanent positions in the garden.

Make the right choice

Flowering heaths and heathers for every season

Provided your soil is suitably acid, heathers are a wonderful way of adding colour to the garden. Choose varieties with different flowering times to extend the season.

Variety	Flowering time	Pointers
Calluna vulgaris	July to November	Hundreds of varieties, with different flowering times
Erica australis	April to May	Can reach 2.4m (8ft) if grown against a high wall
E. carnea	November to April	The hardiest of lime-tolerant heathers
E. cinerea	June to October	Hardy with white, red, maroon or mahogany flowers
E. × darleyensis	December to April	Lime-tolerant with long white, pink or purple blooms
E. erigena	December to April	Usually quite hardy, tolerates limy soil
E. vagans	July to October	Vigorous native heath, pale purple, pink or white flowers

Hedgehogs

A welcome visitor

Hedgehogs are great devourers of snails, slugs and insects and are, therefore, welcome visitors to the garden. Encourage them by putting out bowls of food, such as muesli mixed with water, nuts, sultanas, cake with honey drizzled over it, and cat or dog food. Water is the best drink for a hedgehog, but goat's milk will do no harm. There is a risk that cow's milk will upset the hedgehog's digestive system if put out on its own, so only give it if you are offering the creature a mixed diet.

Help with hibernation

Leave a pile of leaves in a corner of the garden to provide temporary shelter for hedgehogs during cold snaps. Hedgehogs will hibernate in leaves at the base of a hedge but in an exposed spot, rain will eventually soak the leaf pile, making it too damp for hibernation. You will then need to provide a more permanent dwelling (see **below**).

A winter home

To make a hibernation box, you will need an untreated wooden box, roughly 45cm (18in) long, 30cm (12in) high and 30cm (12in) wide. Saw an entrance 10cm (4in) square in the centre of one end. Place the box, upside-down, over a pile of leaves for bedding. Lay six bricks on their sides (three in each row) to create a tunnel leading to the entrance, and cover this with a plank secured with masonry nails. This will prevent foxes and badgers from disturbing the nest.

Protective camouflage

Cover the box with black polythene to keep it dry. Make it look more natural and attractive by adding a pile of brushwood and leaves, held down on top with a few stones.

Poison pellets

The hedgehogs that live in or visit your garden won't eat slug pellets as they are extremely bitter and distasteful to them. But they will have less to eat, if you poison the slugs .

Hazard warning

Potential hazards include garden ponds, particularly those that have steep sides. Construct ramps or slipways round the edge of the water or hang chicken wire over the edge to serve as an escape route. Tennis nets, too, pose a problem, as hedgehogs can become entangled in them. Always roll up nets at night.

Hedges

Plant through plastic

Before planting, lay a length of black plastic sheeting on the ground and anchor it with pegs or bricks. Cut crosswise slits in the plastic and insert the plants through the holes. Camouflage the plastic with crushed bark and dead leaves. The sheet will keep the weeds down, protect the roots from frost in winter and reduce evaporation during the summer.

Trouble-free choice

For a fast-growing, view-blocking evergreen hedge that is easy to maintain, try *Chamaecyparis lawsoniana* 'Green Hedger' or *Thuja plicata* 'Atrovirens'. Buy young trees, 46cm (18in) high, in March, and plant them 61cm (2ft) apart. They do not require support. Give the young hedge a dressing of fertiliser every February, and trim once a year between July and September. Other hedges that require little maintenance include beech and hornbeam (both deciduous trees that retain their brown leaves during winter) and yew. Yew is slow-growing at first, but its rate of growth increases after a few years.

Colourful privacy

The golden-flowered *Berberis* x *stenophylla*, which grows to 1.8–2.4m (6–8ft) in six years, is a handsome, evergreen means of blocking out the world. So, too, is *Escallonia rubra* var. *macrantha*, which does well in the milder areas of the south and west. This has bright, pinkish-red flowers and grows to between 1.8m (6ft) and 3m (10ft). If you prefer a deciduous hedge, try one of the many forms of *Chaenomeles speciosa* (japonica) with

flowers in red, pink or white. Clip *Berberis*, *Chaenomeles* and *Escallonia* once a year, immediately after flowering. For an intruder-proof barrier, plant dense, thorny blackthorn, hawthorn, holly or pyracantha.

Conifer hedges

Conifers make handsome, dense hedges. Shape *Tsuga* (hemlock), *Thuja* (arbor-vitae) and *Taxus* (yew) by clipping the young shoots, leaving about 5cm (2in) of new growth. The hybrid *Cupressocyparis leylandii* (Leyland cypress) is probably the most commonly planted conifer hedge. It grows very rapidly, making it a popular screening plant, but its speed means it needs two or three cuts a year to maintain it as an

effective, manageable hedge. The first cut should be in April, the second in July or August and the third in September or October.

Rosy summer

For a summer-flowering hedge that is about 1.2–1.5m (4–5ft) high, choose large or cluster-flowered roses, such as 'The Queen Elizabeth' (pink, cluster-flowered), 'Chinatown' (yellow, cluster-flowered) and 'Alexander' (vermilion, large-flowered). Space them 61cm (2ft) apart and prune to 15cm (6in) above the ground. Feed each spring with a rose fertiliser and prune in autumn and early spring to ensure even growth. (See also **Romance of the Rose pp.250-1**)

Winter spring-clean

On a mild day in winter, take the opportunity to give the hedge an annual tidy. Cut off any dead twigs close to the main stems. Pull up weeds and seedlings that have invaded the base of the hedge, but leave any dead leaves that have accumulated and add more, if you have them available, to act as a mulch. This will help the hedge cope with a summer drought. If you find a bird's abandoned nest during your clean-up, do not remove it from the hedge. It may acquire a new family of residents in the spring.

The right height

The top of a tall hedge can be difficult to trim, and balancing on a stepladder while operating a hedge trimmer requires utmost care. For ease of maintenance and for safety, keep the hedge to a maximum height of about 1.5m (5ft).

Angle on cutting

To keep your hedgerow full and bushy, graduate its vertical trimming so that the plants are thicker at the bottom than at the top. To ensure uniformity throughout the length of the hedge, make a wooden template to help you to keep a check on the angle of cutting.

A tapestry hedge

Create a natural tapestry with a mixed hedgerow. Alternate green and purple-leaved beeches, carefully pruned, to produce a formal

look. For a less regimented style, plant shrubby *Cornus* (dogwood), Ilex (holly) and *Rosa eglanteria* (eglantine). Native hedge mixes have also become popular because they attract wildlife to the garden.

Dealing with leggy privets

If a privet hedge becomes leggy at the base, prune it back to a few centimetres from its main branches and trim to just below the required height. Remove any weeds from the base, apply a 2.5–5cm (1–2in) layer of compost and fork in a general fertiliser.

See also **Box, Pruning, Wind, Yews**

Hedge trimmers

The tool for the job

When cutting a small-leaved hedge, a hedge trimmer is fine. On large-leaved hedging plants, secateurs are better. Hedge trimmers can damage large leaves and leave the hedge untidy and ragged. (See also **Secateurs**)

Essential maintenance

Ensure that the hedge trimmer cuts cleanly, by having the blades sharpened in winter. After use, remove dried resin and sap from the

blades with a cloth soaked in white spirit, then apply a thin film of oil.

Orange for safety

When using an extension cable with an electric trimmer, make sure the cable can be seen easily – orange stands out well in the garden. Work with the cable draped over your shoulder, and always use a residual current device (RCD).

See also **Safety**

Herbs for flavour and aroma

Herbs have been cultivated for thousands of years, chiefly for their culinary and medicinal properties, although many make attractive specimen plants in their own right.

Where to grow herbs

Herbs are so adaptable that they can be grown in any number of ways, although almost all of them enjoy plenty of sunshine. You can grow them in the traditional way, in their own self-contained herb garden, or plant them in the border among your flowers where their foliage provides contrasting, cooler tones among the bright colours. Put them in pots or tubs on a patio, or in window boxes or hanging baskets. You do not need an especially rich soil or compost, as long as it is reasonably fertile and free-draining. Ideally, site your herb garden near the kitchen door where the leaves can be picked easily.

Planning your herb garden

Before planting an ornamental bed of herbs, sketch a plan so that you make the best use of contrasting leaf shapes and colours to give an attractive appearance.

Plant with care

Remember to place taller herbs such as angelica, dill and fennel at the back of the herb garden. Plant smaller ones – chives, marjoram, parsley and thyme – near the front.

Ease of harvesting

Make sure your herbs are within easy reach for picking. For instance, you can place stepping-stones in an ornamental bed, or use a chessboard design in which different herbs are placed in the 'black' or soil squares, with paving or gravel filling the 'white' squares. In a smaller garden, lay paving slabs in the form of a cross and plant the quarters that lie within the arms of the cross. Alternatively, make a cartwheel design in which bricks form the dividing 'spokes' of the wheel.

1 Sweet cicely (*Myrrhis odorata*)

A perennial with an agreeable aniseed scent. Grow in a shady spot and cut or pick the leaves throughout spring and summer. Regular watering ensures foliage stays tender.

The culinary properties are like those of chervil. Preserve the leaves by freezing.

2 Chervil (*Anthriscus cerefolium*)

An easy-to-sow hardy annual. Chervil often re-seeds itself if you let a few plants go to seed. Select a shady spot and pick the leaves six to eight weeks after sowing.

Use the leaves raw and chop them finely just before serving. They will give a good aroma to salads, soups and grilled fish or meats. Preserve the leaves by freezing.

3 Lovage (*Levisticum officinale*)

A hardy, herbaceous perennial that is rather like a huge celery plant. It grows best in rich soil and in sun or partial shade.

Chop up the leaves and put them in salads and soups. They will add a delicious taste of celery.

4 Mint (*Mentha*)

A perennial that loses most of its leaves in winter. The many varieties all grow well in cool, shaded soil, or moist soil in sun.

Use the leaves to season salads, hors d'oeuvres, certain sauces, grilled lamb, strawberries and fruit salads. The spicy flavoured *Mentha × piperita citrata* 'Basil' goes well with oriental dishes.

5 Sorrel (*Rumex acetosa*)

A perennial that crops for a very long period in late spring. It grows best in well-drained, fertile soil and in partial shade. Use only the young leaves as these are the most tender and least bitter.

Sorrel gives an agreeable acidity to soups, sauces and omelettes. Cook like spinach or purée to serve with rich meats and fish.

6 Chives (*Allium schoenoprasum*)

A perennial herb with rose-pink flower heads. Grow in a good, rich soil and in sun or partial shade, where it will provide many leaves between March and October.

The chopped leaf gives a subtle onion flavour when added to omelettes, soups, cheese and potato dishes and salads.

7 Lemon balm (*Melissa officinalis*)

A perennial that loses its leaves in winter. Balm thrives in well-drained soil in partial shade. Plants need to be regularly cut back as they are quite invasive. Harvest the leaves and young shoots in summer.

The lemon flavour adds zest to soups and marinades but use sparingly. Lemon balm can also be used as a substitute for lemon peel in cakes and fruit dishes and to make a refreshing cold drink.

8 French tarragon (*Artemisia dracunculus*)

A hardy perennial that requires light soil and prefers full sun. Harvest fresh leaves from mid June to the end of September.

Chop the leaf into salads or use it to flavour chicken and other white meats. Tarragon's bitter-sweet taste makes it a good flavouring for vinegar.

9 Parsley (*Petroselinum crispum*)

A biennial that likes cool, partially shaded soil or rich soil in sun. Sow it each year during spring. Pick the leaves when they are young.

Raw and finely chopped, they add a distinctive, mildly spicy flavour to salads, hors d'oeuvres, grilled meats, stuffings and butter. Also used in fines herbes and in bouquets garnis. For cooked dishes, add parsley at the last minute so that it keeps its flavour.

10 Wild celery (*Apium graveolens*)

A hardy biennial grown for its parsley-like leaves with their celery flavour. Grow like parsley, in rich soil, in full sun and keep well watered.

Cut up the leaves and add them to salads and soups.

11 Horseradish (*Armoracia rusticana*)

A hardy perennial that spreads rapidly. Plant it in any rich soil and it will continue to grow there for many years. Harvest the roots in autumn and winter.

Grated, it serves as a hot and piquant condiment. Make a sauce of it to replace mustard. The young leaves have a bitter taste.

12 Shallots (*Allium cepa* Aggregatum Group)

Although strictly a vegetable, shallots still have a place in the herb garden. Plant the bulbs in a light but cool soil. Harvest them in summer when the foliage has turned yellow and let the bulbs dry. The shallots will keep for several months.

Chop shallots finely to use raw in salads or cooked in sauces for meat and game. They are ideal for pickling.

1 Hot pepper (*Capsicum annuum*)

An annual that can be reliably grown only in the greenhouse in Britain. Water regularly and harvest the fruits as they ripen.

Raw or cooked, peppers can be used to season Mediterranean, South American, Caribbean and oriental dishes.

2 Savory (*Satureja hortensis* and *Satureja montana*)

S. hortensis is an annual and re-seeds itself every year; *S. montana* is a hardy perennial. Both grow well in light soil in a sunny position.

The leaves of both species have a slightly bitter, peppery taste. Use them with dried vegetables – beans in particular – and meat. Add them at the end of cooking.

3 Lemon-scented verbena (*Aloysia triphylla*)

A small, rather tender, perennial shrub. Grow it under glass in pots in cold areas. Check it every day during warmer weather to ensure that it does not dry out.

The lemon-scented leaves can be used to replace lemongrass (*Cymbopogon citratus*) in oriental dishes or infusions.

4 Dill (*Anethum graveolens*)

A hardy annual plant resembling fennel. Sow the seeds in April in a sunny spot. Pick the foliage as you need it. Harvest the seeds in summer and use when the supply of fresh leaves has ceased.

Use the leaves to add an aniseed-like flavour to potatoes, beans, soups, poultry and fish. The dried seeds have a stronger flavour than the leaves – use them in pickling vinegar and in sauces.

5 Hyssop (*Hyssopus officinalis*)

A small, hardy evergreen shrub with pretty blue, pink or white flowers. Grow in full sun. Harvest the leaves from early summer

The leaves have a minty but slightly bitter taste. Use them sparingly to season salads and vegetables, white meat and fish or to add flavour to fruit salads.

6 Rosemary (*Rosmarinus officinalis*)

A reasonably hardy evergreen shrub which thrives in a sunny spot. In cold areas, plant in a sheltered position. Pick the leafy shoots throughout the year.

Use the leaves, dry or fresh, to flavour savoury dishes – especially those containing lamb.

7 Sweet marjoram (*Origanum majorana*)

A perennial usually grown as an annual that thrives in rich soil and in full sun. Its foliage gives off a peppery scent of menthol.

Use the chopped leaves in stuffings, stews, soups, cheese dishes and salads, and to flavour meat, poultry and game before roasting.

8 Basil (*Ocimum basilicum*)

A half-hardy annual that should be sown under glass in March, and planted in late May in a sunny spot. Water regularly and harvest the leaves as you need them.

In cold dishes, add basil at the moment of serving. Its clove-like flavour adds spice to omelettes, salads and tomato and fish dishes.

9 Oregano (*Origanum vulgare*)

A hardy perennial, that can be treated in the same way as sweet marjoram.

10 Sage (*Salvia officinalis*)

A hardy evergreen shrub that thrives in dry, sunny conditions.

Harvest the leaves throughout the year and use them with fatty meats such as pork, and white meats such as veal and chicken. The distinctive, slightly bitter aroma of sage blends perfectly with these meats and enhances their flavour.

11 Fennel (*Foeniculum vulgare*)

Hardy perennial that does best in a warm, sunny position. Pinch out flowers unless you want seeds.

Use the leaves for their subtle anise flavour in salads, sauces and with fish. Seeds have a much stronger flavour and can be used in soups and pastry.

12 Bay (*Laurus nobilis*)

An evergreen tree that should be grown in the shelter of a south-facing wall or, in colder regions, in a pot under glass in a greenhouse or conservatory.

Use the leaves in pâtés, marinades, with grilled fish and meats, and in soups and stews.

13 Thyme (*Thymus vulgaris*)

A hardy dwarf shrub that comes in a variety of shapes and scents. It needs sun and warmth to be at its best.

Harvest the fine-leaved shoots throughout the year to season bouillons, stews and grilled dishes. Thyme also form an important component of the ever-useful mixed herb container.

14 Garlic (*Allium sativum*)

A bulbous perennial herb, although usually replanted annually. Plant out bulbs in November. Pinch off flower heads as soon as possible to divert nourishment to the bulbs. Harvest them in summer and tie them into decorative strings to hang in the kitchen.

Whether cooked or raw, garlic is used in many dishes, especially Mediterranean and oriental recipes.

15 Coriander (*Coriandrum sativum*)

A tender annual. Sow it in early summer, in full sun. Pick the leaves when young. Harvest seeds when ripe.

Fresh leaves lend flavour to Middle Eastern dishes and Cantonese rice. Use the seeds to season marinades and roast meats, and to flavour chutneys.

Herbs

Fragrant sun-lovers
Many aromatic herbs, such as lavender, rosemary and sage, grow wild in Mediterranean regions and this indicates the conditions that they will enjoy best in the garden. Plenty of sunshine helps to keep their growth compact as well as increasing the production of the essential oils that give herbs their distinctive flavours and fragrances. A well-drained soil ensures that the roots do not become waterlogged and rot during wet winter months.

Winter protection
A hedge of lavender, hyssop or box will provide protection for herbs in winter. Tall herbs will need staking against strong winds.

Keep the wanderers in check
Some herbs, whose roots put out runners such as mint and lemon balm, will take over in the garden if they are not constrained. Planting them in terracotta pots, troughs or other containers is an ideal way to curb their exuberance. Mint will grow well in an old butler sink as its roots do not require soil that is more than 15cm (6in) deep. (See also **Container gardening, Containers**)

Drying methods
Dry herbs by hanging them in bunches or placing them on drying trays. Herbs that dry well include bay, lovage, marjoram, rosemary, sage and thyme. To make a drying tray, stretch muslin or fine netting over a wooden frame and secure with galvanised nails. Place the tray in a well-ventilated, warm place and lay the herbs on the muslin. When brittle, they are ready to store.

Promoting bushy growth
Pinch back basil shoots to promote bushy growth. Do not allow the flowers to develop as these sap energy and reduce the production of leaves. Both *Ocimum basilicum* (sweet basil), which has dark green leaves, and *O. b. var. minimum* (bush basil), which has smaller, paler green leaves, respond well to this.

Tidying up time
In early autumn, lift and divide robust perennial herbs, such as *Saponaria* (soapwort) and *Artemisia* (wormwood). Prevent frost damage to shrubby herbs, such as thyme and lavender, by pruning back new shoots. Pot up herbs, such as basil, chives, marjoram, mint and parsley, to grow indoors and provide herbs for the kitchen in winter.

Wheel them in
If you have room for only a small herb garden, an old cartwheel, treated with preservative, makes an ideal frame for culinary, aromatic or medicinal herbs. In each space formed by the spokes a different variety can be planted. For the kitchen garden try chives, oregano, parsley, rosemary, sage, thyme and winter savory. Alternatively, you could plant taller herbs, such as rosemary, close to the hub, with creeping thyme in front, and then edge all round with curly leaved parsley.

An indoor herb garden
Although the most convenient place indoors for culinary herbs is the kitchen window ledge, constant fluctuations in temperature and moisture levels in the kitchen can be detrimental to the plants. Basil, chives, marjoram, mint, parsley and thyme survive these conditions best. If possible, keep pots of herbs in a daytime temperature of about 15°C (59°F) and do not expose them to sudden draughts of cold air. A south or west-facing window is best.

Seed collection
Collect the seeds from coriander, dill, fennel and lovage to use in cooking. Select a dry day when the flower heads are turning brown. Turn them gently upside-down and shake the seeds into an open paper bag. Store fully dried seeds in airtight containers, in a cool place out of direct sunlight.

Freeze for winter
Freezing preserves the flavours and colours of herbs, making it especially useful for those, such as coriander, chervil, dill and parsley, that do not dry well. Either freeze whole leaves, in polythene bags, in the quantities that you will need for recipes, or chop them finely and freeze them, in a little water, in ice-cube trays.

Hoes

On stony ground
When you are hoeing a piece of ground that is covered in stones, the job will be made much easier by using a Dutch hoe, the blade of which fits to the shaft from a single, rather than a double, point of attachment.

The long and short of it
Hoes are available in a choice of lengths so shop around to find one that suits you. A hoe that is too short will cause you to stoop, while

Make the right choice

The tool for the job
The hoe is one of the most useful, and ancient, of garden tools and has evolved in a number of different directions. Make sure that you always choose the right one for the job. The flat-bladed Dutch hoe (top) cuts off surface weeds without damaging the roots of surrounding plants. The scuffle hoe has cutting edges at front and back. A draw hoe (middle) is for chopping weeds and drawing soil up round plants. The short-handled onion hoe (bottom) is useful for working between onions and on rock gardens. A three-pronged hoe or cultivator will break up compacted soil.

one that is too long will be awkward to manipulate. As a rule, when held upright, the top of the hoe should be level with your eyes.

See also **Tools, The right tool for the job, pp. 294–5**

Holidays

Time off for the garden
Try, if possible, to take your annual holiday at a time when the garden is at its least demanding and productive. That way, your plot will be at its best when you are at home to appreciate it.

A welcome-home crop
If your holiday comes at a time when the garden is overflowing with vegetables and fruit, ask a neighbour to pick them and to water the beds. If no one is available, then pick all the ripe produce before you leave, water the vegetable garden well, and apply a mulch to keep the soil moist. On your return, there will be more ripe fruit and vegetables ready for you on repeat-croppers, such as strawberries, beans and tomatoes.

Postpone delicate tasks
Pot plants need extra care and attention immediately after repotting so never do the job in a hurry just before going away. Leave it until a time when you will be at home.

Caring for young plants
If you are planning to be away for any length of time, bury young pot plants in a bed of moist peat or in the garden soil. Alternatively, you can wrap the pots in strips of damp cloth or in layers of moist newspaper and leave them in the coolest and shadiest part of the garden.

Keeping containers moist
Help your patio planters to conserve moisture during your absence by placing them in a shady corner of the garden. Even better, you can bury them in the compost bin, plunging the pots into the compost so that it reaches up to their rims. Then, just before you go away, give the plants a good soaking. Alternatively, if you are going away for more than a few days, keep the plants cool and healthy by burying the pots in a shaded, empty bed or border.

Trim the hedge
Privet or *Lonicera nitida* (honeysuckle) hedges should be trimmed before you go away to prevent straggly growth. A normally neat hedge, that has become overgrown may indicate to burglars that the householder is absent.

Let the grass grow
Even if you mow the lawn just before your holiday, two weeks' neglect will make it grow faster than is good for it. On your return, mow in stages over the first three weeks. Remove the top of the grass only for the first cut. Reduce the height for a second cut and cut to the recommended height three or four days later. (See also **Lawn mowing**)

A farewell tidy
Before you leave, spend some time weeding and hoeing your beds. By removing competitive weeds, you reduce the need for watering while you are away.

Floral homecoming
Remember to remove the blooms on repeat-flowering plants, together with any buds that are on the point of opening, just before you go on holiday. This will have the effect of redirecting the plants' energies towards producing new flowers, which will then be in bloom when you return.

Humidity in the bag
Indoor plants, such as marantas, ferns and other leafy specimens, can be protected from drying out by being placed in transparent plastic bags. Spread a small amount of gravel or a few small stones on the bottom of the bag to keep the base of the pot away from the plastic. Put the plant in, having first made sure that it has been thoroughly watered. You can provide essential carbon dioxide by blowing into the bag, then tie at the neck to seal the plant in its mini-greenhouse.

Bottle up before you leave
If you do not have a friendly neighbour who will take care of indoor plants while you are away, you will need to set up a watering system. Collect plastic bottles of various sizes and cut off the bases. Pierce a small hole in the stopper, or remove the stopper and stuff the neck with cotton wool. Push one bottle, neck downwards, into the soil of each pot, using the larger bottles for larger pots. Attach each bottle to a stake to keep it steady, then fill with water. While you are away, the water will seep through the punctured stopper or cotton wool plug, keeping the soil moist.

Bath-time treat
Create a humid atmosphere for house plants by lining the bath with a piece of capillary matting, which is sold in garden centres by the metre. Dampen with water and stand your pot plants on top. Do not close bathroom blinds or curtains; your plants need light.

Specimens from abroad
It is often tempting to bring back cuttings or plants from abroad, especially those not usually grown in British gardens. There are regulations governing which plants, and how many, you can import. Pick up a leaflet at the port or airport as you leave, or apply to the Department for Environment, Food and Rural Affairs (DEFRA) for one before you go. See your local directory for their telephone number and address.

Plant collecting
When travelling abroad, avoid digging up wild plants or gathering seeds. In the past, plant populations have been decimated by indiscriminate collecting and most countries today have strict laws protecting their rare plants against disturbance. The vast majority of plants that you are likely to find are already grown in Britain and can be purchased easily from specialist nurseries if necessary.

Holly

A bushful of berries

With very few exceptions, a solitary holly will produce no berries. Male and female flowers are produced on separate plants, and the pollen from one must pass to the other before berries will develop. Therefore, to enjoy a Christmas glow in the garden, it is necessary to plant two bushes – a female (*below*, right) for the berries and a male (*below*, left) to provide the pollen. Most garden centres provide plant labels that specify whether hollies are male or female but there are some rather strange contradictions. 'Golden Queen', for example,

Stately bush This variegated holly bush has been clipped neatly into a topiary pompom. Hollies bring stately form, polished foliage and bright berries to the garden.

is a male and will produce no berries while 'Golden King' is female and will fruit well only if there is a male holly nearby.

Safely spineless

If you are reluctant to grow prickly holly because you fear children may be hurt on it, try a variety with spineless leaves such as *Ilex* x *altaclerensis* 'Camelliifolia' and *I. aquifolium* 'J.C. van Tol'. Both are female.

Remember next year

Do not be greedy when cutting holly for Christmas. When you cut the branches that bear berries, you are removing next season's flower buds and to take too many could result in a berryless bush next year. Take branches from all round the bush, maintaining the shape and being careful to retain some with berries, not only for next year but also for the birds. Or you could grow several bushes and take just one or two branches from each.

A lasting display

Holly for Christmas displays will last much longer if leaves are sprayed on both sides with a preparation that reduces moisture loss. These sprays are available at garden centres.

A brief history

A Christmas garland

The association of holly with Christmas probably goes back to the wreaths that decorated the rowdy Roman feast of Saturnalia, which took place in December. However, it was the Christian connection that decreed that a sprig of Christmas holly placed in the byre would ensure that the cows thrived throughout the year, while a holly hedge grown round the house provided sure protection against poison, the evil eye, storm and fire. That holly is still viewed with respect in some country districts is apparent from the fact that some people still believe that it is unlucky to cut the plant. This explains why one often sees a holly standing tall and wild above an otherwise immaculate hedge.

Honeysuckle

Repel red spider mites

If you have honeysuckle growing against a wall and the spring and summer are particularly dry, spray the plant regularly with water. This will discourage red spider mites, which are attracted by the warm, dry conditions and cause damage to the foliage.

New life for a neglected climber

Old, tired honeysuckles that have been left unpruned for years will produce few leaves and flowers, and will develop a mass of dried-up branches. They can be rejuvenated by a severe pruning. In March or April, cut back all stems to about 51cm (20in) above the ground and redistribute the plant's new shoots on a trellis, tree or wall. To avoid the danger of severing stalks that you may wish to keep, use secateurs rather than shears.

Non-scrambling varieties

Not all honeysuckles are climbers – some are evergreen or semi-evergreen shrubs. Though their flowers are not usually considered as

Sweet honeysuckle Wafts of sweet fragrance and its distinctive delicate-looking flowers have made honeysuckle a favourite with many British gardeners.

attractive as those of the climbers, many produce bright fruits and are useful for making low hedges (*Lonicera nitida*) or as ground cover under trees (*L. pileata*).

Horseradish

Keeping roots straight

Grow horseradish in drainpipes, pushed vertically into the ground and filled with a mixture of compost and soil. The plants will develop straight, thick roots. This technique will also prevent the invasive roots spreading.

Year-round relish

During summer, lift horseradish roots as required. In early winter, before the frost sets in, lift the remainder and store them in boxes of soil or peat to use until next year's crop is ready. For continued production, replant a few of the smallest roots in March or April.

House plants

Aide-mémoire

Always retain the label of any plant you buy or receive to remind you of its botanical name, the situation it prefers, and its watering and feeding requirements.

Settling-in period

Help a new house plant to settle into a new situation by placing it in a draught-free spot, out of direct sunlight, for at least two weeks. It can then be moved to its permanent home.

Providing humidity

Plants that dislike a dry atmosphere should be placed on a waterproof tray half-filled with pea shingle or clay balls. Then pour a shallow layer of water over the bottom of the tray to create some humidity.

Light seekers

Some plants and germinating seeds require a lot of light during winter when the light quality is low. To ensure they receive the maximum available, choose a south or west-facing window ledge for them and keep feeding to a minimum to prevent the plants from becoming spindly.

Homemade reflectors

To increase the light that reaches a plant during the dull winter months, position a mirror, or a sheet of kitchen foil mounted onto some card, behind the plant or to one side of it. The light reflected by the mirror or foil will encourage plants to grow more upright and less spindly.

Bud preservation

Avoid moving pots of indoor camellias, gardenias, hoyas and hibiscus once the buds have appeared. Otherwise the buds may fall off and you will be left with a flowerless plant. However, rotating the pots by a half-turn every few days is a good idea as it will help to ensure even leaf growth.

Group benefits

Healthy plants that enjoy the same conditions will benefit from being grouped together, particularly during winter when they are in centrally heated rooms. Moisture that evaporates from the compost will help to provide a humid atmosphere.

Indoor attraction

Climbing indoor plants such as *Cissus*, *Rhoicissus* (grape ivy), *Philodendron* and varieties of *Hedera* (ivy) can be trained to grow against a wall in any room. Make an invisible climbing frame from strong colourless nylon thread or fishing line attached to fine nails hammered into the wall.

Showing off trailing plants

Make the most of trailing house plants by using a hanging container or placing the pot in a suspended basket. The flowers of *Hoya bella* (miniature wax plant) in particular are seen to their best advantage from below.

Essential stability

Refrain from constantly moving house plants about. Not only could a plant be damaged, for example a move to bright sunlight could lead to leaf scorch, but changes in temperature, light and humidity can also affect growth. For

Garden secrets

Clearing the air

After painting and decorating, banish paint smells by placing pots containing azaleas, ivies and mother-in-law's tongue in the room. Their leaves absorb and break down toxins.

example, a reduction in temperature could chill and shock a plant. As a result, the plant's growth could be retarded.

Fortnightly feed

Growing house plants soon absorb nutrients from potting compost. Add a slow-release plant food to the compost when repotting or feed frequently in the growing season. If flowers are disappointing, you can feed the plants with a tomato fertiliser. Many of the house-plant fertilisers are formulated for foliage plants and encourage the production of leaves at the expense of flowers.

Growing know-how

House-plant maintenance

Bear in mind a few basic points to help to ensure your house plants have a long life.

- Regularly remove faded flowers, and damaged or dried leaves.
- Do not overwater your plants; let the compost dry out before re-watering.
- Feed plants frequently during the active growth period (usually between late March and late September).
- Do not use leaf-polishing products too often as they may clog leaf pores. Wipe the leaves with a damp sponge instead.

To each according to its needs

Follow the guidelines on the plant's label or consult a specialist book on the care of house plants if you are in any doubt about its needs.

Carrier bag protection

If you have to carry a newly-bought house plant for any distance in cold weather, place it inside several carrier bags. This will prevent any wind chill or change in temperature adversely affecting the plant – cold can, for instance, cause leaf fall.

Water signals

Use one of the many products, widely available from garden centres, that can be inserted into the pot and which gradually change colour as the soil dries out. Treat it as an indication only, and water according to the individual needs of the plant.

Small is best

To make sure the water goes directly where it is needed, round the base of the plant, use a small watering can with a long, slender spout. This prevents splashes on the plant's leaves and on your furniture.

Test the temperature

A sticky deposit on your furniture or window ledge may be a sign that a plant is infected with one of the common insect pests such as scale insects or greenfly. Inspect the plant carefully. If it is affected spray it with a systemic insecticide.

Thirst-quencher

If the potting compost has dried out, immerse the plant pot in a bucket of water until bubbles have stopped coming to the surface. Drain well, and place the pot on a saucer or drip tray.

Watering African violets

Place pots of African violets in a bowl of shallow water. Do not wet the leaves as they are easily marked. Keep the compost moist but not soggy.

Freshening up

Give glossy-leaved plants an occasional light shower of tepid water to remove dust. Wipe the leaves individually with a sponge to remove surplus water.

Repotting plants with chlorosis

Plants badly affected by chlorosis – due to watering with hard tap water – should be repotted. Wash the compost away in tepid rainwater and then repot in a suitable compost.

Gardener's potpourri

Blue blood

According to Greek mythology, the god Apollo formed a passionate attachment to Hyacinthus, a handsome young athlete. Zephyr, the west wind, fell for him too but his love was unrequited. One day, in a fit of jealousy, Zephyr blew the discus thrown by the lovers off course straight into Hyacinthus, who fell, mortally wounded. Inconsolable, Apollo transformed the blood of his beloved into the fragrant flower that now decorates forests and gardens.

Hyacinths

Small is good enough

When buying hyacinth bulbs for the garden, do not be influenced by size. Small bulbs grow just as well, and are considerably cheaper than the larger ones. Their flowers tend to be more in proportion and are less likely to be damaged by wind and heavy rain.

Flowers for Christmas

Flowering hyacinths make attractive Christmas presents. The specially prepared bulbs that are on sale from the beginning of August have been treated to hasten the development of the bud inside the bulb, shortening the period between planting and flowering. Plant these hyacinths as soon as possible, and not later than the first week in September for Christmas flowering. If the bulbs are left exposed to the air, they are unlikely to flower early. If a delay in planting is unavoidable, wrap the bulbs individually in newspaper and place them in the vegetable compartment of the refrigerator for up to two weeks.

Water purifier

Add a piece of charcoal to a vase in which you are growing a hyacinth – it will help to keep the water clear and odour-free.

Growing on air

To grow a hyacinth in a glass of water, remember to leave a 1.3cm (½in) gap between the surface of the water and the bottom of the bulb. This will prevent the base of the bulb from rotting, which frequently happens if it comes into contact with water.

Second time round

Do not throw away forced hyacinths after they have flowered. They will bloom again but will need time to flourish. The following year, the stalks will be feeble but they will thicken over the years, and the hyacinths, although producing thinner flowers, will regain much of their former beauty.

A scented spring

Ensure a scented start to spring by planting hyacinth bulbs in the autumn. Place them 15cm (6in) apart if they are to flower alone, or farther apart if other plants are in the bed. After the first flowering in a spring bedding scheme, dig up the bulbs and replant them in a new spot where they can be left to bloom undisturbed for many years to come.

First-aid for bulbs

It is all too easy to damage bulbs when forking over the ground. If the wound is superficial, dust it with flowers of sulphur or powdered charcoal and let the bulb dry for a few hours before replanting. If the bulb has been cut in half, pot it up in a 13cm (5in) pot of well drained compost, and nurture it in a cold frame. New bulblets may form on the cut areas, or the bulb may recover. If the soil is wet during winter it is better to lift any damaged bulbs and put them into a container of well-drained compost and overwinter them in a cold frame before planting out again during the following autumn.

Heady hyacinths Fill the spring garden with the intoxicating scent of pink, blue and white hyacinths, planted at the front of a low border. Tulips, with their bell-shaped flowers and sword-like leaves, make charming companions.

A garden in the home

The indoor gardener can create a colourful and ever-changing display to be enjoyed throughout the year.

House plants, whether grown for their foliage or flowers, bring the outdoor world right into the home, providing gardeners with the opportunity to exercise skill and imagination whatever the weather.

Like garden varieties, house plants have differing needs for light, food, humidity and water. Some thrive in full sun while others may wilt unless shaded from bright light or sited away from the window. Equally, while many plants respond to regular watering, a few will flourish only if the potting compost is kept almost completely dry.

Understanding these differences is the key to succeeding with house plants. Armed with a little knowledge and applying plenty of care, the indoor gardener can tend tropical species, such as the striking *Aphelandra squarrosa* (zebra plant), as well as old favourites like the delicate *Primula malacoides* (fairy primrose).

The choice is vast. Foliage plants offer an array of leaf shapes, colours, markings and textures, which is complemented by the seasonal diversity of flowering plants. Together, they can be used by the gardener to create a versatile, living show.

Plants in their places

Full sun: on a window ledge facing south or west. The plant will need to be shaded from the midday sun in summer.

Bright light: behind a south or west-facing window shaded by sheer curtains, or on a window ledge facing east or north.

Partial shade: on a window ledge facing north or east, or 2m (7ft) from a bright window, out of direct sunlight.

Shade: in a shaded corner of a bright room or 3m (10ft) away from a north-facing window.

Flowering plants

Aeschynanthus speciosus (basket plant)

A trailing plant with pale leaves. It has tubular orange flowers between June and September.

Normal room temperatures are suitable throughout the year.

Water plentifully and mist foliage during the growing season; always keep compost moist but ensure it is well drained. During winter, allow the surface of the compost to dry out between waterings. Apply a high-potash liquid fertiliser once a month during active growth.

Tip Keep an eye out for aphids, particularly on young leaves.

Aphelandra squarrosa (zebra plant)

Shrub that has a flower spike composed of yellow bracts (modified leaves). Yellow flowers appear from them between July and September. The large leaves have ivory-coloured veins.

Requires a minimum temperature of 10°C (50°F) in winter.

Do not allow the compost to dry out; keep barely moist during the winter resting period. Apply a general liquid feed once a week during the growth period.

Tip Check the plant regularly for signs of aphids, mealy bugs or scale insects.

Beloperone guttata (shrimp plant)

Evergreen shrub, also known as *Justicia brandegeeana*, which has red-brown or pink, shrimp-like bracts. White flowers emerge from April to December.

Thrives in warmth during growth period; requires a cool temperature – at least 7°C (45°F) – in winter.

Water sparingly, allowing the potting compost to dry out partially between waterings. From late winter to early autumn, apply a general liquid fertiliser once a week.

Tip Cut back up to half the growth each spring; pinch out the tips of straggly stems.

Clivia miniata (kaffir lily)

Popular plant with trumpet-shaped orange or red flowers between March and August.

Requires warmth, but keep at just below 10°C (50°F) for six to eight weeks in early winter to encourage flowering later.

Keep compost just moist in spring and summer; reduce watering in autumn and let the compost almost dry out for six to eight weeks in early winter. Increase watering when flower stalks form. When half-grown, apply a general liquid feed every fortnight, until a month before reducing watering.

Tip After flower trumpets fall, cut off embryo fruits and withered flower stalks. Otherwise, the plant may not flower next year.

Echeveria derenbergii (painted lady)

Succulent plant the fleshy leaves of which have a white bloom. Curved stems bear orange-red flowers in spring and early summer.

Normal room temperatures are suitable but the plant prefers to be kept at 13–16°C (55–61°F) during winter.

In summer, water regularly, letting the surface of the compost dry out between waterings. In winter, water enough to prevent the plant from shrivelling. Use a half-strength general liquid fertiliser each week in summer.

Tip Do not water from above as splashes on the leaves can cause rotting. Instead, stand the pot in a saucer of water, then drain thoroughly.

Epiphyllum (orchid cactus)

Large-flowering cactus with flattened stems that blooms from May to June.

Thrives in a minimum temperature of 15°C (59°F) from spring to autumn, 10°C (50°F) in winter.

Water plentifully in spring and summer but ensure good drainage. Mist plants daily and stand them on trays of damp pebbles or clay balls. After flower buds form, apply a tomato fertiliser every two weeks until buds have opened. In autumn and winter, water enough to keep compost barely moist, then water moderately, allowing the top half-inch of the compost to dry out between waterings.

Tip This cactus flowers best when pot-bound; repot only when it becomes top-heavy.

Euphorbia pulcherrima (poinsettia)

Popular Christmas shrub that produces attractive red, pink or white bracts in winter.

Keep at normal room temperatures, at least 13°C (55°F), in winter and at a minimum of 18°C (64°F) from April.

Water regularly, allowing the surface of the potting compost to dry out between each watering.

Tip To encourage a poinsettia to flower for a second year, prune to 10cm (4in) above the base and allow the compost almost to dry out. In April, resume watering and repot, using fresh compost, to restart growth. Feed each week from June to September with a half-strength general fertiliser. From the end of September, give the plant 14 hours of total darkness each day for eight weeks, by covering it with a box or black plastic bag. Your poinsettia will bloom again for Christmas, but will be taller.

Exacum affine (Arabian violet)

Short-lived perennial that flowers profusely, producing fragrant, pale blue blooms. Treated as an annual and discarded after blooming.

Flourishes in temperatures between 13°C (55°F) and 16°C (61°F).

Keep moist at all times. Stand pot on a tray of moist pebbles and mist leaves when watering. While the plant is flowering, feed with a general liquid fertiliser every two weeks.

Tip Pick off any fading flowers. The plant will continue to produce blooms in an effort to set seed, thus prolonging the blooming period.

Hibiscus rosa-sinensis (rose of China)

Indoor hibiscus that flowers from late spring until summer. Blooms are orange, pink, red, white or yellow.

Grows well at normal room temperatures for most of the year; keep at a minimum temperature of 10°C (50°F) over winter.

Potting compost should be kept moist except in winter, when it should be watered just enough to keep it from drying out. Apply a high-potash liquid fertiliser once every two weeks between May and September.

Tip In spring, keep growth bushy by pruning stems and branches to within 15cm (6in) of the base of the plant, or prune the top third and shorten side shoots to 7.5cm (3in).

Phalaenopsis (moth orchid)

Easy-to-grow orchid the arching flower stalks of which carry up to 30 large blooms. Each flower can last for up to three weeks.

This plant needs to be placed in a minimum temperature of 16°C (61°F) throughout the year.

Use soft water and allow the compost surface to dry between waterings; keep it just moist from November to March. Stand on a tray of moist pebbles and mist daily. During growth, feed with a general fertiliser at every fourth watering.

Tip Don't leave drops of water on the leaves as this could cause fungal infection or rotting.

Primula malacoides (fairy primrose)

Indoor perennial with delicate flowers that is usually discarded after its first season.

 Grows best in temperatures between 10°C (50°F) and 13°C (55°F).

 Keep the potting compost moist throughout the year and, if the plant is kept in a warm room, mist the foliage every day. Apply a general liquid fertiliser every two weeks during the flowering period.

Tip Prolong the blooming period by picking off any fading flowers.

Rhododendron simsii (Indian azalea)

Winter-flowering shrub that grows to 46cm (18in) in height and spread when kept in a pot. Its large flowers are funnel-shaped and come in a wide range of colours.

 Requires a cool room, between 7°C (45°F) and 16°C (61°F).

Water plentifully, using soft, lime-free water, and spray foliage daily. If you are keeping the plant for a second season, apply a lime-free liquid fertiliser once a fortnight from late spring to early autumn.

Tip To encourage a second year of flowering, move the plant to a cool room after blooming. Water the compost moderately and do not allow it to dry out. Repot if necessary. When all danger of frost has passed, move it to a shady spot outside and keep the potting compost moist. The plant should be brought back inside in September and should be kept in a cool place until the flowers start to open.

Saintpaulia ionantha (African violet)

Compact and popular plant that blooms for up to ten months a year.

 Temperatures of 18–24°C (64–75°F) are required, but the plant will tolerate 13°C (55°F) in winter if the potting compost is kept on the dry side.

 Water when surface of potting compost is dry. Pour tepid water into saucer to avoid splashing leaves. At every watering during the growing season, feed with a general liquid fertiliser containing nitrogen, phosphate and potash in equal quantities.

Tip Repot every other year, removing any outer leaves that have been compressed against the rim of the pot and have become damaged.

Solanum pseudocapsicum (Jerusalem cherry)

Bushy shrub that produces small flowers in summer and brightly coloured but poisonous berries throughout the winter.

Temperatures should not exceed 15°C (59°F) in autumn or winter; Jerusalem cherries can be placed outside during late spring and summer.

Maintain moist compost by watering frequently, and mist leaves daily during winter. Feed every fortnight with a general liquid fertiliser, except during the rest period.

Tip A Jerusalem cherry can be kept for more than one season. Once berries start to wither, water sparingly for four to five weeks, keeping compost just moist. Then, repot and place out of doors from June until the autumn when it should be brought in.

Spathiphyllum wallisii (peace lily)

A stemless plant with arrow-shaped flowers and glossy leaves.

Thrives in a room temperature of 13–16°C (55–61°F).

Water moderately, allowing the compost surface to dry out between waterings. Feed between spring and late autumn with a general liquid fertiliser.

Tip Stand on a tray of moistened pebbles and mist the leaves regularly to deter red spider mites, which are common pests. Sponge the leaves occasionally to keep them free of dust.

Streptocarpus (Cape primrose)

Cluster-flowered plant, with stemmed or stemless leaves, which produces trumpet-shaped blooms between spring and autumn.

 Grows well in a warm room. It needs a temperature of at least 13°C (55°F) to maintain active growth, but will tolerate 10°C (50°F) during winter.

 Allow the top half-inch of the compost to dry out between waterings while the plant is growing actively; the top inch when dormant. During the growth period, feed every fortnight with a half-strength general liquid fertiliser.

Tip During the growing season, provide extra humidity by standing the pot on a tray of moist pebbles. To avoid mildew, make sure the plant receives adequate ventilation. Repot every other year, using a shallow pot.

Foliage plants

Adiantum raddianum (maidenhair fern)

Popular fern with dark green, drooping fronds and fine, shiny leaf stalks.

Can tolerate a range of temperatures, from a minimum of 10°C (50°F) to 24°C (75°F).

Water moderately, ensuring that the root ball does not dry out. During the growth period, apply a general liquid feed once a fortnight if the compost is peat-based, once a month if it is soil-based.

Tip If the temperature rises above 24°C (75°F), spray the foliage daily and stand the plant on a tray of moist pebbles or clay balls.

Asparagus densiflorus (asparagus fern)

Fern-like plant, related to the lily family, which has attractive, feathery foliage.

Prefers normal warmth but can also tolerate a temperature as low as 7°C (45°F) in winter provided that the compost is kept fairly dry.

Maintain a thoroughly moist soil from spring to autumn; water just enough to keep the potting compost from drying out in winter. During the active growth period, feed with a general liquid fertiliser every two weeks.

Tip Thick asparagus roots tend to force soil upwards so keep the compost well below the rim of the container. Pot on annually or as necessary.

Aspidistra elatior (cast-iron plant)

Tolerant species that has dark green, leathery leaves 38–51cm (15–20in) long.

Does equally well in hot or cold rooms and will cope with a position in a dark corner or hallway.

Allow the top third of the compost to dry out before watering; brown marks appear on the leaves if the plant is overwatered. Feed with a high-nitrogen or balanced liquid fertiliser every two weeks during active growth.

Tip Sponge the leaves regularly to rid the plant of dust.

Ceropegia linearis ssp. woodii (rosary vine)

Trailing succulent with heart-shaped leaves and flesh-coloured tubular flowers.

Keep at normal room temperature throughout the year.

Water moderately in spring and summer, allowing the surface of the potting compost to dry out between waterings. In winter, water just enough to keep the compost from drying out. Feed mature, healthy plants with a general liquid fertiliser once a month during active growth.

Tip When planting rosary vines in a hanging basket, place the tubers 4–5cm (1½-2in) apart to create an effective display.

Cissus rhombifolia (grape ivy)

Quick-growing climber, related to the grapevine, with tooth-edged leaves.

Thrives in warmth but can tolerate a temperature of 13°C (55°F) for a short time in winter if necessary.

Water freely in summer and just enough to keep the plant from drying out in winter. From spring to autumn, feed once every two weeks with a general liquid fertiliser.

Tip In spring, trim back side shoots, leaving them about 2.5cm (1in) long, and cut the main stems by about a third. Pinch out growing tips to promote branching.

Codiaeum variegatum var. pictum (croton)

A bushy shrub with different colours and markings on the leaves according to cultivar.

Requires a temperature of at least 13°C (55°F) throughout the year.

Water plentifully with tepid water during the growth period, allowing the surface of the compost to dry out between waterings, and just enough to keep it from drying out in winter. Stand the plant on a tray of damp pebbles and mist frequently in summer. Feed with a general liquid fertiliser every two weeks during the growing period.

Tip If a codiaeum outgrows its allotted space, cut it back in spring and dust wounds with powdered charcoal to stem the flow of latex.

Cordyline australis (cabbage palm)

Single-stemmed shrub with sword-shaped, leathery leaves, up to 1m (3ft) long and arranged in a loose rosette.

Tolerates a temperature as low as 4°C (40°F). It can be kept outside in summer and early autumn.

Water as often as necessary to keep potting compost well moistened but not saturated; in winter, water just enough to prevent it from drying out. Apply a general liquid fertiliser every two weeks during growth.

Tip Pull off lower leaves as they dry and mist foliage regularly to promote healthy growth.

Cyperus alternifolius (umbrella plant)

Moisture-loving house plant with long, narrow bracts radiating from thin stems. Can grow up to 76cm (2½ft) in height.

Will withstand a minimum temperature of 10°C (50°F) and does well in normal room warmth.

Water plentifully and stand the pot in a deep saucer of water so that soil is kept moist at all times. Apply a general liquid fertiliser once a month during the active growth period.

Tip Mist the foliage regularly, using warm water, to provide the plant with the extra humidity it needs.

Dieffenbachia (dumb-cane)

Striking plant with thick stems and large, fleshy leaves with decorative markings. Grows up to 1.5m (5ft) tall.

Grows best at temperatures of 15°C (59°F) or above.

Stand pot on a tray of moist pebbles and keep the potting compost damp throughout the year, allowing the surface to dry out between waterings. During the active growth period, feed the plant every two weeks, using a general liquid fertiliser.

Tip The sap of a dieffenbachia is poisonous so always wash your hands after taking cuttings or removing faded leaves.

x Fatshedera lizei (ivy tree)

Popular hybrid of *Hedera helix* and *Fatsia japonica*, which has shiny, five-lobed leaves up to 20cm (8in) wide.

Grows best in cool temperatures but will survive in heated rooms at not more than 21°C (70°F).

Place the pot on a tray of moist pebbles if the room is warm. Allow the top half-inch of the compost to dry out between waterings during the growing season and water just enough to keep compost from drying out completely in winter. Apply a general liquid fertiliser every fortnight during the active growth period.

Tip A fatshedera will grow to a height of up to 1.2m (4ft). Insert a stake into the potting compost to give the plant support. Pinch out leggy side shoots in March.

Hypoestes phyllostachya (polka-dot plant)

Dense, bushy, shrub-like plant with pink, red or white-spotted leaves.

Grows best in a room temperature of at least 15°C (59°F). Its markings will fade if the plant is moved out of bright light.

Water moderately between spring and autumn, and just enough to moisten the potting compost in winter. Feed once every two weeks during the active growth period, using a general liquid fertiliser.

Tip Encourage bushy growth by pruning regularly. If an old plant becomes straggly, either take cuttings in spring or summer, or replace it with a new one.

Lobivia, Mammillaria, Rebutia (desert cacti)

Popular flowering cacti with rounded stems.

In winter, keep in a cool but bright place at about 5°C (41°F) to encourage flowering. Shade only in the hottest months.

Treat desert cacti like ordinary house plants in spring and summer, watering when the surface of the compost begins to dry out. Water very little in winter, just enough to keep the plant from shrivelling. In spring and summer, feed with a high-potash tomato fertiliser once a fortnight if the plants are grown in a peat-based compost, once a month if they are grown in a soil-based one.

Tip Open windows in summer to give cacti some fresh air.

Nephrolepis exaltata 'Bostoniensis' (Boston fern)

Popular indoor fern that has long, arching fronds. It looks most attractive when displayed on a pedestal.

 Grows well in temperatures of 15–21°C (59–70°F) but can withstand a temperature as low as 10°C (50°F).

Always keep potting compost well moistened but not saturated but if the temperature is less than 13°C (55°F), allow the top third of the compost to dry out between waterings. Stand on a tray of pebbles and mist regularly. Feed an actively growing plant with a general liquid fertiliser once every four weeks if it is grown in a soil-based compost, once every two weeks if in a peat-based compost.

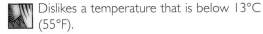

Tip Repot in spring as necessary, taking care not to bury the crown.

Philodendron scandens
(heartleaf philodendron)

Small-leaved climber or trailer, and one of the easiest house plants to grow.

Dislikes a temperature that is below 13°C (55°F).

During the growth period, water moderately, allowing the surface of the compost to dry out between waterings. In winter, water sparingly. Stand on a pebble tray or mist regularly. In the growing season, feed with a general liquid fertiliser every two weeks.

Tip Encourage bushy growth by pinching out the growing tips.

Platycerium bifurcatum (staghorn fern)

Rain-forest fern with spreading, drooping fronds that resemble a stag's antlers.

 Prefers temperatures of 21°C (70°F) in summer, 13°C (55°F) in winter.

To water, immerse the pot, or base of the plant and bark support, in water for a few minutes whenever fronds start to droop. Mist regularly if the room is warm. Feed the plant with a general liquid fertiliser two or three times during active growth.

Tip A staghorn fern thrives when grown on a piece of bark, suspended from the ceiling of a humid, shaded greenhouse. Wrap the root mass in sphagnum moss and peat or coir. Tie this carefully to the bark with either strong cotton or nylon thread. Keep both the bark and root mass moist until the plant has adhered firmly to the support.

Scindapsus aureus (devil's ivy)

Climber, also known as *Epipremnum aureum*, with attractive, bright green and yellow, heart-shaped leaves.

 Likes warm temperatures but needs a winter resting period at 10–13°C (50–55°F).

 Water moderately during the active growth period, allowing the top of the potting compost to dry out between waterings, and sparingly in winter. Feed with a general liquid fertiliser every two weeks during the growing season.

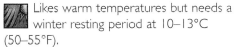

Tip If leaves turn green, place the plant in brighter light to stimulate the variegation.

Syngonium podophyllum
(arrowhead vine)

Tropical climbing and trailing vine with mid-green, rounded leaves.

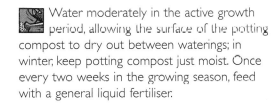

Grows well at normal room temperatures.

Keep soil moist during the active growth period. Give the plant a short winter rest by reducing watering but do not let the potting compost dry out. Apply a general liquid fertiliser every two weeks in spring and summer.

Tip Spray foliage frequently and, in warm rooms, stand the plant on a tray filled with moist pebbles to increase humidity.

Tolmiea menziesii (piggyback plant)

Plant with large, mid-green, heart-shaped leaves that arch downwards.

Prefers cool or unheated rooms and thrives in a temperature of 10°C (50°F).

Water moderately in the active growth period, allowing the surface of the potting compost to dry out between waterings; in winter, keep potting compost just moist. Once every two weeks in the growing season, feed with a general liquid fertiliser.

Tip Grow tolmieas in a hanging basket to show off their attractive, arching leaves.

Hydrangeas

Early frost warning
With the exception of the climbing varieties, which prefer a north-facing aspect, hydrangeas do best in a west-facing situation. Do not plant either type against an east-facing wall, where early frosts and the morning sun may cause scorching. Leave enough space between the shrubs to allow them to develop – 1.5–2m (5–7ft) is ideal. Underplant with perennials and bulbs.

Bluer blues
There are two ways to make pink hydrangeas blue. Either spread aluminium sulphate round the roots, or water with a blueing agent obtainable from garden centres. Gardeners of old believed that burying a few rusty nails or a piece of copper wire near the roots did the trick. The colour of your hydrangeas is an indication of the pH value of your soil. Blue flowers mean the soil is acid, pink that it is alkaline.

Winter cover
When hydrangea flowers fade and die, do not deadhead them but leave them on the plant. They look attractive and will also give next year's buds some protection from frost and snow. Leave pruning until April when the plants should be cut back to a point just above the large, uppermost buds that are swollen with sap.

Hydrangea choice
The mop-headed hortensias and flat-headed lacecaps of *Hydrangea macrophylla* (common hydrangea) are worth growing for their showy clusters of star-shaped flowers. They are best grown in a sheltered position in a sunny or partially shaded area of the garden. Both flower in midsummer on shoots made during the previous growing season.

Popular and pyramidal
A popular hydrangea that is hardy in the north is *Hydrangea paniculata* 'Grandiflora', which produces massive, pyramidal panicles up to 46cm (18in) long during August and September. Unlike *H. macrophylla*, it flowers on the current season's shoots.

Protection for a dwarf
Plant the dwarf *Hydrangea macrophylla* 'Pia' well away from other vegetation. Competition for nutrients could retard the shrub.

Up the wall
For superb cover on a north-facing wall, try *Hydrangea anomala* ssp. *petiolaris* (climbing hydrangea), which produces masses of creamy-white flowers in June and can grow 18m (60ft) high. For best results, plant in soil enriched with well-rotted manure. Like ivy, it clings to the wall and needs no support.

A brief history

A cold beauty
The hydrangea's name comes from the Greek *hydor* meaning water and *angeion* meaning vessel, because of the resemblance of the seedpods to drinking cups. The 23 known species include lacecap hydrangeas that grow to 9m (30ft), and the oak-leaf type, the foliage of which turns wine-red in autumn. Because the flowers have beauty but no scent, they represented coldness or boastfulness in the Victorian flower language. Nevertheless, they are long-lasting, making them much in demand as floral decorations in Derbyshire well-dressings.

Hydroponics

Something completely different
Experiment with an alternative form of gardening by growing hydroponically. This method of growing greenhouse crops and indoor ornamentals uses expanded clay granules instead of soil to support the plants, which are fed on a nutrient-rich water solution. Instead of growing in conventional pots, the plants are cultivated in watertight containers, each of which has a float that indicates when the growing solution should be replenished. Special kits, containing granules, nutrient powder, a float and full instructions, are available from garden centres. Although initially expensive, once installed the system is relatively maintenance-free.

In the greenhouse
If previous seasons' conventionally grown crops have suffered from disorders, such as blossom-end rot, that are caused by erratic watering, or if soil-borne pests and diseases have built up in the greenhouse, hydroculture can be worthwhile. Plants that respond well to this technique include aubergines, cucumbers, lettuces, melons, peppers, strawberries, tomatoes and watercress.

Hydroponic house plants
To grow a house plant hydroponically, in spring, take a strong, healthy stem cutting from a conventionally grown plant and stand it in a jar of water in a well-lit place. When roots have developed, transfer the cutting to a hydropot and grow on according to the manufacturer's instructions. Plants grown in hydropots can be propagated in the same way. (*See also* **Cuttings**)

The right fertiliser
It is claimed that hydroculture can produce greater yields than conventional growing methods. However, it is essential to follow the instructions and to use only the nutrient solution specially manufactured for hydroponic growing. Ordinary fertilisers are not suitable and should never be used.

Impatiens

Raising from seed

Growing from seed is the cheapest way of obtaining a mass of *Impatiens* (busy lizzie) for your summer bedding. Fill a seed tray or other container with seed compost and sow the seeds on top, making sure that they are not covered by the compost. Place the container in a clear polythene bag and put it in a warm room, out of direct sunlight. The extra humidity created in the bag will encourage the seeds to germinate quickly.

Secure roots

Busy lizzies cope badly with root disturbance. Transplant the seedlings into pots or divided trays as soon they are large enough to handle.

Colour for shade

Use the New Guinea hybrids to bring strong bursts of colour to a partially shaded site. In late May, plant seedlings in well-drained soil where they will flower in summer.

Doubling up

Although double-flowered busy lizzie seeds are on sale, only about a quarter of the plants that subsequently develop will have double flowers. Buy 'Confection', which produces the most, and take cuttings. Overwinter the plants in a frost-free greenhouse and take more cuttings in spring. You will soon have enough plants to fill the bed.

Quick cutting

Nothing could be easier than propagating busy lizzies. Between April and September, take a cutting below a leaf joint, remove the tips of the bottom leaves, put the cutting in water and stand it in the light. (*See also* **Cuttings**)

Insects

Good insects

Do not think of all insects as pests. Some, such as bees, may pollinate flowers; others are predators and help out by feeding on garden pests. These predators include black-kneed capsid bugs, lacewings, ladybirds and hover flies. Soil-living centipedes, which are closely related to insects, break down plant debris. They have one pair of legs on each body segment and should not be confused with millipedes, which

Busy border An exuberant mass of *Impatiens* turns a shady border into an eye-catching focus of summer colour.

are pests that feed on plant roots and have two pairs of legs on each segment. (*See also* **Bees**, **Ladybirds**)

Basil barrier
In India, basil is a sacred plant, while in Ancient Greece it signified royalty. Among other attributes, it has a clove-like smell that repels many insects, including mosquitoes and flies. Discourage these pests from entering the house during summer by placing pots of basil plants on window ledges. (*See also* **Mint**)

Protect the predators
As some insecticides kill useful insects as well as pests, do not use them unless absolutely necessary. If possible, choose non-persistent soap-based insecticides or pirimicarb, which kills only aphids. Reliance on insecticides can be reduced if you set out to encourage insect predators into the garden. *Convolvulus tricolor, Limnanthes douglasii* (poached egg plant), *Phacelia* and other nectar or pollen-rich plants all provide food for the predators.

Choosing an insecticide
Systemic insecticides, which are absorbed by the plant, are employed against sap-sucking insects such as aphids. Contact insecticides coat the surface over which insects move or are applied directly to the pests and are effective against chewing insects such as beetles, caterpillars and earwigs.

What form to use
Insecticides are available as liquids, powders, dusts, baits or smoke formulations. Sprays – more effective against sap-suckers – are the most expensive but are easy to apply. Dusts and baits are best for controlling ants and other types of crawling insects.

Elder repellent
Rub elder leaves onto your skin and this will act as an effective insect repellent during warm evenings.

Irises, bearded

Making the most of irises
The golden rule is to plant a single variety of iris in a group rather than dotting single plants round the garden.

An undemanding plant
Irises are easy-going plants. All they need is a sunny, free-draining position and a spring dressing of slow-release fertiliser.

Positioning rhizomes
Align rhizomes north to south, with leaves to the north. This prevents the foliage from casting shadows across the rhizome and affecting its development.

Planting on heavy soil
Before planting a bearded iris on a damp, heavy soil, create a small hillock of soil. Mix in a little coarse grit or sand to improve the drainage, then plant the rhizome on top.

Sunlight for the rhizome
Make sure that the top of each rhizome is exposed after planting. Check them regularly to ensure they remain clear of the soil while the plants are establishing themselves; otherwise flowering will be affected. You can help to prevent wind rock after planting by using secateurs to reduce the foliage by half.

Careful weeding
When weeding round your bearded irises, do the job by hand to avoid damaging the exposed rhizomes and the fragile roots. Alternatively, you may find it worth investing in a tool, such as an onion hoe, which can be used in confined spaces.

When to divide
Divide rhizomes every three to five years, after flowering, before the irises become crowded and blooming is inhibited.

Controlling rust
In spring, check the leaves for orange, brown or yellow spores – the signs of rust. Spray any affected plants frequently with a systemic fungicide.

Removing unproductive growth
When dividing bearded irises, cut out and discard the old centres of the rhizomes, keeping just the healthy, outer parts, which produce new growth. Replant 30–40cm (12–16in) apart.

Post-winter grooming
If winter frost lifts recently planted rhizomes out of the soil, make a small ridge of well-drained soil or sharp sand round them to hold them in place, but do not bury them. Remove any dry or damaged leaves with a sharp jerk, leaving a straight break.

Irises, bulbous

Help dwarf irises to thrive
Dwarf irises sometimes flower well in the first year after planting, then slowly fade away. The secret for long life is to plant them in a sunny place, in well-drained soil. Bulbous irises also do well in the warm conditions of a raised bed or in pockets of soil on top of a dry, retaining wall. A liquid feed every fortnight from when the flowers fade until the leaves turn yellow also helps.

Dwarf spring irises
Small, spring-flowering bulbous irises are ideal companions for rock plants. The blue and purple-flowered forms of *Iris reticulata* and the yellow *I. danfordiae* are attractive choices. Plant them 7.5cm (3in) deep, sitting the bulbs on a 2.5cm (1in) layer of grit. For the best effect, plant in clumps of at least half a dozen.

Dutch irises
Lift Dutch and English irises annually if your soil is heavy clay, or if they are planted in a boggy area. Wait until the foliage has died back – about July – then dig up the bulbs. Place them in an airy shed or garage to dry off, then brush off any soil. Store in a net suspended from the roof until October, when they can be replanted.

Bulb division
Yellow, drying foliage during the active growth season is a sign that bulbous iris clumps need to be divided. Lift them carefully and separate the bulbs, taking care not to break the roots, especially those of *Iris orchioides*. Replant the bulbs individually, in small groups.

Fight ink spot
Never plant bulbous irises that have black spots on their skins – they have ink spot. Lift and burn any plant that has black patches on the bulb or blackened foliage.

Irises, waterside

Growing water irises
Unlike bearded irises, water irises grow best in damp conditions, such as in a bog garden or round the shallow edges of a pond. These attractive, dainty plants prefer a neutral or slightly acid soil, especially one that is rich in plant foods – as many waterside soils are. Transplant the irises from their pots in spring, just as the green shoots are starting to develop from the rhizome.

In the water
To grow water irises in deep water, plant the rhizomes in a mesh basket filled with rich garden soil and covered with a layer of pea gravel. The gravel will protect the soil from being washed out and prevent any fish from uprooting the plants. Place some bricks on the base of the pond and lower the basket on top. Make sure that the rim of the container is no more than 7.5cm (3in) below the surface of the water.

Triple advantage
Help to limit weed growth as well as retain moisture and provide nutrients for water irises grown in a bog garden by covering their bases each spring with a generous amount of mulch or compost.

Longest lasting
To grow water irises that can be cut for the house, choose the prolific *Iris sibirica* (Siberian flag). This species produces the longest-lasting cut flowers.

By summer ponds
Delicate Japanese irises can withstand cool conditions provided that they are planted in large plastic pots. In summer, bury the pots to the rim along the water's edge. Since these irises will not thrive in damp cold they cannot be left by the water in winter. Transfer them to an unheated greenhouse or frame, where the dry, cold conditions are more suitable.

For modest waters
If your pond is small, plant *Iris laevigata* and *I. versicolor*, which have a compact growth habit. Do not plant the yellow iris 'Golden Queen'. This is unsuitable for a small pond since it tends to produce luxurious growth that is invasive.

A brief history

Flag Royal
The three falls on the flower of the wild iris – the yellow flag – are said to symbolise faith, wisdom and courage. Perhaps for this reason, the flower was carried by the Frankish kings when they were proclaimed and later, during the Second Crusade, a stylised version was adopted by Louis VII as a device for his banner. Not surprisingly, the flower became known as *Fleur de Louis*, a name that was quickly corrupted into *fleur-de-luce* or *fleur-de-lys*.

When Edward III laid claim to the French throne in the 14th century, he quartered the English royal arms with the device, which his countrymen came to call 'flower-de-luce'. Hence the dire prophecy in Shakespeare's *Henry VI*, Part I:
Cropp'd are the flower-de-luces in your arms:
Of England's coat one half is cut away.

Ivy

Filling awkward areas

Ivy thrives in any soil and almost any situation, making it an ideal plant to fill awkward spots in the garden. It is one of the few plants that will thrive on an exposed, east-facing wall. However, do not choose a variegated ivy for very exposed situations. Although hardy, it will be less tolerant of poor conditions than would a green ivy.

Coat for a wall

A garden wall can be made into a feature in its own right or into a colourful backdrop for other plants if contrasting variegated and green ivies are trained to scramble up it. Before planting ivy, it is essential to inspect the wall thoroughly and renew any defective pointing. Ivy will find its way through cracks and faults but will not harm a wall that is well maintained.

Decorative berries

Cut shoots of ivy to form part of your Christmas decoration, or use them as a contrasting component in winter flower arrangements. Do not cut ivy shoots after early March however; the blue-black berries will be overripe then and will fall off. Wear gloves when you are handling the plants as ivy sap can irritate the skin.

Versatile ivy The adaptable *Hedera* finds a place to grow in almost every garden. Use it to cover a shady wall, or as an unusual form of ground cover round a pathway.

Growth control

Ivy on house walls looks attractive, but make sure it does not grow under eaves and roof tiles, as it could pull them away from their settings. Keep ivy trimmed away from doors and window frames to prevent it penetrating the wood and cut it back in summer to 60cm (2ft) below the gutters.

Ivy versus trees

Do not let ivy take over a living tree. Unless you control it, the ivy will get the upper hand on its host, covering and smothering the foliage. Another danger is that snow and ice will collect on the ivy in winter and this extra weight may be enough to break the branches. When growing ivy up a tree, use it as a decoration for the lower part of the trunk only, letting it climb to the first fork of the tree at most.

An ivy hedge

Grow an easy-to-maintain hedge that will reach 1.5m (5ft) in height by taking cuttings from ivy in summer. Make sure these are taken from the flower and fruit-bearing adult ivy growth and not from the runners, which are juvenile growth. Plant the cuttings in pots containing a mixture of equal parts of sand and peat. Then, place them in a cold frame for one year. They can then be planted out to grow, using supports, into a hedge. (*See also* **Hedges**)

Express topiary

For an attractive topiary structure, plant a variegated ivy and erect a rough wire and wood pedestal, pyramid, column or cone over it. Cover this with wire mesh, bent into a simple shape. As it grows, the ivy will climb up and through the mesh, following the lines of your construction and developing into an eye-catching feature. Cut back the ivy each spring to keep it in shape. (*See also* **Topiary**)

Quick carpet

Create a handsome, weed-smothering green carpet to brighten up a dull, sunless corner of the garden by planting the Irish ivy *Hedera hibernica*, or one of the other ground-covering ivies. Use one plant to every 1m² (1sq yd) of ground for total cover in three or four years.

Gardener's potpourri

A bush of ivy

Though widely considered to be a harbinger of misfortune if brought into the house at any time other than Christmas Eve – and even then it must be removed by Twelfth Night – ivy nevertheless had many uses in the countryside. Water in which ivy leaves had been boiled was used as a light starch on wash days, and a poultice made of the leaves stewed in vinegar was a certain cure for corns.

Because the plant was sacred to Bacchus, a bush or garland of ivy over the door was the usual indication that a building was a tavern. Hence the old saying 'A good wine needs no bush', meaning that if the vintage is noble enough, it requires no advertising to sell it.

Japanese gardens

Low-maintenance paradise
A patio or terrace about 10m (32ft) square is about the right space in which to make a Japanese garden, a style that draws its inspiration from the landscape. Plants, water and natural materials are combined in simple patterns to create an atmosphere of harmony and tranquillity. Year-round interest is achieved by a careful choice of plants.

An oriental corner
Add a talking point by introducing Japanese characteristics into a secluded corner, which you can devote to an exploration of oriental style. To define it as a special place, surround it with a rendered wall, an undulating border of evergreens or perhaps a bamboo fence.

Cool, clear water
An essential element in a Japanese garden is water, whether running or still. A fountain, a small pond, a simple basin, such as a birdbath, or a bamboo pipe waterspout would make the necessary contribution. (See also **Birds**, **Fountains**, **Ponds**)

Natural sculptures
Structure the background of a Japanese garden with an arrangement of distinctively shaped, large stones, using them upright and flat. Raked pebbles or gravel are an important Japanese feature and are easy to maintain.

Achieving simplicity
Choose plants with distinctive leaves and in all shades of green to clothe the foreground of your garden. Restrict flowering plants to a distinguished and strategically placed few.

Eastern ornamentation
Enhance your garden's oriental character by adding a well-positioned small pavilion, snow lantern, stone bowl or an enigmatic Buddha statue.

The right furniture
Bamboo, rattan, or wooden furniture in simple styles will harmonise well with the vegetation and ambience of a Japanese garden. (See also *Garden furniture*)

Zigzag or straight?
Japanese paths wind or zigzag through the garden to maximise interest and invite attention to the various features. Set stones in, or on, the ground to follow the route most often taken. If you prefer a straighter path, align each of the stones carefully.

Stepping-stones
To supplement, or even replace, paths, the Japanese frequently install stepping-stones. To

Oriental harmony Arresting stands of waterside plants are reflected in the pool's tranquil surface.

make sure that you space these to best advantage, walk with your usual stride across the garden and mark each footfall with a small stick or a handful of sand. The ideal distance between the stones is usually 30–46cm (12–18in).

Walk with interest

Stepping-stones should be level, stable and at least 30cm (12in) square. Lay them either level with the soil or on, or level with, a bed of raked sand and gravel.

Non-slip selection

The stones should be non-slip and solid. Natural or reconstituted stone or small pavers are all suitable. Dig out the soil to a greater depth than the thickness of the stone and lay each one on a bed of hardcore and sand to prevent it from sinking. (See also **Paving**)

Jasmine

Beware of the morning sun

The hardiest of all jasmines is *Jasminum nudiflorum* (winter jasmine), but the flowers can be tender. If the jasmine is planted where it gets the morning sun, the warmth will bring a quick thaw after any winter frost and will bleach out the flower colour. It is best planted on north and west-facing walls with a slow, safe thaw.

Tie with care

Because it does not grow twining shoots to attach itself to a screen, winter jasmine will need careful tying back with plant ties to any trellis on which it is being grown.

Annual pruning

Winter jasmine needs fairly severe pruning every year after flowering. Cut out all old and straggly growths and prune back branches that have flowered. The young shoots that remain will receive all the plant's energy.

Penalty for forgetfulness

Always remember to prune winter jasmine each year. If you forget, by the second year you will find that old wood is choking the young, and drastic surgery will be necessary to streamline the tangled mass of dead shrub.

Longer-lasting sprays

Sprays of jasmine for indoor decoration can be made to last longer by immediately putting the newly cut stems into 2.5cm (1in) of boiling water in a heat-resistant jug. Leave them for a minute, then fill the jug with cold water and let the jasmine stand for an hour before taking it out to arrange it.

A scented frame for summer

Jasminum officinale (summer jasmine or white jasmine) is an easily cultivated climber that will provide a pretty framework for a window or doorway. Its evening-scented white flowers are set off by glossy foliage and will bloom from summer to early autumn.

Perfect for pergolas

Summer jasmine is an ideal shrub for growing up walls and the sides of pergolas. Avoid severe pruning – simply thin the plant's green stems in April or early May.

Creative climber

As well as being a graceful alternative to climbing plants such as clematis and roses, summer jasmine can be grown to form a fretwork of vigorous shoots and white flowers in the vicinity of other climbers.

Fragrance in the greenhouse

The wonderfully fragrant half-hardy climber *Jasminum polyanthum* blooms in winter and spring under glass. It is a perfect addition to a cool greenhouse or conservatory. Plant it in a large container. In very mild, protected locations, it can also be grown outside in a sheltered spot where it will flower in spring and summer.

The time to take cuttings

Propagate jasmine by taking semi-ripe cuttings in early July. Simple layering can be used if only one or two plants are needed.

Jerusalem artichokes

Two good reasons

Jerusalem artichokes are grown chiefly for their edible tubers, which are delicious in either a white sauce or a soup. An added bonus is that they grow to a height of at least 3m (10ft), providing a screen for the vegetable bed. In exposed areas, it is best to support them with wire stretched between two posts.

Repeat performances

Be certain that you enjoy Jerusalem artichokes because, once planted, they are liable to stay with you. A new plant will grow from even the smallest fragment of tuber that has been left in the ground.

Garden secrets

Confused identity

Jerusalem artichokes are not artichokes and they have nothing to do with Jerusalem. They are a species of sunflower, and are native to tropical America. However, the flavour of the tubers does somewhat resemble that of true artichokes. This was first recognised in Rome, where the plant made its European debut in 1617, and was consequently named *girasole articiocco* (sunflower artichoke), from which its present name is thought to be derived.

Junipers

Softening the look of a rock garden

Do not plant prostrate junipers just on level ground. With their interesting colour and texture, they make excellent cover for banks. And, if used next to dwarf shrubs, they can soften the flat look at the top of a rock garden.

Ideal for a patio

Dwarf conifers, including species of juniper such as *Juniperus communis* 'Compressa', do well in containers and always look good on a patio, where their foliage makes an ideal contrast to nearby plants and flowers.

Getting off the ground

Junipers are the only conifers that provide flat ground cover. But they also come as medium-sized shrubs and small trees. For two unusual junipers of upright habit, grow the greyish-green dwarf tree *Juniperus communis* 'Compressa' in the rock garden – a juniper that takes a decade to grow to 61–91cm (2–3ft) – and the pencil-like blue-grey *J. scopulorum* 'Skyrocket' as a specimen plant in the lawn. It will reach a height of 1.8m (6ft) after ten years.

Tied up against the snow

Junipers thrive in most soils but prefer those with some lime or chalk. And while they need little attention – no pruning other than a light trim in the summer if they begin to look untidy – the foliage of erect forms should be tied together fairly tight in winter with several bands of string to prevent branches being pulled out of shape by snow.

One for the shade

A juniper bush such as *Juniperus* × *media* 'Pfitzeriana' is one of the most popular of all conifers. It has good, year-round dense foliage, and is very useful for filling any spaces in the shade of taller trees.

Brightening borders in winter

Give borders winter colour with *Juniperus conferta* (the shore juniper). Its carpet-like, apple-green foliage has a bronze tint in winter, a contrast to the prostrate *J. horizontalis* and the spreading *J. communis* 'Depressa Aurea'.

Kiwi fruits

A plant for warm seasons

It is perfectly possible to grow kiwi fruits in a sunny, sheltered area with good rainfall, such as parts of west and south-west Britain, and the plants will tolerate several degrees of frost when dormant. They like a deep, well-drained soil, enriched with compost and fish, blood and bone fertiliser. Frost protection may be needed in spring. Provide a cover of horticultural fleece kept clear of the plants with bamboo canes.

Balancing the sexes

Kiwi fruits are dioecious, that is, the plants bear either male or female flowers. One male plant can fertilise up to seven or eight female plants, but for the average garden and consumption of kiwi fruits, one of each should be sufficient. Insects attend to the pollination and the female begins to bear fruit three to five years after planting.

Self-sufficient varieties

In recent years, self-fertile varieties have been introduced which do not need additional plants to ensure good fruit set. These are slowly becoming more widely available. Look out particularly for the variety 'Jenny'.

Giant vine

Kiwi plants need not only warmth and shelter, but plenty of space too – the vines grow to at least 7.5m (25ft). Support them on a post-and-wire framework, trellis or pergola on which the long stems will make a shady summer canopy. Prune dormant wood in December or January.

A brief history

Change of name

Chinese gooseberries, as the name implies, originated in China, though an edible variety developed in New Zealand has been grown commercially in that country for many years. When, in the 1960s, the fruits began to be exported to the United States, they became known as kiwi berries or kiwi fruits, after New Zealand's national bird. This was a promotional exercise and a recognition of the fruit's place of growth.

Storing the fruits

Store kiwi fruits in the salad compartment of the refrigerator or in a cool, dry, frost-free place, such as a garage or attic, on a bed of straw or in small crates. The higher the temperature at which the fruits are stored, the sooner they must be eaten.

Leave the stems

Pick kiwi fruits as soon as they begin to soften, retaining a little of the stem. Keep them cool until you want to eat them. At a temperature of 0°C (32°F), they will last for several months.

Keeping cats off

A semi-circle of wire netting or a few thorny branches placed round each young kiwi fruit plant are good ways to prevent cats from rubbing up against the plants and impeding their growth.

Labelling

Quick reference
When your seeds have been sown, impale the packets on small sticks or thin garden canes and cover each one with a transparent polythene bag. Secure the bags with an elastic band or twine, then push the stakes into the soil at the end of each row. They will provide a means of location and identification of the plants, and growing instructions too. Alternatively, you can use purpose-made packet holders.

Stone inscription
Collect a few small, attractively marked, flat stones from a beach or quarry and wash them thoroughly. Using waterproof paint, inscribe plant details with a fine brush and press the stones into the soil beside the plants.

New use for old plastic
Hang on to rigid, straight-sided, plastic food containers and cut them up into narrow strips to make weather-resistant plant labels. Fashion one end of each strip into a point, so that it can be pushed into the soil easily. With a permanent marker pen, inscribe the labels with the names and colours of your perennials, so that when plants die back at the season's end, you will know where they are and will not plant on top of them. On the backs, you could write the planting dates and where the plants were obtained.

Lettering on lolly sticks
Use flat ice-lolly sticks as plant labels in the greenhouse. The lettering will stand out more clearly if you paint the sticks with white emulsion paint first. If you are using plastic pots, paint stripes of emulsion paint on the rims and write the names on those.

That rustic look
To make labels that will mingle harmoniously with plants, split a thin bamboo cane in half lengthways, then cut across each half on the diagonal to produce short, pointed lengths. Inscribe plant names and colours on the bamboo with a permanent marker pen.

Blending with the background
Saw a branch, of about the same diameter as a baguette, into thin slices, smoothing one side of each with a sander. Drill a hole through the upper edge of each piece and thread string through it. With the plant name and planting date painted on them, use the wood pieces as labels for shrubs and young trees.

Dahlia ID
When dahlia tubers lifted in autumn have dried, write the name and colour onto each one with a waterproof felt tip pen before storing them away for winter. You will bless your foresight when you come to plant the tubers out again in spring and want to work out a colour scheme.

Ladybirds

Voracious visitor
Ladybirds, equally at home in woods, meadows and cities, are especially welcome in the garden, where they and their larvae are voracious devourers of aphids. Their large numbers are partly due to the fact that they have few natural enemies: their striking coloration serves as a warning to birds that they are evil-tasting and poisonous.

Organic control
A female ladybird lays about 200 eggs on aphid-infested plants. Her slate-blue larvae eat hundreds of aphids in their three-week lives. Providing your garden is not completely overrun with aphids, ladybirds can provide an efficient and organic way of controlling these pests.

Garden secrets

Colour coding
Use differently coloured permanent marker pens when inscribing plant names on labels. You might, for instance, use yellow for bulbs, white for perennials and blue for biennials. Then, seal with a coat of clear nail varnish.

Gardener's potpourri

Spotting ladybirds
There are some 40-odd species of ladybird in Britain, plus a few more that migrate annually from the Continent. They are mostly distinguished by their coloration and the number of spots on their wing-cases. There is a vegetarian 24-spotter, for example, and a totally black race of ladybirds that live in Glasgow and Merseyside, whose hue is claimed by the locals to be due to lack of sun. All are very much the friends of gardeners.

Lavatera

Colourful trumpets

Lavatera trimestris (mallow) is a bushy annual that showers a bed or border with prolific trumpet-shaped flowers during late summer and autumn. It is particularly effective at the back of a border because it grows 1m (3ft) tall. 'Silver Cup' produces glowing pink flowers while those of 'Loveliness' are a shade of deep rose. In contrast, 'Mont Blanc' has dazzling white flowers.

Sowing know-how

Sow annual lavatera seeds in March under glass, or in April in a sunny spot where you want them to flower, just covering them with soil. Do not sow in over-fertile soil, which encourages excessive leaf growth.

Pink profusion

Lavatera olbia, a vigorous shrubby mallow, can grow 2.4m (8ft) tall and flower exuberantly, with powdery pink flowers from May to November. Positioned carefully – it is not a tidy plant – lavatera is an asset in the garden. *L. arborea* (tree mallow) grows into a neater shape. 'Variegata' is an attractive cultivar.

Lavender

A good home

Warm, dry conditions suit lavender best. Plant in any well drained soil, in a sunny position where the roots will seek moisture deep in the soil, adding pot pieces to aid drainage. Lavender often does well in heavy soil for a while, but any winter waterlogging may well shorten its life. Take cuttings early in September from which to grow replacement plants.

New plants

Take 7.5–10cm (3–4in) heel cuttings from semi-woody non-flowering lavender shoots in August or early September. Insert in pots of cutting compost and overwinter in a cold frame. They can be moved to their flowering positions early in spring. Or try putting them straight into the garden. (*See also* **Cuttings**)

Cutting for drying

If you want to dry lavender, pick it when the flowers show colour but before they are fully open. Cut off the full length of the flower stalks, tie them together in small bunches and hang them upside-down in a cool, airy place, such as a shed, to dry.

Scented pathway

Plant *Lavandula angustifolia* (old English lavender), which has a height and spread of about 1m (3ft), beside a path. The silver-grey foliage exudes as much scent on sunny days in midwinter as the blue-purple flowers do from July to September. You will be able to pluck a leaf or flower as you pass and enjoy its unique scent all the year round.

Deep purple

The 'Hidcote' variety of old English lavender is more compact than others and reaches a height of up to 61cm (2ft). Its deep purple

Subtle shades A billowing bush of silvery blue lavender lends scent as well as style to the summer scene.

flowers combine well with delicate pink roses, such as the sweetly scented 'Warm Wishes'. *Lavandula angustifolia* 'Twickel Purple' has slender, purple flower spikes of up to 10cm (4in) long.

A flowering hedge

To create a fragrant and informal hedge with a profusion of softly coloured flowers in summer, plant different lavender species that will produce flowers in shades of purple, mauve, pink and white. The size and spread of the different species will vary, so you will need to clip the hedge to a uniform height.

Trim neatly

If you have left lavender to flower fully on the bush, cut off the dead flower stems and lightly trim the plants in late summer. Straggly plants may be cut back hard in March or April to promote bushy growth and encourage new shoots. However, lavender plants are inclined to grow leggy with age and are best replaced after five or six years.

What the law says

The boundaries of your garden will more than likely be shared by neighbours. To live happily side by side and enjoy the flourishing haven you have created, you need to know what your rights and responsibilities are according to the law.

A small problem in the garden may bring about a breakdown in good relations between neighbours if they are not aware of their obligations. Who pays for fence repairs? Can you trim a neighbour's tree that is spreading into your garden? Can you light a bonfire on your land? A friendly discussion can prevent a problem turning into a legal issue.

Planning permission for buildings

Talking to your local planning office before you begin any construction (or demolition) work could save you time and money. If the structure you build breaches the rules, you may have to remove it. You do not need to seek local authority approval to erect a greenhouse or a small shed within your property in which to store garden equipment and furniture. This is usually 'permitted development'. Most small changes – such as adding a porch or patio – fall into this category, but check your deeds for any special restrictions. A conservatory, however, is regarded as an extension to the house and may need permission. Much depends on its size and proximity to a boundary.

Boundary fences and walls

The upkeep of fences or walls is not generally shared – if the supporting posts or brick piers are on your side, the fence or wall is usually considered yours. It is a common error to believe that each property owner in a row of houses owns only one of the enclosing fences or walls. If in doubt, check the title deeds and plans of your property. A T or H-shaped mark is used to denote fencing or boundary responsibilities and is usually explained in the deeds. Title deeds or local regulations may oblige owners to keep walls and fences in good repair. Apart from these cases, there is no onus on you to repair boundaries. When

Consult first Neighbours can object to your plans, so ask for their approval.

responsibility is shared, you cannot make your neighbours repair their side. If you cannot persuade your neighbours to repair a wall or fence you could offer to pay half the cost. Negotiation costs less than legal fees. A wall or fence built or changed to more than 2m (6ft 6in) high, or 1m (3ft 3in) if adjacent to a highway, must have planning permission. Listed buildings are subject to different criteria.

Problems with trees

If you are considering chopping down or pruning a tree, first find out if there is a Tree Preservation Order (TPO). These orders, created by the local planning authority, make it illegal to prune, fell, uproot or lop a particular tree. The order applies to all subsequent owners of the land – if you do not know a TPO exists and damage the tree, you can be fined. The maximum fine for felling a protected tree is £20,000 or up to twice its timber value (whichever is the greater) while the maximum for damage (pruning, lopping) is £2,500. In addition, trees are subject to special laws in conservation areas. They require that you give the local authority six weeks' notice before felling, uprooting, lopping or pruning a tree, so that they can decide whether to make a TPO. The penalty for carrying out tree work without giving notice is the same as for a breach of a TPO.

Prune carefully You can trim a neighbour's tree, but you must check for a preservation order and return any fruit.

Roots and overhanging branches

The law gives you the right to cut off branches overhanging your property. However, you must return what you have cut off (including fruit) to your neighbours.

You are entitled to remove any roots growing into your garden that are damaging foundations and hindering the growth of plants. If the roots are very deep or particularly awkward to remove, you may be able to reclaim through your household insurance policy the costs of getting the work done professionally.

If a tree growing in your garden falls down or sheds branches either through old age or disease – causing damage in the process – you are liable. Regularly check all trees within your boundaries for danger signs.

Bonfires

When garden rubbish collects, you have the right to burn it as long as the fire is watched while alight and kept under control. If fires cause a nuisance to neighbours – for instance, if they are regular occurrences or material other than garden rubbish is burnt – they can ask the local authority environmental officers to restrict your actions. If possible, use a shredder to break up garden cuttings, which can then be taken to your council dump or composted. This is more neighbourly as well as more environmentally friendly than lighting a fire.

Keeping an eye Make sure that you have the tools to control a bonfire's size.

Ponds and water

Landowners are legally, as well as morally, responsible for seeing that their land is reasonably safe for all those entitled or likely to use it. For example, if you have a pond, cover it with wire netting to prevent small children falling in.

If you have a rock garden with, say, a fountain and a fish pond, you are choosing to 'store water on the land'. This would make you liable should the supporting walls give way, allowing water to escape into your neighbour's property. You would have to compensate the neighbours if an accident occurred. The same would be true if oil for central heating were to escape from an outdoor tank and ruin a neighbour's garden, even if it was not the tank owner's fault.

Safety first For peace of mind if you have young children, keep water covered.

Water companies can increase the annual rates if you use a hose or sprinkler or draw water from an outside tap even if a hose is not used. During water shortages, temporary bans on the use of hoses and sprinklers are backed up by fines.

Weeds and pests

Under the Weeds Act 1959 a householder can be ordered to prevent the spread of certain damaging weeds. These include spear thistle, creeping or field thistle, curled or broad-leaved dock and ragwort. Failing to do so may incur a fine. Rats, mice, moles, voles, foxes and rabbits can create problems in the garden. Your local authority will be able to give advice on dealing with them; if a pest control expert is suggested, there may be a fee involved. Cold will kill off wasps but in warmer seasons the local council will be able to direct you to an approved contractor who will clear a wasp nest for a fee. If bees swarm into your garden, the only action you can take is to find a beekeeper who will direct the swarm to a suitable hive. Your council should be able to provide you with the name of a local beekeeper. If you find serious pests or diseases in your garden such as Colorado beetle or *Xanthomonas fragariae*, a disease of strawberry plants, report them to Defra's Plant Health & Seeds Inspectorate.

Invaders Animals such as rabbits may appear harmless enough but they can wreck your vegetable plot.

Entry into your garden

Several authorities have the right to enter your garden without notice or consent, including police officers in an investigation, firefighters and customs officials looking for contraband or illegally imported animals or plants. Water company officials can also come in to find out if water is being wasted, misused or polluted. Local authority officers can enter to investigate breaches of health, planning or environmental laws. In Scotland, water companies and the local authority must give 24 hours notice.

Neighbours are allowed in to repair or maintain common services or walls. Reasonable notice must be given and force must not be used. Neighbours can enter your garden to retrieve any fruit that has fallen – in law it remains their property. In Scotland, there is no general right to access your neighbour's land. In individual cases, access may be granted in specific circumstances, sometimes listed in the title deeds.

Lawn care

Homemade seed dispenser
A seed dispenser is a useful aid to even sowing over a large area. Punch holes in the bottom of a large, empty can and use it to sprinkle grass seed at an even rate. Also use it to control the flow when spreading powdered fertiliser.

Grass types
Select grass seed according to whether you require a smooth showpiece lawn, a place where children and pets can play, or a meadow-like lawn where wild flowers grow.

How much seed?
Check the advice on your packet of grass seed before sowing as different blends are sown at different rates. Add a little more at the edges of the lawn, which need a denser coverage. If you are not used to sowing grass seed, help to ensure even sowing by first marking out an area 1m² (1sq yd), then weighing out and filling a container with the quantity of seed specified on the packet to cover that space. Sow half the seed across in one direction and then half across in the other direction. Use garden lines or string for larger areas.

Turf without tears
When laying turfs to make a lawn, lay them close together on a well-prepared, level soil bed. Fill any crevices with sandy soil, then firm gently, using a tamper (a thick board with a vertically attached pole handle) or the back of a shovel. Lay turf in late autumn.

Growing mats
Garden centres sell grass-seed impregnated fibre mats, which are light in weight and easy to lay. They are ideal for replacing a single turf and the fibre will disintegrate in time.

Spiking the lawn
Aerating the lawn is a vital, if wearisome, task. Once a year, in early autumn, spike the grass by pushing the prongs of a garden fork into the ground to a depth of at least 7.5cm (3in), moving the fork backwards and forwards to increase the size of the holes. The insertions should be no more than 15cm (6in) apart. After this treatment, sprinkle fertiliser over the lawn and – unless it rains – water the grass thoroughly within two days.

The right way to water
As a rough guide, water the lawn thoroughly at weekly intervals in dry spells in summer. Regular, thorough watering will help the grass to develop deep roots. Avoid frequent shallow waterings, which encourage shallow rooting. The weather and your garden's soil type will determine whether the lawn needs watering more or less frequently. To cut down moisture loss from the lawn by evaporation, it is best to water in the evening.

Green it up
Epsom salts add magnesium and iron to the soil and will feed the grass, making your lawn the greenest on the street. Add 2 tablespoons to 4 litres (1 gallon) of water and spread it on your lawn. Water it well with plain water to make sure the mixture soaks into the grass.

Seasonal feeding
Be sure you use the right fertiliser on your lawn. Spring and summer lawn fertilisers have a high nitrogen content to promote lush, green growth. Autumn lawn fertiliser is low on nitrogen but high in phosphates. This stimulates root growth and helps the grass to survive if the winter is severe. Both types also contain some potassium – essential for healthy year-round growth.

Dead centre
If a bald patch develops in the middle of your lawn – perhaps the result of a mower petrol spillage – do not re-seed it. You are unlikely to find seed to match the surrounding grass and, in such a conspicuous spot, the new grass will stand out like a sore thumb. Cut out a turf surrounding the bare patch and replace it with one of the same size and shape taken from a less obvious part of the lawn. Make the repair in autumn when the turf will blend in imperceptibly. It is unlikely to root well in summer. Fill in, level and re-seed the place from where you took the turf.

Nitrogen warning
Apply nitrogen-rich spring and summer lawn fertiliser to grass only when the ground is moist. If applied to dry soil, the fertiliser will burn the grass.

Spreading the burden
When attending to plants in beds bordering the lawn, use a kneeling board. This will distribute your weight evenly, help to preserve the grass from compression and bruising, and protect lawn edges.

Damaged lawn edges
If an edge of your lawn is damaged, cut out a rectangular section of grass that includes the spoiled area. Slide a spade underneath it, lift the turf and reverse it so that the bare patch is turned inwards to the lawn. Line the turf up with the edge and firm gently. Sift some soil on the patch to level it with the lawn, sprinkle on a little grass seed and water the area thoroughly.

Instant turf
Ensure that you have an emergency supply of turf to repair damage to the lawn by making an occasional grass path across the vegetable garden. Part of the path can be removed for repairs, then resown later.

Spring flourish
Splash the lawn with colour in spring by planting drifts of bulbs – snowdrops, crocuses, daffodils. However, you would be wise to restrict them to a single area, perhaps near the edge of the lawn, since you will be unable to cut the grass until the foliage dies down in summer.

Lawn alternatives

In shady areas, try ground-cover plants such as dead nettle, ivy, pachysandra, periwinkle or St John's wort instead of grass. If only grass will do, sow a grass-seed mixture designed for shady sites. You may need to re-sow annually.

A wild-flower lawn

A lawn studded with wild flowers is appealing if you have space. Prepare the ground as for a lawn: treading it flat and raking the earth. Sow a mixture of grass and wild-flower seeds. Some garden centres have suitable collections with cornfield annuals like cornflower and field poppy for colour in the first summer. When the lawn has grown, cut paths through it and mow regularly. Mow the entire lawn in July or August when flowering is over and seeds have scattered. (*See also* **Wild-flower meadows**)

Correct aftercare

Never apply fertiliser to wild-flower lawns and take care to remove cut grass from the paths to ensure no nutrients are returned to the soil.

See also **Scarifying**

Lawn mowers

Safety first

When using an electric lawn mower, plug a circuit breaker into the socket. Plug the mower lead into the circuit breaker – it will cut off the power instantly if the lead gets caught in the blades. Never use an electric lawn mower when the grass is wet. When mowing the lawn, drape the cable over your shoulder to avoid cutting through it as you work; it also keeps it out of your way. Never pull a mower towards you, always push it away. Keep the mower switched off and unplugged when not in use; that way, it cannot be started accidentally. Before examining or cleaning an electric mower, make sure it is unplugged. By the same token,

remove the lead from the spark plug of petrol-driven mowers before working on them.

Protecting young trees

Large trees may be fairly impervious to knocks from the lawn mower, but smaller trees may be more easily damaged. If they are located in a vulnerable position, protect the stems with lengths of hot-water pipe insulation. For its first four or five years, a young tree will grow best in a small well-mulched bed with no grass round its base.

Mind your feet

Wear stout shoes or boots when you are mowing. This simple measure is often forgotten in summer, even though failure to wear the correct footwear is a very common cause of painful garden accidents. Another good, practical reason for changing into heavier footwear whenever you mow is that grass stains can prove extremely difficult, if not impossible, to remove from summer shoes made of canvas and other fabrics.

How to make stripes

If you want your lawn to have a distinguishing finish of alternate dark and light stripes, remember that only a mower with a rear roller can supply this effect. Choosing a model that you find easy to manoeuvre will also help you achieve neat stripes.

Routine maintenance

After using your lawn mower, disconnect the power and clean the motor and blades, but be sure to put on protective gloves and to use a brush for the task. Take care to remove encrusted grass mowings from the underside of the mower. Dry the machine, then wipe it over with an oily rag.

Make the right choice

A mower to suit your lawn

When selecting a mower, bear in mind your lawn size and the finish you require

Manual mowers

If your lawn is small and well maintained, a manual mower is all that is required to keep it in trim. The side-wheel models are light and easy to push but are not ideal when it comes to cutting the edges of the lawn. Rear-roller mowers, on the other hand, cut edges very well, and will put stripes on the lawn too.

Powered cylinder mowers

Cylinder mowers with rear rollers produce stripes on the lawn, and the cut made by the moving and fixed blades is close and clean. Electric cylinder mowers are much quieter than petrol-driven machines.

Powered rotary mowers

Rough or long grass will be tackled effectively by the blade of a rotary mower, which spins at high speed. For large areas of lawn a petrol-driven rotary mower is more suitable than an electric one. Rotary mowers with grass-boxes offer the additional advantage of clearing fallen leaves in autumn.

Powered hover mowers

Hover mowers that, like rotary mowers, cut grass with a spinning blade, are light and easy to manoeuvre beneath overhanging shrubs. They can manage gentle slopes as easily as flat ground.

Lawn mowing

The perfect lawn
To achieve a striped effect, mow the lawn in parallel strips of equal width. If you want to give a lawn a really velvety finish, mow up and back along the same strip.

Reaching awkward places
An electric or petrol-driven trimmer, which cuts by means of a rotating nylon line, is useful for cutting grass in places that a mower is too big to reach, as well as for trimming edges. Wear goggles when using a trimmer because stones and dust are often thrown up by the high-speed action.

Making a start
Begin by mowing a double strip across each end of the lawn, to ensure that when turning, no grass is missed, or scuffed, by the mower.

Getting a straight run
Limit the number of obstacles in the middle of the lawn to one or two. Mowing will be more of a pleasure if features like statues or benches are positioned at the edges.

Give the grass a lift
Before the first mowing in spring, gently lift the grass with a spring-tined rake. But do not mow wet grass. The finish will be uneven and the grass will clog the mower. During autumn, dew

Garden secrets

Clippings in dry weather
In hot, dry weather, remove the mower's grass-box. Uncollected clippings will shade the soil, reducing moisture loss and the risk of the grass being scorched and turning brown.

may persist on the grass all day. If bright or windy conditions are forecast, use a besom to 'switch' off the dew, to help the grass to dry.

Trimmer tip
Use a nylon-line trimmer to tidy round trees growing out of grass. But have a plastic pipe handy, cut in half length-ways, to lean against the tree and protect the bark from scarring.

Fertiliser rule
During summer let two days elapse after mowing before applying fertilisers or weed killers. During periods of slower growth, wait four days after mowing before applying them.

Timely trim
During late spring and early summer, mow a fine lawn closely every three days, a utility lawn every week and a rougher lawn every ten days. Double the intervals during slower growth periods. Mowing is not beneficial in winter, except in unusually mild periods.

Variable height
During summer, cut a fine lawn to a height of 1.3cm (½in), a utility lawn to 2.5cm (1in) and a rougher lawn to 5cm (2in). On the first spring cut, remove the top of the grass only, then lower the level of the blade on successive mowings. (See also **Drought**)

Slope safety
Always mow across a slope. This will ensure effective cutting and will also give better control of the mower. To stand above the mower and cut down the slope is exhausting, for you are hauling on the weight of the

mower, while if you stand below and cut up, there is a risk that the mower will slip and run over your foot.

Collect or leave?
If left uncollected, grass clippings will provide some nutrients as they decay but if they accumulate, particularly in wetter periods, they look unsightly and encourage moss and worms. Lawn weeds may also be spread. If your mower has no grass-box rake up the clippings, except in hot and dry weather.

The wrong kind of stripes
If pale stripes appear on blades of grass after mowing with a cylinder mower, it means that the grass is being squeezed instead of cut. Use the adjusting nuts to move the mower bottom plate closer to the cylinder blades.

A wrapper for cuttings
When mowing a large lawn, spread a polythene sheet over a convenient area and empty the grass-box onto it. All the grass clippings will then be in one place and easily carried away when you have finished.

Layering

Choosing the stem
Select a pliable, low-growing stem, preferably from this year's growth, but certainly no older than last year's.

The right conditions
A layered stem roots much faster and produces more, and stronger, roots in a well-drained environment. Insert it in a mixture of equal parts of garden soil, leafmould and coarse sand.

Speeding the rooting
Encourage a shrub stem to root by making a slanting cut and dusting it with hormone rooting powder before bending and planting the stem. Alternatively, tie a wire or strong nylon thread tightly round the part to be planted. Natural rooting hormones will accumulate there in two to three months.

Strip leaves first

When layering plants, it is important to strip leaves from the part of a stem that is to be bent down and inserted in the soil to form a new plantlet. Leaves left on the stem will rot and inhibit the formation of roots. Secure the stem in the soil with a stone or a bent wire. A flat stone will keep the soil cool and moist during dry, warm spells.

Create something new

If you notice that one of your plants has grown a stem of a different colour or shape to the others, you could experiment by layering it to create a new type of plant.

Mass production

Serpentine layering is used on the young, trailing, pliable shoots of climbers such as honeysuckle, clematis, jasmine and wisteria. Make slanting cuts not more than halfway through the shoot close to three or four leaf joints, leaving two pairs of leaves between each cut. Dust rooting powder over the cut joints, then bend and plant them, securing them in the soil with U-shaped pieces of wire.

Timely separation

Shoots layered in spring should form plantlets at the cut joints by autumn or the following spring. Separate them from the parent plant, and from one another, and plant out. Do not let plantlets become too well established – it will be hard to uproot them without damage.

Loganberry lore

Bend down a new season's loganberry shoot at the end of July and plant the tip. Cut off the rooted tip just above a bud in October but do not move the new plant until November.

Transplanting made easy

A stem layered in a plastic pot is particularly easy to transplant once a new plant has formed. Cut a 10cm (4in) slit down the side of the pot, insert the stem and fill the pot with soil. When the plantlet has formed, you will then be able to separate it from the parent plant without causing any disturbance to its immediate environment.

Sleeve on a stem

If a stem cannot be layered at soil level, take the soil to a stem. This process is called air layering. First, choose a stem and strip the leaves from a portion of it. Then, make a slanting upward cut halfway through the stem from just below a joint, dust the cut with hormone rooting powder and keep the cut open with a matchstick. Pack moss into the cut, then wrap an opaque polythene sleeve over the stem, tying the lower end in tightly, 7.5cm (3in) below the cut. Pack the sleeve with a moistened mixture of moss and potting medium before closing the top to make the sleeve airtight. Check the inside of the packed polythene sleeve for roots at regular intervals. When they appear, remove the layered section from the parent plant and pot it up.

Leeks

Prolonged crop

Leek varieties are divided into three groups, early, mid-season and late, so it pays to grow a variety from each group so you can be sure of a long succession. The season starts with 'King Richard' and 'Lyon Prizetaker', while 'Albinstar' and 'Giant Winter Carina' are good mid-season varieties. For late leeks, look for 'Toledo' or 'Musselburgh' – the latter is the traditional favourite.

Growing know-how

Successful leek crops

Prepare the soil to give leeks the right conditions and they will thrive.

- Between December and February, prepare the bed in a sunny spot. Dig the ground well and incorporate well-rotted compost or manure. Leave the ground rough for frost to break down
- Sow maincrop leeks in March, in rows 15cm (6in) apart and 1.3cm (½in) deep drills. Thin to 3.8cm (1½in) apart.
- In May, before transplanting, work into the top few centimetres of soil in the main bed, 30g (1 oz) superphosphate and 15g (½oz) potassium sulphate for every square metre (square yard).
- Transplant the seedlings to the main bed when they are about 20cm (8in) long and as thick as pencils, in June or early July. Allow 23cm (9in) between holes and 23cm (9in) between rows.
- Hoe between rows and weed by hand between the leeks. Water well if dry.
- A month after transplanting, put a collar round each leek stem to assist blanching.

Winter harvest

Before the first frosts, cover the spaces between the rows of leeks with a layer of dead leaves or ferns, at least 5cm (2in) thick. This will prevent the soil from freezing – unless, of course, it is exceptionally cold – and you will then be able to harvest your leeks in any type of weather.

Going for growth

There are several factors that govern the size of the leek crop. The young plants should be as large as possible when they are planted. Sow seeds in March and plant out seedlings 10–12 weeks later when they are pencil thick in order to ensure that they have a long growing season. The soil must be rich and fertile and the leeks

Blanch with collars

If the technique of blanching leeks by planting the seedlings in furrows or deep holes does not appeal, plant the stems just 7.5cm (3in) deep. When the leeks are 15cm (6in) above the ground, cover each one with a tube of corrugated cardboard or a length of plastic drainpipe 5–7.5cm (2–3in) in diameter. The collars will exclude light and blanch the crop.

should be planted out with a spacing of 23cm (9in) all round. This growing pattern results in the heaviest yield of leeks. If you wish to grow even larger individual leeks, however, the spacing all round can be increased to 30cm (12in).

Mini-leeks

Some cooks like the tenderness of mini-leeks, which are grown by sowing the seeds about 1.3cm (½in) apart in rows 15cm (6in) apart where the leeks are to mature – they are not transplanted like other leeks. Mini-leeks are ready three to four months after sowing, when they are about the thickness of a pencil. The varieties 'King Richard' and 'Lavi' respond best to this treatment.

Blanching the stems

To blanch leeks properly, it is necessary to plant them deeply (see also **Garden secrets**, above). Make a furrow 7.5cm (3in) deep, then make 7.5cm (3in) holes with a dibber and drop in the seedlings. Water gently to wash some soil over and through the roots. The holes will fill up when the bed is hoed.

Beat severe cold snaps

To ensure an uninterrupted leek supply when severe frost is forecast, dig up some of your leeks and lay them on the floor of the shed or garage. Cover the roots and stems with sacking or other protective material, leaving the tops uncovered.

Lemons

In a cold climate

Lemons are reasonably tough and can withstand quite low temperatures, though not frost. Therefore, plant them in tubs of rich, well-drained soil that can be brought indoors for the winter and, during the growing season, water them frequently, preferably with rainwater, and give them a weekly feed of liquid manure. Prevent chlorosis with a springtime dose of sequestrene. The end result is a delightful tree with aromatic leaves, wonderful flowers and brilliant fruit.

Hardy choice

For hardiness, try the hybrid cultivar 'Meyer', which flowers and fruits at intervals during the course of the year.

Pollinating flowers

Increase fruit yield by transferring pollen between flowers with an artist's brush. Do so in the middle of the day when pollen is ripe.

The far-travelled lemon

Lemons seem to have originated in central India, reaching the Mediterranean in about AD 300. They were marvelled at in various southern European courts in the 12th and 13th centuries, but were not widely known until about 1500. In the ensuing decades, lemon trees became a feature of great gardens, where they were grown in wheeled tubs and pushed indoors on chilly days; they were as much valued for the scent of their flowers as for their fruit.

As early as 1601, lemon juice was recognised as a preventative of scurvy, and not long after was being dabbed on fashionable skins to whiten them. By the early 18th century, lemonade and lemon barley water were popular drinks.

Lettuces

Pace sowings

Make staggered small sowings of lettuces to avoid a row bolting – that is, running to seed before they are ready to harvest. When you see one sowing start to germinate, you should make another sowing immediately. This should give you a long succession.

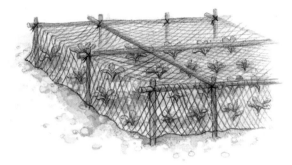

Protect seedlings from birds

Remove the bottom leaves from lettuce seedlings before transplanting them to promote strong growth and prevent birds from pulling them up. Place netting on low supports over the seedlings if they need further protection.

Getting ahead

To grow lettuces quickly, buy strips of young seedlings from a garden centre, plant them out about 20cm (8in) apart in a moist, fertile soil, and water well.

Avoid bolting

Lettuces are particularly prone to bolting. This problem is caused by a check to growth at some stage during their development; delay in transplanting is frequently a cause, as are hot weather, fluctuating temperatures, overcrowding, and dry roots resulting from insufficient watering. Always plant lettuces in light shade if possible and at the recommended planting distance. Try to ensure they are well watered.

The best for the smallest space

The way to obtain the largest continuous supply of lettuces from the smallest area is to grow them by the leaf lettuce technique. Any lettuce may be used, but cos varieties such as

Make the right choice

Know your lettuces

New lettuces from all over Europe give greater variety than ever before.

Batavian Thick-leaved, tasty crisphead, often with red-tinged leaves. Good are 'Regina dei Ghiacci', 'Rouge Grenobloise'.

Butterhead The traditional soft-leaved, hearted lettuce. Good varieties include 'Avondefiance' and 'Debby'.

Cos Tall, with a distinctive flavour and firm heart. Good varieties include 'Corsair' and 'Lobjoits Green Cos'.

Crisphead Flat hearts of crisp leaves, slow to bolt. Good varieties include 'Pennlake', 'Sioux' (red) and 'Webbs Wonderful'.

Greenhouse Outdoor varieties rarely succeed if sown in autumn to grow in the greenhouse. Good greenhouse varieties are 'Kwiek' (butterhead), 'Marmer' (crisphead).

Iceberg Crisphead lettuces that make large hearts, depending on spacings. 'Malika' and 'Saladin' are good varieties.

Loose-leaf Cos lettuces grown at very close spacing to produce a large yield from a small area. 'Lobjoits Green Cos' and 'Valmaine' can be grown like this.

Mini-lettuces Small-headed lettuces. Good varieties are 'Little Gem' and 'Tom Thumb'.

Picking Do not develop a heart, leaves are picked over a long period. Good varieties include 'Red Salad Bowl' and 'Salad Bowl'.

Winter Few are tough enough to be sown in autumn/harvested in spring, but include 'Valdor' (butterhead), 'Winter Density' (cos).

'Lobjoits Green Cos' and 'Valmaine' would do particularly well. Sow the seeds every week for two months from April, thinning the plants to 5cm (2in) apart. After four to eight weeks when the plants are about 10–12.5cm (4–5in) high, harvest by cutting them off 1.3–2.5cm (½–1in) above the soil. They will re-sprout and be ready for cutting again seven to eight weeks after the first cut. This can be repeated two or three times before the plants deteriorate. Keep them well watered and give weekly liquid feeds.

Filling the gaps

If your vegetable garden is overcrowded during May, sow lettuce seeds in trays and when the first gaps appear in the vegetable plot in July, slip in the seedlings.

Keeping a neat edge

Keep the symmetry of lettuces grown as a decorative edging to a flowerbed by picking alternate plants only.

Harvest time

Cut lettuces early in the morning while the dew is still on them. Select first those with firm, well-filled hearts and cut with a sharp knife just below the bottom leaves.

Constant supply

For a constant supply of lettuce leaves, grow loose-leaf lettuces that produce plenty of tasty leaves but no hearts. Harvest this type by regularly picking the best leaves from each plant

in a row. As the leaves are picked from the outside, more leaves develop in the centre. 'Salad Bowl' and 'Red Salad Bowl' have intricately curled leaves that add an interesting texture to salads. Sow in spring and thin the seedlings to 30cm (12in) apart each way. Surplus can be harvested and stored in a polythene bag in a refrigerator.

Dealing with diseases

Lettuces are prone to attack from a number of fungal diseases but, rather than using chemical sprays, look for varieties that are resistant to disease. They are being improved all the time, so check the latest catalogues for the newest and most resistant varieties.

Helpful hoeing

Hoeing will bring cutworms (large, grey-brown caterpillars), which sever lettuce stems, to the soil surface for birds to eat.

Growing know-how

A timetable for lettuces

For sowing times, see the chart below and, to ensure a steady supply of lettuces from April to October, sow seeds at fortnightly intervals, rather than all at once.

Type	Sow	First thinning	Second thinning	Harvest
Summer varieties	Mid March to August	When big enough to handle	When plants touch	June–October
Spring varieties	September	When big enough to handle	March	April–May

Lichen

Easy removal
Lichen does no harm to trees – it takes its nourishment from the air rather than from its host. If it grows on trees with ornamental bark, however, you may wish to remove it, and this is done quite easily with a stiff scrubbing brush and water. On paving and tiles, it can be more of a problem since it makes them slippery. Remove it with bleach and a stiff broom, taking care to keep the bleach away from your plants. Alternatively, buy a proprietary moss control from the garden centre.

Encouraging growth
Walls of raw, new brick can be made to look more mature by encouraging lichens to grow upon them. Do so by painting the wall (or stone garden ornament) with liquid seaweed fertiliser or with yoghurt.

Lilac

A wealth of choice
Single, double and semi-double varieties of the fragrant, lilac flowers of *Syringa vulgaris* (common lilac) hybrids all have cottage-garden charm. Choose, for instance, a single-flowered variety from lilac-blue 'Firmament', deep purple 'Massena' and the largest single, white-flowered variety 'Maud Notcutt'. All bloom in May. Among the double varieties, grow the purple-lavender flowers of 'Katherine Havemeyer', which are heavily scented, and the alabaster-white flowers of 'Madame Lemoine'. The rose-pink buds of semi-double, scented 'Madame Antoine Buchner' open to rose-mauve flowers, the blooms of 'Belle de Nancy' are purplish red when they open from lilac-pink buds, and the scented red flowers of 'Mrs Edward Harding' are outstanding. May and early June are the lilac's flowering times.

Pruning policy
Lilacs can get rather leggy unless an effective pruning policy is adopted. Plants should be multi-stemmed from the base and should have a total of five to seven stems. Cut out one of these main stems each autumn in order to achieve a succession of new growth from the base. After pruning, apply a tree and shrub fertiliser to the plant to encourage the new growth.

Energy conservation
Deadhead lilac bushes after flowering, unless you have picked all the flowers already. This will direct the shrub's energy into making new shoots rather than it being wasted on producing seeds.

Autumn pruning
From October onwards, cut weak lilac branches back to the main stem, even if they have produced plenty of flowers. Leave only the strong, healthy branches to grow, otherwise straggly growth will result instead of a well-shaped tree.

Climbing companion
After flowering, add another dimension to lilac foliage by growing a non-invasive flowering climber beside the shrub. Try a rose-purple perennial sweet pea, such as *Lathyrus latifolius*, a variety of *Clematis texensis*, or orange *Eccremocarpus scaber* (Chilean glory flower). (*See also* **Climbing plants**)

Lilies

What to look for
Lily bulbs must never be allowed to dry out completely. On individual bulbs, look for closely packed scales and reject any that have dry, flaky scales or scales that are too damp.

Care and attention
When buying bulbs at the end of the season, some may have become dry. Sink them into trays of moist peat or coir for a few days to help to plump them up before planting out.

On light, chalky soil
Fork some leafmould, or compost with a little bone meal, into light, chalky soil before planting the bulbs.

On heavy, moist soil
In addition to enriching the soil, line each planting hole with coarse sand, and put coarse sand round each bulb. Lilies dislike dry soil, but are also sensitive to excess moisture.

When to plant
Plant lily bulbs between October and March in sun or in partial shade. *Lilium candidum* (madonna lily) is an exception and should be planted just before the end of August, so that its winter rosette of leaves will have time to grow. Transplant lilies in autumn, when the flowering period is over.

Check the depth
Basal-rooting lilies will be happy with 5cm (2in) of soil covering them, but stem-rooting lilies – those that have roots on the stems as well as on the base of the bulbs – should be planted to a depth of three to four times the height of the bulbs. An exception is *Lilium candidum*, which should be planted with the nose of the bulb just below the ground.

Beware slugs
If the growing tips are eaten, lilies will not flower, so it is vital to protect them from attack by slugs early in the year. (*See also* **Slugs and snails**)

No hoeing

Do not hoe round lilies at the time when the growing tips are emerging from the soil. It is very easy to damage them.

Enrich depleted soil

Lilies are hungry feeders and exhaust the nutrients in soil. Every three or four years, in autumn, remove the soil on top of and around the bulbs and replace it with an equal-parts mixture of good garden soil and leafmould. In heavy soil, first pour a few handfuls of sand directly over the bulb.

Stake tall lilies

In spring, provide each lily that will reach a height of over 1m (3ft) with a bamboo cane support. This should stand just below the eventual flowering height of the stem. Tie the stem into the cane as the lily grows.

A bright addition

You can cheer up dull hedges or shrubs by placing a few pots of lilies in front of them. The bright flowers will liven up a summer view and you can then remove the pots and put them in an out-of-the-way corner of the garden when the blooms have faded.

Health control

Botrytis, a disease which occurs in warm, damp summers, may cause distortion of lily flowers and foliage if it becomes established. To control it, spray lilies regularly with a systemic fungicide during spring and summer.

Watch out for lily beetles

The red lily beetle and its larvae devour lily leaves, stems and flower buds. Spray holes in any of these parts with fenitrothion, permethrin or the systemic insecticide heptenophos.

Plenty in a pot

Potted lilies look best in a crowd, so plant four or five bulbs of a basal-rooting variety – those whose roots grow from the bottom of the bulb – in a 30cm (12in) pot. Start with at least 2.5cm (1in) of gravel in the bottom of the pot to ensure good drainage, then add 7.5–10cm (3–4in) of peat-based compost. Tap the pot on

the ground to settle the compost and gently firm it down. Be sure to space the bulbs about 2.5cm (1in) apart; it is crucial that the bulbs do not touch either the sides of the pot or each other. Top up with compost and gently firm it down so that you leave about 2.5cm (1in) clear between the soil and the rim of the pot. Place the pot in a sunny position, never let it dry out, and feed the bulbs regularly with a liquid fertiliser.

Ahead of schedule

A good many lilies can be persuaded to flower at much earlier times than those advertised in the catalogues. Pot them up in autumn and bury the pots in the garden beneath 10cm (4in) of sand. Sprinkle slug pellets round the pots to prevent damage. When the top growth appears, gradually bring the plants into full daylight. Keep the compost moist and move the lilies to a greenhouse or living room with a temperature of about 16°C (61°F). After flowering, plunge the pots in a shady spot, keep the bulbs well watered and let the foliage die down naturally. Repot the bulbs annually or plant them in the garden.

Growing from seeds

Most lilies can be grown from seed, but new plants raised from seed that was collected from hybrids or named varieties rarely resemble the parents. Allow the seeds to ripen on the plants, then sow them immediately. Stand the pots in a

Flame-coloured flowers Clumps of orange lilies create a spectacular blaze against a green, leafy backdrop.

cold frame for the winter, then bring them into a warm greenhouse in spring. Most lilies will germinate and grow by this method but may not flower for five years.

Bulbs from the stems
Small bulbs, known as bulbils, form on the stems of some lilies just below ground level and can be detached in early autumn. Carefully remove the soil and plant the bulbils where wanted. Protect them during the first winter with a thick mulch.

Planting aerial bulbils
Some lilies, such as *Lilium bulbiferum* and *L. tigrinum* (tiger lily), produce bulbils at the base of leaves next to the stem. Detach them at the end of the season when the foliage begins to yellow. Plant them about 2.5cm (1in) deep in compost in a seed tray. Place the tray in a cold

frame and plant out the young lilies the following autumn. Do not plant the bulbils directly into the garden. Their young shoots might be demolished by slugs.

Bulbs from scales
Lilies are unusual in that the scales that make up the bulb can be removed and planted to form new bulbs. Do this in autumn, by gently detaching healthy and undamaged outer scales from the bulb. Wash them well and soak them in fungicide for half an hour. Place the scales in a polythene bag with enough vermiculite to keep them separate, tie the top and put the bag in a warm cupboard, or in a propagator. After about six weeks new bulbils will form on the scales, when the bag should be transferred to the salad drawer of the refrigerator for three months. In spring, plant the scales with the bulbils in pots or carefully detach and plant the bulbils individually. Keep them in a cool greenhouse where they will flower in three to five years.

Speed up spring flowering
In early March, water lilies of the valley if the ground is dry, then place cloches over them to hasten their growth. In frosty weather, give them extra protection at night by covering the cloches with newspapers and anchoring with bricks. When the leaves begin to appear, you can remove the cloches during the daytime.

Alternative varieties
For a change, grow an alternative to the traditional white, bell-shaped lilies of the valley. The variety 'Plena' has double flowers, and 'Rosea' has pink flowers, while the rare 'Albostriata' has distinctive green and gold striped leaves.

Gardener's potpourri

Battles long ago

Once upon a time – according to legend – there dwelt a fearsome dragon in St Leonard's Forest in Sussex, who made regular forays into the neighbouring countryside to capture maidens and to lay waste generally.

However, he did not have things entirely his own way, for the Sussex people had a champion in Leonard, a blacksmith who also lived in the forest. For years the district rang with howls and the clash of steel as the two fought up and down the glades. At last Leonard overcame the dragon and, for his struggles, was made a saint.

His reward, by divine intervention, was that henceforward no adder would bite in the forest, no nightingale would sing, because the bird had disturbed his slumbers, and wherever the good man's blood had been spilled, lilies of the valley would grow. And there they grow still, to this day.

Lilies of the valley

A touch of spring in winter
If you have a clump of lilies of the valley in your garden, dig up a few crowns in autumn. Plant these in pots filled with a mixture of loam and leafmould. Stand the pots in a cool greenhouse or a cold frame. At the beginning of the year, bring a pot of lilies of the valley into the house each week to enjoy a succession of flowers that bring spring into winter. Water them regularly to ensure they grow rapidly.

Magnolias

Room for expansion

Large magnolias are among the most beautiful of flowering trees, but those that are grown as freestanding specimens need a good deal of space to develop their elegant forms. For example, *Magnolia salicifolia* grows to 6m (20ft)

Magnificent blooms The beautiful white and rose chalice-shaped flowers of *Magnolia x soulangeana* emerge well before the leaves begin to unfurl.

with a spread of 3m (10ft), and the hybrid *M.* 'Heaven Scent' can be about the same. To appreciate their beauty, it is wise to plant them about 5m (17ft) from the house and about 7m (24ft) from any other tree. Some large magnolias grow happily against a house wall and benefit from the protection. *M. grandiflora* is an example. It grows to 4.6m (15ft) and produces creamy, fragrant floral bowls from July to September.

Beware rabbits

In winter, in some rural areas, rabbits take a fancy to young magnolias. To protect the bark, wrap wire mesh round the trunk's base, or cut the top and bottom off a plastic bottle, slit it lengthways down one side, and wrap it round the trunk. A multi-stemmed tree can be protected with a wire mesh framework.

Protection from frost

Protect the small magnolia, *Magnolia stellata*, from icy winds by planting it in a position that is sheltered and protected from the early-morning sun. Otherwise the fragrant, white flowers, which open in March and April, may suffer from frost damage.

Spring dressing

For the first year, support young magnolias with stakes. Each April top-dress them with leafmould or well rotted compost.

Propagating methods

Magnolias can be difficult to propagate from cuttings. Try taking ripe heel cuttings in July and rooting them in a heated propagator. Layering is more reliable. Peg low branches securely into a fertile soil in autumn. They should be ready to transplant a year later.

Manures

Farmyard manure

Traditionally considered to be the best type of organic matter, good farmyard manure, often referred to as FYM, can be hard to come by even if you live in the countryside, and is

well-nigh impossible to obtain if you live in a town or city. There are, however, several alternative natural manures that are equally suitable for the garden and which are usually more readily available.

Horse manure

Riding schools and stables often have large quantities of manure that they need to dispose of, and which they will sell relatively cheaply, and may even be prepared to deliver. Many advertise in the classified sections of local papers. The best horse manure comes from establishments that bed their horses on straw. Manure from horses bedded on wood shavings takes much longer to rot down. Examine the manure carefully, and if there is a large proportion of shavings in relation to dung and urine, it is wise to stack it for at least a year before spreading it over beds in the garden.

Pig manure

To ensure that the pig manure you are obtaining will be beneficial to the garden, check that it is straw-based and well rotted. If it is neat pig dung that has not been mixed with straw, it will be of little value to the soil.

Goat manure

Goat manure has a similar proportion of minerals and trace elements as horse manure, so it is well worth seeking out someone who keeps a goat and who would be able to supply you with some from time to time.

Poultry manure

If you have the space to keep a few chickens, you will have a ready supply of manure, as well as a daily delivery of fresh eggs. If, however, lack of space or, in some cases, local bylaws make this impossible, manure can be obtained from free-range poultry farms or, provided you do not object on ethical grounds, from deep-litter poultry houses.

Sheep manure

To obtain sheep manure you will probably have to be prepared to collect it yourself, with the permission of the landowner, in small quantities from the grazing areas. Although it is unlikely to be free of charge, the droppings are excellent for making liquid manure, so the effort and cost are probably well worth while.

Pigeon manure

Pigeon fanciers are often faced with a disposal problem when they clear out their pigeon lofts, and are pleased to find a gardener to whom they can give or sell the bird droppings. Pigeon manure is an excellent compost activator and can be shovelled on each time that a new layer of material is added to the heap.

Leave it to rot

Fresh animal manure must be allowed to rot down before it is applied, otherwise it will scorch the plants. If you can collect only a small amount of manure at one time, add it to the compost heap. Stack large quantities on a solid base, and water well if it is dry. Cover with polythene to keep moisture in and rain out.

Green manure

If you are short of manure, you can grow your own. For many years farmers have done exactly that by planting field lupins, mustard, grazing rye, winter field beans and other plants. These are not cash crops but green manures that are ploughed in to fertilise the fields. Their seeds are now available to gardeners. Sow them when you have lifted your vegetables or summer bedding and, when the plants have grown, dig them in to add humus and some nutrients to the soil.

Dry is sweeter

It is wise to buy dried poultry or farmyard manure in bags from a garden centre. This is just as nutritious as the raw equivalents but does not need time to decompose and has little odour. Simply scatter the manure on flower and vegetable beds or use as an activator on the compost heap.

Homemade liquid manure

A good liquid manure can be made cheaply and easily in the garden. Half fill an old hessian sack with animal manure (sheep is best) and tie the top tightly with string, leaving enough string to make a loop. Fill a butt or other large

container with water and immerse the sack by suspending it by the loop on a sturdy piece of wood laid across the top of the butt or container. After about two weeks, remove the sack of manure and cover the butt or the container. Draw off the liquid manure as required. The liquid can be given neat to well-watered plants or diluted with equal parts of water as a foliar spray.

Preserving the goodness

If applying well-rotted manure to the soil in autumn, prevent the winter rains from washing away the nutrients by covering it with polythene sheeting.

Manure-go-round

If you garden on a rotation system, make sure that you always have enough well-rotted manure to cover the section of the plot where you will grow beans, celeriac, celery, garlic, leeks, lettuces, onions, peas, shallots, spinach and tomatoes. As these crops move round from year to year a different part of the soil is fed and enriched regularly.

Maples

All shapes and sizes

Among the 200 species of maple are trees and shrubs ranging from the 1.5m (5ft) high *Acer palmatum* var. *dissectum* to the stately 'Norway maple', *A. platanoides*, which can reach heights of over 9m (30ft) in less than 20 years. Choose from columnar, conical, erect, mop-headed, pyramidal, rounded and spreading shapes.

Something for everyone

Before buying a maple, check the conditions that it needs to grow. Some species, such as *Acer palmatum* (Japanese maple), need humus-rich soil and a sheltered spot, while others, such as *A. pseudoplatanus*, will tolerate windy or waterlogged sites. Similarly, there are acers that prefer acid soils, such as *A. ginnala*, and others that thrive in chalky soil – for example, *A. campestre* (field maple).

Under the boughs

Most maples are shallow rooted and some, consequently, have dense canopies of foliage. Shrubs or perennials will not grow successfully underneath them. Try a tough, ground-covering plant, such as periwinkle or ivy, instead. Either species prospers in shade and among greedy maple roots. Spring-flowering bulbs can also be grown, with winter aconite and snowdrops being particularly successful.

Growing from seed

Gather ripe maple seeds in autumn. Put them into a small container with a little sand, cover with wire netting to protect them from mice, and leave the container outside to preserve the seeds throughout winter. In spring sow in pots of seed compost, or directly into the ground in a well-drained, sunny seedbed.

Marigolds

One for the pot, two for the plot

The name marigold is commonly used to refer to two totally unrelated species of plants. African and French marigolds are *Tagetes*, while those known as pot marigolds are *Calendula*. In both cases, the colour spectrum of the flowers ranges from pale yellow to deep orange and some varieties of tagetes produce flowers that are very similar in appearance to calendulas. In Britain, calendulas have been used in cooking as a substitute for saffron since the 14th century, and it was not until the arrival of their lookalikes, the African and French marigolds 200 years later, that calendulas became

A brief history

What's in a name?

Despite their names, African and French marigolds are neither African nor French. They were brought to Spain from Mexico by the conquistadores and the variety now called African was first known to southern Europeans as 'rose of the Indies'. In 1535, Emperor Charles V defeated the Moors in Tunis, where the plant was naturalised, and it was subsequently renamed 'flos africanus'. By the time it reached northern Europe, its Mexican origins had largely been forgotten and it was assumed, because of its name, that it was African. The 'French' variety was so named because, according to tradition, it was introduced to the British Isles by Huguenot refugees from France in 1572.

known as pot marigolds. It is only the pot marigolds that are edible. African and French marigolds are grown purely for their ornamental appearance.

Green guardians

Organic gardeners have long sung the praises of French marigolds (*Tagetes patula*), which, they say, have the ability to protect plants in their vicinity from whiteflies. Although there is no scientific proof of this, it may well be that there is something in the rather strange scent of the flowers and foliage that whiteflies dislike. At any rate, it is well worth planting groups of them in borders near roses, and round the greenhouse door, where they will also add some long-lasting colour.

Seedless display

Try the prolific Afro-French marigolds, which are hybrids of *Tagetes erecta* and *T. patula*. They offer an unusually colourful display and, since they produce no seed, provide more flowers. Zenith Series in shades of yellow, orange and gold and Solar Series, which produces 7.5cm (3in) flowers, are good examples.

Curiouser and curiouser

For a plant guaranteed to get the conversation going after dinner on the patio, seek out the seeds of *Calendula officinalis* 'Prolifera' (hen-and-chicken marigold). The flower head of this variety is encircled by tiny, secondary blooms that grow on little stalks beneath the petals of the main flower. In his *Herball*, the 16th-century botanist John Gerard noted that this plant was referred to 'by the vulgar sort of women' as 'Jack-an-apes on horsebacke'.

Marjoram

Sweet marjoram

Origanum majorana (sweet, or knotted, marjoram) is a half-hardy annual in all but the warmest climates, and grows to 51cm (20in). In early spring, mix the tiny seeds with fine sand and sow in a tray of moist seed compost in a greenhouse or indoors on a window ledge. If necessary, mist spray the compost surface until the seedlings germinate. In early summer plant in a sunny, sheltered spot, or grow on in containers and bring indoors in autumn. They may survive the winter. This herb has a sweeter flavour than its two perennial cousins.

Pot marjoram

Origanum onites (pot marjoram) has clusters of pink flowers and grows to a height of 46–61cm (18–24in). Sow the seeds outdoors in a sheltered spot in early spring in light, well-drained soil, or in containers on the patio or balcony. It also grows well in pots indoors. Pot marjoram is less sweet than sweet marjoram.

Wild marjoram

Origanum vulgare (wild, or common, marjoram), referred to as oregano or rigani in Italian and Greek recipes, is the strongest, spiciest marjoram. It is easy to grow from seed, and reaches about 61cm (2ft). Its aromatic leaves make it ideal to edge paths, where it can be touched gently and encouraged to release its aroma. Once it has spread, it can be divided and replanted. Its taste is much stronger when grown in full sun.

Marrows

Water well

Once the fruits have set, marrow plants need at least 9 litres (2 gallons) of water a square metre (sq yard) each week when it is dry and sunny. To make sure this quantity of watering is effective, leave a shallow hollow when you fill the planting hole. This will help to direct water to the roots of the plant where it will do most good. Also, when you plant the marrow, put a cane into the hole. It will enable you to see where the centre of the roots lies after the plant has grown and spread over the ground.

Make the right choice

Marrows

Marrows come in two types: trailing varieties produce long scrambling shoots; the relatively modern bush marrows are much more compact.

Varieties	Descriptions
Trailing marrows	
Butternut	Cylindrical marrow with a bright orange flesh
Long Green Trailing	Traditional green marrow with cream stripes
Long White Trailing	White marrow; good cropper
Bush marrows	
Badger Cross	F1 hybrid. Disease-resistant; prolific, attractive striped fruit
Long Green Bush	Well-established, economical variety
Tiger Cross	F1 hybrid. Early, disease-resistant; green with cream stripes

Pick and store

At the beginning of autumn, harvest all the remaining marrows, leaving a long stalk on each. If possible, leave them in the sun for a few days to dry and to allow the skins to harden. Fruits must not be touched by frost as this will impair the quality of the flesh and the storage potential. Store in individual nets hung from the ceiling of a cool, airy, frost-free place, such as a garage, where they should last for several months, though it is wise to check them frequently. Marrows can also be stored in a garage, side by side but without touching, on straw-lined shelves. If a hard frost is forecast, cover them with sacking.

Ripe and ready

To ascertain whether a marrow is ready for eating, feel the skin and, if it is quite hard, rap the fruit with your knuckle. A ripe marrow gives off a hollow note.

See also **Courgettes**

Measuring aids

Marking length

Make marks using a permanent marker every 15cm (6in) along the handle of a rake. Then lay the rake on the ground – pressing the prongs into the soil for safety – to produce an easy-to-read planting scale. A narrow strip of wood, about 1.5m (5ft) long, could be similarly marked.

Question of depth

Graduate a dibber and the blade of a trowel with marks every 5cm (2in). This will help to ensure that your bulbs and plants are put in at the recommended depths. When you are digging deeper holes, it is worth noting the depth of the spade blade as an aid to assessing the depth of holes.

Capacity check

If graduated measurements are not marked on your watering can, check its capacity by using a kitchen measuring jug to fill it up. Common capacities are 7 litres (1½ gallons) and 9 litres (2 gallons). If the can is plastic and the water level is visible through it, use a permanent marker pen to note measurements on the outside. Watering requirements vary according to soil and weather, but for a leafy or fruiting crop in summer, give 11 litres a square metre (2 gallons a square yard) each week; this may have to be upped to twice a week in hot weather.

Area guide

With successional sowings, intercropping and close planting, a 100m² (120sq yd) plot should serve a household of four relying on home-grown vegetables, apart from maincrop potatoes, winter cauliflowers and brussels sprouts, which all need a lot of room. In a small garden, grow baby vegetables in a raised bed, interplant among flowers or use pots and tubs.

Growing know-how

Vital statistics

You are already armed with a highly practical instrument of measurement – your own body. By memorising a few of its measurements, you will be able to make swift and reasonably accurate assessments in the garden when, for example, you want to find a cane or stick of a particular length, or the correct distance when planting out seedlings.

- Hold together your index finger, middle finger and ring finger, and measure the distance across the knuckle joints.
- Spread out the fingers of one hand on a ruler or tape measure, and note the distance from the tip of your thumb to the tip of your little finger.
- Measure the length of your index finger.
- By measuring from the heel to the toe, find the length of one of your gardening shoes or wellington boots.
- Lay a long ruler on the ground and take a step to find the length of your normal stride. Experiment to see by how much you must adjust that stride to cover 1m (3ft 3in).
- Extend one arm fully and ask a friend to measure the distance from the fingertips on one hand to the shoulder on the opposite side, then extend both of your arms and ask your friend to measure the distance from the tips of the fingers on one hand, straight across your back to the tips of the fingers on the other hand.

Medicinal plants

A pharmacy in your garden

Many common garden plants have medicinal properties, and herbal teas, tinctures and syrups are simple to prepare in the kitchen. Most gardens, for example, will include a few dandelions, a rose bush or two or a lavender bush spilling over a path. These plants, and many hundreds more, can be used to make safe, simple remedies for a multitude of common minor ailments.

Wise precautions

When gathering plants for medicinal use, avoid any that have been treated with chemical insecticides, or those that are growing close to a busy road and exposed to traffic pollution. Never use any plant that you cannot positively identify. If you have any doubts about a plant's properties, consult a qualified herbal practitioner or a reputable book on herbal medicine before taking it or administering it to others. Be particularly careful when treating young children and pregnant or nursing mothers. Do not delay in consulting your usual medical adviser if illness or symptoms persist.

Calming camomile

After a hard and stressful day, a cup of camomile tea at bedtime can help you to relax and enjoy a deep, untroubled sleep. Camomile's relaxant properties can also be effective in the relief of the after effects of overeating. Try to use the fresh flowers as soon as they open.

Pep up with peppermint

Wake up to a cup of stimulating and refreshing peppermint tea, and start the day feeling bright and alert. Long known to be a good stimulant, peppermint can also be effective in the treatment of chills, fevers, hiccups and heartburn. Use a handful of fresh leaves or a few young sprigs.

Antiseptic mouthwash

A tincture of fresh or dried thyme makes an excellent mouthwash and can help to relieve the discomfort caused by mouth ulcers and inflamed gums. Thyme should be gathered just before the flower buds open. With a good crop, you should be able to make enough tincture to meet the family's needs throughout the year (see *below*, **Medicinal Preparations**).

Out with gout

Parsley is a diuretic, as well as being an effective treatment for premenstrual fluid retention. It may also be taken to relieve the symptoms of arthritis and gout. Its high vitamin C content enhances the body's ability to absorb iron and it is therefore often prescribed as a treatment for iron-deficiency anaemia. Chewing the fresh leaves will, as an added bonus to its curative properties, remove the smell of onions or garlic from the breath. However, as parsley can stimulate the muscles of the uterus, the herb should not be taken during pregnancy.

Garlic for good health

Despite its distinctive odour, which some people may find unpleasant, garlic could be described as the panacea of the plant kingdom. Extract the juice from the cloves and take a teaspoonful with honey from time to time throughout the day to soothe a sore throat or ease a cough. Its antiseptic action on the liver and digestive system is effective against stomach disorders, and it is also known to be able to lower blood sugar levels and reduce blood pressure. Applying crushed garlic will relieve stings, bites and sprains.

Coffee break

Best known to country folk as 'pee-the-bed', dandelion leaves have long been recognised as a remedy for urinary infections and fluid retention. The roots can be roasted and ground

Make the right choice

Medicinal preparations

There are three basic methods of preparation for medicinal plants, depending on the plant itself and the purpose for which the remedy is intended. All are easy and require no special equipment. Do not use aluminium utensils for herbal preparations.

Type	Method
Decoctions	Use this process to make teas from woody plants. Crush or chop the plant and put 60g (2oz) into a small saucepan. Add 570ml (1 pint) cold water and bring to the boil. Reduce the heat, cover the pan, and simmer gently for 10 minutes, strain into a cup and serve, sweetened with honey, if required.
Infusions	This method is best for teas made from flowers, leaves or young stems. Put 60g (2oz) of the fresh herb into a warmed teapot and add 570ml (1 pint) boiling water. Cover the pot and leave to stand for 10 minutes, then strain into a cup. Use honey to sweeten the tea, if required.
Tinctures	Put 200g (7oz) of the herb into a large, screw-topped jar and add 1 litre (1¾ pints) of vodka or other spirit Put the top on the jar and shake vigorously, then store in a warm, dark place. Shake the jar thoroughly twice a day for 14 days, then strain the tincture through a piece of muslin or a jelly bag. When all the liquid has been strained, squeeze the herb tightly to extract the last drops. Bottle the tincture in dark-coloured, screw-topped bottles and add the herb to the compost heap.

to make an excellent caffeine-free coffee. Never give dandelion juice to children because it may make them sick.

Rose hip teas and syrup

Gather the hips from wild roses and make your own wonderfully aromatic and uplifting rose hip tea or syrup. Because the hips are very high in vitamin C, rosehip preparations make an excellent tonic. In addition, mixed with other medicines, the flavour will help to mask the taste of less pleasant herbs.

In the Victorian spirit

No Victorian lady would have dreamed of leaving home without her smelling bottle, for fear that she might be overcome by giddiness or a fainting fit. It is quite easy to make the same spirit of lavender that was contained in those smelling bottles. Simply put some lavender flowers into a bowl, then add a little brandy or gin, cover the bowl and leave to soak for a day or two. Finally, strain the mixture into a small bottle. Inhaling the spirit, or applying a small drop to the pulse points, helps to ease tension and relieve anxiety.

Medlars

Cold-weather friend

Dense and spreading medlars are more often grown today for their ornamental appearance and russet autumn leaves than for their fruit. Their noted hardiness can be turned to advantage by planting two or three on the north side of other fruit trees where they will protect their more delicate neighbours from any chill winds.

Garden ornament

If you are seeking a focal point for a medium-sized garden, consider planting a medlar tree. Its spreading pattern of interwoven branches gives interest in winter, while in early summer it offers white, saucer-shaped flowers that are followed by autumnal leaves turning russet red before they fall. The medlar has the additional

virtue of being repeat blooming and in August or September will often produce a second flush of flowers among the fruits.

The right choice

If you are buying a medlar for its fruits, be sure to purchase one of the named varieties, such as *Mespilus germanica* 'Nottingham' or *M.g.* 'Dutch'. These produce fruits the size of large nuts, unlike wild trees whose fruits rarely exceed the size of marbles.

Pick and blet

The fruits of the medlar ripen in early November, at about the same time as the first frosts. But they cannot be eaten freshly picked as the taste is too sharp. The fruits must first be 'bletted', that is, left to ripen to the point where the flesh softens and starts to rot. They can then be eaten raw, but are better used to make jellies and preserves.

Melons

Right way up

In late March or early April, plant three melon seeds, pointed end down, in a pot of seed compost. Water well, cover with cling film and stand in a warm part of the greenhouse. When the seeds have germinated, usually within two or three weeks, remove the cling film and retain the strongest seedling for planting out.

Greenhouse supports

Insert a cane to support each plant's main stem then attach horizontal wires to the greenhouse glazing bars at intervals of 30cm (12in). Tie in lateral growths. When the main stem reaches the top wire, pinch out the tip. Pinch out lateral shoots when they have five leaves.

Hurry up the harvesting

Speed up the harvesting of melons grown in frames by pruning the young plants three times. First, when they have four large leaves, cut off the stem above the first two; second, cut off the new stems above the third leaf; finally, when the first fruits appear, count two leaves above each fruit and cut the tips off the stems. Remove all shoots that do not bear any fruit.

In the frame

If you do not have a greenhouse, canteloupe varieties of melons can be grown in frames. Do not plant them out in the garden until early May in the south and about a month later in the north. Because south-facing frames will become quite warm during later, sunny weather, causing scorched foliage, remember to open them during the day. Always close them when a shower comes; the growing compost should be rich and permanently damp, but too much moisture can encourage stem canker.

Weed control

You can help to control weeds as well as retain moisture in the soil by growing the melon plants through holes that have been cut in sheets of black polythene or in corrugated cardboard.

Help with pollination

Artificial pollination is necessary to make fruits set. To do this, strip the petals off a male flower and push the pollen-bearing centre into the centre of a female flower, preferably when the weather is dry. Female flowers are distinguished by having a swelling like a small melon behind the petals.

Support small melons

Keep small melons, such as cantaloupes, off the ground and free of pests and disease by using legs cut from old tights as protective sleeves. As the young melons start to develop, slide each one into the foot section of a leg and tie it to a stake to suspend the melon above the ground. The 'hammocks' will stretch as the melons mature and will keep them from sagging to the ground.

Keeping them clean

Lift fruits clear of the soil by slipping tiles or boards under them when they reach the size of oranges. Tiles are better as they attract and give out more heat from the sun. The moist soil under the tiles encourages slugs so sprinkle some slug pellets round the plant.

Mint

Rampant grower

Mint is so rampant that its roots can spread through a herb bed in a matter of weeks. Check its exuberance by planting a clump in a large pot. Sink the pot into the bed, leaving the top 5cm (2in) above the surface. Each autumn,

dig up the pot and trim off any roots that have grown through the drainage holes. Repot every three years. Another way to restrict the roots is to push slates into the ground round the clump.

Aromatic selection

Mint grows in sun but prefers partial shade and is not fussy about soil as long as it does not dry out. If you have the space, it is fun to try several varieties of this useful plant. Lemon mint pleasantly flavours tea, eau de cologne mint can be added to the bath water, ginger mint adds zest to salads if used sparingly, peppermint makes mint tea, pineapple mint looks good in hanging baskets, while apple mint and spearmint – the commonest variety – are used for mint sauce and jelly, as well as being good in iced drinks.

New beds

To establish a new mint bed, dig up or obtain a few mint roots and replant these. The roots will quickly colonise the area. Do not harvest large amounts of leaves from the mint in the first year as this may weaken plant growth.

Freezer flavour

A pot of apple mint or spearmint growing beside the kitchen door looks attractive and is very convenient for culinary purposes. Both varieties can be used to make mint sauce or jelly, or can be added to iced drinks or vegetables, especially peas and potatoes. Add a sprig of mint to dried peas before storing and pop a sprig into the bag with fresh peas before freezing.

Unusual and useful

Pennyroyal is a low, spreading member of the mint family with an unusual aroma that some may find unpleasant. A handful of fresh or dried leaves, rubbed gently into the fur of cats or dogs, is reputed to repel fleas.

Rock garden choice

Plant tiny Corsican mint in the rock garden. In a scented arbour, you could grow it through gravel round a garden seat, where light treading will release its delicious aroma.

Mistletoe

Grow a kiss for Christmas

You can grow your own mistletoe, though it may take years for the plant to establish itself and bear berries. A parasite on trees, mistletoe grows best on apple, hawthorn and lime. Choose a young and vigorous branch in February or March and make a number of shallow slices in the bark on the underside. Press a ripe mistletoe berry beneath each flap; the sticky substance that is released will harden, firmly cementing the seeds into place. Seeds take a long time to germinate, putting out roots that draw nourishment from the tree. It may take several tries before plants are produced and it is rare for a plant to fruit in under seven years. Berries and plants are either male or female; a single plant will not therefore bear fruit.

Decoration not for propagation

The berries on mistletoe sprigs that are hung up as Christmas decorations will dry out and shrivel and will not germinate. To grow the plant successfully, stand berried sprigs in a vase of water and implant the berries on the chosen host tree in February or March, as described above. As the germination rate is very low, sow plenty of seeds, ideally on the same type of tree that hosted the parent mistletoe plant.

Moles

Battle against intruders
Suggested ways to get rid of moles are mostly based upon the animal's sensitivity to sound and scent. The wind thrumming across the open top of a bottle buried in a mole's run, or a plastic bottle rattling against a stake are supposed to upset them, as is the smell of a rag soaked in creosote. Putting brambles or chemical cat deterrents in the runs may be effective, or you could try planting caper spurge. These remedies have a variable success rate. Proprietary smokes will work, but only, of course, if you can find the mole's run.

Deadly deterrent
The most effective method of dealing with moles is to acquire a cat or, better still, several cats. They will happily patrol the garden by night, killing moles and any rodents that might be damaging your crops.

An organic repellant
If moles have invaded your vegetable garden or lawn , try using a fertiliser that contains castor oil meal. This organic, but poisonous, product enriches the soil and discourages rodents of all sorts. Distribute several handfuls per square metre (square yard), water it in, and it should last for several months. Or mix 120ml (4fl oz) of castor oil with 8 litres (2 gallons) of water and drench the molehill.

Chase with bad smells
Moles hate the smell of soiled cat litter even more than you do, so pour some down their tunnels. Some gardeners even drop mothballs down mole runs to deter them.

Looking on the bright side
Despite the havoc they wreak, moles do have some redeeming features. They help to maintain a balance by feeding on many of the garden's enemies, including click beetles, cutworms, leatherjackets and wireworms. In damp areas, the moles' tunnelling helps to drain the soil, and the soil from the molehills themselves makes an excellent top dressing for the lawn.

Moon lore

Grafting guide
It has long been a part of gardening tradition that when grafting fruit trees at the end of winter, it is best to carry out the task when the moon is new. The period when the moon is waxing (between new and full) is said to stimulate the circulation of sap and make for more vigorous buds. By the same token, shield grafting, which is done in summer, is believed to take better if it is carried out when the moon is precisely full or new.

Prune with the moon
The pruning of fruit trees during February and March will awaken the buds, making them more susceptible to frost damage. There is a time-honoured belief that this tendency can be offset if the fruit trees are pruned when the moon is waxing.

Waxing and waning
Old-time gardeners recommend that most vegetables should be planted when the moon is waxing. The only exceptions are those vegetables that form a head – lettuces, cabbages and sprouts, for example – which might then quickly run to seed. Plant these instead when the moon is on the wane.

Lunar power Adherents claim that planting and sowing according to the moon's phases improves results.

Quick weather check
The moon itself has little direct effect on the weather but, by observing changes in the skies about it, some surprisingly accurate forecasts can be made. If there is a halo round the moon, or its outline is blurred, take it as a strong indicator that rain is on the way. The halo is an effect of cirrostratus or altostratus clouds, which are always associated with approaching wet weather. On the other hand, if in winter the moon is seen clearly and distinctly, then there are no insulating clouds present and frost is likely. When the moon's outline is blurred once more, the frosty spell is coming to an end.

Gardener's potpourri

The moon in the garden
The notion that you should garden 'with the moon' is a venerable one. While there is no scientific evidence that the moon influences plant growth, many gardeners believe it does. Their opinions were distilled more than 2,000 years ago by the Roman poet Virgil when he wrote in his farming books, the *Georgics*, 'the moon herself has made some days ... favourable for certain tasks'. Find out if it is true by following the lunar planting chart below.

Timing	Action	Plant
Full moon	Sow	Brussels sprouts, cabbages, carrots, onions, parsnips, radishes, spinach
	Plant	Potatoes, tomatoes
	Harvest	Fruit, herbs, vegetables
Two days before a full moon	Sow	Beans, herbs, peas, sweetcorn

Weeding in the dark

Some German botanists claim that if you hoe a garden bed by artificial light when the moon casts shadows, fewer weeds will reappear than if you carry out the same operation by daylight. They say, too, that weeding under a full moon is more effective than that done at other times in the moon's cycle.

Moss

Eliminate a lawn problem

Moss on a lawn is a clear sign that the ground is poorly drained and that the grass has been ill-treated. Moss killers based on dichlorophen and iron sulphate are available, but no matter how often you use them, the moss will return unless you cure the underlying problem. First apply the killer then, when the moss is dead, vigorously rake it up. If you do this when the moss is alive, you simply spread the spores.

Aerating action

Prevent moss from growing on a lawn by improving drainage. Spike the lawn with an aerator. For a small area, a garden fork will do. Drive it 7.5cm (3in) into the soil, allowing about 15cm (6in) between each spiking, then scatter a top dressing of dry horticultural grit or sand at 1kg a square metre (2lb a square yard). On a larger lawn a roller-type aerator will save time.

High-pressure help

Moss thrives in damp places, particularly on paving stones and roofs sheltered from the sun. Check gutters at the end of winter and clear moss deposits so the water flow is not blocked. Hire a high-pressure hose to remove moss from drives, patios and low roofs. Work down from the top of the roof to avoid lifting the tiles or slates. Then spray the area with a moss killer that does not contain iron sulphate, which leaves a stain. Brush patios frequently to discourage moss and algal growth.

Safety measures

Wear safety glasses when preparing and scrubbing moss and algae killer into paving and when spraying it onto a roof.

Waste not, want not

Collect the moss washed off the roof or gathered from elsewhere. Leave it to darken and die, then spread it on the garden as an acidifying mulch. Azaleas, camellias, heathers and heaths in particular will benefit.

Nest for a pot plant

Moss makes a useful cushion for house plants. When it is placed as a lining between the holder and the pot, its moisture-retentive qualities create a humid atmosphere and stop the pot drying out. Moss also helps to insulate the plant roots from extremes of heat and cold.

That antique look

This old method may help you to give new ornaments an antique look. In a bucket, mix a few handfuls of moss with beer and sugar and churn them together with a blender. Brush the mixture onto new brick walls or fence panels, birdbaths, reconstituted stone pots, or any similar garden furniture to which you wish to impart a weathered or mellow appearance. The mixture will encourage algal growth, making the object look as if it has been gracing the garden for several decades.

Save the peat bogs

If you do not believe that there is an aesthetically pleasing alternative and you decide to buy moss, perhaps to line a hanging basket, avoid buying sphagnum moss. It is removed in vast quantities from the country's peat bogs, leaving them exposed to erosion and extensive damage. Try to persuade your local garden centre to stock Highland moss instead. This grows freely in conifer plantations where its regular cropping is actually beneficial to other plant life and it poses no threat to the environment.

Lining baskets

If Highland moss is not available for lining hanging baskets, after a damp winter you can always rake up moss from your lawn or flower borders and use that instead.

Mulberries

Old fruit

Mulberries have been harvested in Britain for centuries, often from the same tree. There is, for example, a mulberry tree at Syon Park in south-west London that was planted in 1548 and is still producing fruit. Such longevity makes some gardeners believe that it takes an age before the trees will bear fruit, but in fact most will start to do so between their sixth and eighth years. A tree will add a pleasantly antique touch to a garden, whether grown against a wall or as a gnarled specimen on the lawn.

Venerable fruit producer *Morus nigra* (black mulberry) is the species grown for its edible fruits.

Cooks' choice

The best and largest fruits for culinary purposes are produced by the black mulberry. Stew them with other fruits for a dessert or make them into jam. In the latter case, strain them through muslin to get rid of the pips.

Grow a handkerchief

Of the three main kinds of mulberry tree – black, white and the rare ornamental red – silkworms prefer the leaves of the white fruiting type, though they will tolerate those of the black, which is the best for fruit. Silkworms can breed only in controlled temperatures; in Britain they have to be kept indoors and fed on chopped mulberry leaves two or three times a day. A youngish mulberry tree would not feed more than a dozen caterpillars which, between them, might produce enough silk for a handkerchief. Children find silkworms fascinating, but some may be upset by the boiling of cocoons and worms together to obtain silk.

Making their mark

Do not park your car under, or near, a mulberry tree. The stains made by the fruit are very difficult to remove from paintwork

Mulching

Natural or artificial

Soil can be mulched with natural materials such as chipped bark, lawn mowings or compost, or with manmade products including polythene, newspaper and cardboard. It is also possible to use a combination of manmade and natural materials. The type of mulch that you use will depend on the site and on what you wish to achieve. The box on the right gives a general guide to mulch types.

Winter warmer

Increase the life expectancy of newly planted trees and shrubs by watering them frequently and giving them a bulky mulch of moisture-retentive, well-rotted manure or garden compost. In addition to enriching the soil the mulch provides valuable warmth in winter.

Make the right choice

Choose your mulch

Mulches come in a variety of forms and are a boon to all gardeners, especially to those short of time. A good mulch will do much of the work, but it is important to pick the right one for a particular task.

Type	Description
Animal manure	When well rotted, manure will mingle with the soil and enrich it. Even before it has entirely decomposed, although not when it is raw, it makes a fine mulch. It should be stacked for at least three months before use.
Bark (ground to different sizes)	Pleasing to look at and extremely durable, bark keeps weeds at bay and eventually, when it breaks down, adds humus to the soil without compacting it. However, as it contains no nutrients whatsoever, plants surrounded by ground bark will need feeding.
Black polythene	This warms the ground and suppresses weeds in flower and vegetable beds. Set out plants through slits cut in the plastic. Remember to anchor it round the edges with bricks or pegs or by burying it in the soil.
Coffee grounds/ tea leaves	In areas where the soil and tap water are alkaline, these add a little acidity as well as nitrogen and phosphate. But since the supply is small, keep them for azaleas and other acid-loving plants grown in pots.
Conifer needles	Resistant to windy weather, they stay in place well and help to acidify the soil. An excellent mulch for rhododendrons and heathers.
Garden compost	This is composed of grass cuttings, deadheaded flowers, exhausted bedding plants, weeds and kitchen waste that have been collected and stacked over several months. It makes a superb mulch but be careful that the components have not been treated with herbicides. Adding a sprinkling of dried blood or any other high-nitrogen fertiliser between each 20cm (8in) layer of waste will hasten the rotting-down process.
Mushroom and growing-bag compost	Commercial mushroom growers sell the compost in which a crop was grown after harvesting. It makes an excellent mulch for lime-loving plants, as does the compost from growing bags used for tomatoes.
Stones, pebbles and gravel	Not only decorative when spread round tree trunks or potted plants, these also help to retain moisture. A stone or pebble layer is highly effective against weeds if perforated black polythene sheeting is stretched beneath it. The perforations allow rainwater to drain through into the soil.
Straw	Though it may harbour the seeds of weeds from the fields, straw is a good mulch. A layer 10cm (4in) deep is recommended. If chopped up, by running the lawn mower over it a few times, it will repel slugs and snails.

Pretty and practical

In the ornamental garden, a mulch of chipped bark spread round the plants will retain moisture, suppress annual weeds and, eventually, rot down to feed the soil and the plants. It will also look attractive. In the vegetable garden, where appearance is rather less important, soil that has been cleared of crops for the season can be mulched with black polythene sheets to prevent weed growth and the leaching of nutrients by winter rain and snow. Unlike natural materials, artificial mulches add nothing to the soil because they do not rot down.

Perennial problem

If it is spread sufficiently thickly, a natural mulch will suppress the growth of shallow-rooting annual weeds, but it is essential, before applying it, to dig out all traces of perennial weeds that, in the same way as cultivated plants, will thrive in the improved conditions. Alternatively, where possible, cover the soil with perforated black polythene sheets or porous fabric and spread the natural mulch on top – the polythene must be perforated to allow for drainage, or the natural mulch will float away in the first heavy rain. This will dispose of the perennial problem and cut costs because it will not be necessary to lay the natural mulch so thickly.

Mushroom compost

Provided it is not used for acid-loving plants, spent mushroom compost makes an excellent mulch and soil conditioner. If you buy from a

Garden secrets

Quick mulch

If you do not have a compost heap, or you want to produce mulching material quickly, fill a black polythene bag with garden and kitchen waste and let it stand in a sunny place for six weeks or so. After this time, the contents will have rotted down sufficiently to be spread on top of the soil where the worms will gradually pull it down. The mulch can be covered with cardboard or polythene sheets, but as it is not fully rotted, it should not be dug in.

mushroom farm, leave it to rot down until it is dark and has the consistency of peat. Most prepacked varieties can be used immediately.

Count the cost

When buying commercially produced, prepacked mulches, such as chipped bark or coco fibre, do not assess value for money by weight alone, as some materials are much lighter than others. If the coverage is not stated on the pack, ask what area you might expect to mulch with a given amount.

Shredded stems

Woody stems and other garden waste can be used as a mulch, but they should first be put through a shredder. This shredded material

can be used straight away, but first add a dressing of base fertiliser to the ground because it will take nutrients from the soil before it breaks down.

Floating fleece

A floating mulch of lightweight porous material such as spun bonded fleece can be laid over newly sown seeds or young plants to protect them from the cold. The plants will simply push the fleece up as they grow.

See also **Sawdust**

Mushrooms

Morning fresh

To grow mushrooms is not difficult, but much depends on the weather. Dry days during the growing season, followed by mornings of heavy dew, are ideal. Begin in late May and June by finding an open site not shaded by trees and digging out a turf 46 x 30cm (18 x 12in). Take out 15cm (6in) of the soil underneath and fill the hole with well-rotted horse manure. Lay mushroom spawn, available by mail order, on top and replace the turf, treading down firmly. Water lightly. With ideal weather, mushrooms should appear within 12 weeks. Avoid soils freshly disturbed or treated with chemical fertilisers. The use of artificial fertilisers, too, would virtually rule out success.

Fungi kit

Mushroom enthusiasts can raise their favourite fungi without leaving the house. Kits available from specialists will provide regular crops over 8–12 weeks. A kit comprises mushroom spawn, coarse compost, a growing container and a bag of 'casing' – a mixture of peat and chalk, or peat and lime. Mix the spawn with the compost; add the 'casing' two weeks later and lightly water during the final stages of growth. The first crop should be ready eight to nine weeks after the spawn and compost are mixed, provided the temperature does not drop below 16°C (60°F).

Growing know-how

Mulching – why and when

Mulching, the practice of covering the soil round plants with vegetable matter or other material, organic or inorganic, is carried out for a number of reasons. One of the most important is to conserve moisture and to help the roots to maintain an even temperature. Another purpose is to improve the fertility of the soil with garden compost or well-rotted manure, and a third is to smother emerging weeds.

In addition, mulching attracts centipedes, which prey upon many garden pests. Although mulching can be carried out at any time of the year, it does most good in late spring when the ground has been warmed by the sun but still holds winter moisture, and when weeds are yet to become established. Fork or hoe the ground just before spreading the mulch.

Make your own growing medium

For something a little more adventurous than prepacked mushroom kits, you can prepare your own growing medium, such as logs, bags filled with sawdust or straw, or a patch of lawn. This will allow you to purchase spawn of some of the more exotic mushroom varieties, which are not available in kit form.

Bags of taste

To grow mushrooms in a bag of sawdust or straw, first sterilise the growing medium by soaking it in a solution of 1 teaspoon of bleach to 1 litre (1¾ pints) of water for 2 hours. Alternatively, you can mix it with water and cook it in a pressure cooker for 45 minutes, then drain and leave to cool. Add the spawn to the cooled growing medium and mix thoroughly, then transfer the mixture to a polythene bag through which a few holes have been made with a skewer or nail. Tie up the top of the bag and keep it at a temperature of between 20°C and 25°C (68°F and 77°F) until growth appears on the straw or sawdust, when you should move the bag to a cool, moist, well-lit place out of direct sunlight. You should be able to harvest the first crop of mushrooms after two or three weeks.

Proper picking

When picking mushrooms, snap them off at the base or twist them free of the soil; do not take the heads alone. Also, to minimise rot, do not cut the stems. Remove any stumps, pieces of stem and other debris to minimise the growth of moulds that might prevent new mushrooms forming. To encourage further cropping, fill any holes in the compost.

Growing on logs

The most suitable logs for mushroom growing are those cut from beech or oak trees. They should be about 46cm (18in) long, with a diameter of not less than 10cm (4in). Cut the logs in winter and store them stacked on sheets of polythene spread on the ground, in a cool, damp place. In spring, drill large holes along the logs, fill the holes with mushroom spawn and seal them with wax. The spawn needs to be kept warm and moist until it begins to grow, so wrap the logs in a thick covering of old carpeting, newspaper, cardboard or polythene. After a few months (the length of time will depend on the variety of mushroom), check for signs of growth and as soon as you see any, line the logs up in rows in a cool, shady place such as under trees or in a garage or cellar, and wait to harvest your first delicious crop of truly home-grown mushrooms.

Take no chances

Be wary of folklore tests for edible fungi such as 'If the cap peels, you can eat it'. Many such tales have proved to be wrong – sometimes fatally so. To be safe, you should never eat any fungus unless it has been positively identified as edible.

Myrtle

A hint of spice

There are few shrubs that demand so little but give so much as *Myrtus communis* (common myrtle). Its small, shiny, evergreen leaves have a distinctive, spicy fragrance throughout the year, and during July and August it is covered in a profusion of white flowers which are followed in autumn by small, purple berries.

Compact choice

If a hardy myrtle is required, *Myrtus communis* ssp. *tarentina* is the hardiest and has an attractive compact form. 'Glanleam Gold' is a good variegated hybrid but is less hardy than either *M. communis* or *M. c.* ssp. *tarentina*. All grow best in well-drained soils.

Sprays and bouquets

For summer brides, myrtle's white flowers make a delightful, fragrant spray that can be bound simply with a white satin ribbon. Alternatively, the blooms can be included to great effect in a more formal bouquet.

Easy come, easy grow

Semi-ripe cuttings taken in July and August from an established myrtle will root readily in pots of equal parts of sand and leafmould, or sand and peat. The shrubs are hardy to −23°C (−10°F) and will grow well in any soil, including chalk. They are tolerant of high winds and sea spray, and are rarely attacked by pests or diseases. They can also be grown in containers in a conservatory or on the patio. In areas where winters are severe, it is best to grow them in the shelter of a wall or fence to protect the leaves from frost.

Make the right choice

Home-grown mushrooms

For a fresh supply of mushrooms all year round, choose some of these varieties.

Variety	Growing medium
Coprinus comatus (shaggy ink cap)	Bags of straw or on the lawn
Flammulina velutipes (enokitake, or velvet shank)	Bags of sawdust or on logs
Lentinus edodes (shiitake)	Bags of sawdust or on logs
Pholiota nameko (nameko)	Bags of sawdust or on logs
Pleurotus ostreatus (oyster mushroom)	Bags of straw or sawdust or on logs
Stropharia rugosoannulata (stropharia)	Bags of straw or sawdust or on the lawn

Narcissi

A host of golden ...

Gardeners tend to use the name daffodil to describe the spring flowers with long trumpets, while the word narcissus is reserved for those with short, cup-like trumpets. There are, in addition, jonquils, Lent lilies, poet's narcissi and hundreds of garden varieties with all sorts of names. All, botanically, are narcissi, for they belong to the genus *Narcissus*. But whatever they are called, they are the true harbingers of spring, so be generous with your planting. A few bulbs spread round the garden look miserly, but a crowd of 50 or 100 blooms is a stunning way to welcome the new season.

Dividing the clump

When the number of flowers produced by a clump of narcissi begins to decline, it is likely that the bulbs have become overcrowded. From time to time, lift the clump when the foliage has turned yellow, separate the bulbs and replant them immediately.

Cut flowers

If you are growing narcissi for cutting, lift the clumps every three or four years. Separate the bulbs, discard any that are damaged and leave the remainder to dry in a cool place. Remove leaves, skins that are loose and roots as soon as they are dry and brittle. In September, when the soil is moist, replant them and scatter a dressing of slow-release fertiliser round them.

Plant early

It is advisable to plant narcissus and daffodil bulbs as soon as they are on sale in early autumn. They will root more quickly in soil that is still warm from the summer and, by getting them off to a good start, they will last for many years.

Deadheading daffodils

Make sure that you deadhead faded daffodils and narcissi. Not only do the dying blooms look straggly and unattractive but they also drain the valuable energy reserves that are needed by the bulbs if they are to flower again the following year. You can use secateurs or your fingers to remove the faded flower heads, leaving the stems to die down with the foliage.

Cover up

If you do not want to move fading narcissi out of the border, plant something round them that will camouflage the dying leaves and, when they have finally withered, will conceal the empty spot. Perennial geraniums and day lilies make excellent screens in sunny spots, while hostas are perfect for areas of partial shade that are damp.

The importance of foliage

When the bulbs have finished their growing cycle, the foliage will begin to yellow. This may look untidy but it is very important that you do not cut the leaves down immediately because they are needed to replenish the bulbs' energy reserves. You should leave them for at least six weeks. Do not tie up the leaves because this damages the tissues and, by reducing the area exposed to the sun, diminishes the plants' ability to build up food reserves. It is much better to let the foliage die down naturally.

Making room

When narcissi have ceased to flower and the leaves have begun to turn yellow, make room for other plants in the border by lifting the bulbs carefully and replanting them in an out-of-the-way part of the garden. When the leaves dry out, lift the narcissi, remove leaves, loose skins and roots and store them in a cool place. Replant them in autumn.

Gardener's potpourri

Unrequited loves

Narcissus, in one version of the Greek legend, was a youth of great beauty who, because he rejected the advances of the nymph Echo, was condemned by the goddess Nemesis to fall in love with his own image reflected in a pool. Echo pined away until only her voice was left, while Narcissus gazed on in self-adoration. Other versions relate that it was the love of the youth Ameinias that he spurned, or that he yearned upon his reflection to recall the beloved features of his dead twin sister. Whatever the cause, the result was a love that could not be fulfilled, for which he died or killed himself. And where he fell beside the pool a flower sprang up that still bears his name. In all its versions, the tale is perhaps an embodiment of the Greek belief that to look upon your own reflection was unlucky, or even fatal.

The natural look

A lawn scattered with clumps of daffodils and narcissi is a delightful sight, but you will be unable to mow it for at least six weeks until the bulbs' leaves have died down. Instead, plant a small, naturalised area in a corner of the garden, or create a sylvan glade where there is a backdrop of two or three young trees. To avoid a regimented look, scatter the bulbs haphazardly in these areas, adding, perhaps, snowdrops and crocuses for variety. Using a bulb planter, plant them where they fall. They will make a bright show early in the year, and such a small patch will not be conspicuous if it remains rough until summer.

Poor mixers

If you cut narcissi for the house, do not put them straight into a vase with other flowers. The stems of narcissi emit a toxic sap that shortens the life of other blooms, particularly tulips. Cut 2.5cm (1in) from the bottom of the stems and stand the narcissi in a vase of water for 24 hours. The bases of the stems will then become sealed and, once rinsed, they can be safely combined with other flowers. (See *also* **Cut flowers**)

The joys of spring A container fully planted with narcissi makes a bold, early-season statement.

Nasturtiums

Time and money savers

Nasturtiums are fast-growing, they prefer poor soil and require no feeding. In summer, use them to brighten up a dull corner of the garden, to make a colourful screen of flowers to hide the compost heap or rubbish bins, or to fill a gap in the hedge. In April, sow two or three seeds in each planting hole, then thin out the young plants as they start to grow. Or, you can sow the seeds in small pots of gritty compost in March and plant them out when the seedlings reach a height of about 5cm (2in).

Bright and useful

Cabbage white butterflies like to breed on nasturtiums, which makes these plants as useful in the garden as they are attractive. Plant them

in the vegetable patch near your brassica plot, where they will entice the butterflies to lay their eggs away from the vegetables.

Helmets of gold

Nasturtium flowers, like the leaves, are edible, which is one reason why they were grown on the earth roofs of air raid shelters during the Second World War. The plants arrived from the

Make the right choice

The wide range of nasturtiums

Nasturtiums come in a wide range of types, both bushy and climbing, and are ideal for borders, pots, containers and hanging baskets. Choose from the following:

Type	Variety	Description
Trailing or climbing	Climbing Mixed	Colours: cerise, cream, orange, yellow; 1.8–2.4m (6–8ft)
	Golden Emperor	Green leaves with large flowers in deep shimmering gold. Good as climber or ground cover; 1.8m (6ft)
Semi-trailing	Double Gleam Mixed	Mixed colour, semi-double flowers, orange, red and yellow; 30cm (12in)
	Jewel of Africa	Green foliage splashed cream and white. Flowers in orange, red and yellow shades; 1–1.2m (3–4ft)
Bushy	Alaska Mixed	Marbled cream and variegated foliage. Flowers held above leaves; 25–30cm (10–12in)
	Empress of India	Deep crimson flowers above dark foliage; 20cm (8in)
	Salmon Baby	Dark foliage, semi-double salmon flowers; 23cm (9in)
	Whirlybird Mixed	Semi-double, upward-facing flowers of cream, gold, mahogany, orange, rose and scarlet; 30cm (12in)

West Indies in the 1590s, when they were known as Indian cresses, because their peppery flavour resembled that of watercress. The seeds, too, can be eaten – pickled in vinegar they can be used as a substitute for capers. When the plants gained a botanical name, it was *Tropaeolum*, meaning 'trophy', because of their shield-like leaves and the flowers, which resemble golden helmets. Together they look rather like some ancient battle trophy. Interestingly, the botanical name *Nasturtium* – 'nose stinger'– actually refers to a group of yellow-flowered cresses.

Meat and new veg

Make a break with tradition and try something new with the Sunday roast by growing *Tropaeolum tuberosum* (tuberous nasturtium). Apart from its abundance of spectacular red and gold flowers, its ability to scramble up trellises unaided and its total indifference to cold, wet summers, this nasturtium produces a delicious tuber that can be eaten raw like a radish or cooked like a potato. The tubers, which have red stripes that turn blue when they are cooked, form part of the staple diet in many parts of South America, where it is known as *ysaño*. (See also **Edible flowers**)

Floral 'big top'

Fill a wooden half-barrel with a mixture of potting compost and coarse grit, and drive a stout stick through the centre of the compost. Cut a groove round the stick, near the top, and then attach 12 pieces of string to it. With drawing pins, secure the other ends at regular intervals, round the edge of the barrel. Sow nasturtium seeds beside each string and, within a few weeks, you will have a display of flowers in the shape of a circus 'big top' tent that will brighten a terrace or patio.

Nettles

Stinging remedies

Attempting to remove a large nettle by grasping it firmly in your hand is not generally a good idea because, unless your wrists and arms are well protected, you risk being stung by the upper leaves. Fold a plastic dustbin liner or several sheets of newspaper and wrap them round the plant to enclose the leaves, then grasp the nettle firmly and pull sharply to remove it from the ground. If you are stung, traditional remedies that will soothe the irritation include rubbing the affected spot with a dock or sorrel leaf, a slice of onion or a crushed clove of garlic.

Sanctuary for desirable insects

If a patch of nettles grows in the garden, it is not necessarily a bad thing. In a sunny spot, butterflies may be drawn to lay their eggs, while ladybirds are also attracted by nettles, and these carnivorous beetles should certainly be encouraged, as both they and their larvae have an almost insatiable appetite for aphids.

A clue to fertility

If you are planting a new garden, look out for clumps of nettles. Because they grow most readily on nitrogen-rich soil, these weeds are an indication of fertility, a fact that leads archaeologists to regard their presence as a sign of possible ancient human habitation. Dig or pull up the nettles and in their place grow leafy vegetables, which do best in a soil that is rich in nitrogen.

A natural fertiliser

Nettles make an excellent fertiliser. Put the leaves and stems into a water butt or other container and for every 1kg (2lb 3oz) of nettles add 10 litres (17½ pints) of water. Leave to soak for a month, then use the solution to water your plants. Though nettles make excellent accelerators in the compost heap by adding minerals and speeding up the breakdown of materials, make sure you remove the seed heads from annual nettles and cut the roots from perennials before adding them. Seeds are likely to germinate, and roots may continue to grow in the heap.

Garden secrets

To ripen fruit

Slightly under-ripe apples and pears will ripen and soften more quickly if laid on a bed of nettles. Or fill a paper bag with nettle leaves and add the unripe fruits. Check each day and remove the fruits as they ripen; it is advisable to wear gloves.

Gardener's potpourri

Nettle bed

They may not delight most gardeners but nettles have a long and respectable history. Mary, Queen of Scots vowed that sheets woven from nettles were the smoothest she had ever slept in, and fishing nets and ropes were also spun out of the fibres. A green dye was obtained from the leaves, which were also brewed to make tea and beer, and medicinal uses of the plant were legion. Early recognition of the nettle's iron content led to it being prescribed for blood disorders, and nettle ale was said to be good for jaundice; only, however, if the leaves were picked before May Day. After that, the Devil required them as raw material for his shirts. Rheumatism can reputedly be relieved by beating the affected area with bunches of nettles; they would undoubtedly make an effective counter-irritant.

A garden haven for wildlife

Don't be too rigorous in your quest for an immaculate garden – a small patch left untended is attractive in itself and will soon become home to an entire community of wild creatures.

Tadpoles in the pond, greenfinches swooping in to feed at the bird table and butterflies fluttering among summer flowers – a garden that is alive with wildlife is a never-ending source of pleasure for all.

Even a garden in the most urban of areas can become a wildlife haven. Animals, birds and insects will not only visit but may make a town garden their permanent home if food and shelter are provided by an unobtrusive owner.

In the wildlife garden, 'untidy' areas are prized. An old tree or a weathered wall makes an ideal shelter; clumps of weeds provide food for birds in the form of seeds and the insects that they attract; and a patch of unmown grass can be turned into a miniature meadow of wild flowers. Other places in the garden can be designed to attract different kinds of wildlife. A bed of nectar-producing flowers will draw butterflies and bees, a pond makes a natural breeding ground for dragonflies and damselflies, frogs and toads, while berry-bearing shrubs and trees will attract birds from miles around during the lean winter months.

Key to plan, left

1 An old wall
Sanctuary for birds and insects

2 Pile of rocks
Toads' resting place

3 Tree table
Focus for birds

4 Protective thicket
Berries and shelter

5 Water garden
Home to fish and amphibians

6 Summer meadow
Area for native plants

7 Butterfly border
Nectar-producing flowers

1 Welcoming refuge

The reflected warmth of an old wall attracts butterflies, while robins, great tits, redstarts and, possibly, spotted flycatchers may nest in natural holes or in nesting boxes, and spiders, beetles and woodlice shelter in crevices. Plants, including moss and lichen, may take root on the wall surface, while a little soil will encourage other plants to grow from the cracks. Perennial alyssums, arabis, aubrietas, *Campanula portenschlagiana*, helianthemums, ivy-leaved toadflax, *Saponaria ocymoides*, sedums and wallflowers make a colourful show; ivy and native ferns are useful if the wall faces north.

2 Rocky hideaway

In a corner of the garden, a pile of rocks set in leaf litter serves as a quiet and private hideaway for slow-worms and toads.

3 Feeding time

A bird table, adapted from a tall tree stump, is a charming point of interest, especially in winter. Bullfinches, chaffinches, greenfinches, robins and sparrows may pay regular visits, while the tit family, nuthatches, siskins and even the greater spotted woodpecker will cling to a nutfeeder or half a coconut hanging down. Blackbirds, fieldfares, starlings, thrushes and yellowhammers appreciate nuts and seeds left on the ground. A birdbath placed nearby provides a place for drinking and bathing.

4 Berried border

Closely planted trees and shrubs offer birds the safety of dense branches in which to nest as well as berries to eat. Butterflies and other insects, as well as small animals such as hedgehogs, will also visit a thicket or hedgerow of mountain ash, blackthorn, cotoneaster, elder, guelder rose, hawthorn, holly, honeysuckle, hornbeam or field maple.

5 Water world

A pond provides a home for frogs, toads and aquatic insects. Among the plants that offer shelter, food and oxygen are *Potamogeton crispus* (curled pondweed) and *Myriophyllum spicatum* (spiked water milfoil), while the leaves of water lilies provide shade and so control algae. Waterside plants such as *Caltha palustris* (marsh marigold) and *Iris pseudacorus* (flag iris) complete the water garden, providing cover for frogs and toads. Dragonflies, diving beetles, pond skaters and whirligig beetles may make their way to the pond naturally, though amphibians may have to be

introduced from a garden centre.
Unexpected visitors too may arrive in the
form of birds, hedgehogs and foxes that
come to quench their thirst.

6 Meadow magic

Create a summer meadow in a sunny corner of the garden. Plant native
grasses and wild flowers as a magnet for birds and insects. Butterflies and
bees will feed on the nectar of clover, knapweed, scabious and thistles,
while finches and other birds will be drawn to dandelions and teasels.
Insects and small animals may take up residence in the grasses attracting
in turn bats, dragonflies and owls.

7 A bed of nectar

One of the most enjoyable signs of summer is the sight of bees and
butterflies collecting nectar, and it is worth dedicating a sunny border to
these insects. Early nectar-producing flowers include arabis and honesty
while foxgloves, golden rod and Michaelmas daisies will be an attraction
later in the summer. A buddleja is so attractive to these insects that it is
commonly known as the butterfly bush.

Newspaper

Cold frame insulation
If spring frosts are forecast, insulate your cold frame by covering it with several sheets of newspaper held down round the edges with bricks or stones. Cover the frame before the sun sets so that some of the day's warmth is trapped inside.

Protection for an orchid
The orchid *Bletilla striata* will survive in a sheltered spot outdoors, provided it is protected from frost. At the onset of cold weather, lay a newspaper over the plant and cover it with 10cm (4in) of soil.

Weekend watering device
Many people go away for long weekends during the summer, at a time when plants in containers can dry out very quickly. You can give them a little extra protection using old newspapers. Before you go away, cut a circle of newspaper several pages thick and the same diameter as the top of the container. Cut a slit from the edge of the circle to the centre, and shape to fit round the stem of the plant. Water the plant thoroughly, wet the newspaper, then fit it round the plant on the surface of the compost. This will slow the evaporation rate and help the plant to conserve moisture until you are back at home.

Old news is good to use
Make newspaper pots for sowing seeds of plants such as tomatoes and courgettes that will later be planted out in the garden. Cut the paper into rectangles about 20 x 30cm (8 x 12in) and fold in half lengthways. With one narrow end towards you, fold up the bottom third of the paper, then fold down the top third and tuck one edge inside the other. Open out the middle and fill with seed compost. Pack the filled pots into seed trays to keep them upright, and sow in the usual way with one seed to each pot. At planting time, plant out the seedlings, still in the pots.

Make them wet
Newspaper makes an excellent mulch anywhere in the garden. In the ornamental garden, for aesthetic reasons, it can be covered with bark chippings. Where appearance is less important, cover it with grass mowings or use it uncovered and held down securely with stones. Make sure that the paper is thoroughly wet, because it is extremely difficult to dampen layers of newspaper once they are on the ground, as the water does not soak through all the sheets. Soak in a bucket of water or a trough used to wet ready-pasted wallpaper.

Boost beans and peas
When you are planting beans and peas, try layering the bottom of the trenches with a mixture of garden compost and strips of newspaper that have been thoroughly soaked in liquid manure. This will help to conserve important moisture and warmth, so promoting growth of the plants.

In the compost heap
When you are building a compost heap, add a layer of shredded newspaper on top of every 15cm (6in) layer of other materials. You should try to mix the paper with soft green weeds or grass clippings as they will help it to break down more quickly.

Warming a window ledge
The area behind the curtains on a window ledge can be an extremely cold place at night. Push a few layers of newspaper down between the plants and the glass, letting the paper hang loosely over the foliage to stop the plants from becoming chilled.

Nicotianas

Midnight's summer dream
For a little magic, try growing a clump of *Nicotiana* (tobacco plant) close to the place where you sit out on warm summer evenings, and another beneath your bedroom window. The aroma that wafts from this half-hardy annual on summer nights is exquisite. The flowers of some varieties of this plant open only in the evenings when their sweet scent attracts night-flying moths. The white flowers of *N. sylvestris* (woodland tobacco), however, remain open throughout the day and night. For something a little out of the ordinary, experiment with *N. alata* 'Lime Green', which blooms with vivid, greenish yellow flowers in late summer and autumn.

Grow your own tobacco
Nicotiana was so called after Jean Nicot, the 16th-century French ambassador to Portugal who introduced the French to tobacco. *Nicotiana tabacum*, the true smoking tobacco, is a magnificent ornamental plant that reaches a height of 1.8m (6ft). It has pale pink flowers and huge leaves.

Nitrogen

An essential element

Nitrogen is essential for plant development. It encourages leafy growth and sturdy stems as it builds protoplasm, protein and other plant cell constituents. If your soil is starved of nitrogen, plant growth will be stunted, foliage pale and plants vulnerable to attack from pests and diseases. As nitrogen is washed out of the soil quickly by rain, it must be replaced constantly. Dig in plenty of well-rotted compost or manure then add a top dressing of dried blood or slower-acting hoof and horn. But too much nitrogen in the soil can result in plants producing foliage at the expense of blooms.

Feathering your beds

Since time immemorial, Chinese farmers have made a nitrogen-based fertiliser by steeping poultry feathers in water. To do the same, place feathers in a water butt or other container and fill it with rainwater. Put a piece of strong netting or board on top then add a layer of heavy stones. Leave the container in a shady place for about two months while the feathers soften into a mash that can then be spread as a mulch. Take care as feathers can induce asthma attacks.

See also **Spinach**

Growing know-how

Nitrogen sources for the soil

Dried blood and hoof and horn are excellent sources of nitrogen, but dried blood acts faster than hoof and horn. Garden compost and manure contain only small percentages of nitrogen but are rich in humus. However, there are other ways of providing this vital garden nutrient. Many proprietary brands of fertiliser are formulated with the emphasis on nitrogen. Check the label; the number under N (nitrogen) should be higher than those under P (phosphorus) and K (potassium). Chicken manure is another good source of nitrogen and can be bought from poultry farms. It is very strong and should be composted for several months before being used. After harvesting peas and beans, cut off the stems at soil level. As the roots rot, the nitrogen in the root nodules will be released into the ground.

No-dig gardening

Preparing the ground

To prepare a plot for no-dig gardening, the ground needs to be dug deeply in its first year, incorporating generous amounts of organic matter. Take out any weeds, making sure you remove all the roots of perennial ones, as even the smallest piece will regrow. Mark out the area into 1.2m (4ft) wide beds surrounded by paths. Always work from planks to avoid compacting the ground.

Dealing with annual weeds

If the ground is likely to be full of annual weeds, it may be best to leave it fallow for a while so they can be dealt with before any crops go in. By hoeing the soil weekly, you will kill any that have germinated and bring seeds to the surface where they will grow, for dealing with later.

Clearing overgrown areas

If a plot has become overgrown with weeds, it can be cleared either by covering the area with black polythene to exclude light so that any growth beneath it dies out, or – for quicker results – by burning off surface growth with a flame gun, used with extreme care. Whichever you adopt, however, roots below ground will not be destroyed and must be removed by hand.

Rotation of crops

It is still an advantage to follow a rotation plan in your no-dig vegetable garden. If you grow the same crop in the same place year after year, there is always a risk of the crops passing on pests and diseases from one season to another. And a crop such as brassicas following peas and beans will be able to take advantage of the nitrogen that has been left in the soil. (*See also* **Vegetable gardens**)

Sowing and mulching

Although many no-dig gardeners mulch their beds before sowing and sow through the mulch, initially you may find it easier to sow first, in the usual manner, and apply the mulch when the seedlings are established. If you have recently changed to a no-dig system and your soil is still of a consistency that makes it difficult to cover the seed drills after sowing, use, instead, a little potting compost or leafmould to cover the seeds, firming it down gently with the back of a rake.

Transplanting technique

Cabbage, courgette and tomato seedlings are easy to plant out in beds that have already been covered with a mulch. Draw back the mulch with your hand, to expose a circle of soil 15–20cm (6–8in) in diameter. Using a trowel, plant the seedlings in the usual manner. Firm

Garden secrets

Covering up potatoes

Growing potatoes under black polythene cuts down on a lot of hard work. Just lay the seed potatoes in rows on the surface of soil that has been heavily mulched and cover them with black polythene, pulling it taut and anchoring it down round the edges. As the potatoes start to grow, they will push the polythene up. Cut X-shaped slits above each potato to allow the new growth through. The one disadvantage of this method is that it makes watering – particularly important when growing maincrop varieties – more difficult. If you do not wish to spend time watering each plant by hand, you can lay lengths of porous pipe between the rows before putting the polythene in place.

Make the right choice

A green goodness for the garden

Green manures are useful crops for sowing in vacant places to give a protective cover to soil. In spring, they can be dug into the soil to release important nutrients.

Type	Crop name	Soil preference
Annual green manures	Fagopyrum esculentum (buckwheat)	Any, even poor
	Lupinus angustifolius (bitter lupin)	Light, acid
	Phacelia tanacetifolia (phacelia)	Any
	Secale cereale (grazing rye)	Any
	Sinapsis alba (mustard)	Good loam
	Trifolium incarnatum (crimson clover)	Light, sandy loam
	Trigonella foenum graecum (fenugreek)	Heavy, well-drained
	Vicia faba (winter field beans)	Heavy, moisture-retentive
	V. sativa (winter tares)	Moisture-retentive, neutral to alkaline
Biennial Perennial	Medicago lupulina (trefoil)	Light, neutral to alkaline
	Medicago sativa (alfalfa)	Well-drained, neutral to alkaline
	Trifolium hybridum (alsike clover)	Any
	T. pratense (Essex red clover)	Good loam, neutral to alkaline

the soil gently round the roots and replace the mulch, leaving a gap of about 5cm (2in) round the stem of each plant.

Bed covers

The secret of successful no-dig gardening lies in continuous growing. Never allow the soil to lie fallow and exposed to the elements. As soon as one crop has been harvested, sow a follow-on crop, or a crop of an annual green manure such as *Trifolium incarnatum* (crimson clover) in spring, or *Vicia faba* (winter field beans) in autumn. The green manure can be chopped down when it has grown and left on the soil as a mulch.

Make more compost

Finding sufficient raw materials to provide an adequate supply of compost can be a problem for many gardeners. Collecting household and garden waste from friends and neighbours, and discarded vegetable matter from local greengrocers and market stalls, can help, but if

you can afford to devote part of the garden to growing perennial green manure such as *Medicago sativa* (alfalfa) you will have a constant supply of material for the heap.

See also **Deep beds, Manures, Mulching, Organic gardening**

Noise

Soundproofing the garden

If you live near a busy street, a railway or some other source of noise, you may benefit from natural soundproofing. A carefully placed dense hedge or line of trees can reduce noise levels by up to 50 per cent. (*See also* **Hedges, Wall planting**)

Sitting quietly

Plant a hedge of yew, conifers or privet in a semi-circle round a garden bench. In a few years, with careful pruning, the hedge will be tall and thick and you will have a quiet, peaceful and secluded spot in which to sit.

Lazy sunny afternoon

If lounging in the garden on a sunny afternoon is your idea of heaven, add an extra dimension to the peaceful atmosphere by installing a water feature such as a millstone fountain. The sound of water gurgling gently over cobblestones is surprisingly relaxing.

Rude awakening

If you like to start work in the garden early on summer mornings, spare a thought for the neighbours, whose pleasure it may be to sleep late. Restrict your gardening to quiet activities such as weeding, hoeing or pruning and leave the lawn mower and shredder in the shed until midday at the earliest.

Make the right choice

Hedging out the decibels

Choose evergreen rather than deciduous plants. It is the foliage that blankets sound, and you will want to shut it out in winter, as well as in summer. A broad band of planting is required to make a significant reduction in noise levels, and this may not be possible in a small garden. However, even a dense garden hedge provides a good psychological barrier. Ideally, choose a mix of large-leaved and small-leaved evergreens because those with larger foliage will suppress deeper sounds while smaller-foliaged plants will eliminate higher tones. A double barrier of rhododendrons, on acid soils, or *Viburnum rhytidophyllum*, with its huge evergreen leaves, on alkaline soils, makes a good foundation. Couple these with hollies or conifers such as x *Cupressocyparis leylandii* (Leyland cypress) or *Thuja plicata* 'Atrovirens' (western red cedar).

Blowing in the wind

If you are enchanted by the sound of wind-chimes tinkling in the breeze, make sure that you hang them where their chiming will not disturb your neighbours. The wind can carry sounds a long way in the garden, and some people find the constant jangling of wind-chimes most unpleasant and distracting.

Nursery areas

A practical feature

A plant nursery is something no serious gardener should be without, and it is quite easy to create one. In a nursery, you can raise new plants from seeds and cuttings, and propagate trees, shrubs and ornamental plants to keep your garden well stocked, and have some over to give to friends.

Choosing a site

If you have space, turn part of your vegetable garden into a nursery. Choose an area with some shade and easy access to water. Since the young plants may need to be moved about, raise them in containers and to reduce the need for weeding, stand these on a heavy-duty black polythene sheet or piece of old carpet. In colder areas you may need to move them into a cold frame to protect young plants from frost.

Small is cheap

Young trees, shrubs and perennials are much less expensive than mature plants, but they may be too small to plant out in the garden immediately. Keeping them in the nursery for a year or two will give them time to become acclimatised to their surroundings and to grow large enough to make an impact in the garden when they are eventually planted out.

Label your plants

To avoid confusion later, always label the plants you grow in your nursery. The most secure types of labels are plastic or metal tags that loop round the stems of the plants. These cannot be removed easily or become lost. Use an indelible laundry marker or a freezer pen to write on the labels. (See also **Labelling**)

Chestnut giant Distinctive fruits adorn the *Castaneo sativa* (sweet chestnut), which can grow to 30m (100ft).

Nuts

The beauty of almonds

Prunus dulcis (sweet almond) is a tree of modest size that makes an excellent lawn specimen. It flowers in late winter and early spring, before the leaves appear. Almond trees are worth growing for their ornamental value alone but, because they flower very early, to produce a crop of nuts they must be planted against a south-facing wall where frost cannot destroy the blooms. In October, when they fall to the ground, you should harvest the almonds, remove them from their shells and spread them out to dry thoroughly in a well-ventilated place such as a shed or garage. Once dry, the almonds can be stored somewhere cool and dry or, still in their shells, in an earthenware jar in a mixture containing equal quantities of moist coconut fibre and coarse salt.

Sweet chestnuts

A 20-year-old *Castanea sativa* (sweet, or Spanish, chestnut) may be as tall as 10.5m (35ft), and a mature specimen can reach up to 30m (100ft). They can, therefore, be grown successfully only in large gardens. If you have the space, however, the tree is worth growing for both its ornamental value and its delicious nuts. 'Marron de Lyon' is the best variety, with large, sweet nuts. Once established, sweet chestnut trees require little pruning and are rarely troubled by pests or diseases. Gather the nuts as soon as they fall to the ground in October. Remove the husks and spread the nuts out to dry in a warm place, turning every other day. When they are thoroughly dry, pack them in jars between layers of sand in a frost-free place.

Onions

Spring sowing

Growing onions from seeds sown in spring is more economical than growing them from sets – small, immature bulbs – but it is essential to use only fresh seeds from a reputable supplier. As the seedlings begin to become overcrowded, thin them and use the thinnings in salads, in the same way as spring onions.

Heat treatment

To reduce the risk of bolting, make sure when you are buying onion sets that they have been heat treated. This process kills the flower bud in the centre of the bulb while the bulb itself remains unharmed.

Strengthening sets

To prevent birds from pulling up newly planted onion sets, put the sets in trays of seed compost about two weeks before setting them out in the vegetable garden. Plant them out when the green shoots appear, taking care not to disturb the compost round their newly formed roots.

Cut back on nitrogen

Onions planted in nitrogen-rich soil will put out lush foliage at the expense of bulb growth. If the nitrogen content of your vegetable bed is high, interplant the onions with leafy vegetables such as lettuces, which will help to absorb the excess nitrogen in the soil.

Gentle weeding

Do not use a large hoe to weed between rows of onions; you may damage the bulbs and expose them to attack by pests and diseases. Always weed by hand or, alternatively, use an onion hoe, which is small and specially designed for work between the rows.

To bend or not to bend

Once it was common practice to bend onion leaves over before lifting the bulbs from the ground, as it was believed that this allowed more sunlight to reach the onion and thus the ripening process was hastened. Research has shown, however, that this can damage the onion and shorten its storage life. Leave the foliage to die back naturally instead, then, without uprooting them, ease the onions gently to the surface of the soil to increase the area that is exposed to the sun. After two weeks, lift the onions and spread them out on the soil to dry.

Watering sense

As the plants start to mature, the foliage begins to turn yellow and bends over. At this point, stop watering the crop altogether as this allows the bulbs to ripen fully, ensuring better storage quality.

Make the right choice

Summer onions

Enjoy spring onions in early summer salads, and grow sufficient maincrop varieties to eat in summer and to store for use in winter.

Variety	Description
Spring onions	
White Lisbon	Standard variety
Winter-over	For autumn sowing
Maincrop onions	
Bedfordshire Champion	Traditional variety, strong flavour
Brunswick	Red onion, sweet flavour
Buffalo	For autumn sowing
First Early	Sets for autumn planting
Hygro	Excellent modern onion
Jet Set	Among earliest from sets
Paris Silver Skin	Cocktail onion
Red Baron	Red sets, sweet and strong
Sturon	Dependable from sets
SY 300	Traditional pickling variety
Turbo	Bolt-resistant, stores well

Drying time

It is most important to dry onions thoroughly after lifting them, otherwise there is a danger that they may rot in storage. If no rain is forecast, they can be left to dry naturally in the sun. Otherwise, it is best to spread them out carefully on trays or pieces of sacking and dry them in an airy room. When they are dry, remove the dead leaves. Before storing, separate any damaged onions from the others and use them immediately.

Onion stretcher

Nail four pieces of wood together to make a frame, then attach a piece of plastic netting or wire mesh to cover the centre. Spread out the onions on the mesh and leave them outside to

Sets are easier

Make lighter work of onion growing by planting sets rather than sowing seeds. Sets are easy to handle, eliminate the need for thinning out and can be planted in early spring, when it may still be too cold for seeds.

dry in the sun. At night, or in the event of rain, lift the frame, stretcher fashion, and carry the onions into a covered place such as a carport, shed or garage.

Mulch with newspaper

A few weeks before sowing onions, cover the plot with a layer of newspaper, held down with stones. Provided that you keep it damp, the newspaper will act as a mulch, helping to warm up the soil and preventing weed growth. Remove the paper when you want to sow the seeds, then replace it until the first shoots appear. (See also *Newspaper*)

Beat neck rot

It is unwise to store onions with large, thick, fleshy necks; they are prone to neck rot and will deteriorate quickly. Burn any bulbs in store that develop grey fluffy mould on the foliage just above the bulb.

Tying up onions

You can store onions in old stockings or a pair of tights. Tie a knot between each onion to reduce the risk of rotting onions infecting their neighbours. The tights can then be hung over beams or attached to a hook in the ceiling of the garden shed. As the onions are required, remove them by cutting below the knot.

Rope trick

A rope of onions is both traditional and decorative. It is also the best means of storage, since it permits air to circulate all round the bulbs. When the onions have dried, trim off the roots and flaky outer skins, but leave what remains of the foliage. Tie two onions to a string to form the base of the rope, then tightly tie in more onions, two or three at a time, keeping the foliage pointing upwards. When the rope has reached the required length, tie a string round the topmost bulbs and hang the onions in a cool, dry place. Beginning at the top of the rope, remove the onions as you need them, by cutting through their necks.

Tops for salads

To have a fresh salad ingredient all year round, place an onion, about 18–20cm (7–8in) in circumference, in the neck of a carafe or jar of water. The roots will grow down into the water and green leaves will develop from the top of the bulb. Snip off the foliage and use it in salads. When the bulb is exhausted replace it with another.

Tearless peeling

You do not have to suffer when peeling onions. To avoid tears, open a window and breathe away from the bulb or place the onion under water during peeling. Alternatively, unless the onion is to be eaten raw, blanch it in boiling water for 2 minutes then harden by dropping it into cold water for a further minute. This also makes strong onions milder.

Oranges

Worth trying

Orange trees are a little hardier than lemon trees and can even withstand a degree or two of frost. In Britain it is better to grow them in a greenhouse or conservatory in tubs that can be moved outside when the weather is fine; otherwise they will not thrive, even in milder areas. Nevertheless, they are well worth growing, as much for their scent and decorative value as for their fruit.

Mantelpiece orangery

The mini-orange trees complete with mini-oranges that are sold in florists are, in fact, calamondins – Chinese citrus trees that reach a height of 46cm (18in) and make excellent house plants, although they demand a winter temperature of at least 13°C (55°F) to thrive. The fruits, which are produced at any time of the year, are edible but very bitter. However, they make a good marmalade and a delicious dessert if stewed with sugar and served with whipped cream.

Plants from pips

Oranges are grown easily from pips and make good house plants. Plant them in individual pots of damp seed compost in spring, providing a temperature of at least 15°C (60°F) to aid germination. When the plants are 2.5–5cm (1–2in) high, repot them in 9cm (3½in) pots of potting compost. The plants will be attractive, but they will not flower or fruit for seven or eight years and it is unlikely that the fruit will be flavoursome.

Scenting the room

Instead of discarding orange peel, allow its stimulating scent to permeate a room. Peel it in a continuous strip and leave it to dry on the radiator or in the fireplace. Replace frequently.

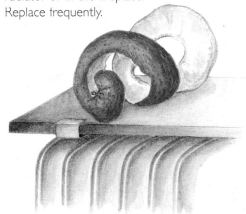

Orchids

Paying for quality
Orchids can be expensive plants so check carefully before buying. Look for healthy leaves and a flower spike that has some unopened flowers. You will be able to propagate further orchids from your plant so it is well worth investing in good stock.

Use soft water
Use rainwater for orchids whenever possible or, as a second choice, cooled boiled water. Alternatively, save the water from a defrosted refrigerator. Bring it up to room temperature before using it to water the plants.

Long display
For a long-lasting profusion of white orchids indoors, choose *Phalaenopsis*, the moth orchid. To prolong the blooming period, which can be initiated at any time of the year, wait until the flowers have faded, then use secateurs or sharp scissors to cut back the stems to the point from which the first blooms appeared. Side shoots will then develop and produce new flowers between six and eight weeks later.

Health check
Many orchids have aerial roots; keep an eye on them, because they are an excellent indicator of the plant's condition. If the ends of the roots are white or green, the orchid is healthy, but if they are yellow or brown, the plant is in need of attention. Check the position of the orchid – ventilation is essential to its well-being but a cold draught may cause it to die. Other causes of unhealthiness could be too much sun, an excess or lack of food or water, or too low a temperature.

The right humidity
Orchids need a humid environment to thrive but roots can rot if plants are overwatered. To increase humidity, stand the pots in trays filled with moist clay balls or gravel and spray the plants with rainwater in the mornings.

A delicate balance
All plants should be kept moist from April to September but very good drainage is vital. Epiphytic orchids such as *Phalaenopsis* should be watered by soaking the pot in a bucket of water once a week, increasing this to twice weekly in hot weather. Terrestrial orchids such as *Cymbidium* should be watered over the surface of the compost until excess runs out of the base. If, by accident, the compost dries out too much, give the orchid a good soaking and it should recover. Less water is required after repotting. Do not water for seven to ten days, then do so sparingly for two weeks to encourage new root growth.

Preserve bulb strength
During the orchid's first flowering season, to preserve the strength of the bulb, remove the flower spike once the flowers have developed. The cut flowers will last for several weeks if they are put into a vase of soft water. Every two or three days, trim the ends of the stems and change the water.

Care with feeding
Some orchids respond to feeding in the growing season, while others do not. Consult the nurseryman about the special needs of the species you intend to buy. Many treasured orchids have been killed by overfeeding.

Potting on
Repot orchids after they have flowered or when new leaf growth appears. Use orchid compost and a pot one size larger than was previously used. To help to promote healthy growth, be sure to brush away or wash off the old compost from around the roots before repotting, and use scissors to trim off dead roots.

Exotics for the garden
If you have little or no space at all to spare in the greenhouse, or the demands of the more glamorous orchid species deter you from attempting to grow them, you could try a hardy type in the garden. More than 50 species of orchid grow in the British countryside, and although it is illegal to collect them from the wild, some, such as *Dactylorhiza maculata* (spotted orchid), can be bought from specialist suppliers. More generally available is the pink-flowered *Bletilla striata*, which requires a sheltered spot, and *Pleione formosana*, which can be grown to add a touch of splendour to a sheltered rock garden.

Growing know-how

Tips for beginners
Follow this guide to increase your chances of success with orchids grown in the greenhouse.

- Grow hybrids that have been specially bred for the greenhouse.
- When your orchids first bloom, remove the flower spikes when the flowers have developed so that they do not sap the plants' strength.
- Some orchids may not flower unless there is a marked drop in temperature at night.
- Leave a little ventilation in your greenhouse but avoid draughts.
- Insulate the greenhouse with bubblewrap stretched tightly about 5cm (2in) away from the inside of the glass to reduce heat loss in winter.
- Dampen the floor of the greenhouse in order to maintain humidity.

Organic gardening

No half measures

Begin by getting rid of any chemical weapons that you have stockpiled in the garden shed or elsewhere, making sure that you dispose of them safely. To be successful, you must adopt the organic system throughout the garden. Banning chemicals from only the kitchen garden may provide you with vegetables that are free of pesticide residues, but it will do nothing to restore the balance of nature that is essential in the control of pests and diseases. If you continue to spray insecticide on your roses, for example, you risk killing not only greenflies, but also the beneficial insects that were on their way to pollinate your vegetables. (*See also* **Chemicals**)

Help plants to stand up for themselves

Healthy, well-fed plants that are grown in the situations best suited to their needs are more able to withstand pests and diseases than those that are forced to struggle for survival in poor, undernourished soils. Check the pH of your soil and provide plants with the conditions they need, or grow only those that require what you can provide. To improve soil fertility and structure, apply well-rotted compost and manure each year and protect the soil from the elements by growing green manure on plots devoid of other crops. (*See also* **Soil analysis**)

Supplementary benefits

If you are starting with poor, badly fed soil, you may need to add extra nutrients in the form of organic fertilisers until the soil improves. The state of the plants is an excellent indicator of deficiencies in the soil. Alternatively, a soil test will reveal which minerals and trace elements, if any, are missing. Depending on your findings, apply either a compound organic fertiliser, like blood, fish and bone meal, or one that will provide a specific element – such as hoof and horn meal, which is high in nitrogen. These fertilisers should be used only when absolutely necessary and only as supplements to, rather than substitutes for, manure and compost. (*See also* **Trace elements**)

A rich source

The leaves of *Symphytum* x *uplandicum* (Russian comfrey), particularly the variety 'Bocking 14', contain a large amount of potash. Vigorous and full of nutrients, it is available from organic nurseries. The leaves can be cut three or four times a year and laid in potato drills, runner bean trenches, and wherever else potash is needed.

Liquid manure

There will be enough leaves on six plants of *Symphytum* x *uplandicum* 'Bocking 14', which should be planted 61cm (2ft) apart, to make a liquid manure to feed potash-loving plants for a season. Cut the leaves, using a pair of garden shears, and stuff them into a water butt or large bucket. You may prefer to wear gardening gloves as comfrey is slightly prickly. Add 22.5 litres (5 gallons) of water to every 1.6kg (3½lb) of leaves and cover the container. When the leaves have fully decomposed, strain off the liquid and use it undiluted on your plants.

Concentrated alternative

As well as being used to make a large quantity of liquid manure, comfrey can also be made into a concentrated manure. Make a hole in the bottom of a container, such as an old oil drum, and stand it over a large bucket. Put a pile of freshly cut leaves into the drum and weigh

Growing know-how

Safer sprays for the organic gardener

Organic gardeners do not use chemicals to deal with pests and diseases, but there are some sprays that are approved for use – even though they may also kill beneficial insects.

Ingredient	Origin	Problems controlled
Copper	Naturally occurring element	Diseases including potato blight and damping off
Pyrethrum	Made from the flowers of *Tanacetum cinerariifolium*	Wide range of pests including aphids and caterpillars
Quassia	Derived from the bark of a tree, *Picrasma quassioides*	Many leaf pests, especially aphids
Rotenone (derris)	Made from powdered roots of a number of tropical plants	Wide range of pests, including aphids, caterpillars, sawfly and thrips
Soaps	Made from organic fatty acids	Wide range of pests, including aphids, red spider mite and whitefly
Sulphur	Naturally occurring element	Fungus diseases. (May damage some plants)

them down with a heavy stone. The leaves will produce a dark brown, bad-smelling liquid that will drip through the hole into the bucket below. The liquid should be diluted in ten parts of water before use.

Rotating your crops
Moving annual crops round the garden on a rotation system is essential to good organic growing. The more years you are able to leave before returning a crop to its original site the better. This helps to maintain a balance between soil fertility and the needs of the plants. (*See also* **Vegetable gardens**)

Protective collar
Maggots of the cabbage root fly feed on the roots of cabbages and other brassicas. Prevent an attack by placing small rounds of carpet or heavy cardboard flat on the soil, to fit tightly round each plant stem, or use brassica collars available from garden centres. These prevent the female fly, active from April to September, from reaching the soil to lay her eggs.

Make the right choice

Soil treatments
This guide will help you to meet the needs of your soil and plants.

Element	Source
Calcium (Ca)	Dolomite limestone
	Gypsum
Nitrogen (N)	Dried blood
	Fish meal
	Hoof and horn meal
Phosphate (P)	Bone meal
	Rock phosphate
Potassium (K)	Rock potash
	Wood ash
Trace elements	Calcified seaweed
	Dried animal manures
	Liquid animal manures
	Liquid seaweed
	Seaweed meal

Pest and disease control
In a well-balanced and established organic garden, pest and disease control is, for the most part, carried out by natural parasites and predators such as beetles, birds and parasitic wasps. Encourage these creatures into the garden by growing plants, such as lavender, rosemary or thyme, that will provide them with food, shelter and breeding places.

Innocent until proven guilty
Learn to distinguish between friends and foes. Never assume that an insect or other creature that appears in your garden for the first time is the scout of an invading army. It is much more likely to be a friend that has come to protect you from invasion and to enjoy the safety of your pesticide-free garden.

Playing your part
Help the beneficial insects to gain and maintain control of garden pests by practising companion and mixed planting and, when possible, by growing plant varieties that are resistant to pests and diseases. Introduce biological control agents into the garden and greenhouse, hang up sticky traps and use barriers round single plants or whole crops to protect them from attack. Be meticulous about garden hygiene and always clear away plant and other debris that could harbour pests or spread diseases. (*See also* **Biological controls**, **Companion plants**)

A little help for your friends
Initially, while predators and parasites are assembling their troops, you may need to help them to keep pests under control. Do not be tempted to resort to chemical pesticides that will kill friends and foes alike. Instead, spray affected plants with an organic control such as insecticidal soap, pyrethrum or rotenone. (*See also* **Growing know-how**, p. 205)

Dealing with diseases
As prevention is always better than cure, grow only certified virus-free plants. Always check any seedlings or cuttings given to you by other gardeners, as you could be importing pests or diseases into your garden. Be watchful for the first symptoms of disease and take quick action

by removing and destroying the affected plant parts. As a last resort, use an organic fungicide.

See also **Biological controls, Companion plants, Deep beds, Insects, Manures, No-dig gardening**

Oriental vegetables

Chinese artichokes
Although *Stachys affinis* (Chinese artichoke) is a member of the mint family, it has no scent and is grown for its tubers rather than its leaves. Plant large tubers 30cm (12in) apart each way, or start them off in pots indoors and plant out when they have sprouted. They can be harvested after seven months but are sufficiently hardy to be left in the ground until required. Prior to use, tubers need only scrubbing. Serve raw or boil gently until soft, or stir-fry.

Shungiku
A familiar vegetable in Japan, shungiku is *Chrysanthemum coronarium* (edible, or garland, chrysanthemum), also known as chop suey greens. In early spring shungiku can be sown in a cool greenhouse or frame and planted out when it is about 5cm (2in) high. Or sow directly outdoors in mid spring. Serve raw, young leaves, sparingly, in salads and use older leaves in soups. Steam or stir-fry the stems.

Climbing spinach
As climbing spinach is a native of Sri Lanka it will grow only in warm conditions. It can reach a height of 3m (10ft) and is an ideal climber for a conservatory or large greenhouse. Sow the seeds in a tray of seed compost in May and pot up the seedlings into small pots. When they are 10–12.5cm (4–5in) high, plant them in their permanent positions, 30cm (12in) apart, and provide supports for the plants to climb on. Pick the leaves frequently to encourage new growth, and cook in the same way as spinach.

See also **Cabbages**

Ornamental grasses

A grass for every border

Soaring and spiky, or willowy and arching, ornamental grasses bring waving life and eye-catching height and mass to borders. Leaf colours include blue-grey, bronze, bright green, green-grey, reddish-green, silver or yellow. The more unusual examples must be grown from seed or bought from specialist nurseries.

Touch of grandeur

Tall perennial grasses such as slightly arching *Helictotrichon sempervirens*, decoratively leaved *Miscanthus sinensis* 'Zebrinus' and silvery plumed *Stipa gigantea* will bring a touch of grandeur to the herbaceous border.

Plumed profusion The waving heads of *Pennisetum orientale* will brighten a border from July to October.

Annual ornaments

Hardy annual grasses are easy to grow and bring interesting variety to the garden in summer without hiding other plants from view. The white fluffy heads of hare's tail grass are a great visual asset dancing on slender 30cm (12in) stems in a flowerbed from June to September, while *Agrostis nebulosa* can be planted to surround bright annuals with showers of tiny florets. The more ungainly squirrel tail barley (*Hordeum jubatum*) waves feathery flower heads from June to August and pearl grass, which reaches 46cm (18in) high, rustles pendent silver-green, heart-shaped spikelets from May to July.

Stunning choices

Some striking annual or half-hardy grasses, which can be grown from seed, have bold or vividly coloured flower heads. Try ruby grass (*Melinis repens*), tender fountain grass (*Pennisetum setaceum*) and feathertop (*P. villosum*). Cut grasses before the seeds ripen if they are for dried flower arrangements.

Arresting arrangements

Ornamental grasses make striking additions to fresh and dried flower arrangements. For dried displays, it is best to pick the grasses just as the flower spikes begin to bloom, to ensure the heads remain intact after drying. (See also **Dried flowers**)

Window boxes of distinction

Ornamental grasses will add distinction to window boxes. For a summer display, sow pearl grass with golden pot marigolds, French marigolds and Californian poppies. (See also **Window boxes**)

Pampas grass

To be seen at its best, pampas grass needs careful placing. A backdrop of dark foliage will set off the dramatic plumes that appear in late summer, but the graceful clumps can also be seen to advantage when the plant is grown as a lone specimen. Grow one in a lawn or gravelled area, in a corner of the garden or near to, but well above, water.

Spring trim

Cut back ornamental grasses to the ground in spring rather than in autumn. As well as protecting the roots from frost, the leaves can bring a decorative note to the winter garden.

Quick division

In early spring, lift a cluster of ornamental grass roots, divide into smaller clusters of three or four and replant in pots. Water regularly until autumn then plant out.

Make the right choice

Grass shades

Overall leaf colours or variegations, such as cross banding or stripes, make dramatic contributions to the garden scene.

Blue
Festuca glauca
Helictotrichon sempervirens
Koeleria glauca
Sesleria caerulea

Red, especially in autumn
Carex buchananii
Imperata cylindrical 'Rubra'
Panicum virgatum 'Rubrum'
Stipa arundinacea 'Autumn Tints'

White
Glyceria maxima var. *variegata*
Miscanthus sinensis 'Variegatus'
Phalaris arundinacea var. *picta* 'Picta'

Yellow
Hakonechloa macro 'Aureola'
Miscanthus sinensis 'Zebrinus'
Spartina pectinata 'Aureomarginata'

Palms

Growing a tropical paradise
A palm tree can add an exotic touch to a garden or patio but palms are only really successful in the mildest areas of the country – the extreme south-west and those western regions warmed by the North Atlantic Current. Elsewhere, it may be worth trying to grow two of the hardiest varieties of palms, *Cordyline australis* (cabbage tree) and *Trachycarpus fortunei* (Chinese windmill palm). Both need to be positioned in a sunny, sheltered spot but they may still die during a severe winter.

Trees from seeds
In mild regions of the country where palm trees flourish, you can try growing them from seeds. Remove the fleshy seed coats, then soak

the seeds in a bowl of lukewarm water for 24 hours. Viable seeds will sink to the bottom of the bowl during this time. Discard the floating seeds and push the others into a mixture of equal parts of sand and compost in a seed tray. Put the tray into a warm greenhouse and keep the compost moist at all times. Germination will take at least a month and possibly as long as a year.

The time to transplant
The most effective time to transplant a palm is during the growing season. Water the soil well before transplanting and make sure that you bury the base of the tree a little deeper than it was planted originally. Firmly anchor a palm that has a clean stem and is taller than 1.5m (5ft) by inserting two or three stakes into the soil outside the rootball and linking them with ties at 46–61cm (18–24in) above ground level. Make sure that you water the palm copiously and frequently.

Good pruning
When pruning faded leaves from a palm tree, use a pruning saw. Cut the stems flush to the trunk and this will help give the palm a neat, trim appearance.

Papyrus

Giant sun-worshipper
Cyperus papyrus (Egyptian paper rush) is a tender plant which grows up to 1.5–2.4m (5–8ft) and requires a temperature of 18–21°C (64–70°F). Plant it in a large container, such as a half-barrel, of rich, very moist compost. The plant produces unusual, sulphur-green, fluffy flowers on globular heads from July to September.

One of the family
Because *Cyperus papyrus* – the true papyrus – is quite a difficult plant to grow in Britain, unless you have a conservatory or a sunny, glass-fronted stairwell, you might want to grow the hardier *C. involucratus* (umbrella grass) instead. Related to the true papyrus, its stiff, upright stems are topped with arching, leaf-like bracts that resemble the ribs of an umbrella. Keep the compost moist and stand the pot in an outer container filled with water.

One for outdoors
A good-sized garden pond with fairly shallow edges presents an opportunity to grow the highly decorative *Cyperus longus* (sweet galingale). The plant has wide, olive-green leaves and produces red-brown plumes with shiny green bracts in August and September. It makes an attractive edging plant for the pond but it can be invasive. In a small pond, grow a single specimen and restrain its roots in a container.

Dividing the roots
Use a cleaver to divide *Cyperus* roots, which are extremely tough. Place the plant on a wooden block, position the edge of the cleaver at the point of division and strike it sharply with a mallet.

See also **Cuttings**

Parsley

Sowing seeds in the ground
When sowing parsley seeds directly into the ground, germination will be more reliable from sowings made in warm soil in May and June than from sowings made in March and April.

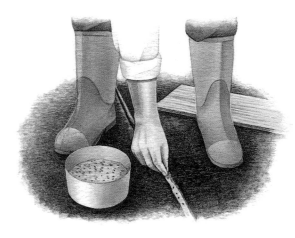

Using a garden cane, draw a shallow drill, about 6mm (¼in) deep. Mix the seeds with a handful of dry sand to aid even spacing, and gently trickle the mixture along the drill. Spread 6mm (¼in) of finely sieved soil over the seeds. Water the drill and cover with black polythene. Lift the cover at regular intervals to check on growth. Remove it when the first leaves appear.

Getting moving

Parsley seeds take a long time to germinate – about four weeks in warm soils and much longer in colder ones. Speed up the process by soaking the seeds in lukewarm water for several hours before sowing. This will help to soften their tough outer shells. Parsley is also available as 'primed seed' – seeds that have been partially germinated, then held in suspended animation, so that when they are sown and watered, they grow quickly.

Holiday care

Before going on holiday, cut back parsley plants and include a general liquid fertiliser in the last watering. When you return, they will have sprouted a rich supply of new leaves. Treat chervil, sorrel and tarragon in the same way. Chop up newly-cut parsley leaves immediately, put them into a bag and store in the freezer. When you use them, they will be as fresh and aromatic as the day they were cut.

Parsley in winter

Parsley is invaluable in the kitchen throughout the year. To ensure a winter supply, make a late sowing outdoors in July or August; the parsley will be ready to pick from autumn onwards. As winter advances, protect the plants from frost with a cloche. To be doubly sure of a sufficient supply during winter, lift a few seedlings from the late sowing and grow them on in pots in a greenhouse or on the kitchen window ledge. Your garden parsley and the pots should provide a plentiful supply throughout the winter.

Choose from three

There are three types of parsley, of which the most decorative and slowest to bolt is the curled variety with dark green, tightly curled foliage. The flavour of plain-leaved, or French, parsley is stronger, but the leaves are less attractive. The dual-purpose Hamburg parsley provides plain leaves and a parsnip-shaped root that offers an alternative to parsnips and has good winter hardiness. 'Par-Cel', although similar in appearance to plain-leaved parsley, is a subtly flavoured variety of celery. (See also **Celery**)

Remove flowers

When a parsley plant enters its second year it will begin to produce greenish flowers. Remove the flowering stems as soon as they appear – if they are not removed, the plant's leaf production will be reduced and it will run to seed quickly.

Gardener's potpourri

Sinister parsley

Perhaps it is the uncertain germination of parsley that has given rise to so many stories about it: the devil takes a tithe of all seeds sown; the plants go seven times to hell before growing; or they should be planted only on Good Friday. Other legends insist that parsley must never be transplanted or given away; if it is, death of the donor will follow within the year. And if parsley does grow well, it will do so only where the wife is master of the house.

Parsnips

Start afresh

Parsnip seeds rapidly lose their viability, so do not buy more than you require and buy fresh seeds every year. It is not worth trying to use the previous year's supply because it will probably have a poor rate of germination.

Fly-away seeds

Parsnip seeds are winged and light. Keep your hand close to the ground when sowing, and avoid sowing on windy days.

Success in sowing

Parsnip seeds should never be sown into freshly manured soil as this is likely to cause the roots to fork. Sow the seeds along the drill in groups of three and lightly rake over the soil to cover them. When the seeds germinate, gently pull out the two weakest seedlings from each group, leaving the strongest to develop into a good-sized plant.

Doubling up

Parsnip seeds can be sown earlier than most other vegetables – from early March in the south, and two or three weeks later in northern areas, although May sowings result in a higher germination rate and healthier roots. Since parsnips are not harvested until the following winter, the crop occupies the ground for much of the year. This is an extravagant use of space, especially in a small garden, so sowing lettuces between the rows will mean you get more out of the plot. The lettuces will be ready to harvest long before the parsnips take over.

Marking the rows

Parsnips seeds are slow to germinate – so slow that weeds often start to sprout before the seedlings appear. To ensure that the parsnip seeds that have yet to germinate remain undisturbed while you deal with the weeds, sow a few radish seeds in the drills between each group of parsnip seeds. Radish seedlings emerge quickly and will indicate the positions of the parsnip seeds.

Patios

Choosing the site

Before beginning work on a new patio, consider the options. What aspect will it have? If the garden is south-facing, you can build as close to the house as you like knowing that its shadow will not be cast on the patio. If the aspect is northerly, it may be better to site the patio far enough from the house to prevent the building's shadow falling across it.

Levelling up

If the patio is to adjoin the house, the level of the paving must be at least 15cm (6in) below the damp course. If the site slopes sharply from the house you may need to build a low retaining wall to contain the soil and hard-core needed to raise the patio's outer edge. If it slopes towards the house, you will need to level the ground and build a retaining wall at the outer edge to hold back the soil.

Rain and the patio

Good drainage is vital. When laying the patio, allow for a fall-away from the house of about 2.5cm in every 1.5m (1in in 5ft). If the fall is towards the house and levelling the site is impossible, you must construct a drainage channel between the edge of the patio and the house wall. This drainage channel can lead into either an existing drain or a specially constructed soakaway.

Weed prevention

If the patio is to be built of timber decking rather than stone, check that the timber has been pressure-impregnated with preservative. Before positioning the decking, lay down heavy-gauge polythene sheeting that has been perforated to allow water to drain away. This will prevent weeds from growing up through the slats. On paved patios, joints between the stones are usually filled with mortar that obstructs the weeds. But if the gaps are filled only with sand, it is advisable to treat them occasionally with a proprietary weedkiller, making sure that it does not stray onto borders nearby. (See also **War on weeds pp. 324–5**)

Welcome wall

A low, surrounding wall or a low, double wall for plants can enhance a patio. So, too, can planting pockets or a small pond. Allow space for them at the planning stage.

Size and shape

When planning a patio, relate its area to the size of paving slabs that you intend to use. This will reduce the need for slab cutting. If the slabs are square-edged, allow for joints between them. Plan your design on paper to calculate how much paving is required.

The next best thing

Ground and reconstituted stone, moulded to resemble the original rock, is cheaper than buying natural stone and is made in standard sizes, making it easier to calculate the quantity required.

Stain away with lemon juice

If you get plant or even nasty rust stains on your concrete patio, get rid of them by mixing natural lemon juice with hot water. Scrub till the stain comes out.

Harmony in brick

If you are constructing brick paths near the patio, use bricks of a single colour. A mixture of colours will detract from the patio and from the garden's unity and harmony.

A romantic touch

If the patio adjoins the house, use bulkhead lights, supplemented by lanterns, to illuminate it. Hire a qualified electrician to install mains-powered lighting. You can do the job yourself using low-voltage lighting from a transformer, which is plugged into the mains and reduces the 240-volt supply. For special occasions, burn flares and outdoor candles. Add a touch of romance with soft lighting by installing dimmer switches in rooms looking out onto the patio. (See also **Garden lighting**)

Garden secrets

Local stone for a natural effect

If you are lucky enough to live in an area where rock occurs naturally, think about constructing your patio, paths and walls from local stone. The colour of the rock will be in harmony with the soil and, because it is quarried nearby, transport costs will be reduced.

Dressing the patio Grouping your containers and changing their positions frequently will keep a patio bright throughout the year.

Space considerations

Restrict the number of potted plants to a minimum on a small patio. Hanging baskets and window boxes are just as colourful, and will not overcrowd the patio. Where space is plentiful, all types of containers can be planted up to provide spring and summer colour so that your patio becomes a delightful, changing tableau reflecting the successive seasons. (*See also* **Container gardening**, **Containers**)

Planting on patios

Because a patio is really an extension of the living area of the house, it should be planted to look attractive all year round. For a show of bright winter berries, but without the danger of fallen fruits staining stonework, choose *Gaultheria mucronata* or *Vaccinium*.

See also **Paving**

Paving

Slabs or blocks?

Paving slabs – flagstones – are the most usual materials for paths and patios, although in recent years there has been an increase in the popularity of smaller stone or concrete blocks. Both slabs and blocks are laid on a bed of sand, but slabs are secured with mortar while blocks are laid dry, directly onto the sand. Blocks are small enough to be kept firmly in place by their neighbours. A little sand brushed into the cracks will also help.

Stability for the drive

Blocks are best for drives and parking areas. If paving slabs are used for a drive, they need a firm foundation and must be well anchored, to prevent them from rocking or cracking.

Working with paving

Paving slabs come in a variety of finishes, colours and shapes. Sizes vary and, as a general rule, the larger the slab, the better it will bed down, although it will be heavier and more difficult to handle. Depending on the manufacturer, slabs are produced in both metric and imperial sizes, so decide on the slabs you want before drawing up plans and calculating the number required. The thickness of the slabs should also be taken into account when working out the height of the path or patio, especially if it is to abut the wall of the house. To prevent rising damp, any paved area should be at least 15cm (6in) below the level of the damp course.

Making a plan

Paving manufacturers' brochures show the choice of materials, sizes and patterns available. They may also provide squared grids on which you can plan your design. It may be best to avoid diagonal patterns, as they involve a lot of cutting at the edges. Use the information in the brochures to calculate how many slabs or blocks of each size are required. Add a few extra to allow for breakages as it may be difficult to obtain an identical match at a later date.

Pegs, string and spirit level

Use string to mark out the area to be paved. To ensure that the paving will have the correct fall, you will need a hammer, wooden pegs, a measuring tape, a spirit level, a length of timber and a small block of wood. For a fall of 2.5cm in 1.5m (1in in 5ft) the wooden block should be 2.5cm (1in) thick and the timber not less than 1.5m (5ft) long. Allowing for the thickness of the slabs, hammer in a peg at the highest point of the area to be paved, then measure off 1.5m (5ft) and hammer in another peg. Place a 2.5cm (1in) thick block of wood on top of this peg, then lay the length of timber from peg to peg and stand the spirit level on top of the timber.

Hammer the second peg down, or raise it if necessary, until you can see they are level. Continue in this way down the slope. Use the spirit level at right angles to the line of fall to check that the slabs are horizontal.

Laying the foundations

Site preparation is vital. Remove any turf, and ram rubble into soft areas to provide a firm base. Where traffic will be light, a layer of sharp sand about 4cm (1½in) thick on top of this rubble is enough. Weight-bearing areas will need deeper excavation and a sub-base material, such as fine rubble, bedded down firmly. Allow a 10cm (4in) deep sub-base for main paths that will support wheelbarrows or garden rollers, and 15cm (6in) for drives and carports. Then add the layer of sand. If the area to be covered is large, first construct a wooden frame to the required size and depth, then tip the sand into it and spread it out with a shovel or rake. To level the surface, lay a length of timber across the former and draw it across the top of the sand.

Secure paving

Paving slabs should never be laid directly onto a bed of sand. Rainwater can seep underneath them, displacing the sand and making the slabs unstable. To ensure that the slabs are laid securely, place five blobs of mortar on the sand before laying each slab, one for each corner of the slab and one for the centre. Lay the slab gently on top and tap, with a mallet or other wooden implement, until level. Or, if the slabs are thin, spread a layer of mortar, 2.5cm (1in) thick, onto the sand, then lay the slab on top.

Mortar mix

To make the mortar for bedding paving slabs, use one part cement to four parts sharp sand and just enough water so that when a little mortar is squeezed in the hand it retains its shape. If too much water is added, the mortar will be soft and will become compressed under the weight of the slab.

Putting in the pointing

When filling the gaps between slabs, make up a dry mixture of one part cement to two or three parts of sharp sand. Brush the mixture into the gaps, pressing down firmly with the edge of a trowel, then brush off the surplus. Wet the joints lightly, using a watering can with a rose and, just before the mortar sets, hollow it slightly by pressing it down with a rounded stick. These indented joints will help any rainwater to drain away. Then, remove any crumbs of mortar from the surface of the paving before it dries.

Cutting know-how

The tools required for stone-cutting are a wide-bladed cold chisel called a bolster, and a club hammer. Lay the slab on a bed of sand to prevent the shock of the blows from breaking it, then cut a V-shaped groove across the stone where you want to cut it. Turn the slab over and repeat the operation on the other side. Now place the bolster in the groove and give one hard blow; the slab should break neatly. If a large number of slabs is to be cut, you may be able to hire a stone-cutting tool from your local DIY or tool-hire shop.

Keeping it clean

During the winter, algae, slime and moss can accumulate on paving, making it dangerously slippery. Remove them with a proprietary path and patio cleaner, or use a high-pressure hose. Do not use a hose if the joints between the slabs are filled only with sand.

Laying blocks

If you have chosen blocks as a paving material, you must make sure that the paved area is surrounded by a firm edge to prevent the blocks and sand from creeping. The edge can be a narrow border of concrete or it can be constructed from planks impregnated with preservative. Lay a base layer of rubble and tamp it down well with a sledgehammer or other heavy object. Alternatively, hire a plate-vibrating tool and run it over the area two or three times. Then, spread a layer of sand on the rubble and lay the blocks directly onto the sand, working inwards from a firm edge and butting them close together. Use portions of cut blocks to fill in gaps round the edges. Finally, brush fine, dry sand into the joints between the blocks.

Plants for paved areas

Add colour and interest to paved areas by omitting a few slabs or blocks. Dig out the soil from these areas and refill the holes with a mixture of loam and compost. These small beds are ideal for low-growing rock garden plants and herbs, whose colours will be set off by the surrounding paving.

See also **Patios**

Peaches

Protective planting

Peach trees are hardy and need no protection from cold weather. The blossom comes out so early in the year, however, that it is often damaged or killed by frosts. For this reason, in most parts of Britain, the best way to grow peach trees is to train them against a south or west-facing wall. The wall will radiate warmth, which will help to protect the peach blossom from frost damage. (*See also* **Fan-training**, **Frost**)

Peaches for Britain

When choosing a peach tree that is suitable to grow in the conditions prevailing in your area, bear in mind both ends of the season. The blossom requires a reasonable chance against spring frost, and the fruit needs an opportunity to ripen before the weather turns chilly. In northern districts, buy varieties that ripen by late July or early August – 'Amsden June', 'Duke of York' and 'Hale's Early'. Farther south the choice can include varieties, such as 'Peregrine' and 'Rochester', on which the fruits ripen by mid to late August. Not all these varieties are available from garden centres, but you will find them in specialist fruit-tree nurseries.

Peach for a patio

Lack of space is no bar to growing peach trees, and it is by no means uncommon to find them growing in pots on patios. All varieties of peach can be grown in this way if they are grafted onto St Julien A, a dwarfing rootstock. Naturally dwarf peaches, including 'Bonanza' and 'Garden Lady', which grow to no more than 1.2m (4ft) in their pots, are available. Their flavour is not quite as good as that of some traditional varieties and they are less hardy.

Getting into shape

In the early years of nurturing a fan-trained peach tree it is important to build up a good branch structure. In late winter shorten each leader by about a quarter; this will encourage the development of the side shoots that will eventually form part of the fan structure. In summer select and tie in shoots to build up the fan. Cut out close to the base any that are growing directly upwards or downwards or that are growing towards or directly away from the wall, leaving branches to develop exactly where they are needed. (*See also* **Fan-training**)

When to prune

Do not prune your peach tree until the fruit buds are on the point of opening. The benefit of pruning at this stage is that you will be able to identify which branches are the ones that will carry fruit. Additionally, because the tree is at the beginning of a new growing season and the sap is rising, the pruning wounds will heal rapidly. If necessary, peach trees can also be pruned in August after fruiting.

Prevent peach leaf curl

Peach trees are prone to a fungal disease – known as peach leaf curl – that causes large red blisters to develop on the leaves; later, these turn white and the leaves fall. To keep the disease under control, prevent rain from splashing spores onto the tree by frequently raking up and burning fallen leaves.

Earwig patrol

Trap the earwigs that will damage your chrysanthemums. Release them instead near your peach trees, where they will devour the larvae of codling moths.

Pears

Pairing up for pollination

To ensure successful pollination, you must plant more than one variety. Apart from 'Conference', which is partly self-fertile, pear trees need a pollination partner. 'Beth', 'Beurré Superfin', 'Conference', 'Joséphine de Malines' and 'Williams' Bon Chrétien' will cross-pollinate, as

will 'Louise Bonne of Jersey' with 'Packham's Triumph' and 'Doyenné du Cornice' with 'Onward'. Seek advice about other varieties at your nursery or garden centre.

Helping the insects

Pear trees flower early, and the young trees need a windbreak – especially if they are on exposed sites – to prevent spring winds from discouraging the important pollinating insects from flying. Solid walls and fences increase air turbulence so it is better to plant the trees in the shelter of a hedge. This will reduce the force of the wind without creating turbulence. (*See also* **Hedges**)

Pear care

Pear trees should be fed annually, otherwise they may drop their crop prematurely. Beginning in the trees' second year, in January or February, give the soil around each a dressing of sulphate of potash at the rate of 25g per m^2 (1oz per sq yd). In March apply the same amount of sulphate of ammonia. Double this amount if the trees are growing in grass. Each spring, add a mulch of well-rotted compost or manure. To ensure a good crop, give 45 litres (10 gallons) of water weekly in dry growing seasons

Three-year treat

Every third year, in January or February, scatter 50g per m^2 (2oz per sq yd) of superphosphate round each tree, covering an area of soil just larger than that overhung by the branches. Keep it clear of the trunk.

Minimal pruning

Plant dwarf pyramid pear trees if you wish to avoid heavy pruning in the years

ahead. These trees will crop well even without being cut back, and a harmonious shape can be maintained easily with a little light pruning. During the summer months, trim back branches that are hanging down too much to just above an upward-pointing lateral branch. Shorten long laterals of the current season's growth to one leaf from the basal cluster of leaves in early to mid August.

Thinning out

In most years, pears will need to be thinned out to ensure that those which remain on the tree develop to a good size. The best time to do this thinning is in June, after the tree has naturally cast off some of its smaller, superfluous fruits and the remainder have started to turn downwards. Thin each of the clusters of young pears to just one fruit, or two if there are plenty of leaves round the cluster. Use secateurs or small, sharp scissors to remove the surplus fruits. (*See also* **Fruit drop**, **Fruit trees**)

So succulent For a juicy crop, pick pears when they have reached full size but before they are fully ripe.

Support for young trees

Once a young pear tree produces fruit, the weight of the fruit can result in broken branches. To prevent this, tie lengths of strong string to the tree's main supporting stake. Lead a length of string down to each branch and tie securely. This technique is called 'maypoling'.

Pears in a small space

If you have only a small garden or a balcony, select a Minarette pear tree. This upright form can be grown in a container. The variety 'Concorde', which is self-fertile, produces well-flavoured, juicy pears. (See also **Balcony gardens**, **Container gardening**)

Storing pears

Once picked, pears should be stored, unwrapped, on slatted trays in a cool, dry place. A few can be put in the bottom of the refrigerator. Check often for signs of ripening – a slight softening of the flesh round the stalk – then bring them into a temperature of about 18°C (65°F) for two or three days before eating. One variety of pear that never ripens, however long you store it, is 'Catillac'. These are the best pears for cooking or bottling. A key virtue is that theyy stay firm, even if they are stored until the following spring.

Prolong storage life

To extend the storage life of pears, dip the stalks in molten candle wax and leave them to dry. This will slow the ripening process.

Peas

An early crop

Peas can be harvested in May if the seeds are sown during October or November. The plants will need to be grown under cloches in deeply cultivated, fertile, free-draining but moisture-retentive soil. The best type of peas for autumn sowings are the round-seeded varieties, such as 'Douce Provence' and 'Feltham First'. If mice are a problem, prevent them from stealing and eating the seeds by placing mousetraps inside the cloches.

Beware of mice

Take care to protect all pea seeds from the ravages of mice. To deter them, you can either lay prickly stems, such as those from holly or roses, in the trenches alongside the seeds, or, before sowing, soak the seeds overnight in paraffin, the smell of which mice cannot abide. Protection of the seeds is essential because if mice find just one, they will swiftly devour the whole row.

Ensuring a good crop

Better crops will be obtained from soil in which peas have not been grown for at least two seasons, because planting in a different area each year helps to prevent the build-up of soil-borne pests and diseases. In autumn or early winter spread a 5cm (2in) layer of well-rotted manure or garden compost in trenches where the peas are to be sown. (See also **Newspaper**, **Vegetable gardens**)

Gilding the peas

Sow cornflower and poppy seeds with maincrop peas. The flowers will brighten up the vegetable patch and attract butterflies and beneficial insects. The cornflowers will enjoy the support of the pea sticks and if you grow *Papaver nudicaule* (Iceland poppies), which also need support, you will have fine cut flowers for the house. However, once picked, these poppies are very short-lived.

Sturdy support

Support for peas is essential. Without it, the plants collapse onto the ground, attracting slugs and dirt, and you may lose much of the crop. Use sturdy twigs to support the peas, spacing them at 20cm (8in) intervals. Dwarf varieties need stakes that are 40cm (16in) long. For climbing varieties they should be 1.2m (4ft) long. (See also **Stakes and supports**)

Climbing frame

Traditional twig supports can occupy a large amount of space. On a small vegetable plot, it may be more efficient to use a simple climbing frame that will be suitable for all types of peas. To make the frame, you will need three stakes, each about 1.5m (5ft) long. Screw two together to make a T shape and drive the upright firmly into the ground. Lay the third stake on the ground, screw it to the upright and anchor each end with wire hoops. Screw six eyelets, spaced an equal distance apart, into each of the horizontal stakes and link pairs of eyelets with stout twine, so that it is strung vertically between all 12. Sow a pea seed at the foot of each string. When the plants have grown to about 7.5cm (3in) in height, guide the tendrils by curling them carefully onto the strings.

Peat

Protecting peat

Until recently, peat was widely used as a soil improver. However, there is now a growing awareness that it is a diminishing natural resource and must be used sparingly. Eke it out in seed and potting composts, then reuse the composts. For example, it can be used first in seed and potting composts when sowing, pricking out or potting up, then used compost can be spread over the lawn as a top dressing. Good alternative soil improvers, which can be used in bulk, include coir and composted bark.

Different types of peat

Two types of peat are available for use in horticulture: sphagnum moss peat and sedge peat. Sphagnum peat is best for most cultivation tasks, while sedge peat is used in the manufacture of peat blocks for commercial plant propagation.

Absorption

Plants in clay pots that have been overwatered can be saved if they are put into plastic bags filled with dry peat. Push the pots well in, pack the peat tightly round the sides and stand in a shady place. The peat will dry out the pots and draw excess moisture from the plants.

Dehydration

When growing plants in peat-based compost never allow the compost to dry out completely. It can be extremely difficult, or sometimes impossible, to wet again.

Moisture for clay pots

Prevent plants in clay pots from drying out in summer by standing the pots in larger containers and filling the space in between with damp peat. Check carefully to ensure that the peat does not dry out completely.

Insulation

In winter, you can protect plants that are sensitive to cold by encircling them with plastic sheeting held in place with some wire netting. Fill the space inside the sheeting with a layer of dry peat. This will help to protect the plants from frost. This additional insulation is particularly beneficial for plants such as fig trees, fuchsias and hydrangeas.

Words of warning

Chemical compost bases and starters that are formulated for mixing with peat should not be mixed with any other medium. Peat is acidic and the compost bases have added lime, which neutralises this acidity. Peat substitutes, such as coir, are neutral, so mixing them with the alkaline compost bases will produce an alkaline and unbalanced compost.

Peat-free compost

Test out first

Increasingly, manufacturers are turning to substances other than peat as the main ingredient of multi-purpose and specialist growing composts. Various raw materials are constantly being tried, including coir, composted garden waste and wood byproducts. Some are more successful than others, and what may suit one gardener may not please another, so if you want to grow without using up valuable peat resources, it is worth trying several products, even if at first you do not get on well with one brand of peat-free compost. Buy a small quantity only of any product you are unfamiliar with to avoid being left with a compost that gives you unsatisfactory results.

Try again

Peat-free composts have been around for many years, and some of the first products were inconsistent and gave disappointing results, which meant many gardeners gave up on them. If you had this experience when you first tried a compost without peat, now is the time to try again, as those available today bear little resemblance to the products that were around a couple of decades ago.

Ask a friend

If you have always used a peat-based compost and feel that now is the time to change, ask among your gardening friends for brand recommendations and tips that will get you off to a flying start.

Reduced version first

A good way to learn how to manage peat-free composts is to start by using one that is described as peat-reduced. The multi-purpose composts of most major manufacturers are, in fact, peat-reduced these days – some more so than others – and once you have adapted to one of them, try a completely peat-free version from the same manufacturer and you should find the transition much smoother.

Commercially developed

Commercial growers are increasingly using peat-free composts in their production of young plants, and their feedback to the compost manufacturers is an important part of the development of a reliable, consistent and effective substitute. What is good for the grower today is equally good for the amateur and home gardener.

Well-known may be best

Well-known, branded names of compost, even if more expensive, are likely to be more reliable than those from unknown manufacturers. A great deal of research is put into developing formulae that resemble most closely the properties of peat, and the larger companies generally have the resources to investigate the subject most thoroughly.

What's the difference?

Cultivation methods vary widely according to the basic ingredients of a peat-free compost, so always read the instructions on the bag. Feeding, in particular, may be different from what you are used to. In general, peat-free composts do not hold nutrients as well as those that are based on peat, so it is likely that you will need to give a liquid feed more often. Composts based on coir and wood byproducts may need a more nitrogen-rich fertiliser, and some manufacturers make particular recommendations for their specific product.

Water matters

You may need to relearn your watering techniques when you change to peat-free composts. Those based on coir can dry out more quickly, while some developed from recycled garden waste, on the other hand, can be easy to overwater. Many manufacturers are aware of these problems, however, and may compensate by adding water-retaining substances or extra drainage materials to help overcome such difficulties.

Sow the seeds

Unless a peat-free, multi-purpose compost is recommended for seed sowing, it is better to use a specific seed compost, as often the particles are too large and the incorporated fertiliser is too strong to make a good medium for germination.

Best of the bunch

The best peat-free composts are those developed for planting trees and shrubs in the open ground. Their humus-rich composition ensures easy establishment of young stock in their permanent places by opening up the soil to make it easier for the roots to grow out and retaining extra moisture in the planting area until the specimens are established sufficiently. Always wash your hands thoroughly when handling peat-free composts, especially before eating.

Make the right choice

Pelargoniums for scent

The leaves of scented pelargoniums can be used to create potpourris and perfumed pillows, or to make an infusion for flavouring jellies and jams. They can also be added to savoury dishes or crystallised to create cake decorations. Pick them just before the flowers open. These are among the best leaves, for use dried or fresh.

Species	Scent
Pelargonium capitatum	Rose
P. Fragrans Group	Nutmeg, with a hint of pine
P. 'Graveolens', *P. tomentosum*	Peppermint
P. odoratissimum	Apple
P. praemorsum 'Prince of Orange'	Orange
P. quercifolium	Incense
P. radens	Rose-lemon

Pelargoniums

Get the name right

When is a geranium not a geranium? When it's a pelargonium. The names of these plants are often confused, despite the fact that they belong to two different genera. The familiar house and bedding plants are, botanically, *Pelargonium*, and are divided into three groups: ivy-leaved, regal and zonal. Ivy-leaved pelargoniums are always trailing in habit. Regal pelargoniums have plain green leaves with serrated edges, while zonal pelargoniums take their name from the zones of bronze or maroon on their leaves. *Geranium*, often called cranesbill, includes several native wild flowers, most of which are hardy.

Know the colour

When buying pelargoniums, look for sturdy specimens with one or two flower buds already open, so you can see what colour they are and select the shade of your choice.

Penny-wise pelargoniums

Save money by growing zonal pelargoniums from seeds. During late February, sow them in a tray of peat-based seed compost and leave them to germinate in a propagator or airing cupboard. As soon as the first shoots appear, move the seed tray to a well-lit place where the night temperature does not fall below 13°C (55°F). Then, when the first true leaves appear, prick out the seedlings into 8cm (3in) pots. As the plants develop, encourage bushy growth by pinching out the tips of the young shoots.

Small pots for more flowers

Grow mature pelargoniums in pots that are no larger than 13cm (5in). Do not be tempted to use larger containers – they will encourage the production of leaves at the expense of flowers.

Frost danger

The tenderness of ivy-leaved, regal and zonal pelargoniums makes them highly vulnerable to frost damage. Do not put them outdoors until all danger of frost is past.

Overwintering

Pelargoniums can be lifted before the first frosts and left to overwinter in a cool, frost-free place. Do not water them, and allow the foliage to die back naturally. As the leaves fade, pull them off, then cover the roots with a little damp peat. Without enclosing it completely, put each plant into a polythene bag and hang it upside-down. In spring, pot up the plants and water well. Take cuttings from the young shoots and replant – but wait until there is no longer any danger of a night frost.

Food and drink

Pelargoniums are of South African origin and do not react well to overwatering. Water the plants only when the surface of the compost is dry. To encourage flower production, add a little tomato fertiliser to the water, following the manufacturer's instructions.

Deadheading

Remove the flowers from pelargoniums as soon as they fade. Snap off the flower stems by pulling them downwards gently. Regular deadheading improves the plants' appearance and also encourages them to continue flowering. This is because, when the flowers are removed, the energy the plant requires for the formation of seeds is redirected to the production of blooms.

Cascading pelargoniums

The best pelargoniums for hanging baskets and window boxes are the F1 hybrid cascading varieties, such as 'Breakaway Red' and 'Breakaway Salmon'. Both varieties will produce flowers throughout the summer. (See also *Hanging baskets*, *Window boxes*)

Holiday hint

If pelargoniums are in full flower just as you set off for two weeks' summer holiday, harden your heart and cut off all the blooms before you go. When you return, the plants will be looking their best once more. If you will be away for more than two weeks, remove the buds as well as the flowers.

Winter schedule

To overwinter potted pelargoniums, cut them back by about half and stand the pots in a frost-free place. Give only enough water to prevent the plants from drying out completely and remove leaves as they turn brown and die. Increase watering gradually when new growth begins to appear in spring.

Taking cuttings

Carefully select healthy, non-flowering shoots and cut them off cleanly below a leaf joint. Divide the cuttings into short sections, severing just below a leaf joint each time. Remove the lower leaves and insert five or six cuttings round the edge of a pot filled with cuttings compost. Cover the pot to retain moisture and warmth. In two or three weeks, the cuttings should be established and able to resist a gentle pull, and white roots may appear through the drainage holes. Transfer to 9cm (3½in) pots of potting compost. (See also **Cuttings**)

Hormones

Do not use hormone rooting powders, gels or solutions for pelargonium cuttings. The hormones in them have been shown to inhibit rooting in pelargoniums.

Peonies

Peony types

There are two distinct types of peonies, both of which produce beautiful flowers. Herbaceous peonies are hardy and suitable for growing in a border. They reach a height of 51–76cm (20–30in). Tree peonies are deciduous, woody-stemmed shrubs that can reach up to 2m (7ft) in height.

Wilting

Peonies, particularly those growing on badly drained soil, can be susceptible to peony wilt. A symptom of this disease is a velvety coating on the buds, while the stems may collapse at ground level. To prevent the problem from spreading, pull up and burn infected plants.

Standing up to the rain

Young peonies may be beaten down by heavy, early-season rains. You can protect them by cutting out pieces of plastic mesh, each one large enough to cover an area where a crown has been planted, and anchoring it with a stake pushed through the centre of the mesh and into the ground. When the peony shoots appear, they will grow up through the mesh.

Dazzling display Tree peonies, such as this *Paeonia suffruticosa* with flowers that are 15cm (6in) or more across, make a superb show.

As the plant grows, raise the mesh to within a few centimetres of the top to keep the stalks erect, and continue to raise it as the plant grows taller. Depending on how tightly the centre stake fits the mesh, you may have to provide additional support round the edge to prevent the mesh from sagging. You can do this by pushing thin stakes or canes into the ground.

Multiplying peonies

Herbaceous peonies can be propagated by division. This is best done in early autumn so that some new root growth can be made before winter. Dig up a plant carefully and divide the crown with a sharp knife, making sure that each division has roots and a dormant bud. Replant the pieces in 8cm (3in) pots of compost, or larger if the roots are long, and water them well. Tree peonies, which have only a few stems, are best propagated by replanting rooted suckers. (See also **Division**)

Growing know-how

Why peonies fail to flower

If your peonies fail to flower, check for these possible causes:

- The roots are buried too deeply. The maximum depth should be 5cm (2in). Lift the whole clump carefully and move to a new position.
- They are in too much shade. Peonies are sun-loving plants that tolerate only light shade. Replant them in a sunny corner of the garden.
- Your garden soil is too dry. Peonies prefer a well-drained soil that is rich in humus. Adding well-rotted manure or compost will help.
- The plants are young. Newly planted peonies may take a year or two to settle down and they will eventually flower in their third year.

Establishing new plants

A division may not flower for two to three years. Plant it no deeper than 2.5cm (1in), mulch in spring and water well in dry spells.

Cold storage

If peonies that you intend to use in a display for a special occasion begin to flower too early, cut them while they are in bud, wrap them in damp newspaper and store in the refrigerator. They will keep for up to two weeks.

Peppers

A warm start

Sow sweet peppers in trays in March. When the first true leaves appear, pot up into individual pots of compost. In milder areas, they can be planted out in early June. In cooler areas, grow them on in the greenhouse. Cultural conditions for sweet peppers are similar to those required by tomatoes. (See also **Tomatoes**)

Picking your peppers

Sweet peppers are the large, rotund peppers, also called capsicums, that can be stuffed and cooked or sliced in salads. Before they ripen, they are usually green and mild in flavour. Depending on variety they may turn red, yellow or purple as they ripen. They have a sweeter flavour when fully ripe. 'Gypsy' and 'Redskin' are good red varieties, 'Luteus' ripens to yellow, 'Mavras' turns almost black. For a colourful display choose assortments such as 'New Carnival Mixture'. In warm, sunny areas, sweet peppers can be grown outdoors, either in the vegetable garden or in growing bags on a patio or balcony. Chilli peppers, the fiery fruits used in curries, chutneys and pickles, are tender plants and, for best results, should be grown in a heated greenhouse. The variety 'Hero' is easy to grow and disease-resistant. 'Apache', which is a little less fiery in flavour than other chillis, may succeed on a sunny patio.

Outdoor peppers

Peppers originated in the tropics so they do best in a greenhouse, where the higher temperatures encourage good growth and heavy crops. Nevertheless, they look good outdoors and will be reasonably successful if planted out against a south-facing wall in early June, when all danger of frost is past. Spray daily with water during the flowering period, to encourage the fruit to set, and give a weekly feed of tomato fertiliser. Tall varieties should be staked. The fruits, which should be ready to harvest from July until the first frosts, are best eaten freshly picked.

Protecting peppers

If growing outdoors, do not plant peppers in soil where cucumbers, marrows, potatoes or tomatoes were grown the previous year. All of these plants share a susceptibility to the same diseases. So if last season's crops suffered from one of them, there is a danger that it could be transmitted to your newly planted peppers.

Sturdy growth

To encourage strong, bushy growth, pinch out the growing tips of sweet pepper plants when they reach a height of 30cm (12in).

Mulch with black bin liners

For healthy, productive peppers, mulch around the plants with black plastic – rubbish bags that have been split open are fine. It warms the soil for these heat-loving plants and protects against soil-borne fungal diseases transmitted by splashing water.

Balancing flavour

The amount of water that sweet peppers receive can affect fruit flavour. In hot weather water plants well until harvesting. Otherwise, reduce watering two weeks before harvesting for a strong flavour. For a milder flavour, water well until a week before harvesting.

Gentle harvesting

Use scissors or secateurs when harvesting peppers. Do not pull the fruits away from the stems, as this may cause damage and provide an entry point for diseases.

Blossom-end rot

Although more commonly seen on tomatoes, blossom-end rot can also occur on sweet peppers. It appears as a brown, dead patch at the base of the pepper. Help prevent it by never allowing the compost in containers to dry out.

Chilli production

Pick chilli peppers as soon as they are fully formed, and place them on a piece of paper on a window ledge to dry. The plants will continue to produce if the fruits are harvested regularly.

Perennials

What are they?

Perennials are long-lived plants with flexible, rather than woody, stems that grow each year from hardy rootstocks. The parts above ground are usually cut down by winter frosts. Because they flower year after year in the same spot, they are the backbone of the herbaceous border. Annuals and bedding plants can be planted among them.

Country garden colour

Use perennials for a traditional show from spring to late summer. Pulmonarias will flower in April, followed in May by London pride, Canterbury bells and columbines. Some will still be in bloom when delphiniums, foxgloves, lupins, peonies and shasta daisies bloom in June. In July, follow with hollyhocks and pinks to continue the display.

Autumn glory

Even at summer's end there are plenty of perennials to serve as curtain-raisers to the flaring autumn hues of trees and shrubs. Michaelmas daisies provide a range of colours, from pink to deep carmine, which will last until November. The perennial chrysanthemums, too,

have much to offer, particularly those such as the bright crimson *Dendranthema* 'Duchess of Edinburgh'. Just right for the season are sedums, whose flowers darken to bronze in the autumn. *Zauschneria californica* produces scarlet blooms in late September.

Sweet peas for ever

Lathyrus latifolius (everlasting pea) lacks the colour range and scent of annual sweet peas, but the flowers are spectacular enough in their own way and the plants are easy to grow. Reaching up to 3m (10ft) in height, they have rose purple, white or red flowers in summer and early autumn. Plant them among tall shrubs and let them scramble through the branches. Cut back the plants in autumn and they will regrow the following spring. (*See also* **Climbing plants**, **Sweet peas**)

Drawing-board beginning

Before planting perennials, draw a plan on graph paper, based on plant height, shape, flowering time and colour. For a long-lasting show, the flowerbed should be at least 1.8m (6ft) wide and 4.6m (15ft) long. Place brightly coloured plants at the centre and make a gradual transition to paler, pastel-hued plants at the sides. To get the right balance of plants, it is best to plant in groups – five to seven identical specimens of small perennials, and clusters of three to five taller ones. Dominant plants, such as campanulas, delphiniums and peonies, are important in the structure of a flowerbed, but should be placed carefully.

Damp places

If your garden has heavy, badly drained soil, select plants from the bog garden section of your garden centre, not the herbaceous area. These are better suited to wet conditions.

Eye-catching The green and yellow of *Alchemilla mollis* (lady's mantle) in the foreground leads the eye to elegant perennials of varying heights and colours.

Looking ahead

Most perennials are quite small when they are sold in pots at the end of winter but, within two or three months, some may have grown to 1m (3ft) or more. When buying, check in the catalogue or with the garden centre for eventual sizes, to ensure you plant your new purchases where they will not obscure other plants.

Planting potted perennials

There is no hurry to plant out pot-grown perennials. Leave them for a few days and water thoroughly to give both roots and stems a boost. When planting out, soak the bottom of each planting hole, especially during dry weather. Make sure that the crown of the plant is level with the surface of the soil.

Starting times

If the soil in your garden is heavy and damp, plant your perennials in spring when the ground is warming up. Conversely, plant them in the autumn if the soil is light. Divide plants with fleshy roots, such as irises and peonies, in July and August, so that they can establish themselves during the autumn.

Self-sown for savings

Increase your plant stock at no cost by growing self-seeding perennials. Among these are dwarf campanulas, columbines, fennel, foxgloves, geraniums and lupins. When tidying up the herbaceous border, collect seedpods from the plants and either sow them elsewhere in the garden or grow them in pots to give to friends.

Feeding time

Give all perennials a general fertiliser in March. Plants that are slow to flower benefit from liquid feeds of potash during the summer months, until late September.

Increasing flower power

For strong, bushy perennials that produce more flowers, pinch out the main stems of the plants in the spring when they are 15–20cm (6–8in) high. This will encourage the plants to develop more flowering stems.

Light watering

Many perennials have flexible stems and large flower heads that become heavy when wet. When watering, use a perforated pipe, or a seephose to avoid spraying water on the plants.

See also **A year of glory in the garden** *pp.108–11*

Make the right choice

Perennials for difficult places

Many gardens have areas of poor soil that may not merit the time or costs involved in improving them. These perennials are among the toughest and most tolerant of poor conditions, but even these have their preferences.

Season	Species	Description	Preferences
Spring	Alyssum	Yellow flowers	Sun, best on lime
	Aquilegia	Mixed flower colours	Shade, limy or acid soil
	Digitalis	Spikes of white/purple/ pink flowers	Shade, best on acid soil
	Doronicum	Early-flowering yellow blooms	Partial shade, limy or acid soil
	Iris	Sword-like growth	Sun, best on lime
	Lamium	Ground-hugging plants	Shade or partial shade, any soil
	Pulmonaria	Hairy foliage, purple/pink/ blue blooms	Shade, limy or acid soil
	Vinca	Arching stems, prostrate habit	Shade, limy or acid soil
Summer	Acanthus	Spiky foliage, purple flowers	Sun or shade, best on lime
	Geranium	Low habit, pink/blue/ lavender flowers	Sun or shade, limy or acid soil
	Hemerocallis	Broad, grass-like foliage	Sun, limy or acid soil
	Hosta	Bold, handsome foliage	Shade, most soils
	Hypericum	Large yellow flowers	Sun or shade, best on lime
	Nepeta	Silver foliage, blue flowers	Sun, best on lime
	Saxifraga	White/yellow/pink starry flowers	Sun, best on lime
	Veronica	Blue flowers, neat growth	Sun or shade, best on lime
Autumn	Anemone japonica	Pink or white flowers	Partial shade, best on lime
	Solidago	Erect growth habit, yellow flowers	Sun, best on lime

Pergolas

A seat in the shade

A pergola is a framework of columns and beams designed to carry climbing plants and provide a sheltered walkway or a shaded place in which to sit. It can be freestanding or attached to a wall. (*See also* **Shade**)

Timber treatment

The most common material for a pergola is timber, which can be planed or rough-sawn. If rough-sawn, sand the surfaces to remove splinters. Use sections at least 7.5cm (3in) square, and select timber that is free of splits or loose knots and which is neither warped nor bowed. Make sure that you choose timber that has been pressure-impregnated with preservative or, otherwise, treat all sections with a preservative before erection; you should pay particular attention to the end sections. Preservative may be clear, or stained to blend with the surroundings.

Spike support

You can buy metal spikes with sockets to support the posts of your pergola. Use a sledgehammer to drive each spike into the ground, making sure it enters vertically. Drop the post end into the socket and tighten the bolt to lock the post in place. A version without a spike can be fixed to a concrete surface using metal anchor bolts. However, these should not be used on paving slabs that may not be firm enough to provide sufficient support. Instead, lift the slabs, use a spiked support, and repave round the posts when they have been erected.

Erecting posts

Posts may be set directly into the ground, in which case a post-hole borer, which can be rented from a local hire shop, may prove useful. Line the base of each hole with a layer of rubble then cement the post in, making sure that no gap is left between the wood and the cement where rain can enter and cause the post to rot.

Fixing crossbeams

The best way to secure beams to posts is with bolts. Because of the thickness of the wood, it may be necessary to use bolts that are more than 15cm (6in) long, and which may be difficult to obtain. If you cannot find bolts of that length, buy threaded rod and nuts and cut your own to size. Use a washer between timber and nut, and grease the bolts to protect them and to ease removal.

Beam support

Where the pergola meets a wall, joist hangers can be used to support the crossbeams. As an alternative, fix a beam to the wall with anchor bolts, having first cut recesses in the timber to house the ends of the crossbeams. Bolts are not necessary for smaller sections of timber. They can be nailed or screwed.

Fruitful labour

Use apple trees to create an attractive covering for a pergola with strong wooden or metal supports. The arch of blossom that appears in spring is breathtaking and is followed by a tunnel of easy-to-pick fruit in late summer or autumn.

Sound barrier

A pergola erected on a terrace or balcony will reduce noise to a surprising degree. Having built the frame, place a large tub at the foot of each upright and grow annual or perennial climbing plants. When they are fully grown their foliage will muffle traffic noise and sounds from neighbouring houses.

Gale warning

If part of a pergola is to be attached to the house, make the framework strong but light, and the foundations firm. When fully grown, the foliage of clematis, climbing roses and wisteria, can exert a weighty pull, which increases in intensity in high winds.

Pergolas with a purpose

If you are constructing a pergola to support a specific plant, give some thought to size. If it is not to catch the hair of passers-by, a climbing rose requires an arch that is at least 2m (7ft) high and, to avoid brushing against wet clematis shoots after rain, allow a width of 1.2m (4ft).

Horses for courses

In a large garden, you may find room to construct a traditional pergola with pillars of brick or stone and crossbeams of stout timber. It could support a leafy tunnel of laburnum or wisteria with a single, annual display of drooping racemes. On a small pergola, it is best to grow several smaller climbers to provide a succession of colour.

Persimmons

Mellow, but inedible, fruit

The tomato-like fruits produced by *Diospyros kaki*, the Chinese persimmon tree, rarely ripen in Britain. But the tree, which reaches 10m (32ft) and spreads up to 7m (23ft), is worth growing for its autumn colour, when its large, lustrous, dark green leaves turn orange, red and plum-purple. After the leaves fall, countless large, round, red-gold fruits remain.

No need to prune

Allow persimmons to grow their own way. In time they will build crowns, like those on old-fashioned apple trees. Then, simply cut off dead branches, as well as any that are spoiling the tree's shape.

Ripeness is all

If your persimmon grows against a warm wall, you may find that, after an exceptionally hot summer, you are able to harvest the fruits. Put them into a bag and keep it in a warm place until the tough skins become translucent and feel soft to the touch. Then, cut off the tops of the persimmons and scoop out the flesh, which can be eaten raw or cooked in pies and cakes. The unripe fruit tastes unpleasantly astringent.

Perspectives

Getting it together

In larger gardens, natural perspective makes the distance between parallel lines appear to narrow in the distance. If the garden is very large, the lines may appear to merge completely. In smaller gardens, mimic the effect by using tricks that will deceive the eye into believing that the garden is longer and narrower, or shorter and wider than it is.

Create an illusion

The technique of false perspective is simple to master. One trick to make a garden seem longer is to position large plants near the house and ones of decreasing size progressively down the garden. Another is to use the garden's sight-lines, which usually run from doors, windows and seating places towards an interesting plant, ornamental object or view some distance away. By slightly narrowing paths, flower borders or the spaces

between clumps of plants along the sight-lines, you can give the impression of greater length.

Increase with a pond

The eye-catching qualities of a pond – no matter how small – will make a garden look bigger. If your patch is small, construct a pond in the foreground, shaping it to follow the longest line of the garden.

A turn for the better

A garden will seem bigger if it is not seen all at once but discovered gradually. Plan lawns and paths so they meander round the corners or curves of borders or groups of plants, perhaps under arches and tunnels, to disappear into hidden areas. These will create an impression of further, unquantifiable spaces beyond. There should always be something of interest to be discovered in these secret places, whether it be a bower, a seat, a wall fountain or pond, or a statue. Perhaps best of all in a small garden is a doorway, real or false, that hints of wonders beyond and invites further exploration.

All done with mirrors

If well placed, a large mirror can add considerably to the apparent length of the garden. Position it to back a pergola at the end of the garden, or place it on a wall with its edges concealed by climbing plants. A mirror can also be used to good effect if it is placed near a pond where it can reflect the surface of the water. Outdoor mirrors must have a lead foil backing to protect the silvering from the effects of the weather.

Flaunting the view

If you have a garden with a view, exploit your good fortune by maximising the enjoyment the view can provide. Keep the foreground as uncluttered as possible – a smooth sweep of lawn or a simple path will lead the eye satisfactorily towards a landmark, such as a church steeple, a shapely hill or, perhaps, a gleam of distant water. Further enhance the view by framing it in some way, perhaps with a gate, or a handsome tree or a clump of shrubs planted on each side.

Something borrowed

Even if your garden has no view of its own, sometimes one can be 'borrowed' from a neighbouring garden or a nearby street. Frame a beautiful tree, an interesting architectural

Growing know-how

Phosphate fertilisers

There are several kinds of phosphate fertilisers, including organic and chemical forms, quick-acting and slow-release. All are available from garden centres.

Bone meal

Made from animal bones that have been ground and sterilised. It is organic and breaks down slowly to release nutrients over a long period.

Farmyard manure and garden compost

A heavy application of farmyard manure or garden compost, about 4.5kg per m² (10lb per sq yd), will provide the same amount of phosphorus as 30g per m² (1oz per sq yd) of triple superphosphate.

Liquid forms

Liquid phosphate fertilisers are rich in phosphate, quick-acting and convenient.

Rock phosphate

This natural ground rock fertiliser is exceptionally long lasting and excellent for soils that are deficient in phosphate. It should be applied at the rate of 175–225g per m² (6–8oz per sq yd).

Superphosphate

Superphosphate of lime, as it is correctly known, is an inorganic chemical made in a factory. It can be bought in two strengths: 'single', and the more common 'triple' superphosphate. The nutrient is fairly quick-acting, yet remains active in the soil for one to two years.

---

detail, or one or two old-fashioned chimney pots with carefully positioned plants or a wrought-iron gate, or an archway or moon window in a wall or fence. The feature will appear to be a part of your domain, and will help to make the garden seem larger than it actually is.

On reflection

Mirrors, in shapes and sizes to suit most garden settings, can be made to order, ready-cut and foil-backed, from most glass and mirror specialists. They should also be able to supply suitable adhesive for the back and a clear sealant for the edges. Stick the foil-backed mirror to a backing of exterior-grade plywood that has been screwed to battens against a wall or fence. If possible, position the mirror at an angle that displays the garden to the greatest effect but does not reflect the viewer directly.

Phosphates

The importance of phosphate

Phosphorus is an essential nutrient for plant growth and one of three principal elements in some fertilisers; the other two are nitrogen and potassium. Phosphate, which contains phosphorus, aids fruiting and stimulates early root formation and growth. If the soil lacks phosphate, initial growth may be weak and the resulting plants will be poorly developed. In addition, newly planted or transplanted subjects will be slow to become established.

Essential for roots

Because phosphate is essential for plant root development, it is traditional to add bone meal to the planting holes of trees and shrubs, and to work some into soil after planting. By stimulating root growth, phosphate ensures plants establish quickly. Bone meal is slow-acting and an

---

application at planting time will last two years. After this time, apply as a top dressing in alternate years if general fertilisers are not used.

A feed for fruit trees

When planting fruit trees, mix bone meal into each planting hole. To boost fruit production, feed established trees with bone meal or superphosphate every two or three years.

Photography

Basic equipment

There are a few points worth bearing in mind that will help you to achieve a professional standard when photographing gardens and plants. Your equipment should be as simple as possible. A good-quality digital SLR camera, which can be fitted with a variety of lenses and with a built-in light meter, is perfect. The fewer gadgets the better – you do not need to have a flash or motor drive, which can be counterproductive.

A choice of two lenses

No more than two lenses should be necessary. Ideally, one should be a medium to long lens, with a focal length of between 80 and 110mm. The other should be a standard 50mm lens that incorporates a macro function. Zoom and wide-angle lenses are neither necessary nor suitable for photography where quality and precision are required. There is no need to use lens filters unless you wish to achieve a particular effect. A simple and inexpensive extension ring is useful, because it allows you to take close-ups using a long lens.

A solid tripod

It is worth investing in a good, stable tripod. This will help you to take well-composed, sharp photographs of gardens or plants.

Which aperture width?

For close-ups, fit either a macro lens or a long lens with an extension ring; use a long lens for views. Choose the highest 'f number' possible, f22 or f32. This narrows the lens aperture, giving greater depth of field and a sharper image. Such high 'f numbers' are only possible with slow shutter speeds of 1/15 and 1/8 of a second or slower, hence the need for a tripod to avoid 'camera shake'.

The ideal conditions

Choosing the best conditions for garden photography is largely a matter of experience. As a general rule, do not take pictures on windy or rainy days. Equally, avoid bright sunshine, which can create problems of contrast, or 'bleach-out'. Ideal days for photography are those that are windless, with hazy or no sunshine.

The right time

One of the best times to capture a plant or garden feature on film is early in the morning, when there is a light covering of dew.

Close call For greater accentuation, eliminate all background detail and let the subject fill the frame.

Alternatively, choose a summer evening: most gardens will look most attractive when bathed in the diffused golden light of the western sky.

Coping with direct sunlight

If you have to take photographs on bright, sunny days, do not photograph subjects with the sun shining directly upon them. Plants will appear dull and flat in the harsh light. Face the sun when taking photographs; the light will shine through the plants and illuminate their natural translucency.

Framing your picture

The subject of your photograph is really a matter of taste – based on your sense of composition, of what 'looks right'. However, the most successful pictures are those that fill the frame. Photographs with too much lawn at the bottom and too much sky at the top lack interest. Often, pictures that exclude the sky turn out best. Portraits where the photographer has failed to go in close to the subject, leaving a flower surrounded by an excess of foliage, or worse, an untidy background, can be unsatisfactory and uninformative. Be daring, decide on your subject and make it fill the frame.

Bold experiment

Remember, however, that rules are made to be broken. Some of the finest photographs of gardens and plants have been taken when the photographers have broken the rules, stretched the capability of their equipment and, above all, used their imagination to produce something entirely different.

Pinching out

The kindest cut

The pinching out of annual bedding plants and herbaceous perennials should be done early in the season before the plants grow too tall. Early pinching out encourages strong basal growth and will result in compact, bushy plants. In the long term, this will lead to the production of many more flowers and the improved quality of the blooms.

Pinching-out time

Trailing varieties of courgettes, marrows, pumpkins and squashes can grow so large that they can be unsuitable for smaller gardens. If you wish to grow these in a limited space, pinch out the tips of the main shoots when they are 61cm (2ft) long. When further side shoots grow to 61cm (2ft) pinch them out in the same way.

Chrysanthemums for show

Large blooms on chrysanthemums and dahlias are practically guaranteed if you pinch out the lateral flower buds in the leaf axils – where the leaf stalks join the stems – the moment they appear. This will concentrate the plants' reserves on the terminal bud on each branch, providing much larger flowers than usual.

Shapely fruit trees

Train fruit trees by removing young, unwanted shoots that, if left, will develop into an untidy tangle of branches. Pinch back any strong shoots that grow from spurs to encourage the development of more fruit buds.

Better aubergines and peppers

Aubergines and peppers produce many flowers, not all of which yield fruit. To strengthen the crop, remove some of the flower buds as they form, leaving no more than six to eight on each plant.

Bigger tomatoes

To ensure that the tomato plant's energy is directed into fruit rather than leaf production, remove all side shoots that develop in the leaf

Plants to pinch

A number of plants will benefit and produce better, sturdier growth if the main shoot is pinched out and the side shoots are left to develop.

Flowers
Abutilon, Antirrhinum, Chrysanthemum, Dahlia, Dianthus, Fuchsia, Lathyrus, Pelargonium, Penstemon

House plants
Begonia, Campanula, Coleus, Hypoestes, Impatiens, Poinsettia

Vegetables and herbs
Aubergines, basil, peppers, tarragon

axils, except on bush varieties. Do not remove the main growing point of the plant.

When not to pinch
During damp weather, faded flowers can develop grey mould. Rather than pinching out, trim these off with scissors, to leave a neat wound. Pinching out may squash the stem, leaving it susceptible to reinfection.

Pinching out pests
Prevent aphid colonies forming by pinching out the ends of stems where the pests gather. This simple, ecological method is effective on broad beans and many ornamental plants too.

Good standards
To prevent suckers developing on the stems of standard roses, pinch them out at an early stage. Secateurs will be required if the shoots are allowed to grow.

Pips and stones

Pick your pips
To grow fruit trees from pips or stones, collect the pips and stones when the fruit is fully ripe and select the healthiest fruit from strongly growing plants. Lay the pips and stones on paper towels and leave them to dry, then rub off any flesh that adheres to them and sow in pots of seed compost.

Keeping them fresh
If, when the pips or stones are dry, you are unable to sow them straightaway, you can keep them fresh for a short time by putting them into a jar of moist sand. Store the jar in a cool place, such as the salad compartment of a refrigerator.

Unpredictable pips
Growing fruit trees from pips can be great fun but the results are unpredictable. In most cases, the tree will not be identical to the one from which the seed came. For example, if you sow pips from a 'Cox's Orange Pippin' apple, you will not get another Cox. You may get something quite good, but it is unlikely that it would resemble its parent. It may also develop into a large tree before it bears any fruit. Most seedlings develop strong growing points. If you want a tree with a bushy habit, remove the growing point when the plant is 7.5cm (3in) tall.

Shortening the odds
To increase the chances of producing a plant from a pip or stone, sow three or four in the same pot. If they all germinate, leave the healthiest one in place and remove the others.

Pips for pectin
Dry the pips from apples, pears and citrus fruits. They will provide the necessary pectin for homemade jams made from fruits, such as cherries, peaches, plums, and strawberries, which have a low level of natural pectin.

Planting

Planting with forethought
If your planting scheme involves a number of plants, use pegs to mark where you want to position them and move them round until you are satisfied. Dig the holes, forking over the base of each. Make sure that there is sufficient room for the roots of each plant to be spread out comfortably. Water in each plant thoroughly.

The risk of facing east
Plants that flower in early spring or late autumn should never be planted facing east. On a clear, frosty morning the sun's early rays could bring about a quick thaw that would cause the cells in buds, flowers and young leaves to swell and burst. When planted in another aspect, where warming is slower, damage should not occur.

Planting a bare-rooted tree
Before planting bare-rooted trees, soak the roots in water overnight. Fill the planting holes with water and leave to drain, then plant the trees and water them in well.

Heeling in
Never attempt to plant bare-rooted trees when the soil is frozen or waterlogged. Dig a trench, lay the roots in it at an angle and cover them with soil until conditions improve.

Tree-planting help
If you have ever tried to plant a tree without assistance, you will know how difficult it is to hold it in place and shovel soil into the hole at the same time. The problem can be overcome by cutting a length of wood that is longer than the width of the hole and firmly tying it to the tree at the exact point where the trunk will emerge from the ground (as indicated by the soil mark). Place the tree in the hole, resting one end of the wooden support on each side. Use a spirit level to check that the tree is vertical. Next, shovel the soil gradually into the hole, treading it down to eliminate pockets of air, then remove the support and water the tree well.

Plums

Cross-pollination

Plums, greengages and damsons, like most other fruit trees, will bear heavier crops if they are pollinated by another variety. Some varieties, including 'Czar', 'Denniston's Superb', 'Early Transparent Gage', 'Marjorie's Seedling', 'Merryweather Damson', 'Oullin's Golden Gage' and 'Victoria' are either self-fertile or partially self-fertile and carry reasonable crops without a pollinator. The best pollinating partners are 'Denniston's Superb' with 'Coe's Golden Drop', 'Czar' or 'Victoria' with 'Merryweather Damson', and 'Old Green Gage' with 'Marjorie's Seedling'.

Pruning plums

Although regular pruning of plum trees is neither necessary nor desirable, branches that are diseased, or those that come in to contact with infected areas, must be removed. Do so immediately after the crop has been harvested: between late July and September the cuts should heal quickly.

Keep the grass off

Do not allow grass or flowers to grow round the trunk of a plum tree – its shallow roots dislike competition. Leave the soil bare and keep it weeded and hoed. To prevent root damage, which could result in suckering, work on only the top few centimetres or inches of soil.

Back to the roots

If your long-established plum tree produces neither fruit nor flowers, the fault may be an overdeveloped root system, which causes foliage to grow at the expense of fruit. If this is the case, the roots will need to be cut back. Wait until winter, when the tree is dormant, to do this. Then, dig a shallow trench round the tree, 1–1.5m (3–5ft) from the trunk, and slice through the thickest roots with the edge of a spade, taking care to avoid damaging thin roots. Fill in the trench immediately the work is completed to prevent the exposed roots from drying out. If the tree is large, do the work in two stages, digging half during the first winter and the other half the following winter. Spread a mulch of well-rotted manure or garden compost over the treated area.

Plums into prunes

When you have a glut of plums, turn the surplus into prunes that you can enjoy eating throughout winter. Cut the plums in half lengthways – without completely severing the

Mouth-watering 'Czar' self-pollinates but produces an even better crop when crossed with another variety.

two halves. Then, put them in an open box or tray. Put the box against a south-facing wall and cover it with a sheet of glass. After it has been in the sun for several days, complete the drying process by placing the plums on racks in an oven set at the lowest heat possible for an hour or two. Keep the oven door partly open and turn the plums from time to time to ensure that they dry out evenly.

Silver leaf

Silver leaf is a descriptive name for a common disorder of plum trees. The disease causes the upper surfaces of some leaves to separate from the lower surfaces, creating air spaces that look like silver. The best way to avoid silver leaf is to prune only in July, August or September, removing any dead, diseased or damaged branches.

Giving support

Plum tree branches can break easily if they are overladen with fruit. Use a long prop to hold up each weak branch until the fruit is ready to be harvested. Put the supports in place by the end of May, before the fruits swell. (See also **Stakes and supports**)

A brief history

Food for the afterlife

Most plums are probably descended from a cross between sloe or blackthorn and the myrobalan or cherry plum, both now largely relegated to hedgerows. Plums were well known to the ancient Egyptians, as were prunes, some of which were found, as provisions for the afterlife, in Theban tombs. On a less spiritual plane, they were valued by the Romans as laxatives. Of the dessert plums popular in Britain, the greengage has one of the longest pedigrees. Sir William Gage popularised it in about 1725 when he brought it from France, where it was named Reine Claude, after the 'good and sweet' queen of Francis I. The excellent 'Coe's Golden Drop' has been grown since the late 18th century, but the 'Victoria' is of more recent date, probably gaining its name about the time of the Queen's coronation in 1837.

Poisonous plants

Keeping things in perspective
Poisonous plants are much less of a threat to children's safety than traffic. But it makes sense to instil in youngsters' minds the idea that some plants in the garden represent a danger, and that berries and fruits should not be eaten without parental approval.

Cover up
Be aware of plants that may irritate the skin and cover up with long-sleeved clothing and gardening gloves before handling them. Never wear shorts when working in strong sunlight among plants known to be irritants.

Safe placing
Plant shrubs with bright berries at the backs of borders, out of reach of children. Do not plant privet, yew or *Prunus laurocerasus* (cherry laurel)

within reach of grazing animals or leave prunings in paddocks. Ban the house plant *Dieffenbachia* if you have children or pets. (*See also* **Trees**)

Quick action
If a child shows symptoms of poisoning – which may include vomiting, diarrhoea or stomach pains – telephone a doctor immediately. Alternatively, take the child to the nearest accident and emergency department of a hospital, together with leaves and fruit from the suspected plant to show to the medical staff.

Growing know-how

The possible effects of contact with poisonous plants

Many familiar plants have irritant or toxic properties. Some can be fatal, but many will cause only minor skin irritations. The most common are listed here:

Plant	Poisonous part	Symptoms
Aconitum	All parts	Even small amounts, if eaten, cause severe or fatal poisoning.
Aesculus	All parts	Respiratory paralysis, mild gastro-intestinal effects if eaten.
Alstroemeria	Foliage	Irritation to skin if handled continuously.
Colchicum	All parts	Burning in the mouth and throat, vomiting and diarrhoea if eaten.
Daphne mezereum	All parts	Eating berries causes severe or fatal poisoning.
Delphinium	All parts	Nausea, vomiting, blurred vision if eaten.
Dieffenbachia	All parts	Sap dangerous if it enters mouth or eyes.
Digitalis	All parts	Headache, convulsions, vomiting if eaten.
Euonymus	Berries	Diarrhoea, vomiting, sleepiness if eaten.
Euphorbia	All parts	Burning in mouth and throat, vomiting, diarrhoea if eaten.
Hedera	All parts	Irritation to sensitive skin.
Helleborus	All parts	Irritation to skin if handled. Digestive upsets if eaten.
Hyacinthus	All parts	Diarrhoea if eaten. Sap causes dermatitis.
Ipomoea	Seeds	Stomach ache, nausea, blurred vision if eaten.
Laburnum	All parts	Vomiting, drowsiness, headache, increased heartbeat if eaten.
Ligustrum	Berries	Vomiting, diarrhoea if eaten.
Lupinus	Seeds	Nausea, vomiting, dizziness if eaten.
Narcissus	All parts	Vomiting, convulsions if eaten. Irritation to skin if handled.
Primula	Foliage	Dermatitis if handled, digestive disturbances if eaten.
Prunus laurocerasus	Berries	Vomiting, convulsions, can be fatal if chewed.
Ruta	All parts	Dermatitis if handled in bright sunlight.
Taxus	All parts	Vomiting, diarrhoea, dilated pupils, low blood pressure if eaten.
Wisteria	All parts	Nausea, vomiting, headache if seeds eaten.

Pollination

Single parents
In a garden where there is room for only one tree, plant a 'family tree' on which two, or sometimes three, mutual pollinators have been grafted together. An alternative is a self-fertile variety, but the choice is not large and the harvests are often mediocre.

Planting the pollinator
When planting fruit trees – apple trees, for example – check that they are capable of mutual pollination or, if not, that they can be pollinated by the addition of a single tree to the group. In a small garden, place the pollinator in the centre of the group if possible. In a larger garden or in an orchard, it is advisable to place the pollinating tree at the end of a row – it must be the end that faces the prevailing wind. Planting in this way will assist the distribution of pollen and encourage pollinating insects to move along the rows in the right direction.

Pollution

Breath of fresh air
Keep indoor plants strong and healthy by opening doors and windows now and then, even in the winter. An unrelieved smoky atmosphere, or one that is dried by central heating, can do considerable damage, especially to begonias, cyclamens and ferns.

A quick rinse outdoors
Outdoor plants are particularly susceptible to atmospheric pollution during spells of warm, dry weather. Spray small trees, bushes and hedges to invigorate them and to give a bright, new look to their foliage.

Hedge your bets
A garden close to a busy road will benefit if a hedge is planted along the boundary nearest the road. The hedge will help to filter out toxic materials that could damage plants. Suitable plants include *Aucuba japonica*, *Euonymus japonicus*, *Ilex aquifolium* and *Ligustrum ovalifolium*. (*See also* **Hedges**)

Pomegranates

Flowers, not fruit
In Britain, plant a pomegranate shrub for its novelty value and for its attractive flowers – it is not hardy and its fruit will be most unlikely to ripen. To ensure reasonable longevity, choose the variety 'Nana', which is small enough to grow in a pot and so can be moved indoors when the weather turns cold.

Best chance of success
Grow pomegranate shrubs in well-drained, loamy soil and against a south or west-facing wall. They flower from June to September and can be propagated by cuttings. However, only in the mildest areas will they survive the winter. If you have a greenhouse that can be heated throughout the winter, it may be worth attempting to grow the variety 'Nana' in the border.

Ponds
Making plans

Call for help
Unless you are particularly fit, or can call on family and friends for assistance, do not try to excavate a pond by yourself. The work can be extremely arduous. If the pond is to be a large one, hire an earth mover and someone to operate it from a plant-hire company. If you plan to have a small pond, find a jobbing gardener from your local paper or, even better, by personal recommendation. Explain in detail what you require and negotiate a price for the job.

Choosing the site
Site the pond well away from overhanging trees and shrubs. Aquatic plants need plenty of light if they are to flourish. Also, scooping out autumn leaves, which will rot and contaminate the water if they are not removed, can be a time-consuming task. Even evergreens may shed some leaves, while the foliage of some shrubs, if allowed to rot in the water, will give off toxins that are harmful to fish and other pond life. In addition, the roots of some shrubs and trees may puncture a pool liner.

Choosing the shape
The shape of your pond should be in keeping with the style of your garden. Near the house, a formal pond with simple straight lines, such as a square or rectangle, is ideal. Farther away from the house, an informal design with gentle curves may be more appropriate.

The right depth
A pond that is to be stocked with fish should be not less than 46cm (18in)

deep at the centre. This will ensure that an area of water at the bottom of the pond remains unfrozen throughout the winter, providing a safe sanctuary beneath the ice for the fish. When you are excavating the site, remember to leave a shelf about 23cm (9in) from the top and 30cm (12in) wide on which to grow shallow-water (marginal) aquatic plants. The shelf can be all round the inside of the pond or on one or two sides only. In larger, deeper ponds, a second, wider shelf about 30cm (12in) deep and wide may also be constructed.

As you dig out the soil, separate it into heaps, one of subsoil, which is light-coloured, and one of topsoil, which is darker. Dispose of the subsoil and stack the topsoil in a vacant area of the garden. It can be added to beds and borders during the following winter.

Creating curves
To construct a curved pool, mark the outline on the ground with a garden hose, and move the hose round until you are satisfied with the shape.

Untroubled waters Position a pond well away from trees to avoid the problem of falling leaves in autumn.

Hold the hose in place with wooden pegs, then, using a half-moon edger or a spade, mark the outline of the pond in the turf or soil. If the pool is to have a flexible liner, make the curves gentle because the lining material will not fit round sharp corners.

Coping with a slope

A preformed, rigid glass-fibre shell is best used to construct a pond on a sloping site. The upper edge can be sited at ground level, and the lower one can be supported by a low wall of bricks or stones. Make sure that all parts of the pond are supported from below by backfilling with sand or soil. Otherwise, when the pond is filled, the weight of the water may cause the glass fibre to crack.

Nitrate warning

Take care when siting a water feature at the bottom of a slope. Nitrates in the soil can be washed into the pond, and will turn the water green. A plastic barrier at the foot of the slope is the easiest way to avoid this problem.

A pond in a lawn

If the pond is to be sited in a lawn it will need a paved edge. The paving stones should be set a little below the level of the grass to ensure that the blades of the mower can pass over them. When marking out the shape of the pond, remember to include the width of the paved edge.

Getting started

A choice of liners

The life-expectancy of both rigid and flexible liners varies according to the materials used in their construction. Preformed plastic liners are cheap but will last for only a few years. Glass fibre, although more expensive, should last for at least ten years.

There are several types of flexible liners – butyl, EPDM, LDPE, polythene and PVC. Butyl is made from synthetic rubber and is by far the best material to use. It has an anticipated life span of 50 years and is usually guaranteed for up to 20 years. EPDM is very tough, but less flexible than butyl. LDPE is sold in several

different grades; the toughest is constructed from several bonded layers. Liners made from LDPE should carry a ten-year guarantee. Polythene is weak and is not suitable as a liner for a permanent pond, but it can be used to make a bog garden. PVC is fairly strong and is about half the price of butyl. A heavy-duty PVC liner should last for up to 15 years.

Calculating the size of the liner

To establish how much flexible liner you will require, first measure the maximum length and maximum width of the hole. To each of these measurements add twice the maximum depth. The resultant figures give the length and width of liner you will need to buy. These measurements include sufficient liner to provide an overlap round the pond and to mould round the marginal shelves.

Colour effects

A black or brown liner creates an illusion of depth. White will make the pond appear to be shallow. Other colours, such as pale green or blue, can look harsh and artificial and may clash with the colours of aquatic plants.

Fine weather for a good fit

If you are fitting a flexible liner, do it on a sunny day. The warmth will make the material more pliable and easier to handle.

Filling up

Stretch the liner over the hole, leaving an overlap of at least 15cm (6in) all round and weigh it down with stones. Use a hose to fill the pond, gently pleating and tucking the liner into the curves as the water level rises. If you need to stand in the pond to do this, remove your shoes to prevent damage to the liner.

Topping up

The water in your pond will need to be topped up frequently, especially in summer when the evaporation rate is high. If possible, avoid using tap water. Rainwater from a butt is best. Stand the butt at a higher level than the

pond, or raise it on bricks so that the water can flow downwards. Use a jubilee clip to attach one end of a hose to the tap on the butt. If filling from a garden tap where water pressure is high, soften the impact of the water as it fills the pond by putting the hose outlet into a bucket. Alternatively, put an old sock over the end of the hose and hold it in place with a rubber band. This will reduce the flow of water and prevent mud from being stirred up.

Repairing damaged liners

Occasionally, a flexible liner may be punctured accidentally, either while it is being installed or after the pond is established. Puncture-repair kits can be bought from water-garden suppliers. Drain the pond to below the puncture then use the repair kit according to the manufacturer's instructions. Leave the repair patch to dry for a day before refilling the pond.

Concealing the edge

When edging a pond with either paving slabs or stones, lay them so that there is an overhang of about 5cm (2in) to hide the top of the liner from view. The paving will protect the liner from damage as well as shielding it from sunlight, which can cause deterioration. In the interests of safety, when you are choosing the materials from which to construct the edging for the pond, check with the supplier that the surfaces of the paving slabs or stones will not become slippery when wet.

Planting and maintenance

Netting scoop
A recently filled pond, where plants are not yet established, can acquire a green film of algae very quickly. Remove with a garden fork whose tines have been thrust through a square of wire netting. Use the algae to fertilise the garden.

Algae control
Algae thrive on sunlight and mineral salts. A week after filling a new pond, introduce oxygenating plants, such as *Elodea canadensis* (Canadian pondweed), which will absorb these salts. In spring, plant a water lily to provide shade on the surface.

Ice-breaker
Glass-fibre ponds may be damaged by ice. In winter, tie a stone to the neck of an empty plastic bottle and float it in the water. When the pond freezes, the pressure of the ice will be absorbed by the bottle.

Room to breathe
Marginal plants, which grow in the shallow waters at the edge of a pond, should not be planted too close together on the pond shelf. Tall plants, such as loosestrife, should be spaced at least 46–61cm (18–24in) apart and smaller ones, such as marsh marigolds, should have a minimum of 30cm (12in) between them.

Keep plants in proportion
Ornamental rhubarbs such as *Gunnera manicata* and *Rheum* look spectacular round a large pond but out of place by a small one. When choosing plants to grow in and round the pond, bear in mind its dimensions and choose ones that will be in proportion to their surroundings.

Good housekeeping
Use a small fishing net to scoop debris out of the pond. If not removed, debris sinks to the bottom where it rots and contaminates the water. In autumn, when falling leaves can cause a problem, stretch a strawberry net over the pond and peg the ends to the surrounding soil. The net will prevent dead leaves from falling into the water and will help you to remove them easily and quickly.

Preserving nature's balance
It is neither necessary nor advisable to clean out and refill a small pond more often than once every four or five years and a large one every nine or ten years. Frequent changes of water prevent a natural balance from being achieved in the pond. If, however, the pond has become polluted and is foul-smelling, it should be emptied immediately and cleaned thoroughly before being refilled.

Stocking with fish

Allow plenty of room
Before choosing ornamental fish, such as golden orfe or koi carp, with which to stock the pond, you will need to calculate the number that the pond can accommodate. As a rough guide, allow 5cm (2in) of fish to every 90cm^2 (1sq ft) of surface area of water. Initially, however, it is better to understock rather than overstock to allow for growth of both fish and aquatic plants.

Which fish?
It is, however, unwise to buy ornamental fish such as golden orfe or koi carp if you wish to attract wildlife to the pond as these fish are also predatory. It would be better to choose i minnows and sticklebacks instead.

Bird barrier
Use wide-mesh netting to discourage herons from fishing in the pond. Peg the netting in place in the surrounding soil. Raise it above the water by running strings across the pond under the net and tying these to the pegs.

Gentle introductions
When introducing new fish to the pond, protect them from the shock of a sudden change in temperature. Float the bag that contains them in the water for an hour or two until the temperature of the water in the bag reaches that of the pond water. Open the bag and submerge it so that the fish may swim out.

Cold fish
When a pond freezes over, fish take refuge at the bottom. Unless the ice is broken, their oxygen supply can become rapidly depleted. Make a hole by standing a saucepan of hot water on top of the ice until it melts through. Repeat the process while freezing lasts.

Feeding times
There is no need to feed fish in summer. They will eat insect eggs, larvae, seeds and minute plants. In winter they are semi-dormant and do not need to be fed. From February–May and from end September–end November, feed sparingly. Uneaten food can pollute the water.

Food for thought
Lawn fertilisers and weedkillers can be harmful to fish if splashed into the pond. They may also upset the chemical balance of the water and encourage algal growth. When treating grass round the pond, protect the water with polythene sheeting. Lawn mowings, even from lawns not treated with chemicals, may also contaminate the water. When mowing near the pond, fit the mower with a grass-box.

Accommodating wildlife

A user-friendly pond
Make sure that creatures, such as hedgehogs, have safe and easy access to your pond. Make a gently sloping beach of cobblestones or gravel or pile up some stones in one corner of the pond. This will allow them to drink easily, and help birds to bathe and frogs to hop in and out.

Clean up with snails
When your aquatic plants have become established, introduce a couple of water snails. They will act as tireless housekeepers, constantly patrolling the sides and bottom, cleaning up algae and fish waste. It is unwise, though, to allow them to live in the pond while plants are young as they may damage tender leaves.

Spawn, baby frog and toad care

A child's fishing net can be used to scoop up spawn to give to friends who also have ponds. Spawn should never be taken from the wild. If your pond is surrounded completely by paving, make sure that plants trail across the stones at some point. This will provide a safe passage for froglets and young toads and newts that may fry on sunbaked paving stones.

A home for ducks

If you have a large garden and a large, deep pond, wild ducks and other wildfowl may be attracted to your garden. You can encourage them to take up residence by constructing an island in the middle of the pond, inaccessible to cats and other predators. Wildfowl may choose to nest in the spot and rear their young in safety. The surface area of the pond should be at least 15m² (18sq yd) and the water should be deep enough for the wildfowl to be able to submerge themselves.

See also **Fountains, A garden haven for wildlife pp. 196–7, Water gardens**

Potash for salad vegetables

Potash is important for fruit formation. For annual plants, such as tomatoes and peppers, use liquid tomato food that is rich in potash. Feed regularly once the first flowers have set and continue at weekly intervals. Stop feeding when night temperatures begin to fall.

Natural source

Wood ash, a form of potash, is a good source of potassium but, to be effective, the ashes must be kept dry until they are spread over the soil. The benefits will be lost rapidly if the ashes are left outdoors and exposed to the rain before they are used. (*See also* **Ashes**)

Old-fashioned boost

Potatoes require a potash-rich soil. Chop up the leaves of *Symphytum × uplandicum* (Russian comfrey) and spread them on the bottoms of the trenches, or put a handful into each hole before planting out seed potatoes in spring.

A healthy mulch

Azaleas, fuchsias, rhododendrons and winter cabbages will all benefit from a little potassium fertiliser sprinkled over the soil during autumn.

See also **Organic gardening**

Potash

The importance of potash

Potassium, found in potash, is a crucial element in photosynthesis, the chemical process by which plants use sunlight to fuel growth. It also helps to protect them against disease, improves the colour of flowers and fruits and ensures a balanced use of the main plant food, nitrogen. There is also some evidence that potassium helps to move nutrients round the plant, thus ensuring that all parts are well supplied.

Healthier fruit

Too much foliage and not enough blossom on a fruit tree could be a sign that it is suffering from an excess of nitrogen. Correct this imbalance by sprinkling potassium fertiliser, in the form of potash (see **panel, right**) on the ground round the periphery of the roots — roughly that of the outer reach of the branches. This also helps to sweeten the fruits and brighten up their colour.

Make the right choice

Sources of potash
Potash does first-rate work in the garden. It is available in a number of forms.

Comfrey
Comfrey is rich in potash. Organic gardeners grow crops of it to use as a fertiliser. Use the leaves fresh, as a mulch or in planting holes, or soak them in water to make a liquid feed.

Muriate of potash (potassium chloride)
Now used less than it once was, this is a cheap form of potash but is not suitable for beetroot, potatoes and soft fruits.

Nitrate of potash (potassium nitrate)
This is convenient if there is a need to provide nitrogen and potash at the same time. Very quick acting.

Sulphate of potash (potassium sulphate)
This is the safest and most widely used potash fertiliser. It provides a quick source of potash soon after being applied and also remains in the soil for some time.

Wood ash
The potash content of wood ash varies enormously depending on the source and whether it has been exposed to the elements. Nutrients wash out of wood ash quickly, but they will last longer if the ash is added to the compost heap.

Potatoes

Chitting

To obtain higher yields from your potato crops, you should chit them. In February, place the tubers, thicker end uppermost, in shallow trays in a well-lit, frost-free place. After six weeks, when the shoots are 2–2.5cm (¾–1in) long, the tubers can be planted out. To produce large early potatoes, remove all but two or three shoots from each tuber.

Harvesting earlies

Early potatoes are ready to harvest about 13 weeks after planting. Insert the fork carefully, close to the haulm (leafy stems), and lift it gently. Shake the fork gently to remove the soil. This will help to prevent the potatoes from becoming impaled on the fork.

Towards bumper crops

You will grow a larger crop if you cut large seed potatoes in half at a point where the number of eyes is equal on each side. Leave the tubers for at least a week before planting out. This will allow time for the wounds to stop 'bleeding', thus lessening moisture loss and protecting the cut surfaces from infection. Although this method will produce a larger crop, each potato produced from a cut tuber will be smaller than usual. Be sure to buy only certified virus-free tubers.

Time your planting

To ensure a continuous harvest from late June until October, plan in advance the planting times for potatoes (see *panel, right*). First earlies, such as 'Arran Pilot' and 'Home Guard', should be chitted for about six weeks, then planted in late March in the south or early April in the north. They will need to be covered with horticultural fleece to protect them from frost. They should be ready to harvest from late June, about 13 weeks after planting. Second earlies, such as 'Carlingford' and 'Estima', can be planted from early April onwards and should be ready in July, about 15 weeks after planting. Maincrop potatoes, such as 'Golden Wonder' and 'Pentland Dell', are planted from mid April onwards and are usually ready to harvest in late summer, about 20 weeks after planting.

Christmas crop

As soon as the first earlies have been harvested in July, plant specially prepared seed potatoes, available from seed merchants, that will be ready to harvest at Christmas.

Continental flavours

Be adventurous and try some continental or salad potatoes. Good garden centres and mail-order suppliers should stock the seed potatoes of, for example, 'Belle de Fontenay', an early and delicious old French variety; 'Ratte', the first choice of many French chefs; and 'Pink Fir Apple', which will keep its flavour until well after Christmas.

Best for baking

Many cooks agree that the best variety to grow for baked potatoes is the early 'Duke of York'. It is good for boiling when small, and develops into a superb baking potato if it is left to grow larger. Other good varieties for baking are the maincrop 'Maris Piper' and 'Pentland Squire'.

Use a bulb planter

Potatoes do best if planted in a series of individual holes about 30cm (12in) apart for earlies, 38cm (15in) for maincrops. Use a bulb planter, which will make holes of exactly the

Make the right choice

Potatoes for all occasions

There are potatoes to suit all tastes and culinary needs.

First early
Plant March, harvest June–July.
Arran Pilot Heavy cropper; does well in light soil.
Home Guard Oval, white flesh, good in heavy soil.
Pentland Javelin Waxy, oval with white flesh, good flavour. Resistant to diseases, such as scab, and to eelworm strains.
Ulster Chieftain Floury texture, good for roasting. Resistant to blight.
Vanessa Red-skinned, heavy yields, good for boiling or roasting.

Second early
Plant April, harvest July–August.
Carlingford Round/oval white flesh.
Catriona Purple-eyed, floury flesh.
Estima Oval, pale-yellow, waxy flesh.
Linzer Delikatess Medium-sized, excellent flavour. Eat hot, or cold in salads.

Maincrop
Plant mid–late April, harvest August; harvest September–October for storage.
Desirée Crops well. Red-skinned, yellow flesh. Good flavour. Low resistance to scab. Unsuitable for sandy or gravelly soils.
Golden Wonder Best of all for roasting or making chips.
Kerr's Pink Good in wet and heavy soil. Floury flesh, makes excellent chips.
King Edward Reliable cropper. Old favourite giving quality rather than quantity. Excellent all-purpose potato.
Maris Piper Oval, white, floury flesh, very heavy yields. Excellent for baking.
Pentland Crown Oval, well-flavoured, heavy cropper. Good all-purpose potato.
Pentland Dell Disease-resistant.

right depth for potatoes. Add a light sprinkling of general fertiliser to each hole. After each row is completed, drop in the seed potatoes. Fill the holes, but do not pile the earth high. Earthing up will be required later. (*See also* **Earthing up**)

Hoeing caution

Do not hoe the ground or earth up potatoes when overnight frost is likely. Disturbing the soil will increase the risk of frost damage. This applies particularly in May when the plants are starting to put out tender leaves. Wait until the weather is warmer. Cover the plants with fleece to prevent frost damage.

Beware of blight

In summer, if the leaves on potato plants develop brown blotches and a white furry coating on the underside, it is an indication that the crop has been attacked by blight. This serious disease affects both potatoes and tomatoes and, unless dealt with quickly, will cause leaves and stems to rot, and the crop will be lost. Stand on the ridged-up earth with one foot on each side of the affected plant. This will prevent disturbance to adjacent plants. Take hold of the affected stem and pull the entire plant carefully from the ground. Burn all of the infected plants as soon as they have been removed, but do not put them on the compost heap as this could lead to reinfection. Do not grow potatoes or tomatoes on the same site for at least three years. Reduce the risk of blight by spraying plants once in June and again in July with a copper fungicide.

Barrel of potatoes

If your garden is small and you do not have room to grow potatoes in the vegetable plot, you can grow them in a large barrel or oil drum instead. The container should be about 1.2m (4ft) deep. Drill some holes in the bottom and cover them with a 5–7.5cm (2–3in) layer of stones to aid drainage. Cover the stones with a 12.5cm (5in) layer of well-rotted compost and add 115g (4oz) of a general fertiliser. Top this up with a 23–25cm (9–10in) layer of potting compost and you are ready to plant your potatoes.

Growing a mini-crop

When planting potatoes in a barrel, lay four 85g (3oz) first early seed potatoes on the compost in late March, leaving 15cm (6in) of space between them and the sides of the container. Then, cover the potatoes with a further 7.5cm (3in) of potting compost. As the potato stems lengthen, add further layers of compost, which has been enriched with a general fertiliser, to each 15cm (6in) of stem height. Water frequently, giving 4.5 litres (1 gallon) each time. When the foliage begins to show above the rim of the barrel, insert stakes to give the plants some support. The potatoes will be ready for harvesting when the plants have flowered, which is usually from late June.

Storing regime

Lift potatoes on a dry day and leave them lying on the soil for a few hours to absorb sunlight and lose some moisture. Then spread them out on newspaper in a dark area of a shed or garage, at about 15°C (59°F), for two weeks. Rub off any dried soil, then store them in a dark, cool, dry place in paper sacks.

Temperature and taste

If your potatoes have a sugary flavour, you are storing them at a temperature that is too low – below –2°C (28°F). They are also in danger of becoming frosted, which will turn them black. Raise the temperature of their storage place, or move them to a warmer spot, and the problem will be solved. Check them frequently and remove any potatoes that are damaged.

Potpourri

Deadheads into potpourri

When deadheading roses, collect the petals in a basket. When they are completely dry, but still supple, put them into a bowl with alternate layers of cooking salt. After two or three weeks, you will have a scented cake. Crumble the mixture with your hands. Add a fixative such as powdered orrisroot, which is available from herbalists and health food shops, at about 50g (1¾oz) to a salad bowl of petals. Add a few spices and dried, ground citrus-fruit peel. Seal the bowl with cling film and leave it for two to six months before use.

Fragrant collection

To make a colourful potpourri that looks attractive and smells delightful, collect the flowers on a dry day when the early morning dew has evaporated. They are at their most fragrant then. Dry the flowers in bunches and remove the heads when dry, or remove the petals before drying and spread them on trays. Put the dried petals and flower heads into a bowl and add ground orrisroot and a few drops of an essential oil of your choice. Stir gently but thoroughly, then transfer to an airtight container and store in a warm, dry place, such as an airing cupboard, for about three months. For extra colour you can incorporate pine cones and the dried petals of colourful, unperfumed flowers.

Spread the joy

Be adventurous with potpourri. As well as putting it about the house in attractive bowls, put some into small cloth bags and hang them on radiator taps, on clothes hangers in the

Colourful quartet The mingling of colours in a potpourri can be as important as the blend of floral scents. This brilliant, sweetly perfumed collection includes Roman camomile, cornflowers, pot marigolds and rose buds.

wardrobe and on hooks in the kitchen and bathroom. It is pleasant, too, to place sachets of potpourri inside cushions or between pillows and pillowcases.

A heady mixture

Make an attractive potpourri with seed heads instead of petals. Clematis, honesty, larkspur, love-in-a-mist and poppies are all suitable. Other, more exotic seed heads can be bought from a florist. Bring seasonal interest to the potpourri at Christmas time by adding small pine cones, cinnamon sticks tied in small bunches, cloves and pieces of dried peel from clementines, mandarins and satsumas.

Potting compost

Set up a sieve

Achieving a fine texture is essential when making potting compost. Make a sieve by replacing the bottom of a wooden crate with a piece of fine-mesh wire netting. Two layers of netting will sift the compost more finely.

Stocking up

Composts for seeds, cuttings and potting are always needed, so keep some in reserve. Make up a small amount of each and store them in clearly labelled plastic bags, Use them within six months while they are still fresh.

Loam-based potting composts

John Innes loam-based composts are available in a choice of mixtures; one is suitable for sowing seeds and the others are for seedlings and more mature plants. As the plants grow, their demand for fertiliser increases. Start with John Innes No. 1, which is low in nutrients. As the season progresses, pot on into John Innes No. 2 or No. 3.

Peak condition

Make sure that you store all potting composts, whether homemade or bought, in a cool, dry place. Otherwise the nutrient balance may be affected. When buying composts, reject bags that have been faded by the sun, or appear to have been stored in wet conditions – water may have seeped in through the ventilation holes and caused the compost to deteriorate.

Fresh compost only

The shelf life of potting compost is usually about six months. After this the nutrient level begins to drop, so do not buy more than you can use within this time. If you discover that you have some compost that has been stored for longer than six months, you can use it in the planting holes when planting out shrubs and trees. Alternatively, you could add it to beds and borders.

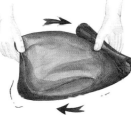

Mix well

When you prepare your own potting compost, ensure it is well mixed and that any added fertilisers are distributed evenly by shovelling it into a large, strong plastic bag. When the bag is half full, close the top securely. Lift the bag in both hands and shake it vigorously, then let it stand for a few minutes to allow the dust to settle before opening it. This action will mix the compost and ensure a well-balanced growing medium for seeds, plants and cuttings.

Primulas

Mixed blessings

Planting different strains of primulas together will result in new specimens of different colours the following year. Primulas hybridise easily. In later years, the plants will bear little resemblance to the original varieties, but the results could be most attractive.

Handle with care

Primula obconica, which flowers from December until May, makes a delightful pot plant for the window ledge, but wear gloves when handling it. Like some outdoor species, it may cause a painful allergic reaction.

From tub to garden

Large-flowered polyanthus primulas look good in tubs and, when they have finished blooming, can be dug up and replanted in the garden border where they will flower again the following year.

Happy marriages

Early-flowering primulas make fine companions for such delicate spring flowers as forget-me-nots and lungworts, and for bulbs such as narcissi and grape hyacinths. Moisture-loving *Primula japonica* flowers later and will look best when grown with ferns, plantain lilies and *Rodgersia*.

Taking cuttings

To propagate old plants of *Primula denticulata*, cut off 5cm (2in) long portions of the roots. Lay them horizontally in a box filled with peat and sand and cover with a layer, about 1cm (⅜in) thick, of the mixture. Keep the root sections in a cold frame during the winter. New shoots will be produced quickly, but do not disturb the plants at this stage because rooting will not occur until the spring. The new plants will flower the following season. Most other types of primulas can be propagated by division. (See also **Division**)

Outdoor types

Primula vulgaris (primrose) and the many strains of polyanthus primulas will grow indoors. However, they are happier outside, in borders or tubs, and will flower for longer.

On chilly windowsills

Shelter primulas growing in a window box to encourage them to continue flowering in cold weather. Protect the plants from any sudden night frosts by covering the container with either cardboard, horticultural fleece or a plastic lid. Remember to remove the cover each day.

Keeping them in flower

Indoor potted primulas will flower for longer if you keep them in a room where the temperature reaches no more than 12–16°C (53–60°F). Failing that, put them in a sheltered place outside overnight. Every two weeks, give them a little house-plant food that has been diluted to half the strength recommended by the manufacturer.

A moist environment

Primulas grown indoors need humidity. Place each pot inside a larger one and fill the space between the two with damp moss peat. Water the peat often, but not excessively.

A prop for primulas

Keep the stems of cut primulas from bending over by standing them in a tall, slender vase. As an alternative, you can tie the stems loosely together below the flowers.

Shapely show Auricula primulas come in many colours. They do best when grown in loam-based compost to which plenty of grit has been added

Pruning

The right season

Generally, the best time to prune trees is not during the winter months, but at the beginning of the growing season – March or April, depending on where in Britain you live. At this time of year, the tree sap is rising and pruning wounds will heal more quickly. The exceptions are trees which have an intense circulation of sap, such as birches, cherries, maples, and walnuts. These should be pruned at the end of summer when the sap is descending.

Collect the trimmings

Before you begin pruning, spread an old sheet or piece of polythene on the ground below to catch the trimmings, making it quick and easy to dispose of them. When pruning a tall hedge or tree near a shrub border, prevent trimmings from becoming lodged in the shrubs by draping the sheet or polythene over them.

Safety sling

It may be advisable to hire a qualified tree surgeon to deal with the removal of branches from large trees. If you choose to do it yourself though, first secure the branch that is to be removed by tying a rope round it and then passing the rope over a strong branch above. Cut the branch in sections and use the rope pulley to lower each one gently to the ground. Remember that, even when cut into sections, branches can be heavy. (*See also* **Safety**)

Lopping branches

Never remove large branches with a single cut. It is much safer, and easier, to saw them off in manageable sections until you are left with a stub that is about 30–46cm (12–18in) long. When removing this last stub, you can prevent it from snagging the bark on the trunk by making the first saw cut in an upward direction one-third of the way through the stub, then cutting down through the stub. Trim any ragged edges from the wound with a sharp knife.

Keeping in trim

Few plants are of more long-lasting, ornamental value in the garden than the small-leaved shrubs such as heathers and lavenders. Although they require little attention, they all need a trim once a year. The dead flowers of callunas and summer-flowering ericas are decorative and may be left until spring, when they should be cut back close to the foliage. Winter and spring-flowering varieties and tall heathers should be cut back after flowering in spring. Dead lavender flowers should be clipped off in late summer, and lavender hedges pruned into shape during March or April. When pruning small-leaved shrubs, it is much easier and quicker to use shears instead of secateurs, but they must be sharp as blunt shears will cause damage to the stems. (*See also* **Heathers**, **Lavender**)

Cut correctly

Pruning cuts should be made about 6mm (¼in) from a healthy bud. If the cut is too close, there is a risk of damaging the bud; if too far away, the useless portion of stem beyond the bud will wither and invite disease.

Wear oven gloves

Although oven mitts may be a bit awkward to use for weeding or planting seedlings in your garden, if you do not have any heavy-duty gardening gloves or gauntlets, they can come in very handy when the time comes to prune trees, hedges and bushes. This is particularly true when dealing with thorny devils such as holly and rose bushes.

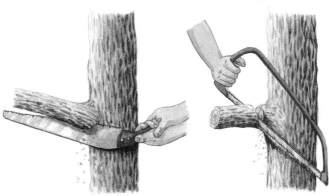

Help sap to circulate

Always prune above a lateral shoot. This will ensure that the sap is channelled towards the living part, otherwise the stumps that are left may produce unsightly growths. If these stumps die they can become infected and the disease may then spread back into the healthy plant.

Encouraging a hedge

One year after a new hedge has been planted, it is beneficial to cut back the new growth severely. The hedge will thicken up much more quickly this way because each shrub will then push out vigorous new shoots.

No pruning on conifers

Firs, cedars, pines and most of the other conifer varieties, unlike broad-leaved, deciduous trees and shrubs, do not respond well to pruning and often fail to produce healthy new shoots if pruned too severely. The yew tree is an exception – it can withstand vigorous pruning.

Back in line

To restore a tall, pyramid-shaped tree that through age or lack of attention has lost its original shape, prune the ends of branches above a bud that is turned inwards. New shoots will grow towards the trunk rather than away from it. Repeat this pruning every two years and the tree will soon regain its shape.

Pumpkins

Growing under glass

If you do not have a greenhouse, sow pumpkin seeds in the garden in late May. Place three seeds, pointed ends upwards, 2.5cm (1in) deep in the bottom of a 10cm (4in) deep planting hole. Place a sheet of glass over the hole. When the first leaves appear, thin the plants out to leave the strongest seedling. If the weather is mild, remove the glass during the day, but replace it at night until all danger of frost is past. Keep the soil moist by watering round the base of the plant. Do not water the foliage. When the fruit begins to swell, feed every two weeks with a tomato fertiliser.

Decoration with a difference

A small-fruited pumpkin can make an unusual display on a pergola. Like most of the gourd family, these pumpkins send out long stalks that can be trained up a trellis support. On a pergola, the flowers and, later, fruits will make an eye-catching decoration that will last through until the autumn.

Shapely show

To create an interesting harvest festival display, grow a selection of the many shapes and sizes of pumpkins that are available. These include bun shapes, squat fruits with striped skins, marrow-shaped varieties and 'Turk's Caps'.

Pumpkins to your taste

If you find that the flesh of most pumpkins is too 'floury' for your taste, try growing 'Red Kuri'. This pumpkin has a sugary, chestnut flavour and can be served either as a vegetable or as a fruit. Other popular varieties in Britain are 'Buttercup', 'Golden Hubbard' and Gem', a black-green pumpkin the size of a cricket ball, which matures from mid August.

Autumnal sacrifice

Large-fruiting pumpkin varieties risk succumbing to frosts before the fruits have ripened. One trick is to nip off half the fruits before they reach full size to direct the plant's energies into ripening the remaining fruits earlier.

High rise

If the ground – or the season – is damp, make mounds about 10cm (4in) high on which to plant your pumpkins and place a layer of compost round the roots to keep the weeds down. This helps to protect the developing fruits from the damp soil, which could cause them to rot.

Ground support

The fruits of ground-hugging varieties of pumpkins are particularly susceptible to rotting if left in the damp soil. To protect them, upend four flowerpots, lay a board or tile on them and place the pumpkin on this. It is best to do this while the fruit is small. If you move a large, heavy pumpkin, it may cause the stem to snap.

Garden secrets

Going for gold

Competitions to find the largest pumpkin are popular at horticultural shows. If you want to compete, try 'Hundredweight', 'Mammoth' or – the biggest – 'Atlantic Giant', which can grow to more than 200kg (440lb). You'll need patience – at least four months of nurturing with compost, fertiliser, water and warmth. In the early stages, allow the plant to form three fruits, then cut off the two weakest. As the pumpkin develops, push a large board underneath it and let it continue to grow on that. This makes it easier to transport the pumpkin when it is fully grown.

Hallowe'en lantern

Choose a large pumpkin. Cut off the top, scoop out the flesh and carve a face in the skin. Put a lighted nightlight inside and replace the top.

Store in nets

Never leave pumpkins out in the cold once they have been harvested. They should be stored at a temperature of 10–18°C (50–65°F). Suspend them in netting in a garage or attic and make sure that they have plenty of light. Alternatively, you can put them on show in the kitchen. Many gardeners assume that their sheds are frost-free but this may not be the case and pumpkins stored there may freeze during a cold spell.

Straw protection

Lay marrows, pumpkins and summer squashes on shelves covered with straw. They will keep there for two to three months as long as there is no damage to the skins. Winter squashes stored in this way will keep for up to six months.

See also **Gourds**

Purchases

No need to rush

The first sunny day does not mean that spring has arrived and the delicate plants on sale at garden centres may well succumb to late frosts. Unless you have a greenhouse or cold frame, do not buy tender plants until it is safe to plant them out without protection.

Things to look out for

When buying a container-grown plant, pay particular attention to the roots – they are the indicators of the plant's future success or failure. Check that the soil in the container is neither too dry nor too moist and that the crown of the plant is firm. If the roots appear to be matted together and forming a knotted mass, or if they are growing through the bottom of the container, the plant may have difficulty in becoming established when it is planted in the garden.

Buds before blooms

Choose a plant that has many buds rather than one that is in full bloom. One slightly opened flower will confirm colour. The flowers of a plant in full bloom will wither quickly when it is planted out.

Medium is best

When selecting a container-grown shrub, try to choose a medium-sized specimen. You may find that large plants have difficulty in becoming established, while very small plants may be recently rooted cuttings, which could take several years to develop and produce a reasonable display.

Before you decide

Before buying any potted plant, lift it up by its stem. If it lifts easily out of the container, it is an indication that, due to lack of water, the compost has shrunk away from the sides of the pot. As it may be difficult or, in some cases, impossible to wet it again sufficiently, it is unwise to buy the plant. Reject plants that have strong roots growing through the bases of their containers. This means that they are pot-bound. Plants with scorched, withered or distorted leaves or damaged stems should be rejected too. Foliage should be healthy and a few fine roots, which indicate that a plant is well established, should protrude from the bottom of the pot.

Best buys for early birds

Garden centres usually replenish their stocks on Thursdays and Fridays, in preparation for the weekend rush. By shopping on these days, you will have the best choice of plants.

Bare-rooted specimens

Bare-rooted trees and shrubs are usually cheaper than container-grown plants, but they should be chosen with care. Select those that have healthy, well-formed root systems. Do not buy any that have distorted, shrivelled or discoloured stems. This may indicate a diseased or badly grown plant. Bare-rooted trees and shrubs should be planted only between November and March.

When a plant lets you down

A plant that dies soon after you have planted it out, or one that does not grow according to the description on the label, should be returned to the place from where it was bought. Reputable garden centres should be willing either to replace the plant or to give you advice on correct cultivation, to avoid further disappointments.

Getting the best deal

Shop around before you purchase tools and larger items for the garden, such as shredders, lawn mowers, greenhouses or sheds. Department stores and DIY superstores often sell these at prices lower than those charged by garden centres.

Quince trees

Which quince is the phoney?

Among gardeners, there is much confusion about quince trees. The true quince, *Cydonia oblonga*, has crooked branches and dark green leaves that are grey on the underside. It is grown mainly for its fruits, which can be cooked with meat or made into delicious, fragrant jelly. Plants of the genus *Chaenomeles* (Japanese or flowering quince) are quite different plants. They are much smaller than the true quince and are grown for the ornamental value of their flowers, which resemble apple blossoms, and their fragrant but tasteless yellow fruits.

Shapely fruit

Depending on the variety of *Cydonia oblonga* that you choose, you can have either apple or pear-shaped fruits. Both are equally tasty. In colder areas, avoid the variety 'Portugal', which has large, pear-shaped fruits but is less hardy than other varieties, such as 'Vranja'.

Feed and mulch

Cydonia oblonga grows to 4.6m (15ft) and does best in good, moist loam but survives in any soil type. In colder areas, plant it in a sheltered, sunny place, such as a corner bounded by two walls. Keep the tree healthy and productive by working bone meal into the soil around it in February at a rate of 130g per m² (4½oz per sq yd). Apply a mulch of well-rotted compost in May.

Watch out for disease

In summer, examine the trees carefully for signs of brown or black spots on the leaves. This is leaf spot, a fungal disease that can cause leaves to fall prematurely. If your quince tree is affected, remove and burn the diseased leaves, then spray it with a fungicide containing mancozeb.

Picking and storing

The fruits of *Cydonia oblonga* should be harvested in October, before the first frosts, by which time, depending on variety, they

Obliging oriental Native to China and Japan, the Japanese quince is adaptable and grows in a wide range of conditions. It can also be grown from seed, however buy a grafted plant if a specific colour is required.

will be either yellow or green. Store them in a dry, frost-free place, such as a shed or garage. Within four to eight weeks, those that are green will ripen and turn yellow. Store them away from other fruits, which can become tainted by the quinces' strong aroma.

Obliging oriental

You can grow the Japanese quince in any soil, in sun or shade, in a border or as a hedge. It gives year-round value in form, flower and fruit. Alternatively, cook the fruits in syrup and then freeze and use them as a delicious filling for pies and tarts.

Colour for a shady wall

Chaenomeles japonica makes an excellent wall shrub and will tolerate shade. *C.* x *superba* 'Knap Hill Scarlet' has large, orange-red flowers from March to May. If the weather is fairly mild, it may produce a second flush of blooms on its leafless branches in winter. The small, yellow fruits ripen in late summer and can be harvested to make preserves or left on the tree, where they will remain to brighten the garden throughout the winter.

Make the right choice

Quince trees

Quinces can be cooked with meat, used to enhance the flavour of apple pies, or made into preserves and jellies. These are the best varieties.

Champion Delicately flavoured, apple-shaped fruit.

Meech's Prolific Bright yellow, pear-shaped quinces. Fruits well, even when young.

Portugal Tall, vigorous tree. Produces large fruits with a mild flavour. Does best in warmer districts.

Vranja Large, pear-shaped fruits. The most widely grown variety.

Aromatic air freshener

Although the fruits of *Chaenomeles japonica* are tasteless, they have a sweet lingering fragrance. Place a few ripe fruits in bowls and distribute them round the house. The fruits will last for up to four weeks, and spread a delightful scent.

Rabbits

Keeping flies from the hutch

If you keep a rabbit in a hutch, plant mint round the outside. This will help to keep flies away in the summer.

A mobile hutch

An ideal way to give a pet rabbit the freedom of the lawn while preventing it from running away is to allow it to eat the grass from the confines of a large, bottomless wire-netting hutch. Move the rabbit and hutch to another part of the lawn when one area of the garden has been grazed. The rabbit and hutch can be similarly moved about on a weedy patch in the garden.

Sheltered position

In summer, do not position a rabbit hutch with the door facing south as the hutch will become too hot. In addition, keep the entrance turned away from the direction of the prevailing wind throughout the year.

Natural barriers

To keep rabbits out of your garden, border it with plants they dislike, such as asters, catmint, globe thistles, lupins and poppies. Alternatively, a border of clover provides a meal so appealing to rabbits that they may have no appetite for eating any of your vegetables.

A good source of nitrogen

Rabbit droppings will provide nutrients for the plants in your garden. Add them to the compost heap to help to boost the supply of nitrogen and other plant foods.

Rabbit guards

Prevent rabbits from nibbling newly planted trees by surrounding the stems with spiral plastic rabbit guards, which can be bought by mail order or from garden centres. These protect the bark without strangling the tree.

Rabbit-proof fence

Dig a trench 46cm (18in) wide and 30cm (12in) deep. Erect a 1.5m (5ft) high wire-netting fence in the trench on the side nearest the garden. Bend the bottom of the wire across the base of the trench. This underground barrier will help to prevent rabbits from burrowing into the garden.

Make cabbages less attractive

Protect cabbages from rabbits by planting members of the onion family (garlic, leeks, onions and shallots) between the cabbage rows. Rabbits dislike the strong smell of these vegetables and will stay away.

Radishes

Healthy growth

Sow radishes at 1.3cm (½in) intervals, in 1.3cm (½in) drills, leaving 10cm (4in) between rows. This will give the radishes enough room to grow, making thinning out unnecessary and helping to ensure that spindly radishes do not develop. Water the bottom of the drills and allow them to drain before sowing. This promotes fast germination and early growth.

Radishes to mark the rows

Sow radish seeds where you are growing carrots, corn salad, onions, parsley and parsnips in March and April. Radishes grow quickly and will mark the vegetable rows within a few days. Pull the young radishes four to six weeks after sowing, to make space for the other vegetables.

Successional sowing

For continuous cropping of this quick-maturing vegetable, make small sowings at intervals of between ten days and two weeks. Harvest radishes no later than eight to ten weeks after sowing or their tender texture and delicate flavour will be lost.

Shade provision

During summer, sow radishes in a shady place in the vegetable garden. You can use the spaces between rows of bean or tomato plants whose leaves will provide the radishes with dappled shade from the sun.

Weekly watering

If the weather is dry when radish seedlings emerge, water them once a week. Use about 9 litres (2 gallons) per metre or yard of row. This will help to maintain a steady rate of growth. Do not overwater, because this will have the effect of promoting foliage development at the expense of roots.

Harvest and store

During the summer months, radishes will tend to ripen all at once. Harvest them daily and store those that you do not use. Washed and placed in a refrigerator, they will keep for up to a week.

Tops as well as roots

Rather than throw them away, add a few young and tender radish tops, mixed with tender turnip or mustard leaves, to your green summer salads. As well as having a spicy flavour, radish

leaves are rich in mineral salts and vitamins. Older radish tops can be cooked and included in soups. In addition, the immature seedpods of bolted radishes can be included in summer salads.

Raspberries

The right spot

Like most dessert fruits, raspberries do best in full sun, which not only aids ripening but assists pollination. Raspberries may tolerate a little shade, but it will not improve the fruit. Late summer and autumn varieties in particular need as much sun as possible.

Depth for planting

A planting depth of 5–7.5cm (2–3in) is sufficient for raspberry canes. Any hoeing that is done later to remove weeds between the canes must be shallow to avoid damaging the roots. Mulching is a safer way to deal with weeds.

Early treatment

Cut down any newly planted canes to 5cm (2in) above soil level. This will stop excessive twiggy growth, encourage a few strong stems and promote the development of the root system.

When plants deteriorate

If crops become less heavy and some of the leaves on the plants become mottled and brittle, the canes are probably under attack by raspberry mosaic virus, or one of the other viruses to which raspberries are peculiarly susceptible. There is no cure, and the only thing to do is to dig up the entire row, burn the plants and start again in the autumn. If possible, avoid planting on the same site, because if even one or two of the old roots remain in the ground, they can put out suckers that will soon infect new canes.

Pest control

A number of the most virulent raspberry diseases are spread by aphids. When you see them, immediately spray canes and foliage with aphid-specific insecticide to eliminate the pests but spare helpful insects. (See also **Chemicals**)

A space-saving method

If you only have a small garden, use a corner of it for your raspberries and plant three canes round each stake to save space. The stakes should be 2.4m (8ft) long and knocked 61cm (2ft) into the ground. As the canes grow, tie them loosely to the central stake with lengths of raffia.

Compact grouping

At knee and chest height, stretch two parallel galvanised wires between two 2.4m (8ft) high solid wooden posts with 1.8m (6ft) of their height above ground. Fix a second set of wires 61cm (2ft) away and tie string across from wire to wire at 61cm (2ft) intervals. Ensure that all the raspberry canes grow inside the wires and pull out any that grow outside.

Shelter from wind

Where raspberries are grown in exposed areas, good support is required to prevent damage. Erect a fence or plant a hedge to provide protection and to encourage pollinating bees, which dislike windy spots. To make a robust support, drive 2.4m (8ft) posts into the ground at the ends of rows, leaving 1.8m (6ft) above ground. Strain galvanised wires 76cm (2ft 6in), 107cm (3ft 6in) and 168cm (5ft 6in) above the ground between the posts. Tie strong string to one post then thread it round and along the wire. Loop it round each cane to tie them to the wire at 7.5–10cm (3–4in) intervals. Knot

Make the right choice

Extend the raspberry crop season

There is now an increasing range of raspberry varieties on the market. It pays to grow a careful selection rather than sticking to just one, which will give only a short season of fruit. You may need to go to a specialist fruit nursery to find them all, as garden centres often stock only a limited range.

Season	Variety	Description
Early	Glen Moy	Large tasty fruits; good for freezing; thornless canes; vigorous
Early–mid	Mailing Delight	Large pale berries; not suitable for freezing; vigorous
Mid	Glen Prosen	Very tasty fruits of moderate size; good for freezing; heavy cropper; thornless
Late–mid	Mailing Admiral	Excellent fruits; good for freezing; very heavy cropper; prolific and vigorous; disease resistant
Late	Mailing Joy	Large, tasty fruits; good for freezing; tall, vigorous canes
Very late	Leo	Large, bright orange fruits; slightly tart flavour; good for freezing; good cropper; slow starter, eventually vigorous
Autumn	Autumn Bliss	Large, tasty fruits; heavy cropper; canes almost self-supporting

the string to the wire every metre or few feet to ensure it remains tight in case of breakages.

Yellow and purple raspberries

Yellow-fruited raspberries are often more tangy than red raspberries. Varieties include the early fruiting 'Summer Gold', midsummer fruiting 'Golden Everest' and autumn fruiting 'All Gold'. 'Purple Glencoe' produces tasty raspberries that turn deep purple when fully ripe.

Water well to swell the fruit

In summer, while the raspberries are ripening, water the plants during the evening in dry weather in order to swell the fruits. A seephose laid along the rows is the most efficient method of watering, while mulching in spring when the soil is still moist will also help to retain moisture.

Look ahead

If you plan to be away in summer when raspberries usually ripen, cut the canes that are going to flower down to soil level in spring. As a result the energy of the plants will go into

producing a superior fruit yield at the end of the summer to greet you on your return.

Effective pruning

On raspberries that are summer-fruiting, cut down canes that have borne fruit to just above soil level between August and October. Remove dead wood and broken or darkened canes. Tie in the canes, trimming them 5cm (2in) above the top wire; canes of especially vigorous varieties can be bent over and tied in to boost the crop.

Pruning autumn-fruiting varieties

Cut back autumn-fruiting canes to ground level in February. Tie all new canes into the wires; these canes do not need to be thinned.

See also **Birds**

Record-keeping

Gardening Domesday

Maintaining a gardening diary helps you to keep track of what was planted where and also serves as a reminder of which species and varieties did particularly well and which were disappointments. It also helps you to forecast, from year to year, when a particular rose variety will bloom or a climber come into flower and if they fluctuate spur you on to find out why. The record can be as elaborate as you please, but an exercise book, ruled into columns, will do. Columns could be headed 'Species', 'Variety', 'Planting' or 'Sowing Date', 'Flowering Period' and 'Comments' – which might include any treatment needed to improve performance next time. Five-year gardeners' record books are also available from garden centres.

Fruit and vegetable records

Similar records can be kept for edible plants as for other plants but here additional information would be useful. As well as species, variety and planting date, it would be good to have a record of harvest times, yields and flavours. To help your awareness of the improvement or otherwise of your crops, you may also like to add entries on the application of mulches, fertilisers and insecticides, together with the results. This could save you money over the years. In addition, by consulting your records you will get to know which varieties of fruits and vegetables suit your garden – and your palate – best.

Weather eye

There are few long-term records more useful to the gardener than those of rainfall and temperature. First and last frosts and periods of drought should also be recorded, together with their effect on your plants. Note how your very localised observations compare with the weather forecasts for your area. Gradually you will build up a scheme for planting and harvesting that suits your plot. You will be able to see, too, how performances vary between exceptionally fine or wet years and those of average weather. You can then assess what really constitutes an average year in your garden.

Staking to the right height

If you like to grow quite a large number of perennials, keeping a record of the height of each variety can be an enormous help when you come to stake them early in the season while they are still developing. This will ensure that your canes or brushwood are neither so tall that they overtop the flowers nor too short to do the job properly.

Timing propagation

Cuttings of some shrubs such as clematis, daphnes and rhododendrons root better at certain times of the year than others. Sometimes even a few weeks can make a big difference to the success rate. Recording exactly when you take cuttings and noting the percentage that root will soon give you the necessary information about the best time to propagate these shrubs.

Recycling

Using foil again

Aluminium foil has many uses in the garden. Attach strips to strings to make bird scarers; lay squares round the base of plants to deter flying insect pests by 'scrambling' their guidance systems; wind 15cm (6in) long strips round brassica stems to minimise damage from cutworms, and round the stems of runner beans and marrows to deter snails; use sheets as light reflectors to prevent seedlings raised on a window ledge from becoming leggy.

Bags of ideas

Reuse polythene food bags to keep cuttings from drying out, both before and after potting. Small paper bags and used envelopes make excellent containers for home-produced seeds. Save larger bags for filling with dried herbs or for storing overwintering bulbs.

Net protection

Drape old net curtains over your fruit bushes to protect them from birds. Alternatively, they can be placed over slightly tender plants to protect them from frost.

Eliminate weeds

Lay old carpets, rugs or underfelt over weed-infested land to smother existing weeds and prevent seeds from germinating. Use them between rows of beans, peas and soft fruit to keep the soil weed-free and retain moisture.

Cleaners' compost

Unless your carpets are made mostly from synthetic fibres, add the contents of the vacuum cleaner bag to the compost heap.

Liquid manure

Place some fresh manure in a hessian sack, tie the top with strong twine, suspend it in a water butt and move it up and down daily. The water is ready to use on your plants when it has turned the colour of weak tea.

Portable path

Make a portable, roll-up path from old cratewood or offcuts of planks. Cut the wood into pieces about 10cm–15cm (4in–6in) and drill a hole in each corner about 1.3cm (½in) in from the edge. Lay two pieces side by side and join their long sides together by threading short lengths of wire through each of the two adjacent holes and twisting them into loops. Join a third piece of wood in the same way, and

repeat until all the pieces have been used. The length of the 'path' will depend on how much scrap wood you have available, and it can be unrolled wherever you need to stand on wet or newly dug soil.

Feathery food

Feathers from old pillows and quilts provide a high-nitrogen food for soft fruit bushes and strawberries. Put a 10cm (4in) layer in the bottom of the hole when planting young fruit bushes and dig them into strawberry beds before planting.

Riches from rags

Old clothing made from natural fibres, such as pure wool or cotton, can be added to the compost heap. Make sure all buttons and zips are removed, then cut or tear the garments into small pieces.

Handy bands

Cut old, unlined rubber gloves, crossways, into narrow rings of assorted widths and use them, like rubber bands, round the tops of pots to hold polythene bags in place.

Seed-savers

Use the plastic containers from 35mm films to store home-produced seeds, or surplus seeds from opened packets.

Pots for plants

Use washed yoghurt pots, plastic cups from vending machines or milk cartons instead of plastic plant pots. Pierce drainage holes in the bottom with a knitting needle or skewer.

Chitting cartons

Empty egg cartons are the perfect shape for holding seed potatoes while they are chitting. Alternatively, you can fill them with compost and use them to sow seeds in.

Sowing rolls

Fill the inner cardboard tubes from toilet rolls with potting compost and sow seeds of runner beans and sweet peas. Longer tubes can be cut in half or into three.

Bottling plant

With a little ingenuity, empty plastic bottles can be used in a multitude of ways. Cut large ones in half and use as mini-cloches; remove the bottoms, pierce holes in the tops and upend them in the soil close to plants to make an irrigation system; use the bottom halves as plant pots by piercing holes for drainage; cut smaller bottles, or plastic beakers, into rings to make slug guards round stems; opaque bottles can be cut up to make plant labels.

Inner-tube ties

Bicycle tyre inner tubes, cut into lengths of between 30 and 46cm (12 and 18in) can be used as tree ties. To protect the trunk from rubbing on the stake, use the ties in the shape of a figure of eight.

Window cloches

Old windows make ideal tops for temporary cold frames, or you can remove the panes of glass to make cloches. You can buy special clips to hold the panes together.

Red and white currants

Currant affairs

Currants will thrive in most of Britain and in a wide range of soils, provided that the soil is moisture-retentive but well drained. Red currants may be shorter lived on dry, sandy soils. Both types do best in open, sunny positions that are not subject to late spring frosts. They are tolerant of partial shade. Water them only in long, dry periods.

Correct planting

Plant red and white currant bushes to the same depth as they were planted in the nursery in order to provide a 'leg' or clear stem of 10–15cm (4–6in) below the lowest-growing branches.

Easy-going fruit

Both red and white currants are amenable to being trained against a wall or fence, where it is usual to coax them into a U shape. Red currants will even fruit well on a north-facing wall.

Training double cordons

In the bush's first season after planting, remove all but two main shoots that are growing in opposite directions. Train them out sideways and then vertically onto horizontal wires set 30cm (12in) apart along the wall. In early winter, cut back all new side shoots to about 5cm (2in) to encourage the spurs on which the fruit grows. Prune new growth on the two main shoots by a third for a few years until the required size is achieved.

Growing know-how

Winter pruning of red and white currants

Prune red and white currants in winter but if they are prone to bird attack, postpone the operation until February – though no later – when the buds begin to swell and you can prune back to an undamaged bud. Red currants in particular bear most fruit on spurs of old wood. Both types should be pruned back to a bowl-like shape to allow air through the branches and to facilitate harvesting.

First winter pruning

Buy sturdy, one-year-old bushes from a reputable nursery between October and March and, immediately after planting, cut each branch back to four buds from the main stem, above an outward-pointing bud.

Second winter pruning

1 Shorten new growth on leaders by half (by two thirds if growth is weak), cutting back to an outward-pointing bud.
2 Cut laterals to one bud from their base to form spurs.
3 Cut out any shoots spoiling the bush shape flush with the stem.

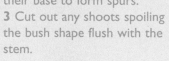

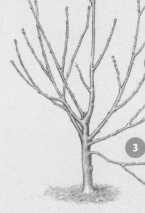

Red and white currants

These can be grown as bushes, cordons, standards or against walls.

Laxton's No. I Early and heavy cropper with bright red berries.

White Versailles Moderate grower with early, pale yellow berries full of flavour.

Red Lake Mid to late-season variety with large fruit.

White Dutch Mid-season cropper with creamy yellow fruit

Rovada A compact variety that produces huge, excellent quality fruit in the minimum space.

Blanka Large, sweet, translucent white berries on long strings. Long cropping period.

Keep birds away

Net currant bushes as soon as the buds start to swell to protect them from birds. Put empty tins upside-down on stakes among the bushes. They will clink whenever there is the slightest breeze, which may scare the birds away.

Space economy

Make the most of the space in your garden by growing currant bushes as 1.2m (4ft) standards, with room for lettuces beneath.

Red spider mites

Susceptible plants

Red spider mites attack apple, peach and plum trees, cucumber, strawberry and tomato plants, some perennials, such as montbretias and primroses, and some shrubs, including roses. Plants that are grown indoors, in a greenhouse, cold frame or polythene tunnel are the most susceptible.

Identifying the pests

Droplets of water suspended on almost invisible webs between plant stems and leaves after watering indicate a severe infestation of red spider mite. Shining a torch on the webs in the evening will show them more clearly.

Telltale signs

Although the tiny red spiders are invisible to the naked eye, the damage they do to plants is unmistakable. Leaves become lightly mottled, lose colour and curl at the edges. Leaf-fall may follow and the plant may die.

Keep the atmosphere humid

Red spider mites flourish in dry heat, so frequent watering of soil and misting of plants, including the undersides of the leaves where red spider mites breed, discourages their development.

Give plants a good airing

Stand indoor and greenhouse plants outdoors on fine days to remove them from the dry, hot conditions that attract the mites.

Destroy their homes

Eliminate overwintering sites and clear out plant debris in late autumn. Empty flowerpots should be washed with disinfectant.

Call in the bugs

Treat an infested greenhouse with the mites' predator *Phytoseiulus persimilis*. It can eat five adult or 20 young mites in a day and breeds faster than the mites, which are soon outnumbered. Having consumed their food supply the bugs die and, if needed, have to be replaced the next year. They are usually sold by mail order – garden centres and gardening magazines have addresses of suppliers.

Repotting

To repot or not to repot

Tap out a plant from its pot by first spreading your fingers across the compost and turning the pot upside-down. If the roots are wound round or densely massed, repot the plant.

Preparing the pot and plant

Use a clay or plastic pot one size larger than the one the plant has been growing in and wash it. Cover the drainage hole with broken crocks and add a layer of compost. Water the plant an hour before repotting, then tap the bottom of its pot sharply to release it with the soil. If the plant is stuck, turn it upside-down and tap the rim of the pot on a firm surface.

A new home

Position the plant on the compost, holding it upright at about the same height as before. Fill the space between the pot and the roots with compost, tap the pot on a hard surface to settle it, then firm it gently to 1.3cm (½in) below the rim of the pot. Water the plant and place it in the shade for a week before moving it to its permanent place.

Rejuvenating touch

Just before repotting, encourage new growth by combing the roots at the base and sides of the rootball with a small hand fork to remove the old, worn-out soil and to encourage new roots to grow.

Feed after repotting

Check the compost bag label to see how much plant food the compost contains. The food in some composts may last for six weeks and in others for six months. Start liquid feeding when the plant food in the compost is running out or add an extra controlled-release food.

Rhododendrons

A share of the sun

The natural habitat of most rhododendrons is light woodland, so find a semi-shaded position to plant them. Large-leaved species require more shade than others and do best in gardens that have plenty of trees. In general, exposure to sun for about half the day promotes abundant flowering. Deciduous azaleas in particular prefer an open sunny site. However, scorching sunlight and dryness at the roots are bad for the plants.

The right situation

Most rhododendrons will grow solely in a lime-free soil. There are one or two exceptions, however, such as *Rhododendron hirsutum* or *R. rubiginosum*. The ideal situation for most of these shrubs is a well-drained, sandy loam. Light soil should be enriched, and heavy soil lightened with bark, well-rotted manure or leafmould.

Ruby Red The flowers of *Rhododendron* 'Coccineum Speciosum' add a vibrant note to a sheltered, sunny corner.

Growing in containers

Where soil is too limy to grow rhododendrons successfully, the best solution is to grow them in containers or raised beds. Choose large tubs or half-barrels and fill them with lime-free compost. The best varieties for tubs are the smaller, slower-growing types such as the Yakushimanum hybrids, which have foliage and flowers in lilacs, pinks, purples and white. Water rhododendrons with rain water; if your soil is limy, your tap water will be too. If you cannot collect enough rain water, add a splash of vinegar to a watering can of tap water. Never let the compost dry out.

Long and short of it

Remember to check labels and catalogues carefully before buying rhododendrons. Some species, such as *Rhododendron impeditum*, reach only about 30cm (12in) in height and are suitable only for small beds. The majority of plants grow to 1.5–2.4m (5–8ft) and will grace many different locations. But a few, such as *R. macabeanum*, can grow up to 9m (30ft) and will dwarf many gardens.

Limit competition

Do not plant rhododendrons near surface-rooting trees, such as birches, elms, limes and poplars. Both trees and rhododendrons will suffer in the competition between the roots. Pines or deep-rooting trees, such as oaks, will not compete.

Big and beautiful

On an acid soil, the best evergreen shrubs for structure and background are often the tree rhododendrons. Tall species such as *Rhododendron arboreum* and *R. macabeanum* can grow to 6–9m (20–30ft) in mild, wet areas, or 3–6m (10–20ft) in less ideal conditions. *R. augustinii* and *R. loderi* retain a fairly bushy habit and are spectacularly colourful and sweetly scented in flower.

First aid for frost damage

Immediately you notice that frost has caused the bark to split, wrap the injured part with strips of cloth to encourage the shrub to repair the damage. Ridge up round the base of the rhododendron with a generous layer of lime-free mulch.

Winter wonders

When looking for shrubs for the winter garden, try winter-flowering rhododendrons. Both *Rhododendron dauricum* and *R. mucronulatum* have rosy purple flowers from January to March, and 'Emasculum' is lilac pink. For growing in a container, try 'Praecox', which has purplish pink blooms.

Foliage as background

Rhododendrons flower fleetingly but their eye-catching foliage provides an attractive background for later-flowering plants. Select plants that do not compete with the rhododendrons. Oriental lilies, for example, give superb splashes of colour when growing through rhododendron leaves. Roses, too, look well with the dark, shiny leaves as a backdrop and, if you choose colours close to those of the rhododendron blossoms, will help to prolong a rich display well into the summer.

Growing know-how

Rhododendron or azalea?

The genus *Rhododendron* is composed of about 1,000 species, and many more thousands of hybrids and varieties. Azaleas are a large group within this community. Once they were classified as a separate genus, but botanists then decided that the points of resemblance were greater than the differences, and so placed them within *Rhododendron*. There are few deciduous rhododendrons whereas the majority of azaleas are deciduous. Even those that are called evergreen have only a cluster of summer leaves, at the shoot tip, which are retained over winter; those leaves that form in spring fall in the autumn. Rhododendrons vary in size, ranging from prostrate shrubs a few centimetres in height to forest trees, while most azaleas are shrubs 0.3–1.8m (1–6ft) in height.

No first feed

Putting fertiliser directly into the planting hole is not good for rhododendrons. Wait until the plant is established – usually one year – before you begin feeding.

Top dressing

Rhododendrons are surface-rooting plants and enjoy a regular top dressing of leafmould or composted bark. As well as reducing moisture loss and weed growth, it evens out the root temperature and promotes better growth.

Fine foliage

Although most rhododendrons are grown for their flowers, some also have beautiful leaves that, because they are evergreen, give them appeal all year round. The leaves of *Rhododendron haematodes* are dark green with rusty brown backs, those of *R. lepidostylum* are a gorgeous sea-blue, while in *R. campanulatum* the young shoots and leaves have a beige woolly coating. The kidney-shaped leaves of *R. williamsianum* are chocolate brown when unfurling, giving additional interest to this plant.

Deadhead carefully

Remove fading blooms, otherwise they will produce seed and reduce the quantity and quality of next year's blooms. Avoid damaging the buds that grow just below the old flower heads on rhododendrons. Snap off this year's faded blooms gently between finger and thumb once the new buds appear.

Light pruning

Rhododendrons do not need to be pruned regularly. However, to promote bushy growth, lightly prune young plants after they have flowered.

New life for old plants

When old rhododendrons lose their shape or become straggly, prune the stems back to 30cm (12in) from the ground and you will be rewarded by new, bushier growth. Alternatively, prune over a three-year period, cutting back a third of the branches each year. Prune in early spring, before new growth starts. Beware of early frosts as this can damage new and tender foliage.

Easily moved

If azaleas or rhododendrons outgrow their spaces in the garden, relocate them rather than prune back. Shallow roots make these plants among the easiest to move. If possible, move the plant in early autumn so that its roots can establish themselves before winter.

Propagating from cuttings

Take cuttings from new shoots: from evergreens, August to October; from deciduous in June. Remove the lower leaves and plant the cuttings in sand under a cloche. When rooted, pot them up.

Rhubarb

Removing flower stalks

Flowering stalks weaken rhubarb plants by absorbing energy and food to the detriment of the edible red stalks. Although they can look dramatic, cut them off as soon as they appear in April.

Winter protection for crowns

Protect crowns in winter by keeping the leaves in place. They will wither at the first frost. Augment this natural cover with a dry mulch in a severe winter. (*See also* **Mulching**)

Acid free

Most rhubarb varieties are fit to eat only early in the season; later the oxalic content of the stems makes them unsuitable for consumption. An exception is 'Glaskin's Perpetual', which not only stays edible right through the season but, when raised from seed by sowing in early spring, can even be harvested late in its first year.

Forced food

To be sure of tender sticks for an early crop, force rhubarb by mounding the crowns with straw, dry leaves or bracken in December or January and then covering with a large bucket or traditional forcing pot. The sticks should be ready to cut two to three weeks before unforced crowns.

Rock gardens

Siting a rock garden

Select a spot with plenty of sun but include a lightly shaded area, if possible, to provide situations in which the greatest variety of plants can grow.

Avoid trees

Do not site a rock garden beneath trees; the tree roots may push up the rocks, while small plants could be smothered under a wet mattress of fallen leaves in autumn.

Start with a slope

Make use of any existing slope in your garden when creating your rock garden. For instance, you may be able to exploit a sloping border beside the descent to a garage. If there is no natural slope in your garden, construct a shallow mound of earth in a corner. A rock garden that rambles across a wide and slightly raised mound will be much more visually effective than one that clambers up the slopes of a prominent hillock in an otherwise flat garden.

A rock garden in a lawn

To introduce a rock garden into a lawn with a natural slope, dig an area 40–51cm (16–20in) deep, distribute a 10–15cm (4–6in) layer of drainage material, then fill with soil mixed with leafmould and coarse sand. Place a few large rocks sloping into the ground and plant your chosen alpines.

Selecting the stone

For many years, waterworn limestone pavements have been a favourite source of stones for rock gardens. Unfortunately, waterworn limestone is a scarce material compared with other types of stone and its use in gardens has led to the destruction of precious wild habitats. It may be possible to obtain stocks of the stone that have been reclaimed from old rock gardens. Otherwise, quarried rocks are widely available from large garden centres.

Try to imitate nature

Examine rocks before positioning them to avoid a regimented line-up. Grooves and fissures in the stones will help you to achieve an arrangement that resembles a natural rocky outcrop.

From the bottom upwards

Start by positioning rocks at the bottom of a slope, laying big flat rocks down on the flattest side, inclining them slightly backwards for stability. Ram down soil behind, between and underneath the rocks as you position them, so that pests, such as ants, slugs and mice, cannot take up residence in air pockets.

A natural landscape

Balance large and small rocks when constructing a rock garden, and evoke a natural formation with a few large, flat stones. Large rocks have the advantage of being more stable than small ones.

Pebbles to create an illusion

If your rock garden has only a few large rocks, enhance its visual impact by covering the soil between plants with a 2.5cm (1in) layer of pebbles. They are good for any rock garden, as they discourage weeds and keep plants healthy.

An easily constructed alternative

With large blocks of natural stone becoming scarce and expensive, a raised alpine bed contained in a low stone or brick wall can make a delightful alternative to a real rock garden. The smaller pieces of stone used are easier to find and a raised bed can be made to fit exactly the space available on a patio or in a small town or city garden. It is also ideal for creating an alpine-friendly environment if the soil in your garden is heavy. Spread a layer of rubble over the bottom of the bed, then fill it with gritty soil to suit alpines.

Making imitation rocks

To make your own large rocks, mix together two parts coarse sand, two parts sieved peat and one part cement (measured by volume). Add water until you obtain a stiff mixture – an essential consistency for success. Dig irregular holes in garden soil, pour a layer of the mixture 5cm (2in) thick, over the bottom and sides. Leave it to dry for several days before extracting, cleaning and arranging the rough-faced imitation stones in a rock garden.

Pause before planting

Delay planting for about two weeks after building your rock garden. This will allow time for the soil to settle and for rain to reveal any imperfections in the structure. There is an exception – crevice plants, which can be put in straight away.

Plants in crevices

Place small rosette-forming plants, such as houseleeks, in vertical cracks and crevices in the rocks, firming in the soil above and below each plant. These protected positions will prevent rain from settling in the rosettes and causing them to rot.

Space for alpine plants to flourish

Keep delicate alpine plants with slow-growing domes, such as rock jasmine and gentian, well away from mat-forming plants such as aubrieta and alyssum, as these will quickly smother them.

A rock garden for all seasons

Extend the flowering season by planting alpines that bloom in late summer and autumn. *Erodium* (stork's bill), autumn gentians, sedums, like the purple-leaved Vera Jameson, the purple-leaved, blue-flowered *Veronica peduncularis* 'Georgia Blue' and orange and red zauschnerias are all worth growing in sunny spots. In shadier corners, try the dainty blue *Cyananthus lobatus*, the dwarf *Gaultheria myrsinoides*, which has deep blue berries, or *Saxifraga fortunei* with its white, star-shaped flowers.

Focus on the highlights

Plant an upright dwarf conifer in front of a rock garden to help to create the illusion of a miniature alpine scene. You can highlight any mat-forming prostrate plants by placing them in soil near the top of rocks so that they will gradually cascade down and cover the rocks.

Controlling the weeds

Prevent weeds from competing with delicate rock-garden plants for moisture and nutrients by constantly uprooting any that appear.

Give a boost to growth

At the end of winter, take soil that has been enriched with leafmould, sand and a slow-acting fertiliser such as bone meal, and heap it round the bases of any plants the roots of which have been exposed by frosts. (See also **Frost**)

Annuals for the rock garden

Serious growers of alpine plants may refuse to use annuals but there are some dainty species that self-sow and produce flowers in unexpected crevices. *Ionopsidium acaule* (violet cress) has violet flowers on plants 5–7.5cm (2–3in) high. *Saxifraga cymbalaria* has starry yellow flowers and grows 10cm (4in) high. *Iberis umbellata* has narrow leaves and white, pink or purple clusters of flowers and grows 15–30cm (6–12in) high. Pink or white *Erinus alpinus*, the fairy foxglove, is short-lived but self-sows freely.

See also **Alpine plants**

Rodents

Protecting bulbs

Protect bulbs such as tulips and crocuses from mice by planting them under a covering of fine-mesh wire. The shoots will grow through the holes and flower normally but the wire will prevent mice from digging down to the bulbs.

A garlic barrier

An effective way to disguise the smell of flowers or vegetables that are favourites with the mice in your garden is by planting rows of garlic round them. Mice dislike the strong smell of this plant and will rarely brave it to try to get at the tasty plants that lie within the cordon.

Mice work

A family of mice can wreak havoc in a vegetable plot, especially in the pea and bean trenches where they take delight in nibbling newly sown seeds. Outwit them by sowing seeds of early varieties indoors, in lengths of plastic guttering filled with seed compost or garden soil. When the seedlings have emerged and formed sturdy roots, thoroughly water the compost or soil and slide the plants, en bloc, out of the guttering and into the prepared trenches.

Security guards

Harvested vegetables in store do not escape the attention of mice. Unless they are well protected you may find your stock of potatoes or apples diminishing at an alarming rate. Sprigs of holly placed over stored apples can be an effective deterrent, while wrapping sacks or boxes of potatoes in fine-mesh wire will protect against all but the most determined mouse.

Safe traps

If you set traps for mice and voles, take a little trouble to protect the garden birds by sliding the traps into lengths of drainpipe where only the rodents can reach them. As an alternative, cover each trap with a pot, roof tile or seed tray propped up on stones that will allow just the mice underneath.

Growing know-how

Identifying a rodent

The following guide will help you to identify any rodents or similar-looking animals that you see in your garden.

If the creature has a long, pointed nose and tiny eyes (see right), it is not a rodent but a useful insect-eating shrew. The minute harvest mouse, which eats grain and insects, has small ears, a blunt nose and a long tail used for grasping. Big black eyes, large ears and a long tail denote a seed-eating wood mouse, also known as the long-tailed field mouse (see right). A large rodent is likely to be a brown rat that eats anything, including stored vegetables. The brown rat's fur can be black, but its small ears and thick, scaly tail – which is shorter than the head and body – distinguish it from a black rat. Black rats are rare in Britain. A young brown rat can be mistaken for a mouse but large feet and a thicker tail are its identifying features. A short tail, small eyes, a rounded nose and barely visible ears identify the vole (see right).

Romance of the rose

Every gardener dreams of growing a mass of roses. But the range of species, varieties and hybrids, as well as of styles and colours, must be approached with forethought if the display is to work.

Rose of all my days, the last rose of summer, a rose by any other name… our language is rich with the literary blooms planted by poets and lyricists. They reflect the national preoccupation with this loveliest of flowers, equally at home and generous with its favours in the gardens of cottage, castle or villa.

Part of the joy of the rose lies in its infinite variety, its vast range of forms, perfumes and colours. Climbers and ramblers create beautiful backdrops; beds of old and species roses, large-flowered and cluster-flowered bushes (traditionally called hybrid tea and floribunda roses) offer a proliferation of opulent blooms, while miniatures provide splashes of colour in the smallest spaces.

Developing a garden dedicated solely to these flowers is, however, a difficult art. As many lovers of the rose have discovered, it is best to combine a variety of its forms with complementary shrubs, such as lavender and rosemary, and perennials like hardy geraniums, delphiniums and irises. These help to do justice to the rose, setting off its beauty and providing interest when it is not in flower.

Climbers and ramblers

This group includes a vast number of scrambling and ascending roses. Some climbers, derived from species roses, flower once and, due to their extreme vigour, do best when clothing walls or growing through old trees. Others, less rampant, and derived from hybrid tea roses, are more suited to screens and fences and flower recurrently. Ramblers, vigorous but supple-stemmed, can be trained over arbours and pergolas where they produce delicate clusters of flowers in June and July. Other climbers, such as clematis, can be grown among them to bloom when the roses are not in flower.

Recommended varieties:
Climbers Compassion, Antique, Mme Alfred Carrière, Clg Arthur Bell, Penny Lane
Ramblers Albéric Barbier (vigorous), Dorothy Perkins, Golden Showers, Kiftsgate (vigorous, see left), Seagull (vigorous), Wedding Day (vigorous)

Seagull This multi-flowered rambler, left, has trusses of sweetly scented white flowers with golden stamens.

Roses for small spaces

Happy array Dwarf roses blend with other small plants, such as irises and lavender.

The neat, compact shape and prolonged flowering of dwarf bush and shrub roses means that they are the perfect choice for the small garden or for pots and patios. In the border, or indeed on a balcony or in tubs about a town house, these handsome roses are shown to their best advantage when they are mingled with other small shrubs, such as potentillas, santolinas and weigelas.

Recommended varieties:
Baby Bio, Bright Smile, Kent, Lilli Marlene (see left), Rose de Meaux, The Fairy, Trumpeter

Pots and tubs

While climbers and ramblers can clamber through tall trees, miniature roses are at the other end of the range. They rarely grow higher than 51cm (20in) and will thrive in a pot. Miniatures are long-flowering, blooming from May until the first autumn frost. Their size makes them ideal for adding colour to such corners as the rock garden, a flight of steps, a low retaining wall or, during flowering, a sunny spot indoors.

Recommended varieties:
Angela Rippon, Baby Masquerade, Letchworth Centenary, Magic Carousel, Starina, Suncharm, Sweet Fairy

Flattery Miniature roses grown indoors deserve the best container possible to do them justice.

Carpet of flowers

Prostrate roses are a small group widely used as ground cover since they sprawl to form a thick carpet of flowers. Some make dense hummocks, others, like 'Nozomi', can be trained to clamber over walls and tree stumps. These plants thrive in the sun and are a delightful way of adding interest to an embankment, camouflaging a manhole cover or softening the edges of a paved terrace. They can also go in tubs, where they will tumble attractively over the rims.

Recommended varieties:
Flower Carpet, Magic Carpet, Max Graf, Nozomi (see left), Wiltshire

Ground cover Prostrate roses make an attractive way of uniting formal and informal areas.

Classic beds

A flowerbed devoted to roses makes an eye-catching feature in the garden, especially if bushes are combined with standard and weeping standard forms. Cluster-flowered (floribunda) bushes will give continuous colour throughout the summer and autumn, while the large-flowered (hybrid tea) varieties, which bloom in distinct flushes, are loved for their incomparable flowers and scent. Bush roses will also look good in a herbaceous bed that, with a little careful planning, can provide colour and interest even when the roses are not flowering.

Recommended varieties:
For mass bedding – Warm Wishes, Silver Jubilee, Elina, Royal William
For specimens in mixed borders – Chinatown, Rhapsody in Blue (see left), Octavia Hill, Jacqueline du Pré

Full colour Bush and species roses such as *Rosa moyessi* blend with weigela and other early summer shrubs.

The flowering hedge

Modern shrub roses are too large for flowerbeds in many small gardens but they can make an attractive hedge, particularly when mixed with other flowering shrubs such as dogwood, forsythia, honeysuckle, Japanese quince, snowy mespilus or viburnum. Bigger varieties of hybrid tea roses, with their large blooms, and the cluster-flowered (floribunda) bushes also make effective and attractive hedges that will reach up to 1.5m (5ft) in height. *Rosa rugosa*, with its large, pink, scented flowers and autumn bounty of orange-red hips – not to mention its savage prickles – is quite unbeatable if a thick, dense barrier is required to deter the neighbourhood's wandering dogs and cats from invading your garden.

Hedging bets When mature, a rose hedge is not only beautiful but an effective deterrent against prowlers of all kinds.

Recommended varieties:
Ballerina, Graham Thomas (see left) Maigold, Prosperity, Queen Elizabeth, *Rosa rugosa* 'Alba' and 'Scabrosa'

Bouquets from the garden

As cut flowers, all roses will add grace and splendour to the house but if you yearn for long-stemmed, classic bouquets, you need to grow large-flowered bush roses (hybrid tea roses). These produce big, shapely flowers, often one to a stem, from early summer to autumn. Their restricted growth makes them an excellent choice for rose beds but they may be too stately and formal for some garden schemes. An alternative is to grow them in a separate place – perhaps in the vegetable garden – where they can be groomed to produce exceptional blooms for the house.

Recommended varieties:
Double Delight, Elina, Fragrant Cloud, Ingrid Bergman, Just Joey, Pascali, Warm Wishes, Wendy Cussons (see left)

Still life A group of hybrid tea roses makes a focal point in any room.

Rosemary

Grow a rosemary hedge
Rosemary makes an effective and attractive hedge. Its fragrant, evergreen foliage becomes dotted with decorative blue flowers in spring and summer. It will grow in any well-drained soil in full sun, including chalky, rather dry soil.

An asset in the vegetable garden
Cabbages, carrots and turnips can be protected from attack by root flies by growing rosemary nearby. The scent of the herb is claimed to confuse the female flies as they hunt for places to lay their eggs. The troublesome carrot fly, in particular, detests the scent of rosemary.

Refreshing rosemary
Enjoy a delightfully fragrant bath by running the hot water over a small bunch of fresh rosemary. Wash first to remove any insects.

Mediterranean gardens
Rosemary is one of the most common shrubs in the Mediterranean region and is an important component of Mediterranean-style planting in Britain. Choose a sunny spot and well-drained soil to plant a range of rosemary varieties along with cistus, euphorbias and lavenders to make the basis of a Mediterranean garden to remind you of your holidays or just to capture a different mood.

Not just blue…
Most rosemary varieties have blue flowers but for something different try *Rosmarinus officinalis* 'Majorca Pink' or the white *R. o.* var. *Albiflorus*. There is also 'Aureus', the leaves of which are splashed with yellow.

Roses

Roses bought by mail order
If the roots of roses ordered by mail are a little dry, soak them overnight in a bucket of water before planting. Add a little liquid feed to the water to help to give them a good start. If planted directly into the soil when their roots are dry, roses may die back and will certainly be very slow to establish and develop into healthy plants. Any roots that have shrivelled totally should be removed with a pair of sharp secateurs. Cut back to where they are plump and firm.

Add colour to a rose bed in spring
Precede rose blooms in a rose bed with bulbs that flower in spring. *Anemone blanda* in mixed colours, blue and white *Chionodoxa*, crocuses, vibrant blue grape hyacinths, golden narcissus, and *Puschkinia scilloides*, with its pale blue flowers, for

example, will give a brilliant show and then vanish from the scene as the roses come into flower. This allows normal cultural operations, such as hoeing, to take place without any harm to the bulbs. Plant bulbs a little deeper than is normal practice.

Planting at the correct depth
In prepared soil, make a generous hole for a new rose and mound the soil slightly before positioning a bare-rooted rose on top and spreading the roots out carefully. Place a cane across the top of the hole before filling it, to ensure the rose will be planted with the bud union a little below the soil surface when the hole is

Make the right choice

Colouring up with autumn roses
The rose has been Britain's favourite flower since medieval times. To ensure a colourful show of roses in September and October, deadhead your blooms regularly, mulch annually, keep black spot and mildew at bay and give a supplementary feed of rose fertiliser as the main flush of flowers is fading. Some varieties are more likely than others to continue blooming into the autumn. Some also exchange their flowers for colourful hips. For your autumn selection, choose from the following (C or R indicates climber or rambler).

Pink flowers
Ballerina
Cornelia
Felicia
Galway Bay (C)
Many Happy Returns
R. × *odorata* 'Pallida'

Red flowers
Glad Tidings
Guinee (C)
Ingrid Bergman
Little Buckaroo (min)
Loving Memory
Royal William

White flowers
Blanc Double de Coubert
R. fedtschenkoana
Iceberg
Nevada
Sally Holmes
Swan Lake

Yellow flowers
Allgold
Arthur Bell
R. banksiae 'Lutea' (R)
Elina
Golden Showers (C)
Peer Gynt

Other flower colours
Antique
Buff Beauty
Félicité Perpétué (R)
Julia's Rose
Mutabilis
Prosperity

Hips
R. davidii
R. glauca
R. macrophylla
R. moyesii forms
R. pimpinellifolia
R. rugosa single forms

filled. This appears as a swollen area between the stem and root of the plant.

Modern planting

To promote early growth, dig plenty of organic matter into the soil when planting a rose. Instead of applying a granular feed, mulch with a porous material like landscape fabric, then, once growth begins, add a liquid tomato feed every three weeks in the first season.

Training time

To grow ramblers or climbers up poles, train the stems in a spiral round the support, bending them almost horizontally to encourage flowering all the way up. Tie them into the support regularly to keep them in place and prevent wind damage.

Effective watering

Rose bushes survive periods of drought quite well but flower poorly unless they are kept well watered. If you are using a sprinkler, water only in the evening or early morning, as droplets of water on the petals in hot sun can cause scorching. Better still, water the base of each plant with a hosepipe or use an automatic trickle system, which waters the soil round each plant from small nozzles. Ensure that each plant receives 9–18 litres (2–4 gallons) each week. Mulching will help to conserve moisture.

A natural fertiliser

Soak nettles in water for three to four weeks to make a liquid fertiliser. Use on your roses after rain or watering.

Making a contrast

Complement upright and formal rose bushes by planting flowers with softer outlines among them. Catmint, hardy geraniums, gypsophila, lady's mantle or rosemary are all suitable.

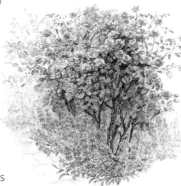

When to feed

Mature roses need feeding during February or March and then again in July. Garden centres

stock granular fertilisers that have been specially formulated for roses and flowering shrubs. If your soil is poor or your roses do not thrive, give them a boost with a liquid tomato fertiliser.

Deadhead for a second flowering

Encourage a second flush of flowers on large-flowered (hybrid tea) and cluster-flowered (floribunda) roses by prompt and frequent deadheading. Cut each faded flower stem with secateurs just above the fourth leaf below the flower. The dormant bud in the joint of the leaf will develop and flower.

Prolonging the life of cut roses

When the first petals have opened on rosebuds picked from the garden, slice the bottom off each stalk again, making an angled cut. Carefully lift off the thorns from the part of each stem that will be standing in water. The small wounds provide additional openings through which the roses can draw in water. A vertical cut into each rose stem or gentle crushing with a hammer blow also help roses to take in more water. If the flowers droop, place the bottom few centimetres or inch of each stem in boiling water to revive them. (*See also* **Cut flowers**)

Removing suckers

Shoots that grow from the rootstock of a rose, rather than from the variety grafted onto the rootstock, are called suckers. Twist and pull off suckers at the point of origin on the root, below the soil surface; otherwise the grafted rose will be weakened and may die.

Early control of disease

When buds begin to swell but before leaf development, prevent black spot and other fungal diseases by applying fungicides every two weeks from February. It is too late to eliminate the problem when symptoms appear in June. Early in December, rake up and burn dropped leaves. The use of a thick, 7.5–10cm (3–4in) mulch will benefit the plant and prevent spores being splashed up by rain onto the stems and reinfecting the plant.

A brief history

'Roves back the rose'

There are fossil roses that date back to more than 30 million years ago. Their descendants are joyously depicted in a wall painting in the palace of Minos in Crete and on murals in Pompeii, while at least one faded, withered garland has been found in an Egyptian tomb.

The Romans associated roses with courage on the battlefield, with funerals and with wine and merrymaking – chaplets of the flowers were worn at feasts. It was generally considered, however, that the Emperor Heliogabalus (AD 204–22) had gone too far when he poured vast quantities of rose petals upon his guests at his coronation banquet. Some of them smothered beneath the weight.

In early Christian times, the rose became a symbol of the Virgin Mary and St Dominic instituted the rosary with especial dedication to her. But by the Renaissance, the flower had lost its religious significance and became a symbol of royal power. Most famously, it was the badge of the Houses of York and Lancaster. The rival factions chose a white and a red rose respectively and wore them as their emblems in the bloody civil war that followed. *Rosa* x *alba* and R. *gallica* var. *officinalis* have been suggested as the relevant species.

Whatever they were, they were combined by Henry VII at the conclusion of the Wars of the Roses and have remained a royal badge ever since.

Resisting disease

If you do not want to use sprays, try growing the totally disease-resistant variety 'Flower Carpet'. This low-spreading rose produces bright pink flowers throughout the summer.

Make more roses

Take cuttings from climbing and bush roses in autumn or early winter. Cut unbranched shoots the thickness of a pencil and about 23cm (9in) long, from the current year's growth. Pinch off the leaves and trim by making a diagonal cut above the top bud and a horizontal cut below the bottom bud. Make a slit in the soil in a sheltered part of the garden and put a 2.5cm (1in) layer of sand in the bottom. Insert the cuttings about 15cm (6in) apart and fill in the slit. The cuttings should have taken root by spring and can be planted out in autumn.

Bright autumn fruits

For colourful hips, choose *Rosa rugosa*, which bears clusters of spherical scarlet hips in early autumn, or *R. moyesii*, renowned for distinctively flask-shaped, glossy red hips.

Victorian solution

If your rose cuttings simply refuse to root, it is worth trying this old trick that was popular with gardeners in Victorian days. Make a cross in the base of the stem with a sharp knife and slip a grain of wheat into the slit. Tie the base with raffia, trapping the wheat, and leave the cuttings to soak in water overnight. The following day place them in a 13cm (5in) pot of cuttings compost in a cold frame. They should root by the spring. Do not be tempted to lift the plant early because this will damage the newly developing roots.

Climbers for a cool aspect

Brighten up a north or east-facing wall with the deep scarlet flowers of 'Danse du Feu', the scented white 'Mme Alfred Carrière' or the yellow blooms of thorny 'Maigold', all of which will climb to a height of up to 3.7m (12ft).

Tree-climbing roses

Choose a vigorous climbing rose to grow up an old tree. Suitable varieties include Kiftsgate and Wedding Day, which have fragrant white clusters of flowers in June. For pink blooms, plant 'Paul's Himalayan Musk'. (*See also* **Climbing plants, Scent**)

Modern pruning

Use a pair of garden shears to cut back both large-flowered and cluster-flowered roses by a third in late October and another third in March. The need to prune to an outward-facing bud is not necessary using this method, which produces a bushy shape. To retain the traditional form, follow traditional pruning practices (see **panel, left**).

Cut back climbers and ramblers

On climbers, cut back weak growth and laterals that have flowered to three or four buds annually. Every few years, prune one or two old shoots back to a few centimetres or an inch above the base. On ramblers, cut out a third of old growth to soil level each year and tie in new shoots.

Growing know-how

Traditional pruning of large and cluster-flowered roses

Prune your roses according to their type and your requirements. It is important that you prune, irrespective of type, to an outward-facing bud.

Pruning	Large-flowered (hybrid tea) roses	Cluster-flowered (floribunda) roses
After planting	Plant in autumn, then cut back hard to about 15cm (6in) above the base in spring.	Plant in autumn, then cut back hard to about 15–23cm (6–9in) above the base in spring and remove all spindly shoots.
Hard	Cut back to 15cm (6in) above the base to rejuvenate old plants and to produce a smaller number of relatively large flowers.	Cut back to 23cm (9in) above the base to rejuvenate old plants.
Moderate	Cut back the strongest growth to about 23cm (9in) and all the less vigorous shoots to about 15cm (6in). This is the classic technique for producing a good garden display.	Prune vigorous one-year-old shoots by between a third and a half, and cut back older growth to 15–23cm (6–9in). As the plant becomes crowded with stems, cut out one or two of the tough old shoots at the base.
Light	Light pruning is not suitable for hybrid tea roses because they tend to become tall and straggly.	A few naturally bushy varieties, such as 'Iceberg', can be pruned lightly by cutting back the whole plant by between one-quarter and one-third to develop a taller, bushier plant.

Shrub, patio and miniature roses

Deadhead shrub roses each year and tidy up more severely every three or four years. A section of very old wood should be removed each year to encourage regeneration. Prune patio roses as described in panel below. Tidy miniature roses with a pair of scissors.

See also **Romance of the Rose pp. 250–251**

Runner beans

A good, space-saving crop

Runner beans are the best for small gardens as they take up little room if grown on a tripod. They are easy to pick and stay virtually pest-free. And, if harvested regularly – at least twice a week – they produce more beans over a longer period of time than dwarf beans.

Supporting runner beans

Hammer two pairs of 2.4m (8ft) high stakes into the ground 2m (7ft) apart (or length of row required). Angle each pair to form an X, 76cm (30in) wide at the bottom. In the top of the two Xs, lay a crosspiece, tying it to each X with garden wire or twine. Push pairs of bamboo canes into the ground at 30cm (12in) intervals, angled so they rest on the crosspiece. Tie them in place. In late May or early June, when the beans have grown in their pots to 15–20cm (6–8in), set them in the ground at the foot of the canes. If you do not have bamboo canes, use strong cords. Stretch them over the crosspiece and secure each end in the ground with wire spikes.

Growing beans on wire

An alternative way to grow beans that will leave you with less tidying up to do in the autumn, is to grow them on wire mesh suspended between two sturdy posts. When the last of the beans have been picked, simply roll up the wire mesh and place it on the bonfire to burn off all the dried vegetation clinging to it. The wire can be saved and reused for next year's crop.

Ways with a wigwam

As a space saver, grow runner beans wigwam-style. Mark out a circle 1.2m (4ft) in diameter. Push six to eight bamboo canes, each 2–2.4m (7–8ft) long, into the ground round the outside. Incline the poles inwards and lash the tops together with garden wire or a strong cord. Set a bean plant into the ground at the base of each pole from late May or when the risk of frost is over. By July, you will have a colourful 'Indian tent' in your vegetable garden.

Watering needs

Water runner beans regularly in hot, dry weather. Unless the roots of the plants are kept moist, beans may not develop. Cold, windy conditions may also prevent beans developing as they discourage pollinating insects.

Helping pollination

Plant some climbing sweet peas near beans. The beans and flowers will grow together round the same stakes. Pollinating insects, attracted by the sweet peas, will visit the bean flowers. (See also **Companion plants, Sweet peas**)

Ornamental uses

Runner beans have ornamental flowers as well as tasty pods and this makes them the ideal cover for bare fences, for example those in new town gardens. As the flowers of most runner beans, including Scarlet Emperor, are red, vary the colours by also planting White Achievement, which has white flowers. If you want to plant only one variety but can't decide which colour you prefer, Painted Lady has attractive red and white blooms – its flower colours are the origin of its other name, York and Lancaster. All these varieties will produce good crops of tasty beans.

Try an alternative

If temperatures are low at flowering time or the garden is exposed, making pollinating insects scarce, runner beans may not set their pods very well Providing shelter for the beans is one answer but if this is difficult, try growing some of the flat-podded climbing French beans instead. These set their pods without pollination – Hunter is an especially prolific variety. (See also **French beans**)

Avoid a surplus

Runner beans can produce an enormous crop from a relatively short row of plants and there are often few takers for free beans during the height of the season. So if you always have a surplus, grow fewer plants and train them as wigwams, which cast less shadow than does a row.

Garden secrets

Climb the right way

If you notice that your runner beans need help to begin climbing, remember that they twine anticlockwise. Plants tied loosely when first planted out usually climb naturally.

Make the right choice

Stringless and dwarf types

Stringless and dwarf varieties of bean are also good to grow. Stringless beans are tender and have no stringy pieces; dwarf types grow to about 46cm (18in). For a varied crop, try the varieties below.

Lady Di	Stringless, lasts well
Mergoles	Stringless, good for freezing
Pickwick	Dwarf, stringless
Red Rum	Early, stringless, heavy yield

Safety

Guard against tetanus
In the garden, tetanus bacteria may lurk in soil at the roots of the finest rose as readily as on a rusty garden fork. Make sure that your tetanus injections are up to date and that you know when the next booster is due.

Wear the right clothing
Never garden with bare feet or in sandals, especially when using machinery or sharp, heavy tools; stout shoes are essential. Always wear gloves when pruning, cutting and trimming. Do not wear a loose-fitting jacket, scarf, tie or any jewellery that might catch in machinery. Ear-plugs or mufflers are advisable if using machinery for long periods.

Ways with wheelbarrows
Never pull wheelbarrows; always push them. It is not easy to maintain balance when pulling a wheelbarrow and, if it topples, it may cause injury, quite apart from damaging the contents and whatever they land on.

Watering cans
Do not leave watering cans near doors, gates or play areas, especially if they are full of water. Children may trip over and hurt themselves. And never leave watering cans containing pesticides or weedkillers anywhere in the garden. Always use up the last of the chemical, then wash the can thoroughly and carefully dispose of any container that has held pesticide or weedkiller.

Eye protection
Goggles should be worn for tasks that send splinters and pebbles whirling. These include brush cutting, chain sawing, hedge trimming, hover mowing and strimming. For jobs such as pruning and working near plants supported by canes, safety glasses are adequate.

Belting up
Do not put secateurs in your pocket between pruning tasks – there are holsters designed to carry them on a belt in safety.

Hidden dangers
Garden canes concealed among growing plants are difficult to see when you are bending down and concentrating upon another task. Guard against eye injury by covering the tips of the canes with ping-pong balls or bright yoghurt pots. A number of decorative, manufactured cane toppers are available on the market.

Cover blades
Keep the blades of garden saws sheathed in protective plastic covers to prevent accidents in transit or in the tool shed.

Tidy sheds
Hang spades, forks and other tools neatly in the garage or tool shed. If tools are merely stacked in the corner, they can easily slide down and trip you up as you pass by. When working in the garden, never leave a rake lying flat on the ground.

In the greenhouse
The damp atmosphere and the possibility of water splashes can make electricity in the greenhouse dangerous. An electrician should install the fittings, using weatherproof plugs and switches. All electrical equipment should be designed for damp environments, and all wiring properly encased. It is a good idea to have the equipment checked every few years.

Plug in for safety
When using electrical machinery, use a residual current device (RCD) or circuit breaker. Available as plugs or adaptors, RCDs are fittings that prevent accidents arising from faulty equipment or wiring.

Switch off
Always ensure that electrical machines, such as mowers, are unplugged before cleaning or maintaining. The on/off switch can easily be knocked while you are working on the machine and serious injury could result.

Make the right choice

Power tool tips
Electrical tools are safe in the garden provided a few basic rules are observed.

- Always attach electrical equipment to an RCD or circuit breaker.
- Loop cables over your shoulder and keep them behind you while working.
- Do not use power tools outdoors when it is raining.
- Always turn off the power supply before adjusting or cleaning a tool. Remove the plug from the socket.
- For safety's sake and to prolong the life of tools, have your electrical equipment regularly checked and serviced by an approved agent. Keep a close eye on cables for signs of damage or wear.
- Use extension leads that have a three-core flex and are connected to purpose-made rubber plugs and sockets. Some leads have their current rating marked on them.
- Do not let children touch electrical equipment or distract you while you are working.

Cable colours

Most garden electrical equipment is supplied with bright orange cable. If you use or make up an extension lead, always use cable of the same colour. The black cable often used for extension leads is more difficult to see and it is more likely to be accidentally cut.

Sage

A useful herb

Salvia officinalis (sage) is one of the most widely used herbs in stuffings and meat dishes. If grown from seed, the results can be variable, so once you get a good cropping plant, sage is best raised from cuttings. If you want to dry and store sage for use later, the young shoots are the best to use. Cut them in early summer before they start to flower.

Sun for sage

Grow culinary sage in full sun so that it stays compact and develops the best aroma. Grown in shade, the herb usually becomes straggly and tasteless and may die off in wet winters.

Sage advice

For the best value from sage in the garden, plant one or two of the more colourful varieties. These have the same flavour as the green-leaved kinds. *Salvia officinalis* 'Icterina' has yellow variegated leaves and the foliage of the Purpurascens Group is dusky purple. Yellow-leaved 'Kew Gold' and 'Tricolor' – the brightest sage with multi-coloured leaves in pink, green and cream – are not so vigorous.

A light trim

If your sage was not cut back by demands from the kitchen during winter, when it is most called upon for stuffings, trim it in the spring to keep the plant dense and bushy. Do not cut back into old wood, which may cause the plant to die, but rather snip back to within 5–7.5cm (2–3in) of it.

Regular renewal

Sage is a naturally short-lived shrub so it is best replaced every three or four years. Sometimes low shoots will layer and root themselves. They can then be detached and replanted to form new plants. Otherwise, take 7.5–10cm (3–4in) cuttings in June or July and root them in pots of gritty compost in a cold frame. Pot up the cuttings before September and plant them out in spring.

Salad crops

Quick and plentiful

Salad vegetables that crop heavily and quickly without demanding a lot of space include lettuces, radishes and spring onions.

Salad medley

Grow a diverse crop from leftover seeds of chervil, chicory, cress, endive, Florence fennel, lettuce and spinach. Sow the seeds fairly densely and cut the leaves when the plants are 10cm (4in) high.

Nurture salad crops

The secret of successful crops is to plant all your salad vegetables in rich soil containing plenty of organic matter and nutrients. They should never be allowed to dry out. Water them well in dry spells, taking care that the moisture soaks down to the roots. Watering is best done in the evening to allow the plants time to absorb moisture before the morning sun hits them.

Provide good drainage

In heavy types of soil, plant out seedlings on 10cm (4in) ridges. It is particularly beneficial to do so if you are growing winter lettuces, which are liable to develop botrytis (grey mould) if they get waterlogged. This may happen even to lettuces that are grown under glass.

Protection for winter salad crops

Protect salad crops that continue to grow in winter, particularly endives and radicchio, and blanch to improve their flavour and texture. Upturn pots or wooden vegetable boxes covered with black polythene over them to exclude all light.

Salvias

Raising half-hardy annuals

Sow half-hardy annual types in seed compost in February or March at a temperature of 21°C (70°F). Pot up into individual pots or space out in a seed tray when seedlings are 1.3cm (½in) high then grow them on in a heated greenhouse. Harden off before planting out in a sunny spot when there is no chance of frost. Space them 25cm (10in) apart.

Stop half-hardy annuals

When young plants are about 5cm (2in) tall, pinch out the growing tips to encourage bushy growth. Alternatively, for earlier colour, allow them to produce the main flower spike but remove it as soon as it starts to fade.

Gardener's potpourri

The plant that protects

'Salvia' comes from the Latin *salvare*, 'to save or protect', confirming the old country saying, 'He that would live for aye, must eat sage in May.' Sage, the herb form of salvia, was also prescribed for the ailments of ague and toothache, in addition to being thought efficacious as a hair restorer, quite apart from its culinary use in a stuffing for 'rosting pigges'.

Winter protection

Most hardy perennial varieties of salvia will tolerate frost but *Salvia guaranitica* and *S. involucrata* should be given extra protection in winter in colder areas. Mulch the soil round the plants with a mix of pulverised bark and pebbles.

Dot plants

Add interest and height to summer bedding by using varieties of *Salvia farinacea* as dot plants.

The flowers are white, light or dark blue, or silver and blue in the case of 'Strata', and easily raised from seed. However, they must be sown in January or February if they are to make decent-sized plants that will not be smothered by surrounding plants. Grow on in individual large pots, then plant them in the desired position during summer. Shelter them in a cold frame or greenhouse in autumn, where they can stay until they are planted out again.

Make the right choice

A host of salvias for a variety of situations

There are some 700 species of salvia, which include annuals, biennials, perennials and evergreen shrubs. Each type can make a very useful contribution to the garden.

Type	Description	Planting time
Salvia officinalis (sage)	A culinary herb of which there are variegated forms with coloured leaves	Spring, in any well-drained soil and in full sun
Hardy perennials	Tough perennials that produce purple blue or pink flower spikes in summer	Autumn or spring, in any reasonable soil in full sun
Half-hardy perennials	Up to 1.8m (6ft) tall, with blue, pink or magenta flowers in summer	Spring, in sun and good soil. May not survive cold winters
Half-hardy shrubs	Low, twiggy shrubs that produce flowers in shades of red, pink or cream in summer	Spring, in reasonable soil with shelter from the wind and in full sun. May be killed in hard winters
Traditional bedding	Half-hardy annual bedding shrubs available in scarlet and mixed colours	February, sowing in the greenhouse, harden off and set out in May
Tall bedding	Tall, elegant bedding plants available in various shades of blue	April or May, in ordinary, well-drained soil and full sun
Biennials	Make a rosette of leaves in the first year and white flower spikes in the second	Summer sowing in full sun and ordinary, well-drained soil

Propagate half-hardy shrubs

Take cuttings of non-flowering lateral shoots with a fragment of the woody stem from half-hardy salvia shrubs at the end of summer. Dip the base of each cutting in hormone rooting powder, then insert it in a pot filled with a mixture of peat and sand.

Sand

Sand for soil improvement

To improve the drainage of heavy clay soil and make it easier to work, dig in coarse, gritty material; sharp sand is ideal. It can be obtained in bulk from builders' merchants, but do not use ordinary soft sand because it is too fine.

Sand as a stabiliser

Stabilise a slender glass rosebud vase with a handful of sand before filling it with water. Layer differently coloured sand in the vase for a decorative effect.

Getting shrub seeds to germinate

The seeds of many trees and shrubs will not germinate unless they are exposed to low temperatures first. Soon after ripening in autumn, place the berries of berberis, daphne, hawthorn, holly and viburnum, for example, between layers of damp sand. A plastic box or a tin with holes punched in the top and base, or a clay flowerpot, would make suitable containers. Cover the container with fine wire mesh to protect the seeds against mice and other small rodents and plunge it in the garden over winter. Remove the seeds from the container in spring and sow them in the normal way, with sand still adhering, in deep boxes or in a nursery bed outdoors.

Maintain the health of cuttings

Before inserting cuttings, put a thick layer of sharp sand on top of a container of well-drained, soil-based seed compost and press it down. Make holes with a dibber and insert the cuttings. The sandy lining will help them to root and prevent them becoming waterlogged. When the roots develop they will push through

Make the right choice

What sort of sand?

Several different kinds of sand are available, each with particular, practical applications in the garden.

Horticultural sand
A coarse sand used in potting mixtures.

Lawn sand
This is a made-up mixture of sulphate of ammonia (a high-nitrogen fertiliser), sulphate of iron and fine sand. To give the lawn a boost and to keep down moss, spread it at the rate of about 115g to every m² (3½oz per sq yd) or as the instructions specify. Do not use lawn sand elsewhere as it may contain too much nitrogen for flowers and vegetables.

Play sand
A non-toxic and non-staining sand used for children's sandpits.

River sand (silver sand)
A fine, lime-free sand used in seed composts and as a top dressing for lawns.

Sharp sand (coarse sand)
Use with equal parts of organic matter to break up clay soil. Between autumn and spring, scatter a bucketful to every m² (sq yd) and work it into the top layer. Sharp sand can be used as an ingredient of potting and seed composts. It can also be used with cement or a stone aggregate to mix concrete for fixing garden posts or laying the foundation of a garden wall.

Soft sand
Made up of small, rounded grains and mixed with cement to make a mortar for brickwork, pointing and rendering.

the sand into the compost, where they will seek out water and nutrients.

Protection for newly sown seeds
After sowing flower or vegetable seeds in rows, sprinkle sharp sand over them to identify the rows and prevent them being trodden on. The layer of sand will also protect the soil surface from heavy rain or watering, which would compact the soil and impede germination.

Sandy soil

The pros and cons
There are pros and cons to planting in sandy soil. Because sandy soil is light and drains well, it warms up rapidly in spring, which allows early sowing and planting. The disadvantage of sandy soil is that essential nutrients are quickly washed out and need to be replaced regularly throughout the growing season.

Adding nutrients
The fertility of sandy soils can be greatly improved by digging in large amounts of well-rotted garden compost, farmyard manure or spent mushroom compost. But remember, you will need to top up the nutrients regularly, as these are quickly leached from the soil by watering or by rain.

Summer bedding plants
Many bedding plants will thrive in free-draining, sandy soil, especially if they are in a sunny position. If alyssums, arctotis, gazanias, mesembryanthemums and portulacas are planted close together so that they overlap, they will spread a carpet of colour over a bed or border. In addition, they will provide a living mulch, stabilising the light soil and helping to retain moisture.

Stabilising and screening soil
Grow plants that will help to stabilise sandy soil, such as hypericums, lyme grass, oleasters, pittosporum and tamarisk. If part of your garden borders onto a beach or other particularly sandy area, prevent sand from being blown onto your plants by creating a low screen from straw. Lay straw across your perimeter line, then dig it in so that it stands vertically. This will help to protect your soil and plants from drifts of sand.

Preventing erosion and water loss
Grow sprawling ground-cover plants such as *Cotoneaster dammeri*, *C. horizontalis* or dwarf hebes to prevent water loss and soil erosion. Mulch between the plants with pulverised bark, partly decomposed straw, garden compost or gravel. (*See also* **Ground cover**)

Vegetables for sandy soil
Sandy soils are ideal for growing carrots, Hamburg parsley, parsnips, salsify, scorzonera and other vegetables with long, tapering roots. The free-draining soil allows the roots to penetrate easily and stay straight and smooth without forking. The roots will also be easier to lift when harvesting. Nor will there be any need to lift them for storing during the winter. Simply cover them up with ridges of soil and, unless the ground is frozen solid, you will be able to harvest them right through the winter months.

Asparagus will thrive
Asparagus grows exceptionally well in sandy, well-drained soil. There is no need to go to the trouble of ridging up the plants, as they will grow on the flat. Dig in plenty of organic matter to retain moisture and mulch the beds with a thick layer of well-rotted farmyard manure in early spring. Plant the two-year-old crowns in early April and you will be able to enjoy your first few succulent spears the following spring.

Sawdust

Sawdust in the garden

Sawmills or cabinet-makers are often sources of sacks of sawdust for use in the garden. Sawdust decomposes very slowly and can take up to two years to break down. It absorbs large quantities of water and so improves the water-holding capacity of light soils and is ideal as a mulch round fruit trees and flowering bushes, including roses. However, as it rots, sawdust takes nitrogen from the soil in the short term before releasing it again in the long term. The addition of a little high-nitrogen fertiliser will keep trees and shrubs supplied with nutrients until the sawdust breaks down.

Speed up decomposition

Spread layers of sawdust and chicken manure alternately in a compost heap, where the acidity of the sawdust will compensate for the alkalinity of the manure. The result will be a soil improver that combines the high nutrient content of chicken manure with the organic bulk of the sawdust. Do not use it until the sawdust has decomposed and the mixture looks like rich, dark peat.

Use as a mulch

Sawdust makes an excellent mulch. Apply it when the ground is moist and it will reduce evaporation and help to retain moisture. Spread it over the surface of the soil about 2.5cm (1in) thick. In addition, it will suppress annual weeds and prevent their seeds from germinating.

Soil improvement

Incorporate any decomposed sawdust into the vegetable plot or flower garden to improve the soil. Mix it in well as you dig, rather than adding it in one thick layer. Alternatively, you can spread it on the surface of the cultivated soil as a mulch during autumn and leave the worms to pull it into the soil. Before you plant in spring, add a general fertiliser to supply the necessary nutrients.

Scarifying

Removing lawn thatch

Hire a powered scarifier to remove thatch from a large lawn in autumn. To be most effective, scarify the lawn in two directions, the second at right angles to the first. A lawn rake can be used to remove the dead grass from small areas. Grass seed can be applied to any areas of the lawn that are left bare by scarifying.

Getting rid of moss

In addition to removing thatch, a scarifier is also an excellent tool for removing moss from the lawn. Do not do this while the moss is green, otherwise the spores will be spread. Treat the area with a proprietary moss killer first, then when the moss has turned black, use the scarifier to rake it out.

Composting the debris

Rather than consigning the material removed from the lawn to the compost heap in a thick layer, pile it up and add it gradually between layers of kitchen waste and manure. This will aid decomposition.

Scent

Fragrance to the fore

All too often, scent is an afterthought or even an accidental inclusion in garden design. Ensure that your fragrant plants are placed well to the fore, and do not waste their sweetness at the back of a border where they are enjoyed only by bees and butterflies. Choose plants, too, the scents of which complement one another and do not clash discordantly.

Scented strategy

Site fragrant plants where they will do the most good – outside a window that is often left open in summer, on a pergola over the path that is most often used or in sunny, sheltered spots where their scent will not be dispersed by the wind. Drape a wisteria over the front door or encourage a really rampant rambling rose such as 'Albéric Barbier' to scramble about the upper windows.

A bower of roses

The number of sweetly scented roses is legion, but for fragrance, charm and variety, you might make a collection embodying some of the following. Among the cluster-flowered roses (floribundas), you could try 'Chinatown', 'English Miss', 'Fragrant Delight', or 'Scented Air'; and among the climbers 'Blush Noisette', 'Compassion', or 'Mrs Herbert Stevens'. Large-flowered roses (hybrid teas) might include 'Crimson Glory', 'Fragrant Cloud', 'Sutter's Gold' and 'Whisky Mac'. For shrub roses, you could choose from among 'Fru Dagmar Hastrup', 'Graham Thomas', 'Maiden's Blush' and 'Queen of Denmark'; while for miniatures you would do very well with 'Angela Rippon' and 'Little Flirt'.

A bouquet of trees

In larger gardens, a fine interplay of fragrances can be obtained by planting trees with scented flowers, foliage or both. The flowers of *Prunus mume* 'Beni-shidori' (Japanese apricot) provide fragrance in March and April; *Magnolia stellata* and *Prunus* 'Amanogawa' (Japanese cherry) in April and May; *Malus coronaria* var. *dasycalyx* 'Charlottae' (crab apple) in May and June; and, *Ligustrum lucidum* (privet) in August and September. For scented foliage, try *Laurus nobilis* (sweet bay) and the apple-perfumed *Thuja occidentalis* 'Fastigiata'.

All through the night

Well, not quite, but you can have a rich fragrance wafting into the house throughout the day and deep into the evening by planting

Make the right choice

Make your garden an aromatic paradise

A careful choice of plants can ensure a sweetly perfumed garden through almost the entire year, though remember that scent output varies according to weather and time of day.

Citrus Sharp, clean scents
Aloysia citriodora
Monarda
Osmanthus
Pelargonium crispum
Rosa ('Madame Hardy')
Skimmia

Flowery Gentle floral perfumes
Convallaria
Cyclamen
Dianthus
Lathyrus odoratus
Lonicera
Rosa
Syringa
Viola odorata

Honey Sweet smells that attract butterflies
Alyssum
Buddleja
Phlox
Pittosporum tenuifolium
Viburnum

Exotic Rich, tropical fragrances
Clerodendrum
Jasminum
Lilium regale
Narcissus jonquilla
Nicotiana
Polianthes tuberosa

Fruity and spicy Rich aromas
Chimonanthus praecox
Lonicera periclymenum
Matthiola bicornis
Myrtus
Rhododendron luteum
Rosa rugosa
Salvia

Vanilla and almond Soft, delicious scents
Akebia quinata
Choisya ternata
Clematis montana
Heliotropium
Laburnum x watereri 'Vossii'
Petunia (some)

Virginian and night-scented stocks outside the back door. The flowers of the night-scented stocks do not open until the evening, and so are not impressive to look at during the day. But those of the Virginian stocks make up for them in attractiveness, as well as providing a heady perfume through the day before they start to mingle with their even more heavily scented partners in the evening.

Summer scents in winter

Mignonette is an annual much valued for the sweet fragrance it provides in gardens through summer and into autumn. But its usefulness can be extended by sowing a few seeds in pots from mid to late summer. Bring them indoors before the first frosts and they will release sweet scents through the winter.

Added pleasure

Someone with fading eyesight will benefit from a gravel path – so they know where they are – bordered with plants of contrasting scents. Try rosemary and thyme, pinks and stocks, phloxes and tobacco plants as well as roses and a mock orange shrub. Supplement the plants with a patch of camomile lawn.

See also **Evergreens**

Seaweed

Preparing seaweed for garden use

Gather seaweed from the upper part of a beach where it has been left by the tide. When sun-dried, it weighs less and is easier to carry. Seaweed contains too much salt to be used as a fertiliser for some sensitive plants, so store it for a few months in a corner of the garden and water it, or allow the rain to do so. Turn the heap several times and water again before use. As seaweed is low in phosphate and nitrogen, add these when fertilising the soil.

Seaweed lovers

Artichokes, asparagus, beetroot, cabbages and sprouts thrive on seaweed, which provides them with a lot of potassium, calcium, magnesium and trace elements, including boron, chlorine, iodine, sodium and sulphur. Rake the seaweed directly into the bed, without first leaving it to decompose. It will have the effect of stimulating micro-organisms in the soil. Seaweed has a similar value in the soil as farmyard manure, with a higher potassium and trace element content.

Boron provider

Add fresh or calcified seaweed annually to rectify any boron deficiency in the soil, which can cause cauliflower curds to develop brown patches and can also cause damage in Brussels sprouts, cabbages and celery.

Garden secrets

Granulated seaweed

Calcified seaweed, available in granulated form from garden centres, is an alternative to fresh seaweed and contains almost the same chemicals and trace elements. When mixed with the soil, dormant bacteria are activated.

Secateurs

Single-bladed or double-bladed
Single-bladed secateurs have a straightedged, hard-metal blade, which must be kept sharp against a soft metal anvil (see below) in order to cut cleanly. The anvil may wear out in time. This type of secateurs is better suited to rough work than delicate pruning. Secateurs in which one blade with a cutting edge slides past a lower blade using a scissor action give a cleaner cut without any danger of squashing the stems you are pruning.

Maintaining secateurs
Clean secateur blades with methylated spirit after use to remove sap. Sharpen them when necessary using an oilstone. Run the chamfered edge of the blade over the stone with a curved motion that follows the shape of the blade. Most makers offer a sharpening and repair service.

Left-handed secateurs
Some left-handed gardeners find it difficult to use normal secateurs that are made for right-handed people. Specially made left-handed secateurs are available in which the blades and the safety catch are reversed. If you have difficulty finding secateurs of this type, make inquiries at a garden centre and they should be able to order them for you.

Long-handled secateurs
Reach and leverage are enhanced by long-handled secateurs, but you need to use both of your hands to operate them. Use them to cut old, hard branches 1.3–2.5cm (½–1in) thick, and thinner stems that are difficult to reach.

See also **Safety**

Seeds

Looking ahead
Do not deadhead all your flowers; allow some of them to go to seed so that you can collect the seeds when they are ripe. But remember that most of the seeds saved from F1 hybrid varieties will not produce identical plants to the parents. This may be disappointing but it can provide some pleasant surprises.

Efficient seed collection
Place paper bags over flowers going to seed and hold each one in place with a small plastic tie. Avoid using polythene bags, which do not let in air. Once the stems are dry, cut each one just below the tie and shake it so that the seeds fall into the paper bag. Label the bag.

Assisting nature
Loosen the soil beneath shrubs or trees where you would like annual and biennial flowering plants to seed themselves, then hang bunches of them from the branches when the seeds are almost ripe. The seeds will fall and scatter in the wind. It is easy to propagate love-in-a-mist, forget-me-nots and poppies in this way.

Seed supplies
Seeds shed by many perennials and annuals after summer flowering will germinate during the following autumn and spring, so look for seedlings in your flowerbeds and transplant them carefully or leave them to grow on.

Test for viability
If you want to sow an old packet of seeds, do a test to make sure you are not wasting your time. Sow a few of the seeds on a piece of damp paper towel laid in the bottom of a clean margarine tub, replace the lid and leave the container in a warm place. Check every day for signs of germination. If none of the seeds germinate on the paper, throw the rest away. If some of the seeds germinate, the proportion showing signs of life indicates how many of the remaining seeds you need to sow to raise the plants you require.

Germination acceleration
The hard coating on seeds of trees, annual and perennial sweet peas and some other perennials can be worn away by shaking the seeds for a few minutes in a tight-lidded jar lined with a medium-grade sandpaper, abrasive side inwards. This will allow water to penetrate the seeds once they are planted, and will permit germination to take place in days instead of months. Alternatively, you can speed up the germination process by soaking hard-coated seeds of broom, cyclamen, lupins and sweet peas between two layers of damp tissue overnight or until they swell to almost twice their size. Any seeds that do not swell should be chipped with a small, sharp knife on the opposite side to the eye.

Sowing seeds of the marrow family
The seeds of courgettes, cucumbers, marrows, melons, pumpkins and squashes should be sown either on their edge or with the pointed end upwards in the compost or soil. This minimises the risk of the seeds rotting before they germinate.

Warm up soil for early sowings
Vegetable seeds will germinate much more readily if the soil in the vegetable garden is warmed with a sheet of black polythene for two weeks before you sow. If the weather is still cold when the seeds have germinated, protect the seedlings with cloches or horticultural fleece.

Seed identification
As soon as you have sown seeds in a pot or seed tray, make sure that you attach a descriptive label or else you

may find that you are unable to identify your plants when the seedlings come through.

Sprinkle compost over seeds

Sift a fine 3-6mm (⅛-¼in) layer of compost over freshly sown seeds through a garden sieve with a 3mm (⅛in) wire mesh. The compost will protect the seeds from the light and prevent them drying out but will not impede their germination.

Storing seed

Leftover seeds in paper packets can be stored if the seeds are wrapped in aluminium foil and then placed in either an airtight container in a cool room or in a screw-topped jar in the vegetable compartment of the refrigerator.

Organising seed sowing

After buying seeds, arrange the packets in sowing order to ensure that you remember seed-sowing times. It can be frustrating to find a favourite has missed its sowing date – or even discover a packet of seeds that has been overlooked altogether.

Keep seeds moist after sowing

When seeds have been sown and watered, cover the seed pots with cling film and seed trays with a sheet of glass to keep the compost moist. If the containers then go into a dark, warm place to aid germination, they must be moved into the light as soon as the seedlings emerge, otherwise the seedlings will become tall and straggly. Remove the glass or cling film the following day.

Surface-sown seeds

Seeds of plants such as begonias, busy lizzies, lobelias and petunias should be sown on the surface of compost, as they require light as well as warmth to germinate well. Once the seedlings have emerged, cover them lightly with a thin layer of seed-grade vermiculite to help them to grow well. (*See also* **Sowing**)

Shade

Effective heat shields

To lower the temperature inside a greenhouse in summer, put up roller blinds on the outside of the sunny, south-facing roof, fastening them to the ridge of the greenhouse roof. On dull days, the blinds can be raised to let in light.

Keep frames and cloches cool

To help to prevent plants becoming too hot during the summer when growing under the protection of frames and cloches, apply a shading paint to the outside when the weather becomes hot. In the autumn, wipe it off.

Light shade

Trees that do not produce dense foliage, such as birches or Japanese maples, can be planted to provide light shade for shrubs that thrive in semi-shaded positions. These include many azaleas and rhododendrons.

Shade calculations

Before planting a large hedge, calculate the amount of shade it will cast ten or more years later. Erect branches or poles of the height you estimate the hedge will reach. Take note of the length of shadow cast throughout the course of a day. Remember that the sun is lower in the sky in winter than in summer and shadows will be longer. (*See also* **Trees**)

Grow instant shade

Enjoy shade beneath a pergola from the first year of planting by interspersing annual climbers, such as *Cobaea scandens* and *Tropaeolum peregrinum*, with clematis and roses that will take longer to establish themselves and

clothe the pergola. Sow the annuals indoors in March and plant them out in a sunny, sheltered position in early June.

Let the light in

Thin out the lower branches of trees to let light and rain filter through so that plants underneath can flourish. In addition, if the area beneath the tree is grassed, raising the canopy will make the grass more accessible for mowing.

Plants for cover

Grow several rows of tall plants in the vegetable garden to shade seedlings and leafy plants, such as lettuces and spinach, that need protection from the sun. Runner beans or Jerusalem artichokes are ideal, or grow flowers, such as sunflowers or dahlias.

Shaded gardens

Shade-loving bulbs
Plant spring-flowering bluebells and lilies of the valley, the summer-flowering Turk's cap lily and the giant lily *Cardiocrinum giganteum* in shade. Winter and early spring-flowering snowdrops and autumn-flowering *Colchicum speciosum* 'Album' prefer partial shade.

Scented plants
Lilies of the valley, primroses and sweet violets bring scent to a shaded garden from early to late spring. To introduce height as well as evening scent to an open or lightly shaded spot in summer, choose a variety of the half-hardy tobacco plant *Nicotiana alata,* which grows to 60–90cm (2–3ft) .

Annuals for partial shade
For vivid splashes of colour, choose profusely flowering busy lizzies to carpet the ground all summer long.

Shade-loving flowers
Make a show in the shade with spring-flowering pulmonarias, early-summer flowering *Smilacina racemosa* and late-winter flowering hellebores

and *Hacquetia epipactis*. Herbaceous plants that grow in partial shade include the spring-flowering *Polygonatum × hybridum* (Solomon's seal) and summer-flowering *Digitalis* (foxglove), *Astrantia major* and *Lythrum salicaria* (purple loosestrife).

Plants to lighten a dark corner
Lighten dark corners shaded by a wall by clothing the wall with a pale-leaved evergreen climbing ivy. Try silver-variegated *Hedera helix* 'Glacier' or yellow-variegated 'Goldheart' – also known as 'Oro di Bogliasco'.

Hostas in pots
Hostas are magnificent shade plants but their large, handsome leaves are a gourmet feast for slugs and snails. Growing hostas in containers generally avoids the worst attacks of these pests, and the plants can be given extra protection by running a band of non-setting insect glue round the rim of the pot.

Variegated plants
Lamium maculatum 'Beacon Silver' will light up a shady corner with silvery leaves, while the leaves of *Polygonatum falcatum* 'Variegatum' (variegated Solomon's seal) have striking cream tips and margins.

Mulch to improve conditions
Where small plants are being grown beneath larger ones, it is particularly important to apply a good mulch every year in order to improve the water and nutrient-holding capacity of the soil. The best time to mulch is during early spring, and materials to use include garden compost, well-rotted manure, spent mushroom compost and chipped bark.

Ground-cover plants
Illuminate shade with *Alchemilla mollis*, the star-shaped yellow-green flowers of which appear throughout summer, or with blue-flowered variegated periwinkle. Another suitable plant is brunnera, with sprays of bright blue flowers in early summer. There are varieties with white-bordered or silver-grey marked leaves. (*See also* **Ground cover**)

Plants for dry shade
The toughest site in which to grow plants is underneath mature trees and shrubs, where the soil is packed with roots and the larger plants take up all the moisture and nutrients. Good specimens for these conditions include *Cyclamen hederifolium*, which forms a carpet of marbled leaves and bears many dainty flowers in autumn, and two summer-flowering perennials with glossy evergreen foliage, *Euphorbia robbiae* and *Iris foetidissima*.

Evergreen shrubs
A number of evergreen shrubs are suitable for a heavily shaded garden: *Aucuba japonica*, which has glossy, oval leaves; *Buxus sempervirens* 'Marginata', the leaves of which are yellow-edged; *Hypericum calycinum* (rose of Sharon); *Lonicera nitida*, a shrubby honeysuckle; *Osmanthus heterophyllus*, the dark green foliage of which is often mistaken for holly; and *Skimmia japonica*, which has oval leaves topped by large bunches of red berries.

Vegetables for shade
Most vegetables will produce a good crop only if they are grown in full sun, but you will find that spring cabbages, hamburg parsley, leeks, winter lettuces and shallots will grow fairly well in slightly shady conditions. (*See also* **Solving the Shade Problem pp. 268–9**)

Shallots

Soil preparation
Shallots need rich, well-cultivated ground to produce a good crop. Add large amounts of well-rotted organic matter into the soil during initial digging and, a few days before planting, apply a generous dressing of base fertiliser to the whole bed. Plant the bulbs 20cm (8in) apart in drills with the tips just below the surface of the soil, and leave 30cm (12in) between each row. (*See also* **Fertilisers**)

Plant shallots early
Shallots should be planted early, while the ground is still cool. If the soil is workable they

can be planted from late December in the milder parts of the country and up to late March in colder areas. The only exception is the variety 'Santé', which must not be planted until the middle of April, wherever you live, to minimise the risk of bolting (running to seed).

Create good drainage

If planting shallots in heavy soils, make a ridge of soil instead of taking out a drill. Plant the shallots with the tips of the bulbs level with the top of the ridge.

Shallots from seeds

Sow seeds outdoors in March. Sow sparingly, about 2cm (¾in) apart, then thin the seedlings to 5cm (2in) apart when they are 5cm (2in) high. Alternatively, sow under glass in February, begin to harden off in mid March and plant out in April. Seed-raised shallots are less prone to disease than those grown from bulbs, because virus and white rot cannot be carried over from one year to the next. They are also highly resistant to bolting. Varieties are yellow 'Creation', red 'Atlas' and 'Matador'.

Monitor moisture levels

If the weather in spring is unusually dry, water shallots well to aid establishment. Left dry, they may cease growing, start to ripen and die down before swelling sufficiently.

Harvest tasty leaves

The tender, green shoots of shallots are ideal for adding to salads – their flavour is similar to that of chives or spring onions. If you plant a small bed with the bulbs as close together as 7.5cm (3in) both ways, you will be able to gather the shoots and use them throughout the spring.

Keep bulbs to plant next year

There is no need to buy in new bulbs for planting every year. You can use some from your own shallot harvest, as long as they are disease-free. Select medium-sized bulbs of a good shape and, before planting them, soak them for an hour or so in a solution of a systemic fungicide. Allow the bulbs to dry again before planting.

Ripening shallots

As soon as the tops start to turn yellow in July, lift shallots slightly with a fork, just enough to break the roots, which will speed up the ripening process. When they have turned brown and started to dry, choose a warm, dry day to lift the shallots completely and spread them out on the soil surface to ripen the bulbs.

Storing shallots

The ripe, dry bulbs can be spread out in thin layers in boxes for storage. Alternatively, you can plait the leaves together to form ropes, wind soft string round the tops and hang the ropes up in bunches, or try to obtain a few old open-weave onion sacks from your local greengrocer to store the shallots in and hang up the sacks in a shed or garage. Whichever method you use, store the shallots in a light, dry and frost-free place.

Speed up drying

A raised wooden support covered with 1.3cm (½in) wire mesh or plastic netting provides an ideal place for finalising the drying of shallots, as it allows air to circulate round them. Place the drying rack outdoors in full sun, turning the shallots every now and again until they are dry and the skins rustle to the touch. Take the shallots back indoors before the temperature drops at night, after which condensation would form on the bulbs.

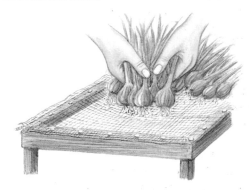

Make the right choice

Know your shallots

Choose the shallots to suit your needs from the various types available.

Yellow shallots
The standard shallots – and easy to grow. 'Giant Yellow' is widely available, although 'Topper' should give you a 30 per cent higher yield and so is becoming very popular. You may prefer the variety 'Golden Gourmet', which produces large, well-shaped, golden yellow bulbs.

Red shallots
Some of these are more of a reddish brown or purple colour than red. The variety 'Pikant' produces small bulbs with a strong flavour, whilst the purple-fleshed Success is slightly larger with a mild flavour. The bulbs of 'Delicato' and 'Santé' are larger and produce heavy crops.

Exhibition shallots
Uniformly sized and shaped shallots that are grown mostly for showing, as they produce a small crop, on average four bulbs to a clump. They are flagon-shaped with deep brown skins. 'Hative de Niort' is the best variety. They are quite expensive, at least four times the price of other shallots, but these are the ones that will win you prizes.

Solving the shade problem

Owners of 'problem' gardens – even those with no more than a few sunless tubs on the basement steps – have gained brightness with a shrewd choice of shade-loving plants.

There are areas of partial or permanent shade in every garden, caused by trees, buildings and walls. Because so many plants are available for the open, sunny parts of the garden, shade is often considered difficult or undesirable by comparison.

In fact, all gardens need the softening counterpoint of shadow that brings richness and depth to the garden through the seasons. Shade presents far more opportunities than drawbacks, if looked at with a creative eye. It can, for example, be used to emphasise those areas of the garden that are in sun, the darkness of the one concentrating attention on the brightness of the other, as in the gardens of great houses where tunnels of yew focus the eye upon some vista beyond.

Green shade Geraniums, lungworts, foxgloves and hostas figure in this well-chosen shade planting.

Go for foliage

Foliage plants, always a key feature in shade, need not be dull. The shapes and textures of their leaves can be put to good effect in positions of low light. Variegated forms of euonymus, fatsias, hostas and ivies are particularly useful. In fact, many yellow-leaved plants prefer semi-shaded positions where their foliage will not be scorched by the sun. Good golden foliage plants for partial shade include the ornamental grass *Milium effusum* 'Aureum', rich yellow *Hedera helix* 'Buttercup', fragrant flowered *Philadelphus coronarius* 'Aureus' and the Japanese maple *Acer shirasawanum* 'Aureum'. The variegated ivy *Hedera helix* 'Goldheart', trained up a trellis, tree or wall, will brighten a dull corner all the year round.

Leafy sculpture Shade-loving hostas handsomely front a group of tall primulas nearer the light.

Trees and their shade

The shade produced by deciduous trees is different from that cast by evergreens. Deciduous trees allow a certain amount of light to reach the ground below them during autumn, winter and for much of spring. The shade of evergreens is permanent, creating a dark, dry desert that would not nourish a blade of grass.

There is a good choice of bulbs and early-flowering perennials that can take advantage of off-season light beneath deciduous trees. Flowers in the wild, such as bluebells, cow parsley, lady's smock and primroses get their flowering over before the leafy canopy overhead becomes too dense to admit direct light. In the garden, you can follow nature's example by planting for a rich spring season of flowers between March and June, followed by leafier plants that lend their sculptural qualities to the scene. Columbines, *Dicentra spectabilis* (bleeding heart), epimediums, hostas and pulmonarias are among the most beautiful plants for this situation.

The underrated fern

Though rather passed over in recent years, ferns are among the most attractive of plants for shady places. There are ferns for both moist and dry sites, though some need frost protection.

The male fern, *Dryopteris filix-mas*, is an excellent 'starter' fern, being almost indestructible. It will grow in almost any soil, except one that is waterlogged, and it will tolerate dry shade.

Silvery tones are unusual in ferns, but *Athyrium niponicum* var. *pictum* unfurls fronds of elegant silver-grey, streaked with aubergine purple along the veins. It requires wind shelter and a rich, well-mulched soil. One of the most dramatic ferns is *Blechnum tabulare*, which thrives in damp, lime-free soils where the winter temperature is not too severe. The fronds are on strong, arching stems, extending nearly 1m (3ft) in length.
The hart's-tongue fern, *Asplenium scolopendrium*, forms clumps of glossy, ribbon-like foliage. It is not fussy about soils, but thrives on limestone. Members of the Marginatum Group have attractively crimped and crinkled edges to their leaves.

Bosky corner
The green straps of hart's tongue fern happily highlight a woody dell.

Bring on the bulbs

Early bulbs make the best use of the temporary light under deciduous trees that have not yet put on their canopy of foliage. In late winter, sheets of *Cyclamen coum*, joined by gold winter aconites and the nodding heads of snowdrops are a breathtaking sight at the foot of trees and shrubs. The mauve carpet of *Crocus tommasinianus* also signals that winter is on the way out.

On rich acid soil, the diminutive *Narcissus cyclamineus*, with its sharply swept-back petals, can be encouraged to flourish round the base of some bare-stemmed shrub. It is a parent of many small daffodils such as 'Peeping Tom', 'Jenny', 'Jack Snipe' and 'February Gold', which can bring spring cheer to areas of ground that will later be suffused with dappled shade. Later spring woodland bulbs such as erythroniums and trilliums relish the low light values of a sunless border, and make excellent companions for ferns and emerging hostas. They need a rich soil full of leafmould or well-rotted garden compost, to emulate the leaf litter of their natural habitat.

Rite of spring Bulbs and blossom make the most of the brief period before leaves burst forth on the trees.

Coping with dry shade

While shade itself need not cause problems for the gardener, the combination of drought and shade can be disastrous. The foot of a sunless wall is often a difficult position because of the dry soil that accompanies the gloom. Painting the wall white or a very pale colour will reflect a little more light into the area, but to enjoy the widest range of shade-tolerant plants, the water-retaining ability of the soil will need to be improved by adding copious amounts of compost and leafmould. With adequate soil moisture, it is possible to grow many desirable shade plants, such as hydrangeas, fuchsias, astrantias, Japanese anemones and the tall, fragrant tobacco plant, *Nicotiana sylvestris*.

If mulching is not enough to retain moisture, it might be worth installing a timer controlled seephose under the mulch.

Wall planting Geraniums, lady's mantle, tobacco plants, fuchsias and Japanese anemones enliven a dry, shady patch.

Shrubs

Reduce the shock of transplantation

If you have to transplant a shrub at the wrong time of year, first reduce its size. Cut it back by a third, then spray it with anti-desiccant before moving it to its new position. Replant the shrub immediately after lifting and water in well.

Mobile shrubs

To avoid positioning a shrub badly and having to transplant it later, pot it up in a large container of John Innes No. 3 compost and stand it in a few selected spots first. Plant it out later when you have decided its ideal position.

Planting a shrub in a lawn

Prepare a planting site in the lawn for a container-grown shrub by first cutting out a neat circle of turf with a diameter three times the radius of the container. Attach one end of a piece of string to a short stake driven into the centre of the site. Cut the string to the same length as the radius of the circle you wish to cut, and attach it to a sharp knife. Keeping the string taut, cut a circle. Cut rectangles in the turf inside the circle and lift them with a spade. Dig a hole for the shrub, depositing the soil on a polythene sheet to avoid making a mess on the lawn.

Hot-weather watering

The roots of newly planted shrubs have a harder time extracting moisture from the soil than those of well-established plants. Each day, wait until the sun goes down, then give all new shrubs a generous soaking until they have settled into their new positions.

Choose a ceanothus

To enjoy showers of minute, star-shaped blue flowers in spring and summer, plant a ceanothus. Most ceanothus survive limited periods of cold, but it is worth making a point of planting them in a sunny, sheltered site in the garden, where they will be protected from the worst of the winter cold. If you want to enjoy panicles of soft blue flowers

tumbling from a height of up to 3m (10ft) from late spring to autumn, plant upright evergreen *Ceanothus* 'Autumnal Blue'.

Scent and colour

For maximum effect in a border, select a shrub that has scented and showy flowers, such as a mahonia or a philadelphus, in addition to attractive foliage.

Specimen plants

Individual shrubs can make superb specimen plants when carefully sited. Choose evergreens with distinctive characteristics, such as a *Fatsia japonica* for shade or the mahonia 'Charity' for a position in the sun.

Brighten up bare stems

Surround bare-stemmed shrubs with evergreen ground-cover plants that will spread and conceal the stems, and provide added colour and interest. Choose from ivies, periwinkles or the gold or silver variegated forms of *Euonymus fortunei*, such as 'Emerald 'n' Gold' and 'Silver Queen'.

Make the most of foliage shrubs

Many foliage shrubs, such as the plum-purple leaved *Cotinus coggygria* 'Foliis Purpureis' (purple smoke bush), golden-yellow leaved *Sambucus racemosa* 'Plumosa Aurea' and silver-grey leaved *Brachyglottis* 'Sunshine' (Dunedin Hybrids Group), often named *B. greyi* or *B. laxifolius*, will produce their best foliage if cut back hard in the spring. Prune to within 7.5–10cm (3–4in) of the base of the previous year's shoots as they start into growth and the result will be a mass of strong shoots with strikingly coloured foliage. You may have to sacrifice the flowers as these shrubs bloom on the previous season's growth. Plants pruned by this method will not achieve maximum height.

A shrub for the shade

Shrubs that thrive in the shade are plentiful. Among evergreens, choose from aucuba, camellia, elaeagnus, euonymus, *Ilex* (holly), *Kalmia*, *Lonicera nitida*, mahonia, osmanthus, rhododendron, *Viburnum davidii* and *V. rhytidophyllum*. Suitable deciduous shrubs include azalea, hydrangea, magnolia, *Symphoricarpos* and *Viburnum* x *burkwoodii*.

Growing know-how

Why a shrub fails to look its best

If a shrub is not growing fast enough, or if it looks sickly, there are numerous possible reasons that could account for it.

- The soil was not properly prepared before planting or it was insufficiently enriched; the planting hole was too small or the soil was dry deep down.
- The shrub was pot-bound and the roots were not well spread out when the shrub was planted; soil was not packed properly round the roots or there were air pockets in the soil.
- The soil is unsuitable for the shrub; the position is too exposed; the shrub suffered from excess or lack of water.
- The shrub was planted during a cold snap, a drying cold wind or it suffered salt burn as a result of a seaside storm.
- The shrub was attacked by pests or a disease or was affected by the run-off from a weedkiller.

Secure shrubs

In spring, firm in any recently planted shrubs that may have been lifted slightly from the soil by the action of frost. Evergreens that may have been rocked by wind and loosened at the roots should also be checked.

Keeping leaves variegated

If you have a shrub – or, for that matter, a tree – in a variegated form, cut out completely any branches on which plain green leaves appear. These branches are vigorous and, if left, will take over from the branches with variegated leaves.

Rejuvenating a shrub

When a shrub is growing slowly and not flowering well it may need radical treatment. First, cut out any dead or diseased wood together with any spindly shoots, then remove the oldest branches, usually the thickest and darkest in colour, cutting them out at the base with a saw.

Finally reshape the plant, cutting back the current growth to within a few centimetres of a strong branch and removing any crossing or rubbing branches. Do all this in spring when growth is beginning. Finally, apply a general fertiliser and finish off with a mulch of organic matter. Ensure that the shrub does not go short of water during the spring after pruning.

Check for dead wood

Spring, when the leaves are just starting to open, is a good time to check shrubs for dead wood. Branches that are not shooting and that are obviously dead should be cut out entirely as they may become infected by coral spot disease. Once the dead wood is infected by this disease, which shows itself in the form of coral-red pustules on the bark, it often spreads to healthy branches and kills them.

Mediterranean magic

In hot and dry situations, especially on sunny slopes, try Mediterranean shrubs, which will revel in these conditions. Rosemary and lavender will grow well, even if the soil is heavy, and on humid or hot summer days the fragrance will be released from their leaves. Plant one of the many pink or white-flowered rock roses and brooms, with their yellow, cream or red blooms shaped like pea flowers, beside them.

Startling stems

Brighten up the winter garden with shrubs grown specifically for their winter stems. A number of varieties of willow and dogwood are grown specifically for their coloured stems. Choose from Cornus alba 'Sibirica' (bright red), C. stolonifera 'Flaviramea' (yellow) and Salix alba vitellina (mustard yellow) – or, better still, plant one of each. Cut back the stems hard every year – cutting back only half in the case of Cornus alba 'Sibirica'. (See also **Bark**)

Winter-flowering shrubs

Utilise the ground beneath winter-flowering shrubs by planting early-flowering bulbs, such as Anemone blanda, Galanthus nivalis, Puschkinia scilloides and Scilla bifolia.

Birds and berries

Birds are attracted to bright berries and help to propagate shrubs by eating their berries and excreting the seeds in another area. Birds seem to prefer some colours to others. Red and orange berries of cotoneasters, hollies and pyracanthas are usually the most popular and are eaten first. Yellow berries of the same shrubs are usually eaten less promptly and the purple berries of callicarpa and the purple, white or mulberry-coloured fruits of gaultheria are sometimes never eaten at all. The least likely berries to be popular with birds are the fat, white berries of Symphoricarpos (snowberry).

Berry drop

Pyracanthas and other fruiting shrubs sometimes drop their berries before they are fully ripe. The problem occurs most frequently when berrying shrubs are planted against a wall, which prevents rain reaching the roots, or near a large tree the roots of which take all the moisture. Help to solve the problem by ensuring that shrubs in these positions are mulched with 7.5–10cm (3–4in) of rich organic matter every year. Make doubly sure that the plant roots have sufficient moisture by soaking the shrubs thoroughly during dry summer spells when the berries are forming.

Handling brooms

There are many attractive brooms, mainly varieties of Cytisus scoparius, with blooms shaped like pea flowers in yellow, cream, red and various bicolours. Brooms can quickly become ungainly and untidy if not pruned regularly so, every year after flowering, cut back the shoots that have flowered to within 5–7.5cm (2–3in) of the old wood.

Welcome sun

Yellow-leaved deciduous shrubs, such as the golden mock orange Philadelphus coronarius 'Aureus' and the yellow currant Ribes sanguineum 'Brocklebankii', produce the best leaf colour when planted in the sun, but too much sun in the heat of summer may scorch the leaves and turn them brown at the edges.

Growing know-how

Why a shrub fails to flower

Provided the shrub has reached flowering age, a lack of flowers may mean buds have not appeared or have been damaged.

- The shrub has been badly pruned or pruned at the wrong time, removing the flower buds.
- The shrub is lacking in the potash that would help it to flower. The foliage has flourished instead of the flowers because a fertiliser too rich in nitrogen has been applied.
- The roots lacked water when the buds were forming.
- The buds were exposed to frost.
- The buds were eaten by birds, rabbits or caterpillars.

Protecting gold-coloured leaves

To prevent leaves scorching in summer heat, plant deciduous golden-leaved shrubs in an open but partially shaded situation. With this amount of protection the shrubs will receive enough sun in summer to ensure that the leaves colour well but not so much that the foliage gets scorched. (See also **Wall planting**)

Multi-season shrubs

In small gardens, make the best use of limited space by choosing shrub varieties that give two or three seasons of colour in a year. One of the most decorative shrubs is *Cornus alba* 'Spaethii', which has red stems in winter, variegated foliage and small creamy flowers in summer, followed by blue-tinted white fruits in autumn.

See also **Pruning, Standards**

Slopes

Dig from the top of a slope

When digging a sloping site, start at the top and work downwards so that any soil that has been washed down will be thrown back towards the top again. Trample the soil down well and it will remain in position longer.

Suitable planting patterns

Always allow for air to circulate properly when planting out a slope. At the top, choose strong deciduous trees and shrubs, such as broom, forsythia, hazel, hornbeam, laburnum, lilac, mountain ash and willow. These will act as windbreaks but still allow wind to whistle through. Lower down, select plants that are shorter, such as *Choisya ternata* and helianthemums.

Ensure proper drainage

Plan a drainage system for water at the bottom of a slope, especially if you live in an area subject to heavy storms. A pond or a pool may be the ideal collection point for water streaming from the slope.

Planting places

To ensure that plants do not dry out, plant them in small hollows dug into a slope. The hollows will collect rainwater and also make it easier to water the plants individually with a can if it proves necessary. A deep mulch round each plant will also help to keep it moist and prevent soil erosion.

A grassy slope

Sow grass seeds on slopes of no more than 15cm (6in) in 1m (3ft). On slopes with a steeper gradient, heavy rain may wash the seeds down to the bottom and it is, therefore, usually preferable to lay turf, which will be more stable than the seeds. If necessary, secure each turf in position using small pegs. On sloping sites, lay turf in winter so that it has time to settle before spring growth begins.

Rocks and waterfalls

Create a rock garden on a slope using firmly placed, substantial stones that will retain the soil. A delightful feature is a series of small waterfalls, using a pump to recirculate the water. (See also **Rock gardens**)

A wattle-retaining structure

To retain earth on a slope in a wild garden, erect a series of wattle hurdles. Hammer 61cm (2ft) stakes into the ground at 61cm (2ft) intervals, leaving 30cm (12in) above the ground. Weave willow or hazel stems between the stakes. The steeper the slope, the closer the hurdles should be

placed to one another – between 1–3m (3–10ft). Planting dwarf shrubs or ground-cover plants will give the soil additional stability.

Binding the soil

On steep slopes where the soil is likely to be washed downward, plants that make a tight carpet of rooted stems help to bind it and keep it in place. Small plants that work in this way include acaena and bugle. Larger suitable plants include the creeping *Cotoneaster dammeri* and *Rubus* 'Kenneth Ashburner'. (See also **Ground cover**)

Right plant, right place

South-facing slopes are ideal for planting Mediterranean shrubs and other sun-loving plants, including many spring bulbs. West-facing slopes are ideal for rock gardens and alpine plants. Ferns and tough evergreens are ideal for north-facing banks, while east-facing slopes, which are often exposed to bitter winds, should be planted with the toughest and most dependable plants, such as *Lamium galeobdolon* (yellow archangel).

Colourful cascades

Climbers, like clematis, provide colourful cover over sloping ground. Peg down shoots so that they grow in the desired direction.

Slugs and snails

Pest control

Sheltering in thick foliage during the day, slugs and snails slide into action at night to devour delphiniums, hostas, lupins, tender emerging vegetable seedlings and cabbage hearts. Since each slug or snail produces 500 offspring every season, it is imperative to control the population in your garden from early spring.

Natural predators

Hedgehogs, frogs and toads eat slugs and snails, so create homes for them with piles of leaves or fallen branches in a patch of wild garden or by installing a small pond. Attract large-beaked, snail-eating birds, such as thrushes, with a selection of berry-bearing trees and shrubs to nest in and to provide food and shelter. (See also **Birds, Hedgehogs**)

Effective barriers

Slugs and snails will not cross a rough-surfaced barrier, such as one made from gravel, crushed eggshells or nut shells. Spread any of these materials round vulnerable plants in the garden – for example, emerging and young flower or vegetable seedlings. Coffee grounds, too, will keep slugs off your plants. You can collect your own or ask a local coffee shop to save their grounds for you to collect once a week. To protect plants in pots, sandpaper discs, sawdust and copper strips are all effective deterrents.

A gritty rampart

Keep slugs and snails away from the larger plants they like to eat, such as delphiniums, hostas and lupins, by surrounding each plant with a ridge of sharp sand, cinders, lime or crushed oyster shells. Ensure that there is no break in the barrier.

Dual-purpose grit

Potatoes may fall foul of the keeled slug, which lives underground. Avoid susceptible varieties, like 'Maris Piper', 'King Edward', 'Desirée' and 'Pentland Crown' and dig the soil in autumn, leaving it rough over winter. Many of the pests will be killed by the cold.

Death by drowning

Slugs and snails find beer irresistible, even if it is flat. Bury a plastic cup half-filled with beer in the soil close to the plants that need protecting. Make sure you do not sink the cup to soil level, otherwise creatures that are beneficial to the garden, such as ground beetles, which eat slugs, will fall in. Cover the cup with an upturned plastic flowerpot with a large hole in the bottom as further insurance against beneficial insects falling in. Empty the cup and renew the beer every three days.

A grapefruit trap

Cut little doorways in empty grapefruit halves to ease a slug's or snail's entrance, then place the halves near threatened plants. Attracted by

the smell, slugs and snails will congregate inside the grapefruit halves, ready for collection and disposal in the morning.

Use slug pellets sensibly

Modern slug pellets are effective. They are usually coloured blue – not a natural food colour – to discourage animals from eating them and also contain a chemical deterrent. The pellets are best used sparingly in the garden; scatter them so that they are about 10–15cm (4–6in) apart. This will provide a sufficient number of pellets to kill the slugs and snails without waste. In wet weather, it is better to use methiocarb rather than metaldehyde as the former is longer-lasting in wet conditions.

Liquid slug-killer

Slugs can cause major damage to newly emerging delphiniums, hostas and peonies. Use a liquid slug killer and spray a solution onto the plants and soil when the growing shoots are just 2.5cm (1in) above ground level. Repeat the application when shoots are 7.5cm (3in) high.

No hiding place

Slugs and snails like to hide in warm, dark or damp places during the day before emerging in the evening to feed. Reduce the number of hiding places by keeping rough grass and weeds cut down in odd corners of the garden, at the base of hedgerows, behind sheds and where susceptible plants – such as lettuces – are being

grown. Ensure that paving stones are well bedded down, and remove large stones and old planks of wood from out-of-the-way corners.

A plastic tower

Cut out the bottoms and tops from transparent plastic bottles, then push each bottle into the soil to encircle a seedling. Remove them before plants become too large.

By torchlight

One of the most effective ways of dealing with slugs and snails is to go out on warm, damp summer evenings when they are most active and collect them by hand with the help of a torch. Put them into a steel bucket or tin and pour in boiling water.

For the soft-hearted

If you cannot find it in your heart to kill slugs and snails, collect and dump the pests on a piece of waste ground. But if a wall separates your garden from the waste ground beware – the wall and any dampness at its base will be attractive to slugs and snails as a place to hide. As a result, they will probably climb back over it to feed on your plants again. If the boundary is marked by a timber fence, they are less likely to climb back over the dry wood.

Organic alternative

If you are an organic gardener or one who prefers not to use slug pellets, apply an aluminium sulphate slug killer or a biological control agent. (See **Biological controls**)

Garden secrets

Big eaters

Teeth-like projections on rasping tongues make slugs excellent at plant devastation. Gastropods ('belly-footed creatures') are able to generate new rudimentary teeth-like projections on their tongues immediately after losing older teeth while feeding on plants, which is partly why so much damage is done so quickly.

Snow

Snow protection

Leave snow where it falls on plants. It insulates them against the intense cold that may follow. Leave snow on the glass panes of greenhouses or cold frames as insulation. However, brush it off if it reaches more than 15cm (6in) deep, at which depth the weight may crack the glass.

Snow weight

Remove thick snow from evergreen shrubs and conifers where its weight, especially if the snow freezes and cannot slide off, could cause branches to break. Use a broom handle or the handle of a garden tool to help to shake off the snow. Camellia buds may be damaged by snow so remove it from them immediately.

Spot the warmest places in the garden

The warmest places in the garden are those where the snow melts first. Take note of where this occurs and plant tender and half-hardy annuals there in the summer. Sow the first seeds of the season there, too. Move containers of tender plants to these spots in the autumn to prolong their season.

Protect conifers from snow damage

The shape of columnar conifers with close, upward-sweeping branches can be ruined by snow, which collects on the branches and causes them to bend outwards. Prevent damage and keep a columnar conifer in shape by wrapping it in plastic pea and bean netting.

The large mesh of the netting will allow the tips of the shoots to grow through and, because it is flexible, will not damage them, so the tree will look natural but be held in shape. Put the netting in place in autumn and carefully remove it in spring.

Clearing pathways

Do not use salt to clear snowy paths. When the thaw begins, the salt may permeate the soil and injure the roots of plants. Sprinkle sand, gravel, cinders or sawdust to melt the snow on paths.

Snowdrops

Plant the bulbs early

There is no need to wait until the autumn before planting snowdrops to appear the following winter. Although you can buy dry bulbs at that time of the year, you will get better results by planting snowdrops while they are still green – that is, immediately after flowering and before the leaves fade. Planting is

best carried out round February or March when garden centres and nurseries will have snowdrops for sale.

Growing snowdrops in the lawn

Many gardeners feel that snowdrops look best when grown in the lawn. Do not be put off by the thought that the plants will have to contend at some stage with the mower. Most of the flowers will have gone by the time the machine is brought out for the lawn's first cut. However,

Garden secrets

Poor displays

Every three to four years, lift your snowdrops immediately after flowering and divide the clumps. Replant five or six bulbs in each new position after applying a sprinkling of bone meal to each planting hole. This will ensure that the plants flower well every year.

A hint of spring A clump of snowdrops is a heart-warming sight at the threshold of a new gardening year. Yellow markings on the inner petals peep through the outer petals of the rare *Golanthus nivalis* 'Lutescens'.

Gardener's potpourri

Promise of spring

Although sometimes seen even before the end of the old year, tradition firmly asserts that the snowdrop is a new year arrival.

'The Snowdrop, in purest white arraie. First rears her hedde on Candlemass Day' – which is February 2, the Feast of the Purification. Once, on that day, it was the custom that maidens, dressed in white, would bring bunches of snowdrops to the church and strew them on the altar, so giving rise to the flower's old country name of Maid of February.

An old legend tells how, after the expulsion from Eden, Eve stood in her wintry garden and wept for the plants that had vanished. A passing angel heard her and, catching a falling snowflake, breathed on it, turning it into a snowdrop. He gave it to her, saying: 'This is in earnest Eve to thee, That spring and summer soon shall be.'

It is a promise that the snowdrop has kept faithfully ever since.

if you delay the first cut for a few weeks and then set the blades high, the leaves will be spared to die down naturally.

Bulbs in the lawn

To plant bulbs in the lawn, undercut a section of turf with a spade and roll it back. Remove about 5cm (2in) of soil, then lightly fork the surface. Firm gently and sprinkle it with a handful of bone meal. Scatter the bulbs at random over the area for a natural effect when the blooms develop. Cover the bulbs with the excavated soil, then replace the lifted section of turf. Tread it down firmly or use a roller.

The best snowdrop for lawns

The best snowdrop to grow in a lawn is *Galanthus nivalis*, the common snowdrop, and its double-flowered form *G. nivalis* 'Flore Pleno'.

Once established, snowdrops will flower reliably every year between January and February.

Snowdrops for autumn

Although we tend to think of snowdrops flowering in early spring, there is also a species – *Galanthus reginae-olgae* – that flowers during October. Plant the bulbs in any areas of the garden that need some autumnal interest.

Soft fruits

Healthy stock

To ensure a good start, buy plants that are certified to be free from pests, diseases or viruses. Certificated clean stock schemes exist for blackcurrants, a number of hybrid berries, raspberries and strawberries.

Keep out the raiders

Construct a metal framework over a bed of fruit bushes and cover it with 2cm (¾in) mesh netting to protect ripening fruit from birds. The fruit cage should be high enough to allow you to stand up while tending the bushes and picking the fruit.

Temporary protection

Keep birds off individual fruit bushes by erecting temporary netting. Insert bamboo canes round the plant and drape plastic bird netting over them. Prevent the net snagging on the canes and allow the net to be removed easily for picking by making slits in ping-pong balls and slipping them over the tops of the canes.

Stopping stains

Small fruits are easily crushed. To avoid staining your collecting basket line it with several layers of absorbent paper or large leaves.

Easy picking

Free your hands when picking small fruits by making a sack from a piece of fabric held open at the top with a hoop of sturdy wire threaded through it. Create a handle to slip over your arm by attaching each end of a semi-circle of wire to the hoop.

Soil analysis

Identify the soil in your garden

Knowledge of soil type is an essential aid to successful planting. Take note of the plants growing naturally in your neighbourhood. An acid soil is indicated by the presence of broom, foxgloves, gorse, heaths and heathers, Scots and maritime pines and speedwell. Cranesbill, various field poppies, juniper, thistles and wild cherry trees grow in alkaline soil.

Growing know-how

Testing soil in the hand

Do a simple hand test to determine soil type in your garden. Lift up and rub a ball of moist soil between your fingers. It may be necessary to moisten the soil slightly.

Sand
If the soil breaks up and feels gritty it contains sand; largish particles signal grit.

Clay
If it smears smoothly and appears slightly shiny, it contains plenty of clay.

Silt
If it feels soapy and sticky it is a silt.

Loam
If it starts to smear then breaks up, it is probably a loam that has been improved over the years. This is suitable for a wide variety of garden plants.

Test the pH level of your soil

It is easy to determine the pH level of your soil, using a simple test kit from a garden centre. Usually, a tablet is added to a soil sample dissolved in water. Any colour change in the solution is compared to colours on a test card to give the pH level on a scale of 1 to 14; below 7 is acid and above 7 is alkaline.

Ensure suitable soil for plants

Certain plants will not adapt to unsuitable soil. Azaleas or rhododendrons will not thrive in alkaline soil. Even if you introduce acid soil as the immediate growing medium, chalk or lime will still seep in through watering. The plant will grow poorly, look yellow and eventually die. The solution is to grow these plants in containers filled with ericaceous compost and to water only with rainwater or water with a little vinegar.

See also Acid soil, Chalky soil, Clay soil, Sandy soil

Sorrel

Sorrel differences

Rumex acetosa (common sorrel) grows best in rich, moist soil in a semi-shaded position. *R. scutatus* (French sorrel) has more succulent leaves and thrives in a dry, sunny spot.

Tasty addition

Use sharp-tasting young sorrel leaves sparingly in salads, soups and sauces, or cook them in the same way as spinach.

Picking policy

Never pick too many leaves from young plants at one time as this will slow down their growth. Pick little and often until the plants are established. When the plants are growing vigorously, a whole plant can be cut just above the neck and it will soon resprout to provide more leaves as long as the soil remains moist.

Sorrel for winter

Sorrel is one of the last plants to die down in the autumn, so pickings should be available until late in the year. It also sprouts early in the spring. To enable picking to continue all winter, cover a few plants with cloches, move roots into the border of a cold greenhouse after any tomatoes have been removed or sow a few seeds in pots in the summer to provide indoor pickings in winter.

Sowing

Spacing your seeds

In the case of large seeds, it is possible to sow them spaced out evenly in a seed tray to germinate. This avoids the need to prick out the seedlings when they have developed. For example, sow cyclamen 2.5cm (1in) apart.

Controlling the flow

Small seeds stick to fingertips with the result that they are sown unevenly and germinate in clusters. Avoid uneven sowing by using a piece of stiff white paper folded to make a channel for the seeds. Use the tip of a knife to push them singly into the drill. Watch the seeds as they slip off the paper onto the soil or compost and move the paper along to ensure even spacing. Seeds will bounce out if the paper is held too high.

Sterile sowing compost

Never use garden soil for sowing seeds in pots. It contains bacteria, fungi, pests and weeds, which will damage your seedlings as they germinate. It is rarely possible to be sure of sterilising garden soil effectively in the oven or microwave, as is sometimes suggested, and can

Garden secrets

See your seeds

If you experience difficulties in sowing seeds because you cannot see them against the dark colour of the compost or soil, take a pinch of unscented talcum powder and put it into the seed packet. Shake the packet vigorously before sowing the seeds in the usual way. The white powder will adhere to the seeds, thus enabling you to see them clearly.

be dangerous. Always buy bagged seed compost from a garden centre to give your seedlings the best possible start.

Ensure germination

When sowing seeds in individual pots, sow two seeds in each pot in case only one seed germinates. If both seeds germinate, gently remove the weaker seedling, leaving the stronger one to develop fully. Do not pinch off the seedling, as leaving the root in place could result in root rot.

Speed germination in dry weather

Seeds sown in dry soil will not germinate until rain provides moisture. Speed up the process by watering the seed drills from the spout of the watering can before sowing, then sow the seeds and return the soil with the back of a rake. Alternatively, if your soil is poor, cover the drill with fresh seed compost and water carefully with the rose on the watering can.

Say goodbye to backache

Sow large seeds at the required intervals, without bending over, by sowing through a piece of plastic drainpipe 2.5cm (1in) in diameter and about 1m (3ft) in length, depending on your height. Cut one end to form a point to insert into the soil. Place the sowing pipe at the start of the drill. Drop a seed in the top end, then move the pipe the required spacing along the drill before sowing a second seed. Continue in the same way to the end of the drill. Cover the seeds and firm the soil with the flat of the garden rake. This method is appropriate for large seeds, such as those of beetroot, broad beans, french beans, peas, runner beans and squashes.

Firming in

Use the back of a rake to return the soil to a drill where seeds have been sown and to firm in gently. The compost in pots can be firmed in with the bottom of another pot. Alternatively, you can use a purpose-made presser consisting of a disc of plywood nailed to a piece of dowel.

Nature's way

Seeds that fall to the ground naturally are buried only to the extent that the wind blows a light covering of soil over them. Imitate nature's way when sowing seeds by covering them with no more than their own depth of soil.

The right temperature

The optimum temperature for the germination of most seeds is 21°C (70°F). After sowing, place the seed trays in a warm place indoors and check them every day. Move them into cooler conditions with good light when they start to sprout – better still, use a thermostatically controlled seed propagator in the greenhouse or on the window ledge to keep the seeds at precisely the right temperature to encourage germination.

Light and dark for germination

Most seeds will germinate in light or dark as long as moisture and warmth are provided. It is usual to cover seeds with a little compost, more to ensure that they do not dry out than to cut out light. A few seeds, including begonias, busy lizzies, lobelias and primulas, need light to germinate, so do not cover them.

A light covering

Seeds should never be covered with an opaque material, as this prevents light reaching seeds that need it and germinating seeds left under the covering become leggy.

Protect early-summer seedlings

Keep seedlings cool and sheltered by spreading a fine white or light-coloured cloth or horticultural fleece over them if you are going away for the weekend. Tie the corners to short stakes. Rain will be able to filter through the cloth or fleece and the seedlings will be protected from cold or heat.

Do not disturb seedlings

Avoid transplanting fragile seedlings. Sow their seeds directly into biodegradable containers, such as newspaper cones, small peat pots or papier mâché egg boxes. These materials disintegrate in the soil and seedling roots are undisturbed. (See also **Newspaper**)

Deal with damping off

Damping off is a fungal disease that causes young seedlings to rot at soil level and fall over. It is common when compost is too wet through firming hard or overwatering. Sowing seeds too thickly, using garden soil or reused seed compost, and using dirty pots and trays also encourage the disease. Gently water the seeds with a liquid copper fungicide and give the seedlings the same treatment when they germinate and after pricking out.

See also **Seeds**

Spices

Grow your own saffron

Plant *Crocus sativus* corms in late summer or as soon as they are available, about 5–7.5cm (2–3in) deep in warm, well-drained soil. When the blue-purple flowers appear in October, cut out the three orange stigmas and the part of the style that comes with them and spread them out carefully to dry. The saffron crocus is not easy to grow – a warm summer is needed to ripen the corms. It is available from mail-order bulb nurseries. However, hundreds of flowers are needed to yield just 10g (¼oz) of saffron.

Tender cumin

Cumin seed, which is widely used in Indian dishes, is produced from a tender annual plant that grows to a height of 15–30cm (6–12in). It requires a long growing season and must be sown under glass from February to April. Not only will cumin produce seeds for use in cooking, but it is also a highly ornamental plant and will be an asset in the herbaceous border.

Provide warmth for aromatic aniseed

Sow aniseed seeds in spring in a sunny, sheltered spot in the garden. Use the leaves in summer salads and add the seeds to breads and savoury dishes. Harvest the seeds, which ripen in autumn, when the tips of the fruits turn from green to grey.

Spinach

Keep spinach cool
During summer, do not sow spinach seeds in dry, unsheltered soils as heat encourages bolting. If you must sow seeds, sow them in the shade of peas, runner beans, or sweetcorn. It pays to grow modern, bolting-resistant varieties such as 'Sigmaleaf' and the F1 hybrid 'Space', which have been developed to produce a long succession of leaves and are slow to bolt, even in hot weather.

Sowing times for summer spinach
In the south, sow summer spinach every three weeks from early March until early August and from late March until mid July in the north. These sowings should give you crops to pick all summer until October or the first frosts.

Sowing times for winter spinach
Make two sowings of winter spinach during September. These sowings should make tiny plants before the onset of winter weather and, if protected with cloches, may provide occasional pickings during late winter and into spring, coming into full leaf production during April and May. Choose specific overwintering spinach varieties such as 'Broad Leaved Prickly'.

Grow a nitrogen supply
In mild areas, sow perpetual spinach at the end of summer in empty vegetable rows. Allow the plants to grow and do not pick the leaves.

In spring, cut the plants down to ground level, then dig them in. Nitrogen, which would otherwise be washed out of the soil during the winter months, is stored in the spinach leaves and, in that way, retained for the following season.

Identify nitrogen levels
Vigorous spinach growth indicates good nitrogen levels in the soil; pale green, limp leaves signal that the soil is low in nitrogen.

Soil for spinach
Spinach grows best in a soil that retains moisture well without being waterlogged, and which has been enriched with well-rotted manure. Starved, dry soils yield bitter, poor-quality leaves and a crop that is more likely to run to seed quickly. Powdery mildew is also more prevalent when the plants run short of water, although some newer varieties have high resistance to the disease.

Water supplies
Spinach benefits from copious watering, particularly in dry weather. Give your crop up to 18 litres per m^2 (4 gallons per sq yd) each week, in two or three applications, to ensure good growth.

A quick crop
Maximise space in the vegetable garden by sowing fast-maturing spinach between crops, such as beans, which take longer to mature. By the time the beans are filling out between the rows, the spinach will have been picked.

Make the right choice

Alternatives to annual summer and winter spinach

Half-hardy annual New Zealand spinach grows best in light, well-drained soil but will not survive autumn frosts. Hardy biennial spinach beet or perpetual spinach leaves have a stronger taste than spinach. Broad white stalks characterise sea kale beet, a form of spinach beet, while the red-stalked variety, 'Ruby Chard', makes a decorative addition to a flower border. Perennial Good King Henry, also known as Poor Man's Asparagus, can be grown as a spinach substitute or the shoots may be forced like asparagus. It used to be a culinary favourite but is less in vogue today.

Spraying

Precision weeding
A systemic weedkiller ready-mixed in a trigger sprayer is useful for killing weeds near bushes or in a flowerbed – the fine jet allows you to spray the weedkiller onto the weeds without harming plants nearby.

Extend the range of a sprayer
Add an extension or telescopic lance – available from garden centres – to your sprayer to help you to treat pests and diseases on out-of-reach trees.

Knapsack sprayer
For controlling pests or diseases, feeding plants or killing weeds over a large area, buy a sprayer that can be worn on the back and pressurised while it is in operation. A knapsack sprayer holds a far greater quantity of liquid than a hand-held one, yet it is easily carried on the back and can be used for some time without the added weight being difficult to manage.

Hose attachment
Instead of carrying a large, heavy sprayer, attach a hose-end feeder to your hose for applying fertiliser as you water your plants.

Spray screen
To kill weeds between plant rows or along a pathway without damaging nearby plants, fit a flat spray attachment or a hood to the end of your lance. This will prevent spray drift.

Fine-weather spraying
If rain is forecast, do not carry out any spraying job in the garden. During showery weather a chemical is likely to be washed away and will not therefore be effective. Wait until the weather is settled. Chemicals require several hours of dry weather to be absorbed by plant leaves or through the body of an insect.

Clean water
When mixing water with garden chemicals prior to spraying plants, do not use rainwater collected in a bucket in the garden or the water

that has been stored in a water butt outside. Water stored outside frequently contains algae, bacteria and foreign particles, which will block the nozzle of a sprayer. Always use tap water for spraying.

Avoid leaf burn
Never spray plants when the sun is fully on them. The fine droplets will act like small magnifying glasses, concentrating the sun's rays, and scorching can easily follow.

Stop spotting
When spraying the leaves of a flowering plant, prevent the petals from being spotted by holding a sheet of cardboard in front of the flowers.

A rain forest in the home
The sprayer has a vital role in helping you to care for plants that, in their natural state, grow on trees in the rain forest. These plants, which include tropical orchids, bromeliads and certain ferns, take no sustenance from the ground, but draw moisture and nutrients from the air. To reproduce these conditions, it is important not to overwater: mist over the leaves now and again, especially in summer, but avoid using water containing chlorine. Add a few drops of liquid fertiliser to the water every few weeks.

The right temperature
When treating house plants, fill a sprayer with the appropriate mixture and let it stand for a few hours to reach room temperature before using it.

Prevent furniture damage
Before spraying house plants, move them either onto the draining board or into the bath. The fine mist from a spray can make a mess on surrounding waxed surfaces if you leave the plants on fine furniture.

War on red spider mites
When fighting red spider mite infestations, spray all parts of the plant twice a day with tepid water. Check the undersides of the leaves; these are favourite places for red spider mites to lay eggs.

Sprayer sense
Keep one sprayer for misting plants and a separate one – clearly labelled – to use solely for applying pesticides.

Foliar feeding
If plants are subject to stress, for example, growing in compacted soils or suffering diseased or damaged roots, they may be unable to take up nutrients and will benefit from foliar feeding. The feeds are devised so that a plant can absorb nutrients through its leaves.

Clean a sprayer after use
Immediately after applying a treatment, part-fill the sprayer with water, then add a few drops of washing-up liquid and shake it well. Wash out with clean water and spray for a few moments to clean any residue that may otherwise obstruct the tube and nozzle in subsequent treatments, then shake the sprayer empty.

See also **Chemicals, Fungicides, Insects**

Stakes and supports

Lasting stakes
The best stakes are those made from ash, chestnut or hazel. These are usually straight and will last particularly well. Unfortunately, though, you may find when you come to buy stakes that the type of wood is not actually specified. In the long term, you could have your own source of stakes by growing the appropriate trees.

Prolong usefulness
Extend the life span of stakes by standing the ends that will be in contact with the soil in a bucket of wood preservative. Make sure the preservative is non-toxic to plants. Immerse them for at least 48 hours before use. When reusing a stake, first clean the bottom end then dip it in wood preservative.

Green stakes
Paint stakes green or buy green stakes so that they blend in with your plants. Alternatively, use a green timber preservative that both colours and protects against rot.

Supporting a young tree
In most gardens, young trees with weak root systems, such as dwarf apple trees, are best staked with a short stake that reaches about a third of the way up the trunk and is tied with a single tie. However, if the conditions in your garden are exceptionally windy, a stout stake reaching higher into the tree is better. It can be secured at three different heights to give the tree firm support.

Staking early
Support trees and shrubs early on as this improves the chances of strong development. Staking ensures that the stem is held firmly in place, which prevents root movement. By preventing such movement, the root hairs, essential for water and nutrient uptake, are not damaged and the plant establishes itself better than if left to rock in the wind.

Staking a bare-rooted tree
Before positioning a tree in a prepared planting hole, drive a 5cm (2in) thick stake 61cm (2ft) into the ground, ensuring first that it is tall enough to support the tree's trunk up to the point where it branches. Putting the stake in first avoids any risk of damage to the roots. Plant the tree and tie it securely to the stake.

Staking a tree in an exposed position
Before planting a tree in a windy position, drive stakes into the ground on each side of the planting hole. Attach the tree securely to the

stakes with strong, flexible ties. This should ensure that the tree will withstand gales blowing from any quarter.

Staking a tree after planting

When staking a tree after it has been planted, avoid damaging the roots by driving two stakes into the ground, one on each side of the tree, nailing a firm wooden crossbar to them, and tying the tree to the crossbar. An angled stake, tied halfway up the trunk, is an alternative means of staking a tree after planting.

A tie for all seasons

Tree ties should be strong enough to resist the force of wind and bad weather but should not cut into the bark. Suitable ties include a plastic or webbing strap with a plastic or rubberised buffer, a pair of old stockings or tights, or a wide rubber or plastic strip held firmly in place with string or wire. If wire is used, it is essential to loosen it as the girth of the trunk increases to ensure that it does not cut through the strip into the trunk. A good homemade tree tie can be devised by cutting a 15cm (6in) piece of hosepipe and threading a length of stout galvanised wire through it. Place this round the tree, then fix the wire to the stake. The wire makes a strong tie and the hosepipe protects the stem.

Ready-made supports

There are numerous ready-made decorative obelisks and tripods available, made from wrought iron, plastic-coated tubular steel, decorative wirework and rustic wood. Most types are best used in a large container such as a wooden half-barrel or in a border.

Flower stakes

Stake tall flowers, such as chrysanthemums, delphiniums, gladioli and irises, by winding string in a figure of eight between a flower stem and a bamboo cane or by adapting a short piece of wire attached to a metal stake to hold a stem.

Trellis fans

A piece of fan-shaped trellis is a good support for a climber or a wall shrub in a container. When planting up a tub, place the piece of trellis so that the 'fan handle' is at the bottom of the container. (See also **Trellises**)

Growing tall

Drive a tree stake – up to 1.8m (6ft) tall – 61cm (2ft) into the ground. Take a piece of 7.5cm (3in) mesh wire netting wide enough to surround the stake, leaving a gap of 30cm (1ft), then cover it with black polythene. Place the netting round the stake with the polythene on the inside and fasten with wire. Fill the gap between the polythene and stake with compost, punch holes in the polythene through the netting and plant up with herbs, busy lizzies and winter-flowering pansies.

Prop appeal

If props support the heavy branches of fruit trees in your garden, plant a climbing annual that does not need to be in an especially sunny position at the foot of each prop for a striking visual effect. Canary creeper or climbing french beans are suitable candidates.

Woven willow supports

Willow twigs are very flexible and can be woven in bands round a tripod of thin rustic stakes to create an attractive climbing plant support for an informal cottage-style garden. Use freshly cut twigs or soak the twigs in water for a few hours before use to make them more flexible.

Removing a stake that is stuck

To remove a stake that is firmly stuck in the ground, drive it in deeper with a light tap of a hammer. This will loosen it and the stake will come out far more easily than if you try to dislodge it by pulling alone.

Natural stakes

Instead of using conventional stakes, choose sticks with appealing shapes to use as stakes in containers. Cut stems from unusually shaped shrubs and trees will make an attractive display. Two good plants for this purpose are *Salix babylonica* var. *pekinensis* 'Tortuosa' (dragon's claw willow) and *Corylus avellana* 'Contorta' (corkscrew hazel). Coloured stems of shrubs such as the varieties of *Cornus alba* (dogwood) can be used as ornamental supports for spring bulbs.

Going geometric

To grow a decorative column of flowers or foliage, position a cylinder of rigid netting in compost in a container after planting, securing it with slender stakes. Alternatively, roll the netting into a cone and position it firmly in the compost, securing the cone shape at the top with small twists of wire.

Securing canes

To keep the base of a tripod or wigwam of bamboo canes close to a pot's rim, carefully drill holes through the rim and thread a circle of wire through the holes. The lower parts of the canes can then be wired securely into the pot.

Discreet stakes

Thin, twiggy branches, usually called pea sticks, make ideal supports for plants that reach a height of up to 1.2m (4ft) and tend to flop over. Push two or three pea sticks firmly into the soil round the edge of the plant. If a plant is inclined to sprawl after heavy rain, try looping twine round the outside of the sticks as additional support.

A perfect finish

For a neat finish to pea stick stakes, break them near the eventual height of the plants, bend them inwards and interlace them.

Standards

Steady standards

When training standards in pots, always use a loam-based potting compost, such as John Innes No. 3. This contains soil and will be heavier than a peat-based compost. The weight will help to prevent the top-heavy plant from falling over in windy weather.

Train a shrub into a standard

Drive a stake into a planting hole outdoors or into a pot filled with compost. Then, plant a young shrub with a straight, sturdy stem. Train the shrub into a standard by cutting off the lowest branches so they are flush with the main stem. When the shrub reaches the desired height, pinch out the tip to make the head branch out and form a ball. Remove all buds or branches that appear on the stem.

Even flowering

If you are growing a standard plant in a container near a wall, hedge or fence, turn the container once a week. This will help to prevent uneven growth and flowering on just one side of the plant.

Desirable bays

Standard 'lollipop' bay trees, which are trained into a ball of foliage on a bare stem, make elegant potted specimens on either side of the front door. Unfortunately, they make an attractive target for thieves in urban areas so chain them to a nearby railing.

Suitable shrubs

Evergreen shrubs make particularly striking standards and look good all the year round. Shrubs that can be easily trained in this way include box, euonymus, holly and yew. The main stem will need support while it is growing and even when it is mature it is wise to provide a discreet stake in case a gale catches the leafy head.

Large shrubs

If you want to grow large shrubs in a small garden, train them as standards. By doing so you can restrict the size of the head and, in addition, have space to grow other plants underneath them.

Exotic standards

To make the most of your space in a conservatory, train a variety of plants as standards. Good choices would be bougainvilleas, *Brugmansia* (angel's trumpets) and pelargoniums in pots. Or grow trailing plants, such as *Lotus berthelotii* and *Plectranthus oertendahlii* at the bases of the standards. None of these is

Fragrant showers Climbing honeysuckle trained into a standard is sweet-smelling and decorative in flower.

hardy so leave them to ornament the conservatory throughout the year.

Decorative stems

Grow three *Ficus benjamina* house plants in the same pot to a height of 36–40cm (14–16in), then remove the lateral branches. Carefully plait the three stripped stems, which will thicken and form a single plaited trunk.

Climbers as standards

Climbers that can be trained into unusual and eye-catching standards include honeysuckle and wisteria. Wisteria makes a spectacular standard but needs lifetime support and regular pruning in both summer and winter to keep it compact and induce prolific flowering. Rambling roses also make colourful standards, but again regular pruning is required to keep them in shape.

Steps

Versatile bricks
Using bricks as your material enables you to make steps of all sizes. Treat the bricks with a clear waterproofing liquid. Build brick steps on firm ground or concrete bedding.

Seasonal considerations
Log, slate and smooth stone steps can become slippery in freezing weather. For a non-slip surface select textured materials, such as raised-pattern concrete slabs. The best treads are made from natural or constructed stone slabs, positioned on stable risers of stone or brick. If slabs wear, lift and turn them over to expose a new surface.

Firm treads
Each tread should overhang its riser by at least 2.5cm (1in) and slope slightly downwards so that rain runs off. Plant mat-forming New Zealand burr, phlox and wild thyme and let them spread over the edges and in between the stones. Trim as required once flowering ends.

Teaming up heights and depths
Make risers a minimum of 10cm (4in) and a maximum of 18cm (7in) high. The lower the height you choose, the deeper each tread needs to be from front to back: team up a 10cm (4in) riser with a tread depth of 46cm (18in) and an 18cm (7in) riser with a tread depth of 30cm (12in). Build steps starting from the lowest and working up.

Slippery steps
Steps made from railway sleepers or timber boards can become slippery, especially when sited under trees or in other shady areas. Prevent accidents by covering the tops of the steps with chicken wire, wrapping it down the sides and stapling it securely in place. This will give a good grip even after frost.

Winding steps
If you are building steps in a steep slope, set them across the slope diagonally rather than straight up. The steps can be made to wind and will look more attractive. Use pegs and line to mark out the direction.

Simplicity and economy
Cut steps directly into the soil, compacting it firmly at each tread and riser position. Cover the treads with a stabilising material – gravel or coarse bark chips would be suitable. Add retaining risers of log roll (split treated logs stapled to stout wire), to complete the steps. Alternatively, large logs, presoaked in wood preservative, may be laid horizontally to form the risers. Layers of roofing tiles cemented together also make attractive risers.

Rock garden steps
Steps facilitate maintenance of a rock garden. Match the steps with the stone in the rock garden so that they will not stand out, and let them wind irregularly through the garden with stopping places to linger in and admire the plants. Apply a waterproofing liquid to the steps to prevent flaking in frost.

Recycled steps
Hard-wearing, secondhand wooden railway sleepers make excellent risers for shallow steps and provide a generous width too. Sometimes they can be bought from a reclamation yard. Get some help when handling them as they are heavy.

Soften the edges
Border concrete steps with fragrant flowering shrubs, such as lavender and rosemary, and colourful annuals, such as nasturtiums, which will tumble over and soften the edges.

Scarcely steps
Make a donkey path on a gentle slope. Dig out a series of shallow, 10cm (4in) steps, adding wooden retaining risers, and making extremely deep treads of 1.8m (6ft).

Landings between steps
For visual effect on a long slope, link a maximum of eight steps with level pieces of ground at least the length of three treads.

Climbers to clothe steps
Give wide steps the appearance of being narrower by planting undemanding climbers, such as ivy and Virginia creeper at the ends, or by training more vigorous climbers – *Clematis montana*, honeysuckle or wisteria, for example – along the rails and edges of the steps.

Brighter basement
If you live in a basement flat, try painting the area walls a bright hue and turning the steps leading down to the front door into a mass of colour with flower-filled containers. Provide height with a climber growing in a trellis-backed planter against the rear wall, or add a touch of dignity with a bay tree grown in a Versailles box.

Stocks

Doubles are best
The best stocks are those with double flowers. Doubles produce the most attractive spikes, which are dense and colourful. The double flowers also last much longer and usually have a more intense scent than single-flowered stocks.

Selecting double-flowered stocks
There are no varieties of stocks in which every seedling produces double flowers but there are two ways to select seedlings that will produce double flowers at an early stage. Most develop dark green seedlings that will produce single flowers and pale green seedlings that will produce double flowers. Only the seedlings with pale leaves are pricked out and grown on. Occasionally, varieties are listed in which seedlings are separated according to whether the young leaves have notched or smooth edges.

Secret stocks
Night-scented stocks have small, insignificant flowers but a wonderful evening scent. Plant them behind more colourful flowering plants, which will provide a good show, while the scent from the stocks is powerful enough to waft all over the garden in the evening.

Seedling care
Stock seedlings are susceptible to diseases caused by overwatering so do not let the compost get too wet. When handling plants, pick them up by the leaves, not the stems.

Make the right choice

Know how to use your stocks
All stocks belong to the genus *Matthiola*, except for Virginian stock whose genus is *Malcolmia*. The scented flowers, in vivid or pastel colours, are clustered in spikes.

Type	Description	Flowering time
Beauty of Nice	Pink, crimson, purple double-flowered stocks, reaching a height of about 46cm (18in).	Summer bedding or winter flowering in a greenhouse.
Brompton	Yellow, white, pink, carmine double-flowered stocks; about 46cm (18in) high.	Spring bedding. Often overwintered in pots.
Column	White, pink, blue, violet single-stemmed stocks, 61–91cm (2–3ft) high, long flower heads densely packed with double flowers. Highly scented.	They can be grown all year round in the greenhouse. Some can be grown outside in summer.
East Lothian	Yellow, white, pink, purple, mainly double-flowered plants, 30cm (12in) in height.	Summer bedding or spring flowering after late summer sowing.
Night-scented	Lilac single-flowered hardy annuals, about 30cm (12in) in height. Evening and night-time scent.	Summer bedding.
Ten Week	White, pink, red, carmine short-term stocks 20–46cm (8–18in) high.	Summer bedding. They usually flower about ten weeks after sowing.
Virginian	Pink, lilac, mauve, white and cream single-flowered hardy annuals, about 23cm (9in) high.	Summer bedding.

Stone

Stone mulch
A light covering of small stones or gravel slows down the evaporation of moisture from the soil and, at night, gives out the heat that it has absorbed during the day.

Protective coating
In a dry, shady place where even grass will not grow, stop weeds taking over by covering the area with black polythene sheeting camouflaged by a bed of attractive pebbles.

Rock mobility
Move a heavy rock more easily by rolling it along on five or six logs or metal pipes. As you progress, move the log or metal pipe at the back to the front.

Bed maintenance platform
Install a paving stone in a flowerbed to stand on when watering, hoeing and spraying and to avoid trampling over the soil and treading on plants. Lay the stone on a bed of sand so that the top is flush with the soil; eventually it will blend in with the foliage.

Keep features to scale
When using a hard landscaping material, such as stone, within the confines of a small garden, bear in mind the scale of the garden and of the existing features to ensure that an overall impression of equal proportions is maintained. Examples of inappropriate scale in a small garden include exceptionally wide steps or a high surrounding wall.

Storage

Clean up storage boxes
Before using wooden boxes for storing fruit and vegetables, brush them clean, wash them with disinfectant, then rinse with fresh, clean water and leave to dry off. Paint each box with a wood preservative.

Growing know-how

Storing vegetables

Many vegetables do not store well but root vegetables store best. Leeks, carrots, parsnips and swedes can be left in the ground in sheltered parts of the country.

Beetroot, carrots, parsnips and swedes
Store these in boxes of slightly moist sand or sieved ash. Place the largest roots in the bottom and the smallest at the top, to be used first. Keep the boxes in a frost-free cellar, garage or vermin-proof shed.

Marrows and pumpkins
Dry marrows and pumpkins in the sun, then store them on slats in a cool, dry, frost-free place or hang them in nets.

Onions and shallots
Plait onions and shallots in ropes and hang them in an airy place just above 0°C (32°F). They can also be stored in nets or tights.

Potatoes
Store potatoes in the dark and above freezing; 4–10°C (39–50°F) is ideal. Half-fill double-thickness paper sacks or lay potatoes in shallow wooden boxes, covered with carpet to keep out the light.

Winter cabbages
Store just above freezing on wooden slats or on a mat of straw.

Fumigate the storage shed
Kill off any germs or fungus spores in your shed before storing fruit and vegetables. Empty the shed in early summer, before the fruit is ripe and after hibernating insects have gone. Seal up any cracks, then use an insecticidal and fungicidal greenhouse fumigant to destroy any pests and diseases. The fumigants are sold in cones and are set off in a similar way to fireworks – by lighting the cone's touch paper. Place a warning sign on the door and leave it closed overnight. Ventilate the shed in the morning by leaving the door open.

Keep it natural
When storing vegetables, make use of the natural preservative qualities of garlic by peeling a few cloves and placing a couple at various points in the cellar or shed. Alternatively, you can use bay leaves, which will also help to keep your crop fresh.

Hard-to-ripen fruit
Put unripe fruit in a plastic bag with a pineapple or banana. These fruits give off the gas ethylene, which speeds up ripening.

Tidy tools
Using shoe holders is a cheap and efficient way of helping to keep the shed tidy. Nail to the wall and use the plastic pockets to store seed packets, small tools and labels.

String holder
Convert a flowerpot into a handy dispenser for garden twine or string. Stand a ball of twine or string in a saucer, turn the flowerpot over to cover the ball and feed one end of the twine or string through the drainage hole at the top. To prevent the string from falling back into the pot every time you cut off a length, secure the end with a clothes peg.

Cloche storage
If you are not using them in the garden during the winter, store polycarbonate or polythene cloches in a dark place. This will prevent the rapid breakdown of the ultraviolet inhibitor that preserves them and will prolong their useful life.

Growing know-how

Storing fruit

Apples, nectarines, peaches and pears are the only fruits that can be stored naturally, although many others can be frozen, bottled or used in preserves.

Apples
Varieties vary enormously in their suitability for storage. Early varieties are best eaten straight off the tree; mid-season varieties can be stored for four to eight weeks; late varieties will not develop their best flavour until they have been in storage for some time and may keep well for several months. Apples are best stored in the dark, in a moist atmosphere with some air movement. The temperature should be as even as possible and while 3–5°C (37–41°F) is best, the temperature in a garden shed or garage – usually about 7°C (45°F) – is also suitable.

Nectarines and peaches
Ripe fruits can be kept for a short period in a cool place, in shallow boxes lined with cotton wool.

Pears
Pears like cooler temperatures than apples: 0–1°C (32–34°F) is suitable. They keep well in the bottom of a refrigerator. Most pears are at their best for only a short period so should be checked frequently.

Storage in small spaces
If your garden is not big enough to house a garden shed, substitute trunk-shaped metal, plastic or wooden containers. Use these to store all your garden implements, including large items such as lawn mowers, strimmers, hedge trimmers and deck chairs.

Strawberries

Planting young plants

When planting strawberries, put them in freshly dug and weeded soil that has been enriched with farmyard manure or well-rotted compost. Plant pot-grown strawberries in rows, with the base of the central crowns level with the soil surface. For plants dug from the open ground and supplied with bare roots, dig out a hole for each plant, mound some soil in the bottom of the hole, then position a plant on top of the mound and carefully spread the roots down the sides before replacing the soil and firming in the plant.

Weed control

To prevent weeds growing and keep fruit clean, cover the soil with a sheet of black polythene before planting rows of strawberries. Bury the edges of the polythene to keep it in position. Using a sharp knife, cut crosses in it at 46cm (18in) intervals. Plant the strawberries through the slits. Firm the base of each strawberry crown level with the soil surface.

Planting in heavy soil

When planting strawberries in heavy soil, first improve drainage by mixing in sand and mounding the soil. Plant in rows on top of the mounds and apply a mulch between the rows.

Growing in barrels, pots and baskets

To grow strawberries on a balcony or terrace, plant them in barrels bored with 5cm (2in) holes or in a strawberry pot. Place broken pots or stones in the bottom of the barrels for drainage. Then build a central drainage core of the same material, retained by wire netting. Another option is to grow 'Temptation' in a hanging basket; it is compact enough to thrive in such an elevated position. (See also **Hanging baskets**, **Watering outdoors**)

Deblossoming

Remove the first blossoms from remontant (perpetual) strawberry plants to ensure abundant fruits in August.

Advance fruiting

From mid February to mid March, cover a bed of plants that have not fruited before – planted during the previous August – with a low polytunnel and pick strawberries up to a fortnight earlier than usual.

Autumn berries

Small-fruited alpine strawberries yield a good crop of fruit in autumn and are pretty enough to grow in a flower border.

Growing healthy strawberries

Keep the soil round strawberry plants cool and the fruit clean and free of grey mould by spreading a layer of straw, untreated by weedkillers, or of bracken, under the leaves after flowering. (See also **Companion plants**)

After fruiting

To keep strawberry plants healthy and vigorous, clear away the straw from between and underneath the leaves and cut off all the old leaves and runners after the fruit has been picked. If you grow a lot of strawberries, run a rotary mower along the rows with the blades set high. Burn all the debris, including the straw, then feed the plants with sulphate of potash at a rate of 15g per m² or ½oz per sq yd and water well.

Future harvests

Ensure that you have a good strawberry crop the following year by enriching the soil in late summer after picking the current crop. Mix 15g (½oz) of sulphate of potash into a bucketful of compost. Apply the mixture in a 5–7.5cm (2–3in) layer and fork it lightly into the soil.

Propagating strawberries

As long as you are sure that the parent plant is healthy, encourage plantlets that form on strawberry runners to root by pegging them into the soil with pieces of wire that have been bent into U shapes.

A brief history

Strawberry fields forever

The plant may have acquired its English name from the early British practice of laying straw beneath the berries to keep them off the ground. The Romans ate the fruits in large quantities but gathered them from the woods rather than growing them. These must have been from the wild strawberry plant, *Fragaria vesca*, the only species available in Britain for centuries after. The musk strawberry, *F. moschata*, was introduced from central Europe in the 16th century and was said to be delicious but is practically unobtainable now. The colonies in Virginia contributed a new species several decades later, and later still, pine strawberries, *F. chiloensis*, arrived from the Pacific coast, where Native Americans had enjoyed them since long before the advent of Columbus. A hybrid of the American species was available by the mid 18th century, and was widely enjoyed doused with sugar and claret, or orange juice. It is the descendants of this American marriage that are still grown today.

Renew strawberry plants

Vigour and cropping of strawberry plants are diminished by virus diseases and pests so the plants should be renewed with virus-free stock after two or three years. Obtain certificated plants from a garden centre.

Keeping birds away

When the fruits begin to colour, stretch plastic 'humming lines' immediately above your strawberry plants, twisting the lines slightly to maximise the bird-deterring vibration in the wind. As an alternative form of protection, push metal hoops into the soil, about 61cm (2ft) apart, above the strawberry bed. Cover the hoops and the plants with 2cm (¾in) mesh netting and secure this to stakes at each end. Weight the sides with bricks so that birds are not able to slip under the net.

Handle gently

Strawberries are particularly delicate fruits. When picking, never pull the fruits from the plant but nip them off by pinching the stem above the hull between the thumb and index finger. The berries will keep for longer.

Sunflowers

The best way to plant

Sunflower seeds should be sown in rich, well-drained soil in a sunny position, in groups of two or three. Space the groups about 61cm (2ft) apart. Thin out to keep the strongest seedling in each group.

Small sunflowers

If you do not have room in your garden for the traditional tall sunflowers, try growing some of the new dwarf varieties. 'Music Box' reaches just 61cm (2ft) and comes in a mixture of shades from cream through bright yellow to mahogany red. 'Sunspot' grows 46–61cm (18–24in) high but produces bright yellow flowers at least 20cm (8in) across, while 'Teddy Bear' grows to about 61cm (2ft) and has fully double flowers like yellow pincushions 15cm (6in) across.

How to grow giant blooms

The attractive heads of sunflowers can be 30cm (12in) in diameter. For the best chance of growing such giants, sow seeds in April, for blooms in August. While sunflowers can be transplanted, sunflower plants will continue to get taller if allowed to grow on from seed sown outside where they are to flower. As they grow taller, stake them to ensure they do not fall over in the wind or after heavy rain, when water retained in the foliage can weigh down the plants.

Protecting young plants

Make sure that your young sunflower plants are adequately protected from slugs and rabbits, which are particularly fond of them. Spread slug pellets round the bases of the plants and sink wire netting into the soil round each plant, which will prevent surface disturbance and uprooting of the plants.

Pollen-free sunflowers

Sunflowers cut for the house can spoil flower arrangements by shedding pollen over the rest of the display and furniture. Some varieties have been developed that produce no pollen – look out for cultivars such as 'Full Sun', 'Prado Yellow', chestnut red 'Prado Red' and the dwarf variety 'Big Smile'.

Moisture-absorber

Although the sunflower is a plant that thrives with its head in the sun, its roots will tolerate damp conditions. You can take advantage of the sunflower's ability to absorb moisture by planting groups at the bases of walls or fences in the garden where there are damp spots. Such are its powers of moisture-absorption that the sunflower has even been planted in the Netherlands to assist in the reclamation of waterlogged land.

Bright and beautiful The sunflower 'Teddy Bear' is a dwarf variety, which is suitable for small gardens.

A brief history

Flowers of the sun

Sunflowers were said by the Incas of Peru to have been sacred to the Sun, whose priestesses wore sunflower crowns of pure gold. It was the flower's resemblance to a stylised representation of the solar orb that gained it its common name. As well as being ornamental, the plant is also very useful. The leaves are used as animal fodder and the petals produce a yellow dye.

Sunflower oil is used like olive oil in cooking – and has the advantage of being flavourless. It is also used as a lubricant and in soap and paint manufacture. The oil cake makes a winter feed for cattle and poultry, while the seeds may be eaten roasted, or ground into flour to make bread. More unusually, they are roasted and ground to make a beverage, said to be akin to coffee.

Swedes

The right soil

Grow swedes in ground that was well manured the previous season for another crop. The roots may fork and have an earthy flavour if grown in freshly manured soil. Allow plenty of space because swede plants produce large amounts of foliage.

Lifting swedes in winter

Although not harmed by being left in the ground during winter, swedes are difficult to lift when the ground is frozen. A layer of mulch, consisting of straw, bracken or newspaper, round the vegetables will absorb frost and allow you to lift them from all but the coldest ground.

Sowing and growing

Sow seeds in early May in the north and in late May in the south in 1.3–2.5cm (½–1in) deep drills, where the swedes are to crop. Thin the plants as they grow, to a final spacing of 23cm (9in) intervals.

Sweetcorn

Early starters

In many areas of Britain sweetcorn is rather a borderline crop; the cobs do not always ripen before the weather starts to cool and the days shorten. They need a long growing season in warm conditions to provide a good crop. In warm areas, seeds can be sown outside in May but in most parts of the country it pays to get one step ahead of the seasons by starting sweetcorn off in the greenhouse. Sow two seeds in 8cm (3in) pots in late April or early May in a warm greenhouse. Remove the weaker seedling once they germinate. Growth is usually rapid, and, after hardening off, the plants can be set out in the vegetable garden in early June.

Extra sweetness

Supersweet varieties of sweetcorn are genetically different from traditional sweetcorn varieties and have at least double the sugar content. They are also less easy to grow and should always be sown in pots. Supersweet varieties, for example, the F1 hybrid 'Dickson', should be grown in isolation from traditional varieties, otherwise their extra sweetness may be lost.

Mini-sweetcorn

Demand is increasing for the attractive and tasty miniature cobs seen in supermarkets and restaurants. Unfortunately, the usual variety, 'Minor', produces rather low yields. You need a lot of plants, which take up a great deal of space, to produce a reasonable crop. A newer variety, 'Minipop', is far more productive than 'Minor', with the result that growing mini-sweetcorn is now worth while.

Perfect picking

It can be difficult to tell when the cobs are ripe. Once the tassels have withered to dark brown, peel back the sheath round each cob and press an individual grain with a finger nail – if the cob exudes a watery liquid it is not yet ripe; a milky fluid signifies ripeness. If no liquid is exuded, the cob is past its best.

Garden secrets

Blockbusters

Sweetcorn is wind-pollinated and without good pollination does not set full cobs. Instead of planting sweetcorn in rows like most vegetables, plant them in more or less equal-sided blocks to give the wind the best chance of pollinating all of them.

From plot to pot

Sweetcorn is a good choice of vegetable to grow in the garden because, apart from Supersweet varieties, it loses its flavour very rapidly after picking. As a result sweetcorn from the greengrocer or supermarket is never at its best. Do not pick sweetcorn, therefore, until you are ready to cook it; then, boil or steam it for about 10 minutes and eat it straight away.

Sweet peas

Help seeds to germinate

Sweet pea seeds will germinate easily if left to soak overnight. Place them between two layers of damp tissue in a plastic container. By the morning they will have doubled in size. Nick any seeds that do not swell up with a sharp knife and soak them for a second night.

Sowing sweet peas

The best sweet peas are raised by sowing six seeds to a 13cm or 5in pot of seed compost in November and placing the pots in a cold frame. The seedlings will grow slowly during the winter and can be planted out in March. Seeds can also be sown outside in autumn in the south of the country but the seedlings may suffer in hard winters. Those that come through will flower very well. Good plants can also be obtained by sowing in pots in March and planting out when the seedlings are about 7.5cm (3in) high. Sowing outside where the plants are to flower in March or April is the easiest method but plants will not usually flower for as long as pot-grown or autumn-sown plants.

Keep seedlings dry

Overwintering sweet pea seedlings should not be overwatered – excess water round their roots can cause more damage than intense cold.

Saving seeds

Cut sweet peas as they flower or fade to promote further flowering, but leave some flowers to set seeds if you want them for the following year.

Creeping peas

For hanging baskets or for edging borders, choose 'Cupid', an old Victorian variety of sweet pea that is now available again. This is a pink and white bicoloured variety that grows to only about 15cm (6in) high but which spreads out to about 46cm (18in) across if grown in borders and trails appealingly in containers. 'Fantasia' is similar but comes in an attractive mixture of colours.

Sweet peas for scent

The best varieties of sweet peas for that gorgeous sweet-pea fragrance are the old-fashioned ones. These are not always available in garden centres. They come under a variety of names, so check mail-order seed catalogues for mixtures like 'Antique Fantasy', 'Old Fashioned Mixed', 'Old Fashioned Scented Mixed' and 'Old Spice Mixed' together with varieties such as 'Matucana' (purple and blue) and 'Painted Lady' (pink and white).

Create a miniature wigwam

Three short bamboo canes angled in compost in a container and tied together at the top make a climbing frame for twining plants such as dwarf sweet peas. Use four or five canes in a large pot and loop garden twine round them halfway up to ensure stability as the plants grow.

Non-climbing sweet peas

Dwarf or semi-dwarf varieties of sweet peas require little or no support. Depending on size,

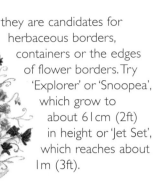

they are candidates for herbaceous borders, containers or the edges of flower borders. Try 'Explorer' or 'Snoopea', which grow to about 61cm (2ft) in height or 'Jet Set', which reaches about 1m (3ft).

Prizewinners

Sweet peas for cutting or for garden decoration can be grown up wigwams but to win prizes at the local show the plants need special treatment. Make a double row of canes 1.8m (6ft) high, in the same way as for runner beans, and place a single sweet pea plant alongside each cane. Train each one up a cane, tying it in regularly, then pinch out all the side shoots and nip off all the tendrils as the plant grows. Pick the flowers as they develop. Once the stems reach the tops of their canes untie them one by one. Lay half of each stem along the ground, then train the other half up another cane farther along the row, so the stems can continue to grow. Water and feed well. Long-stemmed heads with five or six large flowers each will be produced – just the thing to sweep the board at the local show.

The natural way

Use mature spring-flowering shrubs, such as forsythia and flowering currant, or climbers like *Clematis armandii* as supports for sweet peas. Plant sweet pea seedlings beneath the shrubs or climbers. As they develop, guide them up into the branches to provide colour in summer when the shrubs and climbers have finished flowering.

Water supply

In dry weather make sure that sweet peas are well watered or flowering may be restricted. Run a length of seephose along the row and connect it to a hosepipe to ensure that the plants get moisture exactly where it is required. Then leave it turned on for 2 hours.

Tarragon

A shovelful of sand
Tarragon requires well-drained soil if it is to thrive. If you have waterlogged soil, you can improve the drainage by forking a shovelful of sand and one of compost into each planting hole. Alternatively, grow tarragon in pots of good potting compost, clipping the plants to keep them compact.

Question of identity
There is little point in buying tarragon seeds in Britain, as only Russian tarragon seeds are available. This has less of an aroma and a coarser flavour than French tarragon, whose dark green, fragrant leaves are prized by cooks. But French tarragon does not set seed in cool climates, so you will have to buy the plant from a nursery and propagate it either by cuttings or by root division. (*See also* **Cuttings**, **Division**)

Keeping your plants going
Waterlogging is the most widespread cause of fatalities among French tarragon plants, but a sharp, early frost can also cause casualties. For that reason, from autumn onwards, you should protect your plants with cloches. To ensure a continuing supply of tarragon, pot up some 5–7.5cm (2–3in) long cuttings in late summer and keep them in a cold frame during winter. Alternatively, cut the plant down in late autumn, covering with straw until frost risk has passed. Lift, divide and replant the roots every two or three years in spring to provide the best-flavoured leaves.

Theme gardens

Memories of Spain
Provided you have the right site, a Mediterranean-style garden is not all that difficult to create. A sunny, walled corner is the main requirement, and a southern ambience is at once suggested by painting the walls white and topping them with an inward slope of terracotta tiles.

After treating the ground with weedkiller, put down a foundation of crushed hardcore and top up with a 10cm (4in) layer of gravel or shingle, leaving planting holes here and there for silver-leaved shrubs and aromatics such as cistus (rock rose), lavender, rosemary and thyme. Make a shady seating area with terracotta tiles laid beneath a simple, vine-covered pergola. To complete the picture, add a silvery olive tree or a bay, some spiky yuccas, an oil jar or two, plus several pots of bright geraniums (zonal pelargoniums) and other sun-lovers, with a sprinkling of small spring bulbs to provide some early interest.

Roman herb garden
In a collection of formal terracotta containers, grow a selection of the herbs and spices that were essential to Roman cuisine. These included anise, basil, bay, capers, catmint, coriander, dill, garlic, myrtle, mustard, oregano, parsley, rocket and saffron.

Oriental calm
With two or three bonsai trees and shapely boulder islands rising out of a 'pool' of raked gravel, you can create your own Japanese garden. Add a stone stork for effect. (*See also* ***Japanese gardens***)

Tying the knot
Though not a style that can be achieved in a hurry, the Elizabethan knot garden is immensely satisfying in its formality. It is particularly suited to the smaller town plot where it can be looked down upon from the upper storeys of the house. There are several classic patterns of curls and arabesques, which are usually executed in *Buxus sempervirens* 'Suffruticosa' (dwarf box).

A scented patio
Patios are dry, warm and handy for the kitchen. This makes them ideal places to grow pots of scented herbs such as curry plant, fennel, lavender, lemon verbena, mint, rosemary and thyme to perfume the air.

A Shakespearean garden
Draw inspiration from the age of Shakespeare and create a bed that is divided in the Elizabethan manner with low, clipped box hedges. There you could grow some of the many plants that are mentioned in the Bard's plays including, for example, balm, borage, columbine, harebells, larkspur, lavender, musk roses, mustard, myrtle, oxlip, pansies, poppies, primroses, rosemary, rue, thyme, woodbine, wormwood and yarrow.

Elizabethan elegance The formal box hedges of a knot garden bring an air of sophistication to a town plot.

Thinning

Gentle handling
Thinning – the removal of seedlings from beds, pots or trays – helps the growth of plants that remain. When thinning out seedlings, carefully loosen the soil round their roots, then, to protect roots of adjacent plants from damage or disturbance and to avoid pulling the other seedlings out, hold down the soil with the fingers of one hand and remove the seedling with the other.

Watering time
You can make uprooting easier by watering seedlings thoroughly the evening before you intend to thin them out. Thin them in the early morning, if at all possible, then water the remaining plants well, because this will help to settle the soil round their roots.

Easy stages
Always thin out in stages to allow for natural loss from pests or diseases or other disorders. Clear away all the thinnings; their odour may prove attractive to pests. Both carrot flies and onion flies can detect the scent of crushed leaves from a long distance.

Garden secrets

A quick snip
If seedlings are growing very close together, it may be difficult to uproot thinnings without damaging the plants that remain. In this case, a pair of scissors could be used to snip off the surplus seedlings at ground level, leaving their roots in the ground. Without the foliage to sustain them, the roots will soon die, leaving enough room for the plants that remain to expand.

Waste not
When you are making the final thinnings of your carrots and onions, leaving spaces of 15cm (6in) between rows, 2.5–5cm (1–2in) between the carrots that remain, and 10cm (4in) between the onions, do not discard or destroy the thinnings. The young onions can be used as salad vegetables, and the baby carrots are delicious eaten raw. Other thinnings from the vegetable plot, including those of lettuce crops, can also be eaten.

Replanting vegetable thinnings
You can replant thinnings from some vegetable garden crops, including lettuces and onions, provided you handle them gently. To avoid causing any accidental damage to the stem or roots, use a pencil to loosen the soil round the roots, then lift the seedling out with a forked stick. There is no point in trying to replant thinnings from beetroot, radishes and other root vegetables as they are unlikely to become established successfully in a new home. (See also **Transplanting**)

Thistles

Silver elegance
Despite its prickles, *Onopordum acanthium* (Scotch or cotton thistle) is well worth growing in limited numbers. Its broad, silvery leaves covered with fine, cobweb-like hairs are very handsome, as are its purple flowers. Provided you can manage the prickles, it will add an unusual touch to flower arrangements – although it is not long-lived.

Lending stature
Use a few Scotch thistles to give height and stature to groups of smaller summer flowers. Try them with clumps of sweet williams, whose colours will be accentuated beautifully by the thistles' silvery leaves.

Globe thistle
The spherical, steely blue flowers of *Echinops ritro* (globe thistle) make a long-lasting successor for irises in the border. Bees love them, they are non-invasive and they dry beautifully for winter decoration.

Holy herb
An excellent plant for the back of the border or for bringing grace to a wild garden is the tall *Silybum marianum* (holy or blessed thistle). Growing up to 1.2m (4ft) tall, this attractive plant has a flat rosette of marbled, dark leaves with pronounced white veins, and produces handsome, deep violet flowers from June through to September.

Thistle control
Most thistles are invasive and must be controlled, but, on the plus side, they are a rich source of potassium, and their seed heads attract goldfinches as well as other seed-eating birds to the garden. Thistles are tenacious, and timing is everything in getting rid of them. There is much truth in the words of the old rhyme that says:

> *Cut in May/Waste a day*
> *Cut in June/A month too soon*
> *Cut in July/Sure to die.*

A brief history

Prickly problem
There is no doubt that Scotland's adoption of the thistle as her national emblem took place a long time ago, but the precise date is a matter of much debate. According to one legend, it was as long ago as the 11th century, when one of a party of marauding Danes trod barefoot on the plant. His howl of anguish alerted the Scots who fought off and vanquished the invaders, then gratefully took the thistle as their emblem. Other sources date it to the 15th century, when the thistle was added to the Scottish banner of St Andrew's Cross.

Thyme

Success in heavy soil

Thyme grows best in well-drained, poor soil in full sun but, if growing in a heavy or poorly draining soil, fill one-third of the planting hole with gravel or grit. Cover this drainage layer with potting compost, then plant the thyme. Do not apply either manure or fertiliser.

Winter flavouring

Although thyme is an evergreen herb, its leaves have less flavour in winter. In summer, just before the flower buds open, cut some sprigs and hang them up to dry in a warm, dark cupboard. Store the dried herb in paper bags or screw-top jars, until required, to flavour your winter cooking.

Blooming thyme

Cut flower stems back after blooming to encourage new shoots. If left unclipped, thyme bushes become leggy.

Flowers for the butterflies

Close-growing thyme looks particularly good outlining the front of a flowerbed, where its aromatic flowers will help to attract both butterflies and bees into the garden.

Special events

Plant varieties of lemon-scented, variegated or pink-flowered *Thymus serpyllum* in the cracks between paving stones. When crushed underfoot, the herb will release its delightful aroma. Lemon-scented and flavoured *T.* x *citriodorus* can be included in custards and other sweet puddings.

Winter aid

As befits their Mediterranean origins, thyme plants hate cold and wet weather, and tend to die back in hard winters. If they do, leave the dead stalks as some protection against further damage and add a layer of straw for good measure.

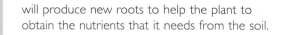

Gardener's potpourri

The wild thyme

As *A Midsummer Night's Dream* points out, banks of wild thyme were a well-known fairy habitat, which may be the reason why gypsies and other country folk would not bring the plant into their caravans or homes. However, no one denied its healing properties. It was good for whooping cough and stomach problems, while an infusion rubbed into the scalp reportedly delayed the onset of grey hair and banished depression. The Elizabethan herbalist John Gerard claims that it 'helpeth against the bitings of any venomous beast, either taken in drinke or outwardly applied'.

Tomatoes

Young and tender

When outdoor tomato plants have produced between three and five leaves, they are ready to be moved from the greenhouse to the garden. Before planting them out, put them outdoors during the day and return them to the greenhouse each night. Plant them out with their lowest leaves at soil level. The stem base

will produce new roots to help the plant to obtain the nutrients that it needs from the soil.

Growing cheap plants

Tomato plants are widely available from nurseries and garden centres but it is much cheaper to raise them from seed. Sow from January if you have a heated greenhouse, in March if it is unheated, and in April if you are growing them outdoors. The seeds can be sown in pots on a window ledge and one variety, 'Totem', can be left there to grow on right up to the fruiting stage.

Fertilise with eggshells

Every week or two, crush eggshells in a blender and add them to the water for your tomatoes – use about six shells per litre (2 pints). The extra calcium aids growth of the leaf tips and blossom ends and prevents blossom-end rot.

Tiles for heating

Tomato plants react badly to extreme changes in temperature. To keep their roots warm at night, especially during their first few weeks outside, lay a terracotta tile on each side of the plant. These will absorb the sun's rays during the day and radiate heat at night.

Remove growing tips

In the greenhouse, pinch out the growing tips of tomato plants in late August, or when six or seven trusses (flowering stems) have developed, whichever is the earlier. On outdoor tomatoes, pinch out the growing tips once three to five trusses have set. Bush varieties do not need to have their young tips or side shoots removed.

Fruit promotion

To encourage good fruit setting, help the plants to distribute pollen by tapping the tomato flowers gently each day and mist spray the flowers to moisten the air.

Nettle food

Line the bottoms of the planting holes with nettle leaves and cover with a layer of well-rotted manure. As the nettles decompose, they will provide a supply of plant food.

A brief history

A love apple

It took some time for the tomato to gain acceptance in Britain. It is a native of South America and was first brought to Spain by mariners, from where it spread throughout Europe, reaching England in the late 16th century. It was known in England as a golden apple – the earliest arrivals were a yellow variety – and a love apple, since it was, rather hopefully, held to have aphrodisiac properties. Some thought the tomato might be poisonous and, for one reason or another, it was grown mainly as an ornamental plant.

The herbalist John Gerard was aware that others felt differently and wrote, rather loftily, in 1596: 'In Spaine, and those hot regions, they use to eat the Apples boiled with pepper, salt and oyle; but they yeeld very little nourishment to the body, and the same naught and corrupt.'

Fast ripening

Ripen the late season's green tomatoes quickly by wrapping them individually in tissue paper, then placing them in either a drawer or cardboard box with a few red tomatoes or a couple of bananas. These fruits give off ethylene gas, which hastens the ripening process. Check the tomatoes daily and remove them as soon as they ripen.

Save your skins

When planting out tomatoes, place two banana skins in the bottom of each planting hole. The skins are a good source of potash.

A free, organic feed

Use the fast-growing comfrey variety 'Bocking 14' to make a high-potash fertiliser. Pack a water butt tightly with the leaves and cover with water. Leave for a week or two, drain, then water your tomatoes with the liquid. The partly decomposed leaves can be used as a top dressing round the plants. (*See also* **Organic gardening**)

Water plentifully

Erratic watering causes tomatoes to split. Water regularly and mulch round the plants; this helps to prevent evaporation, and to control the weeds that compete with the tomato plants. (*See also* **Mulching**)

Feed them Epsom salts

Every week, for every 30cm (1ft) of your plant's height, add 1 tablespoon of Epsom salts to 4 litres (1 gallon) of water and pour it on. The magnesium is a good nutritional supplement.

Boiler room treatment

As an alternative to ripening, pick all the fruit before the first frost strikes. Use the small, green tomatoes to make chutney. If you have lots of fully grown but unripe tomatoes, place them in a basket and hang it in the warmest part of the house – near the boiler, for example – where they will ripen quickly.

Water with sugar

When the fruits begin showing colour, add a teaspoonful of sugar to the water. They will be sweeter and juicier as a result. But go easy – minimising water while fruits ripen enhances their colour.

Patio tomatoes

Choose the right variety and you can grow tomatoes in containers on the patio or balcony. 'Totem' grows to just 46cm (18in) tall, and 'Tumbler' is a trailing plant specially suited to hanging baskets. (*See also* **Container gardening**, **Hanging baskets**, **Wall planting**)

Make the right choice

Top of the tomatoes

Tomatoes come in varieties suitable for growing in the greenhouse, or growing outdoors.

Greenhouse tomatoes
Dombito Large beefsteak variety, the fruits of which can weigh up to 225g (8oz) each.
Gourmet Excellent flavour. Produces a high yield of fruits of uniform size.
Shirley The standard greenhouse tomato, dependable and prolific.
Yellow Debut Yellow-fruited cherry tomato with an excellent flavour. Good disease resistance.

Outdoor tomatoes
Marmande Standard Continental ribbed variety. Large, irregular fruits.
Tornado Easy-to-grow bush tomato, which ripens early and has a good flavour.
Tumbler The hanging-basket tomato. Neat trailing growth, good flavour.

Dual-purpose tomatoes (greenhouse or outdoors)
Gardener's Delight Small, sweet, red fruits packed with flavour.
Golden Sunrise Attractive yellow tomato with a distinctive flavour.
Golden Tomboy F_1 hybrid with small, slightly oblong golden yellow fruits.
Inca Plum tomato with firm texture, this variety is resistant to some diseases. Will ripen by late July in the greenhouse.
Sungold Exceptionally sweet, reliable yellow variety with small fruits.
Supersweet 100 Cherry tomato that produces very long strings of small, sweet tomatoes.
Tigerella Unusual medium-sized fruits, which are red, streaked with orange.

Tools

Bright beacon
Losing small tools among plants and in undergrowth is a frequent annoyance for gardeners. Make the tools more easily seen by painting their handles in bright colours that will stand out from the greenery.

Saw size
When using a bow saw, do not be tempted to tackle branches that are too thick for the saw. A 60cm (2ft) bow saw should not be used to cut branches that are more than 10cm (4in) in diameter.

Choice of spade
There is a wide selection of garden spades to choose from, with different-sized blades, handles that vary in length and differing weights. Although the spades have specific names, such as digging or border spade, they can be used anywhere in the garden.

Work in comfort
There are many garden tools available, but only you can choose the ones that you will find comfortable to work with. When buying, go through the motions of planting, raking and so on to make sure the tool fits your build.

A quick shine
Put a shine on rusty or dirty tools. Add oil to a bucket, or other large container, of sharp sand. Brush the worst of the dirt from your tools then, one at a time, move them up and down several times in the mixture until the abrasive sand has removed the tarnish.

Brush a saw's teeth
If your garden saw is very dirty because, for example, you have used it to cut a branch full of sap, spray it with oven cleaner. Leave the cleaner to act for a few minutes, then remove the dirt with an old toothbrush. To keep the saw in the best possible condition, when not in use, wrap it in oil-coated newspaper.

Clean up after use
Get into the habit of cleaning your garden tools every time you have finished working with them. They will be easier to use and will also last longer. Before you put tools away for winter, remove traces of soil with newspaper or a brush. If you wash tools, dry them thoroughly and apply oil to all metal parts with a paintbrush or soft rag. Treat wooden handles with linseed oil, which should be left to feed the wood until the tools are needed next season.

Handling handles
Metal handles on tools are stronger, but are not as warm to the touch as wooden or plastic ones. Check wooden handles of spades and forks for splits, rough patches and abrasions, as these can cause splinters or blisters. Use sandpaper to smooth them down, then coat with polyurethene varnish for a comfortable grip. The wooden handles of handforks and trowels often have a rough patch on the end. Sand this smooth to prevent blisters.

Safe use of a wheelbarrow
Load a wheelbarrow so that the weight is mainly over the wheel. Bend your knees and not your back to lift and lower a barrow.

Wheelbarrow care
When not in use, stand a metal wheelbarrow on its wheel and lean the handles against a wall, or turn it upside-down. This prevents rainwater from collecting in the barrow and causing it to rust.

Take advantage of quiet winters
Have your lawn mower serviced in winter when you do not need to use it. Mechanics are also often less busy during this period.

Lawn rakes
Although several models of lawn rakes are available with thin metal tines, these tend to clog up quickly with leaves when the garden is being cleared in autumn. Plastic alternatives have wider tines, which do not clog up so readily. Plastic rakes are generally lighter than metal ones and so are less tiring to use.

Scoop up snow
Cut out the base of a 2.3 litre (4 pint) plastic milk bottle, then remove the side beneath the handle. You will be left with an easy-to-hold scoop ideal for small garden jobs, such as removing snow from flights of steps or for filling a container with compost.

See also *Hedge trimmers*, *Hoes*, *Lawn mowers*, *Safety*, *Secateurs*, *The right tool for the job pp. 294–5*,

Garden secrets

On your knees
Avoid backache by kneeling down to plant or weed rather than bending. There are various ways to make a kneeling pad. You can fold an old hessian bag into a pad and cover it with polythene to keep it dry, stuff a strong plastic bag with rags, or fill an old hot-water bottle with sawdust. Do not overfill the bottle, as this will make it rather hard on the knees. Glue a piece of old carpet to the pad to make it even more comfortable. Or make use of old computer mouse mats – these are just the right size to cushion your knees while setting out seedlings or doing other garden chores. Simply kneel on them, or attach them directly to your trouser legs with duct tape.

The right tool for the job

With a bewildering array of tools available, it is difficult to know which are indispensable and which are not. This guide will help you to decide what to buy.

It is best to begin with a collection of basic tools, then add to it as your interest and experience grow. You will need a spade and fork for digging the soil, a Dutch hoe and hand fork for weeding, a lawn rake and lawn shears, a trowel for planting, and pairs of shears and secateurs for trimming and pruning hedges or shrubs. These are the essential tools that will enable you to tackle the majority of tasks in the garden.

As well as meeting the requirements of the job, each tool should be comfortable to use and suit your height and strength. Good equipment will be used repeatedly so it is well worth buying quality products made from sturdy materials. Most will last a lifetime if properly maintained, and cleaned and dried before being put away.

Digging and cultivating

Digging with a spade or fork breaks up the soil and assists penetration of air and water. This speeds up the natural processes of decay and also promotes fertility. At the same time, many less vigorous weeds are destroyed. Digging is also used to alter the character of a soil – for instance, breaking down a clay soil by working in bulky manures, garden compost or leafmould.

Weeding and watering

Weeds compete with cultivated plants for light and nourishment and must be destroyed. Hoeing is a safe, effective method of removing them, and a way of breaking up the surface of the soil to allow air and moisture to penetrate. Moisture is essential for all plants, and supplying them with water is a vital garden task, especially for those grown under glass.

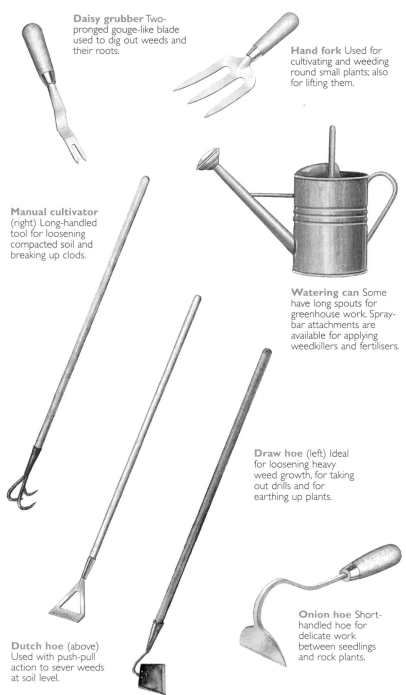

Daisy grubber Two-pronged gouge-like blade used to dig out weeds and their roots.

Hand fork Used for cultivating and weeding round small plants; also for lifting them.

Manual cultivator (right) Long-handled tool for loosening compacted soil and breaking up clods.

Watering can Some have long spouts for greenhouse work. Spray-bar attachments are available for applying weedkillers and fertilisers.

Draw hoe (left) Ideal for loosening heavy weed growth, for taking out drills and for earthing up plants.

Dutch hoe (above) Used with push-pull action to sever weeds at soil level.

Onion hoe Short-handled hoe for delicate work between seedlings and rock plants.

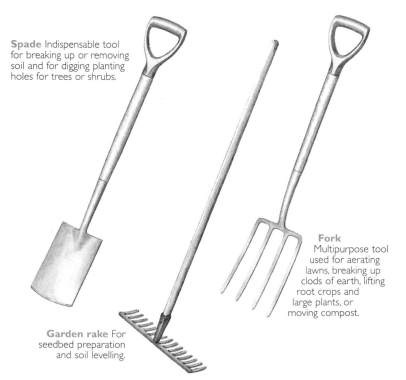

Spade Indispensable tool for breaking up or removing soil and for digging planting holes for trees or shrubs.

Fork Multipurpose tool used for aerating lawns, breaking up clods of earth, lifting root crops and large plants, or moving compost.

Garden rake For seedbed preparation and soil levelling.

Lawns and lawn care

To make a neat job of mowing the lawn, you will need to trim edges and cut the grass in any awkward corners that the mower cannot reach. Autumn is the time for a tidy-up – raking off dead leaves and using a spring-tined lawn rake for scarifying or removing moss and dead grass.

Pruning and picking

Cutting back woody plants such as roses, ornamental trees, fruit trees and shrubs has three main purposes: to regulate growth and shape; to improve the quality of flowers and fruits; and to remove dead, damaged or diseased wood. Pick fruit with care, using a fruit picker if necessary.

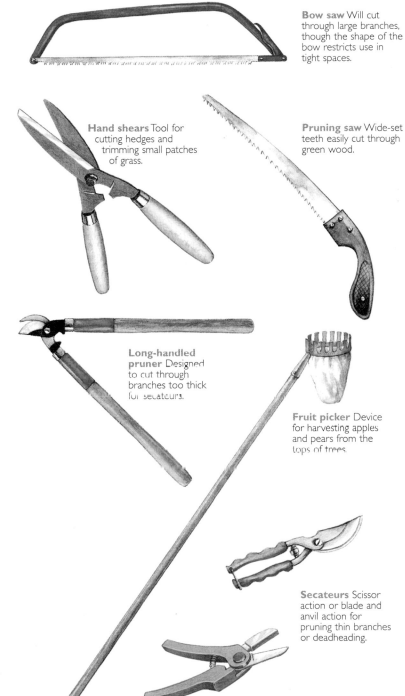

Bow saw Will cut through large branches, though the shape of the bow restricts use in tight spaces.

Lawn shears These have vertical blades for edging, horizontal blades for trimming.

Lawn rake Designed for collecting fallen leaves.

Hand shears Tool for cutting hedges and trimming small patches of grass.

Pruning saw Wide-set teeth easily cut through green wood.

Edging knife Used in conjunction with a garden line for cutting a straight edge in turf.

Long-handled pruner Designed to cut through branches too thick for secateurs.

Fruit picker Device for harvesting apples and pears from the tops of trees.

Planting and sowing

Annuals, perennials and bulbs must be planted carefully if they are to establish themselves successfully. Plants must be correctly spaced to allow them light, air and room for growth. They should also be set at the right depth – roots must not be too deep or too near the surface.

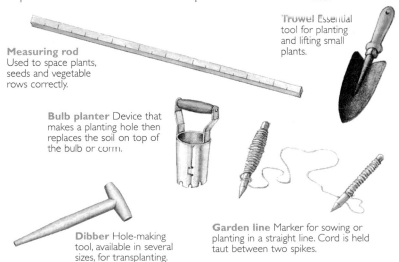

Trowel Essential tool for planting and lifting small plants.

Measuring rod Used to space plants, seeds and vegetable rows correctly.

Bulb planter Device that makes a planting hole then replaces the soil on top of the bulb or corm.

Secateurs Scissor action or blade and anvil action for pruning thin branches or deadheading.

Dibber Hole-making tool, available in several sizes, for transplanting.

Garden line Marker for sowing or planting in a straight line. Cord is held taut between two spikes.

Topiary

Living sculptures

Topiary is no longer the stiff, formal art that it was in bygone days. If you like the idea of living sculptures in the garden, see what can be achieved by visiting gardens that are famous for their topiaries. Abstract shapes, umbrellas and birds can be found at Levens Hall in Cumbria; Hever Castle in Kent has a garden of chessmen; a fox hunt 'runs' through a garden at Knightshayes Court, Devon; and you can see magnificent yew obelisks at Pitmedden in Aberdeenshire.

A protected place

If you want to create a topiary specimen in your garden, choose the site with care. The shrub should be in a sunny, sheltered position where strong winds will not be able to distort its shape. To facilitate initial shaping and subsequent pruning, make sure that you have unobstructed access to all sides of the shrub.

Choosing plants

Evergreens, including hollies, are suitable for topiary when simple shapes are required. If, however, you would like to create more complex sculptures, you will need to use box or yew, which are slow-growing and easy to clip and train. Rosemary makes a fine specimen with its delightfully aromatic foliage, while good small-leaved evergreens include myrtle, *Phillyrea angustifolia*, *P. latifolia* and *Rhamnus alaternus*.

Variegated box

As well as the popular green-leaved *Buxus sempervirens* (box) which is used widely for topiary, there are several variegated cultivars that look most attractive when clipped into small balls or pyramids. These include 'Argenteovariegata', with slightly puckered green leaves that are margined with white; 'Aureovariegata', which has leaves streaked with pale yellow; 'Elegantissima', with dark green leaves that have a wide, silvery border; and 'Marginata', whose leaves are partly edged with gold.

Begin with the basics

If you are a newcomer to topiary, it is advisable to begin with a simple shape such as a cone, pyramid or ball. Buy a ready-made frame, available from specialist suppliers and some garden centres, or make one using wooden stakes and chicken wire. Place the frame over the shrub and, as the shrub grows, use pruning shears to trim all the shoots that protrude through the mesh. In a short time, the shrub will begin to take on the shape for which you are aiming.

Ivy topiary on a frame

Create an attractive topiary specimen in two or three years by training small-leaved varieties of *Hedera helix* (ivy) over a ready-made frame. Ivies make good specimens for containers and will give you a year-round display on the patio. A variegated ivy such as 'Goldheart', which has yellow and green leaves, or 'Glacier', with variegated silver-grey leaves edged with white, will add extra interest to the winter garden.

Green pots for standards

Make a 'pot' for a specimen tree by surrounding it with young hedging plants that will grow fairly quickly, for example, privet or box. Prune the plants regularly to form a low, round, square or octagonal 'pot'.

A bird in the bush

A bird-shaped bush is not as difficult to achieve as you might think. Drive a stake into the ground until the top is at the intended height of the finished sculpture, then plant a box or yew tree close to the stake. Create a bird shape out of chicken wire, making it in several sections. Attach the sections to each other and then to the stake. As the shrub grows, tie the shoots to the wire so that they cover the body. Select one vigorous shoot at each end to create the head and tail. Attach one end of a length of string to the tail and peg the other end to the ground to pull the tail downwards. When the bird has grown, trim the shrub regularly to keep it in perfect shape.

Sheep shears

On small plants, use sharp sheep shears in preference to large hand shears. As sheep shears are held in one hand, clipping and shaping is much easier. They are available from garden centres.

A brief history

The living art of topiary

Topiary was introduced by the conquering Romans – the word is derived from the Latin *topiarus*, 'fancy work' – but did not become a passion for British gardeners until the 16th century. It then remained popular for more than 200 years, especially during the reign of William and Mary (1689–1702). But even during its golden age, this living form of sculpture was not without its critics – Francis Bacon commented that 'images cut out in juniper or other garden stuff be for children'.

Much topiary work was destroyed in the 18th century as natural landscapes became fashionable but, by 1800, the pendulum had swung back. Today interest in topiary is enjoying a resurgence: many garden centres stock basic shapes in box, and amateur as well as professional gardeners enjoy creating these leafy works of art.

Collecting clippings
Remember to put a polythene sheet under a plant before trimming it to shape so that the clippings fall onto the sheet and can then be collected up and removed. Provided the material is disease-free, soft clippings can be put directly onto the compost heap. Thicker, woodier shoots should be shredded first.

Precise but limited pruning
Topiary specimens should be pruned lightly and regularly. While the shrub is taking shape, cut back half of the annual shoots to ensure that new growth remains bushy. Once the shape has been created, keep it tidy by light trimming after the spring growth and again in late summer.

Creating a spiral
Topiary spirals are much admired, and are not too difficult to create. Choose a plant such as *Taxus baccata* 'Fastigiata', the Irish yew, which will make a slim column if it is left to grow naturally. Plant a young specimen and drive a stout stake into the ground on each side, about 15cm (6in) apart. Bend the main shoot round one of the stakes, and tie it firmly in place. As it grows, continue to twist the shoot round each

stake in turn, to form a spiral. Use sharp kitchen scissors to keep the plant in shape when it is young, and garden shears as it matures and the stems become tougher.

Early feeding and regular watering
A straggly piece of topiary is unsightly, so it is essential to ensure that early growth is strong and bushy. Work a slow-release fertiliser, such as bone meal, into the soil before planting and apply a mulch of well-rotted compost or manure round the plant to retain moisture. During the years of active growth, give the shrub an annual spring feed of a general fertiliser at the rate of 85g per m² (3oz per sq yd), and replenish the mulch.

Heading off the competition
Once the shrub is mature, apply a general fertiliser each March. This will ensure that both the shrub and any plants round it receive fertiliser when they start into growth in the early spring. You will need to water the shrub during dry weather. (*See also* **Fertilisers**)

Beware of heavy snowfall
Branches laden with snow may break under the weight – a sad ending for a carefully tended and shaped shrub. If you live in an area where snow falls regularly, place a framework of fine-mesh wire over your topiary when the cold season begins and brush off any snow that falls.

Sheep shape
A sheep is an impressive, yet fairly straightforward, topiary subject. Plant one bush at each of the points where you want the feet of the animal to be, and stake them to provide support. Using wire, wind an oval shape round the stakes, about 30cm (12in) from the ground, then bend a second piece of wire into a sheep silhouette and attach it to the wire oval. As the plants grow, tie the shoots to the wire so that they cover the body, and clip them when they exceed the wire outline. Attach string to a healthy shoot and peg it to the ground to form a tail. Trim regularly with shears to ensure that the foliage grows quickly to fill the wire shape and the sheep shape soon becomes apparent.

Tortoises

Keeping them in
So that a tortoise cannot escape, block up gaps and gateways with firmly secured boards. A greenhouse or conservatory will give shelter in spring and autumn months.

A hearty appetite
Tortoises damage young plants, which should be protected with firmly anchored wire cloches. Grow some plants just for them to eat, such as dandelions and lettuces.

Town gardens

Good neighbours
In town gardens, neighbours can be very close at hand. When erecting a fence, remember that the woven types have gaps that let sound through. A feather-edged board fence gives better soundproofing and, since it has no gaps, provides greater privacy. (*See also* **Fencing**)

Choose your trees
Town gardens, especially if positioned behind terraced houses, tend to be shady. In such conditions it is best to plant small trees or tree-like shrubs that will not add to the gloom. Choose a columnar tree such as *Prunus* 'Amanogawa' (Japanese cherry), or something delicate and feathery that will not resent being cut back hard if it grows a little too large. *Salix exigua* (coyote willow), *Sambucus racemosa* 'Plumosa Aurea' (yellow, cut-leaved elder) and *Acer negundo* 'Flamingo' are all ideal candidates.

All-year evergreens
In a small town garden every shrub must pull its weight for as much of the year as possible. Evergreens are indispensable but must be chosen carefully. Good examples include the variegated form of *Viburnum tinus*, with cream-edged leaves, pink buds and white winter flowers followed by blue-black berries. *Mahonia*

× *media* 'Charity', a striking evergreen with a bold architectural shape, has yellow winter flowers, while the yellow-splashed leaves of *Elaeagnus* × *ebbingei* 'Limelight' will brighten a shady wall or fence with its tiny, fragrant autumn flowers. If you can grow a few deciduous shrubs among the evergreens this will help to ensure that the garden changes with the seasons. (*See also* **Evergreens**)

Banish the lawn

The lawn in a small town garden can develop worn patches very quickly because all the traffic is concentrated in a small area. Consider replacing the grass with paving or gravel, which will withstand wear and tear. Without a lawn, the mower can be dispensed with, leaving storage space for other things.

Make less work

In some town gardens, the whole area may have been concreted over. It can be an enormous task to remove the concrete and then dig over and improve the soil ready for planting. Much hard work can be avoided if you decide on the positions of beds and borders first, then break up the concrete in these areas only. Raised beds for the plants can then be constructed on top. The remaining concrete will serve as paths.

Access through the house

Terraced town houses without separate access to the back garden can present enormous problems when potting compost, plants and other messy garden materials must be carried back and forth through the house. Avoid damage to your carpets, as well as injury to your back, by using the folding frame of a shopping trolley to transport materials to and from the back garden. Garden rubbish can be packed into old compost bags, tied tightly at the top, and loaded onto the trolley to be wheeled safely and cleanly through the house.

Trace elements

How to recognise a deficiency

Plants usually obtain sufficient trace elements from the soil. Occasionally, however, they may suffer from a lack of a particular trace element. The main symptoms of these deficiencies are yellowing between the veins, particularly in young leaves (lime-induced chlorosis); yellowing between the veins of older leaves (manganese deficiency); and yellow bands between the veins that become brown (magnesium deficiency). Less common are problems such as whiptail of brassicas (molybdenum deficiency) and brown cracks in celery stalks (boron deficiency).

Seaweed cure-all

It can be difficult to decide which problem is causing a deficiency. In such cases, water the plant with a liquid feed that is based on seaweed. These feeds contain a wide range of trace elements and will generally cure the problem, whatever it turns out to be. (*See also* **Seaweed**)

Lighten the load

If carrying heavy watering cans of sequestrene solution is difficult, select instead a granular formulation, which is easily handled and can be spread over the soil.

Feed full of goodness

Spray plants suffering from trace-element deficiencies with a foliar fertiliser that is rich in the missing element. These are available from specialist mail-order suppliers. In spring, feed lime-hating plants with a fertiliser designed for azaleas, heathers and rhododendrons. If they develop lime-induced chlorosis, treat with a sequestrene-based tonic. To avoid trace-element deficiencies, garden organically and apply rotted manure or garden compost generously to fruit and vegetables. Mulching with leafmould or composted bark has an acidic effect.

Transplanting

Successful seedlings

Transplant seedlings as soon as they are large enough to handle. If you wait too long, the closely grouped plants will become leggy and may suffer from diseases. To help small seedlings to withstand the shock of the move, water them several hours before, and also immediately after, transplanting them.

Be firm with brassicas

When transplanting members of the brassica family, always ensure that they are planted firmly. This will help to prevent tall plants such as broccoli and Brussels sprouts from being blown over in winter. It will also protect against 'blown' Brussels sprouts and poor quality cauliflower heads.

A gentle touch

It can often be tempting to firm seedlings in well but there is a risk that this can damage the young roots. Once the soil has been replaced round the roots, a thorough watering will settle it sufficiently.

Growing know-how

Vegetable seedlings – how deep?

For best results when transplanting, set seedlings at the appropriate depth.

Deep planting

Plant seedlings up to the base of their first leaves. This depth is suitable for aubergines, cabbages, courgettes, cucumbers, gherkins, melons, peppers and tomatoes.

Normal planting

Bury only the roots, leaving the entire stem above soil level. You may find that the seedling falls back to the ground but it will regain its vigour. This depth is suitable for beetroot, celery, chicory and lettuces.

Tiny seedlings
Because lobelia seedlings are so tiny, it is virtually impossible to prick them out individually. Instead, transplant the seedlings in small clumps and treat each clump as if it were one plant. Each grouping may contain four or five individual plants, which will go on to develop a clump-forming habit of growth when they are planted out.

A corking method
Nail staggered rows of corks onto a board at regular intervals. When you are ready to transplant, press the board, cork side downwards, onto well-worked soil. Your planting holes will be made in one easy step, saving time and leaving the correct distance between the seedlings.

Handle with care
Seedlings need gentle handling. Do not tug the young plants when transplanting. Lift them carefully out of the soil using a small-pronged fork or a plastic plant label as a miniature trowel. As handling the stem can cause damage, hold each seedling by a leaf. A pencil is the ideal size to use as a dibber with which to make the new planting holes.

Take a break
If you are planning a holiday, wait until your return before transplanting seedlings. These young plants need regular watering, and may not survive your absence. (See also **Holidays**)

A year of preparation
If you intend to transplant an established tree, prepare it for the move a year in advance. Dig a narrow, circular trench halfway between the trunk and the outer limit of the branches, and use the edge of the spade to sever any roots that protrude. Refill the trench with well-rotted compost and keep the area well watered. This will encourage the tree to form fibrous roots close to the trunk, which will help it to establish itself quickly after the move.

Wait for a downpour
Always choose a rainy day for transplanting trees and shrubs. This will limit moisture loss and, therefore, the trauma of disturbance.

The right season
If possible, wait until the autumn before transplanting deciduous trees or shrubs. This will give them time to form new roots before the onset of winter. Evergreens should be moved in either October or April, when the soil is moist and warm.

New homes for trees and shrubs
Make sure that the new planting hole is 30cm (12in) wider all round than the root ball of the tree or shrub. Work in a handful of bone meal and some well-rotted compost to provide nutrients. Plant wo that the old soil mark is level with the surface of the soil.

Better safe than sorry
If some of a tree's roots are severed during transplanting, the reduced root system may result in the tree being unable to support all of its foliage. You can rectify this by removing up to a third of the tree's branches. This will prevent wilting or dieback, which could result if the branches do not receive enough moisture from the roots.

From seed to garden
Some plants, evening primroses, for example, do not transplant well. It is advisable, therefore, to raise new plants from seeds. For best results, sow them in small pots, then plant the seedlings directly from the pots into their final positions in the garden.

See also **Layering**, **Planting**

Transporting plants

Moving small plants
Ensure safe transport of small plants or rooted cuttings by laying them side-by-side on a length of damp paper towel. Fold up the lower edge of the paper over the roots, then roll it gently lengthways with the plants inside. Retain moisture by sealing in a clear polythene bag or a sandwich box; keep the container cool.

Car journeys
When transporting plants by car, place them in the boot, which is the coolest part of the vehicle. If you need to move a tree, carry it on the roof rack. It will not suffer damage from the wind if you put the root ball at the front, with the branches pointing backwards. If the branches overhang the rear of the car, tie a bright cloth onto them to warn other drivers. (See also **Cut flowers**)

Plants in a picnic box
Before making a journey during hot weather, place transplanted cuttings, recently taken cuttings and young seedlings in a polystyrene-lined picnic cool box with its ice packs. This reduces the rate of transpiration, and ensures that the plant material rejuvenates quickly.

Long-distance removals
If you plan to transport seedlings over a long distance, grow them in egg boxes with the lid open. For the journey, close the boxes and lay them in the car boot, or put them into a sturdy bag. To ensure that the seedlings recover quickly and to return them to a good growing condition, thoroughly water them right away on arrival.

Silhouettes and styles

A huge variety of trees is available, in every shape and size. Even for the smallest garden, you can find one to add elegance and style.

The 1500 or so species of tree in British gardens are divided into two main categories – broad-leaved and coniferous. The most common broad-leaved trees include ash, beech, chestnut, oak and willow. The only native conifers are juniper, Scots pine and yew.

Nearly all broad-leaved trees are deciduous – that is, they shed their leaves annually – while most conifers are evergreen. This provides you with the first of several choices when selecting a tree – a skeletal, sculptural form in winter or leaves all year round.

The shape and size of the tree is the next most important factor – not only is it a personal choice but considerations of light and space in your garden must be taken into account. Deciduous and coniferous trees are available in many different shapes. The slender birch, for example, bears no resemblance to the bulky silhouette of the oak, and a mature Scots pine is shaped like a parasol, not an inverted cone. A columnar tree such as a birch or poplar will take up less space than a spreading one. And a parasol shape will give a certain amount of shade without blocking out natural light. More solid forms of conifers can act as windbreaks or sound barriers. And for fun, there are oddly shaped trees such as the corkscrew hazel. In any event, find out the eventual spread and height before you make a decision. Remember, you are planting for posterity. The eventual shape of a tree can be influenced by prevailing winds, pruning and speed of growth.

The following pages, with trees listed by shape, will help you to choose.

Rowan tree *Sorbus aucuparia* is widely planted in streets and gardens.

Maidenhair tree In a dry autumn, the leaves of the *Ginkgo biloba* turn a brilliant amber.

Egg-shaped and conical
Deciduous
Acer platanoides (Norway maple)
A. rubrum (red maple)
A. rufinerve (snake-bark maple)
A. saccharinum (silver maple)
Alnus glutinosa (alder)
Carpinus betulus (hornbeam)
Corylus colurna (Turkish hazel)
Davidia involucrate (handkerchief tree)
Fagus sylvatica (beech)
Ginkgo biloba (maidenhair tree)

Ilex aquifolium (holly)
Populus tremula (aspen)
Prunus avium (wild cherry)
Pyrus communis (pear)
Quercus coccinea (scarlet oak)
Salix alba (white willow)
Sorbus aucuparia (rowan)
Tilia × *europaea* 'Pallida' (lime)
T. Tomentosa (silver lime)

Western red cedar The reddish-brown wood of *Thuja plicata* is used for fencing, wall cladding and garden sheds.

Caucasian fir *Abies nordmanniana* grows best in the moist conditions of the west coast.

Conifers
Abies nordmanniana (Caucasian fir)
Cedrus deodara (Himalayan deodar cedar)
C. libani ssp. *atlantica* (Atlas cedar)
Chamaecyparis lawsoniana (Lawson cypress)
Cryptomeria japonica (Japanese red cedar)
× *Cupressocyparis leylandii* (Leyland cypress)
Cupressus arizonica var. *glabra* 'Aurea' (smooth Arizona cypress)
Juniperus virginiana (pencil cedar)
Larix decidua (European larch)
L. kaempferi (Japanese larch)
Metasequoia glyptostroboides (dawn redwood)
Picea sitchensis (Sitka spruce)
Pinus contorta (shore pine)
P. peuce (Macedonian pine)
Pseudotsuga menziesii (Douglas fir)
Sequoiadendron giganteum (Wellingtonia)
Taxus baccata (common yew)
Thuja plicata (Western red cedar)

Columnar
Deciduous
Acer platanoides 'Columnare' (Norway maple)
A. saccharinum pyramidale (silver maple)
Betula pendula 'Fastigiata' (silver birch)
Carpinus betulus 'Fastigiata' (hornbeam)
Fagus sylvatica 'Dawyck' (Dawyck beech)
Malus tschonoskii
Populus alba pyramidalis (white poplar)
P. nigra var. *italica* (Lombardy poplar)
Prunus 'Amanogawa' (Japanese cherry)
P. 'Hillieri Spire' (ornamental plum)
Quercus robur fastigiata (cypress oak)
Robinia pseudoacacia 'Pyramidalis'
    (false acacia)
Sorbus aucuparia 'Fastigiata' (rowan)
Tilia cordata 'Greenspire' (small-
    leaved lime)
Ulmus minor 'Dampieri Aurea' (smooth-
    leaved elm)

Lombardy poplar *Populus nigra* var. *italica* has roots that can block drains in their search for water.

Conifers
Austrocedrus chilensis (Chilean cedar)
Chamaecyparis lawsoniana
    'Grayswood Pillar'
    (Lawson cypress)
Cupressus macrocarpa 'Goldcrest'
    and 'Golden Pillar' (Monterey
    cypress)
C. sempervirens 'Stricta'
    (Mediterranean cypress)
Juniperus chinensis 'Obelisk' and
    'Spartan' (Chinese juniper)
J. communis 'Hibernica' (Irish juniper)
J. scopulorum 'Skyrocket'
    (Rocky Mountain juniper)
Picea omorika (Serbian spruce)
Pinus sylvestris 'Fastigiata' (Scots
    pine)
Taxodium distichum var. *imbricatum*
    'Nutans' (swamp cypress)
Taxus baccata 'Fastigiata Aurea',
    'Fastigiata Aureomarginata' and
    'Standishii' (yew)
Thuja occidentalis 'Europa Gold'
    and 'Smaragd' (American
    arbor-vitae)

Mediterranean cypress *Cupressus sempervirens* 'Stricta' is a medium-sized tree with dark foliage.

Tall rounded
Deciduous
Acer cappadocicum
    (Cappadocian maple)
A. negundo (box elder)
A. opalus (snowball maple)
A. pseudoplatanus (sycamore)
Aesculus × carnea
    (red horse chestnut)
A. hippocastanum (horse chestnut)
Ailanthus altissima (tree of heaven)
Carya ovata (shagbark hickory)
Castanea sativa (sweet chestnut)
Catalpa bignonioides
    (Indian bean tree)
Fraxinus excelsior (common ash)
F. ornus (manna ash)
Juglans nigra (black walnut)
J. regia (common walnut)
Magnolia acuminata
    (cucumber tree)
Malus sylvestris (crab apple)
Platanus × hispanica
    (London plane)
Pterocarya fraxinifolia
    (Caucasian wing nut)
Quercus cerris (Turkey oak)
Q. frainetto (Hungarian oak)
Q. ilex (holm oak)
Q. palustris (pin oak)
Q. robur (common oak)
Q. rubra (red oak)
Salix alba (white willow)
Sorbus thibetica 'John Mitchell'
Tilia × europaea (common lime)
T. platyphyllos (broad-leaved lime)
Zelkova carpinifolia (Caucasian elm)

Conifers
Pinus pinaster (maritime pine)
P. radiata (Monterey pine)

London plane *Platanus × hispanica* was planted extensively in cities, especially London, because of its tolerance to atmospheric pollution.

Common lime tree *Tilia × europaea* is Britain's tallest-growing broad-leaved tree.

Ball

Deciduous

Acer platanoides 'Globosum'
(Norway maple)
Robinia pseudoacacia
'Umbraculifera' (false acacia)

Norway maple *Acer platanoides* 'Globosum' is common in southern parks.

False acacia *Robinia pseudoacacia* honours Jean Robin, who first grew it in 17th-century Paris.

Conifers

Abies lasiocarpa 'Arizonica Compacta'
(subalpine fir)
C. obtusa 'Pygmaea' (Hinoki cypress)
C. pisifera 'Filifera' (Sawara cypress)
Cryptomeria japonica 'Globosa Nana'
(Japanese cedar)
Picea abies 'Clanbrassiliana', 'Nidiformis'
and 'Ohlendorffii' (Norway spruce)
Pinus mugo 'Mops' (mountain pine)
P. sylvestris 'Moseri' (Scots pine)
Thuja occidentalis 'Danica', 'Golden Globe'
and 'Tiny Tim' (American arbor-vitae)

Parasol

Deciduous

Betula nigra (river birch)
Koelreuteria paniculata (pride of India)
Laburnum × *watereri* 'Vossii'
(golden chain)
Prunus 'Kiku-shidare-zakura'
P. 'Shirofugen' (Japanese cherry)

Conifers

Pinus nigra (Austrian pine)
P. pinea (stone pine)
P. sylvestris (Scots pine)

Scots pine *Pinus sylvestris* graces Highland lochs and mountains.

Stone pine *Pinus pinea* grows in the south of Britain.

Weeping

Deciduous

Betula pendula 'Tristis' and
'Youngii' (silver birch)
Cercidiphyllum japonicum
pendulum (katsura tree)
Fagus sylvatica 'Pendula'
(weeping beech)
Fraxinus excelsior 'Pendula'
(weeping ash)
Laburnum anagyroides
'Pendulum' (laburnum)
Malus × *gloriosa* 'Oekonomierat
Echtermeyer' (flowering crab
apple)
Morus alba 'Pendula'
(white mulberry)
Populus tremula 'Pendula' (aspen)
Prunus pendula 'Pendula Rubra' (weeping spring cherry)
Pyrus salicifolia 'Pendula' (willow-leaved pear)
Salix alba 'Tristis' and *S.* × *sepulcralis chrysocoma* (weeping willows)
Ulmus glabra 'Camperdownii' (wych elm)

Weeping willow Some *Solix* × *sepulcralis chrysocoma* grow to over 65ft (20m) high.

Conifers

Cedrus deodara 'Pendula' (Himalayan deodar cedar)
C. libani ssp. *atlantica* 'Glauca Pendula' (Atlas cedar)
Juniperus recurva var. *coxii* (drooping juniper)
Picea abies 'Inversa' (Norway spruce)
P. pungens 'Pendula' (Colorado spruce)
Tsuga canadensis 'Pendula' (Eastern
hemlock)

Weeping beech *Fagus sylvatica* 'Pendula' is a large weeping tree with enormous branches.

Spreading or creeping

Deciduous

Acer palmatum var. *dissectum* (Japanese maple)
Albizia julibrissin (silk tree)
Aralia elata (angelica tree)
Cotoneaster horizontalis
Ficus carica (see right)
Lonicera pileata (honeysuckle)
Malus × *purpurea* 'Aldenhamensis' (flowering crab apple)
Morus nigra (black mulberry)
Prunus sargentii (Sargent's cherry)
Viburnum plicatum 'Mariesii'

Black mulberry *Morus nigra* was introduced into Britain about 400 years ago to found the silk industry.

Fig *Ficus carica* has been grown in Britain since the 16th century, mainly for its fruit.

Conifers

Juniperus communis 'Hornibrookii' (juniper)
J. horizontalis (creeping juniper)
J. sabina 'Tamariscifolia' (Savin juniper)
J. squamata 'Meyeri' (scaly-leaved Nepal juniper)
Picea abies 'Repens' (Norway spruce)
Pinus densiflora 'Umbraculifera' (dwarf Japanese red pine)

Multi-branched with several trunks

Deciduous

Acer davidii 'Serpentine' (maple)
Betula papyrifera (paper birch)
Carpinus betulus (hornbeam)
Cercis siliquastrum (Judas tree)
Corylus avellana (common hazel)
Gleditsia triacanthos 'Rubylace' (honey locust)
Magnolia sieboldii (magnolia)

Hornbeam The tough wood of *Carpinus betulus* was once used to make wheel spokes.

Conifers

Juniperus chinensis 'Kaizuka' (Chinese juniper)
Pinus contorta (shore pine)
Sciadopitys verticillata (umbrella pine)
Taxus baccata (common yew)
Tsuga canadensis (Eastern hemlock)

Common hazel *Corylus avellana*, yellow or purple-leaved.

Bizarre and picturesque

Deciduous

Acer palmatum var. *dissectum* (Japanese maple). Eventually producing a large bush with bronze-tinged leaves.
Arbutus unedo (strawberry tree). Flowers and fruit are produced simultaneously. Has short trunk and naturally twisted branches.
Corylus avellana 'Contorta' (corkscrew hazel). Twisted branches.
Robina pseudoacacia 'Tortuosa' (false acacia). Contorted branches, corkscrew-like shoots.
Salix babylonica var. *pekinensis* 'Tortuosa' (willow). Of conical habit, with twisted and contorted branches and twigs; *S.* 'Erythroflexuosa' (willow). With drooping, spiralling branches.

Japanese maple *Acer palmatum* var. *dissectum* has attractively twisted and contorted branches that are reminiscent of 'willow pattern' designs.

Conifers

Abies homolepis (Nikko fir). Symmetrical, triangular shape, branches at distinct levels.
Araucaria araucana (monkey puzzle tree). Sharp, flat, oval leaves in a geometric pattern.
Juniperus chinensis 'Kaizuka' (Chinese juniper). Small tree, divergent, irregular branches.
Pinus parviflora (Japanese white pine). An ideal centrepiece ofr a large lawn.
P. thunbergii (black pine). A pine with stout, twisted branches and very long needles.
Sequoiadendron giganteum 'Pendulum' (Wellingtonia). Weeping variety, has vertically downswept branches.
Taxodium distichum (swamp cypress). Mature plant; if grown in water it exhibits knee-like growths from the roots.

Monkey puzzle The odd *Araucaria araucana*.

Tree repairs

Rot prevention

Trees that have narrow crotches (points where lateral branches join the main branch structure) are prone to a build-up of debris in this region. It should be removed each autumn to prevent rot setting in, which can result in the loss of large branches.

Canker wounds

Check fruit trees early in the year for signs of canker wounds. Use a sharp knife or pruning saw to cut away all affected bark and wood. Having treated one tree, sterilise knives and saws before treating another.

Torn branches

If a branch of a tree has been broken and a ragged snag is left on the trunk, the snag should be removed as it can become a point of entry for bacteria and fungal diseases that can attack the tree. If the snag is thick, use a sharp pruning saw to remove it. Begin by sawing in an upward direction. If necessary, remove the snag in two or three sections, finishing as close to the trunk as possible. Using a sharp knife, trim any ragged edges that remain round the wound. If the snag has been removed cleanly, it should not be necessary to seal the wound.

Split trunks

There are two main causes of split tree trunks. Sudden, severe late frosts can damage the trunks of some trees. This usually happens in spring after a mild spell has encouraged vigorous growth. Splits can also occur when a long period of hot, dry summer weather is followed by prolonged heavy rain. In many cases the split runs deeper than the bark, and such damage can lead to rotting of the heartwood. It is far better to leave well alone and leave the tree to heal naturally, cutting back any dead wood the following autumn. Although a tree with a split trunk may survive for many years, its life expectancy is usually reduced.

Growing know-how

When lightning strikes

Tall trees are occasionally struck by lightning, though in many cases the only damage is the loss of a few branches from the crown. Remove damaged branches and clean ragged wounds. In a few cases, large parts of the crown may be lost and this will require more substantial repairs. Even when repairs have been done, the shock to the tree may be such that it loses vigour and dies a few years later. Some hardwood trees such as oaks may, if struck, be left with a narrow scar down the trunk, but this is usually superficial. To aid healing, tidy up any ragged parts to leave a clean wound. Very occasionally a whole tree may be blown out of the ground. Small trees can be saved sometimes if replanted and supported, but large specimens seldom retake.

Trees

Take expert advice

Most trees will live and grow for many years, so it is essential to make the right choice before planting one in your garden. Make use of the expertise of the staff at a specialist tree nursery. They should be able to provide information about the most suitable varieties to grow in your area and on your type of soil. They can also advise on the growth rate and eventual height of trees.

Strike a balance

Plant a mixture of evergreen and deciduous trees in your garden. Doing so will provide you with a year-round structure as well as colours and shapes that change with the seasons. A ratio of two thirds evergreen to one third deciduous is a good balance. (See also **Evergreens**, **Town gardens**)

Earning their keep

In a small garden, where there is room for only a few decorative trees and shrubs, maximise on the available space by planting those that will provide variety in summer foliage, autumnal colour, elegance of bark and winter silhouette. Among those that fulfil most of these requirements are the *Acer* (maple), *Amelanchier* (snowy mespilus), *Betula* (birch), *Malus* (crab apple), *Prunus* species (ornamental plum and cherry) and some varieties of *Salix* (willow). For a decorative evergreen that changes colour with the seasons, plant *Photinia* 'Red Robin'. (See also **Autumn colours**, **Bark**, **Flowering trees**)

A pot of tree

If your garden is very small, try growing a tree in a large tub or half-barrel. This may shorten a tree's life but if the tree is kept well watered and fed regularly, it is likely to survive for up to ten years. Trees suitable for large containers include *Acer shirasawanum* f. *aureum*, *Chamaecyparis lawsoniana* 'Columnaris' (Lawson cypress), *Cupressus sempervirens* 'Green Pencil' (Mediterranean cypress), *Juniperus chinensis*

Garden secrets

Use a balloon on a string

If you want to see where the shadow of a tree you intend to plant will fall and do not have a stick long enough to represent the tree's eventual height, use a short stick, a length of string and a helium balloon. Measure a piece of string equal to the height of the mature tree, minus the length of the stick. Thread or glue paper onto the string to increase visibility. Tie the balloon to one end and secure the other end to the stick, then note where the shadows of the paper fall. To prevent distorted shadows, do this on a day with no wind.

'Kaizuka' (Chinese juniper), *Laurus nobilis* 'Aurea' (golden bay), *Malus pumila* 'Cowichan', *M.* 'Crittenden' and *M.* 'Elise Rathke' (crab apple), and *Prunus* 'Kiku-shidare Zakura' or *P. incisa* 'Kojo-no-mai' (Japanese cherry). (*See also* **Container gardening**)

Tolerant of bogs

If your garden contains a boggy but well-drained area, create a sense of drama by planting the moisture-tolerant *Acer palmatum* (Japanese maple). This specimen is especially attractive in the autumn when its distinctive foliage turns crimson. The Japanese maple is a slow-growing tree and is suitable for a small garden.

Tree choice

When buying a young tree, take care to choose one that has only a single main stem. If the plant has two main shoots, they will compete with each other as the tree grows, and will reduce its overall quality.

Small and young

Always buy small, relatively immature trees. As well as being less expensive than larger ones, they are easier to carry, more likely to re-establish themselves successfully and will always grow quickly once planted.

Bare versus covered

Generally, most ornamental trees sold at garden centres are in containers, but fruit trees are often sold bare rooted. Make sure the roots never dry out between lifting and planting – cover with moist hessian or place in a black polythene bag tied round the stem.

Root health

Avoid buying a container-grown tree with roots that have developed strongly outside the container or one in a pot full of weeds. Either condition indicates that the tree has been in the pot for too long. Also reject any tree whose compost has dried out completely.

Prune for healthy growth

Before planting a deciduous tree, remove any weak or bruised branches and roots. A tree can lose a third of these without harm, and pruning encourages new, healthy growth. A sawhorse will ease the task.

Light before foliage

If you plan to install outdoor lighting in the garden at some time in the future, lay the cables before planting trees. Then you will not have to disturb the roots of mature trees.

Loosen the root ball

If the roots of a tree grown in a pot have become compacted while in the container, tease them away carefully from the root ball before planting.

Protect other plants

Tree roots are greedy, soaking up moisture and nutrients. If you are worried that nearby plants could suffer, plant your tree in a properly constructed brick pit with bottom drainage. More sensibly, make sure that plants being grown adjacent to the tree are tolerant of dry soil conditions.

Stake before you plant

Always put a tree's support in place before you fill up the planting hole with soil. This will prevent you from inadvertently damaging the roots of the tree as you drive the stake into the ground.

Uninterrupted services

Do not plant trees where gas pipes and electricity cables run underneath the garden, or where there are drains and inspection covers. Tree roots can obstruct access to, or damage, cables, drains and pipes. Information on the underground routes of these services is available from the relevant authority.

Shallow roots need space

Do not plant alders, birches, ornamental cherries, poplars or willows in a lawn or near a vegetable garden. These trees root near the surface, making it difficult to mow the lawn or work the soil when they have become established after many years. Plant them instead only in a wild area, and do not position them close to buildings, paving stones, fences or drainage pipes, all of which they can damage.

Safety in the small garden

In a small garden, it may be impossible to allow the recommended safe distances between trees and buildings. However, planting too close, particularly if insufficient building foundations have been laid, can result in damage to the buildings. Instead of standard trees, you should choose dwarf or slow-growing varieties that can be planted closer to buildings, or select specimens that have been grafted onto dwarfing rootstocks.

Shade considerations

Do not plant evergreen trees or tall conifers on the west or south boundaries because they will cast shade over the garden.

Growing know-how

Safe planting distances

A survey by the Buildings Research Establishment showed that 79 per cent of insurance claims for subsidence involved trees or shrubs close to the property. Hot, dry summers increase the risk as thirsty roots go in search of water, drawing it from the clay soil round the building's foundations. In time, parts of the foundations will shift, and the walls of the property crack as they are moved out of position. To prevent this, plant a tree at a distance from the property equivalent to at least one-and-a-half times the tree's ultimate height. Many smaller growing trees, however, are fairly shallow rooting and should not interfere with foundations.

Type of tree	Minimum distance from property
Apple	10m (32ft)
Ash	20m (65ft)
Beech	15m (50ft)
Birch	10m (32ft)
Cherry	11m (36ft)
Cypress	17m (55ft)
Elm	30m (100ft)
Holly	6m (21ft)
Horse chestnut	23m (75ft)
Laburnum	9m (30ft)
Laurel	6m (21ft)
Magnolia	5m (17ft)
Maple	20m (65ft)
Oak	30m (100ft)
Pear	10m (32ft)
Pine	8m (26ft)
Plum	11m (36ft)
Rowan	11m (36ft)
Spruce	7m (24ft)
Sycamore	17m (55ft)
Walnut	14m (46ft)
Willow	40m (130ft)
Yew	5m (17ft)

Shady days

See where the shade of the mature tree will fall by placing a stick that is the same height in the proposed planting spot. On a sunny day, take a look at its shadow at various hours, paying close attention to flower beds or seating areas that you wish to keep in the sunshine.

Loosen the tie

Check tree ties regularly to make sure that they have not become too tight. Constriction can damage the wood fibres and weaken the tree trunk, which could then break in a high wind. Remove ties and stakes after about two years when the tree will have rooted firmly.

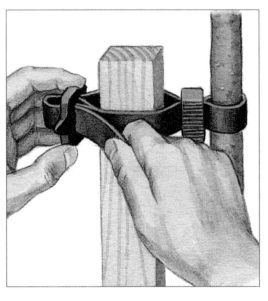

Sizing up your tree

To measure a tree, place a stick nearby and measure the shadows of both. Multiply the length of the stick by the length of the tree's shadow, then divide the answer by the length of the stick's shadow. The figure represents the height of the tree.

Ties from tights

Cut an old pair of nylon tights into strips, twist them together, then wind in a figure-of-eight round the trunk of a young tree and its supporting stake. Knot the ends of the tie securely together. The nylon will not rot, and will hold the tree firmly in place without causing damage.

Autumn planting

Container-grown trees can be planted during most times of the year – provided the ground is not frozen or too dry – but autumn is best. The soil is moist then and will still retain some of summer's warmth.

Protection for a young tree

Put a sleeve protector, made of either perforated plastic or fine mesh wire, round the base of a young tree. Alternatively, if the trunk is not too thick, cut open a plastic bottle, lengthways, and secure it round the trunk with twine. These guards will protect the tree's bark from being eaten by rabbits, and from accidental damage by either lawn mowers or strimmers.

Double decoration

To extend the period of interest, make a larger planting hole than is needed for the tree and put in a climbing plant that will bloom just before or just after the tree. Clematis, climbing roses and, provided the tree is a large one, wisteria are ideal. (*See also **Climbing plants***)

Direct route

Do not let a newly planted or young tree suffer from drought – this weakens the root system. Insert a length of pipe with one end close to the roots, the other just above ground. Water into the pipe to give the roots instant moisture.

Keep trees watered

For a mature tree, it is advisable to water beneath the canopy, where the roots are, rather than close to the trunk.

Feeding a tree

Mature trees growing in their natural habitat are unlikely to require feeding. However, young trees, those grown for fruit, and ornamental varieties will all benefit from a slow-release fertiliser, such as bone meal, in late winter. (*See also **Fertilisers***)

Remove suckers

If your tree produces suckers, cut them off cleanly with secateurs. Any shooting later should be pinched out with finger and thumb.

Action against poor growth

If a young tree appears to make no growth after it has been planted, this may be because it is establishing badly. Make sure that it has the best conditions for growth. Mulch the soil round the roots and water regularly. Also reduce the crown by about a third – pruning can help to stimulate growth.

Tree preservation

Heavy machinery left to lean against a tree can cause damage to the trunk, and a heavy roller left close to a tree can interfere with growth because of pressure on the root plate. Careless use of lawn mowers and strimmers can also damage bark and surface roots.

Dangerous nails

On no account should nails be hammered into trees. They may become embedded and forgotten and could be the cause of a serious accident if a chain saw is used on the tree.

Water supply

An effective way of supplying water is to create a moat, by using a hose to fill a channel round the trunk of a newly planted tree. Mulching will help to ensure the soil round the tree retains this moisture. Do not mulch right up to the stem.

Zap the sap

Tree sap is sticky stuff and often will not come off easily. Don't worry: just rub butter on your hands and the gunky sap will wash right off with soap and water.

Woodpeckers

While it can be a great pleasure to see a woodpecker in your garden, if the bird chooses to build a nest in one of your trees this may indicate that the tree is unhealthy. Woodpeckers usually nest in trunks that are partially rotten in the centre. If you find a woodpecker's nest in one of your trees, plant a replacement as soon as possible. Although some trees have a protective barrier against rot, their survival period will not be for ever.

Keep children safe

Two attractive garden trees can be dangerous to children so think carefully if planting them. Laburnums have poisonous seeds so are best avoided. Yellow-leaved

Robinia pseudoacacia 'Frisia' has vicious thorns; a good alternative is *Gleditsia triacanthos* 'Sunburst'. Other thorny trees to avoid planting are *Crataegus* (hawthorn) and *Prunus spinosa* (blackthorn).

See also **Planting, Pruning, Stakes and supports, Transplanting**

Tree stumps

Removal by hand

Stumps of small trees can be removed by hand, although the job can be arduous. Cut down the tree, leaving about 1.5m (5ft) of trunk. Dig a trench one spade wide round the trunk of the tree and about 60cm (2ft) away from it, cutting through roots with secateurs or long-armed pruners. Use the spade to undercut the tree, and the stump as a lever to help to work the roots free.

Chemical killers

Removing large tree stumps that are still alive is a job for a professional, but they can be treated with a chemical killer. On a dry day, drill holes about 1.3cm (½in) wide, 15cm (6in) deep and 15cm (6in) apart in the stump, then pour in a solution of ammonium sulphamate, made up according to the instructions on the pack. The chemical will be taken up by the stump and will rot it from the inside.

Prevent honey fungus

Always remove or kill the stumps of trees after the trunk and branches have been removed. Honey fungus can infect stumps, then spread through the soil to healthy trees, and may eventually kill them.

Trellises

Add a little distance

Do not place a trellis directly onto a wall. Attach it to vertical 5 × 5cm (2 × 2in) wooden battens fitted to the wall. This allows air to circulate, which helps to prevent mildew from infecting plants.

Up the trellis

Rambling and climbing roses can display their blooms to the best advantage when trained on a trellis. Tie in new shoots before they become so long that they obstruct paths or patios where their thorns may cause injury. Clematis is also ideal when trained on a trellis, because its leaf stems curl round and cling to the wooden struts. On a south-facing wall, the gorgeous annual morning glory, *Ipomoea tricolor* 'Heavenly Blue', in a lovely sky-blue, will twine round the struts and support itself.

Fake the effect

Create an impressive perspective by attaching a mirror to a wall and erecting a trellis arch round it. Alternatively, you can make a *trompe l'oeil* (literally, 'deceive the eye') feature by fixing a piece of specially shaped trellis onto a wall. This trellis is shaped to give the impression of a tunnel, or perhaps an archway, which makes a small garden appear larger. Artistic gardeners could even paint a picture in the centre.

Clever camouflage

Selecting the trellis that is most suitable for a particular plant can be difficult. Unless you want the trellis itself to be a feature, your best bet is to select a colour that will blend into the background.

Make a lasting bamboo trellis

Use bamboo canes to make an attractive trellis for climbing annuals. To prevent the canes from rotting, sharpen the base of each to a rough point, then stand them in a bucket of exterior wood preservative for at least 24 hours. Allow the canes to dry before tying them together securely with rot-proof or wire ties. If properly preserved, the trellis should last for up to five years.

Fashion a fedge

One of the best ways to use trellis is to make a fedge, a combination of fencing and substantial climbing plants, that can be used as a divider within the garden or as a screen between neighbours' properties. Many wall shrubs are suitable, but roses are probably the best choice, as long as their thorny growth is not in danger of catching passers-by. The pink 'The Queen Elizabeth' and yellow 'Chinatown' make dense, vigorous growth but need much pruning to keep them within bounds. *Rosa × odorata* 'Mutabilis' combines rich foliage with peach-coloured flowers that turn crimson as they age. This will need vigorous pruning to encourage more flowers.

Trilliums

Moist rhizomes

When you buy trillium rhizomes, make sure that they are firm and moist and have not been allowed to dry out. Select only those that have plump, healthy, green buds.

Buy plants in flower

When buying trillium plants, purchase them in pots between April and June. Flower size and colours vary, so it is best to buy the plants when they are in bloom. Many trillium species die down after they have been planted, so mark the spot with a cane and be sure to keep it well watered. New shoots will emerge the following spring.

First flush The delicate flowers of *Trillium grandiflorum* (wake robin) and its varieties have three slightly reflexed petals on short arching stems.

Bigger and better

Unlike other perennials, trilliums should not be split regularly but left to mature. They develop slowly into an impressive clump.

Plant in shade

The ideal habitat for trilliums is a woodland floor, where they will be in partial shade. They will tolerate sunlight as long as the soil is kept constantly moist. Plant them in August or September, 7.5–10cm (3–4in) deep, in small groups underneath trees or shrubs, in a well-drained fertile soil.

Splitting up

To propagate a trillium, wait until the foliage has died down in late summer. From then until March, you can lift and divide the plant but make sure that each piece has a growing point. Do not propagate a trillium more than necessary as both plants will take some time to become established after division. (See also **Division**)

Tulips

Easy lifting

Before planting a clump of tulip bulbs, line the planting hole with a piece of wire mesh or plastic netting, or invest in a purpose-made bulb planting basket; these are available from garden centres. Leave the edge protruding slightly above ground level. After the foliage has died back, lift the bulbs by pulling gently on the edges of the liner.

Spring in the window box

To fill your window box with early colour, plant short-stemmed tulips. These will withstand strong winds much better than standard varieties. Try the early-flowering *Tulipa kaufmanniana* 'Ancilla' (pink and white), 'César Franck' (carmine and yellow), 'Stresa' (yellow and orange), and 'The First' (white and carmine), all of which will create a cheerful start to spring and will enchant people passing by.

Correct planting depth

The lighter the soil, the deeper tulip bulbs should be planted. On sandy soil, plant the bulbs to a depth of 18–20cm (7–8in). On heavy soils, do not plant them deeper than 12.5–15cm (5–6in).

Summer space-saver

If necessary tulip bulbs can be lifted as soon as the flowers fade and replanted in an out-of-the-way area. Dig a trench and cover the bottom with a strip of wire netting, leaving each end protruding above the top of the trench. Lay the bulbs on top of the netting and replace the soil, leaving the tulips' leaves exposed. When the leaves have died, pull up the netting and collect the bulbs for storage.

Blind tulips

If tulips fail to flower, there are two possible causes. The young buds may have been destroyed by heavy frosts – in which case, provided the weather is milder next year, the bulbs should flower normally. Alternatively, if the bulbs that you planted were very small, they will need some time before they can produce flowers. Fertilise them well and they should flower normally after a year or two. In the meantime, to ensure a display, interplant the young bulbs with the largest ones you can find.

Small tulips

If your garden is very windy, then growing tall tulips such as the Darwin types can cause problems because they tend to be blown over. Smaller-growing varieties, such as 'Apricot Beauty', or the

species *Tulipa tarda*, *T. tubergeniana* or *T. turkestanica*, all of which attain a height of only 30cm (12in), would be much more suitable for growing in these conditions.

Avoid competition

It is better to grow species of tulips on their own instead of through other spring-flowering plants. The tulips will deteriorate rapidly if their leaves are covered by other foliage and thus prevented from receiving the light necessary to help the bulbs to form flowers for next year.

Garden secrets

Lifting and replanting

Do not leave bedding tulip bulbs in the ground. They will degenerate from year to year and will yield fewer and fewer flowers as time passes. Instead, wait until the foliage has yellowed before lifting them, then store them in a dry place until autumn, when they can safely be replanted. Unless the soil is very wet, wild species, or varieties that are derived from them, can remain in the garden all year round.

Make the right choice

Groups and varieties of tulips

Horticulturists have divided tulips into 15 divisions, each of which has special characteristics.

Division	Description	Varieties
Single early	Good for forcing, for early displays in tubs and bedding in exposed areas	'Apricot Beauty' (salmon pink and orange), 'Colour Cardinal' (red), 'Keizerskroon' (red, edged yellow)
Double early	Longer lasting than singles, these are ideal for containers and bedding	'Peach Blossom' (deep pink), 'Schoonoord' (white)
Triumph	Classic bedding tulips in a vast range of colours, but too tall for containers	'Dreaming Maid' (mauve, edged white), 'Garden Party' (carmine and white), 'Yellow Present' (yellow)
Darwin	Tall tulips with strong stems, ideal for bedding in most areas	'Apledoorn' (cherry red), 'Elizabeth Arden' (deep salmon), 'Golden Apledoorn' (deep yellow)
Single late	The best tulips to plant with wallflowers and for cutting. A large and diverse group	'Georgette' (yellow), 'Maureen' (white), 'Queen of Night' (deep maroon-purple)
Lily-flowered	Supremely elegant flared tulips. Ideal for late bedding or containers	'Ballerina' (blood-red on yellow), 'West Point' (yellow), 'White Triumphator' (white)
Fringed	Single flowers with attractive, frilly edges, good for bedding or cutting	'Fancy Frills' (pink and white), 'Hamilton' (deep yellow), 'Redwing' (deep red)
Viridiflora	Unusual single-flowered tulips with green streaks in the petals	'Artist' (purple and salmon), 'Greenland' (pink), 'Spring Green' (white)
Rembrandt	Single-flowered tulips in a wide variety of colours with stripes or streaks	Usually available in mixtures only
Parrot	Very colourful tulips with deeply cut petals streaked in a contrasting colour	'Estella Rijnveld' (red and white), 'Flaming Parrot' (red and yellow)
Peony-flowered	Double-flowered tulips for containers in sheltered positions, but not for bedding	'Angélique' (pale pink), 'Carnival de Nice' (white and deep red), 'Mount Tacoma' (white)
Kaufmanniana	Dwarf varieties, ideal for small containers and window boxes in windy places	'Ancilla' (pink and white), 'César Franck' (carmine and yellow), 'Shakespeare' (carmine and salmon)
Fosteriana	Relatively short varieties with vivid colours and tall, slim flowers	'Candela' (yellow), 'Princeps' (scarlet), 'Purissima' (white)
Greigii	Attractive mottled leaves. Ideal for small containers and for early bedding schemes	'Cape Cod' (apricot-edged yellow), 'Mary Ann' (deep pink and white), 'Red Riding Hood' (carmine red)
Other species	Including selections and hybrids	*Tulipa praestans* (six scarlet flowers per bulb); *T. sprengeri* (slender green buds open to scarlet); *T. batalinii* (pale lemon flower); *T. clusiana* (narrow flowers, white with scarlet stripe)

A brief history

Tulips from Amsterdam

When Dutch professor of botany Carolus Clusius brought home a collection of tulip seeds from Turkey in the late 16th century, from which he raised bulbs, he started a craze that has lasted until the present day. Within a few years, 'Tulipomania' swept Holland. Precious bulbs changed hands for hundreds of pounds and whole fortunes were wagered on new varieties. Most popular were the striped or blotched tulips, varieties that we now know were created through viruses rather than the skill of growers. Inevitably the frenzied speculation ended, but not before the tulip had become a firm favourite throughout Europe. Tulips are still widely grown and there are more than 100 species and 2,000 varieties to enjoy.

Leave the leaves

When tulip blooms have faded and have been deadheaded, you may dislike the untidy look of the old foliage, but do not be tempted to cut it down. The leaves replenish the bulb's strength and ensure that it will bloom again the following year.

Lifting and replanting

Do not leave bedding tulip bulbs in the ground. They will degenerate from year to year and yield fewer and fewer flowers as time passes. Wait until the foliage has yellowed before lifting them, then store them in a dry place until autumn, when they can be replanted. Unless the soil is very wet, wild species, or varieties derived from them, can remain in the garden all year round.

Turnips

Little and often

You can enjoy a constant supply of fresh turnips from summer through till winter if you sow a few seeds of early varieties in succession every three weeks from March until early July, then sow late varieties during July and August.

Sunshade companions

Sow turnips next to tall plants such as peas, runner beans, sweetcorn or tomatoes. These will all provide some welcome shade for the turnips and prevent them from becoming woody in the sun.

Make the most of your small plot

Interplant turnips and a fast-growing crop such as radishes to make double use of the space. The radishes are harvested young and will not impede the growth of the turnips.

Regular watering for tenderness

Give your turnips plenty of water. This will keep them tender and prevent them from running to seed.

Thinnings for soup

When thinning out maincrop varieties, do not discard the small turnips. These make a tasty addition to soups and stews, and the leaves can be used as 'greens'.

Keep turnips apart

Grow turnips and swedes away from other root vegetables. Despite appearances, both of these vegetables belong to the brassica family and are related to cabbages and cauliflowers. As such, they are susceptible to club root, a serious fungal disease. Grow them instead in the same section of the vegetable plot as other brassicas so that they can all be rotated together from year to year to prevent a build-up of club root in the soil. (See also *Cabbages*, *Vegetable gardens*)

Tops for crops

In August or September, sow quite thickly a maincrop variety of turnip, such as 'Imperial Green Globe', and allow the plants to grow on to provide spring greens in March. When the leaves have reached 10–15cm (4–6in) in length, cut them off close to the stems. They will regrow and, if given a liquid feed, should provide several harvests.

Protection from the sun

To protect turnip seeds from the sun, cover the bed with a piece of sacking after sowing. Keep it moist and check daily until the seeds germinate. Then remove the sacking.

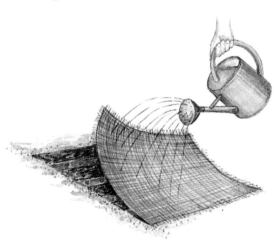

Underplanting

Carpet with periwinkle
In shady spots under bushes, you can make a fine spring showing with *Vinca minor* (lesser periwinkle). It comes in green-leaved and variegated forms and has blue, purple or white flowers. The pale mauve *V. difformis* grows well when used as underplanting and flowers in spring. It may also flower again in autumn.

Violet undercoat
An excellent specimen for underplanting is the rock garden violet *Viola riviniana* Purpurea Group. Its white-throated violet blooms rise above purple-tinged leaves, and it seeds freely and makes good ground cover.

Spreading scent
For scented underplanting, grow the spring-flowering lily of the valley. If grown under deciduous trees, which provide the best conditions, it will spread quickly by means of creeping horizontal rhizomes. An alternative is to plant sweet violets, which thrive in partial shade.

Vegetable gardens

Clues to the right spot
To grow vegetables in a new garden, choose the flattest, sunniest area. Look closely at the weeds growing on it. Creeping buttercups, common chickweed, dead nettles, ground elder and stinging nettles all thrive on rich soil that is eminently suitable for vegetables.

Vegetables for a new plot
However carefully you prepare your new vegetable garden, it is impossible to remove all the weeds and create a good soil structure straightaway. During the first year, plant vegetables that grow well in less than ideal conditions and also smother weeds. Courgettes, marrows, potatoes and pumpkins, for example, produce dense covers of leaves that help to keep weeds down. Do not plant carrots, cauliflowers, parsnips or tomatoes, which are difficult to grow well even in good soil. Grow onions from sets – small, immature bulbs available from garden centres – rather than from seeds. (*See also* **Ground cover**)

Test case
Most vegetables do best at a pH of 6.5 to 8, though potatoes prefer a more acid soil. Regular testing of the soil in your garden with an inexpensive kit will let you know if or when you need to 'sweeten' the soil by adding lime. (*See also* **Acid soil**, **Soil analysis**)

Buy healthy specimens
Vegetable plants bought at garden centres should be well grown and sturdy. Choose those that are grown singly in pots as this will minimise disturbance to the roots when the vegetables are planted out.

Feeding habits
In March, apply a general fertiliser to the vegetable plot before sowing or planting, or give a high-nitrogen feed to overwintered crops. Between March and September, feed crops with appropriate fertilisers. (*See also* **Fertilisers**)

Coarse feeding
Applying bulky organic matter annually benefits vegetable gardens. Use well-rotted farmyard or stable manure or provide nourishment by sowing a green manure crop such as alfalfa, clover, mustard or winter tares. (*See also* **Manures**, **Organic gardening**)

Beware club root
If club root has been a problem in your plot, do not grow mustard as green manure. It can act as a host to the disease.

Planting know-how
Plant low-growing vegetables on the sunny side of tall ones in your vegetable garden to ensure that both receive the light they need and that space is maximised. In addition, intercrop vegetables that reach maturity at different times. For example, shallots will be ready to harvest by the time tall asparagus begins to steal vital moisture and light. (*See also* **Shade**)

Fancy greens
If there is insufficient space to grow kale in the vegetable garden, grow 'Darkibor', 'Dwarf Green Curled' or the F₁ hybrid 'Showbor' in the flowerbed. They will provide an attractive, frilly, green edging.

Tall, vivid screens
Attractive, flowering vegetables help to create a visual link between the vegetable plot and the rest of the garden. As an ornamental divider, it is hard to beat tall, twining runner beans with their attractive scarlet or white flowers or

Garden secrets

Consult the compass
When sowing or planting out vegetables, if possible align the rows so that they run east to west. This ensures that the plants receive more sun than if the rows were aligned north to south, when the growing vegetables would shade each other at various times of the day.

climbing french beans, such as 'Purple Podded Climbing'. Both of these vegetables should also produce an excellent crop of beans.

Pretty peas
Plant a row of bushy asparagus peas along the edge of a vegetable patch close to a flowerbed. The scarlet flowers of these vegetables are followed by attractive, dainty pods.

Eye-catching dividers
The bright red leaf stalks and veins of the spinach beet 'Ruby Chard' and the purplish-red buds of Brussels sprouts 'Rubine', clustered beneath a loose head of large leaves, make attractive, low-growing dividers between a vegetable plot and the rest of the garden during autumn.

Cost-effective vegetables
If space in the vegetable garden is at a premium, you should try to grow crops that will provide fresher, more nutritious and cheaper produce than that available from the greengrocer or supermarket. Such crops include Kenyan (filet) beans, runner beans, chard, mangetout and snap peas, spinach and sweetcorn.

Make the right choice

The best and worst companion crops
Almost all vegetable crops need full light and a good soil to do well. They all benefit from a border of strong-smelling herbs, such as lavender, rosemary, sage and thyme, and from French marigolds planted in their midst. These plants support many beneficial insects and their smells confuse many pests. Many vegetables are prone to pest invasion and disease and if you wish to minimise problems and avoid using insecticides and fungicides, companion planting may be a better way of growing your vegetables than traditional crop rotation methods. Below are some good and bad combinations.

- Plant cucumbers, marrows and squashes with sweetcorn. These plants thrive in rich, moist conditions, and the dappled shade provided by the sweetcorn helps the roots of the cucumbers, marrows and squashes to stay cool.
- Grow maincrop potatoes with sweetcorn. Both do well in rich soil and are cleared at the same time.
- Combine broad beans and peas with potatoes. The legumes shelter the potato shoots, particularly those of early varieties. After cropping, broad beans and peas die away to feed the tubers of the maincrop potatoes.
- Sow tomatoes with basil on the asparagus bed, or with chilli peppers indoors. Each helps to reduce the many pest and disease attacks on tomatoes.
- Interplant the cabbage family and french beans. This significantly reduces pests.

- Grow sweet peas next to runner beans. They grow well together, and the scented sweet pea flowers attract pollinating insects, encouraging early bean pollination.
- Plant carrots, leeks and onions together. Their smells confuse each other's most common pests – carrot and onion flies – attracted by the scents of the vegetables.
- Do not plant beans, especially broad or french beans, with or near any of the onion family. Neither beans nor onion family members will thrive if they are grown too close together.
- Never put tomatoes near potatoes or allow either to follow the other in rotation. They are closely related and suffer from the same pests and diseases.
- Do not grow potatoes near marrows, raspberries, squashes or sunflowers. They make potatoes prone to blight.

Vegetable garden in miniature
Even in a flat or town house, it is fun to produce some nutritious home-grown vegetables. Miniature carrots, lettuces, peppers, tomatoes and other vegetables can be grown in hanging baskets, containers and window boxes. You can also grow miniature varieties in the garden if there is insufficient space for the cultivation of conventional vegetables. (See *also Hanging baskets*)

Fit in other crops
A crop-rotation system ensures that the large plant groups, the onion and cabbage families and root crops, for example, move round the vegetable garden, and are grown in the same area only once every three or four years. This prevents the build-up of pests and diseases and ensures that the soil receives, in turn, balanced amounts of well-rotted bulky organic matter, fertiliser and lime. It can, therefore provide the crops with the nutrients they need. In larger gardens, a four-year rotation cycle is ideal but where space is limited, use a three-year cycle instead. (See *panel, p. 316*)

Slight rotation
Gardeners who grow only small quantities of a few crops have less need to practise a crop rotation system than those who grow large quantities of vegetables. However, if space permits, it is still best to avoid growing the same crop in the same area of the vegetable garden two years in succession.

Vintage vegetable revival

Gardeners are turning towards vegetables relished by our forebears – including some long thought of as weeds. By doing so, old varieties are conserved and a valuable genetic base is maintained for breeding new plants that are resistant to bolting and that preserve flavour and colour.

The gardener's hunger for new plants (and the supplier's commercial need to produce them) has ensured that there is an ever-changing supply of ornamental plants for our gardens. In the kitchen garden, scientific research has developed new vegetables bred to provide pest and disease resistance, greater yield and, sometimes, improved flavour.

New developments that improve the gardener's yield are welcome, but there are also signs that the vegetables of yesteryear are starting to enjoy a revival. Colourful chicories are now widely available in supermarkets and finding favour in British gardens too. A few producers still supply unusual vegetables that were once popular in the walled Victorian gardens of the well-to-do, while the rarer sea kale and cardoon are returning to the seed catalogues, having long been out of fashion.

We can enjoy the novelty of growing some of these vegetables, such as Jerusalem artichokes, salsify, scorzonera and skirret, provided that we know what to do with them in the kitchen. Many old-fashioned vegetables are ideally suited to growing in modern-day small gardens and some are ornamental enough to be slipped into the flower garden.

Classic harvest Traditional vegetable varieties bring timeless style to the kitchen garden.

The root of the matter

Skirret is seldom seen today although it has been cultivated in Britain since at least the 16th century. Botanically known as *Sium sisarum*, skirret was valued as 'the sweetest, whitest and most pleasant of roots'. The fleshy, grey-skinned tubers are harvested after the first frosts. A relative of parsnips and carrots, its flavour falls between the two.

Skirret grows best in an open position in light, rich and well-manured soil that has good moisture retention. Set plants at 20cm (8in) intervals. Seed sown in spring will provide an autumn and winter harvest.

An old-fashioned root that has made a welcome return to greengrocers' shelves is the nutty-flavoured Jerusalem artichoke. Its name has no connection with the Holy City, but derives from its close relationship to the sunflower, known as *girasole* in Italy, meaning 'sun follower'. The flavour of the tubers is a little like that of true artichokes.

Plant Jerusalem artichoke tubers in spring, about 15cm (6in) deep and 30cm (12in) apart. They grow well in virtually any soil but are especially valuable in helping to break up heavy soil with their roots. The leafy stems can grow up to 2.4m (8ft) tall and provide an ideal windbreak in the kitchen garden if planted several rows deep. Cut back the stems to about 1.5m (5ft) in late summer. This will prevent development of the flowers and seeds, and divert energy down to the edible tubers. Harvest them fresh for the kitchen, digging up small clumps of tubers whenever required throughout winter.

Like the Jerusalem artichoke, both salsify and scorzonera belong to the daisy family. They are valued for their long, slender tap roots. Salsify roots resemble a thin, but elongated parsnip, while those of scorzonera have a distinctive black skin. Both vegetables grow best in deep, stone-free, freely draining soil that has not been recently manured.

Sow them in their growing position from mid to late spring for harvesting from mid October onwards. Leave the roots in the soil over winter, to be harvested as required, or lift and store them in boxes of sand or coir compost, in a cool shed or garage. If the roots are boiled, the skins should be left on to preserve flavour. The young flowering shoots (which are called chards) have a sweet flavour and can be used raw in salads, or lightly cooked.

Large-leaved lovelies

Crambe maritima (sea kale), which also grows wild on sandy and shingly beaches round Britain, was used by Victorian gardeners and is becoming popular again. Plant it in fertile, well-drained soil, with both lime and humus added. Crowns should be set 5cm (2in) deep, and 46cm (18in) apart, in a sunny position. Cover the plants in January as soon as they begin to show signs of growth to blanch the young shoots. Terracotta sea kale forcing jars are again being

Tasty roots Skirret (right) is a visual asset and a welcome winter vegetable.

Leafy line-up Grown for their roots, salsify and scorzonera also have edible flowering shoots

made by some potters, but a large, inverted flowerpot with a stone covering the hole will do just as well. Pick blanched stems when about 25cm (10in) long, pulling them from the base and taking care not to damage the crown. Cardoon, too, was very popular in Victorian kitchen gardens. This handsome perennial grows to around 1.8m (6ft) tall and is easy to propagate from seeds sown in spring. Bundle and tie the leaves together in September, wrapping with hessian to blanch the stems. After four weeks dig up the bundle and remove leaves and roots. Use the stems and inner-leaf midribs only; chop and boil in soups for 30 minutes.

Edible ornament Sometimes grown as a feature plant in the ornamental garden, the cardoon's boldly arching leaves make it an attractive addition to the vegetable plot.

One man's weed

The dandelion was highly valued in earlier centuries for its leaves, roots, flowers and even flower stalks. Varieties with large leaves were bred in the 19th century for use in salads, with named forms including 'Ameliore Geant', 'Thick-leaved Improved' and 'Vert de Montagny'. Bitterness in the leaves is removed by covering the plant with a pot to keep out the light. The roots of the dandelion are still grown commercially today for making a coffee substitute.

Blanching for tenderness Sea kale forcing jars are attractive and useful.

Few gardeners will need reminding that the tap roots readily produce new plants if any pieces are left in the soil. As a propagation method, root cuttings are more reliable than allowing the plants to set seed. Were the dandelion not such a rampant weed, it would be treasured for its sunny yellow flowers and general usefulness.

Small and tender

Vegetables are best harvested when they are small and tender. Kohlrabi, in particular, soon becomes woody in texture if it is left to grow too large. Regular picking increases the yield of repeat-cropping vegetables, such as beans.

No home for slugs

Make sure that grass is kept short at the edges of the vegetable garden. Slugs love to hide in long, damp grass that provides easy access to your vegetables.

Plants in harmony

Sow or plant flowers and herbs round the vegetable patch to attract beneficial insects such as ladybirds and hover flies. Dill, fennel, French marigolds and *Limnanthes douglasii* (poached egg plant) are all beneficial additions. (*See also* **Companion plants**)

Suitable deterrents

Do not crisscross nylon threads above rows of vegetable seedlings to deter birds; they will not break if the birds become entangled in them. Also avoid black cotton thread; although it breaks, it could still become tangled about birds' beaks or legs. White or coloured cotton threads are the best to use because birds can see them against the dark soil, and will avoid them. Better still, place cloches, horticultural fleece or galvanised or plastic netting over the rows of seedlings. Available from garden centres, these can be reused again and again.

Aphid watch

If your vegetable patch is surrounded by hedgerows, check them thoroughly in late March and early April for aphids and other pests. Covering your crops with horticultural fleece or cloches helps to prevent the pests from moving onto the vegetables as the soil warms up and the growing season gets under way.

Growing know-how

Three and four-year rotation cycles

Each of these rotation cycles will provide your soil with all the organic matter and nutrients needed and will reduce the build-up of soil-borne pests and diseases.

Three-year rotation cycle

Divide the area into three plots, 1, 2 and 3, and the crops into three groups, A, B and C.

Group A: Beans, celery, chicory, cucumbers, endives, garlic, leeks, lettuces, marrows, onions, peas, radishes, spinach, sweetcorn, tomatoes.
Group B: Beetroot, carrots, parsnips, potatoes, swedes, turnips.
Group C: Broccoli, Brussels sprouts, cabbages, cauliflowers, kale.

	Plot 1	Plot 2	Plot 3
1st year Add	A Compost or manure	B Compost, fertiliser, manure for potatoes	C Lime and fertiliser
2nd year Add	C Lime and fertiliser	A Compost or manure	B Compost, fertiliser, manure for potatoes
3rd year Add	B Compost, fertiliser, manure for potatoes	C Lime and fertiliser	A Compost or manure

Four-year rotation cycle

Divide the area into four plots, and the crops into four groups.

Group A: Broccoli, Brussels sprouts, cabbages, cauliflowers, kale, lettuces, turnips
Group B: Celery, garlic, leeks, onions, potatoes, shallots
Group C: Beetroot, carrots, chicory, parsnips, salsify, swedes
Group D: Beans, cucumbers, endives, marrows, peas, radishes, spinach, sweetcorn, tomatoes

	Plot 1	Plot 2	Plot 3	Plot 4
1st year Add	A Compost and lime	B Manure and fertiliser	C Compost and fertiliser	D Compost, manure, fertiliser
2nd year Add	D Compost, manure, fertiliser	A Compost and lime	B Manure and fertiliser	C Compost and fertiliser
3rd year Add	C Compost and fertiliser	D Compost, manure, fertiliser	A Compost and lime	B Manure and fertiliser
4th year Add	B Manure and fertiliser	C Compost and fertiliser	D Compost, manure, fertiliser	A Compost and lime

Wall planting

Make room to grow

When planting wall shrubs and climbers, dig a hole that is 30–50cm (12–20in) deep, and wide enough to accommodate the roots of the plant without causing restriction. Add plenty of moisture-retentive, bulky organic matter, such as well-rotted compost or manure, to the soil. Then, place the plant at least 30cm (12in) away from the wall. To encourage quick establishment, make sure that the plant leans slightly towards the wall and has its roots pointing towards the garden.

Avoid unwanted noise

A 20–30cm (8–12in) thick row of plants grown against the walls of a balcony, terrace or patio will absorb noise from traffic, garden machinery, local children and neighbours' pets.

Ageing new walls

To give the appearance of age to a new dry-stone wall – and make an eye-catching feature – pack soil between the stones and insert small plants or a few seeds in the crevices. Water these well, using a fine rose on the watering can or hose attachment until established.

Moisture retainer

To create a 'flowering' stone wall, press seeds of aubrietas, forget-me-nots, lobelias, love-in-a-mist, French marigolds and nasturtiums into handfuls of moist soil and roll the soil into balls. Wrap the balls in some moist moss, then gently press them into crevices in the wall. Water the planting area frequently; the moss keeps the soil damp and encourages the seeds to germinate.

Wall game Make the most of a wall, with aubrietas and alyssums scrambling down to troughs of flowers.

Cosmetic cover

Hide an ugly wall by growing evergreen plants with dense foliage on or over it. Camellias, ceanothus, euonymus, *Lonicera japonica* 'Halliana', pyracanthas and certain varieties of rose, such as 'Gloire de Dijon', 'Guinée' and 'Mme Alfred Carrière', are all particularly suitable for this.

Anchor young plants

Young plants growing from wall crevices can be washed out of their places by a bout of heavy rainfall or watering. Anchor them firmly until their roots grow by making small 'sausages' from children's modelling putty and tucking these round their necks. Nylon stockings can also be used.

Get an early harvest

If you have a south or west-facing wall, plant fruit trees and bushes against it. They will benefit from the protection and warmth that they receive, fruiting a little earlier and more regularly than plants in the open.

Make the right choice

Plants to grow in a wall

Fill crevices or holes in a garden wall with some of the following plants, which will provide an attractive cascade of bright colour.

Plants suitable for a sunny wall
Alyssum (dwarf and trailing varieties), *Aubrieta, Campanula* (dwarf and trailing varieties), *Cerastium, Corydalis, Erodium* (stork's bill), *Lewisia, Meconopsis cambrica* (Welsh poppy), *Phlox* (alpine species), *Silene acaulis* (moss campion), *S. uniflora* (sea campion), *Thymus* (thyme), *Valeriana* (valerian)

Plants suitable for a shady wall
Arabis, Asplenium adiantum-nigrum (black spleenwort), *Campanula, Corydalis lutea, Cymbalaria muralis* (ivy-leaved toadflax), *Polystichum setiferum* (soft shield fern), *Saxifraga* (saxifrage), *Viola* (pansy)

Make the right choice

Plants for growing against walls

North, south, east, west ... where do plants grow the best? Use the following plant guide to match shrubs and climbers, fruits and vegetables to the walls in your garden.

For north and east-facing walls
Shrubs
Berberis x stenophylla (barberry)
Camellia japonica
Chaenomeles (Japanese quince)
Cotoneaster horizontalis
Garrya elliptica
Ilex (holly)
Jasminum nudiflorum (winter jasmine)
Kerria japonica (Jew's mallow)
Pyracantha (firethorn)
Ribes sanguineum (flowering currant)

Climbers
Akebia quinata
Ampelopsis glandulosa var. brevipedunculata
Celastrus orbiculatus
Clematis alpina, C. macropetala, C. montana
Euonymus fortunei
Fallopia baldschuanica (Russian vine)
Hedera helix (ivy)
Hydrangea anomala ssp. petiolaris
Jasminum officinale (summer jasmine)
Lathyrus latifolius (everlasting pea)
L. periclymenum (honeysuckle)
Parthenocissus (Virginia creeper)
Pilostegia viburnoides
Rosa 'Danse du Feu'
Schisandra chinensis
Schizophragma integrifolium
Vitis coignetiae (ornamental vine)

For south and west-facing walls
Shrubs
Buddleja fallowiana var. alba
Ceanothus
Choisya ternata (Mexican orange blossom)
Clianthus puniceus
Cytissus battandieri
Daphne odora
Magnolia grandiflora
Viburnum x burkwoodii
V. macrocephalum

Climbers
Actinidia kolomikta (kolomikta vine)
Clematis cirrhosa var. balearica
Humulus lupulus (hop)
Lonicera x brownii 'Dropmore Scarlet'
Passiflora (passion flower)
Rosa
Wisteria

Annual climbers
Cucurbita pepo (gourd)
Lathyrus odoratus (sweet pea)
Thunbergia alata (black-eyed Susan)
Tropaeolum majus (nasturtium)

Fruit and vegetables
Courgettes, cucumbers, figs, french beans (climbing), grapes, peaches and runner beans

Cold comfort The bright berries of pyracantha (firethorn) bring welcome colour to a bare wall in winter.

Promote fruit and flowers
To encourage flowering and fruiting from the base of fruit trees or flowering shrubs or climbers grown against walls, attach lower branches to the wall at 90-degree angles to the trunks or stems.

Shrubs and climbers
To keep them growing close to the wall, the branches of wall shrubs need to be tied in to their supports. Climbers, however, have natural adaptations that enable them to cling to their supports without assistance.

Warm walls
Take advantage of any wall that is backed by a fire or a boiler to grow winter-flowering wall shrubs and climbers such as *Abeliophyllum distichum* and *Chimonanthus praecox*. These plants will thrive in the warmth that is transmitted through the brickwork.

Pot planting below a wall
If there is no soil at the base of the wall, use climbers planted in large tubs or troughs to provide colour and interest. Set the tubs or troughs, which should have drainage holes drilled into their bases, at the foot of the wall. Unless the plants are self-clinging, you will need to provide supports by stretching rows of wires, horizontally, about 30cm (12in) apart, across the wall. Water the plants frequently, particularly in hot weather, and protect them from frosts in winter by wrapping the containers in straw, bubblewrap or other insulating material. By selecting plants with varying flowering or berrying times, you can enjoy a display for several months of the year.

Plant a wall
Where no wall exists, create a floral border by using a trellis to provide a sturdy framework and closely planting climbing shrubs or roses at its base.

Stone wall trailers

Bush tomatoes can be grown as attractive trailing plants. If possible, plant them above a stone wall in a sunny position, which will accelerate ripening. Only certain bush varieties are suitable for this – including 'Tumbler', which is best used for a low wall. If you have a high wall, plant 'Red Alert' or 'Tornado', which both produce extensive growth.

Summer colour

Create a cascade of summer colour by fixing hanging baskets or wallpots to the wall. Fill these with a mixture of bedding plants such as trailing lobelia, petunias and ivy-leaved pelargoniums. (See also *Hanging baskets*)

See also Climbing plants, Trellises

Walls

Helping algae to grow

A thin paste of flour and milk laced with a concentrated liquid seaweed fertiliser painted over the surface of the stones or bricks in a wall will encourage the rapid growth of algae, moss and lichen.

Choice of bricks

Make sure that the bricks you choose to construct a garden wall are frost-resistant; some bricks are intended for internal use only. Engineering bricks are less attractive but a cheaper, durable option – especially if you plan to render the wall and they will not be seen.

Wall warmth

Brick walls absorb heat during the day and release it at night. Consequently, plants close to a wall will be protected from frost.

Trompe l'oeil

Add an attractive extra dimension to your garden by painting an arch or gateway with a rural vista beyond on a boundary wall. This also creates an illusion of space in a small garden.

Walnuts

Frost-free location

Juglans regia, the common walnut, must be grown in a frost-free place. Even so, you can expect to harvest nuts in mild years only, as a late frost can destroy a complete crop.

Stain-free harvesting

When harvesting fresh walnuts, spread polythene sheets on the ground round the foot of the tree when the nuts start to fall. Use a long stick to dislodge any that remain on the tree, then gather together the corners of the sheets. This will stop your hands getting stained.

Storing nuts

Unshelled walnuts will keep for over a year if preserved with salt. Pack alternate layers of nuts with an equal-parts mixture of coarse salt and coconut fibre, well-dried hardwood shavings, bulb fibre or sawdust, in either an earthenware pot or a slatted box. Push each layer down firmly. Then, cover the container and store it in a cool, dark place.

Cleaning the shells

Scrub walnut shells with a clean nailbrush that has been dipped in water. This will remove dirt

and reduce the risk of the walnuts developing mould. Leave them to dry at room temperature before you store them.

Time to prune

While a walnut tree is still small, frost may cause damage to its leading shoot. The young tree may then develop three or four shoots as replacements for the original, and an unsightly and, ultimately, unsafe tree may develop. Select a new shoot to become a replacement for the damaged leader and cut out the others in late autumn. Never prune a walnut tree in spring. This will cause bleeding from the pruning cut, which will weaken the tree and may lead to fungal infections.

Wasps

Protection in the garden

Cut the top from a plastic bottle, invert and replace it to make a funnel. Pour some sugared water into the bottle. Then, use a darning needle or skewer to pierce two holes near the top and thread a string through them. Use the string to hang the bottle from a tree branch. Wasps will be drawn to the sugary cocktail and will be unable to escape from the bottle.

Protecting fruit

Perforated plastic bags tied over unripe fruits will protect them from wasp attacks and hasten the ripening process.

Water gardens

Planting for ornamental effect

When planning a water garden, choose a mixture of aquatic plants with contrasting shapes and foliage colours. Plant water lilies with their soft pads of leaves, irises and grasses that have spiky foliage, and plants with a rounded shape such as kingcups. Include some variegated foliage to create interest when flowering has finished.

A clean-up before planting

Do not place aquatic plants in your pool immediately after buying them because the leaves and roots may contain larvae, eggs, or some undesirable pests. Make sure they are clean by washing them under the cold tap before setting them out.

Potting up aquatic plants

Always sieve garden soil that you want to use for potting up your pond plants. Any twigs, weeds or leaves left in the soil are likely to decompose and foul the water. Selecting heavier soils instead of those rich in organic matter will promote healthy growth of aquatic plants and, in addition, will help to prevent the water from turning green.

Broad picture

To make a pool look bigger than it is, plant shrubby dwarf junipers with silvery-blue foliage such as *Juniperus squamata* 'Blue Carpet' or 'Blue Star' round the edges.

Letting a plant root by itself

When planting a water lily, wrap the rhizome in a piece of turf and secure it with a rubber band or a length of plastic-covered wire, then toss the plant gently into the water. The weight of the piece of turf will cause the plant to sink to the bottom of the pool where it will take root and establish itself. To ensure that the plant will land the right way up and root properly, secure a small but reasonably weighty stone inside the lower part of the bundle.

Using the right containers

Do not use ordinary garden flowerpots for aquatic plants – they need to be planted in special lattice containers that allow the free passage of roots on all sides. Old nylon tights or stockings make good alternatives. Double the material back on itself several times to create a bag several layers thick, then put in the plant and fill with soil. Tie the bag loosely round the neck of the plant to prevent soil from escaping.

Planting where you cannot reach

To submerge a plant in the middle of a large pond, pot it up in a plastic lattice pot, then feed two lengths of strong, nylon string through the holes near the top of the pot, so you can suspend it over the pond. With the help of a friend on the other side, position the plant above where you want it to grow, then lower it into the water. Pull gently on one end of each string to remove it from the container.

Protecting plants from soil erosion

To prevent soil from being washed out of lattice pots, line them on the inside with pieces of material – sacking, gauze or muslin, for example – before potting up the aquatic plants. To prevent fish from disturbing and,

possibly, uprooting the plants before they become established, cover the surface of the soil with a layer of aquatic gravel.

Mini water garden

If you have a small garden, try creating a mini water garden in a half-barrel – you can buy one from a garden centre. Raise the mini pond on a plinth and plant it up with a dwarf or pygmy water lily, a miniature bulrush and other small varieties of aquatic plants.

Beware vigorous floaters

Some floating aquatic plants, such as *Azolla* (fairy moss) and *Lemna* (duckweed) are prolific growers that can become a nuisance; if left unchecked, they can cover the surface of a pond. As well as looking unattractive, they can turn a pond into a hazard as any visitors to your garden may not realise there is water underneath the foliage.

Letting fish make a meal of aphids

To eliminate water-lily aphids on aquatic plants, stretch a piece of mesh over the foliage then, using a hose, add water to raise the level of the pond. The mesh will ensure that the foliage is kept submerged. allowing the fish to eat the aphids. Remove it after a couple of days.

The right lilies for small ponds

Never overstock a pond with water lilies; the aim should be to cover about a half of the pond's surface with floating foliage. In small ponds, grow dwarf or pygmy varieties. Get advice from a specialist water-garden centre, and always remember that water lilies cannot tolerate turbulent water or constant splashes from jet nozzles and fountains.

Acclimatising deep-water plants

Vigorous deep-water aquatic plants such as water lilies can grow in water as deep as 1m (3ft), but they need to be acclimatised gradually to their final positions. To do this, stand the plant first on a stack of bricks so that the leaves are just below the surface, then remove the bricks one by one as the leaf stems develop. In a large pond, where access can be difficult, suspend the plant on ropes held taut by a stake at each side of the pond, and lower it into the water gradually.

Heads above water

If your pool is too deep for some of your plants, simply stand some bricks in the water up to the desired height and place your pots on top.

Protect plants from fish

Some fish, especially larger ones such as koi carp, forage round the roots of aquatic plants, which can hinder their growth. To prevent this, cover the rootballs of the plants with flexible, fine-mesh, plastic netting, or use the netting to fence off an area of the pond to keep exclusively for plants.

See also **Irises (waterside)**, **Ponds**

Watering equipment

Thrifty winder

When not in use, wind your garden hose round a wheel rim and hang it on a large hook or bracket, securely attached to the wall near your outdoor tap, or in the garden shed. This stops any kinks, which can cause punctures.

Perforated hoses

If you have an outdoor tap, investing in a trickle watering system, or seep hose, can save you much time and effort when watering the garden, and will also prevent water from being wasted. These systems can be controlled automatically by a timer or operated manually and are particularly useful in narrow borders where they allow water to penetrate the soil only where it is needed.

To and fro An oscillating sprinkler saves time and effort by watering a wide area with a gentle spray.

Watering cans

Use a separate watering can for applying weedkillers. This should be of a different colour from cans that are used for watering, or clearly labelled with an indelible marker or gloss paint. Wash out the can after use and keep it out of reach of children and animals.

Oscillating sprinklers

These hose attachments are available in various sizes, and most are adjustable according to the width, height and direction of spray needed. They are particularly useful for large areas, such as lawns.

See also **Water sources**

Watering indoors

Rainwater for lime haters

Tap water is suitable for most house plants, with the exception of lime haters. In soft water areas, they can be given water from the tap, but in other areas, the water may cause the leaves to turn yellow. Rainwater is best for lime haters, and should be collected in a bowl. Avoid using stagnant rainwater from a butt because this may contain organisms that cause root disease.

Test the temperature

Never water tender indoor plants with cold water. Let the water stand overnight so that it reaches room temperature, or add a little boiled water that has been allowed to cool.

Watering needs of pot plants

The compost surrounding most pot plants should be kept moist but not saturated, and all plants will require less-frequent watering during their dormant season. Follow the watering guidelines on the plant's label.

The fingertip test

If the surface of the compost appears to be dry, push your finger into the pot to the depth of your fingernail. If your finger remains dry, depending on the needs of the plant and time of year, it is probably time to water.

Water signals

Use one of the products, available from garden centres, that, when inserted into the pot, gradually changes colour as the soil dries out. Treat it as an indication only, and water according to the individual needs of the plant.

Water retention

When repotting, add water-storing granules to the compost. These retain moisture and can help to reduce the frequency of watering. They are particularly useful for vigorous plants in pots, which can dry out very quickly when in active periods of growth.

Small is best

To make sure that the water goes directly where it is needed, round the base of the plant, use a small watering can with a long, slender spout. This prevents splashes of water from landing on either the plant's leaves or your furniture.

Short circuit

Do not place a plant on top of the television. Not only are the changes in temperature bad for the plant but if water spills into the television, it may cause a short circuit.

Water on the surface

If water sits on top of the compost and does not drain through the pot, either the compost has become compacted or a build-up of salts has caused a crust to form on its surface. Break the crust and relieve the compaction by using a small table fork to rake over the surface of the compost.

Water well before feeding

To ensure that plants do not receive overconcentrated doses of liquid feed, which can be harmful, water thoroughly a few days before feeding to ensure that the compost is moist when the fertiliser is applied.

Weekend bath-time

If you will be away from home for a short time, provide humidity for your plants by lining the bath with old towels. Sprinkle water over them, then stand your plants on top. Do not close the bathroom blinds or curtains as your plants will need light.

Pot-grown azaleas

These plants are frequently supplied in clay pots that are prone to rapid drying out. The best method of watering is to plunge the pot into a bowl of water and leave to soak for 2 to 3 hours before removing and draining.

Watering trays and seedlings

Plants in small pots and trays of seedlings need special care while you are away. Buy a length of capillary matting from a garden centre. Lay it on the draining board with 30–38cm (12–15in)

hanging into the sink, wet it thoroughly and stand your pots and trays on it. Fill the sink and place the overhanging matting in the water. The water will be sucked up by the matting and absorbed by the potting compost through the drainage holes in the pots. Large, or clay, pots may need help to draw up enough moisture. Insert wicks made of strips of capillary matting into the drainage holes.

Saucer size

If you water your house plants from below, make sure the saucer under each pot is large enough to hold sufficient water to soak the rootball. If others have agreed to take care of your plants while you are away, provide a large saucer for each pot and fill these with water, thus saving time and trouble.

Avoid waterlogged roots

When watering from below, do not allow the plant to stand in water for prolonged periods, as this may result in root rot. Any water remaining in the saucer an hour or two after watering should be poured away.

See also **A garden in the home pp. 154–9**, *Holidays*

Watering outdoors

Water to every plant

Before planting up a strawberry or parsley pot, cut a length of plastic tubing a little shorter than the height of the pot. Using a heated skewer, make some holes in an upward direction along its length. Block the bottom with a cork, then stand it upright in the centre of the pot and pack the growing medium around it. The top should protrude slightly above the surface of the compost. Fill the tube

with water and allow it to seep slowly into the pot. In this way, the water will reach every planting pocket.

The right time

Water in the morning during spring and autumn. This protects the foliage from the damaging effects of night frosts by allowing it to dry in the relative warmth of the day. During the summer, water in the evening when the sun has gone down. If water is applied in the heat of the day during the summer, much of it is lost to evaporation and your plants may also be scorched.

The right amount

Water the soil copiously every week, applying sufficient water to penetrate right down to the plants' roots. It is a mistake to sprinkle on a daily basis as this merely dampens the top layer of soil and encourages plants to grow roots near to the surface.

Regulating water

Watering through a coarse rose is suitable for established plants but use a fine rose when watering seeds and seedlings. This finer spray of water will not disturb the compost and flatten young plants.

Make the most of it

Mulch well-watered soil with a thick layer of well-rotted compost or bark chips. Provided that the layer is at least 5cm (2in) deep, it will limit evaporation and suppress weeds that steal moisture needed by your plants.

Watering in full sun

If you must water in full sun, be careful. Any droplets that fall on leaves can act as magnifying glasses and may cause scorching.

Over the top

When using a sprinkler to water tall plants, position it a few metres or feet away. This will ensure that the water falls from above the plants, allowing it to run down the stems to moisten the soil beneath the foliage canopy.

Thirsty vegetables

Fleshy vegetables such as marrows and tomatoes should never be allowed to dry out. To ensure that enough water reaches the roots, push a large clay pot or an inverted bottomless plastic bottle, with the top removed, into the soil close to each plant and pour the water directly into it.

Water sources

Know the law

Take care when using water. Most sources of water are the property of the water company. You have the right to use water running beneath your own land unless it connects with the company's supply, in which case you can be prevented from using it. If in doubt, consult your local water company.

Hoses and sprinklers

Check your water company's regulations before using a hose or sprinkler. Regulations vary throughout the country – some companies have abolished the sprinkler licence, others have put water-rate payers on water meters. During a drought, they may ban the use of hoses and sprinklers. Special rates apply for garden swimming pools.

Garden tap fittings

By law, an outside threaded tap should be fitted with a double check valve – this is simple to fit and can be bought from hardware shops. It will prevent the backflow of water from hosepipes that could contaminate domestic water supplies.

Conserving rainwater

Collect and store rainwater if possible. Downpipes on houses, garden buildings and outhouses can be modified to feed water butts or storage tanks. Link several butts together with connecting hoses and use a rain-saver to prevent overflowing. Cover water butts, as direct sunlight promotes the growth of algae. This attracts egg-laying insects and the resulting larvae will contaminate the water.

Weather lore

Garden forecasts

Centuries of observing the manner in which certain trees and plants react to or reflect imminent changes in the weather led plant growers to compose little couplets, many of which contain more than a grain of truth.

Pimpernel, pimpernel, tell me true
Whether the weather be fine or no.
The scarlet pimpernel flowers in June. On fine mornings it stands with flowers fully open, but when humidity is about 80 per cent, it closes its petals to protect the pollen. Other flowers that close on, or before, rainfall include daisies and tulips. Lime leaves cover the flowers before rain and clover leaves contract before a storm.

When the dew is on the grass
Rain will never come to pass.
Dew on the grass at the end of a summer's day indicates a settled atmosphere – dew is caused by the cooling earth condensing moisture in the air. The necessary heat loss from the ground cannot occur if there are insulating clouds.

Ne'er cast a clout till May is out.
Whether the old adage refers to the month or to hawthorn (may tree) blossom does not really matter, for there is sometimes a chilly snap at the end of May that can delay the opening of flowers.

Beware the blackthorn winter.
A spring-like spell in mid March can bring the blackthorn into bloom when often some of the worst weather of the year is still to come.

Spring starts when you can put your foot on
12 daisies.
Daisies, among the earliest of spring flowers, often emerge in clumps on the lawn.

When the leaves show their undersides
Be very sure that rain betides.
High humidity and strong winds before rain make stalks more pliable and toss branches about, showing the undersides of the leaves.

War on weeds

Uncaring of gardening opinion, weeds are simply highly successful plants that will overwhelm all less rampant, but more desirable, species. Unless vigilance is constant, they may quickly take over the garden.

Perennial and annual weeds must be controlled, otherwise they will compete with plants for food and water and eventually overrun a garden altogether. The weeds shown here are among the most common to be found in flowerbeds and vegetable plots and need to be eliminated as soon as possible. There are three ways of getting rid of them: the hard way of pulling them up by hand; the relatively expensive way of using a chemical weedkiller; and, for many of them, the easy way – of hoeing them out as soon as they appear. Much depends on the type of weed.

Perennial weeds

Perennial weeds, including bindweed, dandelion and dock, multiply by invasive rhizomes, tubers, roots and bulbs. Hoeing and digging may only spread the weeds further, so the only answer is chemical weedkillers. There are three main types. Contact weedkillers, such as paraquat, kill leaf growth. Systemic weedkillers like glyphosate work through the leaves to the roots and kill the whole plant. These are selective, in that there are types that work only on broad-leaved or narrow-leaved plants. Sodium chlorate and other residual weedkillers are applied to the soil to attack the roots. Probably the most useful to gardeners are contact and systemic weedkillers, which are inactivated when they reach the soil and will not harm plants nearby. Residual weedkillers tend to creep outwards from the point of application and must be used with care near other plants.

Large bindweed (*Calystegia sepium*) Like small bindweed, can be controlled by spot treatment with glyphosate.

Small bindweed (*Convolvulus arvensis*) Difficult to eradicate by digging. Control by repeated spot treatment with glyphosate or glyphosate-trimesium.

Dandelion (*Taraxacum officinale*) Usually easy to dig up but can be troublesome when growing among the roots of fruit bushes or trees. Control by spot applications of glyphosate or glyphosate-trimesium.

Creeping buttercup (*Ranunculus repens*) Generally most troublesome on poorly drained soil. Control by spot treatment with glyphosate or glyphosate-trimesium.

Broad-leaved dock (*Rumex obtusifolius*) Grows again and again from small pieces of root. Control by spot treatment with mecoprop, MCPA, dicamba or glyphosate-trimesium.

Curled dock (*Rumex crispus*) All docks can be controlled by repeated use of glyphosate.

Horsetail (*Equisetum arvense*) Has spore-bearing single stems in spring and branching, non-fertile branches in summer. Control by repeated applications of glyphosate or glyphosate-trimesium.

Creeping thistle (*Cirsium arvense*) So called because it reproduces by creeping rhizomes, also by seed. Control by spot treatment with glyphosate or glyphosate-trimesium.

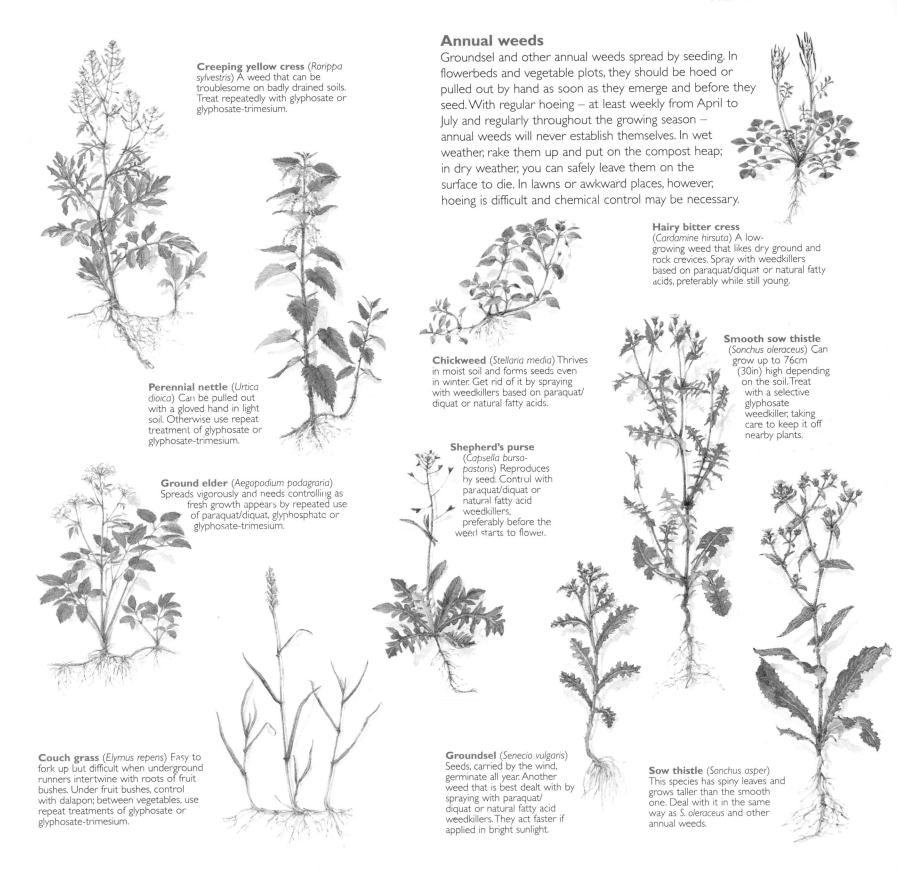

Creeping yellow cress (*Rorippa sylvestris*) A weed that can be troublesome on badly drained soils. Treat repeatedly with glyphosate or glyphosate-trimesium.

Perennial nettle (*Urtica dioica*) Can be pulled out with a gloved hand in light soil. Otherwise use repeat treatment of glyphosate or glyphosate-trimesium.

Ground elder (*Aegopodium podagraria*) Spreads vigorously and needs controlling as fresh growth appears by repeated use of paraquat/diquat, glyphosphate or glyphosate-trimesium.

Couch grass (*Elymus repens*) Easy to fork up but difficult when underground runners intertwine with roots of fruit bushes. Under fruit bushes, control with dalapon; between vegetables, use repeat treatments of glyphosate or glyphosate-trimesium.

Annual weeds

Groundsel and other annual weeds spread by seeding. In flowerbeds and vegetable plots, they should be hoed or pulled out by hand as soon as they emerge and before they seed. With regular hoeing – at least weekly from April to July and regularly throughout the growing season – annual weeds will never establish themselves. In wet weather, rake them up and put on the compost heap; in dry weather, you can safely leave them on the surface to die. In lawns or awkward places, however, hoeing is difficult and chemical control may be necessary.

Hairy bitter cress (*Cardamine hirsuta*) A low-growing weed that likes dry ground and rock crevices. Spray with weedkillers based on paraquat/diquat or natural fatty acids, preferably while still young.

Chickweed (*Stellaria media*) Thrives in moist soil and forms seeds even in winter. Get rid of it by spraying with weedkillers based on paraquat/diquat or natural fatty acids.

Shepherd's purse (*Capsella bursa-pastoris*) Reproduces by seed. Control with paraquat/diquat or natural fatty acid weedkillers, preferably before the weed starts to flower.

Smooth sow thistle (*Sonchus oleraceus*) Can grow up to 76cm (30in) high depending on the soil. Treat with a selective glyphosate weedkiller, taking care to keep it off nearby plants.

Groundsel (*Senecio vulgaris*) Seeds, carried by the wind, germinate all year. Another weed that is best dealt with by spraying with paraquat/diquat or natural fatty acid weedkillers. They act faster if applied in bright sunlight.

Sow thistle (*Sonchus asper*) This species has spiny leaves and grows taller than the smooth one. Deal with it in the same way as *S. oleraceus* and other annual weeds.

Weather stations

Met checks
Rather than putting your trust entirely in published or broadcast weather forecasts, with a few items of basic equipment you can create your own meteorological station. It is worth doing because local weather conditions can sometimes differ greatly from those forecast for a general area.

Frost warning
Remember, when taking temperatures, that a thermometer fixed at 1.5m (5ft) above ground records a temperature higher than that at soil level. Thus, a reading of 5°C (41°F) could mean the temperature is 3°C (37°F) on the ground, and a ground frost is imminent. Also remember that temperatures taken in the shade are more relevant than those in sunlight.

There she blows A weather vane, placed on top of the roof or in an open position away from trees, is a decorative way of showing the wind direction.

Make a rain gauge
A rain gauge can be constructed easily out of a 1 litre (1¾ pint) plastic bottle. Cut off the top quarter and slide it, upside-down, into the lower portion to act as a funnel. Tape the edges together and stick small strips of waterproof tape onto the side of the bottle 5mm (¼in) apart, as a scale. If the base of the bottle is opaque, fill it with water to the point where the clear plastic begins and treat that as zero on the scale. Stand the gauge in the garden and, after it has rained, check how far up the scale the water reaches. Record the measurement and empty the gauge to the zero mark again.

Identify microclimates
Microclimate identification is best done with a maximum-minimum thermometer, obtainable at garden centres. Its purpose is to record the highest and lowest temperatures, over a given period, in the spot where you placed it. For example, to discover if the place where you plan to plant apple trees is a frost pocket, leave the thermometer there for a couple of days at blossom time. As the temperature rises, a marker in the right-hand column is pushed up to indicate the highest reading. When the temperature falls, the left-hand marker is pushed towards the bulb to show the lowest level. Use the thermometer in the greenhouse, or to discover the temperature to which house plants on window ledges are exposed on chilly nights.

Weather prophet
Buy a barometer to help you to predict the weather. It records changes in atmospheric pressure levels. The weather shown on the dial is often not particularly accurate. More important is the speed with which the indicator changes over time. If it remains steady, good weather can be expected, if it drops rapidly, expect unsettled conditions.

Weeding

Return the goodness to the soil
In warm, dry weather, leave small, uprooted weeds on top of the soil where they will quickly dry out. In wet weather, do not leave uprooted weeds on the soil as they will re-root. Gather them up and bury them in the compost heap where they will quickly rot down, but if they have run to seed, dispose of them in the dustbin or at your council tip.

Deadly dandelion
Weeds that have long taproots, such as dandelions, can survive without soil or water for many months. Since it is unlikely that the compost heap will heat up enough to destroy them, it is safer to put them in the dustbin.

Take up the hoe
Frequent hoeing of the soil kills existing and germinating weeds. If left undisturbed, weeds will deprive plants of nutrients and moisture.

Avoid hoeing wet soil
Do not hoe when the soil is wet, because it will result in weeds being transplanted from one place to another unless they are cleared away. After being disturbed they re-root easily in the loose soil. If possible, always hoe in hot, dry conditions.

Weed cycle
Digging brings dormant weed seeds to the soil surface where they will germinate. A couple of weeks after digging, check the site and hoe off any small seedlings that have developed.

Sharp practice
A blunt hoe makes for heavy work and will merely bruise and bend rather than slice through the weeds in your garden. Make sure that you sharpen your hoe frequently, using a coarse stone sharpener or a metal file.

Handle with care
Pernicious perennial weeds such as *Elymus repens* (couch grass), *Equisetum arvense* (horsetail), and *Calystegia sepium* and

Weed before seed

Always remove weeds before they have the chance to flower. Then there is no risk of 'one year's seeds becoming seven years' weeds', as the old saying goes.

Convolvulus arvensis (bindweed) develop vast underground networks of roots. Treat them with weedkiller or remove them carefully by hand, as the smallest piece of root left in the soil quickly throws up new shoots. Dig out all fragments with a fork, and leave them in the sun until they shrivel, then burn or dispose of them at the rubbish tip.

Frosted chickweed

Take advantage of a period of hard frost to get rid of Stellaria media (chickweed) by trampling it down hard while the clumps are frozen. Already weakened by the frost, it will rarely survive such harsh treatment.

Blanket coverage

To clear previously uncultivated land of perennial weeds, cut down any tall specimens, then cover the area with old carpet, thick cardboard or heavy-duty black polythene. Weight down the covering with bricks to prevent it from being blown about by the wind. Total exclusion of light will kill most weeds within a season but some more persistent varieties, such as dandelions, can take up to a year to die out completely.

Potato cleaner

A crop of potatoes will cure a rash of annual weeds. Regular hoeing and earthing up of the crop stops the weeds' roots from gaining a foothold in the soil, while the potato's foliage cuts out light and limits new weed growth.

Green manures

Keep weeds out of fallow land with green manure crops such as buckwheat, tares, or phacelia. These fast-growing crops smother weeds and, when the growing season is over, can be dug into the soil or placed on the compost heap. (See also **Organic gardening**)

Clearing perennial weeds

Before sowing a new lawn, dig over the area and remove perennial weeds. Leave the soil undisturbed to give annual weed seeds time to germinate. Hoe the plot two or three times to kill them off before raking it level.

See also **Companion plants**

Weedkillers

Paths and driveways

Use a brand of weedkiller that attacks weeds at the germination stage as well as those that are already established. Apply it early in the season before the weeds have begun to take hold and your path or drive should remain weed-free for several months.

Creeping weedkiller

Never apply the total weedkiller sodium chlorate near garden plants that you wish to retain. It kills any plants it touches. As it seeps through the soil it can also kill plants some distance away from the area to which has been applied.

Beware of accidents

Take care when applying weedkillers. Should a cultivated plant be treated accidentally, spray the leaves immediately and soak the soil thoroughly with clean water to minimise absorption. Water thoroughly 24 hours later.

Light exclusion

Bulbil-forming weeds such as Oxalis corymbosa and Ranunculus ficaria (lesser celandine) are difficult to eradicate. The tiny bulbils are easily detached from the parent plant and spread when digging. Thick mulches, at least 23cm (9in) deep, can 'starve out' infestations over time, but buried bulbils may survive for several years.

Take care with lawns

Combined weed-and-feed treatments will save time and effort, but take care to apply them only during rainy weather or after thoroughly watering the lawn. Dry, slow-growing grass cannot absorb chemicals and is therefore likely to be scorched. The ingredients will degrade over time so add grass and weed mowings to the compost heap rather than using them as a mulch.

Safety first with weedkillers

Here are seven rules you should follow when using weedkillers:

- Check that you have the appropriate product for the problem.
- Read the instructions and precautions carefully and follow them to the letter.
- Keep all chemicals in their original containers and store them out of reach of children and pets.
- Wear gloves and protective clothing.
- Keep separate watering cans and sprayers specifically for weedkillers and wash them out thoroughly after use.
- Never apply weedkillers on a windy day.
- Never mix products together unless advised to do so on the label.

Watch out for bulbs

Do not use selective weedkillers on lawns where naturalised bulbs are grown, except when the bulbs are dormant. Weeds in these area should be treated with a spot-weeder, which can be painted or squirted directly onto the leaves.

Protection for borders

Cover cultivated plants with plastic bags or cardboard boxes to protect them from weedkillers when you are spraying nearby. To prevent drift, spray only on windless days.

Making a quick killing

A bramble or thistle in the flower border can be killed quickly and safely with the help of a large, bottomless plastic bottle. Without removing all the leafy growth, cut back the weed to a few inches above the ground. Wait until it has resprouted, then slip the bottle over it. Spray a systemic weedkiller carefully through the neck of the bottle, then replace the stopper.

Cleaning up hedges

Perennial weeds, such as brambles and ivy, at the base of a hedge are easier to deal with if the area has first been cleared of all debris such as stones, dead twigs and leaves. Screen the base of the hedge before applying any weed treatment.

See also **Chemicals, Spraying, War on weeds** *pp. 324–5*

Weeping trees

A green hideaway

Create a secluded and shady seating area by cutting away the inner branches from a large, mature weeping tree and constructing a low bench seat round the trunk. For comfort underfoot, cover the soil with timber decking or paving slabs.

Make the right choice

Weeping trees for every garden

A weeping tree adds character, charm and variation of form to the garden. Choose from the selection below.

Betula pendula **'Youngii'**
Young's weeping birch makes an excellent centrepiece for a lawn.

Fagus sylvatica **'Purpurea Pendula'**
The weeping form of common purple beech is clothed in beautiful purple-red leaves throughout the summer.

Laburnum alpinum **'Pendulum'**
Weeping Scotch laburnum is known as the golden rain tree because of its cascades of yellow flowers. All parts are poisonous, so position it with care.

Prunus subhirtella **'Pendula Rubra'**
Beautiful rose-pink flowers are borne in April on this ornamental cherry.

Pyrus salicifolia **'Pendula'**
Weeping willow-leaved pear with silvery leaves and creamy-white flowers in spring, followed by small, inedible pears.

Salix x sepulchralis **'Chrysocoma'**
This willow makes a good specimen tree to overhang a large pond. Suitable only for a large garden.

When the willow stops weeping

Upright growth on a willow is natural. Prune the upright branches to reduce its final height, but if you have room, do nothing, as the tree will soon resume its weeping habit.

Solving the mowing problem

Before cutting the grass beneath a weeping tree, gather the branches together and tie them to the trunk with strong cord or rope. This will enable you to mow round the tree without damaging the weeping canopy.

See also **Silhouettes and styles** *pp. 300–302*

Whiteflies

A yellow trap

Whiteflies find yellow irresistible. To control these pests in the greenhouse, use a proprietary yellow sticky trap, or paint a piece of card yellow and cover it with non-drying glue.

Deter the pests

Plant *Tagetes patula* (French marigold) in the greenhouse borders or in pots near the door. This will help to keep whiteflies away.

Wild-flower meadows

Attracting wildlife to your garden

To create a haven for wildlife in your garden, turn an uncultivated patch of soil into a wild-flower meadow. By recreating the type of habitat found in nature, you will attract butterflies, birds and small animals that rely on flowers and grasses for their food. (*See also* **A garden haven for wildlife** *pp. 196–7*)

Poor soil is best

You do not require any particular type of soil for a wild-flower meadow – in fact, the lower the fertility the better. Remove the top 5–7.5cm (2–3in) from the uncultivated patch and transfer it to your vegetable plot. Rake the exposed surface lightly to form a seedbed, removing any stones. Before sowing, allow a week or two for deep-rooted weeds to grow then either dig them out or treat them with an appropriate weedkiller as soon as they appear. (See also **Weeding**, **Weedkillers**)

Mixing grass and flower seeds

The best time to sow seeds for a new wild-flower meadow is late September when the soil is warm and when there is less chance of the seedlings being dried out by hot sunshine. Use a standard meadow mixture of grass and flower seeds – usually made up of 80 per cent grass and 20 per cent flowers – and sow it shallowly. Water the meadow regularly until the new plants are established.

Mowing a spring-flowering meadow

Plants from seeds sown the previous autumn will be well developed by the spring. Delay mowing until June to give the flowers time to produce seeds. Set the mower blades to a height of 5–7.5cm (2–3in). After mowing, leave the cuttings for one or two days so that any seeds can ripen and drop to the ground to develop, then clear the cuttings so that excess nutrients are not returned to the meadow. Cut the meadow at the same height two or three times during that year. In later years, one or two cuts may be all that is needed, depending on the growth of the plants.

Planting an existing lawn

To establish a wild-flower meadow in an existing lawn, first rake the lawn, then water it copiously and sprinkle the seeds at the rate recommended by the suppliers. To plant the lawn with pot-grown wild flowers, first remove an area of turf equal in diameter to the pot. Using a trowel, dig a hole in the soil, then remove the plant carefully from its pot and place it in the hole. Firm the rootball in and water it well.

See also **Creating a wild-flower garden pp. 332–3**

Willows

Thirsty willows

When selecting a tree for your garden, bear in mind that the roots of a willow may travel a long way in search of water. Water mains and drainpipes are not out of bounds for them. Drains, particularly old ones, leak slightly and the roots will soon head for them and may cause lasting damage. (See also **Trees**)

Small and stunning

The purple-brown stems and silvery white catkins of Salix hastata 'Wehrhahnii' make it a very decorative willow. As it grows to a height of 1.2–1.5m (4–5ft) and has a spread of 1.5–1.8m (5–6ft), it is a suitable specimen for growing in a small garden.

Winter colour

Bring some dramatic colour to the winter garden by planting Salix alba 'Britzensis' (white willow), whose young stems are a vivid orange, and S. daphnoides (violet willow), which has attractive purple-violet stems.

Pruning for colour

To ensure that a willow continues to produce its young, coloured stems, you will need to prune it annually in February or March. If you require a bushy shape, with all the stems growing from soil level, cut it back almost to the ground – a process known as stooling. If, however, you require a taller tree, wait until the young plant has reached 1.2m (4ft) in height, then cut the side and top growth back to the trunk. The result of either of these pruning methods will be a profusion of vigorous, brightly coloured stems that will create a show of interest in the garden throughout the winter months.

Taking cuttings

When cutting back a willow in February or March, use the prunings for hardwood cuttings. Cut each stem into 30cm (12in) sections. Insert these, to a depth of 23cm (9in), in a slit or trench. Leave the cuttings until the autumn when they should have rooted. They can then be moved to permanent positions. (See also **Cuttings**)

Wind

Extra protection

Where there is space, hedges of different heights will reduce the strength of the wind more effectively than one thick hedge. Grow a low hedge of sturdy wind-resistant shrubs, such as Berberis darwinii, holly or beech, as a first line of defence. Next, plant your main hedge, using plants that will grow to between 1.8m (6ft) and 4m (13ft) high. If you have a large garden, add a belt of trees that will reach a height of between 5.5m (18ft) and 9m (30ft). The triple hedge arrangement will provide good protection for delicate plants for a distance of up to 100m (110yd).

Natural barrier

Grow a thick hedge to protect the plants in your garden from high winds. The twigs and foliage of the hedge will act as an effective filter, reducing wind speed and minimising damage to your plants.

Plan hedge height

A reasonably thick hedge will protect an area of five to ten times its height, and reduce the wind speed by 60 per cent. Before choosing your plants, calculate the hedge height needed to protect your garden. If you have a large garden, remember that tall hedges have negative effects too – for example, they cast shade and take nutrients from the soil. Any plants growing on the shaded side of a hedge may lean forwards in their search for light. This can be prevented by staking the plants to keep them upright.

Screen with a view

Where a tall hedge would block an attractive view, trees such as silver birches or *Amelanchier lamarckii* (snowy mespilus), which have fairly light foliage, can be planted to filter out wind.

Protect the young

While a hedge is becoming established, give it shelter from the wind. Attach plastic windbreak netting to posts hammered firmly into the ground. Position these on the windward side of the hedging plants and leave the screen in place during their first two winters. More attractive, but also more expensive, are willow hurdles, which are available from garden centres.

Netting windbreak

If lack of space prevents you from growing a natural hedge in your garden, make a windbreak by attaching special fine-mesh or broad-banded plastic netting to strong posts. This is available in different densities. For very exposed sites, select a mesh or netting that offers a high level of protection.

Caring for young plants

Any young plants in an exposed garden are extremely vulnerable to high winds. Protect them while they are establishing themselves by surrounding them with a screen of plastic netting supported on posts that have been driven firmly into the ground.

Vulnerable vegetables

Tall-growing vegetables such as tomatoes and Brussels sprouts can suffer badly in exposed gardens. Try growing one of the shorter varieties of Brussels sprouts such as 'Peer Gynt' and grow bush, not upright, tomatoes. Continual wind-buffeting and moisture loss can reduce the yield of many vegetable crops significantly.

Strong support

In an exposed site, semi-mature trees may need support. This can be done by triple guying: support the tree using a firm collar around the trunk, attach wires to this, then to stakes in the ground.

Shelter for bees

Bees, which pollinate fruit trees and bushes, do not like flying in wind. It makes sense then to provide effective wind screening in exposed gardens. This is likely to be rewarded by considerable crop increases, because bees prefer open, undamaged flowers to those that have been wind-battered.

See also **Hedges**

Window boxes

A succession of colour

Use liners to ensure that there is no break in floral continuity when removing exhausted plants and changing displays in your window boxes. The liners, which are available from large garden centres, are made from compressed cardboard or paper. Plant the displays early and grow them on so that they are ready to replace the previous ones as soon as they fade.

Evergreen window boxes

There are plenty of compact evergreens to provide winter colour on your windowsill. Choose variegated shrubs such as *Euonymus*, berry-bearing plants such as *Gaultheria procumbens*, and dwarf conifers with green, blue or variegated foliage. The black-leaved *Ophiopogon planiscapus* 'Nigrescens', with its broad, grass-like leaves, provides an unusual contrast of colours. One advantage of using these plants is that after they have spent the season in the window box, they can be planted out in the garden, where they will continue to grow for many more years.

Generous flow A window box brimming with flowers enhances the appearance of your house.

Minimise feeding

Cut down on the chore of weekly liquid feeding during the growing season by using a controlled-release fertiliser. These fertilisers come in granule or pellet form and are coated with temperature-sensitive resin to ensure that nutrients are released only when it is warm enough for the plants to take them up. Add controlled-release fertiliser to the compost when planting. Restart liquid feeds towards the end of the summer, as and when the fertiliser stops releasing its nutrients.

Getting started

Cover the drainage holes in the bottom of your window box with some crocks or gravel before half-filling it with compost. While the plants are still in their pots, water them well. Next, arrange them in various ways in the box until you find a composition that displays each plant at its best. Then turn the plants

out of their pots. Gently loosen the roots and firm in each plant with more compost. To allow room for watering, leave a space between the compost surface and the top of the box.

Neighbourly precautions

If you are a flat-dweller, stand your window boxes on individual plastic drip trays on the windowsills. This will prevent water running down the walls and paintwork of the flat below every time you water the plants.

Made to measure

To maximise your plant-growing potential in a small space, it may be worth having a wooden window box made to fit the exact dimensions of your windowsill. Once you have treated this with a non-toxic wood preservative and lined it with plastic sheeting, you can plant directly into the box. Alternatively, fill the container with a succession of plants in pots for a display that never passes its peak.

Wall-mounted window box

If the projecting windowsill is too narrow for a box, attach brackets, strong enough to hold the window box firmly in place, to the wall beneath the window. If the window opens outwards, take care to leave sufficient space above the box so that the fully grown plants will not obstruct it.

Herbs to hand

Plant culinary herbs, such as thyme, basil, mint and parsley, in a window box to stand on the kitchen windowsill, then enjoy picking and using the fresh leaves as you cook.

Added attraction

Brighten up a plain window box by cutting split canes to length and gluing them to the sides and front of the box, or use beading for a moulded effect, finished with a coat of paint or varnish. Alternatively, decorate the box to complement the plants by painting it with a green exterior wood primer to provide a suitable background, then use

stencils and spray paints to add leaves, stems and flowers, or other patterns of your choice. Bright berries on a dark green background are particularly effective. Boxes painted to match the front door give overall coordination.

Preventing dirty drainage water

Avoid unsightly dribbles of soil coming out of your window boxes at watering time by lining the base with a disposable kitchen cloth. It will let water drain through freely but keeps soil in.

Keep compost off the glass

The tiny particles of potting compost that splash onto window panes when boxes are watered can make frequent window cleaning a necessary chore. Prevent splashing by covering the surface of the compost in each box with a layer of fine grit or small stones. This mulch will have the added advantage of improving moisture retention by reducing evaporation from the compost.

Wire

Fruit picker

Screw a medium-sized wire hook into one end of a broom handle or long pole and use it to bring high branches within reach for pruning or picking the fruit.

Hands free

Fruit picking, particularly from a ladder, is easier and safer with both hands free. Make an S-shaped hook from strong wire and hang the basket from it by its handle. Move the basket as you pick by hooking it on the nearest branch.

Strawberry propagation

Bend wires 7.5cm (3in) long into U shapes. Use them to peg strawberry runners to the soil, or compost in pots, until they take root.

Repairing fruit cages

To make sure it continues to keep out birds, a permanent wire netting fruit cage needs frequent checking for holes. Repair any that you find with thin, galvanised wire.

Creating a wild-flower garden

Despite widespread spraying, many wild-flower species still doggedly occupy motorway verges, headlands, moors, meadows and abandoned quarries. When making a wild garden, leave these beleaguered plants where they are and buy seeds from specialist suppliers instead.

If you have the room, there are few more rewarding or interesting horticultural sidelines to adopt than the creation of a wild-flower garden. There are species to suit every mood, habitat and soil from delicate alpines to lush water plants, from the bright jewels of the high chalk country to the subtler tints of flowers from dappled woodland floors. Other welcome garden immigrants are those that were a common sight in arable land that was regularly turned over, and those whose original habitat was the peat bog or the seashore. As well as attractiveness, wild flowers offer economy. Neither fertilisers, weedkillers, pesticides nor greenhouses are required.

Call of the wild A border alongside the lawn has been transformed into a starry profusion of cornflowers, daisies and poppies.

Flowers of cornfield and meadow

The ordering of set-aside land in farming practice has at least given a boost to our native wild flowers, most especially those of the cornfield. However, they are not so plentiful as to discourage growing a small combination of field headland and meadow yourself.

Start by leaving a small area of grass unmown, and see what comes up naturally. Clover, daisies and plantains may already be present. Supplement these with seeds or nursery-grown meadow plants such as clustered bellflower and cowslip on chalk or bird's-foot trefoil and meadow cranesbill on clay. Add plants from arable land such as cornflowers, corn marigolds and field poppies. Access to your wild flowers can be obtained from one or two paths mown through, but general mowing should be delayed until well into autumn, to allow time for the seeds to develop and disperse.

A woodland garden

Broad acres are not essential to the creation of a woodland dell. In fact, much of the magic of natural woodland can be scaled down and recaptured in a smallish corner where a shady canopy of trees and shrubs will provide an ideal situation for showing off woodland flowers.

Small trees that give dappled shade are best, and should be deciduous, native – or familiar – species. Crab apple, hawthorn, silver birch or wild pear are unfussy about soil type and are easy to grow. Beneath this upper canopy, deciduous flowering shrubs can be planted to form a middle layer. Guelder roses, hazel or *Rosa rugosa* are ideal, or for some constant greenery, put in holly and untrimmed boxwood.

Though many woodland flowers will become established from seed, you will gain a quicker impression of the effect you require by buying potted plants ready grown from a nursery that specialises in wild flowers.

Your display should certainly include drifts of ferns, foxgloves, stinking hellebores, oxlips, primroses, wild daffodils and wood anemones. Bluebells and rosebay willowherb also look well in this setting but are quite invasive, so be prepared to do some maintenance if planting such vigorous colonisers.

Secret dell Rhododendrons, foxgloves and granny's bonnet all brighten up a woodland clearing.

A wild hedgerow

In Britain, it is common practice to hide one's garden behind dense hedges of evergreen. Altogether the mileage of privet and laurel up and down the country must run into thousands, despite the fact that there are far more ancient and beautiful examples for us to choose from. Some of the hedges bordering British fields date back to Saxon times and vary from the fuchsia-filled banks of the south-west to the dense beech hedges of the southern chalk downland. More often they are simply a mix that, if copied in the garden, would take a generation or so to mature, but would nevertheless be attractive in youth. Ash, beech, dog rose, elder, field maple, guelder rose, hawthorn, honeysuckle and oak make solid garden hedges that will be decked in flowers, haws and berries in their seasons and provide a rich habitat for birds and animals. Holly, ivy and yew can be added to lend an evergreen touch to the mix.

Country memories Poppies, heartsease and daisies bring a touch of rural simplicity to a town garden.

An informal hedge This wild hedge has gathered to itself oak, beech, honeysuckle, ivy, hawthorn and wild roses.

Wild flowers in a town garden

Space is always at a premium in town gardens, but you can still find room for wild flowers by interspersing them with cultivated species. A small patch of grass could be devoted to a spring display of cowslips and native wild daffodils (*Narcissus pseudonarcissus*), for example, and ferns and navelworts can be poked into cracks in walls and paving. Like cultivated plants, wild flowers will thrive best in a habitat that suits them. For example, in the shady border of mixed shrubs and flowers that is often a feature of town gardens, there may be room for some cow parsley or sweet cicely, as well as a clump of bluebells, red campion or dusky cranesbill. A sunny flowerbed could include mallows, mauve knapweed and scabious.

Wireworms

A bait made from potato peelings

Fill some old tin cans with potato peelings and bury them just below soil level. After a few days, retrieve the cans and empty them into a bucket of water. The wireworms, having gorged on the potato peelings, will drown.

A dash of mustard

Sow a crop of mustard in late summer to give wireworms an abundance of green manure feed. Eating this hastens their metamorphosis into click beetles and they fly away. Dig in the mustard before first frosts.

Wisteria

Graft is best

When selecting a new wisteria from a garden centre, choose from the grafted plants that are available. These are more reliable and flower earlier than plants that have been raised from seeds.

Small garden

If space in the garden is limited, grow a wisteria in a container. This will restrict its roots and, with careful pruning, it can be trained as a standard. (See also **Standards**)

How to prune

To encourage a wisteria to bloom, establish a regular pruning routine. Cut back long non-flowering shoots to five or six leaves from the base in July or August, then, in December, cut them back to two buds.

Extra warmth

Although wisterias are hardy climbers, their flower-producing wood needs the warmth of the sun to ripen. For the best blooms, plant against a south or south-west-facing wall. However, if you are growing a wisteria from seed, sow it in a pot in autumn and place it at the base of a north-facing wall. This will provide the seed with the cold it needs to germinate. The seedling can be transplanted to a south-facing wall as soon as it is large enough to be moved.

Strong support

A wisteria is heavy, so use strong wire or thick battens on a trellis to prevent it from pulling the framework away from the wall.

Make the right choice

Wisterias for large walls

Wisterias are spectacular climbers for sunny walls, with long racemes of blue, purple or sometimes pink or white pea-like flowers. They need plenty of space in which to develop and regular pruning if they are to give their best. They thrive on most soils but must have plenty of space for their roots as well as their top growth, and they often take a few years to establish before flowering well. Some varieties are attractively scented.

Name	Growing habit	Cultivars and their flowers
Wisteria floribunda (Japanese wisteria)	Longer racemes of flowers than other wisterias, up to 30cm (12in), or even 75cm (30in) in some cultivars. Less vigorous so easier to look after in most gardens, growing to about 9m (30ft). Species bear violet-blue flowers in May and June.	'Alba': white flowers with lilac tint, 61cm (2ft); 'Kuchi-beni': pink opening to off-white, 75cm (30in); 'Multijuga': dark violet-purple, 51cm (20in); 'Purple Patches': violet-purple, 75cm (30in); 'Rosea': pale pink flowers with purple tips, 46cm (18in)
W. sinensis (Chinese wisteria)	Racemes of mauve flowers 20–30cm (8–12in) long in May and June, but more vigorous than *W. floribunda*, reaching 15m (50ft) where there is space for it to climb.	'Alba': white flowers, 23cm (9in); 'Caroline': deep blue, strongly scented, free flowering, 23cm (9in); 'Prematura': mauve, flowers reliably when young, 15cm (6in); 'Prolific': dark purple flowers in both May and August, 23cm (9in)
W. x formosa (Hybrid wisteria)	A cross between the two species above. Often very prolific and sometimes bears unusually long racemes of flowers. Can be hard to find in nurseries. Usually reaches about 9m (30ft).	'Issai': lilac-blue scented flowers, starts flowering when young, 25cm (10in); 'Kokkuryu': dark purple double flowers, 75cm (30in)

Patience is a virtue

Do not assume that a wisteria that has never flowered has failed, and pull it up. Seed-raised plants can take up to 10 years to bloom. Encourage them by applying a weekly feed of potash-rich liquid fertiliser from late March to September, and wait. Avoid using any nitrogen-rich fertilisers as these will encourage growth of foliage at the expense of flowers.

Yews

An easy-trim hedge

Taxus baccata 'Elegantissima' (golden yew) is ideal if you want a dense, labour-saving hedge. Since it puts on no more than 23cm (9in) of growth each year, it requires only a single clipping in late summer. Treated in this way, the hedge will, after 10–20 years, reach a solid 2m (7ft) in height.

Boosting growth

Make sure a yew receives plenty of nutrients in its early life by working well-rotted manure into the ground before planting, then applying a top dressing of bone meal each year. Water regularly for the first two years, applying 22.5 litres (5 gallons) to each plant once a week. This will ensure that the soil round the yew does not dry out.

Planting for hedging

When planting a yew hedge, use plants that are about 38cm (15in) high. Set them out at any time in autumn or spring. Prune hard for the first three or four years to ensure that the hedge develops a solid centre.

Hard pruning

Prune back an old yew hedge hard but cut back only one side at a time, otherwise it may not grow again. Always prune in spring, before new growth begins.

Dangers of yew

Almost all parts of the yew are poisonous to animals, so it should never be used to hedge a field that is home to any livestock. Dry leaves, twigs and clippings are just as lethal and give off toxic fumes when shredded. Keep an eye too on any children in the garden. They may be tempted by the bright red berries, which contain highly toxic seeds.

Yuccas

A touch of the tropics

Of the 40-odd species of yucca, rather less than a dozen are sufficiently hardy to be grown in Britain — and most of those need to be grown under glass. However, to bring a touch of the tropics to your garden, try the hardy *Yucca gloriosa*, which reaches almost 2.4–3m (8–10ft) in flower, or *Y. filamentosa* (Adam's needle), a smaller variety whose late summer glory is an immense 1.2–1.8m (4–6ft) flower stalk covered in creamy-white blooms. Both require well-drained loamy soil and a warm, sunny spot.

Perfect for pots

Plant even the hardier yuccas in pots. Not only do they look attractive in containers but they can also then be moved to the sunniest spots of the garden in the summer and back to more sheltered corners in the autumn months, when the weather starts to become colder.

Winter protection

Except in mild areas, hardy yuccas should be protected from frosts by piling grit over the roots in autumn. Alternatively, apply a top dressing of coarse bark to the compost.

Propagating yuccas

Detach young suckers from the base of the plant in spring and pot them up individually. The new plants may take five years to flower.

Zinnias

When to sow

For early zinnias, sow the seeds in a warm greenhouse in the first week of April. Transfer the seedlings to a cold frame in May, then harden them off and plant out when all danger of frost is past.

A longer run

After making the first sowing of zinnias in April, make a second one outdoors in May. Transplant the April-sown seedlings next to the May sowing and you will enjoy a continuous display of flowers from early July until September.

A page number in **bold** indicates a main entry or feature; a page number in *italics* indicates a picture caption

x y z

Picture credits

All pics © Reader's Digest, except:
Front cover (top left): The Garden Collection/ Torie Chugg
Front cover (top right), spine and back cover: The Garden Collection/Jonathan Buckley
Front cover (bottom left): The Garden Library/ Howard Rice
Front cover (bottom right): The Garden Library/Maxine Adcock

Letter artwork throughout: www.istockphoto.com/Bryan Malley

9 Photo Lamontagne
16 TR Gap Photos Ltd/Neil Holmes
16 BL Gap Photos Ltd/Clive Nichols
17 Gap Photos Ltd/Adrian Bloom
20, 30, 31,37, 38 Photo Lamontagne
64 Photolibrary.com/Stephen Wooster
72 Photo Lamontagne
77 Philippe Perdereau
85 Photo Lamontagne
87 Andrew Lawson
88 Joêlle Caroline Mayer & Gilles Le Scanff
94, 97,106 Photo Lamontagne
108 Photolibrary.com/Ron Evans
122 Photo Lamontagne
124 Photos Annette Schreiner
125 www.thesolarcentre.co.uk
126 Photo Lamontagne
138 Alamy Images/Brian Hoffman
150 Photo Lamontagne
153 Philippe Perdereau
161, 164, 165, 169, 179, 181 Photo Lamontagne
188 ShutterStock, Inc/niderlander
194 Photo Lamontagne
210 Mise au Point/ N & P Mioulane
217, 219, 230, Photo Lamontagne
236 Mise au Point/ N & P Mioulane
237, 239 Photo Lamontagne
241 C.M Walkenden
250 CR, BL Mise au Point/ N & P Mioulane
250 BR Photolibrary.com/Chris Burrows
251 CR The Garden Collection/Nicola Stocken Tomkins
251 BL The Garden Collection/Derek Harns
268 T Photolibrary.com/ Stephen Wooster
268 B Jerry Harpur
269 TR Eric Crichton
269 CL Photolibrary.com/Neil Holmes
281 Mise au Point/ N & P Mioulane
289 Photolibrary.com/Marijke Heuff
300 www.eyedea.fr /Jacana/ D Lecourt
301 R Mise au Point/ N & P Mioulane
301 L BIOS Photos/ Gunther
302 T Mise au Point/ A Descat
302 BL, BR, 303 T Mise au Point/ N & P Mioulane
303 CR, BL Philippe Perdereau
315 TR Photos Horticultural Picture Library
315 C, BL, BR Eric Crichton
317, 318 Photo Lamontagne
321 Mise au Point/ N & P Mioulane
326 Photolibrary.com/Joe Cornish
331 Photolibrary.com/Nigel Francis
332-333 Photolibrary.com/Lamontagne
333 Eric Crichton
336 BL Photos Horticultural Picture Library

All-Amazing Garden Secrets was published by The Reader's Digest Association Limited, London.

First edition copyright © 2008
The Reader's Digest Association Limited
11 Westferry Circus, Canary Wharf
London E14 4HE

Paperback edition copyright © 2009

We are committed both to the quality of our products and the service we provide to our customers. We value your comments, so please do contact us on 08705 113366 or via our website at www.readersdigest.co.uk

If you have any comments or suggestions about the content of our books, email us at gbeditorial@readersdigest.co.uk

All-Amazing Garden Secrets
is based on material previously published in *Reader's Digest 1001 Hints & Tips for the Garden* (1996).

Editorial consultant
Daphne Ledward

Assistant editors
Diane Cross and Ali Moore

Designer
Keith Miller

Proofreader
Cheryl Paten

Indexer
Hilary Bird

For Reader's Digest

Project editors
Alison Candlin
Rachel Warren Chadd

Art editor
Conorde Clarke

Editorial director
Julian Browne

Art director
Anne-Marie Bulat

Managing editor
Nina Hathway

Head of book development
Sarah Bloxham

Picture resource manager
Sarah Stewart-Richardson

Pre-press account manager
Dean Russell

Product production manager
Claudette Bramble

Production controller
Katherine Bunn

Origination
Colour Systems Limited, London

Printed and bound in China

Concept code	UK2462 / IC/UK-A
Book Code	400-423 UP0000-1
Oracle code	250011801S.00.24
ISBN	978 0 276 44532 3